An *Introduction to the* Biology *of*
M*arine* L*ife*

An Introduction to the Biology of
Marine Life

Fifth Edition

James L. Sumich
Grossmont College

Contributions to chapters 6 and 14 by Krystyna Wolniakowski
Coastal and Estuarine Water Quality Specialist

WCB Wm. C. Brown Publishers

Book Team

Editor *Kevin Kane*
Developmental Editor *Margaret J. Manders*
Production Editor *Renee A. Menne*
Designer *Mark Elliot Christianson*
Art Editor *Margaret Rose Buhr*
Photo Editor *Carrie Burger*
Visuals Processor *Amy L. Saffran*

Wm. C. Brown Publishers

President *G. Franklin Lewis*
Vice President, Publisher *George Wm. Bergquist*
Vice President, Operations and Production *Beverly Kolz*
National Sales Manager *Virginia S. Moffat*
Group Sales Manager *Vincent R. Di Blasi*
Vice President, Editor in Chief *Edward G. Jaffe*
Marketing Manager *Paul Ducham*
Advertising Manager *Amy Schmitz*
Managing Editor, Production *Colleen A. Yonda*
Manager of Visuals and Design *Faye M. Schilling*
Production Editorial Manager *Julie A. Kennedy*
Production Editorial Manager *Ann Fuerste*
Publishing Services Manager *Karen J. Slaght*

WCB Group

President and Chief Executive Officer *Mark C. Falb*
Chairman of the Board *Wm. C. Brown*

Cover photo © F. Stuart Westmorland/Allstock, Inc.

Library of Congress Catalog Card Number: 91–71936

ISBN 0–697–05143–9 (Paper)
0–697–13515–2 (Cloth)

Printed in the United States of America by Wm. C. Brown Publishers, 2460 Kerper Boulevard, Dubuque, IA 52001

10 9 8 7 6 5 4

Contents

Preface

An Introduction to the Biology of Marine Life was written to satisfy the demand for an introductory college-level text dealing with the biology of marine organisms. Recent developments in the field of marine biology have shown that courses in this subject provide an exciting and effective framework for illustrating basic biological principles. As a result, marine biology courses for the nonmajor or premajor student have become increasingly popular.

This text is written for the introductory marine biology student. No previous knowledge of marine biology is assumed. However, some exposure to the basic concepts of biology is helpful. Selected groups of marine organisms are used to develop an understanding of biological principles and processes that are basic to all forms of life in the sea. To build on these basics, information dealing with several aspects of taxonomy, evolution, ecology, behavior, and physiology of selected groups of marine organisms is presented. I have intentionally avoided adopting one of these major subdivisions as the framework of this text. Biology is an inclusive term, and a student's initial venture into this field should provide some flavor of the mix of disciplines that constitutes modern biology.

Scope of Subject Matter

This text includes more material than the typical student can assimilate in a semester. Instructors can select and mold the material to match their teaching styles and time limitations. The accompanying instructor's manual provides suggestions for use of this text, with judicious use of outside supplementary readings, in a two-quarter or two-semester course.

Sequence of Topics

As in most textbooks, each topic is developed after all have been first introduced in a general overview. Consequently, the sequence of topics is somewhat arbitrary and is intended to be flexible. The first chapter consists of an introduction to the marine environment. Chapter 2 examines the general features of life in the sea and how it has evolved to the present. Chapter 3, a survey of marine animal groups, is included here to avoid cumbersome definitions and descriptions in later discussions. Chapters 4 and 5 describe marine primary producers and examine the major factors that shape the pattern of marine primary productivity. Chapter 6 discusses estuaries as a reduced-scale analogy of the world ocean, its inhabitants, and their interactions. Chapters 7, 8, 9, and 10 emphasize the roles of marine organisms in divergent marine communities. Chapters 11 and 12 examine structural and physiological adaptations necessary to adequately fill those roles. The final two chapters offer a perspective for understanding the effects of human intervention upon marine ecosystems, including fishing (chapter 13) and pollution (chapter 14).

Student Aids

Each chapter contains numerous illustrations, graphs, and charts to assist students in visualizing the concepts presented. End-of-chapter summaries, questions for discussion, and supplementary reading lists encourage further in-depth exploration of covered topics. Additional references, listed at the end of the text, will be useful to students who have the enthusiasm and communication skills necessary to cope with the challenges of reading original literature.

Supplementary Materials

Instructor's Manual

The Instructor's Manual offers a variety of course schedules, chapter summaries, film and video sources, and sample test questions for each chapter.

Transparencies

Fifty two- and five-color acetate transparencies are available with this text. The transparencies are taken from the text and represent figures that merit extra visual review and discussion. These images can also be ordered as a slide set.

TestPak

wcb TestPak, a free, computerized testing service, simplifies testing while offering you flexibility. Two convenient TestPak options are available:
—Use your Apple® IIe, Apple® IIc, Macintosh or IBM PC to pick and choose test questions, edit them, and add your own questions. We can send you program and test item diskettes for this purpose.
—If you don't have a microcomputer, pick and choose your questions via our call-in/mail-in service. Within two working days of your request, we will put a test master, a student answer sheet, and an answer key in the mail to you. Call-in hours are 8:30–5:00 CST, Monday through Friday.

Materials for Field Study

Since I have avoided regional limitations where practical, this text is not designed for use as a detailed field guide for local marine organisms; however, several regional identification and field guides are listed in Appendix C. A companion text, *Laboratory and Field Investigations in Marine Biology,* by J. L. Sumich and G. H. Dudley, is available for courses emphasizing field or laboratory experiences.

New to this Edition

The widespread and positive reception of the four previous editions of this text continues to be encouraging. This edition represents a continuing effort to better meet the needs of those who use the text. The many suggestions and comments from readers have been considered in the changes that were made. Two new chapters, chapter 9 (Coral Reefs) and chapter 14 (Ocean Pollution), have been added. Information on deep-sea hot springs and their associated bacterial production, primary productivity in polar oceans, air-breathing tetrapod groups, and many other topics have been added or expanded significantly. Most existing illustrations have been revised, and numerous new ones have been added, all with full-color presentation, to better complement the text material.

List of Reviewers

The following critical reviewers provided in-depth analyses of individual chapters and made many valuable suggestions concerning the final shape and content of the text:

Brenda Blackwelder, *Central Piedmont Community College*
Susan Cormier, *University of Louisville*
Sheldon Dobkin, *Florida Atlantic University*
J. Nicholas Ehringer, *Hillsborough Community College*
Robert T. Galbraith, *Crafton Hills College*
Hal M. Genger, *College of the Redwoods*
Lynn Hansen, *Modesto Jr. College*
Lester Knapp, *Palomar College*
Matthew Landau, *Stockton State College*
Cynthia Lewis, *San Diego State University*
Donald Munson, *Washington College*
Joel Ostroff, *Brevard Community College*
Richard A. Roller, *University of Wisconsin–Stevens Point*
Mary Beth Saffo, *University of California–Santa Cruz*
Cynthia C. Stong, *Bowling Green State University*
Jefferson T. Turner, *Southeastern Massachusetts University*
Richard Turner, *Florida Institute of Technology*
Jacqueline Webb, *New York St. College of Vet. Med., Cornell University*
Robert Whitlatch, *University of Connecticut*
Richard B. Winn, *Duke University Marine Laboratory*

Market Research Respondents

We would like to thank the following adopters of the third edition for their help in preparing the current edition. Each contributed greatly to our understanding of the relative strengths and weaknesses of the third edition.

Genevieve Anderson, *Santa Barbara City College*
Jonathon N. Baskin, *Cal Poly University, Pomona*
Paul A. Billeter, *Charles County Community College*
A. D. Brant, *Calvin College*
David B. Campbell, *University of New Hampshire*
James L. Campbell, *Los Angeles Valley College*
Raymond D. Clarke, *Sarah Lawrence College*
S. M. Cormier, *University of Louisville*
Angela Cristini, *Ramapo College of New Jersey*
Sheldon Dobkin, *Florida Atlantic University*
Donald Dorfman, *Monmouth College*
William Fox, *Ventura College*
Harry W. Freeman, *College of Charleston*
Greta A. Fryxell, *Texas A & M University*
Hal M. Genger, *College of the Redwoods*
Malcolm S. Gordon, *U.C.L.A.*
Mark Gould, *Roger Williams College*
G. S. Grantham, *College of the Redwoods*
Philip F–C Greear, *Shorter College*
N. E. Grossnickle, *Grand Canyon College*
James D. Haddock, *Indiana University–Purdue University at Fort Wayne*
E. C. Haderlie, *Naval Postgraduate School*
Bernard F. Hanke, *Brunswick Technical College*
Shelly R. Johnson, *Pasadena City College*
Robert A. Jordan, *Hampton University*
Dennis L. Kelly, *Orange Coast College*
Richard S. Kelly, *SUNY at Albany*
Robert W. Kelly, *Furman University*
William T. Krauss, *Los Angeles Valley College*
David A. Krupp, *Windward Community College*
Jacqueline Lane, *Pensacola Junior College*
Carolyn G. Lebsack, *Linn-Benton Community College*
Alan C. Miller, *California State University–Long Beach*
Harold R. Milliken, *Loma Linda University*
W. J. Menkel, *Santa Clara University*
John P. Manning, *Massasoit Community College*
Michael S. Murray, *Brookdale Community College*
Steve Murray, *California State University–Fullerton*
Phillip A. Nickel, *California Lutheran University*
June K. Ramsey, *Pensacola Junior College*
Brian R. Rivest, *SUNY at Cortland*
L. O. Sorensen, *Pan American University*
Carol A. Stepien, *University of San Diego*
Richard A. Snyder, *University of Maryland*
Susan O. van Loon, *Our Lady of Holy Cross College*
Leland Van Fossen, *DeAnza College*
Thomas A. Wayne, *Lane Community College*
Judith Ann Williams, *Hawaii Pacific College*
P. Kelly Williams, *University of Dayton*
Ray E. Williams, *Rio Hondo College*
W. Herbert Wilson, Jr., *Northeastern University*
Melvin B. Zucker, *Skyline College*

Acknowledgments

Much credit for the development of this text goes to students and instructors who have used previous editions and have offered valuable comments and criticisms. I thank my instructors of the past and colleagues of the present for their contributions to my education and to this book. Special thanks also go to the many individuals and institutions that graciously supplied many of the photographs. Most of the biological illustrations are the work of a fine artist, Steve Haney. Significant contributions to the development of chapters 6 and 14 were made by Krystyna Wolniakowski, specialist on coastal and estuarine water quality. Finally, I thank my present and former students for their interest and enthusiasm in discovering rewarding methods of communicating this information.

James L. Sumich

The Ocean as a Habitat

Chapter 1

A synthetic satellite view of the North Atlantic Ocean Basin

Courtesy National Aeronautics and Space Administration

Figure 1.1
Some important marine features with appropriate time and size scales

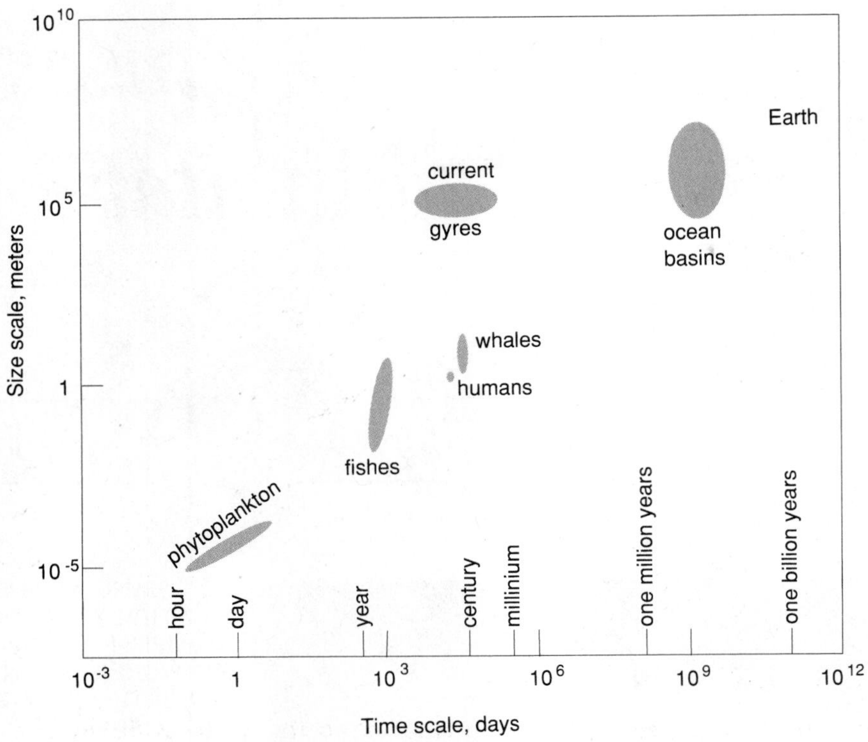

The ocean environment is home to a tremendous variety of living organisms highly adapted to the special conditions of the sea. The general features of these organisms and the variety of marine life itself are products of the many properties of the ocean habitat. This chapter will provide a survey of the developmental history and present geography of the ocean basins and a general discussion of some properties of seawater and of ocean circulation processes.

You need to develop a special perspective to study the oceans. We naturally tend to see the world from a human viewpoint, with human scales of time and distance. To begin to understand the marine environment of earth and how it evolved to its present form, you must broaden your perspective to include very different time and distance scales. Terms such as young and old or large and small have limited meaning unless placed in some manageable context. Figure 1.1 compares space and time scales for a few common oceanic features and inhabitants. Throughout this book, these scales will be revisited and others will be introduced to help you develop a practical sense of the time and space scales experienced by marine organisms.

The Changing Marine Environment

Our solar system, including the earth, is thought to have been formed approximately 4.7 billion years ago. Modern theories on the origin of the solar system suggest that the planets aggregated from a vast cloud of cold gas and dust particles into clusters of solid matter. These clumps continued to grow as gravity attracted them together. As the earth grew in this manner, pressure

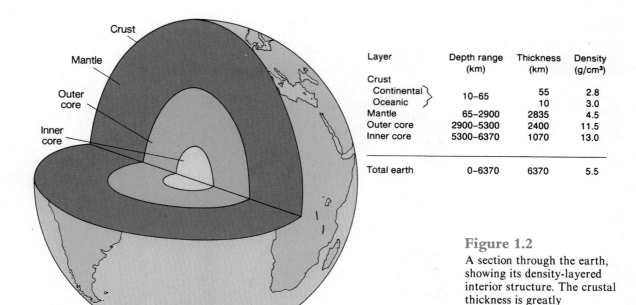

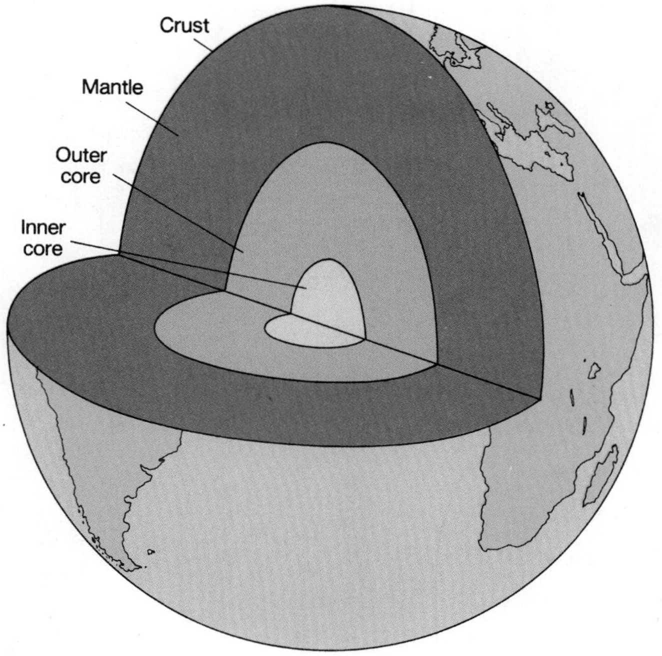

Layer	Depth range (km)	Thickness (km)	Density (g/cm³)
Crust			
Continental	10–65	55	2.8
Oceanic		10	3.0
Mantle	65–2900	2835	4.5
Outer core	2900–5300	2400	11.5
Inner core	5300–6370	1070	13.0
Total earth	0–6370	6370	5.5

Figure 1.2
A section through the earth, showing its density-layered interior structure. The crustal thickness is greatly exaggerated in order to show continents and ocean basins at this scale.

from the outer layers compressed and heated the earth's center. Aided by heat from decay of radioactive elements, the interior of the earth melted. Iron, nickel, and other heavy metals settled to the core, while the lighter materials floated to the surface and cooled to form a thin crust (figure 1.2).

Numerous volcanic vents poked through the crust and tapped the upper mantle for liquid material and gases that were then spewed out over the surface of the young earth, and a primitive atmosphere developed. Water vapor was certainly present. As the water vapor condensed, it fell as rain, accumulated in depressions on the earth's surface, and formed embryonic oceans. Atmospheric gases dissolved into accumulating seawater, and ions, dissolved from rocks and carried to the seas by rivers, added to the mixture, eventually creating seawater.

Since their initial formation, ocean basins have experienced considerable change. New material derived from the earth's mantle has extended the continents so that they are now larger and stand higher than at any time in the past. The oceans have kept pace, getting deeper with accumulations of juvenile water from volcanic gases and of chemical breakdown of rock. Earth's early life forms (represented by fossils older than about one billion years) had a significant impact on the character of their physical environment. Free oxygen (O_2) was produced in increasing amounts by microscopic photosynthetic cells. The O_2 content of the atmosphere 600 million years ago was probably about 1% of its present concentration. It was not much, but it is believed to have been the turning point, the time when organisms utilizing O_2 (in aerobic respiration) became dominant and organisms not utilizing O_2 became less prevalent.

The evolution of more complex life-forms using increasingly efficient methods of energy utilization set the stage for an explosion of marine life forms. By 500 million years ago, most major groups of marine organisms had made

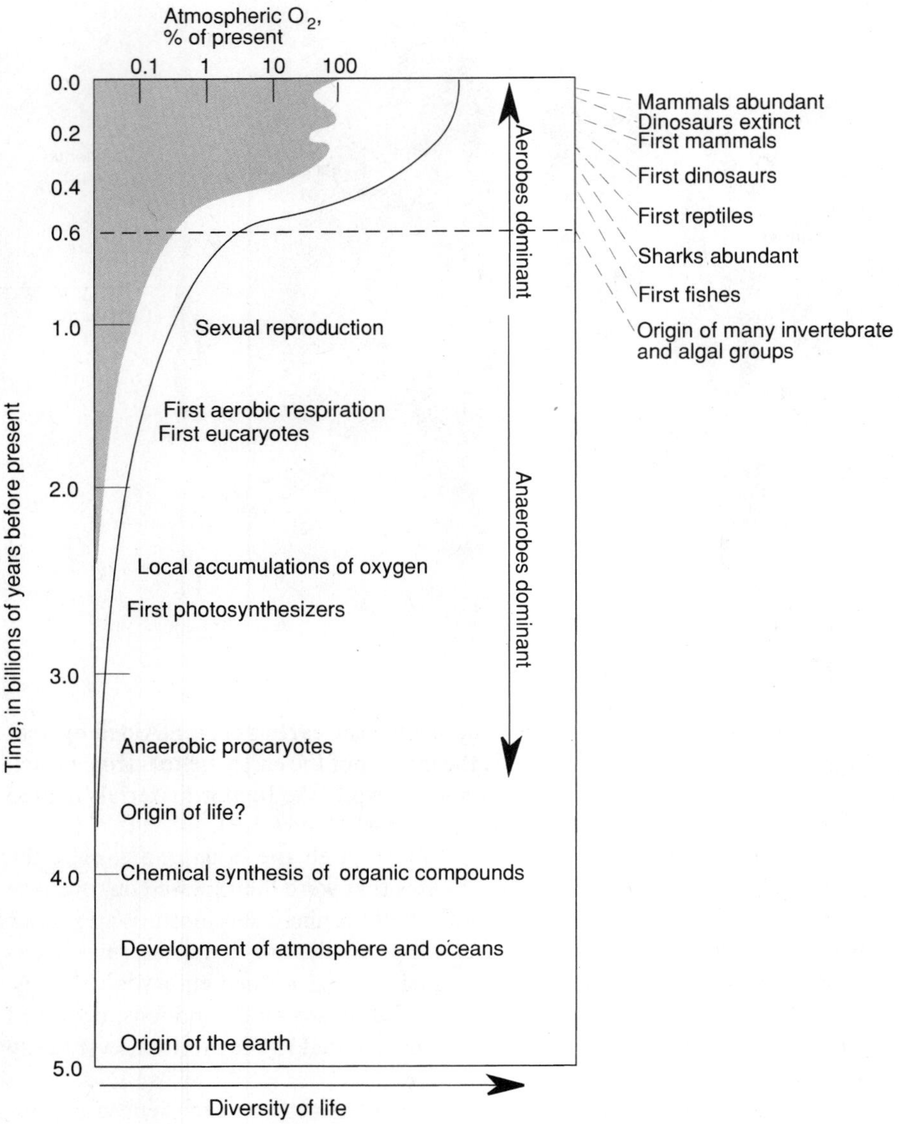

Figure 1.3
A summary of some biological and physical milestones in the early development of life on earth. The lower curve represents the relative diversity of life; the upper curve represents the O_2 concentration of the atmosphere. Several of the terms used here will be defined in Chapter 2.

their appearance. Worms, sponges, corals, and the immediate ancestors of terrestrial animals and plants were abundant. But life could only exist in the sea at that time, where a protective blanket of seawater shielded it from harmful ultraviolet radiation.

As O_2 became more abundant in the upper atmosphere, some of it was converted to **ozone** (O_3). The process of forming ozone absorbed much of the lethal ultraviolet radiation coming from the sun and prevented the radiation from reaching the earth's surface. The O_2 concentration of the atmosphere 400 million years ago is estimated to have reached 10% of its present level. The ozone derived from the additional O_2 screened out enough ultraviolet radiation to permit a few life-forms to abandon their sheltered marine home and colonize the land. Only recently have we become aware that industrialized society's increasing use of aerosols, refrigerants, and other pol-

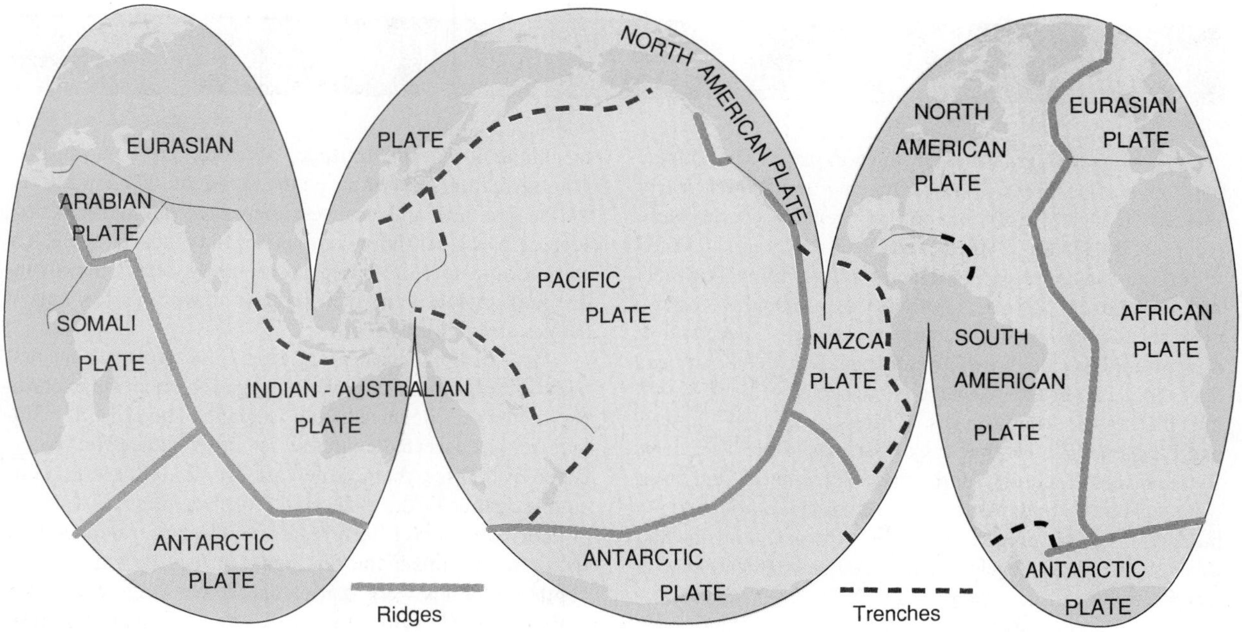

Figure 1.4
The major plates of the earth's crusts. Trenches are shown with dashes, ridges and rises with hatching. Compare the features of this map with those of figures 1.9 and 7.21.

lutants is gradually depleting this protective layer of ozone. Figure 1.3 summarizes significant events of the origin and early development of life on earth.

In the early part of this century, Alfred Wegener proposed that the oceans were changing in other ways. Wegener developed a detailed hypothesis of **continental drift** to explain several global geological features, including the remarkable jigsaw-puzzle fit of some continents (especially Africa and South America). He proposed that our present continental masses had drifted apart following the breakup of a single supercontinent, **Pangaea.** His evidence was ambiguous, and most scientists remained unconvinced. It was not until the early 1960s that new and telling evidence elicited wider endorsement by the scientific community. The early cruises of the *Glomar Challenger* (box 1.1) provided the telling evidence that verified Wegener's hypothesis.

The evidence that supports the closely related concepts of **seafloor spreading** and **plate tectonics** indicates the earth's crust is divided into a number of giant irregular plates (figure 1.4). These rigid plates float on the more dense and slightly plastic mantle material. Each plate is bounded by oceanic trench and ridge systems, and some plates include both oceanic and continental crusts. New oceanic crustal material is formed continually along the axes of oceanic ridges and rises. As the crustal plates grow on either side of the ridge, they move laterally in opposite directions, carrying bottom sediments and attached continental masses with them (figure 1.5).

In 1977, a remarkable discovery of new marine animal communities associated with seafloor hot water vents was made by scientists working in the deep-diving research submersible, *Alvin.* These vents are integral parts of some oceanic ridge or rise systems (figure 7.21). Members of these and other recently discovered deep-sea communities are discussed in chapter 7.

The changes that seafloor spreading and plate tectonics have wrought on the shapes and sizes of the oceans have been impressive. The African continent is drifting northward on a collision course with Europe, relentlessly

Box 1 *Three Voyages in Different Dimensions*

Primitive humans must have explored the marine portion of their immediate environment very early in their history, but few of their discoveries were recorded. By 325 B.C., Pytheas, the Greek explorer, had sailed to Iceland and developed a method for determining **latitude.** About a century later, Eratosthenes of Alexandria, Egypt, provided the first known estimate of the earth's size, its first dimension. His calculated circumference of 45,000 km was only about 12% greater than today's accepted value of 40,000 km. During the Middle Ages, Vikings, Arabians, Chinese, and Polynesians sailed over major portions of earth's oceans. By the fifteenth century, all the major inhabitable land areas were occupied; only Antarctica remained untouched by humans. Even so, precise charting of the ocean basins had to await three key developments, each one associated with its own voyage of discovery.

Between 1768 and 1779, James Cook, the English navigator, conducted three exploratory voyages, mostly in the Southern Hemisphere. He was the first to cross the Antarctic Circle and to understand and conquer scurvy (a disease caused by a deficiency of vitamin C). He is best remembered as the first global explorer to make extensive use of the marine **chronometer** developed by John Harrison, a British inventor. The chronometer, a very accurate shipboard clock, established the **longitude** of any fixed point on the earth's surface. Together with Pytheas's 2000-year-old technique for fixing latitude, accurate positions of geographic features anywhere on the globe could be established for the first time, and our two-dimensional view of the earth's surface was essentially complete. Today, coastal LORAN stations and satellite-based positioning systems permit individuals to determine their position to within a few tens of meters anywhere on earth.

In 1882, one century after Cook's voyages, the first truly interdisciplinary global voyage for scientific exploration of the seas departed from England. The H.M.S. *Challenger* was converted expressly for this voyage. The voyage lasted over three years, sailed almost 125,000 km in a circumnavigation of the globe, and returned with such a wealth of information that fifteen years and fifty large volumes were required to publish the findings. During the voyage, 492 depth soundings were made. These soundings traced the outlines of the Mid-Atlantic Ridge, plumbed the Mariannas Trench to a depth of 8185 m, and filled in rough outlines of the third dimension of the world ocean, its depth.

In 1968, a new and unusual ship, the *Glomar Challenger,* was launched to probe time, the fourth dimension of the oceans. Equipped with a deck-mounted drilling rig, the *Glomar Challenger* was capable of drilling into the seafloor in water over 7000 m deep. Within two years, the *Glomar Challenger* recovered vertical sediment core samples from enough sites on both sides of the Mid-Atlantic

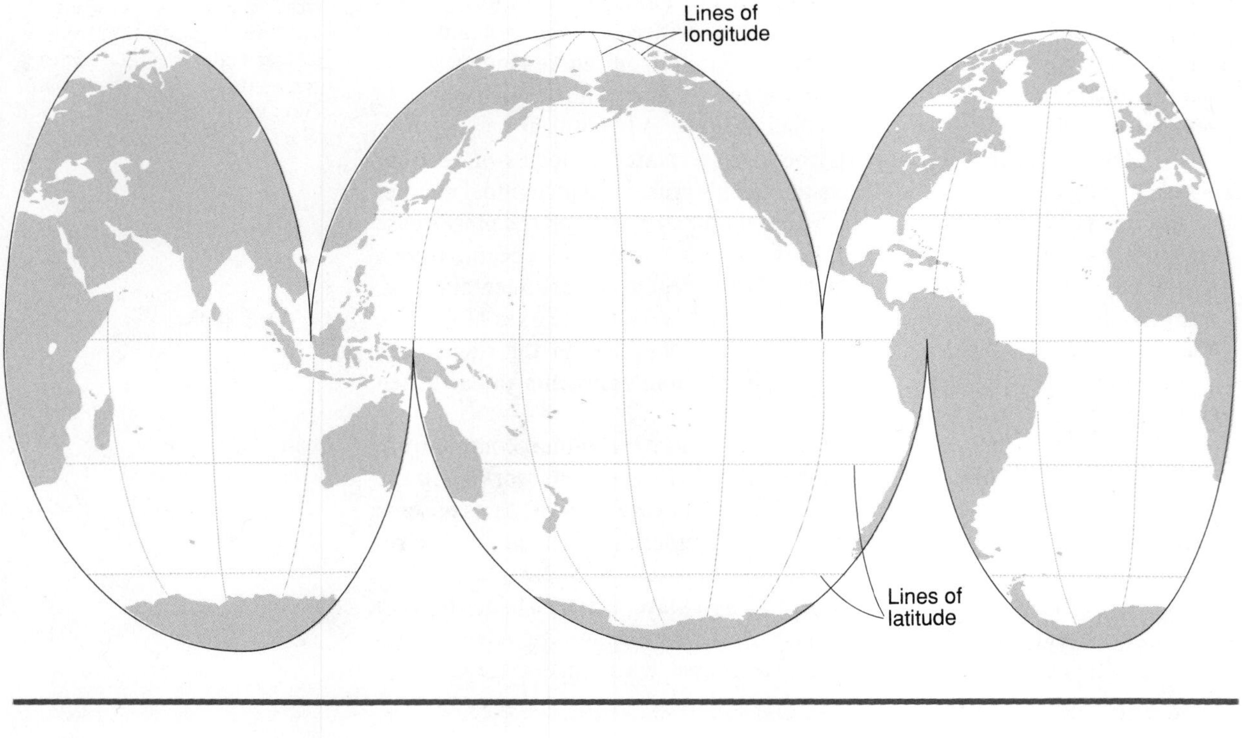

Box 1 *Three Voyages in Different Dimensions*

Ridge to finally and firmly confirm the concept of seafloor spreading and continental drift. Before being decommissioned in 1983, the *Glomar Challenger* traveled almost 700,000 km and drilled 318,461 m of sea floor in 1092 drill holes at 624 sites in all ocean basins. Subsequent analyses of microscopic marine fossils recovered from this tremendous store of marine sediment samples have led to refined estimates of the ages and patterns of evolution of all the major ocean basins.

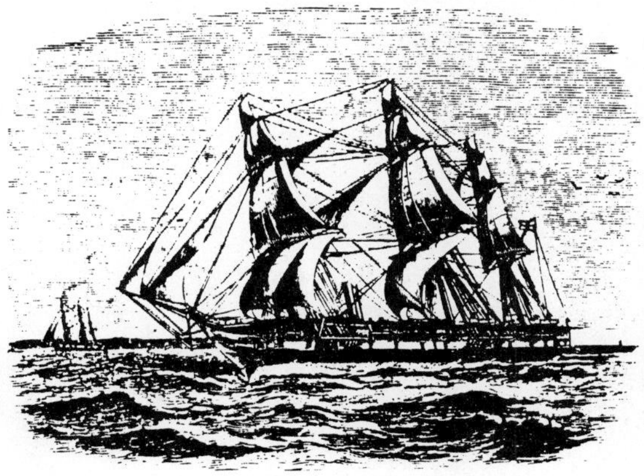

H.M.S. *Challenger*

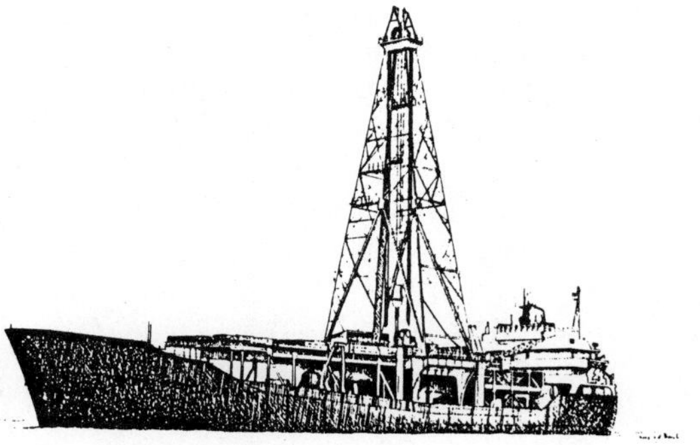

Glomar Challenger

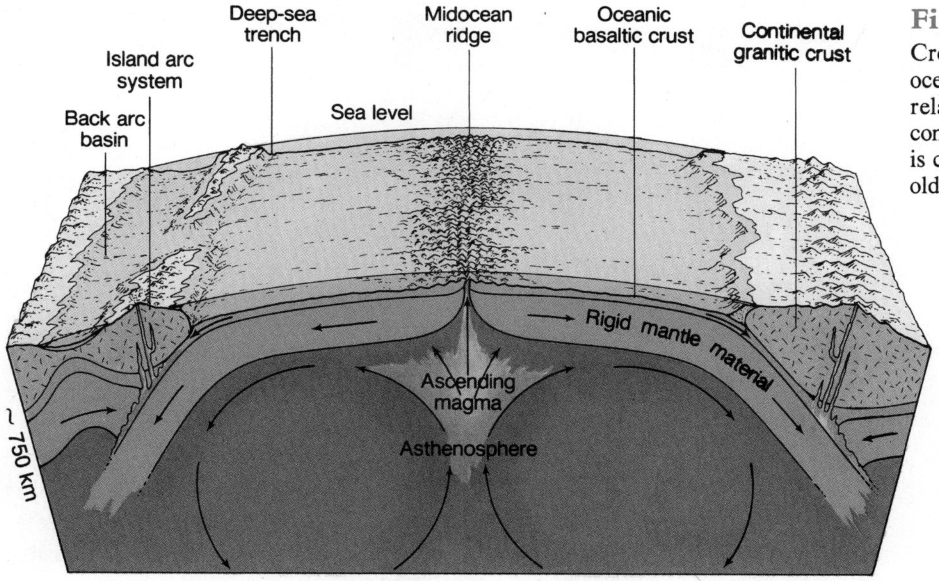

Figure 1.5
Cross section of a spreading ocean floor, illustrating the relative motions of oceanic and continental crusts. New crust is created at the ridge axis, and old crust is lost in trenches.

closing the Mediterranean Sea. The Atlantic Ocean is becoming wider at the expense of the Pacific Ocean. Australia and India continue to creep northward, slowly changing the shapes of the ocean basins they border. Occasional violent earthquakes are only incidental tremors in this monumental collision of crustal plates. The rates of seafloor spreading have been determined for some oceans,

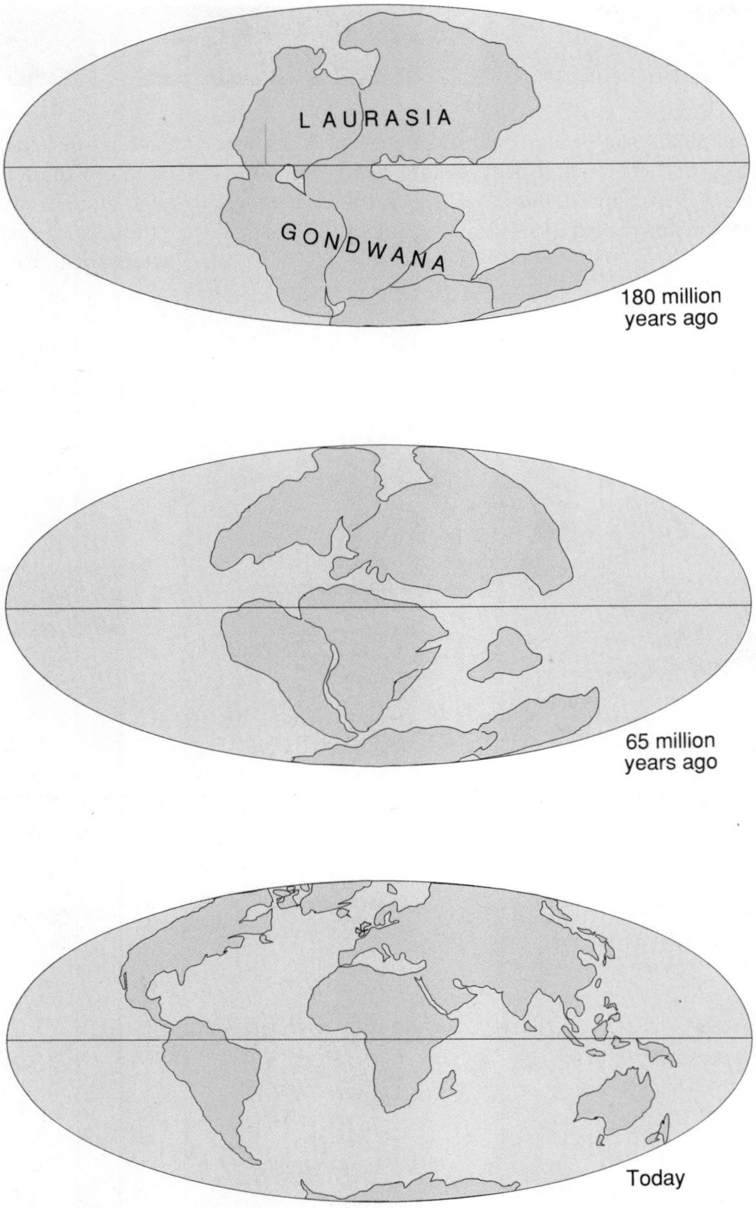

Figure 1.6
About 200 million years ago, Pangaea, the megacontinent, separated into two large continental blocks, Laurasia and Gondwana. Since then, they have fragmented into smaller continents and continue to drift apart. These maps outline the changing past positions of the continents and ocean basins.

Adapted from Dietz and Holden, 1970

and they vary widely. The South Atlantic is widening about 3 cm each year (or approximately your height in your lifetime). The Pacific Ocean is shrinking somewhat faster.

The breakup of the megacontinent, Pangaea, produced ocean basins where none existed before. The seas of 200 million years ago changed size or disappeared altogether. The past positions of the continents and ocean basins, based on our present understanding of the processes involved, are reconstructed in figure 1.6. Excess crust produced by seafloor spreading folds into mountain ranges (the Himalayas is a dramatic example) or slips down into the mantle and remelts (figure 1.5). Unfortunately, most of the fossil deposits of early marine life-forms can never be studied; they too have been carried to

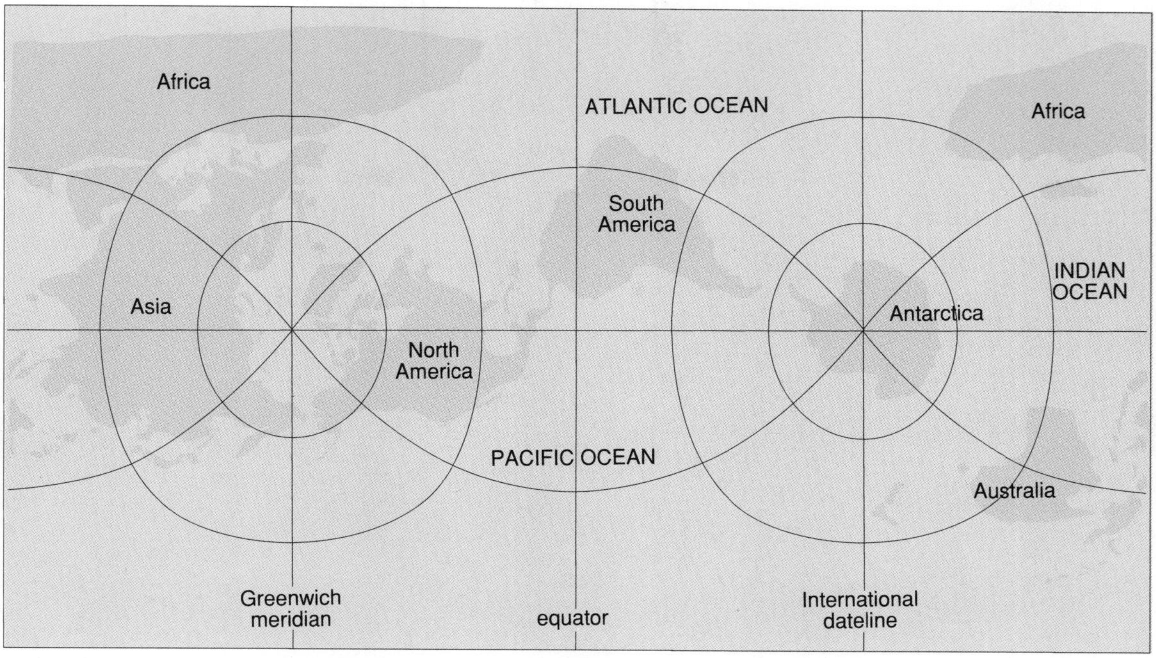

Figure 1.7
A modified polar view of the world ocean, showing the extensive oceanic connections between major ocean basins

destruction in the mantle by the "conveyor belt" of the seafloor crust. It is ironic that the only fossil evidence we have for the first 90% of the evolutionary history of marine life is found on land that was once ancient seabeds.

On a much shorter time scale, other processes have been at work to alter the shapes and sizes of ocean basins. Only 18,000 years ago, northern reaches of Europe, Asia, and North America were frozen under the grip of the most recent "Ice Age," or the **last glacial maximum (LGM).** The massive amount of water contained in those glaciers lowered sea level about 150 m below its present (and also its preglacial) level. Between 18,000 and 10,000 years ago, the shrinking of these continental glaciers was accompanied by a 150 m rise in sea level and the flooding of land exposed during the LGM. Coral reefs, estuaries, and other shallow water marine habitats were modified extensively during this flooding; these topics will be discussed in chapters 6 through 9.

The World Ocean

At the present time, the world ocean covers approximately 70% of the earth's surface and has an average depth of about 3700 m. This may seem like a lot of water, but when compared to the earth's diameter of 13,250 km, the ocean is actually a very thin film of water covering the earth's crust. On the scale of this chapter's front photograph of earth from space, the average ocean water depth is represented by a distance of about 0.04 mm, or slightly more than one one-thousandth of an inch.

Conventionally, the world ocean has been separated into four major ocean basins: the Atlantic, Pacific, Indian, and Arctic oceans. A more realistic approach views the marine environment as one large interconnected ocean system. This can be visualized best from a South Polar view of the earth (figure 1.7). The Antarctic continent is surrounded by an "Antarctic Ocean," which

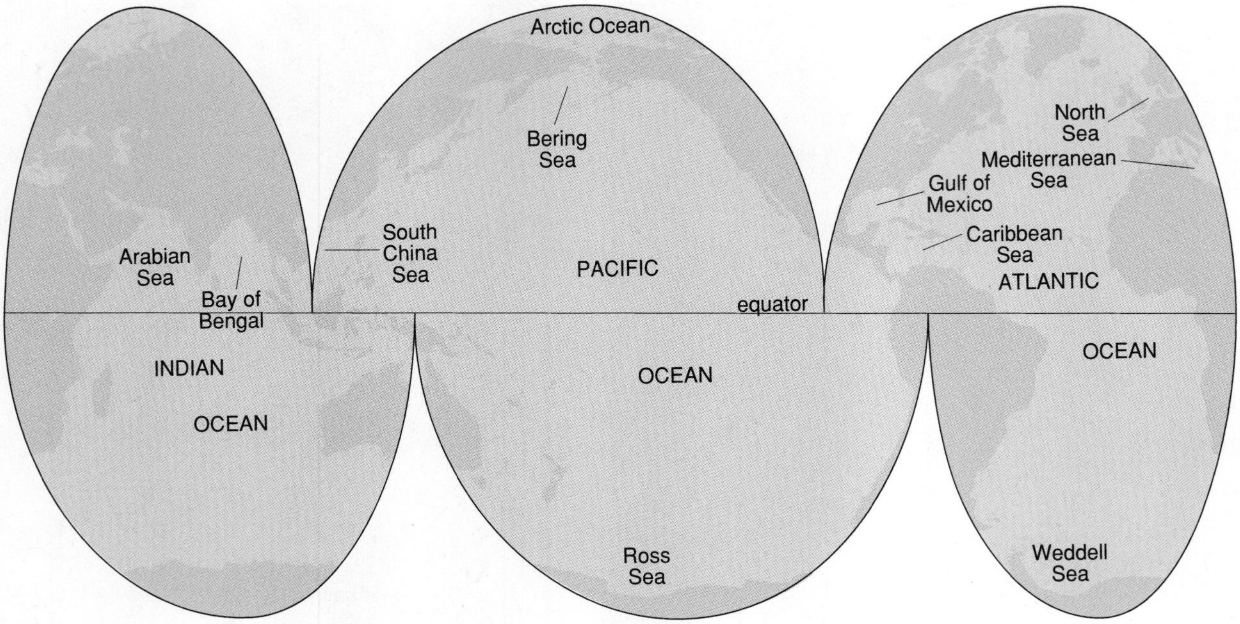

Figure 1.8
An equatorial view of the world ocean

has three large embayments extending northward. These three oceanic extensions, partially separated by continental barriers, are the Atlantic, Pacific, and Indian oceans. Other smaller oceans and seas, such as the Arctic Ocean and the Mediterranean Sea, project from the margins of the larger ocean basins. Connections between the major ocean basins permit exchange of seawater and marine organisms.

Figure 1.8 presents a more conventional view of the world ocean. Note that this type of map does not emphasize the extensive southern connections apparent in figure 1.7. The format of figure 1.8 is often more useful because interest in the marine environment has been focused in the temperate and tropical regions of the earth. In addition, the equator is a very real physical boundary between the northern and southern halves of the large ocean basins, dividing northern and southern current patterns and life zones. The curvature of the earth's surface causes areas near the equator to receive more radiant energy from the sun than equal-sized areas in polar regions. The resultant heat gradient from warm tropical to cold polar regions establishes the basic pattern of atmospheric and oceanic circulation. Surface ocean current patterns display a mirror-image symmetry in the northern and southern halves of the Pacific and Atlantic oceans. This hemispheric symmetry establishes the equator as a natural focus for the graphic representation of these features.

The distribution of continents and oceans over the earth's surface is not symmetrical on either side of the equator. Nearly two-thirds of the land area is located in the Northern Hemisphere. The Southern Hemisphere is an oceanic hemisphere, with 80% of its surface covered by water. The Pacific Ocean alone accounts for nearly one-half of the total ocean area. Some statistics for features of the six largest ocean basins are listed in table 1.1.

Oceanic depths extend to over 11,000 m, but most of the ocean bottom lies between 3000 and 6000 m. An idealized cross section of an ocean basin (figure 1.9) indicates the large-scale features of the ocean bottom.

Table 1.1
Some Comparative Features of the Major Ocean Basins

Ocean	Area $\times 10^6 km^2$	Volume $\times 10^6 km^3$	Average Depth, m	Maximum Depth, m
Pacific	165.2	707.6	4,282	11,022
Atlantic	82.4	323.6	3,926	9,200
Indian	73.4	291.0	3,963	7,460
Arctic	14.1	17.0	1,205	4,300
Caribbean	4.3	9.6	2,216	7,200
Mediterranean	3.0	4.2	1,429	4,600
Other	18.7	17.3		
Total	361.1	1,370.3	3,795	

The **continental shelf,** which extends seaward from the shoreline and is actually a structural part of the continental landmass, would not be considered an oceanic feature if sea level were lowered by as little as 5% of its present average depth. In fact, much of what is now continental shelf was above sea level as recently as 15,000 years ago during the last ice age. The width of continental shelves varies from almost nonexistent off southern Florida to over 800 km north of Siberia in the Arctic Ocean. Continental shelves account for about 8% of the ocean's surface area; this is equivalent to one-sixth of the earth's total land area.

Most continental shelves are relatively smooth and slope gently seaward. The outer edge of the shelf, sometimes called the **shelf break,** is a vaguely defined feature that usually occurs at depths of 120 to 200 m. Beyond the shelf break, the bottom steepens slightly to become the **continental slope.** The continental slope is the boundary between the continental mass and the true ocean basin. The slope is steep, rapidly dropping to depths of 3000 to 4000 m.

A large portion of the deep ocean basin consists of flat, sediment-covered areas called **abyssal plains.** Most abyssal plains are situated near the margins of the ocean basins at depths between 3000 and 5000 m. **Oceanic ridge and rise systems,** such as the Mid-Atlantic Ridge and East Pacific Rise, occupy over 30% of the ocean basin area. The ridge and rise systems are rugged linear features that form a continuous underwater mountain chain that encircles the earth. Isolated peaks of these mountain systems occasionally extend above sea level to form islands such as Iceland and Ascension Island in the Atlantic Ocean.

Trenches are distinctive ocean-floor features that are generally deeper than 6000 m. Most trenches, including the five deepest, are located along the margins of the Pacific Ocean. The Challenger Deep, in the Mariannas Trench of the western North Pacific, extends to 11,022 m, the greatest ocean depth found anywhere. (This is as far below sea level as commercial jets are above sea level.) Trenches account for less than 2% of the ocean bottom area, but they are significant because of the rigorous temperature and pressure regimes they impose on their inhabitants. As discussed in the previous section, trenches (along with ridge and rise systems) are integral parts in the processes of sea-floor spreading and plate tectonics.

Figure 1.9
Large-scale features of the North Atlantic seafloor
Courtesy National Geophysical Data Center

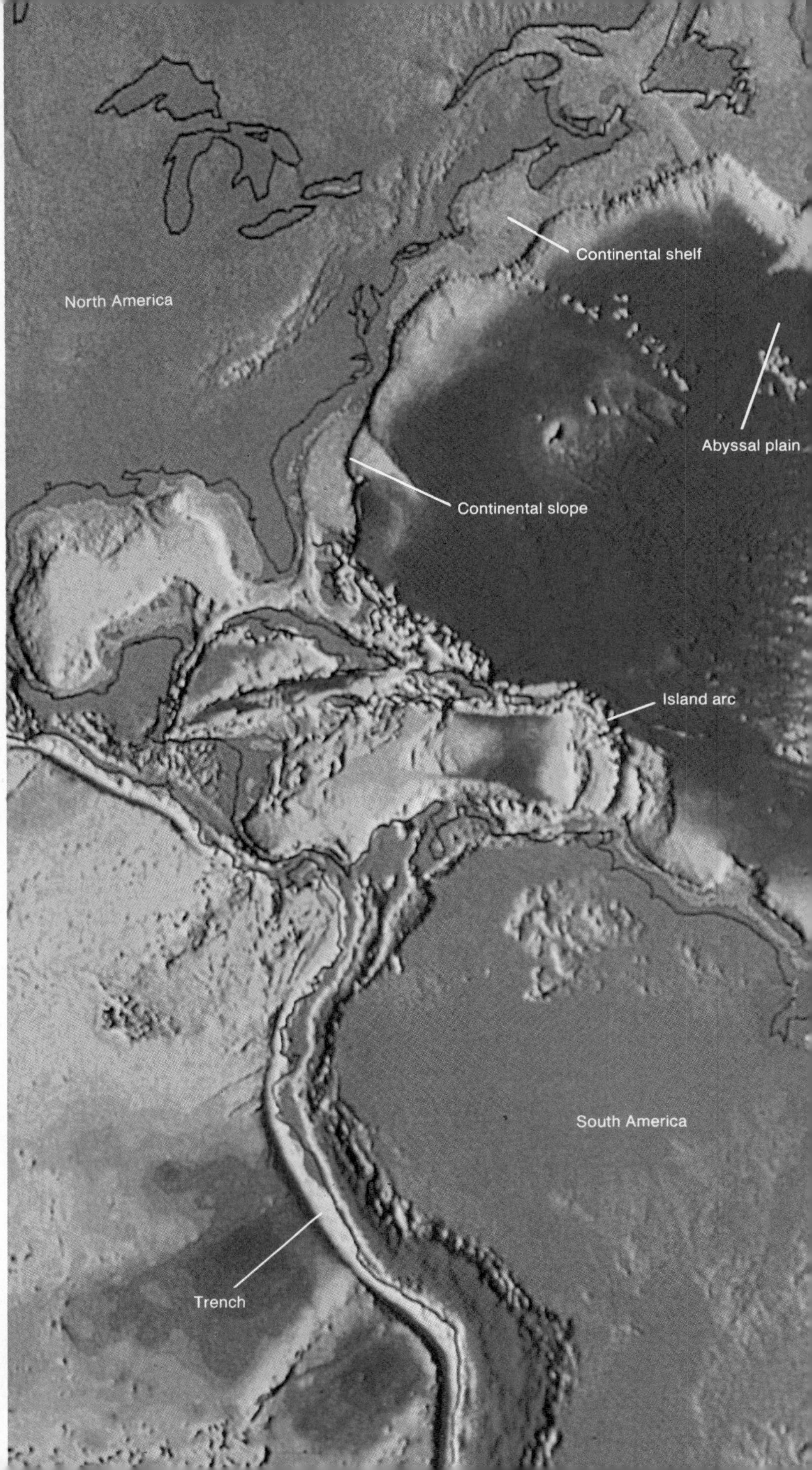

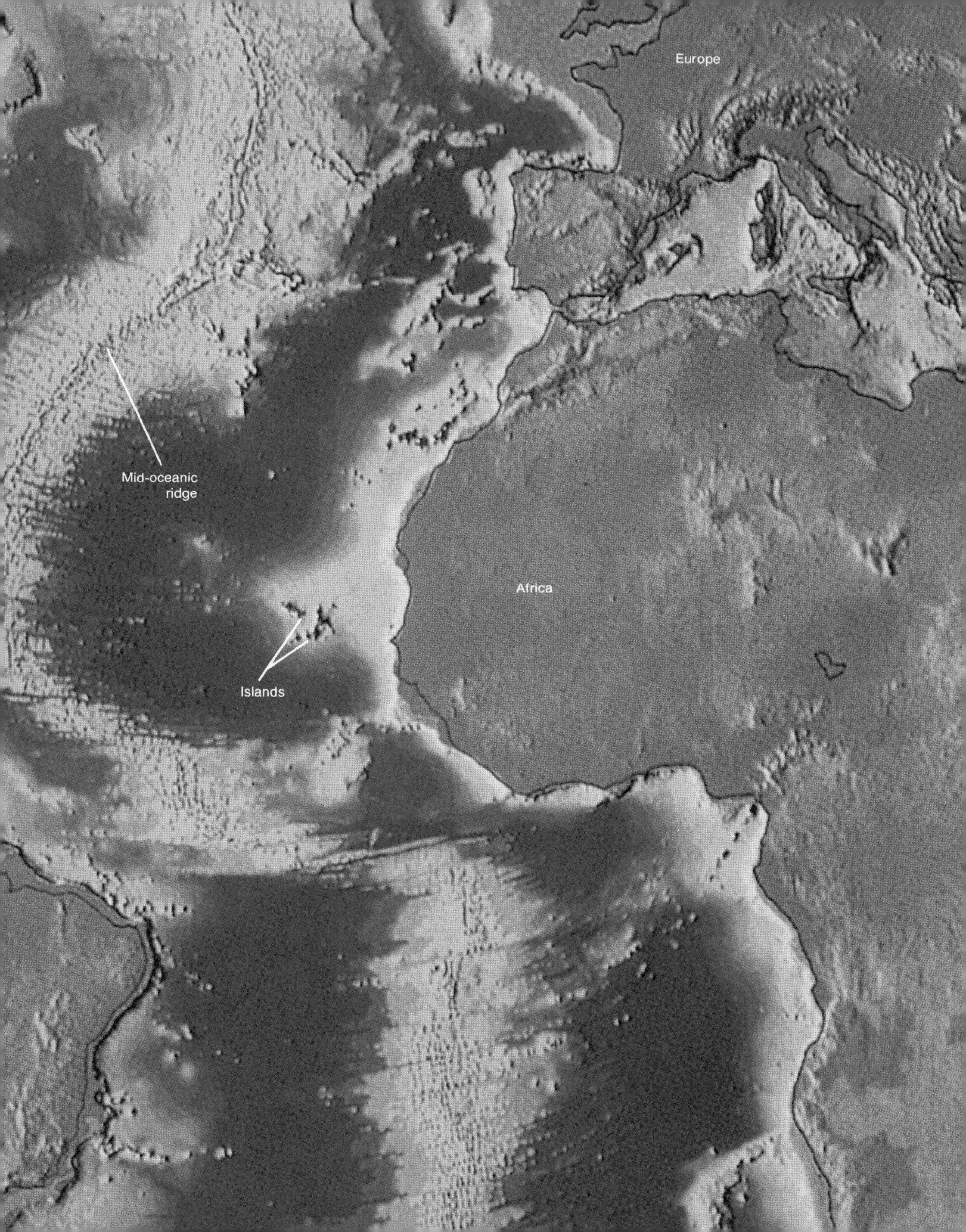
Europe
Mid-oceanic
ridge
Africa
Islands

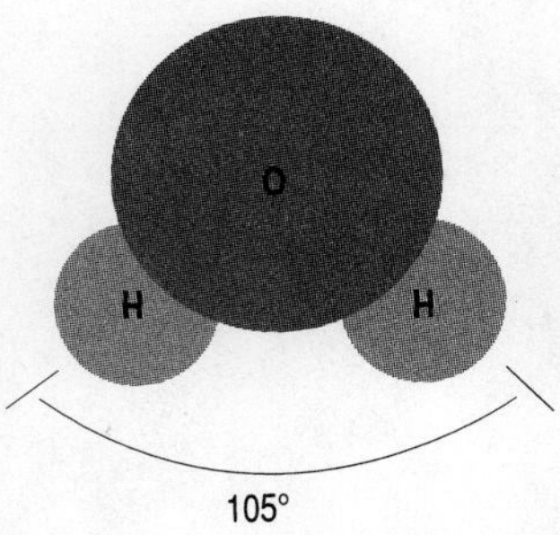

Figure 1.10
The arrangement of H and O atoms in a molecule of water (H_2O). The oxygen end has a slight net negative charge; the hydrogen end has a slight net positive charge.

Most oceanic islands and **seamounts** have been formed by volcanic action. Islands are volcanic mountains that extend above sea level; seamounts are volcanic mountains whose tops remain below the sea surface. The majority of these features are located in the Pacific Ocean. Islands in tropical areas are often capped by coral **atolls** or fringed by coral **reefs.** These reefs, examined in chapter 9, form some of the most beautiful and complex communities found anywhere.

Properties of Seawater

Many properties of seawater are crucial to the survival and well-being of the ocean's inhabitants. Water accounts for 80 to 90% of the volume of most marine organisms. It provides buoyancy and body support for swimming and floating organisms, thereby reducing the need for heavy skeletal structures. Water is also the medium for most chemical reactions needed to sustain life. The life processes of marine organisms in turn alter many fundamental physical and chemical properties of seawater, including its transparency and chemical makeup, making organisms an integral part of the total marine environment. Understanding the interactions between these organisms and their environment requires a brief study of some of the more important physical and chemical attributes of seawater. The characteristics of pure water and seawater differ in some respects and are similar in other respects. Let us consider first the basic properties of pure water and then study the effects of dissolved substances on these properties.

Pure Water

Water is a common, yet very remarkable, substance on the earth's surface. While abundant in its liquid form, large quantities of water also exist as a gas in the atmosphere and as a solid in the form of ice and snow. Although water molecules have a simple structure, the collective properties of many water molecules together are quite complex. Each water molecule has one atom of oxygen (O) and two atoms of hydrogen (H), which together form water (H_2O). (Some properties of these and other biologically important elements are listed in Appendix B.) The many unusual properties of water stem from its molecular shape: Two hydrogen atoms form an angle of about 105° with the oxygen atom (figure 1.10). This configuration produces an asymmetrical, dipole water molecule, with the oxygen atom dominating one end of the molecule and the hydrogen atoms dominating the other end. The bond between each hydrogen and oxygen atom is formed by the sharing of two negatively charged electrons. The larger oxygen atom attracts the electron pair of each bond, causing the oxygen end of the water molecule to assume a slight negative charge. The hydrogen end of the molecule, by giving up part of its electron complement, is left with a small positive charge. The resultant electrical charge separation causes each water molecule to behave like a miniature magnet, one end with a positive charge and the other end with a negative charge. Each end of one water molecule attracts the oppositely charged end of other water molecules. This attractive force creates a weak bond, a **hydrogen bond** or **H-bond,** between adjacent water molecules (figure 1.11). These bonds are much weaker than the covalent bond within a single water molecule and are continually

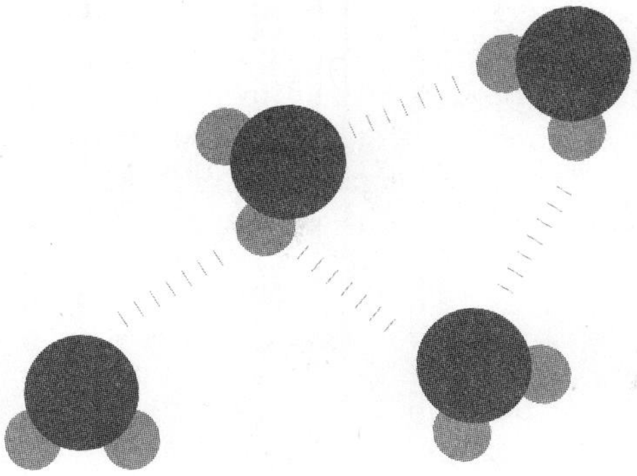

Figure 1.11
Hydrogen bonding between adjacent molecules of liquid water. Blue dashed lines represent hydrogen bonds.

Table 1.2
Some Biologically Important Physical Properties of Water

Properties	Comparison with Other Substances	Importance in Biological Processes
Boiling point	High (100° C) for molecular size	Causes most water to exist as a liquid at earth surface temperatures
Freezing point	High (0° C) for molecular size	Causes most water to exist as a liquid at earth surface temperatures
Surface tension	Highest of all liquids	Critical to position maintenance of sea surface organisms
Density of solid	Unique among common natural substances	Causes ice to float and inhibits complete freezing of large bodies of water
Latent heat of evaporation	Highest of all common natural substances (540 cal/g)	Moderates sea-surface temperatures by transferring large quantities of heat to the atmosphere through evaporation
Latent heat of freezing	Highest of all common natural substances (80 cal/g)	Inhibits large-scale freezing of oceans
Solvent power	Dissolves more substances in greater amounts than any other liquid	Maintains a large variety of substances in solution, enhancing a variety of chemical reactions.
Heat capacity	High (1 cal/g/° C) for molecular size	Moderate daily and seasonal temperature changes Stabilize body temperatures of organisms

breaking and reforming with other water molecules. Without H-bonding between molecules, water would boil at −80° C and freeze at −100° C, making life as we know it impossible. Hydrogen bonding also accounts for many other unique properties of water. Table 1.2 and the following paragraphs discuss some of these properties.

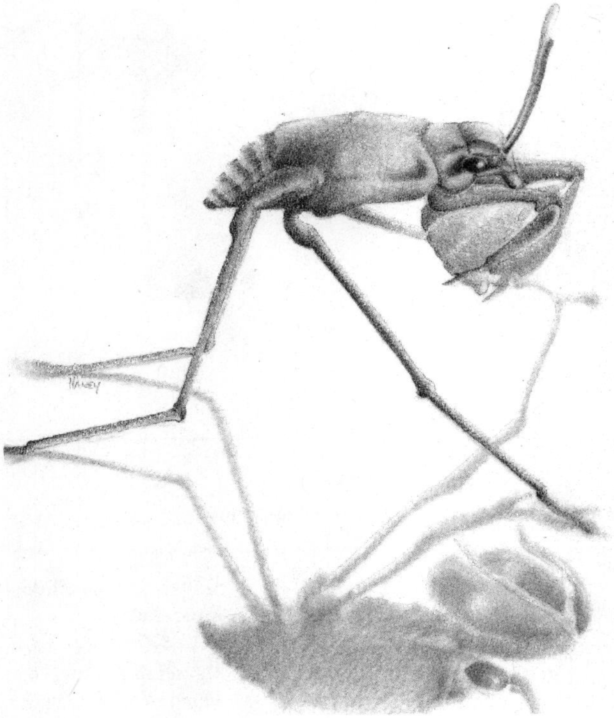

Figure 1.12
A water strider (*Halobates*), one of the few completely marine insects, is supported by the surface tension of seawater.
Redrawn from a photograph by Lana Cheng, Scripps Institution of Oceanography

Viscosity and Surface Tension

Hydrogen bonding between adjacent water molecules within the fluid mass tends to resist external forces that would separate these molecules. This property, known as **viscosity,** has a significant effect on floating and swimming marine organisms. The viscosity of water reduces the sinking tendency of some organisms by increasing the frictional resistance between themselves and nearby water molecules. At the same time, viscosity magnifies problems of drag that actively swimming animals must overcome.

The mutual attraction of water molecules at the surface of a water mass (such as the air-sea boundary) creates a flexible molecular "skin" over the water surface. This, the **surface tension** of water, is sufficiently strong to support the full weight of a water strider (figure 1.12). Both surface tension and viscosity are temperature-dependent, increasing with decreasing temperature.

Density-Temperature Relationships

Most liquids contract and become denser as they cool. The solid form of these substances is denser than the liquid form. The structure of liquid water at low temperatures is not known, but several models have been proposed to explain its behavior. Over most of the temperature range at which pure water is liquid, it behaves like other liquids. At 4° C or above, the **density** increases with decreasing temperature.[1] Below 4° C, the normal density-temperature pattern of pure water reverses. One model suggests that at near-freezing temperatures, less dense icelike clusters consisting of several water molecules form and disintegrate very rapidly within the body of liquid water. As liquid water continues to cool, more clusters form and the clusters survive longer. Eventually

1. The maximum density of pure water is used to define the fundamental metric measurement of mass, the gram. The gram is defined as the mass of pure water at 4° C contained in the volume of one cubic centimeter. Thus the density, the ratio of mass to volume, of pure water at 4° C is 1.000 g/cm^3.

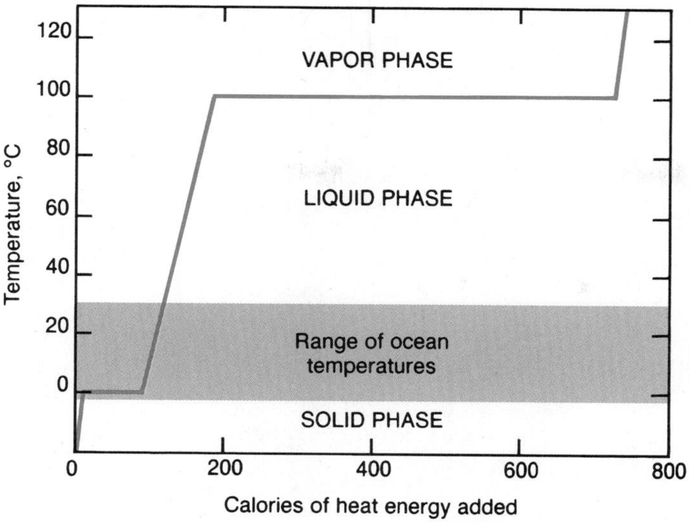

Figure 1.13
The heat energy necessary to cause temperature and phase changes in water

at 0° C, all the water molecules become locked into the rigid crystal lattice of ice. The ice formed is about 8% less dense than liquid water at the same temperature, so ice always floats on liquid water. For living organisms, this is an unusual, but very fortunate, property of water. Without this unique density-temperature relationship, ice would sink as it formed; and lakes, oceans, and other bodies of water would freeze solid from the bottom up. Winter survival for organisms living in such an environment would be very difficult.

Heat Capacity

Heat is a form of energy, the energy of molecular motion. The sun is the source of almost all energy entering the earth's heat budget. At the surface of the sea, radiant energy is converted to heat energy. In the sea, heat is transferred from place to place primarily by **convection** (mixing) and secondarily by **conduction** (molecular exchange of heat). Heat energy is measured in **calories.**[2]

Water has the ability to absorb or give up heat without experiencing a large temperature change. To illustrate the high **heat capacity** of water, imagine a one-gram block of ice at −20° C on a heater that provides heat at a constant rate. Heating the ice from −20° C to 0° C requires 10 calories, or 0.5 calories per degree of temperature increase. However, converting one gram of ice at 0° C to liquid at 0° C requires 80 calories. Conversely, 80 calories of heat must be extracted from one gram of liquid water at 0° C to convert it to ice at the same temperature. This is referred to as the **latent heat of fusion.** Continued heating of the one-gram water sample from 0° C requires one calorie of heat energy for each one degree change in temperature until the boiling point (100° C) is reached. At this point, further temperature increase is halted until all the water is converted to water vapor. For this conversion, 540 calories of heat energy are necessary; this is referred to as the **latent heat of vaporization.** Figure 1.13 summarizes the energy requirements for water temperature changes. The high heat capacity and the large amount of heat required for evaporation enable large bodies of water to resist extreme temperature fluctuations. Heat energy is absorbed slowly by water when the

2. A calorie is a unit of heat energy, defined as the quantity of heat needed to elevate the temperature of 1 g of pure water 1° C.

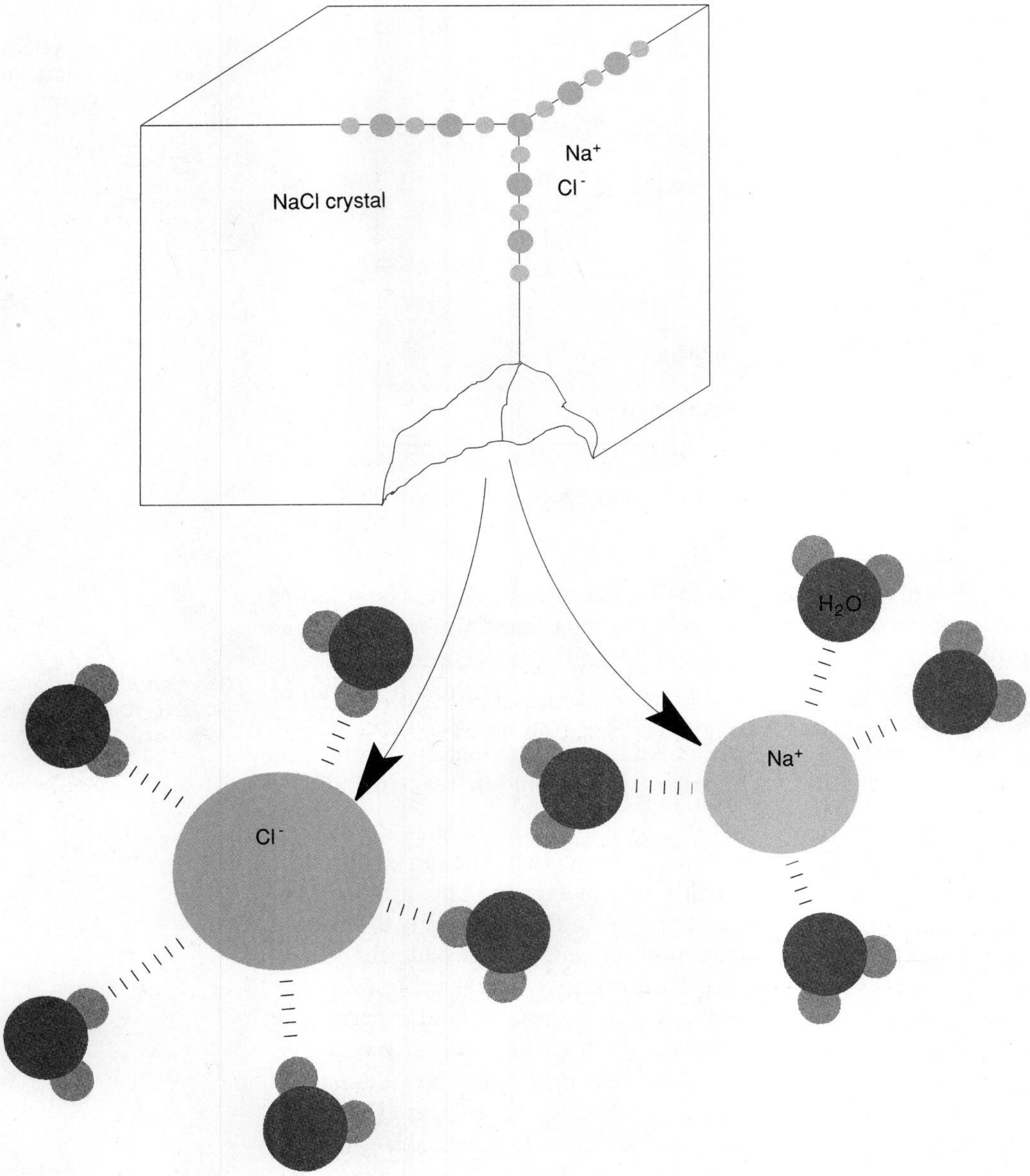

Figure 1.14
A salt crystal (above) and the action of charged water molecules in dissolving the crystal to dissociated Na^+ and Cl^- ions

air above is warmer and is gradually given up when the air is colder. This process provides a temperature-moderating effect for the marine environment and adjacent land areas.

Solvent Action

The small size and polar charges of each water molecule allow it to interact with and dissolve most naturally occurring substances. Crystals held together by **ionic bonds** (bonds between oppositely charged adjacent ions of a crystal, such as salt) are particularly susceptible to the solvent action of water. Figure 1.14 illustrates the process of a salt crystal dissolving in water. Initially, several water molecules form weak H-bonds with each Na^+ and Cl^- ion, and they eventually overcome the mutual attraction of those ions that previously bound

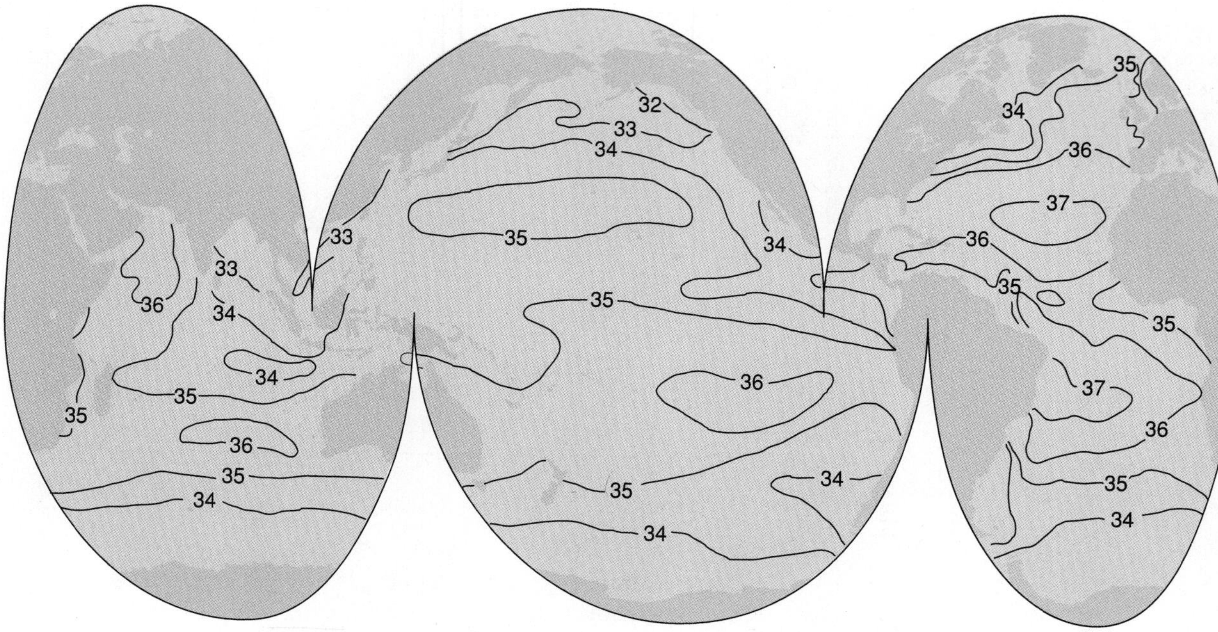

Figure 1.15
Geographic variations of surface ocean salinities, expressed in ‰

them together in the crystalline structure. As more Na^+ and Cl^- ions are removed in this way, the solid crystal structure disintegrates and the salt dissolves. Nonpolar substances like oxygen are generally less soluble in water.

Seawater

Seawater has accumulated during billions of years of eroding action of water on rocks and soil, the breakdown of organisms, and the condensation of rain from atmosphere. About 3.5% of seawater is composed of dissolved compounds from these sources. The other 96.5% is pure water. Traces of all naturally occurring substances probably exist in the ocean and can be separated into three general categories: (1) inorganic substances, usually referred to as salts, including nutrients necessary for plant growth; (2) dissolved gases; and (3) organic compounds derived from living organisms. An adequate discussion of the final category is not within the scope of this text. Organic compounds dissolved in seawater include fats, oils, carbohydrates, vitamins, amino acids, proteins, and other substances. Scientists think that these compounds are an important source of nutrition for marine bacteria and several other types of organisms. Current research indicates that other organic compounds, especially synthetics such as DDT and other chlorinated hydrocarbons that accumulate in seawater, can have devastating effects on some forms of marine life.

Dissolved Salts

Salts account for the majority of dissolved substances in seawater. The total amount of dissolved salts in seawater is referred to as its **salinity,** measured in parts per thousand (‰). Average seawater salinity is approximately 35‰. Salinity values range from nearly zero at river mouths to over 40‰ in some areas of the Red Sea. Yet in open ocean areas away from coastal influences, the salinity varies only slightly over large distances (figure 1.15).

Figure 1.16
Average north-south variation of sea surface evaporation and precipitation

Redrawn by permission of G. Dietrich, 1963, *General Oceanography.* (New York: Interscience Publishers.)

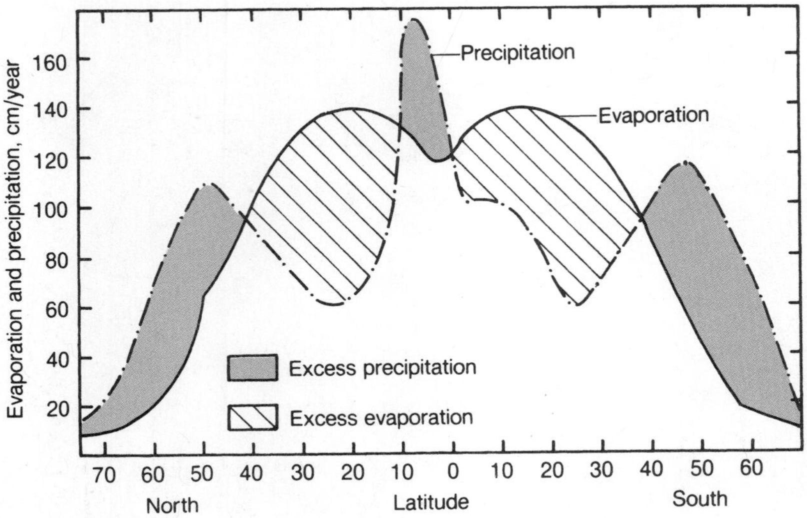

Salinity is altered by processes that add or remove salts or water from the sea. The primary mechanisms of salt and water addition or removal are evaporation, precipitation, river runoff, and the freezing and thawing of sea ice. When evaporation exceeds precipitation, it removes water from the sea surface, thereby concentrating the remaining salts and increasing the salinity. Excess precipitation decreases salinity by diluting the sea salts. Freshwater runoff from rivers has the same effect. Figure 1.16 illustrates the average annual north-south variation of sea surface evaporation and precipitation. The areas with greater evaporation than precipitation (hatched portions of figure 1.16) generally correspond to the high surface-salinity regions shown in figure 1.15. These latitudes also coincide with most of the great land deserts of the world.

When seawater freezes, only the water molecules are incorporated into the developing ice crystal. The dissolved salts are excluded, thus increasing the salinity of the remaining seawater. The process is reversed when ice melts. Freezing and thawing of seawater are usually seasonal phenomena, resulting in little long-term salinity differences.

When dissolved in water, salts dissociate to produce both positively and negatively charged **ions.** For example, table salt (sodium chloride) dissociates to form positively charged sodium ions (Na^+) and negatively charged chloride ions (Cl^-). The more abundant ions found in seawater are listed in table 1.3 and are grouped as major or minor constituents according to their abundance. The major ions account for over 98% of the total salt concentration in seawater. In relation to each other, concentrations of the major ions remain remarkably constant even though their total abundance may differ from place to place.

Seawater is a complete chemical medium for life for it provides all the substances necessary for the growth and maintenance of plant and animal tissue. Magnesium, calcium, bicarbonate, and silicate are important components of the hard skeletal parts of marine organisms. Plants need nitrate and phosphate for the synthesis of organic material. In addition, a vital similarity exists between the chemical composition of seawater and the composition of the body fluids of marine organisms. Most of the more abundant ions enumerated in table 1.3 are important components of the body fluids of all organisms.

Table 1.3
Major and Minor Ions in Seawater of 35‰ Salinity

Ion	Chemical Symbol	Concentration ‰	
Chloride	Cl^-	19.3	Major
Sodium	Na^+	10.6	
Sulfate	SO_4^{-2}	2.7	
Magnesium	Mg^{+2}	1.3	
Calcium	Ca^{+2}	0.4	
Potassium	K^+	0.4	
Bicarbonate	HCO_3^-	0.1	
Bromide	Br^-	0.066	Minor
Borate	H_3BO_3	0.027	
Strontium	Sr^{+2}	0.013	
Fluoride	F^-	0.001	
Silica	$Si(OH)_4$	0.001	
plus traces of other naturally occurring elements			

Marine Temperatures

Temperature, the term we use to measure the condition caused by heat energy, is most commonly recorded in degrees Fahrenheit (°F) or degrees Celsius (°C). It is a universally important factor governing the existence and behavior of living organisms. Life processes cease to function above the boiling point of water and at subfreezing temperatures when the formation of ice crystals disrupts cellular structures. But between these absolute limits, life flourishes.

The high heat capacity of water limits marine temperatures to a much narrower range than land temperatures (figure 1.17). Some marine organisms survive in coastal tropical lagoons at temperatures as high as 40° C. Some bacteria associated with deep-sea hydrothermal vents (figure 7.22 and figure 7.23) experience water temperatures above 60° C. Other deep-sea animals spend their lives in water perpetually less than 0° C. Penguins and a few other birds and mammals well-adapted to extreme cold commonly tolerate air temperatures far below 0° C in polar regions. Penguins even manage to incubate and hatch eggs under these conditions. But these are exceptions; most marine life thrives at water temperatures above 0° and 30° C.

The distribution of various forms of marine life is closely associated with geographical differences in seawater temperatures. Surface ocean temperatures are highest near the equator and decrease toward both poles. This temperature gradient establishes several east-west trending marine climatic zones (figure 1.18). The approximate temperature range of each zone is included in figure 1.17.

Salinity-Temperature-Density Relationships

Seawater density is a function of both temperature and salinity. The density increases with a temperature decrease or a salinity increase. Under normal oceanic conditions, temperature fluctuations exert a greater influence on seawater density because the range of marine temperature values is much greater (−2° C to 30° C) than the range of open-ocean salinities.

Figure 1.17

The range of biologically important temperatures at the earth's surface. The temperature ranges of marine climatic regions are included.

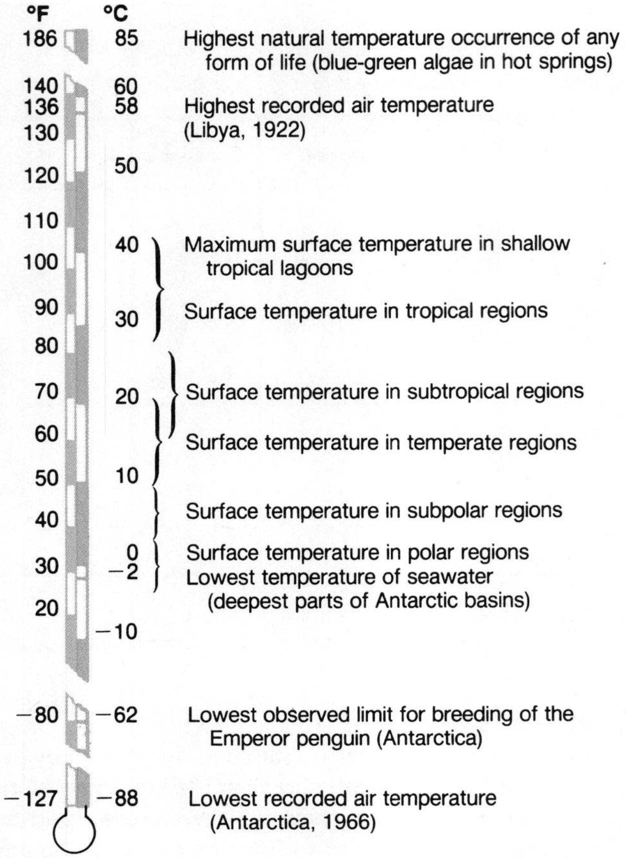

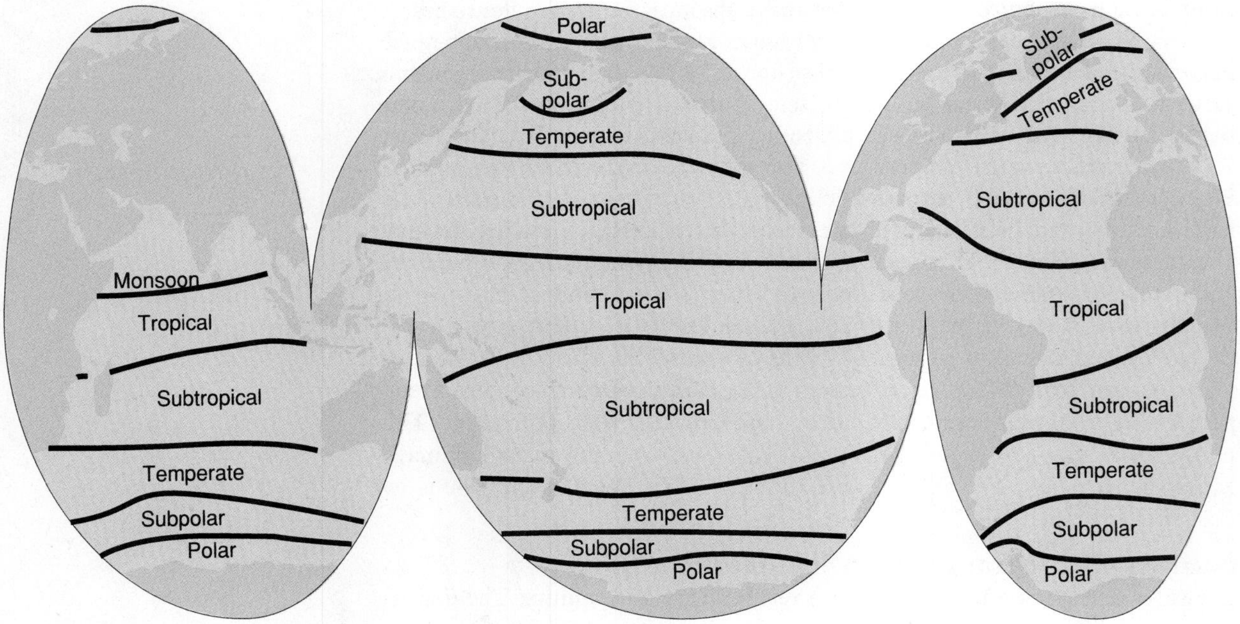

Figure 1.18

Marine climatic zones

Adapted from Bogdanov, 1963

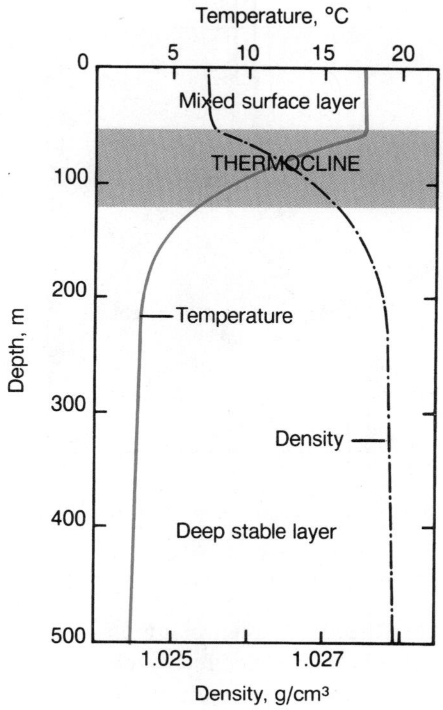

Figure 1.19
Vertical distribution of water temperature and density in 35‰ salinity seawater. The thermocline is the depth range over which temperature and density rapidly change.

Some generalizations can also be made about the vertical distribution of ocean temperature, salinity, and density. The most dense water is found on the bottom; however, the physical processes that create this dense water (evaporation, freezing, or cooling) are strictly ocean surface features. Therefore, dense bottom water must originally sink from the surface. This sinking process is the only mechanism available to drive circulation of water in the deep portions of ocean basins. An obvious feature in most oceans is a **thermocline,** a subsurface zone of very rapid temperature (about 1° c/m) and density change (figure 1.19). The large density differences on either side of the thermocline effectively separates the oceans into a two-layered system: a thin, well-mixed surface layer above the thermocline overlying a heavier, cold, thick, stable zone below. The thermocline inhibits exchange of gases, nutrients, and sometimes even organisms between the two layers. In temperate and polar regions, the thermocline is a seasonal feature. During the winter months, the surface water is cooled to the same low temperature as the deeper water. This causes the thermocline to disappear and allows seasonal mixing between the two layers. Warmer marine climates of the tropics and subtropics are more often characterized by well-developed, permanent thermoclines.

Dissolved Gases and Acid/Base Buffering

The solubility of gases in seawater is a function of temperature. Greater solubility occurs at lower temperatures. Nitrogen, carbon dioxide, and oxygen are the most abundant gases dissolved in seawater. Nitrogen (N_2) is comparatively inert and, therefore, is not involved in the basic life processes of most organisms. (Notable exceptions are some N_2-fixing microorganisms and the occasional careless SCUBA diver who dives too deep for too long.) Carbon dioxide and oxygen, on the other hand, are metabolically very active. Carbon

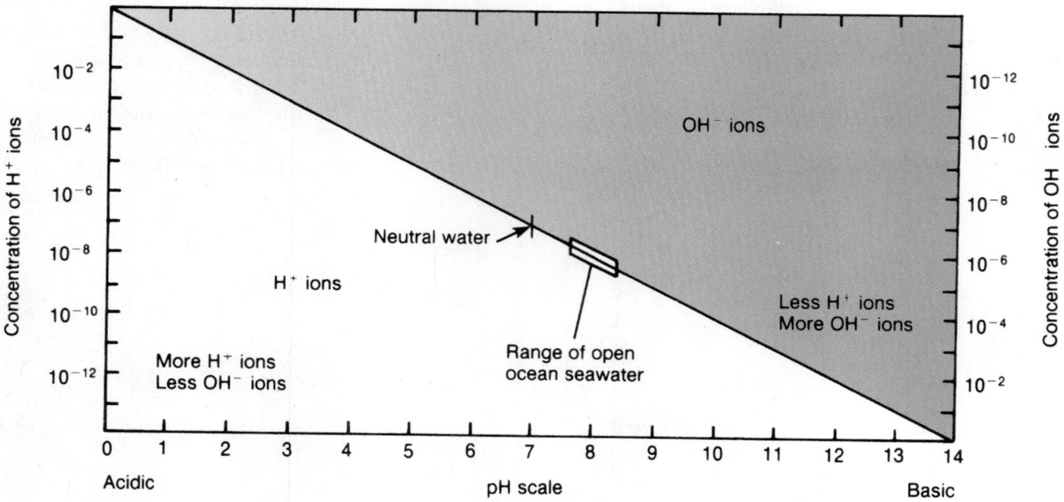

Figure 1.20
The pH scale, showing the concentration of H^+ and OH^- ions at each pH unit, and typical range of open ocean seawater. Note that the concentration scale is exponential.

dioxide and water are utilized by green plants in photosynthesis to produce oxygen and high-energy organic compounds such as carbohydrates and fats. Respiration reverses the results of the photosynthetic process by releasing the usable energy incorporated in the organic components of the organism's food. In contrast to photosynthesis, oxygen is used in respiration, and carbon dioxide is given off.

Carbon dioxide (CO_2) is abundant in most regions of the sea; concentrations too low to support plant growth do not normally occur. Seawater has an unusually large capacity to absorb CO_2 because most dissolved CO_2 does not remain as a gas. Rather, much of the CO_2 combines with water to produce a weak acid, carbonic acid (H_2CO_3). Typically, carbonic acid dissociates to form a hydrogen ion (H^+) and a bicarbonate ion (HCO_3^-) or two H^+ ions and a carbonate ion (CO_3^{-2}). These reactions can be summarized in the following chemical equations:

1. $CO_2 + H_2O \rightleftarrows H_2CO_3$
   carbon dioxide + water ⇄ carbonic acid
2. $H_2CO_3 \rightleftarrows H^+ + HCO_3^-$
   carbonic acid ⇄ hydrogen ion + bicarbonate ion
3. $HCO_3^- \rightleftarrows H^+ + CO_3^{-2}$
   bicarbonate ion ⇄ hydrogen ion + carbonate ion

The arrows pointing in both directions indicate each reaction is reversible, either producing or removing H^+ ions. The abundance of H^+ ions in water solutions controls the acidity or alkalinity of that solution and is measured on a scale of 0 to 14 pH units (figure 1.20). The pH units are a measure of the H^+ ion concentration. Low pHs are very acidic and represent a high H^+ ion concentration. A pH of fourteen is very basic (or alkaline) and denotes

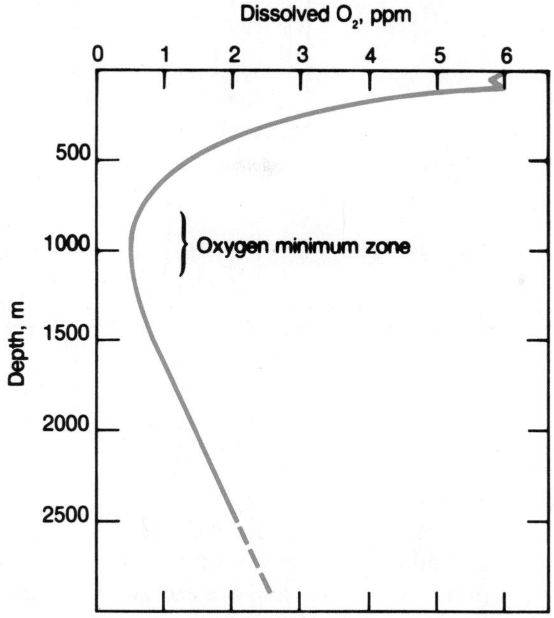

Figure 1.21
Vertical distribution of dissolved O_2 in the North Pacific (150° W, 47° N) during winter
Data from Barkley, 1968

low H^+ ion concentrations. Neutral pH (the pH of pure water) is 7 on the pH scale. The carbonic acid-bicarbonate-carbonate system in seawater functions to **buffer** or to limit changes of seawater pH. If excess H^+ ions are present, the reactions above proceed to the left and the excess H^+ ions are removed from solution. Otherwise, the solution would become more acidic. If too few hydrogen ions are present, more are made available by the conversion of carbonic acid to bicarbonate, and bicarbonate to carbonate. In open-ocean conditions, this buffering system is very effective, limiting ocean water pH values to a range between 7.5 and 8.4. This dynamic system functions as a crucial storage device for accumulating atmospheric CO_2 that is a result of our human activities on land (see box 2.1).

Oxygen in the form of O_2 is necessary for the survival of most organisms. (The major exceptions are some species of anaerobic microorganisms.) The abundance or lack of O_2 in seawater strongly influences the distribution of marine life. Oxygen is utilized by organisms in all areas of the marine environment, including the deepest trenches. However, the transfer of oxygen from the atmosphere to seawater and the production of excess oxygen by photosynthetic marine organisms are the only methods available to introduce oxygen into seawater. Both of these processes are limited to the near-surface region of the ocean. Oxygen consumed near the bottom can only be replaced by oxygen from the surface. If replenishment is not rapid enough, available oxygen supplies may be reduced to critically low concentrations or removed completely. Oxygen replenishment occurs by very slow diffusion processes from the oxygen-rich surface layers downward and also by downward vertical water movements that carry oxygen-enriched waters to deep-ocean basins. At intermediate depths, around 1000 m, animal respiration and bacterial decomposition use O_2 as fast as it is replaced, creating an **O_2 minimum zone.** Figure 1.21 illustrates a vertical profile of dissolved oxygen from the surface to the bottom of the sea.

Figure 1.22
A spectrum of ocean surface waves based on period, generating force, and the relative amount of energy available in each wave type
Adapted from Munk, 1950

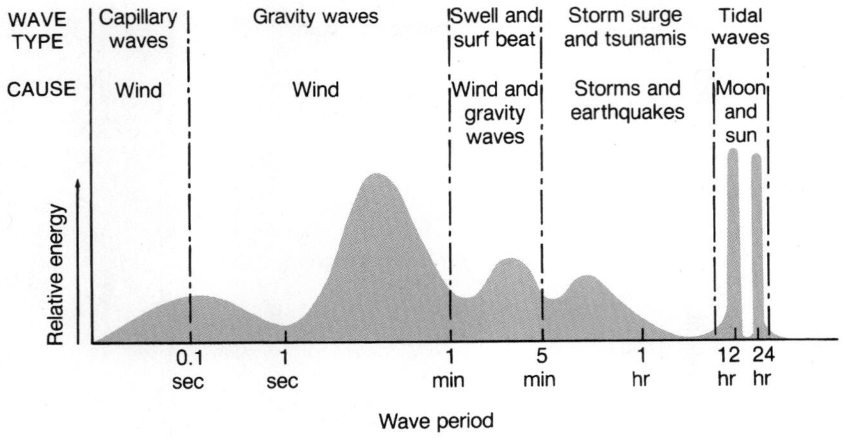

Dissolved Nutrients

Nitrate (NO_3^{-2}) and phosphate (PO_4^{-3}) are the fertilizers of the sea. These and smaller amounts of other nutrients are utilized by photosynthetic organisms living in the near-surface waters and are excreted back into the water at all depths as waste products of the organisms that had consumed the photosynthetic material. This sinking of once living material eventually removes nutrients from near-surface waters and increases their concentrations in deeper waters. (More details concerning these patterns of nutrient distribution appear in chapter 5.)

The vertical distribution of dissolved nutrients is usually opposite that of dissolved oxygen. The opposing patterns of vertical oxygen and nutrient distribution reflect the contrasting biological processes that influence their concentrations in seawater. Oxygen is normally produced by near-surface photosynthesizers and consumed by animals and bacteria, whereas O_2 is consumed and nutrients are excreted by organisms at all depths.

The Ocean in Motion

Ocean water is constantly in motion, providing a near-uniform medium for living organisms. Such motion enhances mixing and minimizes variations in salinity and temperature characteristics. Oceanic circulation processes also serve to disperse swimming and floating organisms and their reproductive products. Toxic body wastes are carried away, while food, nutrients, and essential elements are replenished. Heat from the sun is the driving force behind oceanic circulation processes. These circulation processes, so beneficial to all forms of marine life, are wave action, currents, and vertical water movements. (Tides are considered separately in the intertidal section of chapter 8.)

Waves

Differential solar heating of various regions of the earth's atmosphere produces winds. Winds that blow across the sea surface produce **waves** and **surface currents.** Waves, periodic vertical disturbances of the sea surface, typically travel in a repeating series of alternating wave crests and troughs. The mechanism of energy transfer from the atmosphere to the ocean is not well understood. However, it is known that the size and energy of waves is dependent on

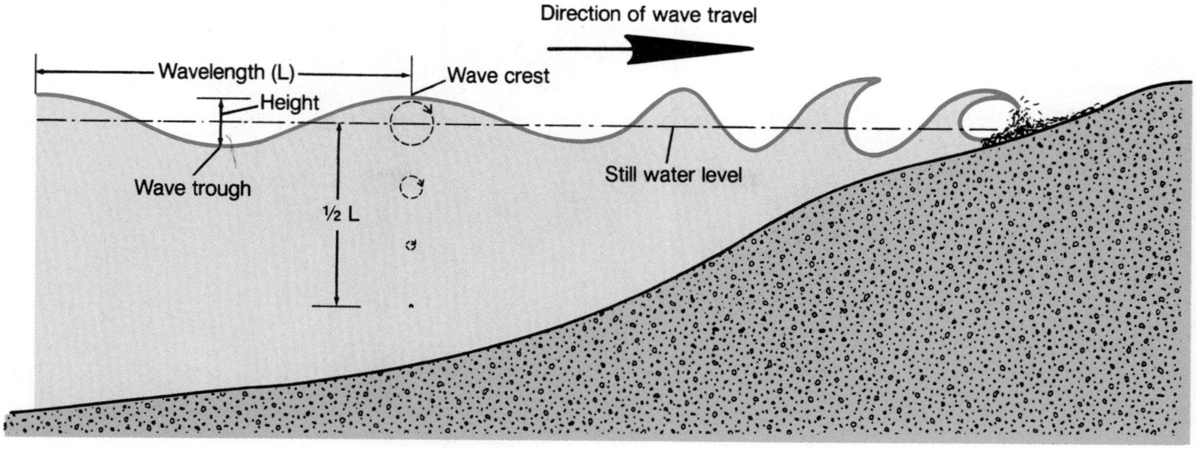

Figure 1.23
Wave form and pattern of water motion in a deepwater wave as it moves to the right in to shore. Circles indicate orbits of water particles diminishing with depth. There is little water motion below the depth of one-half of the wavelength.

the wind's velocity, duration, and **fetch** (the distance over which the wind blows in contact with the sea surface). Ocean waves range in height from a few millimeters for very small capillary waves to over 30 m high for towering storm waves. Waves are commonly characterized by their height, length, and **period** (the time required for two successive wave crests to pass a fixed point). Several types of ocean waves, with their periods, their causes, and their relative amounts of energy, are given in figure 1.22. Regardless of their size, period, or cause, the general features of wave motion apply to all ocean waves.

Once generated, waves move away from the area of formation. However, only the wave shape advances, transmitting the energy forward. The water particles themselves do not advance horizontally. Instead, their paths approximate vertical circles with little or no forward motion (figure 1.23). Waves provide an important mechanism to mix the near-surface layer of the sea. The depth to which waves produce noticeable motion is about one-half the wavelength. As wavelengths seldom exceed 100 m in any ocean, the depth of effective mixing by wind-driven waves is generally no greater than 50 m.

Waves entering shallow water behave differently than open-ocean waves. When the water depth is less than one-half the wavelength, bottom friction begins to slow the forward speed of the waves. This causes the waves to become higher and steeper. At the point where the wave height/wavelength ratio exceeds 1/7, the wave top becomes unstable as they overrun the bottom, and they pitch forward and break. These breaking waves release tremendous amounts of energy on shorelines (and on the organisms living there) and are major forces in shaping the character of the seashore.

Surface Currents

Measurable ocean surface currents occur in regions where winds blow over the ocean with a reasonable constancy of direction and velocity. Unlike wave motion, surface currents represent large-scale horizontal movements of water molecules. Three major wind belts occur in the Northern Hemisphere. The **trade winds,** near 15° N latitude, blow from northeast to southwest. The **westerlies,** in the middle latitudes, blow primarily from the west-southwest. And the **polar easterlies,** at very high latitudes, blow from east to west. Each of these wind belts has its mirror-image counterpart in the Southern Hemisphere.

Figure 1.24
A spiral of current directions, indicating greater deflection to the right (in the Northern Hemisphere), which increases with depth due to the Coriolis effect. Arrow length indicates relative current speed.

Redrawn from H. U. Sverdrup, Martin W. Johnson, and Richard H. Fleming, *The Oceans: Their Physics, Chemistry, and General Biology*, © 1942, renewed 1970. By permission of Prentice-Hall, Inc., Englewood Cliffs, New Jersey.

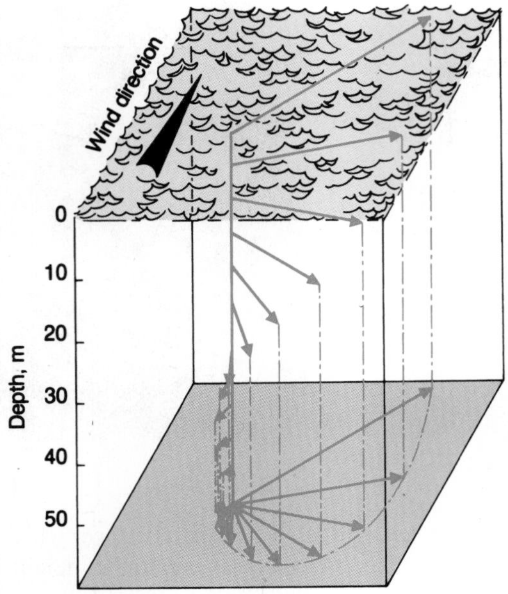

Figure 1.25
Generalized surface-current flow in the North Pacific Ocean. Blue arrows indicate general directions of ocean-surface winds.

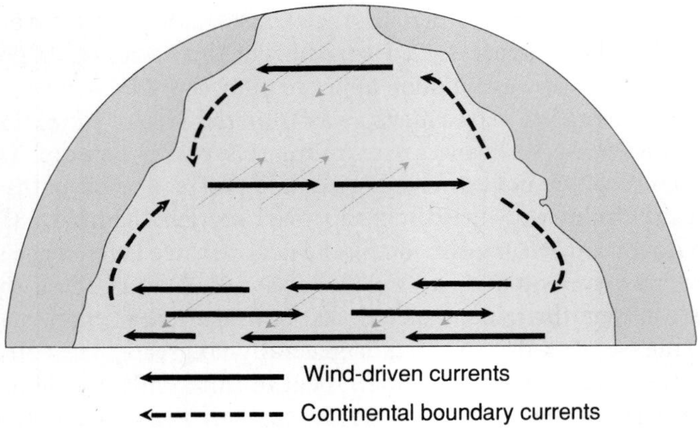

The momentum imparted to the sea by these winds drives regular patterns of broad, slow, relatively shallow ocean surface currents. Some currents transport more than one hundred times the volume of water carried by all of the earth's rivers combined. Currents of such magnitude greatly affect the distribution of marine organisms and the rate of heat transport from tropical regions to polar regions.

As the surface layer of water is forced horizontally by the wind, momentum is transferred downward. The speed of the deeper water steadily diminishes as momentum is lost to overcome the viscosity of the water. Eventually, at depths generally less than 200 m, the speed of wind-driven currents becomes negligible.

The surface water moved by the wind does not flow parallel to the wind direction but experiences an appreciable deflection—a deflection to the right in the Northern Hemisphere and a deflection to the left in the Southern

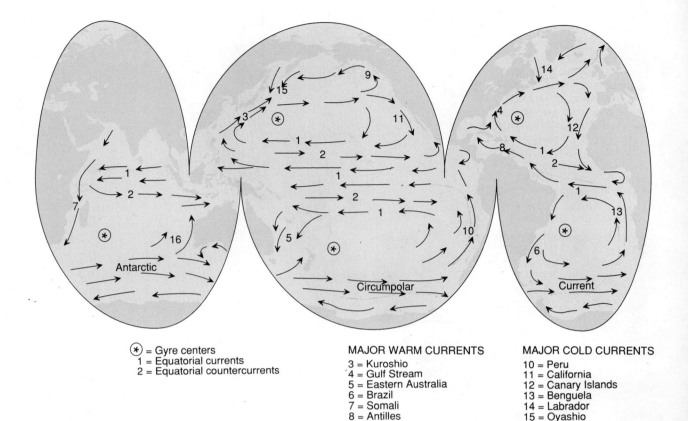

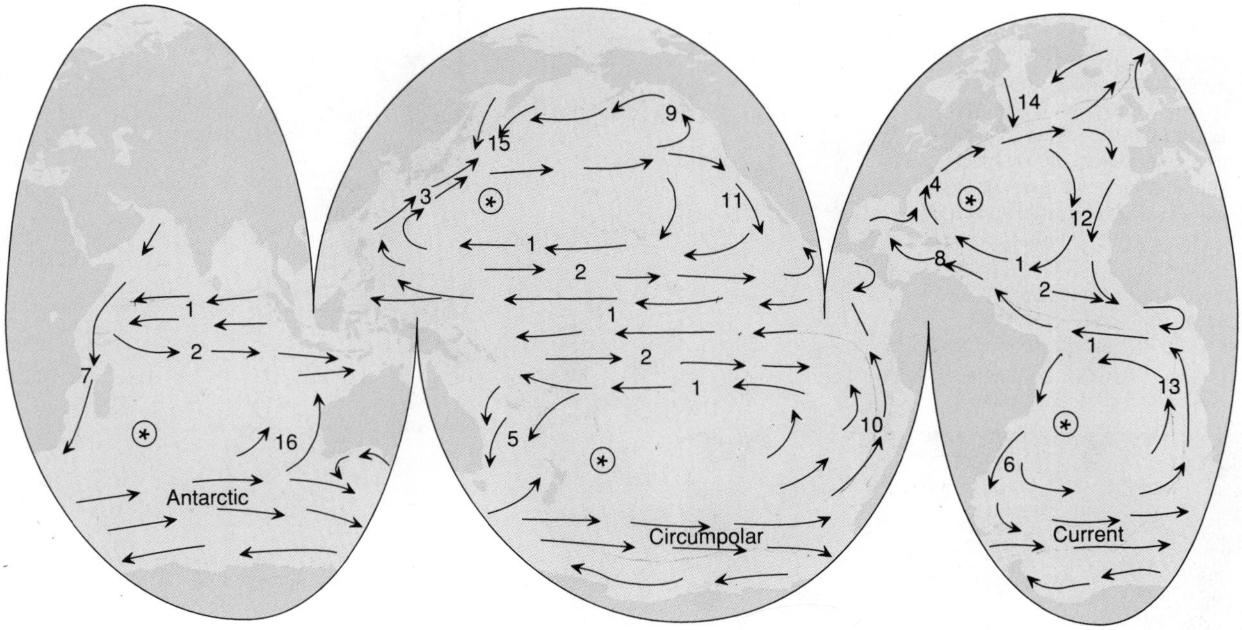

(✱) = Gyre centers
1 = Equatorial currents
2 = Equatorial countercurrents

MAJOR WARM CURRENTS
3 = Kuroshio
4 = Gulf Stream
5 = Eastern Australia
6 = Brazil
7 = Somali
8 = Antilles
9 = Alaska

MAJOR COLD CURRENTS
10 = Peru
11 = California
12 = Canary Islands
13 = Benguela
14 = Labrador
15 = Oyashio
16 = Western Australia

Figure 1.26
The major surface currents of the world ocean
Adapted from Picard and Emory, 1982

Hemisphere. This deflection is known as the **Coriolis effect.** As successively deeper water layers are set into motion by the water above them, they undergo a further Coriolis deflection from the direction of the water above to produce a spiral of current directions from the surface downward (figure 1.24). The magnitude of the Coriolis deflection of wind-driven currents varies from about 15° in shallow coastal regions to nearly 45° in the open ocean. The net Coriolis deflection from the wind headings creates a pattern of wind-forced ocean surface currents that flow primarily in an east-west direction.

Continental masses obstruct the continuous east-west flow of currents. Water transported by these currents is moved from one side of the ocean and accumulates on the other side. The surface of the equatorial Pacific Ocean, for example, is higher on the west side than it is on the east side. The opposite is true in the middle latitudes of both hemispheres, where the east side is higher. Eventually, the water must flow from areas where it has accumulated to regions where it originated. Either the water flows directly back against the established current, producing a **countercurrent,** or it flows as a **continental boundary current** in a north-south direction from areas of accumulation to areas of removal. Both these current patterns exist, but they are especially obvious in the North Pacific (figure 1.25). An east-flowing Equatorial Countercurrent divides the west-flowing North Pacific Equatorial Current. The north-south flowing continental boundary currents connect with the east-west currents to produce large, circulating currents, or **gyres.** Similar current patterns are found in the other major ocean basins (figure 1.26).

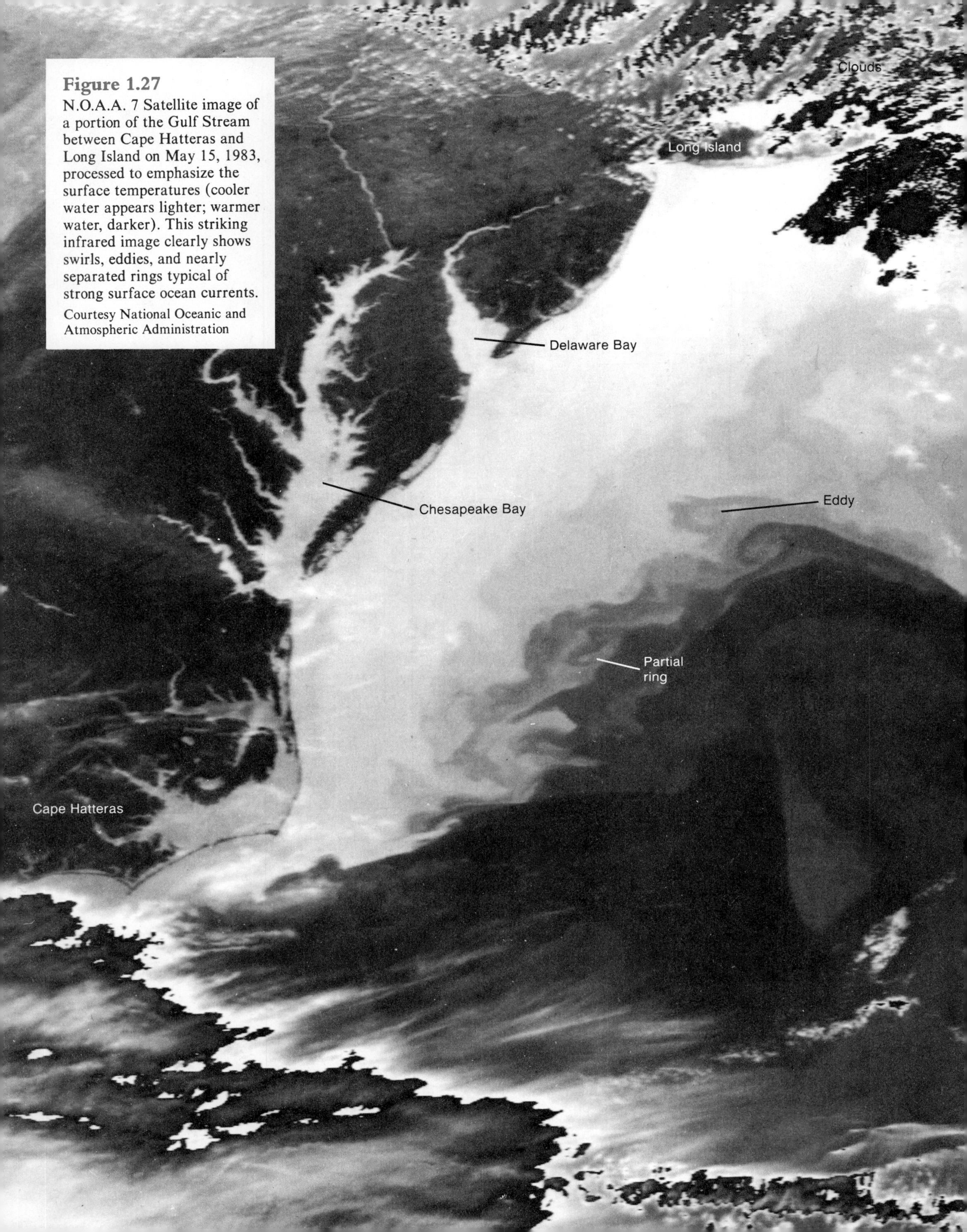

Figure 1.27
N.O.A.A. 7 Satellite image of a portion of the Gulf Stream between Cape Hatteras and Long Island on May 15, 1983, processed to emphasize the surface temperatures (cooler water appears lighter; warmer water, darker). This striking infrared image clearly shows swirls, eddies, and nearly separated rings typical of strong surface ocean currents.
Courtesy National Oceanic and Atmospheric Administration

Maps similar to figure 1.26 are useful for describing long-term average patterns of surface ocean circulation. However, they tend to hide the complexity and even the beauty that exists in these currents at any moment in time. Current maps are analogous to the blurred images taken of a night freeway scene when the camera shutter is held open for hours. The pattern of traffic flow is obvious, yet the details of drivers slowing, accelerating, and changing lanes are completely lost. The recent advent of satellite monitoring of ocean surface phenomena (see box 5.1) has opened a completely new approach for visualizing and understanding global-scale surface current patterns. Figure 1.27 is a satellite image of a portion of the North Atlantic Ocean, including the Gulf Stream. This image emphasizes ocean surface temperature differences and reveals remarkable meanders, constrictions, and nearly detached rings of Gulf Stream water as the current flows north and east along the path shown in figure 1.26.

Several short-term and dramatic departures from the average current patterns shown in figure 1.26 do occur. One departure, El Niño, is characterized by a prominent warming of the equatorial Pacific surface waters. El Niño occurs irregularly every few years, usually around Christmastime (hence the name "El Niño" or "The Child"); each occurrence lasts from several months to over a year. El Niño is associated with the Southern Oscillation, a transpacific linkage of atmospheric pressure systems. Normally, the trade winds blow around the South Pacific high-pressure center located near Easter Island and then blow westward to the large Indonesian low-pressure center. As these winds move water westward, the water is warmed and the thermocline is depressed from about 50 m below the surface on the east side of the Pacific to about 200 m deep on the west side. El Niños occur when this pressure difference across the tropical Pacific relaxes (for reasons not yet known), and both surface winds and ocean currents either cease to flow westward or actually reverse themselves. Although the effects of an El Niño/Southern Oscillation event are somewhat variable, they are often global in extent and occasionally severe in impact. The 1982–1983 event, for example, was associated with heavy floods on the West Coast of the United States, intensification of the drought in sub-Saharan Africa and Australia, and severe hurricane-force storms in Polynesia. Surface ocean water temperatures from Peru to California soared to as much as 8° C above normal. The impact that such severe short-term departures from normal conditions have on local plant and animal populations is considered in chapters 5 and 13.

Vertical Water Movements

Vertical water movements are produced by sinking and upwelling processes. Such processes tend to break down the vertical stratification established by the thermocline. Seawater sinks when its density increases. The physical processes that increase seawater density are strictly surface features. Thus, dense seawater, which is from the surface and usually highly oxygenated, transports dissolved oxygen to deep areas of the ocean basins, areas which would otherwise be **anoxic** (lacking O_2). The chief areas of sinking are located in the colder latitudes where sea surface temperatures are low. Figure 1.28 outlines the general patterns of large-scale deep-ocean circulation. These patterns of water transport are very slow and ill-defined. Time spans of a few hundred to a thousand years are required for water that sinks in the North Atlantic to reach the surface again in the Southern Hemisphere.

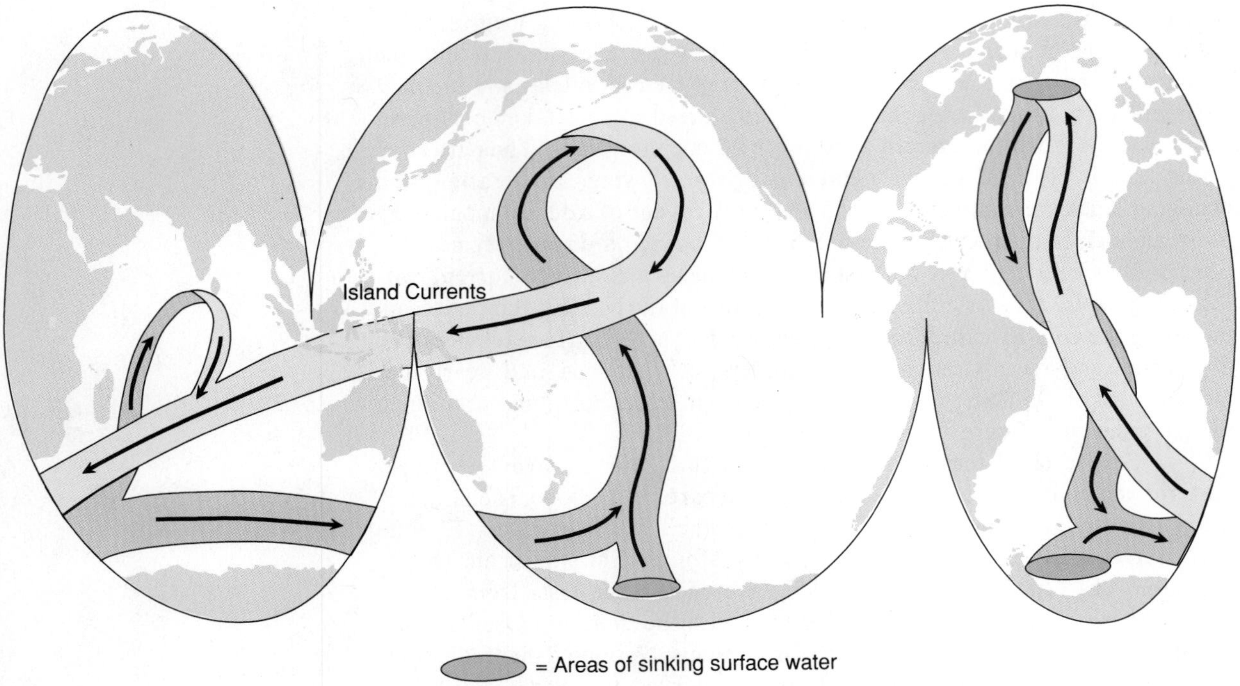

Figure 1.28
The general pattern of deep-ocean circulation in the major ocean basins
Adapted from Broecker et al., 1985

Rising water masses are produced by **upwelling** processes and are considered in chapter 5. Whatever the cause, all upwelling processes bring deeper nutrient-rich waters to the surface. The continuous availability of deep-water nutrients that can be used by photosynthetic organisms accounts for the high productivity characteristic of regions of upwelling. Several of the world's important fisheries are based in upwelling areas.

In the arid climate of the Mediterranean Sea, evaporation from the sea surface greatly exceeds precipitation and runoff. The resulting high-salinity water sinks and fills the deeper parts of the Mediterranean basin. The sinking of surface water provides substantial mixing and O_2 replenishment for the deep water of the Mediterranean and is similar to the deep circulation of the open ocean. Part of this deep, dense water eventually flows out of the Mediterranean over the shallow sill at Gibraltar and down into the Atlantic Ocean. To compensate for the outflow and losses due to evaporation, nearly two million cubic meters of Atlantic surface water flow into the Mediterranean each second. The currents at Gibraltar can be compared to two large rivers flowing in opposite directions, one over the other (figure 1.29).

Like the Mediterranean, the Black Sea is isolated by a shallow sill (at the Bosporus). However, in contrast to the Mediterranean Sea, the Black Sea is characterized by a large excess of precipitation and river runoff. The dilute surface waters form a shallow, low density layer that does not mix with the higher salinity, denser water below but, instead, flows into the Mediterranean Sea through the Bosporus (figure 1.29). For all practical purposes, the water below 150 m in the Black Sea is stagnant. Low salinity, oxygen-rich surface water does not sink, so the more common oxygen-dependent forms of marine life are restricted to the uppermost layer. But the anoxic deep waters

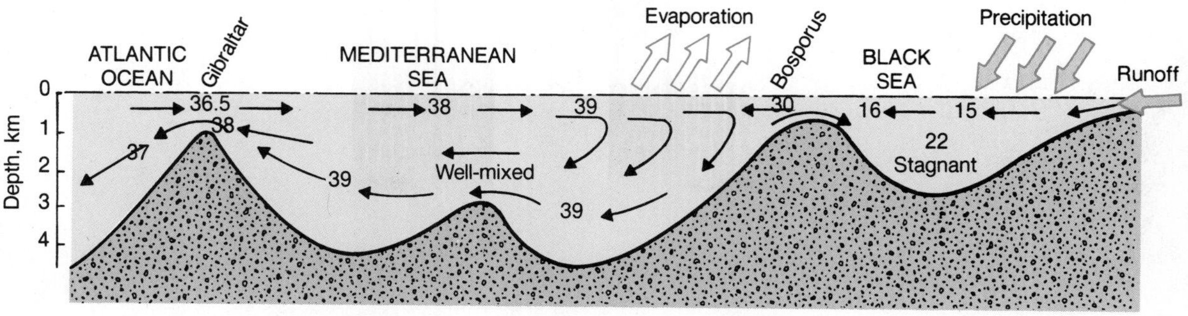

Figure 1.29
A comparison of the deep-ocean circulation patterns of two marginal seas, the Mediterranean Sea and the Black Sea. The numbers represent salinity (°/₀₀).

of the Black Sea (over 80% of its volume) are by no means lifeless. The rain of organic remains from above accumulates and provides abundant nourishment for numerous types of anaerobic bacteria. These bacteria exist without O_2 and in turn produce hydrogen sulfide (H_2S), which is toxic to other forms of life. Thus, the lack of deep circulation in the Black Sea limits the input of O_2 and allows the buildup of nutrients and H_2S. In this sense, the circulation of the Black Sea resembles that of some enclosed **fjords** of Scandinavia and the west coast of Canada.

Classification of the Marine Environment

The size and complexity of the marine environment make it a difficult system to classify conveniently. Many systems of classification have been proposed, each reflecting the interest and bias of the classifier. The system presented here is a slightly modified version of a widely accepted scheme proposed by Hedgpeth. The terms used in figure 1.30 designate particular zones of the marine environment; these terms should not be confused with the names of groups of organisms that normally inhabit these zones. The boundaries of these zones are defined on the basis of physical characteristics such as water temperature, water depth, and available light.

The limits of the splash and intertidal zones are defined by tidal fluctuations of sea level along the shoreline. These zones and their inhabitants are examined in detail in chapters 3 and 8. The splash, intertidal, and inner shelf zones occur in the **photic** (lighted) **zone** where the light intensity is great enough to accommodate photosynthesis. The depth of the photic zone is highly variable and depends on conditions that affect light penetration in water. As a result, the photic zone extends much deeper in clear, tropical waters than in murky, coastal waters of temperate areas. The average depth of the photic zone is 50–100 m. The remaining zones are located in the **aphotic** (unlighted) **zone** where the absence of sunlight prohibits photosynthesis.

The **benthic division** refers to the environment of the sea bottom. The portion of the continental shelf below the photic zone is the outer shelf. The bathyal zone is approximately equivalent to the continental slope areas. The abyssal zone refers to abyssal plains and other ocean bottom areas between 3000 and 6000 m in depth. The upper boundary of this zone is sometimes defined as the region where the water temperature never exceeds 4° C. The hadal zone is that part of the ocean bottom below 6000 m, primarily the trench areas.

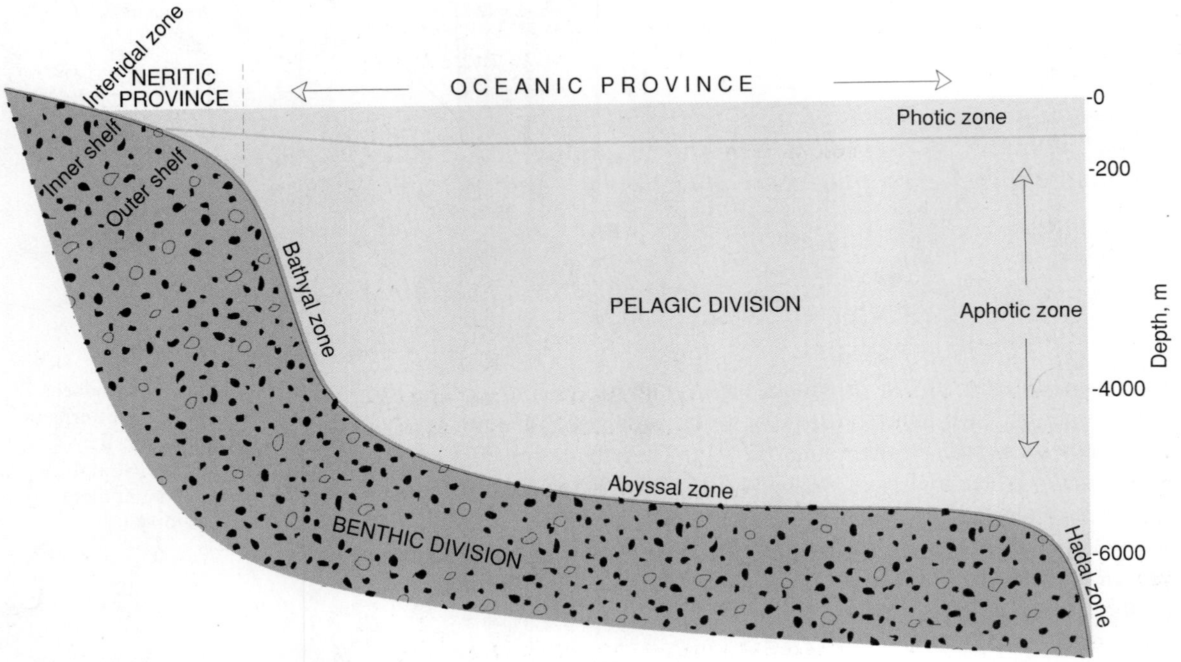

Figure 1.30
A system for classifying the marine environment
Adapted from Hedgpeth, 1957

The **pelagic division** includes the entire water mass of the ocean. For our purposes, it will be sufficient to separate the pelagic region into two provinces: the **neuritic province,** which includes the water over the continental shelves, and the **oceanic province,** which includes the water that overlies the deep ocean basins.

Each of these subdivisions of the ocean environment is inhabited by characteristic assemblages of marine organisms. It is these organisms and their interactions with their immediate surroundings that are the subject of this book.

Summary

The world ocean is a large interconnected body of seawater separated by continents into several ocean basins and marginal seas. The sizes and shapes of the ocean basins as well as their seawater contents are the consequences of a long history of geological processes, including vulcanism, seafloor spreading and plate tectonics, and extensive continental glaciation.

The unusual characteristics of water itself determine most of the basic properties of seawater. The asymmetrical shape of a water molecule creates an electrical charge separation that initiates hydrogen-bonding interactions with adjacent water molecules. Hydrogen bonding, in turn, affects water's basic properties, including viscosity, surface tension, heat capacity, solvent capability, density-temperature relationships, and its stability as a liquid.

Seawater contains, in solution, a variety of salts, gases, and other substances. These dissolved substances affect the density of seawater, its osmotic properties, buffering capacity, and other biologically significant features. This water is constantly in motion, mixed and moved by winds, waves, currents, sinking water masses, and upwelling. The driving force behind these mixing processes is heat from the sun.

The marine environment can be separated into two broad units, the benthic and pelagic divisions. These in turn may be subdivided into smaller, more convenient categories based on water depth, light availability, and tidal exposure.

Review Questions

1. List the processes that occur when ice forms on seawater. Explain why these processes, once initiated, tend to establish conditions that resist further freezing.
2. How are the surface currents of the North Atlantic similar to those of the South Atlantic? In what major way do they differ?
3. A bottle is tossed into the ocean off the northern coast of Peru. Three years later the bottle is recovered on a beach in Norway. Describe the bottle's most likely path from Peru to Norway, assuming it was transported solely by ocean surface currents. Do any other reasonable routes exist?
4. List the two most abundant ions and gases dissolved in seawater.
5. List four major causes of salinity variation in seawater.
6. List three properties of seawater which change with salinity variations, and indicate how those properties change as the salinity *increases*.
7. Name the four continents that border the Indian Ocean.
8. List the names of two major *cold* surface currents found in the North Pacific Ocean and in the North Atlantic Ocean.

Questions for Further Discussion

1. Describe why surface ocean-water temperatures vary less from season to season than do air temperatures over nearby land masses.
2. Explain why both latitude and longitude are necessary to fix the position of any location on the earth's surface.
3. List and describe the major physical and chemical features of seawater that change markedly from the sea surface downward. How do these same features change along the sea surface as one proceeds from the equator north or south to higher latitudes?

Suggestions for Further Reading

Books

Borgese, E., and N. Ginsburg, eds. 1985. *The ocean yearbook.* Chicago: University of Chicago Press.

Cloud, P. 1989. *Oasis in space: Earth history from the beginning.* New York: W. W. Norton.

Duxbury, A. C., and A. B. Duxbury. 1991. *An introduction to the world's oceans.* Dubuque, IA: Wm. C. Brown Publishing.

Elton, L. R. B., and H. Messel. 1979. *Time and man.* New York: Pergamon Press.

Open University. 1989. *Seawater: Its composition, properties, and behavior.* Oxford, England: Pergamon Press.

———. 1989. *The ocean basins: Their structure and evolution.* Oxford, England: Pergamon Press.

———. 1989. *Waves, tides, and shallow water processes.* Oxford, England: Pergamon Press.

Rand McNally. 1987. *The Rand McNally atlas of the oceans.* Chicago: Rand McNally.

Articles

Armi, L. 1978. Mixing in the deep ocean—The importance of boundaries. *Oceanus* 21(3):14–19.

Ben-Avraham, Z. 1981. The movement of continents. *American Scientist* 69:291–99.

Bonati, E. 1987. The rifting of continents. *Scientific American* 256(3):97–103.

Broecker, W. S. 1983. The ocean. *Scientific American* 249 (September):146–60.

Bryan, K. 1978. The ocean heat balance. *Oceanus* 21(3):18–26.

Cloud, P. 1980. Beyond plate tectonics. *American Scientist* 68:381–87.

Edmond, J. M. 1982. Ocean hot springs. *Oceanus* 25(2):22–27.

MacIntyre, F. 1970. Why the sea is salt. *Scientific American,* 223 (November):104–15.

McDonald, J. E. 1970. The Coriolis effect. *Scientific American* 222 (May):72–76.

Vink, G. E., W. Morgan, and P. Vogt. 1985. The earth's hot spots. *Scientific American* 252(4):50–57.

Webster, P. J. 1981. Monsoons. *Scientific American* 244 (February):108–18.

Whitworth, III, T. 1988. The Antarctic circumpolar current. *Oceanus* 31(2):53–58.

Wiebe, P. T. 1982. Rings of the Gulf Stream. *Scientific American* 246 (March):60–70.

Wilson, W. S. 1981. Oceanography from satellites? *Oceanus* 24(3):9–16.

Some Ecological and Biological Concepts

Chapter 2

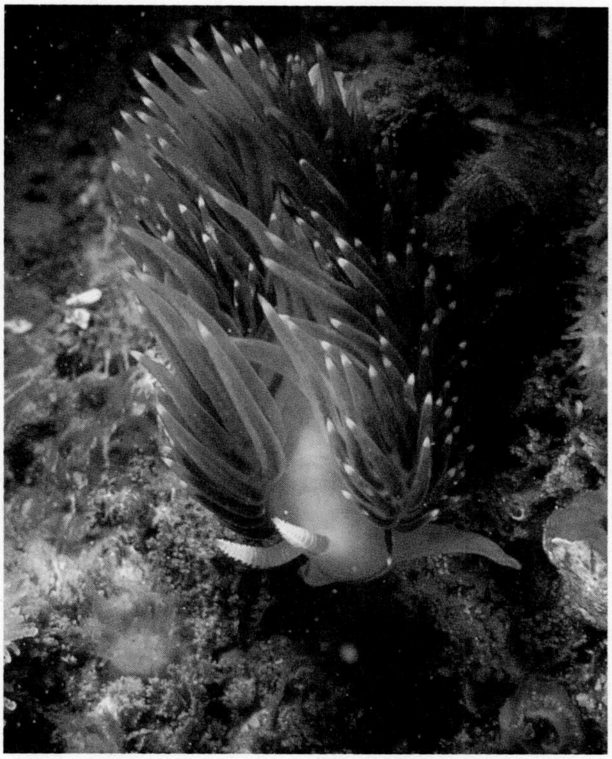

A nudibranch
Photo by T. Phillipp

Figure 2.1
Electron micrograph of a bacterial cell, *Bacillus* (cell wall, CW; the mesosome, M; nucleoid, N; poly-β-hydroxybutyrate inclusion body, PHB; plasma membrane, PM; and ribosomes, R).
Courtesy © Ralph A. Slepecky/Visuals Unlimited

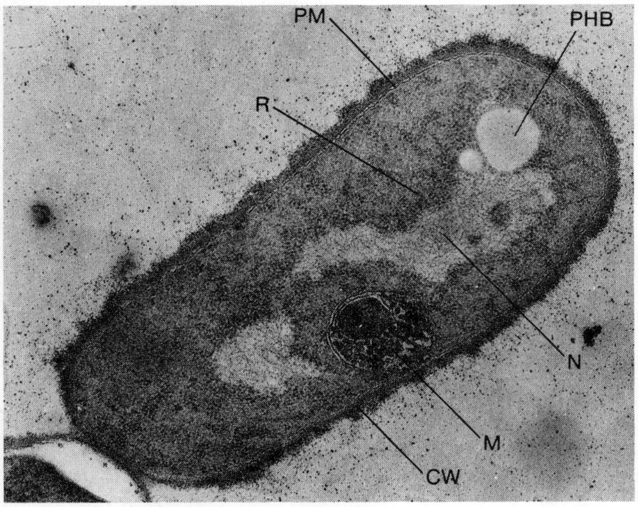

Life is a special phenomenon. We observe, dissect, analyze, and discuss it. We can characterize the attributes of life and can state with a good deal of authority how living systems work. Yet, life remains a difficult term to define. Life forms require energy to break down and resynthesize complex chemical substances. These materials and energy are used by all life forms to accomplish the four *Rs* of living:

Respiration: To obtain, with a series of enzyme-controlled chemical reactions, usable energy from complex high-energy molecules.
Reproduction: To transfer genes to subsequent generations.
Response: To react to and interact with stimuli from their surroundings.
Regulation: To control the exchange of materials between internal and external environments while maintaining a level of constancy in their organized internal environment.

How marine organisms accomplish these life requirements is the recurrent theme of this book.

The Cellular Structure of Life

Living organisms are modular: They are composed of a single cell or a complex assemblage of specialized cells. Fossil evidence of complex life forms older than 600 million years is not abundant. Even so, fossil remains of simple cells over 3 billion years old have been reported from scattered sites in Africa and Australia. These microscopic organisms achieved a level of structural organization strikingly similar to some modern bacteria. Like modern bacteria and cyanobacteria (figure 2.1), these early life forms lacked much of the complex subcellular structure found in other modern cells. Yet, they presumably contained the necessary complement of cellular machinery needed to function as living cells. A **cell wall** provides form and mechanical support for the cell. Inside the cell wall, a selectively permeable **plasma membrane** separates the internal fluid environment (the **cytoplasm**) from the exterior environment of the cell and regulates exchange between the cell and its external medium, with limited movement provided by a whiplike **flagellum.** Internally, the genetic

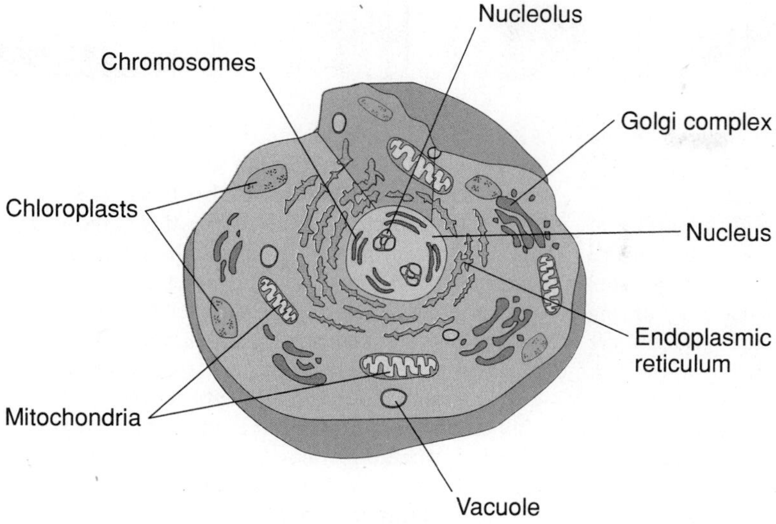

Figure 2.2
Simplified diagram of a eucaryotic cell. In addition to several types of subcellular organelles common to most eucaryotes, photosynthetic cells contain chloroplasts and are typically supported by external cell walls.

information is coded and stored in a single, looped **chromosome.** Small ribosomes use that information to direct the synthesis of enzymes. The enzymes, in turn, control and regulate all other chemical reactions that occur in living cells.

The structurally simple bacteria and cyanobacteria (the **procaryotes)** have been eclipsed in most environments by groups of relatively large and ecologically dominant organisms, the **eucaryotes.** The complexity and diversity of eucaryotic cells are responsible for most of the immense variety of life forms on earth today.

With additional energy to expend, larger cells with increased structural complexity and greater stability evolved. These eucaryotic cells possess a membrane-bound **nucleus.** (Bacteria and cyanobacteria lack a true nucleus and are termed procaryotic cells). Eucaryotic cells are generally larger than procaryotes and house a variety of membrane-bound structures (figure 2.2) not found in procaryotes (figure 2.1).

The chromosomes and their surrounding **nuclear membrane** form a central structure, the nucleus. The enzymes involved in respiration and energy release are associated with numerous small **mitochondria.** Many of the enzyme-synthesizing ribosomes are free in the cyotplasm, but others organize on a membranous **endoplasmic reticulum.** Food particles are ingested through **pinocytosic channels** and stored in **vacuoles** within the cell. Other subcellular structures are involved in excretion of wastes, osmotic balance, and other cellular chores. In addition, photosynthetic eucaryotes typically possess two special features: (1) **chloroplasts** serve as the sites of photosynthesis, and (2) a rigid cell wall provides shape and support in a manner similar to procaryotic cell walls.

From the basic module of the cell, organisms of greater size and organizational complexity have evolved. Yet each level of organization within any living system is derived from one or more components smaller and less complex than itself. Table 2.1 lists and defines some common levels of organization found in living systems.

Box 2 *Our Planetary Greenhouse*

In the past decade, a consensus has emerged among most atmospheric scientists that an increase of atmospheric greenhouse gases will cause (or has already initiated) a general global warming of the surface of our planet. The average temperature of the earth's surface is maintained at its present temperature by a finely tuned global heat engine. About half of the solar energy hitting our upper atmosphere penetrates to the earth's surface where it is converted to heat energy as it is absorbed by water, vegetation, soil, and human structures. If the average temperature of the earth's surface is to remain stable, an equal amount of heat energy must be reradiated from the earth's surface back into space.

Heat energy, however, radiates at longer wavelengths than does incoming visible light, and some atmospheric gases are more transparent to visible light than they are to radiated heat. These atmospheric greenhouse gases (especially water vapor, CO_2, methane, and ozone) serve as a natural part of the global heat budget system by trapping heat near the earth's surface and keeping most of our solar-powered planet well above the freezing temperature of water. Why then is the greenhouse effect considered a problem? We have, since the beginning of the Industrial Revolution, begun to enhance the greenhouse effect by substantially increasing the concentrations of natural greenhouse gases in our atmosphere. Fossil fuel combustion and devegetation of land surfaces (especially burning of tropical rain forests, clear-cutting of temperate forests, and urban development) appear to be the main sources of CO_2. Within the next century, a doubling of preindustrial levels of this gas is a virtual certainty and substantial amounts of industrially produced chlorofluorocarbons (CFCs, another greenhouse gas commonly used in aerosol products and refrigerants) will also make their way into the atmosphere.

What is not yet certain is what effect these greenhouse gases will have on planetary temperatures and ultimately on climate. The most likely eventual response of our climate to increased concentrations of greenhouse gases is a general, long-term global warming, causing deserts to expand, continental ice caps to partially melt, and the sea level to rise. However, the magnitude and geographical distribution of such a warming trend cannot be predicted with confidence using current climate prediction models. We cannot know whether a particular climatic event, such as the 1988 United States midwestern drought, is part of a global warming trend or merely a fluctuation of normal climatic cycles (see box 5.2); but these models do suggest that major droughts will occur more frequently and in more areas over the next several decades.

One reason for the uncertainty of predictions from the best available climate models is the role of the world ocean in both global heat and carbon budgets. Seawater has a high heat capacity, and the temperature of the water filling the deep-ocean basins is substantially lower than surface water temperatures. Can the deep sea serve as an effective sink for excess heat from the surface? One difficulty in understanding the processes governing heat transfer from air to water is the difference in time scales; days or weeks for the atmosphere are years or centuries for the ocean. Any temperature response by the ocean to increased atmospheric temperatures may be too slow to moderate rising earth surface temperatures. Other complications also exist. As water warms, it expands. This thermal expansion of the world ocean could cause average sea level to rise as much as 1m for each 1° C increase in temperature and cause significant worldwide changes in the present pattern of human occupation of low-lying coastal plains.

The world ocean is also a CO_2 sink; it already contains more than fifty times as much CO_2 as the atmosphere and 20 times as much CO_2 as earth's total biosphere. Several features of the ocean govern its capacity to absorb and hold CO_2. First, the rate of vertical circulation and mixing limits the direct exchange of CO_2 between the atmosphere and the ocean. Once in seawater, solubility of CO_2 is much greater than that of other atmospheric gases because it reacts with water to form carbonate and bicarbonate ions (see figure 1.14). In addition, there exists a biological "carbon pump" of organisms that absorb carbonate in surface waters and make hard skeletons of it; these skeletons rapidly sink to the deep seafloor. These features make it exceptionally difficult to accurately predict the behavior of CO_2 exchange between the atmosphere and the world ocean. It is known that only half as much CO_2 as was expected from present rates of industrial emissions is accumulating in the atmosphere. The oceans may be the sink for the missing CO_2.

Some atmospheric pollutants have other effects that further confuse the global greenhouse picture. As CFCs are sprayed from aerosol containers or slowly leak from refrigerating units, they rise to the upper atmosphere, 10–50 km high, where they react photochemically with atmospheric ozone. This thin ozone layer shields the earth from the biologically damaging effects of solar ultraviolet radiation. As the CFCs combine with ozone molecules (O_3), they convert ozone to molecules of oxygen (O_2) and free oxygen atoms, allowing more ultraviolet radiation to penetrate the atmosphere and reach the earth's surface.

In addition to its well-known effects on human skin, ultraviolet radiation inhibits photosynthesis in some near-surface phytoplankton. CFC-induced decreases in strato-

Box 2 *Our Planetary Greenhouse*

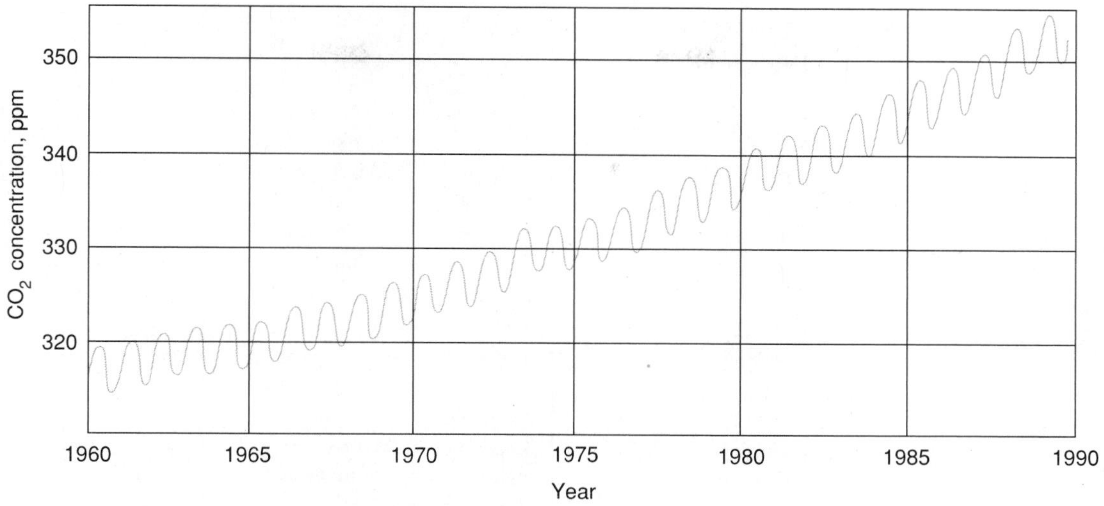

spheric ozone are also being detected. Decreases in the Northern Hemisphere between 1969 and 1986 averaged 0% to 1.9% in the summer months and 2.3% to 6.2% in the winter months. In the Southern Hemisphere, depletions ranged from 2% to 10.6%. The greatest depletion was observed in Antarctica, where the ozone depletion reached 50%. With this trend continuing, global declines in the ozone layer may seriously affect marine ecosystems. Some studies predict that even a 1% decrease in ozone will cause an increase in ultraviolet radiation and a measurable decline in phytoplankton production. Other deleterious effects such as altered community patterns of predation, competition, and diversity may occur as production decreases and species resistant to ultraviolet radiation replace more sensitive species.

Adaptations of Marine Life

All living organisms exhibit varying capabilities for both **ecological** and **evolutionary adaptations** to changing conditions. Ecological adaptations occur within one's lifetime, are accomplished by individuals, and sometimes show immediate results. Evolutionary adaptations are products of the changing response of a population of individuals over many generations. The ultimate effect of ecological adaptations is the ability of individuals to secure sufficient resources so they might survive until they successfully reproduce. By the simplest of definitions, to reproduce successfully means only that an organism must replace itself with an offspring also capable of reproducing successfully (by the same definition).

Most natural populations are characterized by reproductive potentials that exceed those needed to maintain the population size and that are in excess of the number their habitat can support. Eventually, expanding populations outgrow their necessary resources, and competition between individual members of the population intensifies. An individual's ability to survive and

Table 2.1
Levels of Organization in Living Systems.*

Level of Organization	Definition	Examples
Ecosystem	The organisms of a particular type of area and the physical features of the environment in which they live	Coral reef ecosystem
Community	An ecologically integrated group consisting of all the populations living in a given, limited area	Coral reef lagoon
Population	A group of interbreeding organisms coexisting in the same time and place	Barracuda school
Organism	An individual structure of one or more cells capable of reproduction and mutation	Barracuda
Organ	A specific body part consisting of several tissues performing as an identifiable, functional unit	Heart, intestine
Tissue	An aggregation of similar cells, usually with a specific function	Muscle tissue, fatty tissue
Cell	The fundamental organizational unit of living material	Muscle cell, nerve cell
Cellular organelle	A well-defined structure within a cell	Mitochondrion, nucleus
Macromolecule	A very large molecule consisting of numerous simple molecules linked together	Proteins, carbohydrates
Simple molecule	A small chemical unit consisting of two or more atoms bonded together	Amino acids, sugars
Atom	The smallest unit of an element; not divisible by ordinary chemical procedures	C, H, O

*The living systems are listed from the most complex systems to the least complex systems. Each level is composed of numerous units from one or more levels below it.

reproduce is affected by its genetic and physical uniqueness. Natural conditions cause many to perish before reaching sexual maturity. Only those better equipped to compete and survive succeed in passing on their genetic traits to future generations.

The offspring inherit characteristics that, in turn, provide an improved ability to compete and survive. This improved fitness may result from an increased resistance to disease, starvation, or climatic variations; or it may be simply a capacity to reproduce faster. This competition and differential survival is summarized in the overworked phrase "survival of the fittest." However, the rules and conditions for survival change continuously and unpredictably. The selection factor for one generation might be a food shortage, for the next generation, disease. As a result, "survival of the fitter" might be a more appropriate phrase, for organisms seldom evolve to perfectly fit their total environment.

The basic biological units of evolutionary adaptation, then, are populations. Evolutionary adaptation occurs only in populations, never in individuals. Individuals perish regardless of whether or not their populations evolve. When populations cease to adapt and change, extinction becomes inevitable. Of the millions of types of organisms that have evolved in the past 3 billion years of life's history on earth, only a tiny fraction exist today. These are the temporary victors.

In the sea, these winners perpetually confront fluctuations in temperature, salinity, available oxygen, light, and food, as well as attempts by their neighbors to crowd them out or consume them. This chapter examines a few general strategies exhibited by marine organisms for coping with such stresses. In day-to-day ecological time, these stresses mold the structures of communities and ecosystems. Over much longer periods of time, they shape the evolutionary destiny of the affected populations. Ecological adaptations can be reduced to the following three general categories:

1. Adaptations to accommodate the physical environment
2. Adaptations to secure food and avoid being eaten
3. Adaptations to ensure successful reproduction.

An organism's (or population's) success in the first two categories ultimately reflects its capacity to reproduce and endure. This section provides a few examples of strategies to deal with the physical environment and with problems related to nutrition. Other chapters will introduce additional strategies. Finally, successful reproduction strategies are so varied and so specific to individual groups that their discussion is placed with the chapters or sections dealing with other aspects of the biology of those groups. However, this chapter will discuss a few important generalizations regarding reproduction.

The Value of Sex

Although we often refer to reproduction as the process by which we replicate ourselves from one generation to the next, it also can be described as the process by which sets of genes are transferred through generations of organisms. Organisms that reproduce **asexually** (figure 2.3) copy themselves; the products of their reproductive efforts are genetically identical to each other and to their parent. However, it is not accurate to say that sexually reproducing organisms produce replicates of themselves. In fact, the whole point of **sexual reproduction** is to provide a mechanism whereby diverse offspring can be produced by the same parents. The offspring of sexually reproducing parents may coexist better where resources are variable than will the progeny of asexual reproducers simply because offspring of sexual parents are different. They have different resource needs, and competition between individuals for the resources is less severe than it would be between genetically identical offspring. Therefore, the relative advantage for sexual versus asexual reproduction is a function of the resources available to the reproducing population and the size of the population. In small populations (less than one million individuals), the costs of sexual reproduction begin to outweigh the advantages, and asexual reproduction becomes the more advantageous method.

Figure 2.3
Four approaches to asexual reproduction

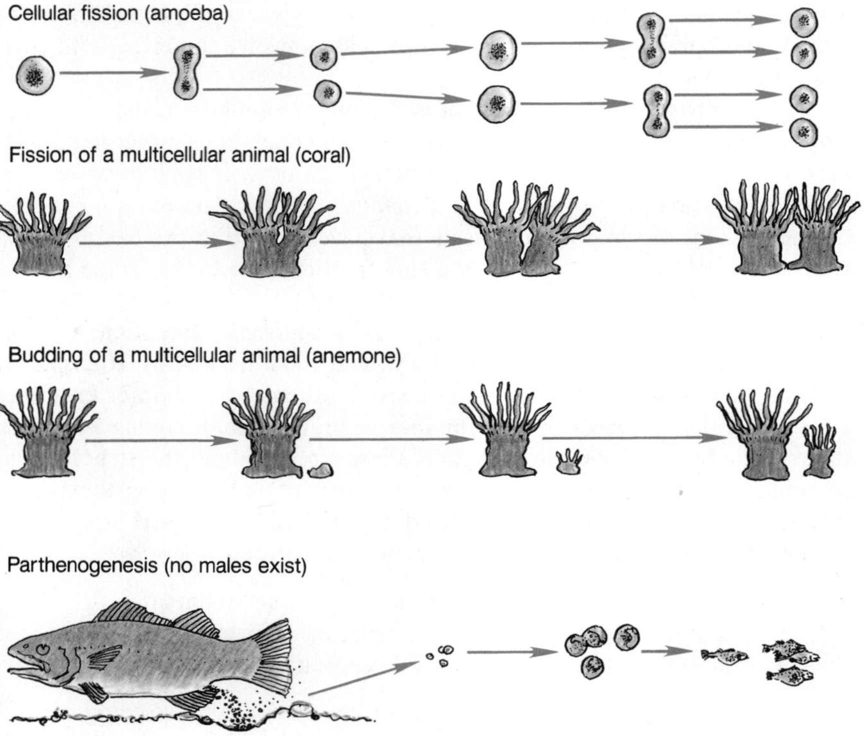

Sexual reproduction is not only more complex than asexual reproduction, it is also more costly. The high costs of sexual reproduction are related to the expenses of producing and maintaining males and to the expenses associated with meiosis. Regardless of the approach taken to accomplish reproduction, all sexually reproducing organisms include the same basic elements in the process (figure 2.4). In **hermaphroditic** animals like barnacles and some fish, all adults function in both female and male gender roles, some at the same time (**simultaneous hermaphrodites**), others function as one gender and then transform to the other (**sequential hermaphrodites**). Most other animals retain the same gender role for their entire lives, with approximately equal numbers of males and females. Plants exhibit different life cycle patterns (see chapter 5), but still express the basic attributes of sexual reproduction: meiosis followed by fertilization.

When mature, sexually reproducing adults produce **gametes** (either eggs or sperm) by **meiosis.** Meiosis is a cell division process in which the chromosomes of the gametes produced include one of each of the pairs of chromosomes characteristic of the other cells of the adult individuals (figure 2.4). This is termed a **haploid** chromosome condition. Halving of chromosome numbers in the formation of gametes is a necessary component of sexual reproduction for gamete production is followed by **fertilization,** the remaining obligatory part of sexual reproduction. In fertilization, the chromosomes carried by the sperm cell are combined with those of the egg to form a **zygote** with double the chromosome number of either of the gametes. This double, or **diploid,** set of chromosomes is carried by all cells in the development to sexual maturity. The process is complex, but it produces variety within a population and within a short time span. Sex in reproduction, then, is the method

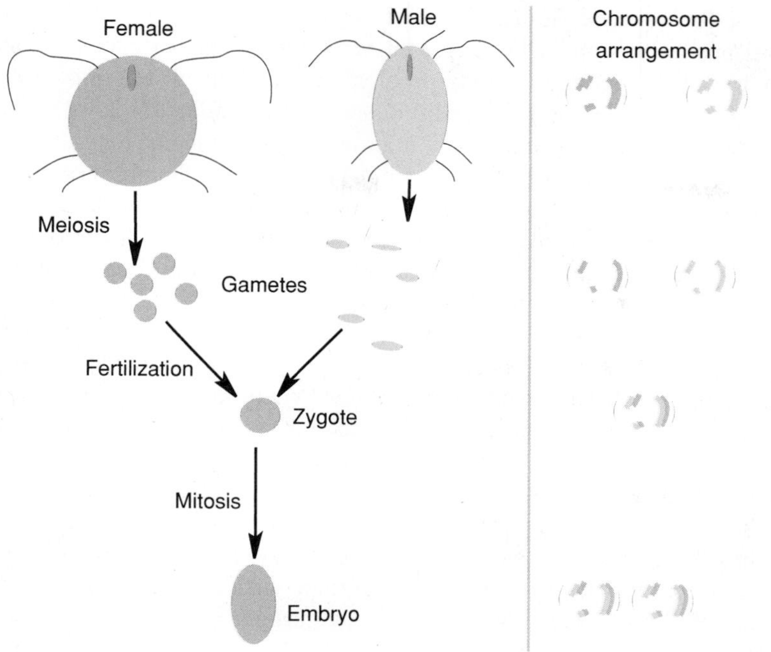

Figure 2.4
The basic components of sexual reproduction. The chromosome arrangement of each cell is shown to the right.

of choice for most multicellular animals and plants. The fusion of the eggs and sperm from two genetically different individuals promotes genetic diversity, the basis for adaptation in evolutionary time scales.

Salinity Effects

It is essential to the well-being of all living things that they maintain reasonably constant internal environmental conditions. **Homeostasis** is the tendency of living organisms to control or regulate fluctuations of their internal environment. Homeostasis is the result of coordinated biological processes that regulate conditions such as body temperature, blood sugar level, and metabolic rate. Homeostasis is not a static situation; it is a situation that varies within definite and tolerable limits. This section describes those processes that affect the homeostasis of salt and water exchange between the body fluids of an organism and its seawater environment.

The body fluids of marine organisms are separated from seawater by boundary membranes that participate in many vital exchange processes, including absorption of oxygen, nutrient intake, and excretion of waste materials. Small molecules, such as water, easily pass through some of these membranes, but the passage of larger molecules and the abundant ions of seawater is restricted. Such membranes are **selectively permeable;** they allow only small molecules and ions to pass through while regulating the exchange of larger molecules and ions. When substances are free to move, as they are when dissolved in seawater, they move along a gradient from regions of high concentrations to regions of lower concentrations. This type of molecular or ionic transfer is known as **diffusion.** Diffusion causes both water molecules and dissolved substances to move along concentration gradients within living organisms and across selectively permeable membranes between organisms and surrounding seawater.

To illustrate the basic problem of salt and water balance in marine organisms, let's examine two representative animals: a sea cucumber and a salmon. A sea cucumber avoids problems of salt and water imbalance by maintaining an internal fluid medium chemically similar to seawater (about 35‰ dissolved salts). It can easily maintain this balance as long as the salt concentrations of the fluids on either side of its boundary membranes are equal and no concentration gradient exists. (This is known as an **isosmotic** condition.) A state of equilibrium is maintained as long as water diffuses out of the sea cucumber as rapidly as it enters and the salt content of the internal fluids remains equal to that of the seawater outside.

However, if the sea cucumber is removed from the sea and placed in a freshwater lake, the salt concentration is then greater inside the animal (still 35‰) than outside (the body fluids are now **hyperosmotic** to the lake water), and the internal water concentration (965‰) is correspondingly less than the concentration of the lake water (1000‰). Water molecules, following their concentration gradient, diffuse across the selectively permeable boundary membranes into the sea cucumber. The movement of water across such a membrane is a special type of diffusion known as **osmosis.** The dissolved salts, now more concentrated within the animal than outside the animal, cannot diffuse out of the sea cucumber because this movement is blocked by the impermeability of the membranes to the salts. The net result is an increase in the amount of water inside the sea cucumber. The additional water creates an internal **osmotic pressure** that is potentially damaging because the animal is incapable of expelling the excess water and so it swells. Most other marine invertebrates and many marine plants, as well as sea cucumbers, have little or no capability for countering such osmotic stress. As a consequence, these organisms are limited to regions where salinity fluctuates little from open-ocean conditions.

In contrast to the limited control that sea cucumbers have over their osmotic situation, bony fish and some other marine animals and plants possess well-developed **osmoregulatory mechanisms.** As a result, some of these organisms are free to move between regions of varying salinities unhindered by osmotic upsets. (Estuarine organisms are discussed in chapter 6.) A salmon (which spends part of its life in seawater and the remainder in fresh water) will serve as an example of how some organisms maintain a homeostatic internal medium regardless of external environmental conditions (figure 2.5).

The salt concentration of a salmon's body fluids, like those of most other bony fish, is midway between the concentrations found in fresh water and in seawater (about 18‰). As such, the body fluids are hyperosmotic to fresh water and **hypoosmotic** to seawater. Thus, these fish never achieve an osmotic balance with their external environment. Instead, they must constantly expend energy to maintain a stable internal osmotic condition different from either river or ocean water. In seawater, salmon lose body water by osmosis and are constantly plagued by dehydration. To counter this, the salmon drink large amounts of seawater, which is absorbed through their digestive tracts and into their bloodstreams. The water is retained in the body tissues, and excess salts are actively excreted by special **chloride cells** located in the gills. Since the kidneys of salmon are unable to produce urine with a salt concentration higher than that of their body fluids, their kidneys are of no use in getting rid of excess salts.

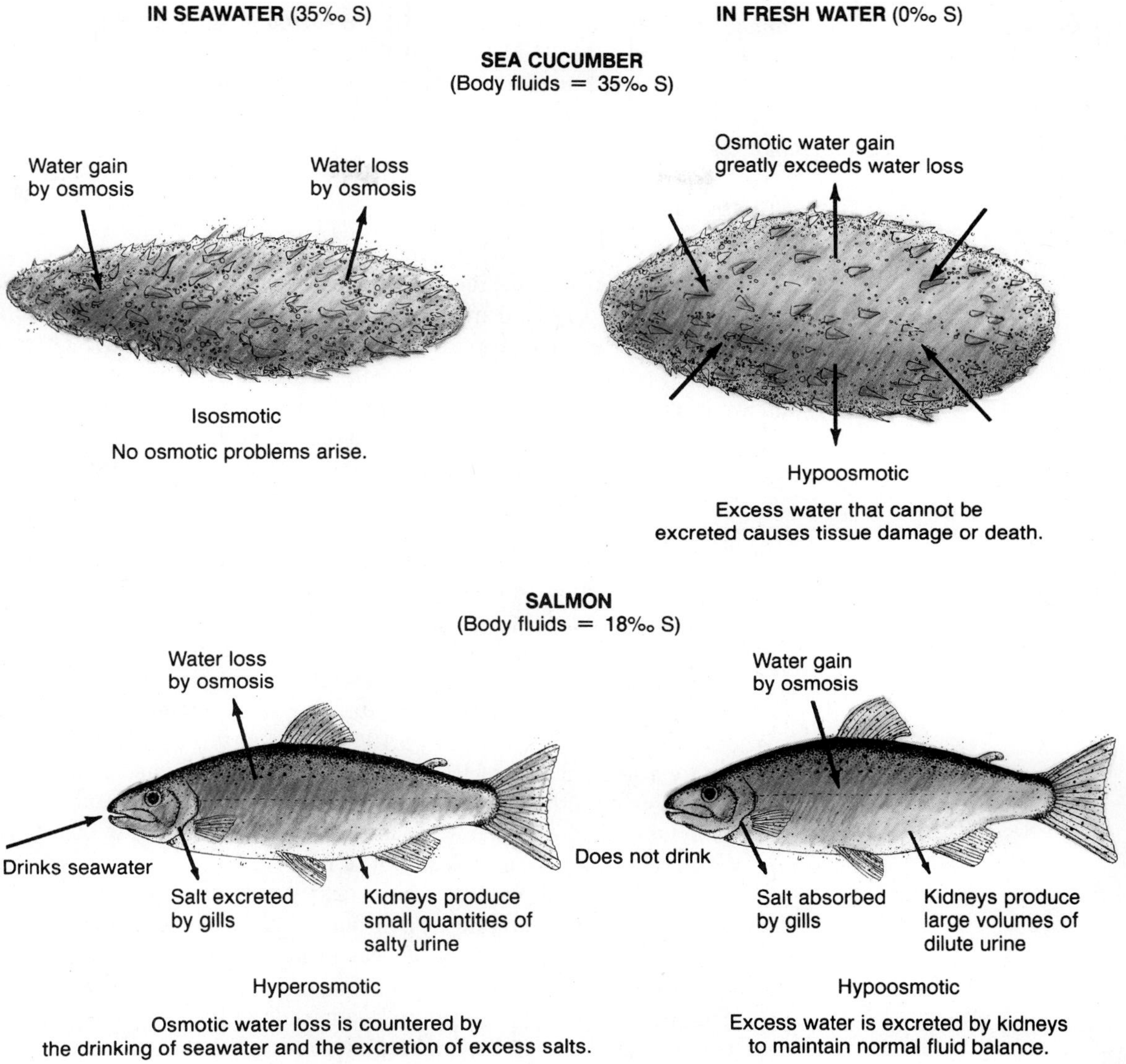

Figure 2.5
A comparison of the osmotic conditions of a sea cucumber and a salmon in seawater and fresh water

The osmotic problems of salmon are completely reversed when they are in freshwater rivers and lakes. Now the problem is one of osmotic water gain across the gill and digestive membranes and a steady loss of salts to the surrounding water. Salmon drink very little fresh water. To balance the inflow of water, the kidneys produce copious amounts of dilute urine after effectively recovering most of the salts from that urine. Needed salts are obtained from food and are actively absorbed from the surrounding water through specialized cells in the gills. Thus, at a considerable expense of energy, salmon maintain a homeostatic internal fluid environment in either river or ocean water. Figure 2.5 compares and summarizes the osmotic effects of fresh water and seawater on the salmon and sea cucumber.

Marine autotrophs also deal with their osmoregulatory challenges in various ways. Like sea cucumbers, many marine autotrophs maintain cell fluids such that little or no concentration gradient exists across membranes. Unlike animal cells, most photosynthetic cells are surrounded by inelastic cell walls that provide structural resistance to the stresses internal osmotic pressures place on fragile cell membranes. Often, cell walls alone are sufficient to deal with pressures generated by ion imbalances across cell membranes. Later chapters will discuss this process.

Temperature Effects

Individual activity, cell growth, O_2 consumption, and other physiological functions collectively termed **metabolism** proceed at temperature-regulated rates. Most animals lack mechanisms for body temperature regulation. These are **poikilotherms** (often inappropriately described as cold-blooded). These organisms are also referred to as **ectotherms;** their body temperatures vary with, and are largely controlled by, outside environmental temperatures. The terms poikilotherm and ectotherm, often used interchangeably, refer to distinct aspects of body temperature control. Poikilotherms do not regulate their body temperatures; external conditions govern the body temperatures of ectotherms. Most organisms are simultaneously ectothermic and poikilothermic.

For marine ectotherms, water temperature is a principal factor controlling metabolic rates. Marine ectotherms generally have rather narrow optimum temperature ranges, bracketed on either side by wider suboptimal, but tolerable, ranges. The temperature-moderating properties of water described in chapter 1 restrict fluctuations of temperatures experienced by marine ectotherms. Within these tolerable temperature limits, the metabolic rate of many poikilotherms is roughly doubled by a 10° C temperature increase. This, however, is only a general rule of thumb; some processes may accelerate sixfold with a 10° C temperature increase, while other processes may not change at all. The actual effect of water temperature on the feeding rate of a typical marine ectotherm, a barnacle, is shown in figure 2.6.

Only birds and mammals have nearly constant body temperatures. They are known as **homeotherms.** Their normal body temperatures are maintained near 40° C by the release of heat in internal tissues. Thus, they are also **endotherms.** Endothermic homeotherms are less restricted by environmental temperatures than are their poikilothermic neighbors. As a result, they often range widely over all thermal regimes present in the sea.

A few large tunas, billfishes, and sharks occupy a thermal position intermediate to the two just discussed. These fishes are poikilothermic, so their temperatures fluctuate with that of the surrounding seawater. However, they are unlike most other poikilotherms since they retain the heat released by their swimming muscles. These animals are endothermic and lack the constant body temperatures characteristic of birds and mammals. Chapter 11 will describe the mechanisms for this heat retention.

Trophic Relationships

Relationships between different organisms can be described by their **trophic** associations. This approach involves determining what an organism eats and what eats it. Living organisms require two fundamental things from their nourishment, matter and energy. Matter is necessary for individual growth and for reproduction. Energy is needed to maintain the ordered chemical state that distinguishes living organisms from nonliving assemblages of similar ma-

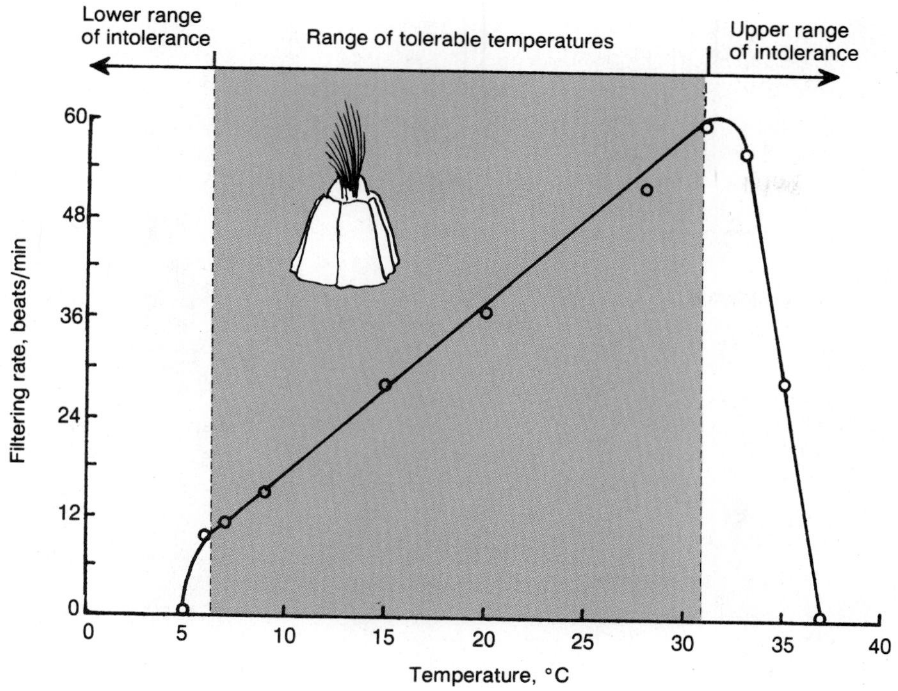

Figure 2.6
Filtering rate of an intertidal barnacle as a function of water temperature. Only within the range of tolerable temperatures is the filtering rate proportional to the water temperature.
Adapted from Southward, 1964

terial. To satisfy their energy needs, all living organisms use **adenosine triphosphate (ATP)** as their fundamental molecule of energy exchange. A molecule of ATP is composed of an adenosine compound with three phosphate groups: [adenosine] — (P) ~ (P) ~ (P). The symbol ~ represents a slightly unstable chemical bond that, when broken, provides the energy necessary for metabolic work. Usually, only the terminal bond is broken to release energy, a P unit, and [adenosine] — (P) ~ (P) (adenosine diphosphate or ADP):

$$\text{ATP} \xrightarrow{\text{enzyme}} \text{ADP} + \text{P} + \text{energy}$$

Photosynthesis is a biochemical process that uses **chlorophyll** pigments to absorb some of the abundant energy of the sun's rays. In this process, ATP and other high-energy substances are made and then used to synthesize sugars, amino acids, and lipids from CO_2 and H_2O. For the present, photosynthesis can be summarized by the following general equation:

$$\underset{\text{carbon dioxide}}{6CO_2} + \underset{\text{water}}{12H_2O} \xrightarrow[\text{chlorophyll}]{\text{sunlight}} \underset{\text{sugar}}{C_6H_{12}O_6} + \underset{\text{water}}{6H_2O} + \underset{\text{oxygen}}{6O_2}$$

Fossil evidence suggests that early procaryotes were the first to capitalize on photosynthesis as a solution to their energy needs. Fossil remains of cyanobacteria nearly 3 billion years old indicate that photosynthesis evolved at an early stage in the development of life on earth.

Most nonphotosynthetic organisms on earth rely directly or indirectly on the energy-rich organic substances produced by photosynthetic organisms. In environments with limited amounts of free O_2 (such as anoxic basins or

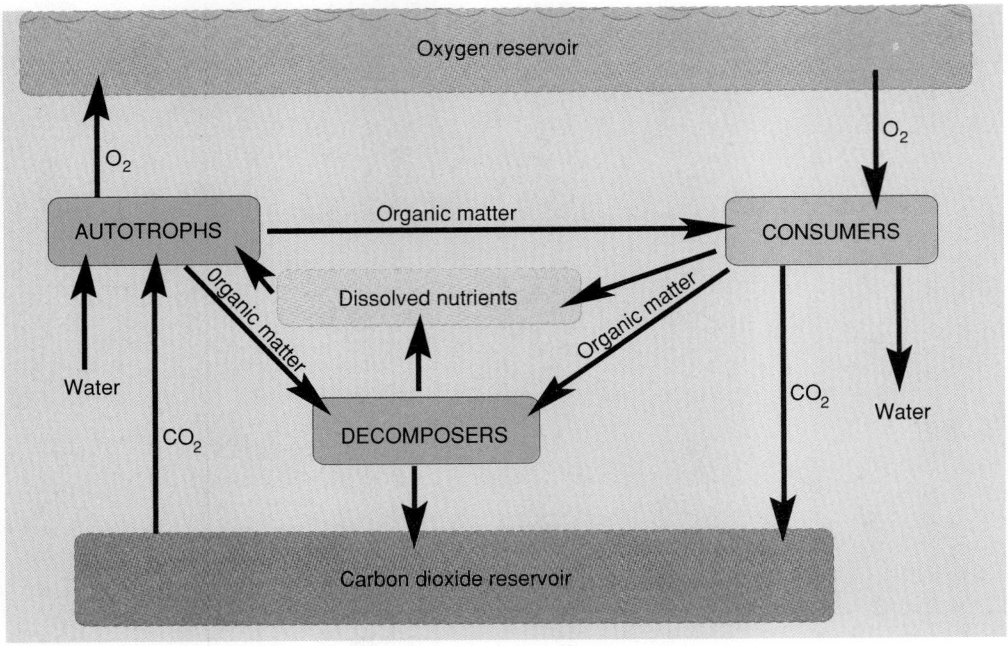

Figure 2.7
Simplified paths of the flow of oxygen and carbon in an idealized marine ecosystem

deep ocean bottom muds) and abundant supplies of organic material, **anaerobic respiration** (respiration without O_2) provides a mechanism to obtain energy for use in cellular processes. Several variations of anaerobic respiration are exhibited by plants and animals, yet all release energy from organic substances without using O_2. In **alcoholic fermentation,** for example, sugar is degraded, or broken down, to alcohol and CO_2. Energy is released in the form of ATP:

$$\underset{\text{sugar}}{C_6H_{12}O_6} \xrightarrow[\text{enzymes}]{\text{respiratory}} \underset{\text{alcohol}}{2C_2H_5OH} + \underset{\text{carbon dioxide}}{2CO_2} + \underset{\text{(equivalent to 2 ATP)}}{\text{ENERGY}}$$

In most eucaryotic organisms, respiratory processes more complex than that of anaerobic respiration completely oxidize high-energy compounds such as sugar to carbon dioxide and water and, in the process, release energy:

$$\underset{\text{sugar}}{C_6H_{12}O_6} + \underset{\text{oxygen}}{6O_2} \xrightarrow[\text{enzymes}]{\text{respiratory}} \underset{\text{carbon dioxide}}{6CO_2} + \underset{\text{water}}{6H_2O} + \underset{\text{(equivalent to 37 ATP)}}{\text{ENERGY}}$$

This process utilizes oxygen and is called **aerobic respiration.** In aerobic respiration, each molecule of sugar yields 18 times as much energy as it would if used in anaerobic respiration. Organisms that metabolize food and oxygen in this manner secure a tremendous energetic advantage over their anaerobic competitors.

The transfer of matter and energy for use in metabolic processes has resulted in a close interdependence of three major categories of marine organisms: **producers, consumers,** and **decomposers. Autotrophs** are self-nourishing organisms capable of absorbing solar energy and photosyntheti-

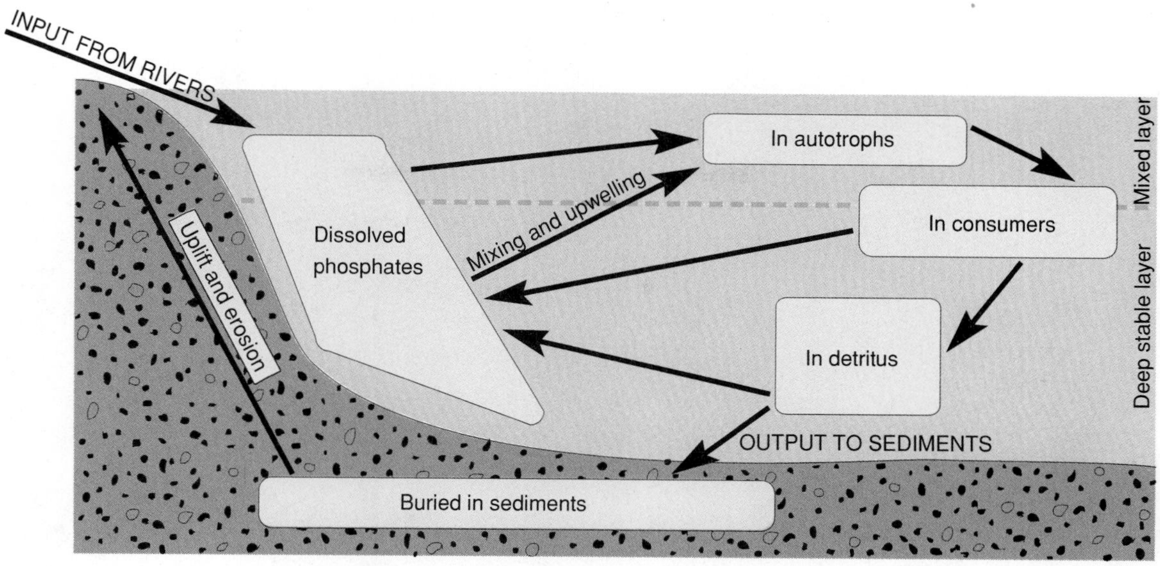

Figure 2.8
Biogeochemical cycle of phosphorus, showing its major marine reservoirs. Little phosphorus is available to autotrophs in the upper mixed reservoirs; much more is dissolved in deep stable waters. Similar cycles exist for biologically important chemicals such as nitrogen and carbon.

cally building high-energy organic substances such as carbohydrates. In the process, autotrophs use inorganic nutrients (primarily nitrate and phosphate), water, and dissolved gases. They are the **primary producers** of marine ecosystems and are placed in the first **trophic level.** Some bacterial autotrophs extract energy from inorganic compounds to build high-energy organic molecules. These autotrophs are **chemosynthetic,** and they will be discussed more in chapter 7. The consumers and decomposers are unable to synthesize their own food from inorganic substances and must depend on autotrophs for nourishment. These are **heterotrophs,** each having some specialization in terms of nutrition. Animals who feed on autotrophs are **herbivores** and occupy the second trophic level, while those that prey on other animals are **carnivores** and occupy the third and higher trophic levels. The decomposers, primarily bacteria and fungi, exist on **detritus,** the excrement and other waste products of all types of organisms as well as the dead remains of the organisms themselves. Whatever their specialized feeding role may be, all heterotrophs metabolize the organic compounds synthesized by primary producers to gain available energy.

Organic compounds produced by autotrophs become the vehicle for the transport of usable energy to the other inhabitants of the ecosystem. A distinction must be made between the flow of essential nutrients and the flow of energy in an ecosystem. The movement of nutrient compounds and dissolved gases is cyclic in nature, going from autotrophs to consumers to decomposing bacteria and fungi back to the autotrophs (figure 2.7). Since there is limited input from outside ecosystems of most of these materials, the materials pass from one ecosystem component to another in cycles known as **biogeochemical cycles.** These cycles link living communities of organisms with nonliving reservoirs of important nutrients (figure 2.8).

In contrast to the cyclic flow of materials, the flow of energy in ecosystems is unidirectional, from the sun through the autotrophs to the consumers and decomposers. Living organisms, like most energy-consuming systems, are not highly efficient in their use of energy. Less than 1% of the

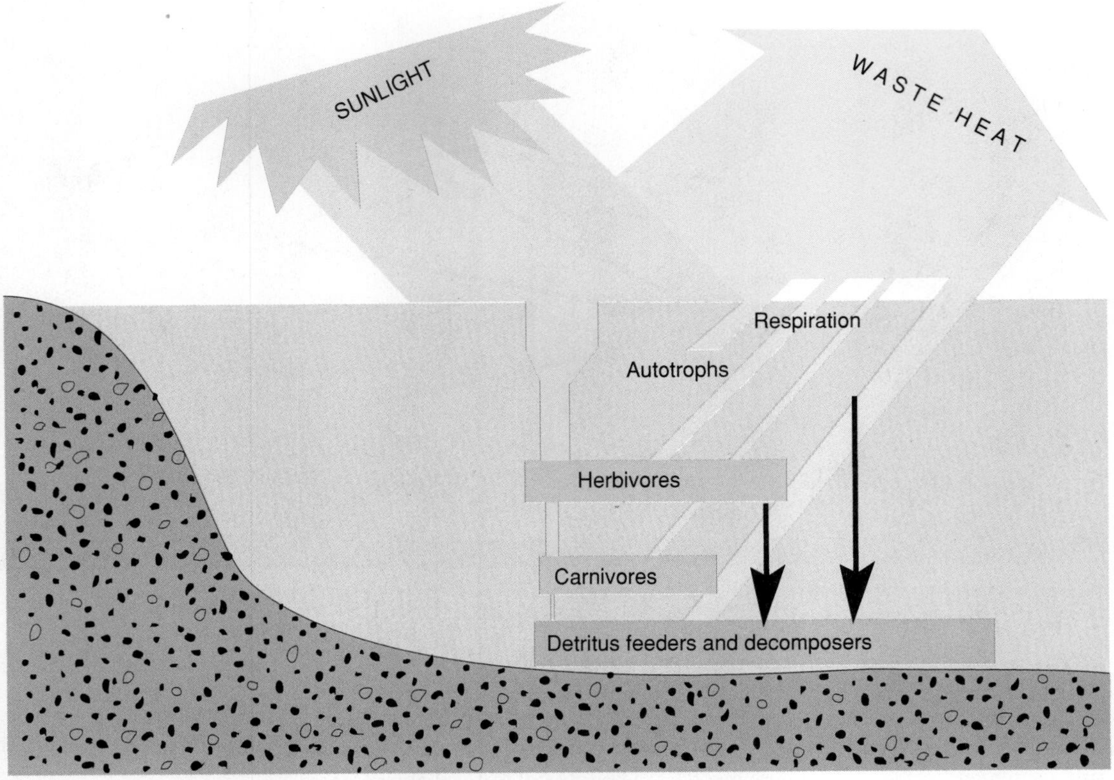

Figure 2.9
Energy flow in a marine ecosystem. Sunlight first captured by autotrophs is eventually degraded by cellular respiration and lost as waste heat.

solar energy available at the sea surface is absorbed by autotrophs. Furthermore, a portion of the energy captured in the photosynthetic process is used for cellular maintenance, growth, and reproduction. Thus, only a small fraction of the energy produced by photosynthesis is available to the consumers.

A similar decrease in available energy occurs between the herbivores and carnivores (figure 2.9). Laboratory and field studies of marine organisms place the efficiency of energy transfer from one trophic level to the next at between 6% and 20%. In other words, only 6% to 20% of the energy available to any trophic level is usually passed on to the next level. A widely accepted average efficiency is 10%; however, recent studies of certain benthic communities and fish populations provide examples of energetic efficiencies significantly higher.

The paths that nutrients and energy follow through the living portion of ecosystems are referred to as **food chains.** They may be grazing food chains, food chains commencing with autotrophs and progressing through a succession of grazers and predators; or they may be parallel **detritus** food chains, food chains based on the waste and death of the grazing food chains. With only a few near-shore exceptions, the first trophic level of marine food chains is occupied by widely dispersed microscopic phytoplankton. The microscopic character of most of the marine primary producers imposes a size restriction on many of the occupants of higher marine trophic levels. Since very few animals are adapted to feed on organisms much smaller than themselves, marine

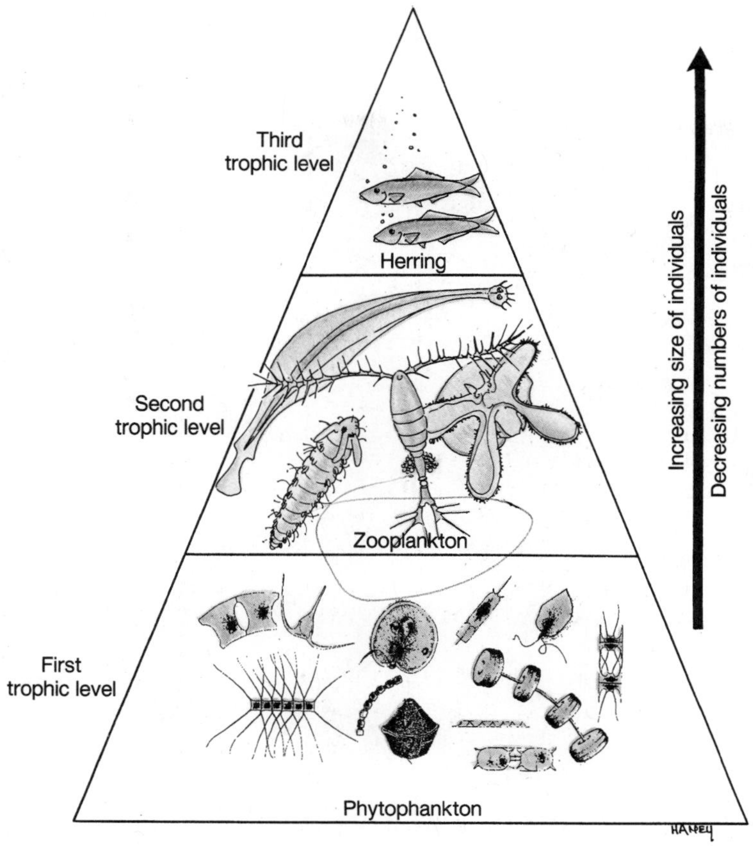

Figure 2.10
Food pyramid that leads to an adult herring

herbivores are usually quite small. Large marine animals are carnivores and usually occupy higher levels in the food chain. In contrast, the plants of the terrestrial ecosystem are generally quite large. As a result, most large land animals are herbivores. Food chains can be arranged in a linear fashion to illustrate the decrease in available energy and material from lower to higher trophic levels. Figure 2.10 illustrates such a food pyramid, proceeding from phytoplankton to herring at the third trophic level.

Marine communities seldom have straight-line food chains. **Food web** is a more descriptive term for the complex feeding relationships of marine organisms. Figure 2.11 outlines the major trophic relationships of the members of a typical marine community. The herring, like many of the other organisms of this food web, is an opportunistic feeder and does not specialize on only one type of food organism. Because of the complex feeding relationships of the herring, it is very difficult to place the herring in a particular trophic level. The adult herring occupies the third level when feeding on *Calanus* copepods, the fourth level when feeding on sand eels, and either the fourth or fifth trophic level when feeding on the amphipod *Themisto*. Even the complex of feeding relationships outlined in figure 2.11 is an oversimplification for it ignores other marine animals that compete with the herring for the same food sources. Such a confusion of interrelated feeding patterns often becomes quite complex; therefore, we must simplify the food web concept for a more easily

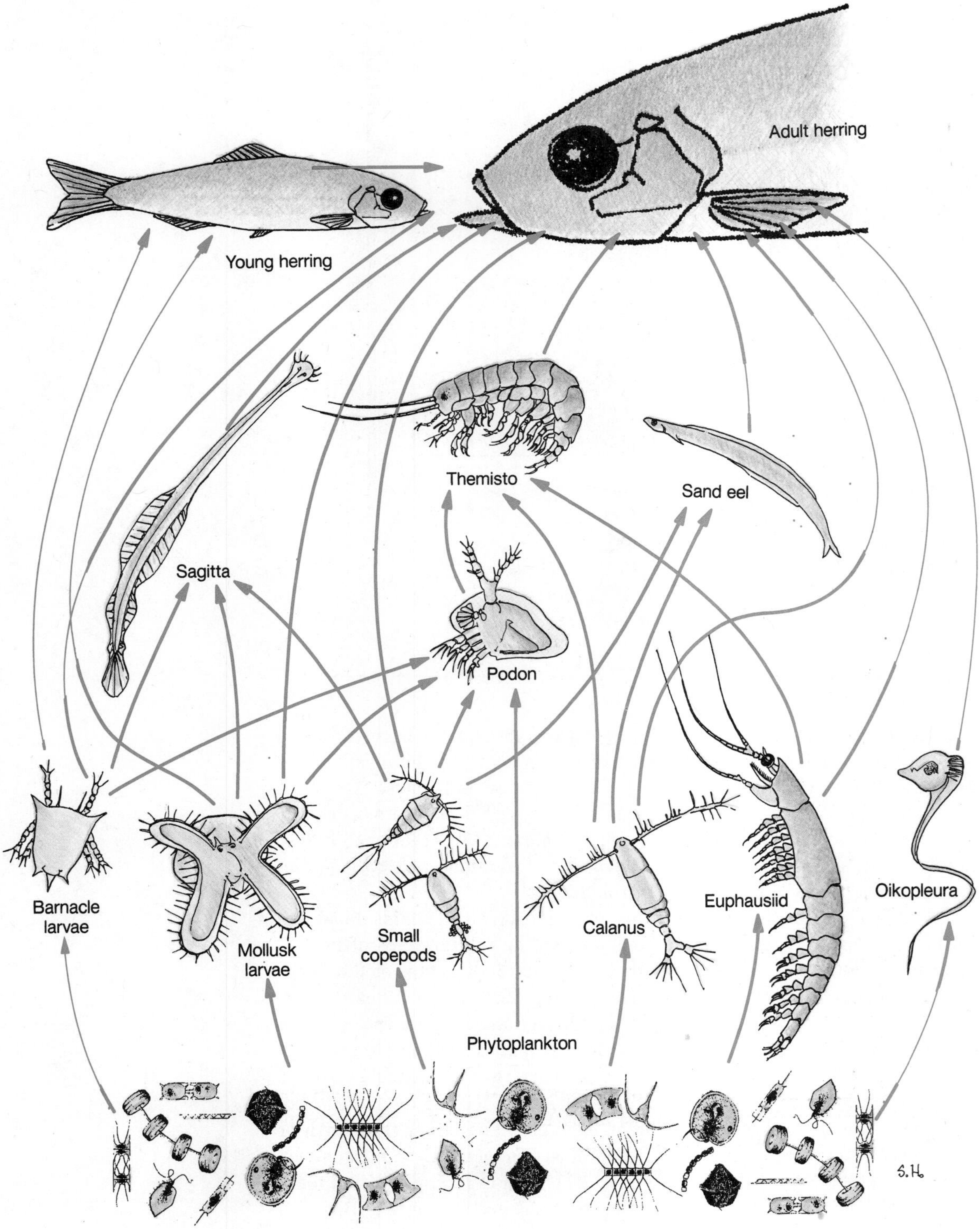

Figure 2.11
A marine food web, illustrating the major trophic relationships that lead to an adult herring
Adapted from Hardy, 1924

understood, though admittedly incomplete, explanation of the trophic relationships of marine organisms. Figure 2.12 outlines some of the more common energy and nutrient pathways of a marine ecosystem.

Many other marine organisms obtain their food by establishing highly specialized symbiotic relationships. The term **symbiosis** denotes an intimate and prolonged relationship between two (or more) organisms in which at least one organism obtains some benefit from the relationship. Most commonly, the benefit is food.

Symbiotic relationships can be reduced to three broadly overlapping categories (figure 2.13). **Commensalism** provides an obvious benefit to one partner (the **symbiont**) without seriously affecting the **host. Mutualism** benefits both the symbiont and the host. **Parasitism** benefits the symbiont at the expense of the host. A parasite lives on or in the host and obtains food benefits from the host. Parasites do not usually kill their hosts (those that do might be considered imperfect parasites or very slow predators), but they make their presence felt by reducing the host's food reserves, resistance to disease, and general vigor. The infected host then is more likely to become a casualty of infection, starvation, or predation, but not of the parasite directly. (Later chapters examine representative food-oriented symbiotic relationships.)

Spatial Distribution

Natural systems are sometimes difficult to consider in their entirety. To cope with this complexity, we often subdivide these systems into smaller, more convenient units and then categorize the units and relate them to the whole system on the basis of certain characteristics. The classification of the marine environment (figure 1.30) is a good example. To be of value, any classification scheme must present the information in a generally accepted manner. This requires an orderly framework to logically classify the available information so that it becomes significantly more meaningful or useful. Whatever forms they assume, all classification schemes have one fundamental purpose: to provide a contrived, but accepted, means of treating information from complex natural systems in a useful and informative fashion.

A simple way to classify marine organisms is according to where they live (figure 2.14). The **benthos** includes the organisms living on the bottom (**epifauna**) or in the sediment (**infauna**). This definition is often extended to include those fish and other swimming animals that are closely associated with the ocean bottom. Benthic photosynthesizers are restricted to the intertidal areas and shallow margins of the oceans. Below the photic zone, they disappear, and animals, bacteria, and fungi survive on organic material drifting down from above.

The large, actively swimming marine animals belong to the **nekton.** This group includes marine mammals, many fish, and a few types of invertebrates such as squid and some crustaceans.

Plankton (derived from the Greek term *planktos* which means 'to wander') are defined by their movements and their small size. Carried about by water currents, they have little or no ability to swim horizontally although some have remarkable abilities to swim vertically. Plankton are usually small, even microscopic organisms; however, some jellyfish have tentacles over 15 m long and a bell 2 m in diameter. Autotrophic members of the plankton are termed **phytoplankton.** They are nearly all microscopic, either a single-cell or

Figure 2.12
The major biotic components of a marine ecosystem with their interconnecting paths of energy and nutrient exchange
Adapted from Russell-Hunter, 1970

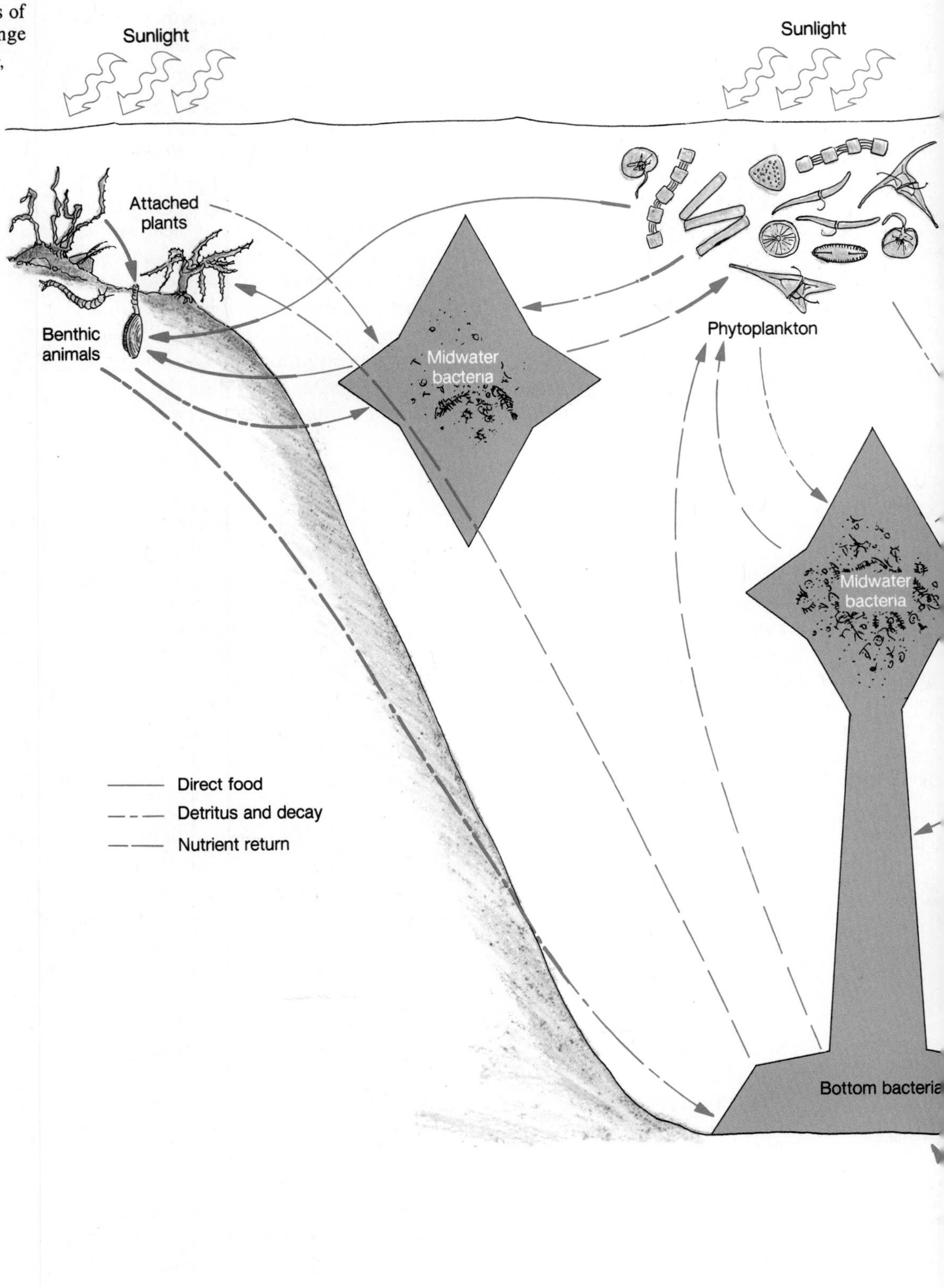

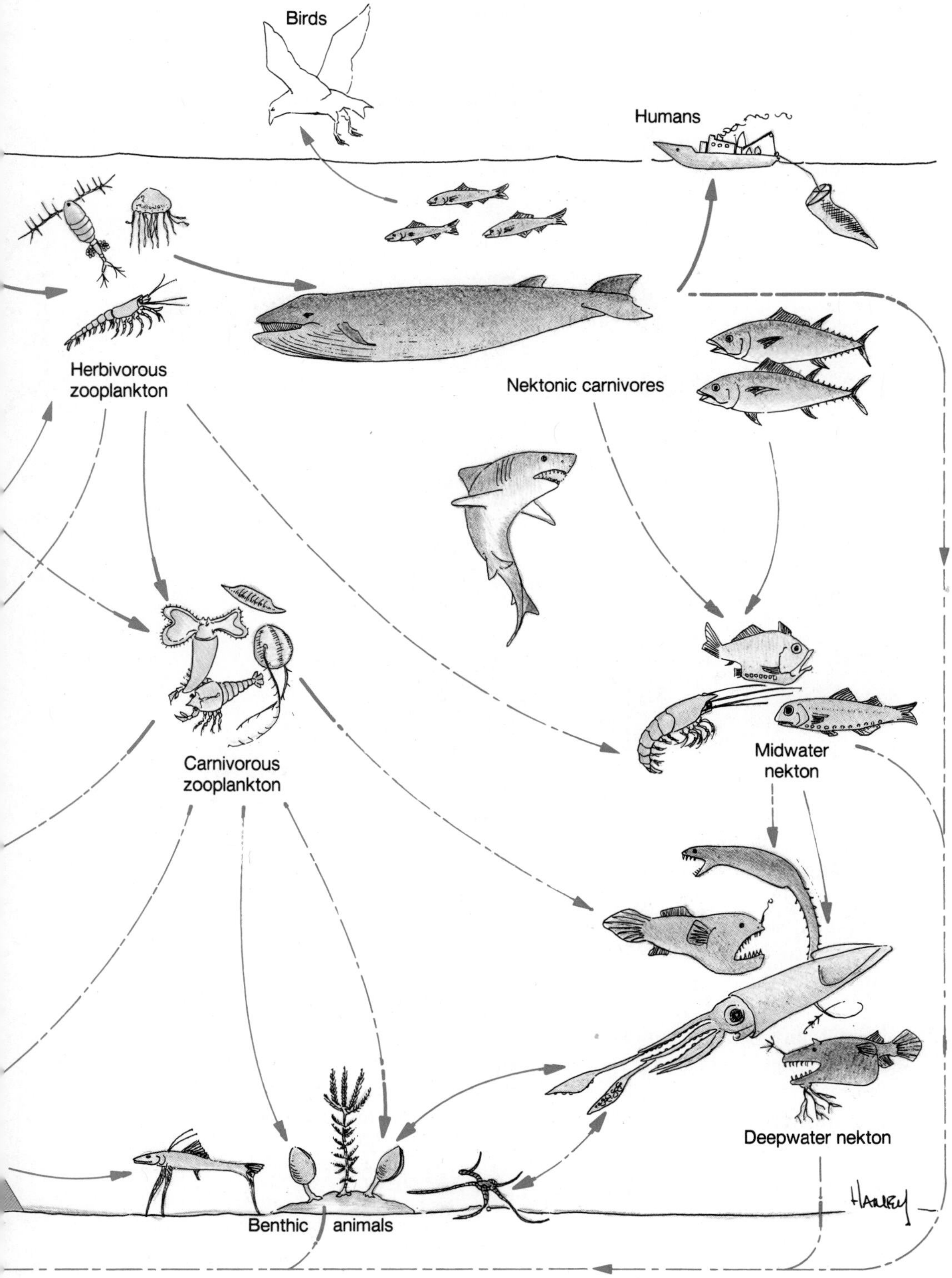
Birds
Humans
Herbivorous zooplankton
Nektonic carnivores
Carnivorous zooplankton
Midwater nekton
Deepwater nekton
Benthic animals
HARVEY

Figure 2.13
The range of common symbiotic interactions between a host and its symbiont

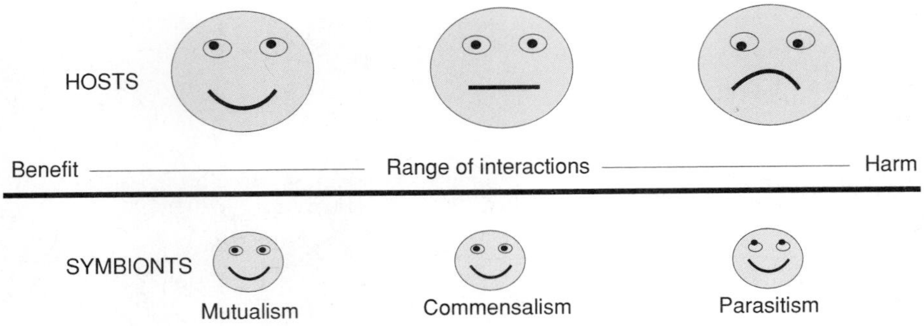

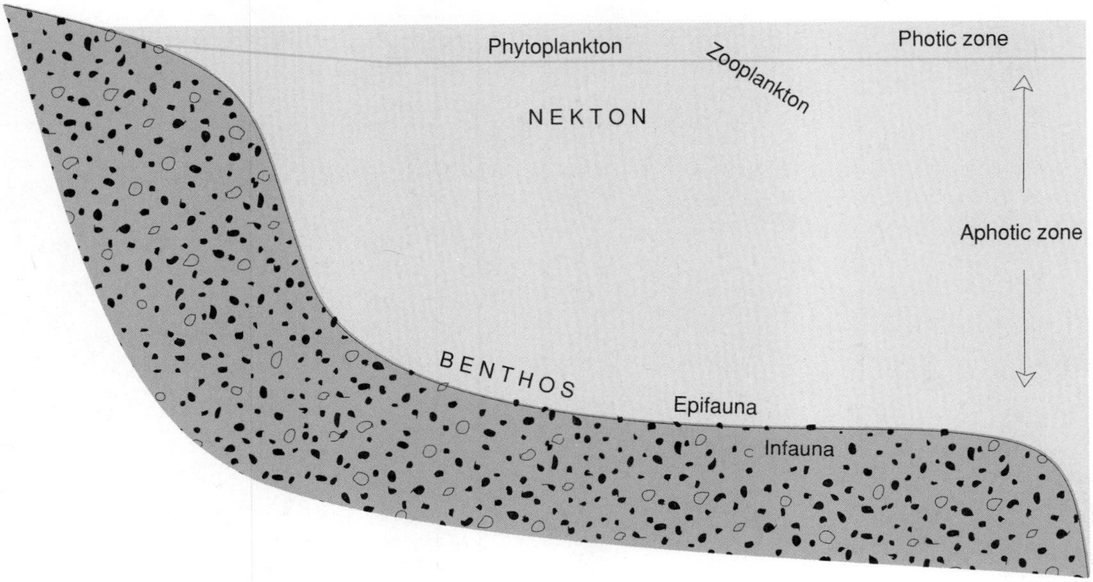

Figure 2.14
A spatial classification of marine organisms. Compare this figure to the classification scheme for the marine environment, figure 1.30.

loose aggregates of a few cells and are restricted to the sunlit, or photic, zones of the marine environment. The **zooplankton** are the heterotrophic plankton. Zooplankton range in size and complexity from microscopic single-celled organisms to large multicellular animals. The zooplankton are distributed throughout the pelagic division of the marine environment.

Sometimes, these clear-cut distinctions between major groups break down. Many fish, for example, hatch from eggs as zooplankton and then gradually develop into nektonic animals as their size increases and their swimming ability improves. Even so, this system is useful for referring to major groups of marine organisms living under similar environmental conditions.

The General Nature of Marine Life

Although modern marine organisms share many basic structural and behavioral characteristics with their terrestrial relatives, marine life is unique in several important ways. Marine organisms exist within a dense, circulating, interconnected seawater medium. The movement of seawater mixes and transports organisms, their food, and their waste products so that few of these organisms are isolated from the effects of other organisms. Populations of even the smallest unicellular planktonic organisms can become widely distributed by moving currents and water masses.

The biology of marine organisms is, to a large extent, the biology of the very small. It is the phytoplankton that initially establish much of the structural character of marine life. Even in very productive areas of the open ocean, the concentration of phytoplankton is thousands of times more dilute than a healthy cornfield. The dispersed nature, extremely small size, and rapid reproductive rates of the phytoplankton limit the size and abundance of other life in the sea. Most of the heterotrophs are congregated near the photic zone and its supply of food. At greater depths, the density of marine populations tends to decrease as the food supply diminishes. Below the photic zone, all marine life is dependent on the rain of detritus from above. Unlike the land, there are few plant-dominated communities in the sea. (A few notable exceptions are depicted in chapters 4 and 6.) Instead, the sea is occupied by coral reefs, mussel beds, and other communities characterized by their dominant animal members.

Many of the substances produced by marine primary producers are not consumed directly by herbivores but are dissolved into seawater. These substances, including lipids and amino acids, are eventually absorbed by suspended bacteria at all depths. The bacteria, in turn, become food for consumers capable of harvesting them. Thus many small marine animals and many large ones are directly dependent on microscopic phytoplankton or even smaller bacteria for their nutrition. These are **suspension feeders** that employ numerous techniques and devices to separate minute food particles from seawater.

The sea provides buoyancy and structural support to many strikingly beautiful organisms. But if these organisms are removed from the water, they collapse into formless masses. It is only with the supportive aid of seawater that these organisms can continue to exist and function. Seawater also supports some extremely large animals. Deep-sea squids over 15 m long have been observed and squids 20 or even 30 m in length are not improbable. Some blue whales approached weights of 200 tons before their populations were diminished by whaling. But these animals are exceptional and stand out in sharp contrast to the generally diminutive nature of life in the sea.

Summary

All life forms are constructed on either a procaryotic or eucaryotic cellular plan. Within either of these cell types, living organisms process energy through cellular respiration for reproduction, growth, response capabilities, and regulatory processes.

Marine organisms exhibit adaptations to numerous aspects of their physical environment, including salinity and temperature fluctuations. These adaptations occur on both ecological and evolutionary time scales and enable organisms to succeed in their reproductive efforts.

The functional structure of marine communities is largely shaped by the trophic relationships that have evolved between community members. These relationships occur as parts of grazing food chains, detritus food chains, or because of specialized symbiotic associations.

The relatively dense fluid environment of marine organisms promotes the existence of microscopically small and dispersed phytoplankton. They in turn influence the general nature of all other forms of marine life. These features stand in sharp contrast to patterns of existence in terrestrial communities.

Review Questions

1. Freshwater crayfish and marine lobsters are closely related; yet, each is incapable of surviving in the other's habitat. List and describe two likely osmoregulatory reasons that would account for this.
2. Describe the fundamental differences between the flow of nutrients and the flow of energy in marine ecosystems. How is most of the energy lost from these ecosystems?
3. List and discuss the general conditions that cause marine food chains leading to large animals to be much longer (have more trophic levels) than terrestrial food chains leading to animals of a similar size.

Questions for Further Discussion

1. Describe conditions in which a small population might live where asexual reproduction would be advantageous over sexual reproduction.
2. What single property of water has limited the number of successful homeotherms in marine habitats? Why?

Suggestions for Further Reading

Books

Allen, T. F. H., and T. B. Starr. 1988. *Hierarchy: Perspectives for ecological complexity.* Chicago: University of Chicago Press.

Groves, D. L., J. S. R. Dunlop, and R. Buick. 1981. An early habitat of life. *Scientific American* (October):64–73.

Articles

Groves, D. I., J. S. R. Dunlop, and R. Buick. 1981. An early habitat of life. *Scientific American* 245 (October):64–73.

Guttman, B. S. 1976. Is "levels of organization" a useful biological concept? *Bioscience* 26:112–13.

Lewin, R. A. 1982. Symbiosis and parasitism: Definitions and evaluations. *Bioscience* 32:254.

An Overview of Marine Animals

Chapter 3

A feeding barnacle amid sea anemones
Photo by T. Phillipp

Biologists estimate that between ten and thirty million different types or **species** of organisms exist on earth today. Of these, only about 1.5 million of them have been identified and formally described. Although the great majority of species that have been described (as well as those still awaiting formal description) are land-dwelling insects, the diversity of life in the sea remains immense. Due to the evolutionary processes that started in the sea and have operated for the past 3 to 4 billion years of earth history, each of these species exhibits some genetic relationship to all other species. It is the purpose of this chapter to outline these relationships and to provide an introduction to the major groups of marine animals.

Taxonomic Classification

Sometimes, evolutionary relationships between organisms are obvious; for example, porpoises and dolphins. At other times, however, such relationships are more obscure (see box 3). The **taxonomic method of classification** deals with this vast and often confusing array of diversity by reflecting these evolutionary, or **phylogenetic,** relationships of organisms. Taxonomic classification categorizes organisms into natural units. It traces the lines of evolution that have led to the diverse life forms of the present and it identifies and describes similarities among existing groups of organisms.

The process of taxonomic classification consists of three basic steps. First, closely related groups of individual organisms must be recognized and described. Next, these groups, called **taxa** (singular, taxon), are assigned Latin names according to specific formal procedures established by international convention. Finally, the described and labeled groups are fitted into a system of larger, more inclusive taxa.

The fundamental and smallest unit of taxonomic classification is the species. A species is a group of closely related individuals that are similar in appearance and that can and normally do interbreed and produce fertile offspring. The free exchange of genetic information between individuals of such groups connects each individual to a common gene pool and steers them along a common evolutionary path, with whole populations adapting to environmental influences over long periods of time.

This widely accepted definition of a species, however, poses special problems for the classification of marine organisms. Due to the environmental extremes occupied by many marine animals, they are quite often difficult, or even impossible, to study alive, and little is known of their reproductive habits. In such cases, another somewhat circuitous definition is used: a species is a group of closely related individuals classified as a species by a competent taxonomist on the basis of body anatomy, physiology, and other characteristics. Whichever definition is used, the species must be regarded as a functional biological unit capable of being studied and identified.

Assigning names to species or larger groups of organisms is a process more regimented than merely recognizing and describing the species. Common names are often used in localized areas, but the lack of standardization in the use of common names detracts from their widespread usefulness and acceptance. To some people, the name "dolphin" refers to an air-breathing porpoiselike marine mammal (figure 3.1a). To others, a "dolphin" is a tasty game fish (figure 3.1b). These common-name drawbacks are eliminated when species and other taxonomic groups are assigned latinized names that are accepted by international agreement as standard group names.

Box 3 *Biochemical Taxonomy*

To assign an organism to its proper taxonomic category, we must interpret what we know of its evolutionary history. This history must be reconstructed from whatever clues are available; typically, the most reliable and widely used clues are general anatomical features (especially shell, bones, or teeth), fossils, and embryonic or larval development patterns. For each organism, it must be established whether a similar structure or developmental state seen in different taxonomic groups indicates a common evolutionary origin (and a common ancestor) or whether that feature has evolved independently in several groups. For example, most people would probably correctly guess that dogs and foxes (placed in the family Canidae) are more closely related than either are to cats (family Felidae). But are bears (family Ursidae) more closely related to dogs or to cats?

A relatively new technique, **biochemical taxonomy,** has been developed to assist in unraveling the complex knot of ancestral information derived from anatomical features, fossils, and developmental studies. Differences in the biochemical structure of proteins, for example, should be at least as meaningful as differences in bone or tooth structures. Recent improvements in the techniques for determining the sequences of amino acids in proteins have enabled researchers to detect and compare differences in proteins of related groups of organisms. Cytochrome *c*, collagen, albumin, hemoglobin, and other blood proteins are frequently used. Cytochrome *c* consists of a chain of 100 amino acids. Twenty-seven are common to all the species studied so far. The amount of difference seen in the other seventy-three amino acids of cytochrome *c* taken from different groups of organisms is a clue to their degree of relatedness. Because the rate of change of a protein like cytochrome *c* is thought to be relatively constant through time, the amount of structural difference in a protein found in different groups of organisms can also serve as a crude clock to estimate the amount of time that has passed since those groups diverged from a common ancestor. For example, elephants and the now extinct mastodons and mammoths (order Proboscidea) appear to have shared a relatively recent common ancestor. But how long ago that common ancestor existed is best answered with chemical taxonomic methods. These methods help to clarify relationships between animal groups where similarities are not apparent, as between elephants, manatees, and dugongs (order Sirenia).

Similar approaches can be used with other proteins and with short segments of DNA. Using these techniques, a few species of mammals, such as cheetahs and northern elephant seals, have been found to possess very little of the genetic diversity thought to be critical to their long-term ability to adapt to changing environmental conditions. Biochemical taxonomic methods are also being used to justify reclassifying larger taxonomic groups. Recent comparisons of DNA sequences of pinnipeds (seals, sea lions, and walruses) with those of cats and dogs have yielded strong evidence in support for a new suborder of mammals, the Pinnipedia, within the order Carnivora. Biochemical approaches to taxonomic questions are one of the latest developments in our understanding of evolution.

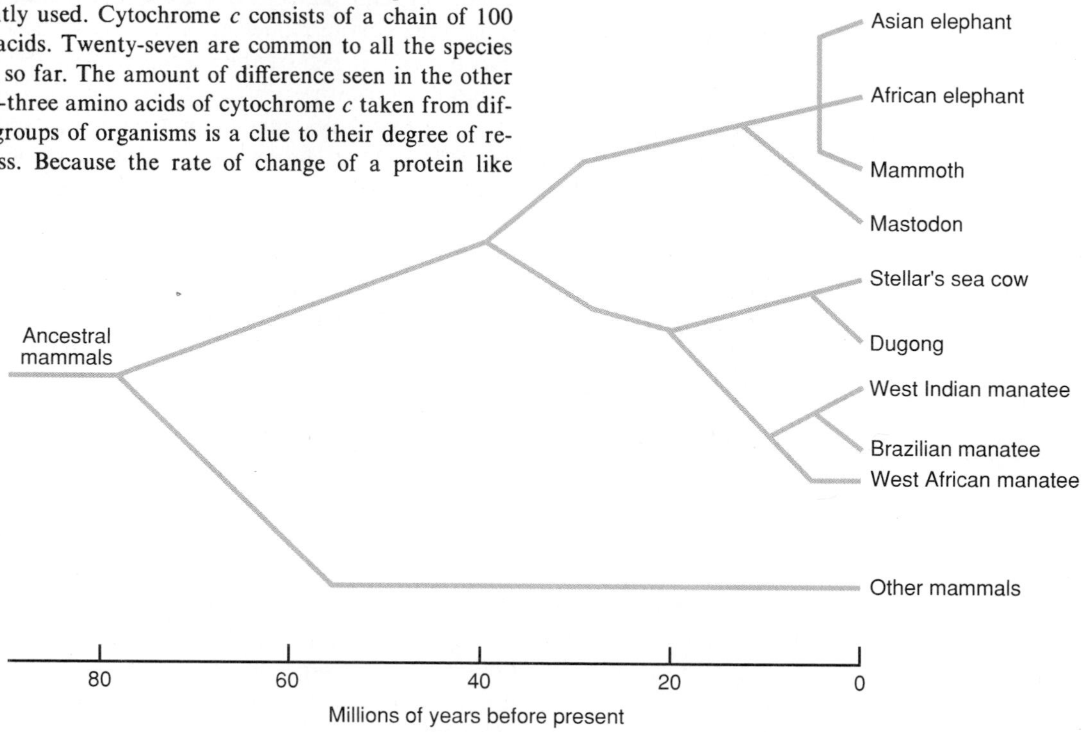

(a)

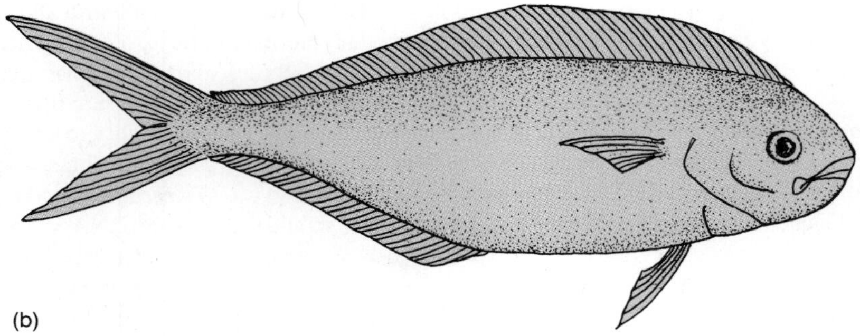

(b)

Figure 3.1
(*a*) Common dolphin, *Delphinus delphis.*
(*b*) Dolphin-fish, *Coryphaena hippurus,* also known as a dorado or mahi-mahi

Following the scheme first introduced by the Swedish botanist Lineaus over two centuries ago, taxonomic names of organisms consist of two terms. The first is the **genus** name followed by the species name. Conventionally, the genus name is capitalized; the species name is not. Both are either italicized or underlined. Each taxonomic name is unique and represents only one species of an organism. Thus, there can be no confusion that *Delphinus delphis,* the common dolphin, refers only to a species of mammals and not to the dolphinfish, *Coryphaena hippurus.*

The naming of a species does not complete the taxonomic classification process. The species is only part of a larger classification scheme that consists of a hierarchy of taxonomic categories:

Kingdom
- Phylum (Division for photosynthetic groups)
  - Class
    - Order
      - Family
        - Genus
          - Species

Each category is constructed so that it encompasses one or more categories from the next lower level. All categories above the species level are artificial; they were contrived for the convenient pigeonholing of similar groups of organisms. These groups are not completely arbitrary, however. Each group reflects the evolutionary relationships known or assumed to exist between its

Table 3.1
Taxonomic Classification of Some Marine Organisms.

	Taxonomic Category						
Organism	***Kingdom***	***Phylum/ Division***	***Class***	***Order***	***Family***	***Genus***	***Species***
copepod	Animalia	Arthropoda	Crustacea	Calanoida	Calanidae	*Calanus*	*finmarchicus*
blue whale	Animalia	Chordata	Mammalia	Cetacea	Balaenopteridae	*Balaenoptera*	*musculus*
mangrove	Plantae	Anthophyta	Dicotyledones	Laminales	Avicenniaceae	*Avicennia*	*germanins*
tintinnid	Protista	Ciliophora	Ciliata	Spirotricha	Tintinnidae	*Halteria*	*grandinella*
dolphin	Animalia	Chordata	Mammalia	Cetacea	Delphinidae	*Delphinus*	*delphis*
dolphinfish	Animalia	Chordata	Osteichthyes	Teleostei	Coryphaenidae	*Coryphaena*	*hippurus*

component taxa, based on its structure, embryology, and cellular chemistry. It is because much of the evolutionary history of life is not known in detail that classification based on this lack of information sometimes tends to become artificial.

Ideally, each genus is composed of a group of very closely related, but genetically isolated, species. **Families** include related genera that have many features in common. The cat family is a familiar example (box 3.1). **Orders** include related families based on generalized characteristics. **Classes, phyla** (singular, **phylum**), and **kingdoms** are increasingly larger categories based on even more general features. The term **division** is used in place of phylum for plants, photosynthetic unicellular organisms, and fungi.

Table 3.1 lists the taxonomic labels of several organisms mentioned in the first three chapters of this book. Dolphins and blue whales are more closely related to each other than to the other organisms listed in table 3.1, so they are placed in the same order, Cetacea, that includes other whales but excludes all other species of organisms. Copepods do not resemble whales or dolphins, yet their evolutionary connections are closer to either dolphins or blue whales (organisms in the same kingdom) than they are to mangroves in the kingdom Plantae. In this way, the taxonomic system of classification serves as a framework to support our understanding of the evolutionary relationships that exist between groups of organisms.

In figure 3.2, the major phyla and divisions of marine organisms are arranged as a **phylogenetic tree** to illustrate the presumed evolutionary relationships of each group. Only phyla or divisions with several free-living nonparasitic marine species are included. Common classification schemes typically group these phyla and divisions into five kingdoms to accommodate groups that cannot be characterized as either plant or animal. The component groups of each of the five kingdoms are separately shaded in figure 3.2. In this five-kingdom system, the procaryotic divisions, Bacteria and Cyanobacteria, are placed in the kingdom **Monera.** The predominantly single-celled eucaryotic organisms, regardless of whether they are photosynthetic or not, are grouped together in the kingdom **Protista. Fungi** form a third kingdom consisting of nonphotosynthetic eucaryotic organisms with chitinous cell walls. Those phyla

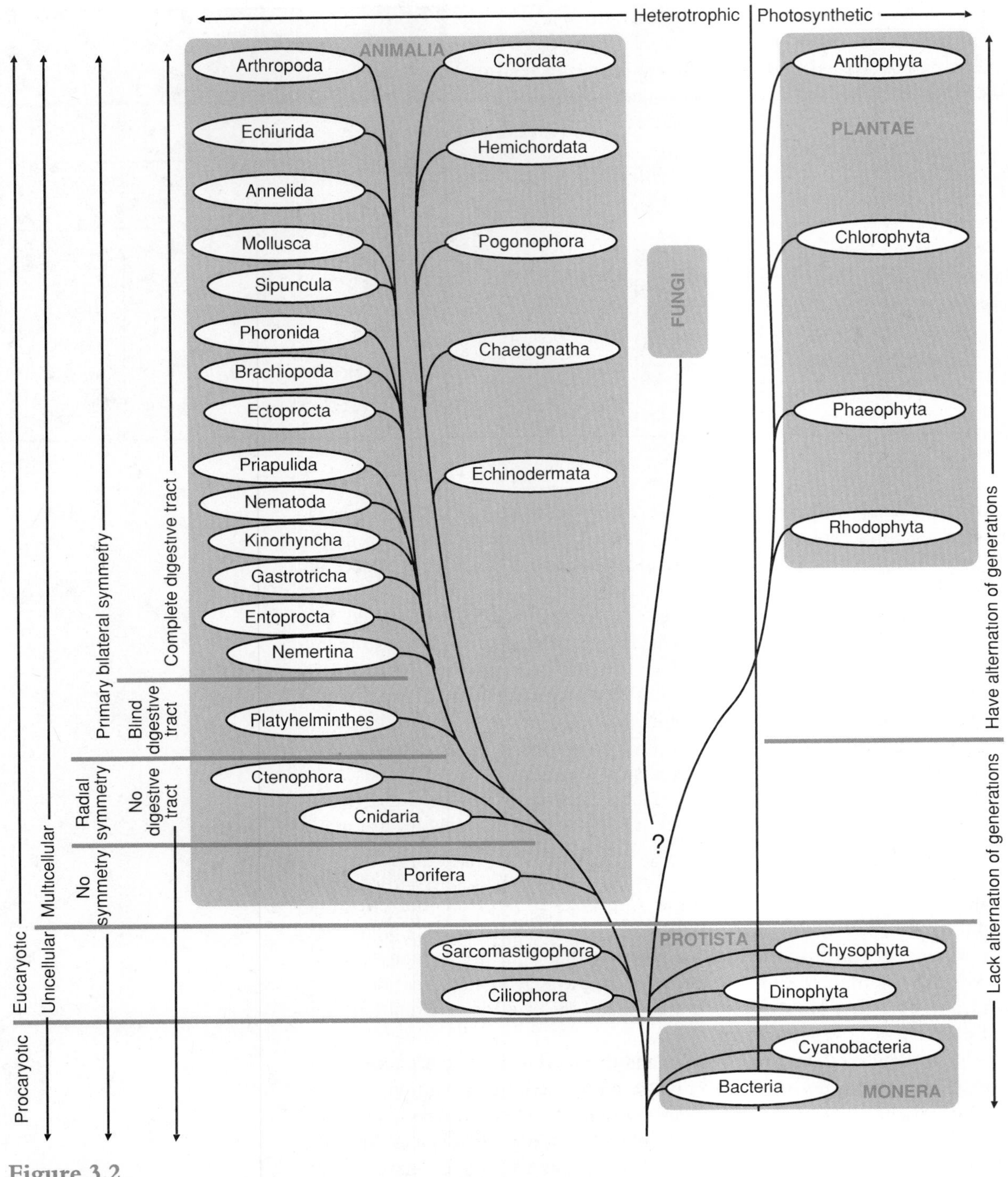

Figure 3.2

A phylogenetic tree illustrates the evolutionary relationships of the major groups of marine organisms. Each phylum and division is listed within ovals. The five kingdoms are shaded in color.

of multicellular organisms that lack cell walls and exhibit some development of nerve-conducting and muscle-contracting capabilities are placed in the kingdom Animalia. The kingdom **Plantae** accommodates the remaining divisions. These are all multicellular, photosynthetic organisms that have cell walls and a life cycle that includes alternating gametophyte and sporophyte generations. (The next chapter describes these life cycles.)

The remainder of this chapter introduces the phyla of the animal kingdom and nonphotosynthetic protistan phyla. Groups that are primarily or wholly parasitic are not included. The chapter emphasizes the more abundant and obvious phyla and stresses the identifying features and habitats of the adult forms. However, it should be noted that many marine animals do produce planktonic larval stages that appear and function quite differently than the parents. The larval stages live at different depths than adults, feed on different foods, and generally experience quite different environmental selection pressures.

Of the many phyla introduced in this chapter, only a few—in particular, protozoans, cnidarians, nematodes, mollusks, annelids, echinoderms, arthropods, and chordates—clearly dominate the composition of and monopolize the energy flow in most marine communities. These phyla are presented in an order that generally corresponds to a movement up the phylogenetic tree (figure 3.2). This sequence represents several significant trends in animal evolution. Increased complexity and specialization of structures are evident, especially in the systems involved in oxygen exchange, excretion, feeding and digestion, circulation, and reproduction. In the more complex phyla, there is a greater dependence on sexual reproduction and less dependence on asexual budding or fragmentation. Improved sensory systems and increasingly complex brains able to integrate sensory information have led to expanding patterns of behavioral responses. Table 3.2 lists these phyla and some of their major taxonomic subgroups.[1]

The Protozoans

The term protozoa encompasses a variety of nonphotosynthetic microscopic members of the kingdom Protista. (The next chapter will describe the photosynthetic protists.) Although protozoans consist of a single cell or loose aggregates of a few cells, some are quite complex structurally. They are included in this chapter for convenience and because many biologists casually consider them "single-celled animals." Asexual reproduction by cell division is common. Sexual reproduction, when it does occur, is often quite elaborate.

Seven protozoan phyla are usually described in modern classification systems. Of these, five are mostly or completely parasitic, and the other two have numerous marine nonparasitic species thriving in both benthic and planktonic communities.

Sarcomastigophora

A large and widespread phylum, these organisms use either whiplike **flagella** or extensions of their cellular protoplasm, **pseudopodia** (figure 3.3), for locomotion. The foraminiferans and radiolarians are members of this phylum, as are a large variety of amoebalike and flagellated forms. Sometimes, the photosynthetic dinoflagellates (considered with other autotrophs in chapters 4 and 5) are also included in this phylum.

About one-half of all named protozoans are foraminiferans. Foraminiferans are shelled amoeba that are mostly marine. They are common in the plankton, but most are benthic or live attached to plants and other animals.

[1]For more detailed taxonomic information regarding local species in your coastal area, see Appendix C for a list of several field-oriented identification guides, grouped by coastal region.

Table 3.2
A Partial (and Brief) Taxonomy of the Marine Animal and Nonphotosynthetic Protist Groups.[2]

Kingdom: Protista

Phylum: Sarcomastigophora (5000, all habitats)—unicellular animals; locomotion with flagella or pseudopodia

Phylum: Ciliophora (5000, all habitats)—unicellular animals; locomotion with numerous cilia

Kindgom: Animalia

Phylum: Porifera (10,000, mostly marine)—simple multicellular animals found attached to solid substrates in benthic habitats; reproduction is sexual and results in free-swimming larval stages

Phylum: Cnidaria (9000, mostly marine)—radially symmetrical animals with mouth, tentacles, nematocysts, and simple sensory organs and nervous system; common in both benthic and pelagic habitats; reproduction is both sexual and asexual (by budding or fission)
- **Class:** Hydrozoa—often colonial, with both polypoid and medusoid forms
- **Class:** Scyphozoa—free-swimming medusoid forms (most jellyfish)
- **Class:** Anthozoa—attached benthic polypoid forms (corals and anemones)

Phylum: Ctenophora (90, marine)—radially symmetrical, pelagic swimming animals with rows of cilia (ctenes)

Phylum: Platyhelminthes (12,700, all habitats)—free-living and parasitic flatworms
- **Class:** Turbellaria—small free-living flatworms with incomplete digestive tracts and ciliated undersides; found in benthic habitats

Phylum: Nemertina (650, mostly marine)—small, inconspicuous wormlike benthic animals with complete digestive tracts

Phylum: Gastrotricha (175, mostly marine)—microscopic, with elongated bodies; in benthic habitats

Phylum: Kinorhyncha (64, marine)—elongated, less than 1 mm in length; in benthic habitats

Phylum: Priapulida (8, marine)—small, benthic worms

Phylum: Nematoda (10,000, all habitats)—parasitic and free-living roundworms a few mm in length; mostly benthic

Phylum: Entoprocta (60, mostly marine)—nearly microscopic benthic animals that form colonial encrustations on solid substrates

Phylum: Ectoprocta (4000, marine and freshwater)—superficially resembles Entoprocta

Phylum: Phoronida (70, marine)—tube-dwelling benthic worms

Phylum: Brachiopoda (260, marine)—benthic animals; bodies covered with hinged shell

Phylum: Mollusca (65,000, mostly marine)—unsegmented body usually covered with external shell of 1, 2, or 8 pieces
- **Class:** Aplacophora—rare benthic mollusks without shells
- **Class:** Monoplacophora—rare, benthic
- **Class:** Polyplacophora—shallow-water benthic animals known as chitons; 8-piece shell
- **Class:** Gastropoda—mostly benthic; shell usually absent or of 1 piece; includes slugs, snails, and limpets
- **Class:** Scaphopoda—benthic; shell of 1 piece and elongated; known as tusk shells
- **Class:** Bivalvia—benthic; shell of 2 pieces; clams, oysters, and other bivalves
- **Class:** Cephalopoda—benthic and pelagic; shell usually absent, foot modified as tentacles with suckers; octopuses and squids

Phylum: Sipuncula (250, marine)—benthic worms a few cm in length; known as peanut worms

Phylum: Echiurida (60, marine)—benthic; cylindrical worms

Phylum: Pogonophora (80, marine)—deep-water benthic, tube-dwelling worms; to several m in length

Phylum: Hemichordata (80, marine)—elongated benthic worms

Phylum: Chaetognatha (50, marine)—pelagic, active predators; a few mm in length; known as arrowworms

Phylum: Annelida (8700, marine, freshwater, and terrestrial)—segmented worms, to several cm in length
- **Class:** Polychaeta—mostly benthic, free-living
- **Class:** Hirudinea—leeches; some parasitic

[2]The numbers in parentheses refer to the approximate numbers of described species in that group. Data mostly from Villee et al., 1984 and Hickman et al., 1984.

Phylum: Arthropoda (920,000, all habitats)—segmented animals with bodies covered by exoskeleton of chitin; most a few cm or less in length; several classes not found in marine habitats
- **Class:** Merostomata—horseshoe crabs; benthic near-shore animals
- **Class:** Pycnogonida—sea spiders; benthic animals with 4 pairs of elongated legs
- **Class:** Crustacea—mostly marine; with 2 pairs of antennae; numerous pelagic and benthic species
  - **Subclass:** Branchiopoda—brine shrimps
  - **Subclass:** Ostracoda—seed shrimps; pelagic animals usually less than 1 cm
  - **Subclass:** Copepoda—abundant animals in pelagic and benthic habitats; microscopic to about 1 cm
  - **Subclass:** Cirripedia—barnacles; larger benthic, attached animals
  - **Subclass:** Malacostraca
    - **Order:** Mysidacea—mysids; benthic and pelagic; size to a few cm
    - **Order:** Cumacea—burrows in mud and sand; size to a few cm
    - **Order:** Isopoda—benthic; body flattened dorsoventrally; size to a few cm
    - **Order:** Amphipoda—benthic and pelagic; body laterally flattened; size to a few cm
    - **Order:** Stomatopoda—mantis shrimps; benthic; size to 30 cm
    - **Order:** Euphausiacea—krill; pelagic; size to several cm
    - **Order:** Decapoda—crabs, shrimps, and lobsters; mostly benthic; several cm to 1 m in size

Phylum: Echinodermata (5300, marine)—5-sided radial symmetry; mostly benthic
- **Class:** Echinoidea—sea urchins, sand dollars
- **Class:** Asteroidea—sea stars
- **Class:** Ophiuroidea—brittle stars
- **Class:** Crinoidea—feather stars, sea lilies
- **Class:** Holothuroidea—sea cucumbers

Phylum: Chordata (39,000, all habitats)
- **Subphylum:** Urochordata
  - **Class:** Ascidiacea—sea squirts; benthic; solitary or colonial
  - **Class:** Larvacea—pelagic; less than 1 cm
  - **Class:** Thaliacea—salps; pelagic; gelatinous
- **Subphylum:** Cephalochordata—slender, laterally compressed; benthic
- **Subphylum:** Vertebrata—fish and tetrapods
  - **Class:** Agnatha—lampreys and hagfish
  - **Class:** Chondrichthyes—sharks, skates, and rays
  - **Class:** Osteichthyes—bony fish; includes about 30 orders with marine species
  - **Class:** Reptilia—marine turtles, iguanas, crocodiles, and sea snakes
    - **Order:** Testudinata—turtles
    - **Order:** Squamata—iguanas and snakes
    - **Order:** Crocodilia—caymens and crocodiles
  - **Class:** Aves—marine birds
    - **Order:** Sphenisciformes—penguins
    - **Order:** Procellariiformes—albatrosses, petrels, fulmars, shearwaters
    - **Order:** Pelecaniformes—pelicans, cormorants, gannets, boobies
    - **Order:** Charadriiformes—gulls, sandpipers, puffins
  - **Class:** Mammalia
    - **Order:** Carnivora—sea lions, seals, walruses, sea otters
    - **Order:** Cetacea—whales
    - **Order:** Sirenia—manatees and dugongs

Figure 3.3
A planktonic foraminiferan, *Globigerina*. (*a*) Drawing of an intact animal. (*b*) Photograph of *Globigerina* test.
(*a*) From Brady 1884;
(*b*) Courtesy of Deep Sea Drilling Project

Most foraminiferans are microscopic, although individuals of a few species are several mm in size. They have internal chambered shells usually composed of either calcite ($CaCO_3$) or cemented sand grains. Penetrating this shell, or test, are numerous strands of cytoplasm called pseudopodia (figure 3.3). The pseudopodia are used for locomotion, for attachment, and for collecting food. Some planktonic foraminiferans, such as *Globigerina* (figure 3.3), are so widespread and abundant that their tests blanket large portions of the seafloor. After thousands of years of accumulation, this **globigerina ooze** may form deposits tens of meters thick. The famous chalk cliffs of Dover, England, are composed mainly of foraminiferan tests that accumulated on the seafloor and were subsequently lifted above sea level.

Radiolarians are entirely marine, and most members are planktonic. They are similar in size to planktonic foraminiferans. An internal skeleton of silica (SiO_2) forms the beautiful symmetry often associated with radiolarians (figure 3.4).

Ciliophora

Members of this phylum possess **cilia** as their chief means of locomotion. Structurally, cilia (figure 3.5) are like flagella; however, cilia move in a coordinated manner with each other and are much shorter and much more numerous than flagella. Tintinnids are probably the most abundant of the marine

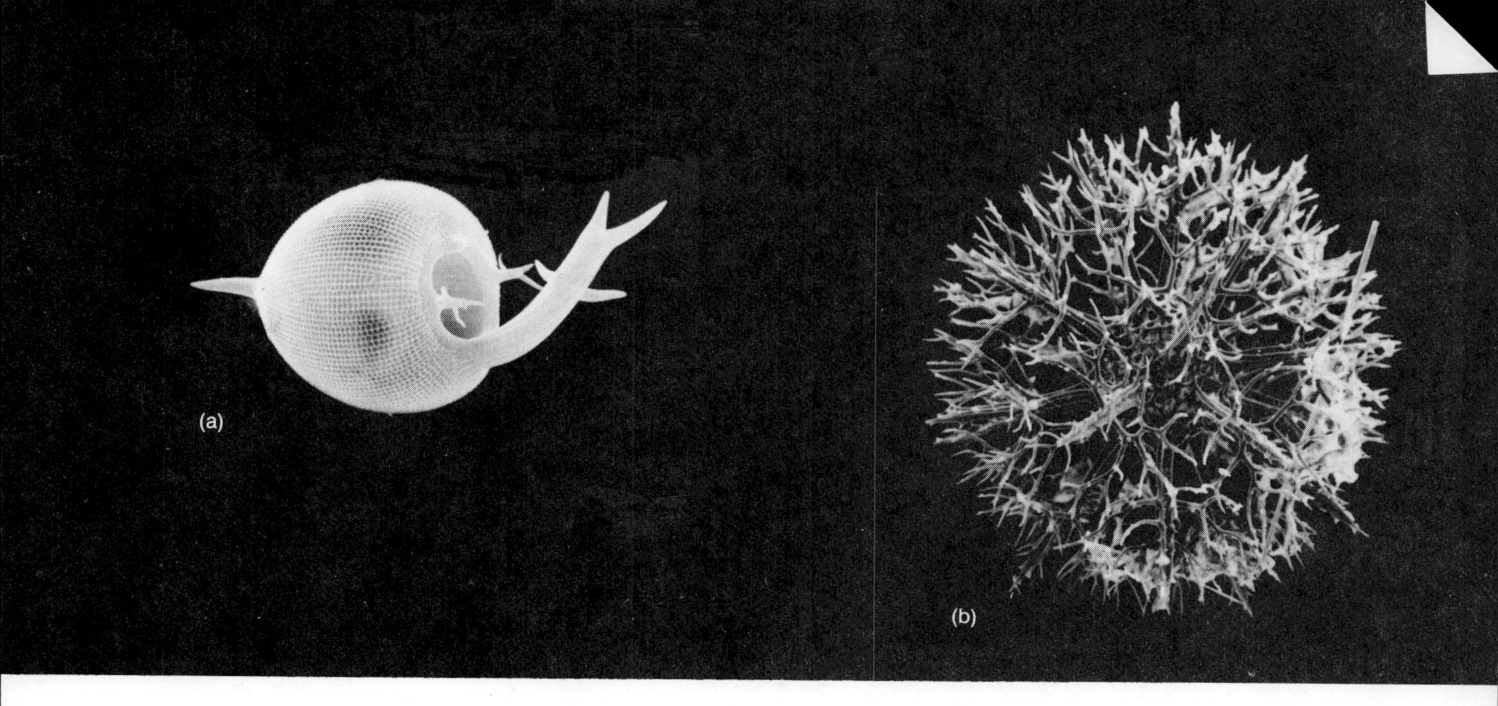

Figure 3.4
Scanning electron micrograph of the silicate skeletons of two planktonic radiolarians: (*a*) *Euphysetta elegans,* 230×; (*b*) *Elatomma pinetum,* 110×
Courtesy Kuzo Takahashi, Scripps Institution of Oceanography

ciliophores. The tintinnid cell is partially enclosed in a vase-shaped **lorica** made of cemented particles or of a material secreted by the cell. Ciliated tentacles at one end of the cell are used for feeding. A large variety of other ciliates exist in the sea, some free-living, most parasitic on or in other marine animals.

An Evolutionary Sideline

Porifera

The Porifera is one of the few animal phyla with a widely accepted common name—the sponges. The sponges are among the simplest multicellular animals. Each sponge consists of several types of loosely aggregated cells but lacks the cellular specialization and organization characteristic of most multicellular animals. Sponges represent an evolutionary sideline not followed by any other group of living animals. In spite of their simplicity, they share several advantages with other multicellular animals. Unlike the single-celled Protista, cells within each individual sponge can divide repeatedly to permit larger size and longer life span. In addition, specialization of the cells can promote more efficient handling of food collection, protection, and other diverse chores of survival (figure 3.6).

The name Porifera stems from the numerous pores, holes, and channels that perforate the bodies of sponges. Water is circulated through these openings into an internal cavity, the **spongocoel,** where food and O_2 are extracted by flagellated choanocytes lining the spongocoel. The water then exits through a large excurrent pore, the **osculum.**

Sponges are mostly marine and are usually found attached to hard substrates such as rocks, pilings, or animal shells. Sometimes they are radially symmetrical, but more commonly they conform to the shape of their substrate or to the sculpting influence of waves and tides. Some sponges are supported internally by a network of flexible **spongin** fibers. (The commercial bath sponge is actually the spongin skeleton with all living material removed.) Other sponges

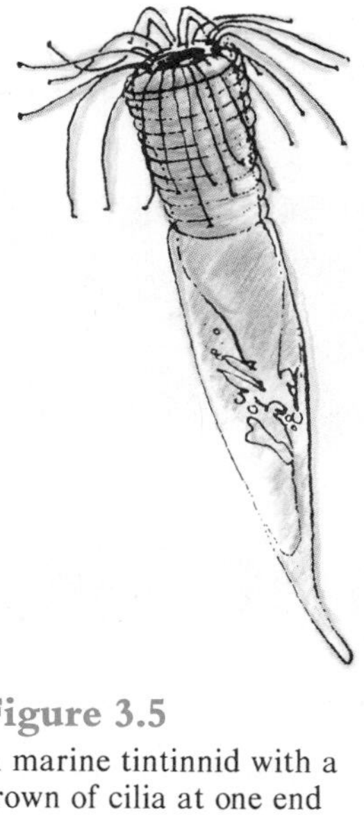

Figure 3.5
A marine tintinnid with a crown of cilia at one end

Figure 3.6
A group of marine finger sponges and several of the specialized cell types that make up the sponge wall

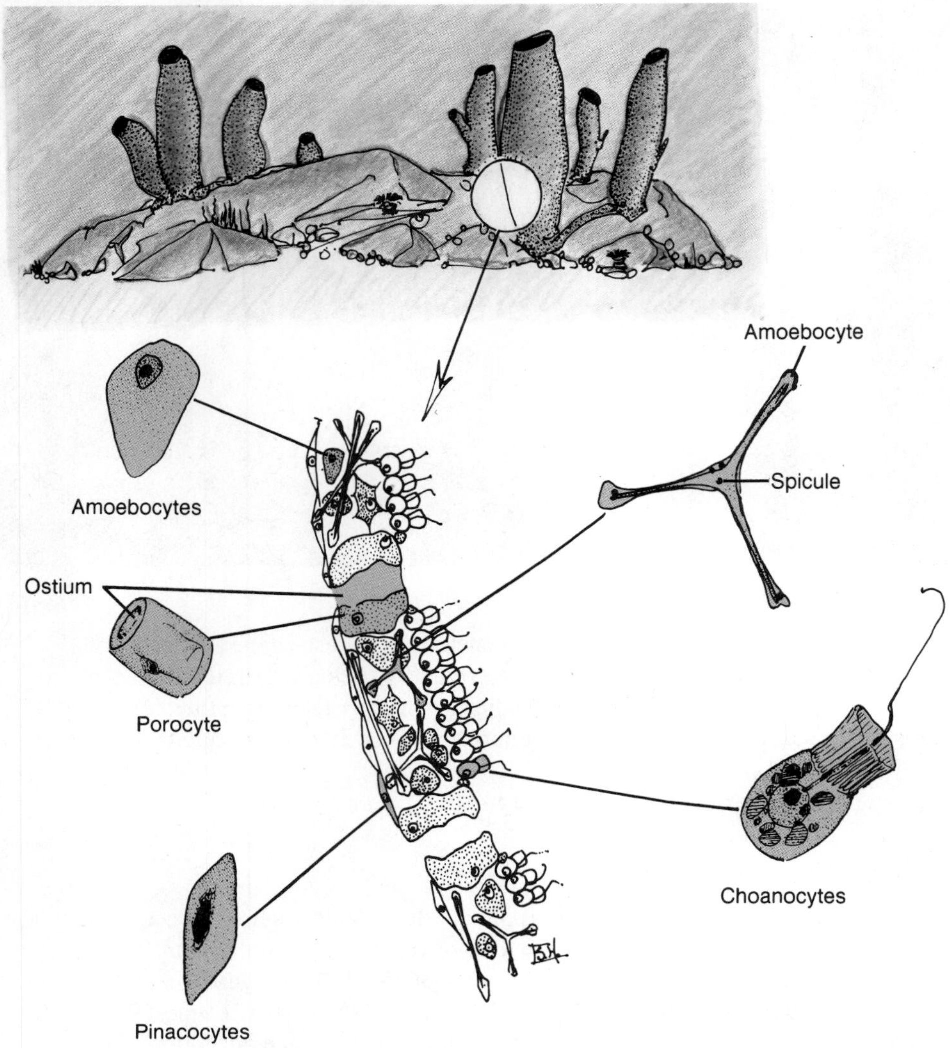

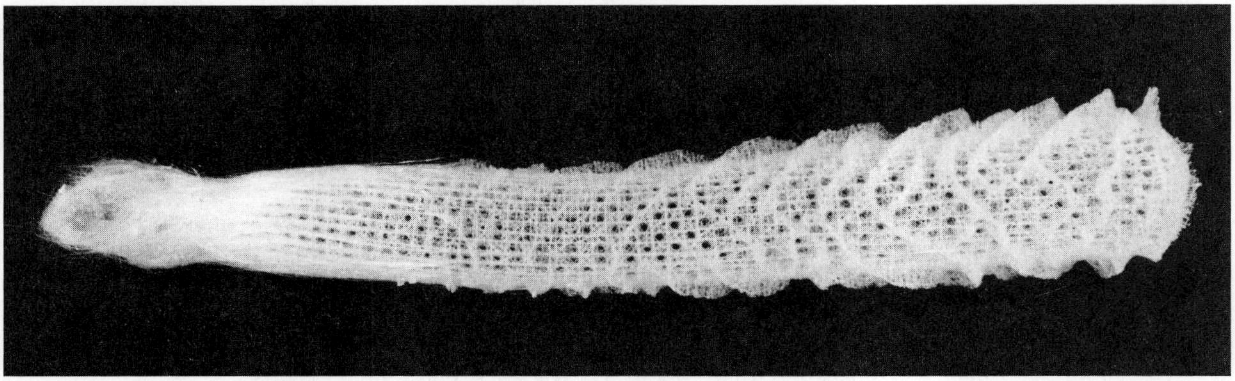

Figure 3.7
Silicate skeleton of a glass sponge, *Euplectella*
Courtesy of J. White

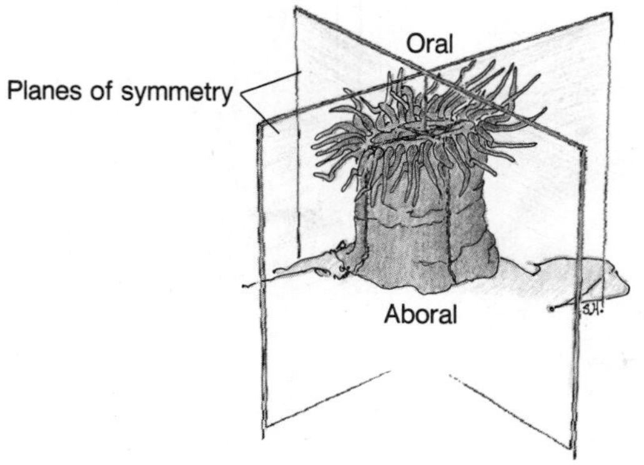

Figure 3.8
Planes of symmetry in a radially symmetrical animal

have skeletons composed of hard mineralized **spicules.** The spicules are either calcareous ($CaCO_3$) or siliceous (SiO_2) in chemical composition. The spicule skeleton of the deepwater glass sponge, *Euplectella,* is one of the most complex and beautiful of all sponges (figure 3.7).

Radial Symmetry

Members of the phyla Cnidaria and Ctenophora exhibit radially symmetrical body plans. The circular shape of radially symmetrical animals provides several different planes of symmetry to divide the animal into mirror-image halves (figure 3.8). The mouth is located at the center of the body on the **oral** side; the opposite side is the **aboral** side. Radially symmetrical animals possess a relatively simple diffuse nerve net that lacks a central brain to process sensory information or to organize complex responses.

Cnidaria

The phylum Cnidaria includes a large, diverse group of relatively simple, yet versatile, marine animals, such as jellyfish, sea anemones, corals, and hydroids. In all cnidarians, the inner and outer body walls are separated by a gelatinous layer called the **mesoglea.** A centrally located mouth leads to a blind digestive tract, the **gastrovascular cavity.** The mouth is surrounded with tentacles capable of capturing and ingesting a wide variety of marine animals. The tentacles and, to a lesser extent, other parts of the body, are armed with batteries of microscopic structures, the **nematocysts.** Nematocysts are produced in special cells, the **cnidoblasts,** and are unique, with one exception (page 74), to this phylum. They are discharged when stimulated by contact with other organisms. Some nematocysts are adhesive and stick to the prey, others become entangled in the prey's bristles or spines, and still others (figure 3.9) pierce the prey and inject a paralyzing toxin.

Cnidarians exist as free-swimming **medusae** or as sessile benthic **polyps.** Both forms have essentially the same body organization. The oral end of the medusa, bearing the mouth and tentacles, is oriented downward. The mesoglea of most medusae is well-developed and is jellylike in consistency, thus earning them the descriptive, if inappropriate, name of jellyfish. In the polyp, the mouth and tentacles are directed upwards. Many species of cnidarians alternate between a swimming medusoid generation and an attached benthic polypoid generation. In a generalized cnidarian life cycle (figure 3.10),

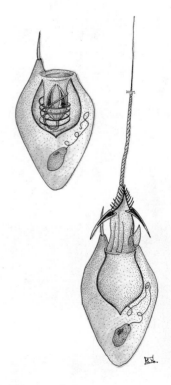

Figure 3.9
(top) Undischarged nematocyst; (bottom) discharged penetrant nematocyst

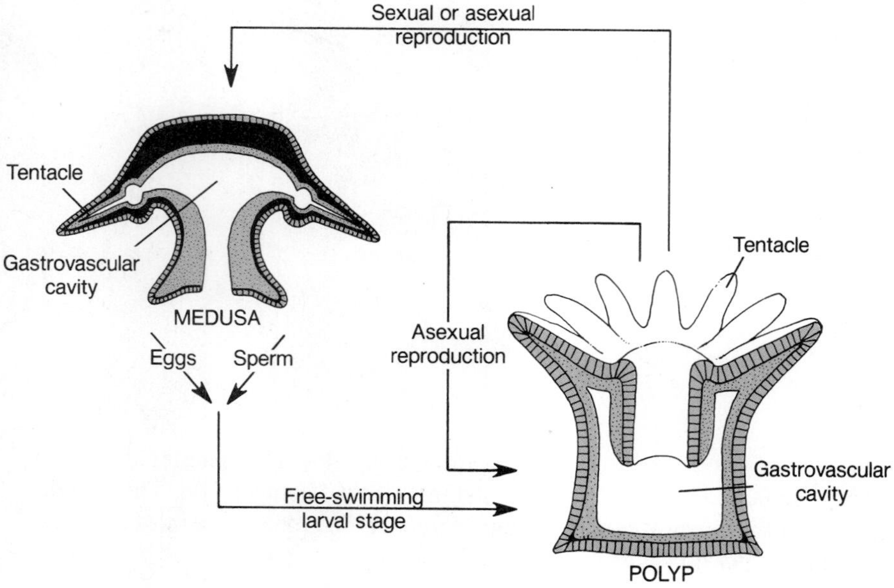

Figure 3.10
Generalized cnidarian life cycle

Figure 3.11
A large jellyfish, *Pelagia*
Photo by T. Phillipp

polyps can produce medusae or additional polyps by budding. The medusae in turn produce eggs and sperm that, after fertilization, develop into the polyps of the subsequent generation.

The phylum Cnidaria consists of three classes, each characterized by its own variation of the basic cnidarian life cycle shown in figure 3.10. The Hydrozoa includes colonial hydroids and siphonophores, such as the Portuguese man-of-war, *Physalia.* Hydrozoans usually have well-developed medusoid and polypoid generations. Various individuals of the polypoid colony are specialized for particular functions, such as feeding, reproduction, and defense.

In the class Scyphozoa, the polyp stage is reduced or completely absent. This class includes most of the larger and better-known medusoid jellyfish (figure 3.11). In the third class, the Anthozoa, the polyp form dominates and the medusoid generation is absent. Many anthozoans, such as corals and sea fans, are colonial, but some anemones exist as large solitary individuals (figure 3.12). Unlike most cnidarians, the corals and some other anthozoans (and a few hydrozoans) produce external, often massive, deposits of $CaCO_3$.

Ctenophora

The phylum Ctenophora consists of about ninety species. All are marine and most are planktonic, usually preying on small zooplankton. Most individuals are smaller than a few cm in size, but one tropical genus (*Beröe*) may be found up to 20 cm in length.

Ctenophores are closely related to cnidarians. Ctenophores have radial body symmetry, a gelatinous medusalike body, and, in some, **colloblast cells** that superficially resemble cnidarian nematocysts but are sticky rather than barbed. In fact, one ctenophore species does possess true nematocysts.

Members of this phylum have external longitudinal bands of cilia, called **ctenes** (figure 3.13), that provide wavelike movements of the ctenes. Tentacles armed with colloblasts capture food.

Figure 3.12
Sea anemones, with nematocysts showing as white bead-like structures on tentacles
Photo by T. Phillipp

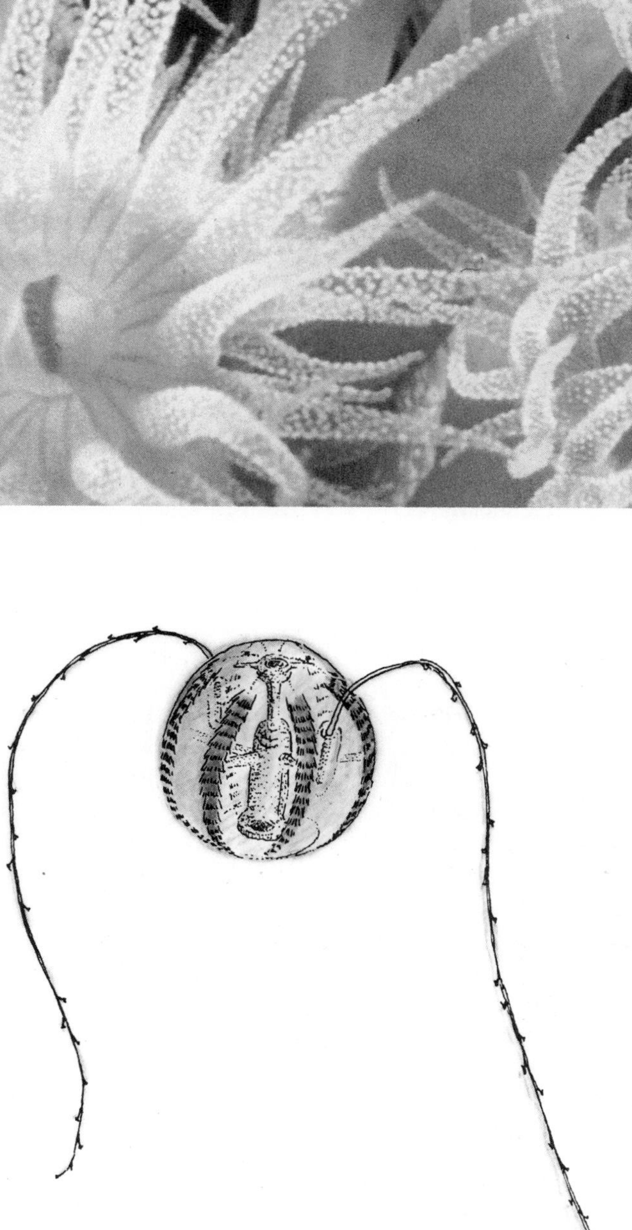

Figure 3.13
A ctenophore, *Pleurobranchia,* with tentacles and four radial rows of visible ctenes

Figure 3.14
Plane of symmetry in a bilaterally symmetrical animal

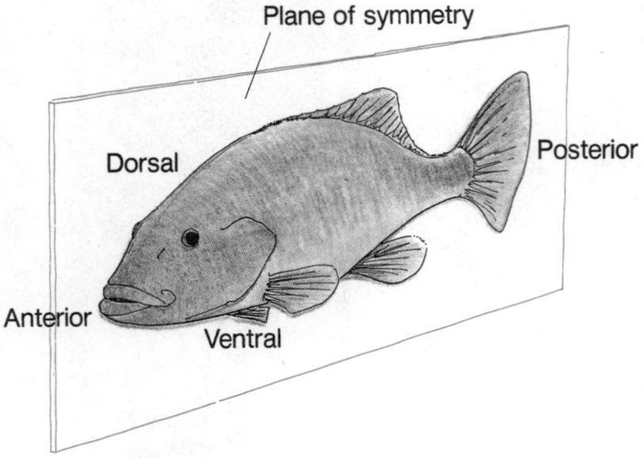

Bilateral Symmetry

With one exception (the echinoderms), the remainder of the animal phyla exhibit **bilateral body symmetry.** Bilateral symmetry refers to a basic animal body plan in which only one plane of symmetry exists to create two mirror-image halves (figure 3.14). Such animals exhibit definite head (anterior) and rear (posterior) ends, right and left sides, and a top (dorsal) and bottom (ventral) surface. These animals possess sophisticated sensory systems capable of one-way conduction of nerve impulses and an increasingly complex mass of nerve cells necessary to process the widening scope of sensory information. Accompanying this evolutionary trend toward an anterior brain has been the development in the head region of specialized sensory receptors for vision, smell or taste, and hearing.

The simplest groups of bilaterally symmetrical animals are composed of small, elongated, mostly wormlike creatures. These animals fall into seven phyla: the Platyhelminthes, Nemertina, Gastrotricha, Kinorhyncha, Priapulida, Nematoda, and Entoprocta. Most members of these phyla, except for the entoprocts, are benthic, living in soft bottom deposits.

Platyhelminthes

Most Platyhelminthes, or flatworms, are parasitic (this group includes flukes and tapeworms). Only in the class Turbellaria are free-living flatworms found. Turbellaria are primarily aquatic and the great majority are marine. There are a few planktonic species of flatworms, but most dwell in sand or mud or on hard substrates (figure 3.15a).

Marine flatworms are usually less than 10 cm long, thin, leaf-shaped, and sometimes quite colorful. Cilia, best developed on the flatworm's underside, covers its outer surface. These cilia provide a gliding type of locomotion for moving over the bottom. The mouth is usually centrally located on the underside and leads to a blind digestive tract. Turbellarians are carnivorous, preying on other small invertebrates.

Nemertina

The nemertines are benthic animals, known as ribbon worms, that are closely related to the flatworms but have more elaborate body structure (figure 3.15c). They have a simple circulatory system, a complex nervous system, and a com-

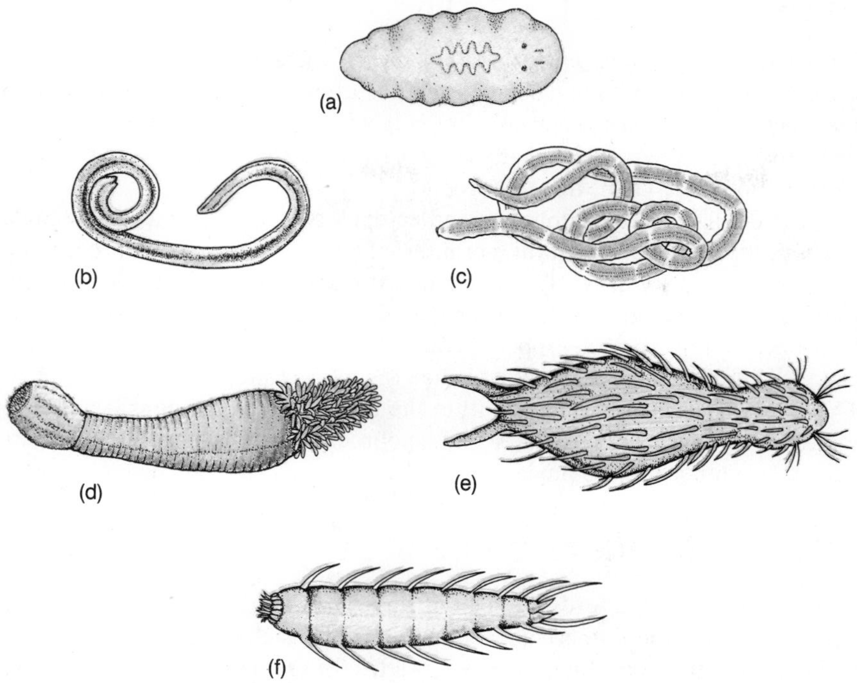

Figure 3.15
Some simple wormlike animal phyla: (*a*) flatworm, (*b*) nematode, (*c*) nemertine, (*d*) priapulid, (*e*) gastrotrich, and (*f*) kinorhynch

plete digestive tract. Individuals of one species are over 2 m long, but most are much smaller. These shallow-water animals are equipped with a remarkable **proboscis** for defense and food gathering. The proboscis can be everted rapidly from the anterior part of the body to ensnare prey. The proboscis of some nemertine worms has a piercing stylet to stab prey and inject a toxin.

Gastrotricha and Kinorhyncha

Gastrotrichs and kinorhynchs include a large variety of marine species, but most are so small (usually less than one mm) that they go unnoticed by most observers. They are cylindrical and elongated, with a mouth, feeding structures, and sensory organs at the anterior end (figure 3.15c and d). Marine gastrotrichs and kinorhynchs inhabit sand and mud deposits in shallow water and feed on detritus, diatoms, or other small animals.

Priapulida and Nematoda

More wormlike in appearance are the priapulid and nematode worms (figure 3.15b and d). Only three species occur in the phylum Priapulida. They live buried in intertidal sediments of polar and subpolar waters and seldom exceed 10 cm in size. Priapulid worms are carnivorous, feeding on soft-bodied invertebrates they capture with their eversible proboscis.

The nematode worms are among the most common and widespread multicellular animals. Some are parasitic, but many are free-living. Most marine nematodes live in the bottom sediments and are found at virtually all water depths. In fact, nematodes are probably the most abundant multicellular animals in the marine benthic environment. Locomotion is not well-developed; nematodes depend on quick bending movements of their small bodies. Cylindrical in cross section and greatly elongated, nematodes seldom exceed a few cm in length.

Figure 3.16
A magnified view of a branched colony of ectoprocts with extended feathery lophophores

Entoprocta

Entoprocts are benthic, living on rocks, shells, sponges, and seaweeds. Most are colonial, secreting thin calcareous encrustations over rocks, seaweeds, and the hard shells of some other animals. Superficially, they resemble small colonial hydroids. Their external appearance is also quite similar to that of members of another phylum, the Ectoprocta.

Until recently, entoprocts and ectoprocts were combined in a single phylum, the Bryozoa. But studies of internal structures have shown that these two groups are only distantly related, and two separate phyla are warranted. Individuals of both groups have U-shaped digestive tracts and a crown of tentacles projecting from the upper surface. The mouth and anus of entoprocts open within the ring of tentacles (hence the name Entoprocta—inner anus). The ectoproct mouth is located within the tentacles, but the anus is not. The crown of ciliated feeding tentacles of ectoprocts, a **lophophore,** is characteristic of two other marine phyla.

The Lophophore Bearers

The lophophore is the feeding organ of three structurally dissimilar phyla of marine animals: the Ectoprocta, Phoronida, and Brachiopoda. These and the other phyla to follow are characterized by a true internal body cavity, or **coelom.** This cavity originates during embryonic development and causes the digestive tract to separate from the body wall. This allows the coelomic fluids to move and aid circulation of oxygen, wastes, and nutrients. With a coelom, the digestive tract has become specialized, and its efficiency improved. Body wall muscles function independently of the digestive tract and have a greater range of specialized actions. The coelom was thus a major step in the evolutionary development of more complex animal phyla.

Ectoprocta

The ectoprocts are a major animal phylum, with 4000 freshwater and marine species. They are primarily members of shallow-water benthic communities, occupying the same general habitats as entoprocts. Like entoprocts, ectoprocts are colonial and form encrusting or branching masses of small individuals (usually less than 1 mm in size, figure 3.16). Ectoprocts and entoprocts provide excellent examples of how the evolutionary pathways of quite different animal groups converge to similar adaptive forms and habits when exposed to similar environmental stresses. Such **convergent evolution** is common in several taxonomic groups, and additional examples will be encountered elsewhere in this book.

Phoronida

The phylum Phoronida consists of about fifteen species of elongated, burrowing animals. All are marine and live in tubes in shallow water. During feeding, the lophophore projects out of the tube, but it can be rapidly retracted for protection. The phoronids seldom exceed 20 cm in length and have no appendages except for the lophophore.

Brachiopoda

The brachiopods, or lamp shells, were very successful in the past, with more than 30,000 extinct species described. Fewer than 300 still survive. *Lingula,* for example, has an unbroken fossil history that extends back over the past one-half billion years of earth's history! All brachiopods are benthic and live attached to the sea bottom by a muscular stalklike pedicle (figure 3.17). The outer calcareous shell superficially resembles that of a bivalve mollusk. However, the symmetry of the shells is quite different. Bivalve shells are positioned to the left and right of the soft internal organs. In contrast, brachiopod shells are not symmetrical and are located on the dorsal and ventral sides of the soft organs.

Living brachiopods occupy a wide variety of seafloor niches, from shallow-water rocky cliffs to deep muddy bottoms. Like the phoronids and ectoprocts, the ciliated lophophore gathers minute suspended material for nutrition from seawater.

Figure 3.17
Brachiopods (*Neothyris*) among scattered shell fragments at a depth of 40 m
Courtesy J. Richardson, Victoria Museum, Melbourne

The Mollusks

Mollusca

The mollusks are among the most abundant and easily observable groups of marine animals because they have adapted to all the major marine habitats. It is difficult to characterize such a large and diverse group as the phylum Mollusca but some common traits are observable. Mollusks are unsegmented animals. Most mollusks have a hard external shell surrounding the soft body and use a large muscular foot for locomotion, anchorage, and securing food. Most mollusks have an array of specialized sense organs in the anterior region of their body near the brain. (This pattern of body organization, known as **cephalization,** is most apparent in squids and octopuses.)

This phylum is composed of seven classes. Representatives of five of these classes are quite common and are shown in figure 3.18. Another class, the Monoplacophora is a rare group that was thought to have been extinct for 400 million years. But in 1952, a few living specimens of the genus *Neopilina* were collected from deep water off the coast of Costa Rica. Since then, additional specimens have been collected and carefully studied. Alone among the mollusks, the monoplacophorans exhibit some body segmentation and are thought possibly to represent an evolutionary link between mollusks and the segmented annelid worms.

Chitons belong to the class Polyplacophora. They are characterized by eight calcareous plates embedded in their dorsal surfaces. These animals, found in rocky intertidal areas, use their large muscular foot to cling to protected depressions in rocks. Chitons feed by grazing algae from rocks with a rasping tonguelike organ, the **radula.**

The class Gastropoda includes snails, slugs (marine, freshwater, and terrestrial), limpets, abalones, and nudibranchs. Although one-piece shells are characteristic of this class, several types of gastropods lack shells. Most gastropods are benthic; only a few without shells, or with very light ones, successfully assume a pelagic life-style. Like chitons, many gastropods graze on algae; others feed on detritus and organic-rich sediments. Numerous gastropods are also successful predators of other slow-moving animal species.

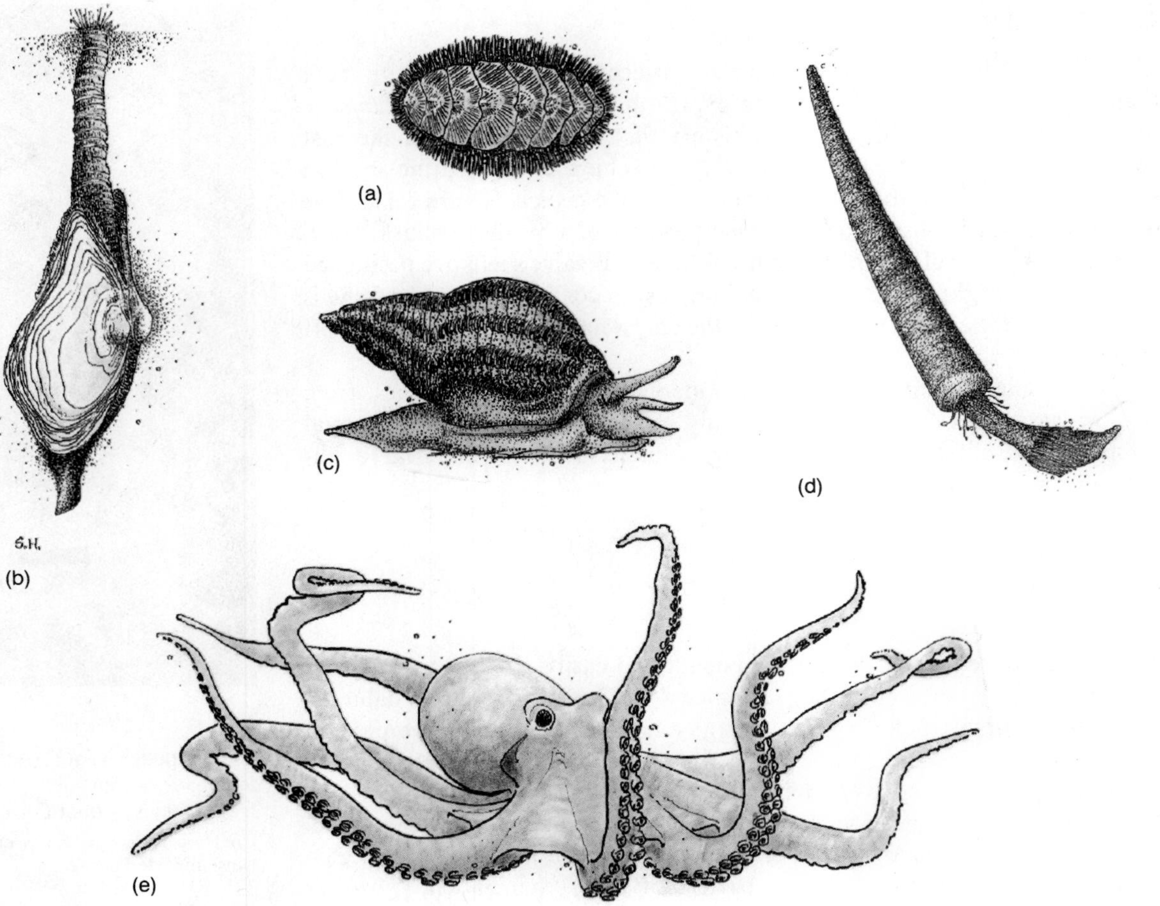

Figure 3.18
Representatives of the common classes of mollusks:
(*a*) Amphineura, (*b*) Bivalvia,
(*c*) Gastropoda,
(*d*) Scaphopoda, and
(*e*) Cephalopoda

The 200 species of tusk shells, class Scaphopoda, are found buried in sediments in a wide range of water depths. As the common name implies, the shells of these animals are elongated and tapered, somewhat like an elephant's tusk but open at both ends. The head and foot project from the opening at the larger end of the shell. Microscopic organisms from the sediment and water are captured by adhesive tentaclelike structures.

The Bivalva, which includes mussels, clams, oysters, and scallops, have hinged two-piece, or bivalve, shells. As adults, most are slow-moving benthic animals. But some, such as mussels and oysters, are cemented to hard substrates. This class has an extensive depth range, from intertidal areas to below 5000 m. Most feed on sediment deposits or on suspended plankton and detritus from the water.

Molluscan evolution has reached its zenith in the class Cephalopoda, the squids, octopuses, cuttlefish, and nautiluses. Members of this class are specialized carnivorous predators with sucker-lined tentacles, well-developed sense organs, and reduction or loss of the external shell typical of other mollusks. A unique propulsion system, using high-speed jets of water, provides speeds greater than those of other marine invertebrates. Cephalopods are also larger than most other invertebrates. The giant squid, *Architeuthis,* may reach 20 m in length, by far the largest living invertebrate species.

Figure 3.19
Sipunculid worms, *Sipunculus*
Courtesy R. Brusca

More Wormlike Phyla

The wormlike body structure of the phyla previously discussed was an extremely successful evolutionary adaptation. We will examine the reasons for this success before introducing the remaining phyla of marine "worms." Most members of the wormlike phyla dwell in soft mud or sand deposits. Their elongated body forms permit effective burrowing movements in spite of a lack of rigid internal skeletons to support the muscles of locomotion. Muscles in the body wall work against the enclosed fluid contents of the body to allow burrowing actions and other body movements. The fluids cannot escape and are essentially incompressible. As such, they provide a **hydrostatic skeleton** for the muscles of the body wall. In the more effective burrowing worms, these muscles are arranged in two sets; circular muscle bands around the body and longitudinal muscles extending the length of the body. Like all other muscles, these muscles can only work by contracting. Thus when the circular muscles of a worm's body contract, its diameter decreases, squeezing its hydrostatic skeleton and forcing the body to elongate. If the rear of the body is anchored, contracting the circular muscles results in a forward movement of the anterior end. The circular muscles resume their precontraction state by relaxing, allowing the longitudinal muscles to shorten the body and make it fatter. These two types of muscles continue to work in opposition to each other to provide an effective sediment burrowing motion for a large variety of marine worms.

Sipuncula

Sipuncula, another major phylum of wormlike creatures, are found throughout the world ocean. The 250 species of sipunculids, or peanut worms, are entirely marine. Most are found in the intertidal zone, but their distribution extends to abyssal depths. Peanut worms are benthic. They live in burrows, crevices, or other protected niches and are often in competition with other wormlike animals. Sipunculids range from 2 mm to over 50 cm in size and have a cylindrical body that is capped by a ring of ciliated tentacles surrounding the anterior mouth (figure 3.19).

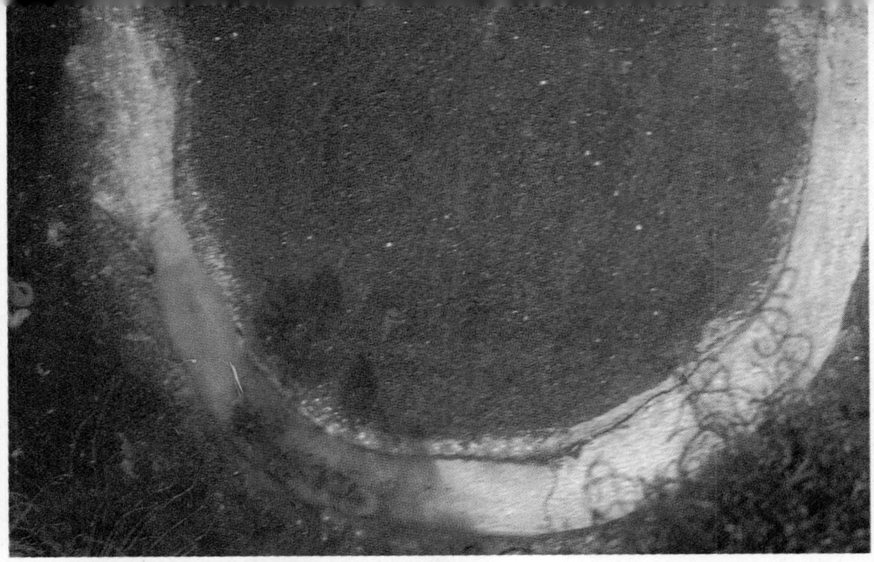

Figure 3.20
The fat innkeeper, *Urechis,* shown within a glass-walled burrow

Echiurida

This small phylum of benthic marine worms resembles peanut worms in size and general shape. Echiurids are common intertidally, but they are occasionally found at depths exceeding 6000 m. Most echiurids live in burrows in the mud. One remarkable feature of echiurids is their extensible proboscis, a feeding and sensory organ that projects from their anterior. In some species, the proboscis is longer than the remainder of the body and is quite effective for gathering food by "mopping" the sediment while the worm remains in the protected confines of its burrow.

Urechis, an echiurid of the California coast known as the fat innkeeper, has a very short proboscis. The proboscis secretes a mucus net from the animal to the wall of its U-shaped burrow (figure 3.20). Usually, the burrow is also inhabited by small crabs, shrimps, or other casual guests. Water is pumped through the burrow by repeated waves of contractions along the worm's body wall. As water passes through the mucus net, extremely fine particles are trapped. When the net is clogged with food, the worm consumes it and constructs another.

Pogonophora

Pogonophorans are almost exclusively deep-water, tube-dwelling marine worms. (Eighty percent of the known species live below 200 m.) This obscure phylum was not even invented until 1900. Since then, about seventy species have been fully described. Adult sizes range from 10 to 35 cm in length. Pogonophorans are noted for their complete lack of an internal digestive tract and are thought to use symbiotic bacteria to provide their energy needs. The remarkably large tube worms recently discovered in deep-sea hot spring communities (figure 7.22) were initially assigned to the phylum Pogonophora. However, a decade of study suggests that they may be sufficiently distinct to warrant placement in a new phylum.

Hemichordata

Hemichordates are a small group of benthic marine worms (acorn worms) closely related to the pogonophorans. They have an anterior proboscis and a soft, flaccid body that is up to 50 cm long. These worms are generally found in shallow water and live in protected areas under rocks or in tubes or burrows.

Chaetognatha

In contrast to the general benthic habitat of most marine wormlike animals, chaetognaths, or arrowworms, are torpedo-shaped planktonic carnivores (figure 3.21). Although they seldom exceed 3 cm in length, they are voracious predators of other zooplankton. Arrowworms swim with rapid darting motions and capture prey with the bristles that surround their mouth. Only about 60 species of arrowworms exist, but they are frequently very abundant in the zooplankton. Certain species of arrowworms apparently respond to and associate with subtle chemical or physical characteristics of seawater. As such, they serve as useful biological indicators of particular oceanic water types.

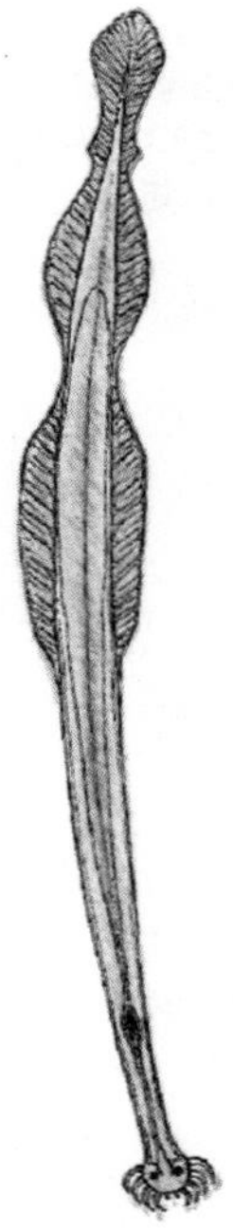

Figure 3.21
Sagitta, a chaetognath

Segmented Animal Phyla

Annelida

The annelids are usually represented by the familiar terrestrial earthworm. However, this phylum also contains a diverse and successful group of marine forms with over 5000 species, the class Polychaeta. Polychaete worms, like other annelids, are segmented, as are members of the next two phyla. The body cavity and internal organs contained within polychaete worms are subdivided into a linear series of structural units called **metameres.** The result of segmentation is a sequential compartmentalization of the worm's hydrostatic skeleton and surrounding muscles. This permits a greater degree of localized changes in body shape and a more controlled and efficient form of locomotion.

Some polychaetes ingest sediment to obtain nourishment, others are carnivorous, and many use a complex tentacle system (figure 3.22) to filter microscopic bits of food from the water. Suspension-feeding polychaetes often occupy partially buried tubes and are common in intertidal areas; however, they are also found in deeper water. One polychaete, *Tomopteris,* is planktonic throughout its life cycle.

Arthropoda

Like annelids, arthropods are segmented linearly. In addition to the advantages of segmentation, arthropods possess a distinctive hard **exoskeleton** that consists of a complex organic substance, **chitin.** This rigid outer skeleton serves not only as an impermeable barrier against fluid loss and bacterial infection but also as a complex lever system for muscle attachment. Its structure resists deformations induced by contracting muscles, allowing faster responses and greater control of movements. Flexing of the body and appendages is limited to thin membranous joints located between the rigid exoskeletal plates. In addition, the exoskeleton cancels the shape-changing advantages of segmentation and hydrostatic skeletons found in annelid worms. The exoskeleton also restricts continuous growth. Periodically, arthropods shed their old exoskeleton and it is replaced by a new larger one as the animal quickly expands to fill it (figure 3.23).

Members of the phylum Arthropoda account for over 75% of all existing animal species identified. Most belong to the class Insecta, whose members are almost exclusively nonmarine. However, three classes of this phylum, the Crustacea, Merostomata, and Pycnogonida, are primarily or completely marine in distribution.

Figure 3.22

The filtering structures of a tube-dwelling polychaete worm

Photo by T. Phillipp

Figure 3.23

Patterns of arthropod and non-arthropod growth. In contrast to the smooth curve of other animals, arthropods rapidly increase their body size in steps following each molt of the exoskeleton.

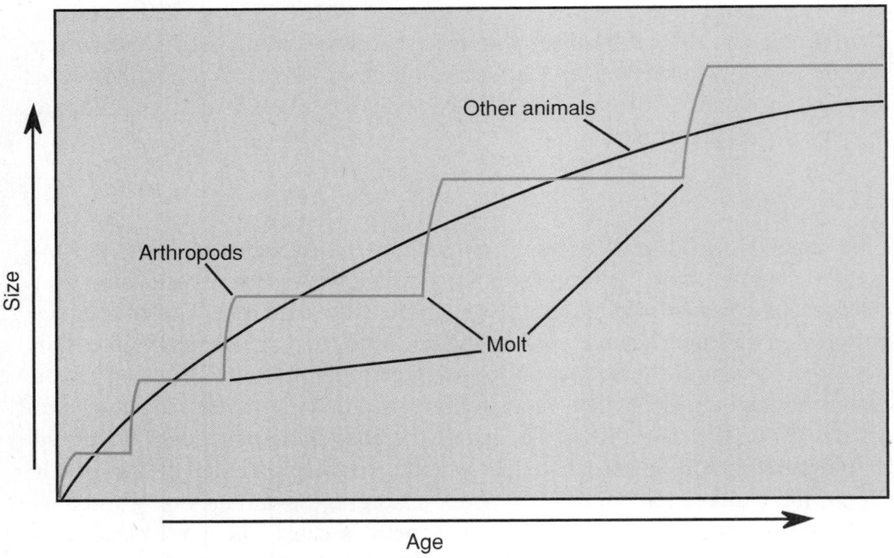

Two classes of arthropods are completely marine, but their diversity is very restricted. The first class, Merostomata, has an extensive fossil history that includes extinct water scorpions 3 m long. Modern representatives include the horseshoe crab, *Limulus,* an inhabitant of the Atlantic and Gulf coasts of North America (figure 3.24). The sea spiders of the class Pycnogonida are long-legged bottom dwellers with very reduced bodies (figure 3.25). Small

Figure 3.24
Two mating horseshoe crabs, *Limulus*
Official photograph U.S. Navy

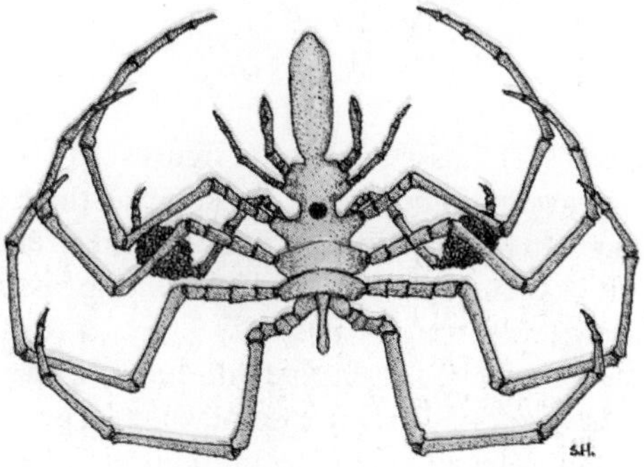

Figure 3.25
A deep-sea pycnogonid with a leg span of about 30 cm

pycnogonids only a few mm in size are quite common intertidally. They can be collected from hydroid or ectoproct colonies or from the blades of intertidal algae. Deep-sea pycnogonids are often much larger and may have leg spans of 60 cm.

The third class, the Crustacea, is an extremely abundant and successful group of marine invertebrates. Obvious and well-known crustaceans include shrimps, crabs, and lobsters. These large, mostly benthic, crustaceans are not representative of the entire class, however. Most marine crustaceans are very small and are major components of the zooplankton.

Crustaceans are arthropods with two pairs of **antennae.** Few other useful generalizations can be made concerning this class. Its members exhibit a tremendous diversity in body structure and mode of feeding (figure 3.26). The range of habitats also varies greatly, from burrowing ghost shrimp to planktonic copepods and parasitic barnacles. Representatives of several of the crustacean subgroups listed in table 3.2 are included in figure 3.26. Two of these groups figure significantly in so many marine trophic associations that they merit special attention.

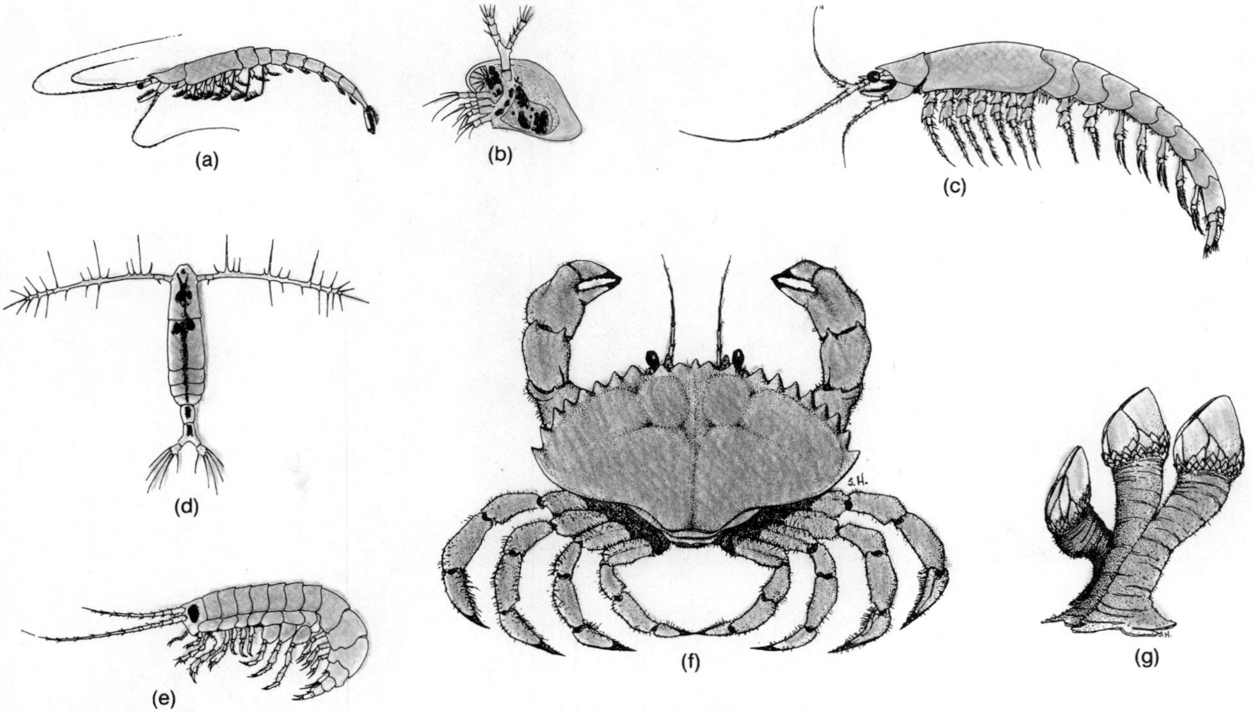

Figure 3.26
A variety of marine crustaceans: (*a*) mysid, (*b*) cladoceran, (*c*) euphausiid, (*d*) copepod, (*e*) amphipod, (*f*) crab, and (*g*) barnacle

The copepods (subclass: Copepoda, figures 2.11 and 3.26g) are small crustaceans, seldom larger than one cm. In spite of their size, their efficient filter-feeding mechanisms (described on p. 277) and overwhelming numbers in pelagic communities dictate that much of the energy available from the first trophic level is channeled through copepods. They, in turn, are consumed by predators as diverse as minute fish larvae and huge right whales.

Euphausiids (figure 3.26c) are somewhat larger than copepods, but they fill similar trophic roles in pelagic communities. These crustaceans have a global distribution (see figure 10.7). The largest species of this group, *Euphausia superba,* grows to 6 to 7 cm. Found in cold waters around Antarctica, this species aggregates in enormous dense shoals sometimes tens of km long. They are a favorite prey of fish, whales, seals, and penguins and are fast becoming the world's largest single-species commercial fishery (chapter 12 examines this topic).

Radial Symmetry Revisited

Echinodermata

The echinoderms, an exclusively marine phylum, are widely distributed throughout the sea. They are common intertidally and are also abundant at great depths. Almost all forms are benthic as adults. Most are characterized by a calcareous skeleton, external spines or knobs, and a five-sided, or **pentamerous,** radial body symmetry (figure 3.27). Because echinoderms develop from bilaterally symmetrical larval stages, radial body symmetry is a secondary condition in this phylum. This and other aspects of their evolutionary history separate them on the phylogenetic tree of animal groups (figure 3.2) from those phyla characterized by primary radial body symmetry. A unique

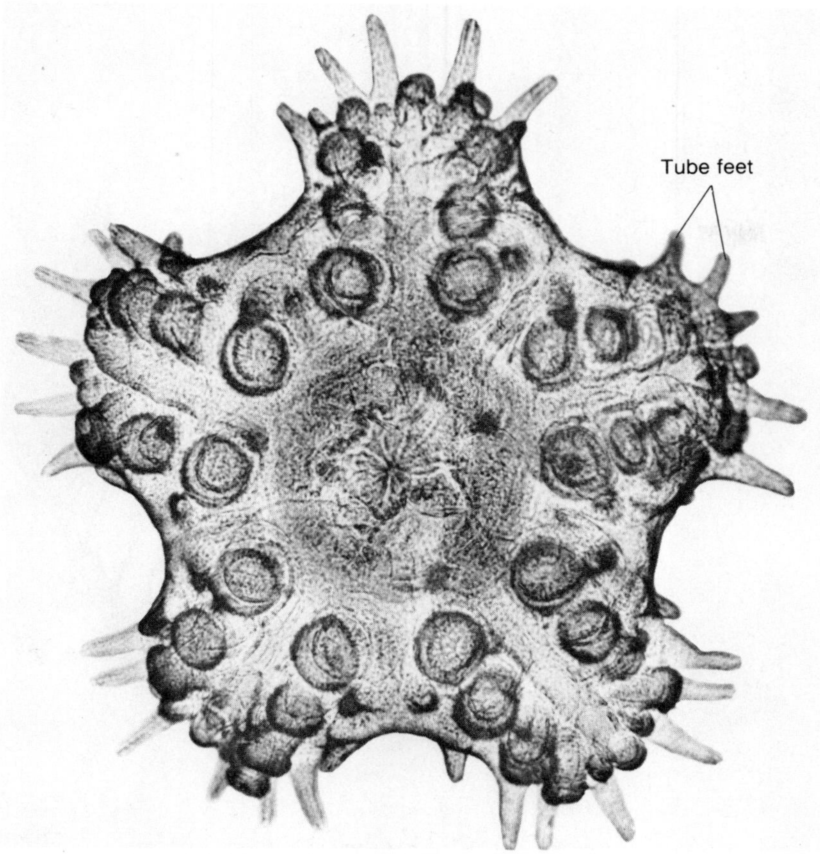

Figure 3.27
A very young sea star with numerous tube feet projecting from its body
Courtesy Carolina Biological Supply Company

internal **water-vascular system** hydraulically operates the numerous tube feet. The tube feet extend through the skeleton to the outside and serve as respiratory, excretory, sensory, and locomotor organs.

Five classes of echinoderms currently exist. Representatives of each are shown in figure 3.28. The Echinoidea are spiny herbivores or sediment ingesters variously known as sea urchins, heart urchins, and sand dollars. The Asteroidea, or sea stars, are usually five-armed, but the number of arms may vary. Six-, ten-, and twenty-one-armed sea stars are known. Most sea stars are carnivorous, but a few use cilia and mucus to collect fine food particles. Feather stars and sea lilies (class Crinoidea), usually attached to the sea bottom with the mouth oriented upward, trap plankton and detritus with their arms and the mucus secretions. Sea cucumbers of the class Holothuroidea are sausage-shaped and have their mouth located at one end of their body. The body wall is muscular, with reduced skeletal plates and spines. A few sea cucumbers feed on plankton, but most ingest sediment. The brittle stars (class Ophiuroidea) are smaller than most other echinoderms, but are very common animals in soft muds, rocky bottoms, and coral reefs.

The Chordates

Chordata

The phylum Chordata exhibits a remarkable variety of body forms. Yet at some stage in their development, all members of this phylum possess a supportive **notochord** (made of a cartilage-like material), a **hollow dorsal nerve cord,** and **pharyngeal arches.**

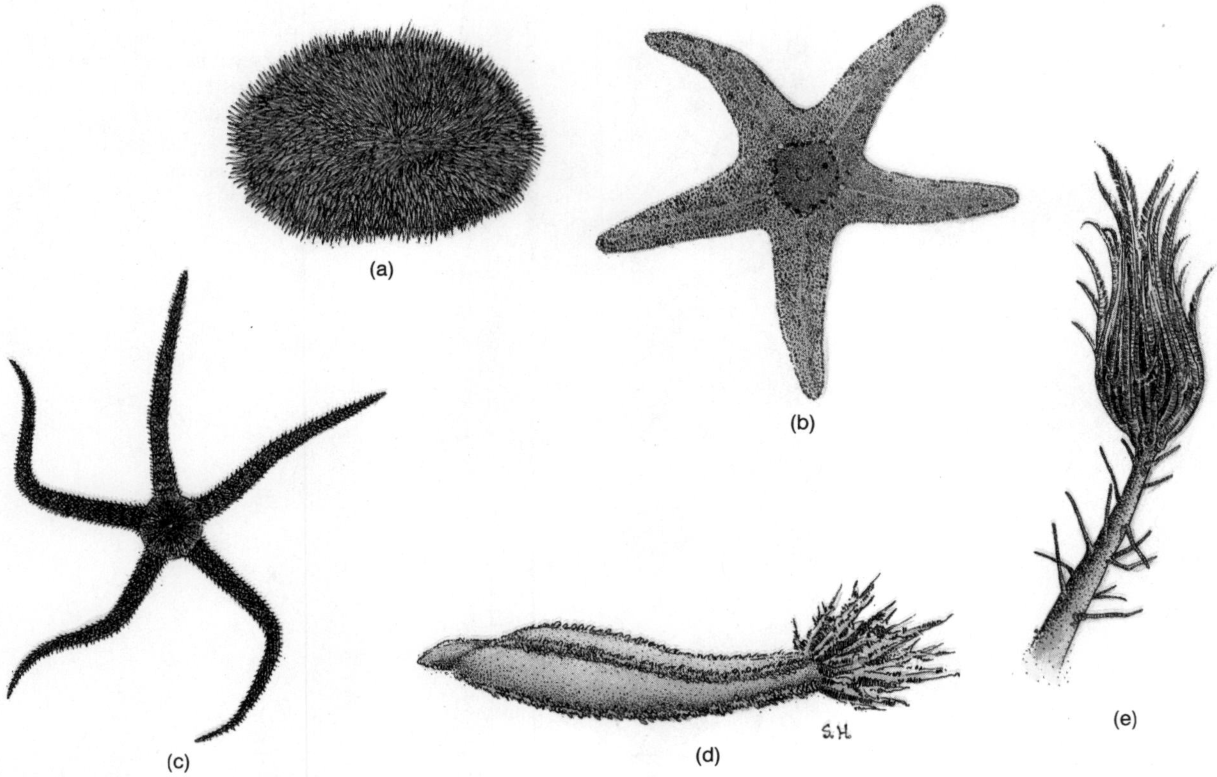

Figure 3.28
Representatives of the five living echinoderm classes: (*a*) Echinoidea, (*b*) Asteroidea, (*c*) Ophiuroidea, (*d*) Holothuroidea, and (*e*) Crinoidea

The subphylum Urochordata includes animals such as benthic filter-feeding sea squirts (figure 3.29) and the planktonic gelatinous salps. Another subphylum of the chordates, Cephalochordata, includes the lancelet *Amphioxus*. These animals are small and tadpole-shaped and live partially buried tailfirst in near-shore sediments.

The unique feature of the third subphylum, the Vertebrata, is the **vertebral column** that extends through the main axis of the body for support. This single feature is often used arbitrarily (and unfortunately) to divide the animal kingdom into two disparate groups, the invertebrates and the vertebrates (animals with a vertebral column). The marine vertebrates (figure 3.30) include three classes of fish as well as three classes of tetrapods. Fish are difficult to precisely characterize; but, typically they grow or live in water, swim with fins, and utilize gills for oxygen and CO_2 exchange.

More species of fish exist than all other vertebrate groups combined, and a large portion of these fish are marine. The members of class Agnatha exhibit a mixture of primitive and specialized characteristics. Agnathans lack paired fins and biting jaws. As adults both types of living agnathans, the lampreys and hagfish, are parasitic or scavengers. The class Chondrichthyes (cartilaginous fish) includes sharks, skates, and rays. Bony fish (class Osteichthyes) account for all other living fish. Chapter 11 examines the cartilaginous and bony fishes in more detail.

Tetrapods are four-limbed, air-breathing vertebrates with a terrestrial evolutionary history. A few species of snakes, turtles, and iguanas from three reptilian orders are succeeding quite well in the sea, as are their nonmarine relatives on land. The same is true for several orders of birds. Penguins, for instance, spend most of their lives in the ocean, leaving only to rear their young. Many other birds are semimarine and use the sea as a source of food.

Figure 3.29
Nearly transparent sea squirts, each with a small incurrent and a large excurrent opening for circulating water through its body cavity
Photo by T. Phillipp

Three orders of mammals are conspicuous in marine habitats. Seals, sea lions, walruses, and sea otters (order Carnivora) are quite agile in the sea, yet all except the otter must leave the ocean to give birth. The other two orders of marine mammals, Cetacea (whales) and Sirenia (manatees and dugongs), need never leave the sea. The sirenians, not a numerous or especially well-known group, are placid herbivores of warm coastal waters. Occupying the apex of marine mammal evolution are the cetaceans—the whales, dolphins, and porpoises. The many adaptations that permit these active, warm-bodied, air-breathing birds and mammals to succeed in a cold and watery environment are the subject of chapter 12.

Figure 3.30
Marine vertebrate classes: (*a*) Agnatha (hagfish); (*b*) Chondrichthyes (shark); (*c*) Osteichthyes (bass); (*d*) Reptilia (turtle); (*e*) Aves (pelican); and (*f*) Mammalia (dolphin)

Summary

The animal and protist kingdoms are well represented in the marine environment. All major and most minor phyla have at least some marine species, and several phyla are found only in the sea. To deal with this diversity, the taxonomic system of classification serves as a framework around which the discussion of these phyla is organized. Each phylum and its major subgroups are briefly described to provide the means for acquiring a working familiarity with marine protozoan and animal groups. The phyla are introduced in an order generally corresponding to an ascent of the phylogenetic tree (see figure 3.2). Multicellularity, bilateral body symmetry, the evolution of a coelom, and cephalization appear as major trends along the evolutionary paths of the animal kingdom.

Review Questions

1. Discuss some of the advantages and disadvantages inherent in grouping living organisms into the classification schemes outlined in this chapter.
2. Many common marine animals have wormlike body forms. What survival advantages does this body shape create for mud or sand dwellers?
3. List and discuss the advantages and disadvantages of the rigid arthropod exoskeleton in comparison to the fluid hydrostatic skeleton of annelid worms.

4. List the genus names of two common local intertidal animals that exhibit radial body symmetry.
5. Use the general approach presented in box 3.1 to construct a phylogenetic tree for the organisms listed in table 3.1.

Cnidaria ; Ctenophora
Physalia ; Pleurobranchia

Questions for Further Discussion

1. What survival advantages and disadvantages might an animal such as a sea anemone with radial body symmetry have over an animal with bilateral symmetry?
2. Why do you think many critical sense organs are concentrated in the head region of "higher" animals rather than in other parts of their bodies?
3. Why are protists placed in the same kingdom (in a five-kingdom classification system) as photosynthetic diatoms and dinoflagellates?

Suggestions for Further Reading

Books

Alexander, R. McN. 1979. *The invertebrates.* New York: Cambridge University Press.

Margulis, L., and K. V. Schwartz. 1987. *Five kingdoms: An illustrated guide to the phyla of life on Earth.* San Francisco: W. H. Freeman.

National Research Council. 1981. *Marine invertebrates: Laboratory animal management.* Washington, D.C.: National Academy Press.

Niesen, T. M. 1982. *The marine biology coloring book.* New York: Harper and Row.

Russell-Hunter, W. D. 1979. *Life of invertebrates.* New York: Macmillan.

Warner, G. F. 1977. *The biology of crabs.* New York: Van Nostrand Reinhold.

Wells, M. J. 1978. *Octopus: Physiology and behavior of an advanced invertebrate.* New York: John Wiley.

Articles

Atema, J. 1980. Senses in the sea: An introduction. *Oceanus* 23(2):2–4. Also see other articles in this issue describing sensory capabilities.

Hadley, N. F. 1986. The arthropod cuticle. *Scientific American* (July) 244:104–12.

Roper, C. F. E., and K. J. Boss. 1982. The giant squid. *Scientific American* (April) 246:96–105.

Valentine, W. 1978. The evolution of multicellular plants and animals. *Scientific American* (September) 239:140–58.

Marine Primary Producers

Chapter 4

Kelp forest
Photo by T. Phillipp

Box 4 *Microscopes—The Small View*

Your eyes are capable of clearly distinguishing visual features larger than 0.1 mm (or 100 μm). Yet almost all eucaryotic cells are smaller than 0.1 mm. Most phytoplankton and marine protozoans are much too small to see without some magnification. The impact of microscopes on how we view life in the sea has been extensive.

In the three centuries since Robert Hooke first described cells from his microscopic observations, cell studies have benefited from the development of two different types of magnifying systems, light microscopes and electron microscopes. The microscopes' names are based on the type of energy beam used to illuminate the sample being observed. Both microscopes have high-magnification versions that pass the energy beams through the sample as well as lower-magnification versions that bounce the illumination beam off the sample. Each microscope has its own strengths and weaknesses.

Light microscopes depend on light beams to illuminate the specimen being observed. In **dissecting,** or **reflected light, microscopes,** magnification is low (up to 50×) and features smaller than 5–10 μm cannot be resolved. These microscopes are useful for observing multicellular or large unicellular specimens. High quality **transmission light microscopes** provide much more magnification (up to 1500×) and finer resolution (to 0.2 μm), but the specimen must be sufficiently thin and transparent to allow the illuminating beam of light to pass through it. The transmission light microscope is typically used to observe single cells or thin slices of multicellular tissues. Thus, it is more limited than the dissecting microscope for use on live organisms.

The maximum resolution of light microscopes is limited by the wavelength of light itself. It is impossible to build microscopes with greater resolving power as long as visible light is being used to illuminate the specimen. A breakthrough was achieved in the middle of this century with the development of the electron microscope. Now, electron beams with much shorter wavelengths than those of visible light can be focused with magnets rather than optical lenses and used to illuminate a specimen. As with light microscopes, both a low magnification **scanning electron microscope** (SEM), using electron beams reflected off the specimen, and a higher magnification **transmission electron microscope** (TEM), using electron beams passed through very thin slices of cells, are in widespread use. The SEM has a resolving power of about 0.01 μm (about 20 times better than the best light microscope) and is appreciated for its clarity and focus in depth of field.

Presently available TEMs have enormous resolving power (0.0005 μm, or about 400 times greater than the best light microscope). Two major drawbacks of electron microscopes limit their obvious advantages over light microscopes. First, they are large, expensive to purchase and maintain, and nonportable. Second, biological materials do not reflect electrons very well, so the specimen being studied must be coated with a very thin film of electron-reflecting metal atoms, such as gold or platinum. This procedure is lethal; consequently electron microscopes can never be used to study live cells or organisms. In spite of this, both scanning and transmission electron microscopes have contributed greatly to our overall understanding of the structures of very small cells.

Within the sunlit surface layer of the sea, marine primary producers thrive, ranging from extremely small cyanobacteria to tree-sized kelp plants. This chapter introduces the major groups of these marine autotrophs and describes their more obvious features.

Members of the abundant plant groups so familiar on land—ferns, mosses, and seed plants—are poorly represented or totally absent from the marine environment. The majority of marine primary producers are quite different in structure and in many functions from their terrestrial counterparts. At the beginning of this century, most marine primary producers were collectively referred to as *algae* and were lumped together in a single division, the Thallophyta. By the 1920s, it was recognized that algae comprised several distinct groups of organisms spanning the boundaries of three kingdoms, the Monera, Protista, and Plantae.

Currently, marine species from approximately a dozen divisions on the photosynthetic side of figure 3.2 have been recognized and described. These divisions are characterized by their unique combinations of photosynthetic

Box 4 *Microscopes—The Small View*

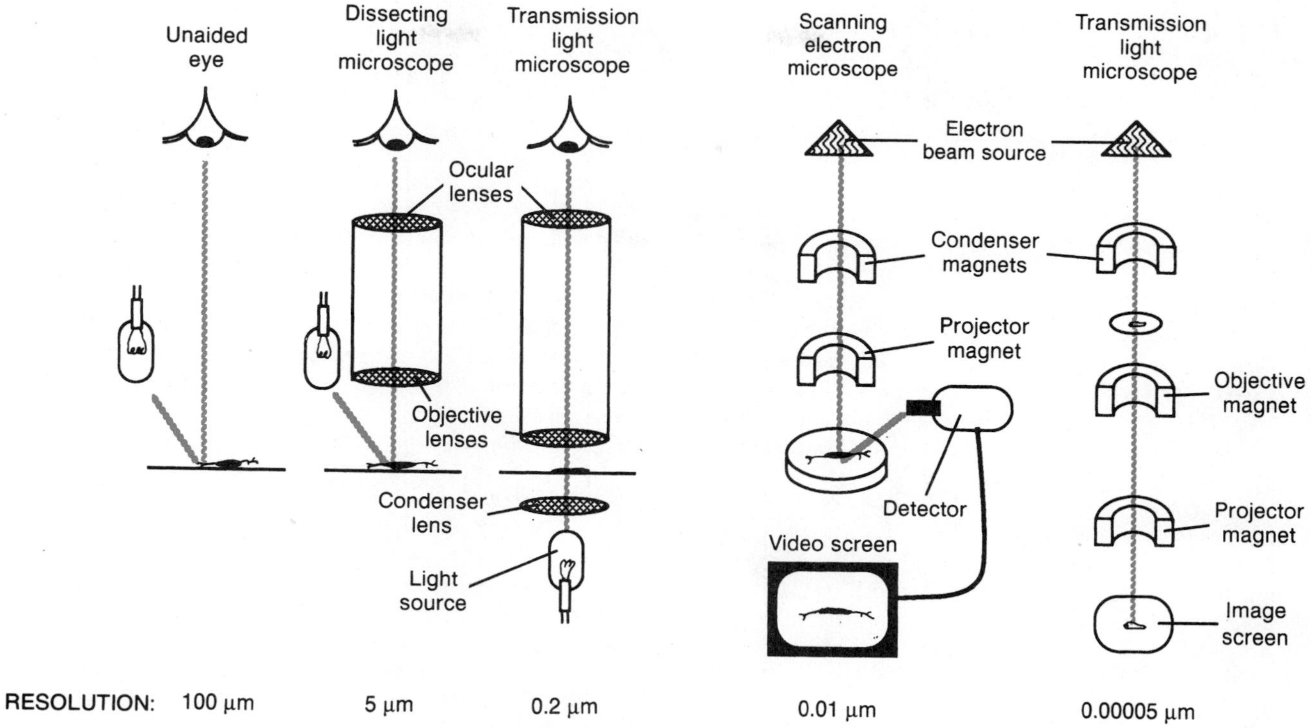

pigments, cell-wall structures, storage products, and growth forms (table 4.1). Of these, only five are predominantly marine: the Cyanobacteria, Chrysophyta, Dinophyta, Phaeophyta, and Rhodophyta. Two other divisions, the Chlorophyta and Anthophyta, are found mostly in fresh water and on land, but they still contribute measurably to some coastal marine communities.

Phytoplankton

Almost all marine phytoplankton belong to three divisions in the kingdoms Monera and Protista. Consequently, they are essentially all single-celled microscopic organisms. They are found dispersed throughout the photic zone of the oceans and account for the major share of primary productivity in the marine environment. Figure 4.1 shows the four size categories into which phytoplankton cells are grouped. Only in the last few years has it been possible to collect representative samples of the exceptionally small **picoplankton** and **ultraplankton.** As our knowledge of these very small phytoplankton groups improves, our understanding of their contribution to marine food webs is increasing. Presently, it is thought that the most important primary producers in all marine environments, but especially in oceanic waters, are **nanoplankton**-sized or smaller.

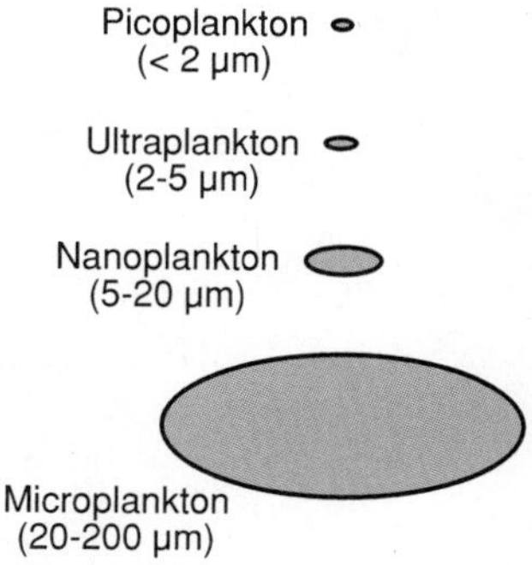

Figure 4.1
Relative sizes of phytoplankton groups. All are enlarged 1000×. At the same magnification, a human hair is as thick as this page is wide.

Table 4.1
Major Divisions of Marine Primary Producers and Their General Characteristics

Division (Common Name)	Approx. No. of Living Species	Proportion of Species Marine (%)	General Size and Structure	Photosynthetic Pigments	Storage Products	Habit
Cyanobacteria (blue-green algae)	200	~75	Unicellular, prokaryotic, nonflagellated, microscopic	Chlorophyll *a* Carotenes Phycobilins	Starch	Mostly benthic
Chrysophyta (golden-brown algae) (coccolithophores) (silicoflagellates) (diatoms)	650 200 ? 6000–10,000	~20 96 most 30–50	Unicellular, often flagellated, microscopic	Chlorophyll *a, c* Xanthophylls Carotenes	Chrysolaminarin Oils	Planktonic and benthic
Dinophyta (dinoflagellates)	1100+	93	Unicellular or colonial, flagellated, microscopic	Chlorophyll *a, c* Xanthophylls Carotenes	Starch Fats Oils	Planktonic
Phaeophyta (brown algae)	1500	99.7	Multicellular, macroscopic	Chlorophyll *a, c* Xanthophylls Carotenes	Laminarin and others	Mostly benthic
Rhodophyta (red algae)	4000	98	Unicellular and multicellular, mostly macroscopic	Chlorophyll *a* Carotenes Phycobilins	Starch and others	Benthic
Chlorophyta (green algae)	7000	13	Unicellular and multicellular, microscopic to macroscopic	Chlorophyll *a, b* Carotenes	Starch	Mostly benthic
Anthophyta (flowering plants)	250,000	0.018	Multicellular, macroscopic	Chlorophyll *a, b* Carotenes	Starch	Benthic

Adapted from Scagel et al. 1965, Dawson 1981, and Kaufman, P. B. et al. 1989.

Cyanobacteria

Marine cyanobacteria have been the object of much recent study. Their small cell size (most are less than 5 μm) makes them very difficult to collect and examine. Their cellular structure (figure 4.2) is typical of procaryotes, with only a few of the complex membrane-bound organelles so obvious in larger eucaryotic cells (see figure 2.2). Unlike photosynthetic bacteria, photosyn-

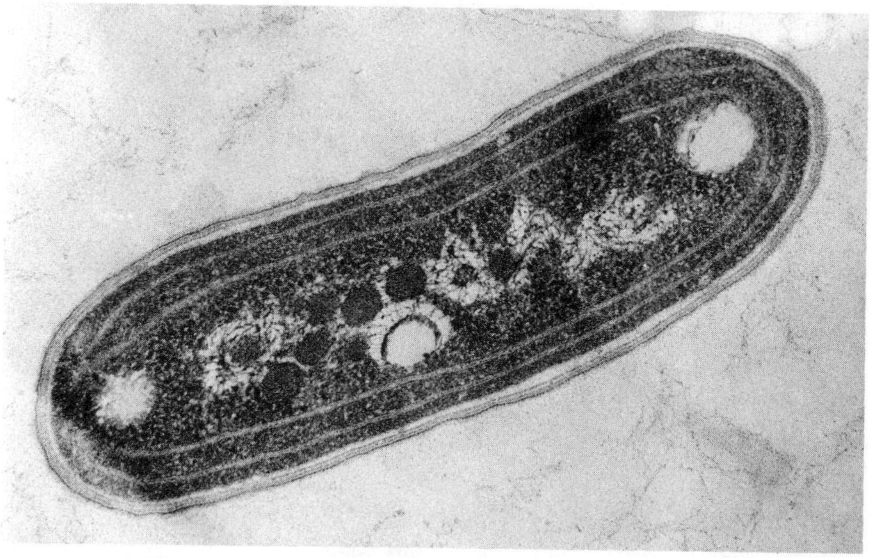

Figure 4.2
A TEM of a marine cyanobacterium, *Synechoccus*
Reproduced by permission from J. B. Waterbury, Canadian Bulletin of Fisheries and Aquatic Sciences 214:71-120, 1986; Eds. T. Platt and W. K. W. Li.

Figure 4.3
Stromatolites, resembling mushrooms one meter high, grow on the shallow sandy bottom of Shark Bay, Australia.
Photo by D. Doubilet

thesis in cyanobacteria is similar to that in eucaryotic autotrophs in structure and function. It is based on chlorophyll *a* and results in the production of oxygen.

Marine cyanobacteria are especially abundant in intertidal and estuarine areas, with a lesser role in oceanic waters. Some species of cyanobacteria produce dense blooms in warm-water regions. The red phycobilin pigment of *Oscillatoria* is responsible for the color and name of the Red Sea.

Cyanobacteria are not newcomers to marine environments. Modern cyanobacteria descend from some of the earliest forms of life on earth. Fossil stromatolites over three billion years old are remarkably similar to modern ones living at the edges of tropical lagoons in Australia (figure 4.3).

Figure 4.4
SEMs of three coccolithophore cells, each showing clearly their dense coverings of coccoliths. (*a*) *Emiliania huxleyi,* (*b*) *Umbilicosphaera* spp., and (*c*) *Anthosphaera* spp. All magnified approximately 4500×.
Courtesy F. Reid, Scripps Institution of Oceanography

Chrysophyta

This division consists of two classes: the Chrysophyceae and the Bacillariophyceae. The marine members of this division are single-celled. Like all other eucaryotic autotrophs, their primary photosynthetic pigment is chlorophyll *a*. In addition, Chrysophyta have accessory chlorophyll *c* and golden or yellow-brown xanthophyll pigments also characteristic of brown algae. Most have mineralized cell walls or internal skeletons of silica or calcium carbonate. Some species possess flagella for motility but, like other planktonic organisms, can do very little to counter horizontal transport by water currents.

Although most species of Chrysophyceae are found in fresh water, two groups, the coccolithophores and silicoflagellates, are relatively abundant in some marine areas. Most marine coccolithophores and silicoflagellates are nanoplankton in size. Only in recent years has the use of membrane filters and fine collection screens and the wider application of scanning electron microscopic (SEM) techniques provided us with a better look at the very small nanoplankton (see box 4).

Coccolithophores have numerous small calcareous plates, or **coccoliths,** embedded in their cell walls (figure 4.4). Coccoliths from seafloor sediments have been studied, but it was not until 1898 that the photosynthetic cells producing them were observed. It has been suggested that coccoliths reflect much of the ambient light in clear tropical waters, permitting these organisms to thrive in areas of very high light intensity. Coccolithophores are found in all warm and temperate seas and may account for a substantial portion of the total primary productivity. In the Sargasso Sea, for instance, a single species, *Emiliania huxleyi* (figure 4.4a), seems to be responsible for most of the photosynthesis. However, the photosynthetic role of coccolithophores in marine primary production is not yet well defined.

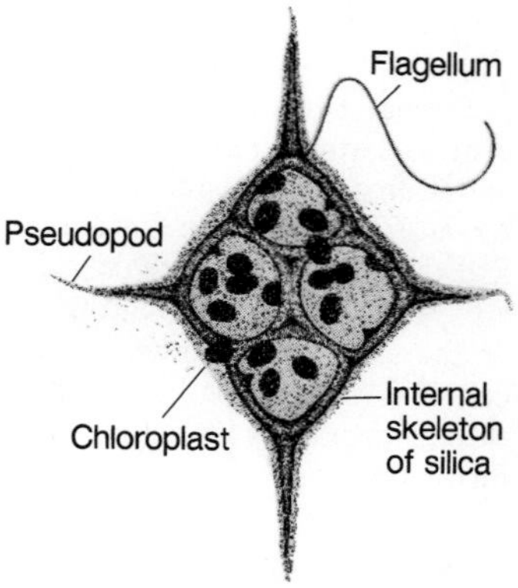

Figure 4.5
Dictyocha, a common marine silicoflagellate

The silicoflagellates, like the coccolithophores, were first recognized and identified from fossil skeletons in marine sediments. Silicoflagellates have internal, and often ornate, silica skeletons. They have one or two flagella and many small chloroplasts (figure 4.5). The significance of silicoflagellates as marine primary producers has not been evaluated, but their contribution is thought to be small.

The most obvious and often the most abundant members of the phytoplankton are the diatoms (class: Bacillariophyceae). Although diatoms are unicellular, they may occur in chains or other loose aggregates of cells. Cell sizes range from less than 15 μm in length to 1 mm (1,000 μm) in length. Most diatoms are between 50 and 500 μm in size and are typically much larger than coccolithophores or silicoflagellates (figure 4.6). Diatoms have a cell wall, or **frustule,** composed of pectin with large amounts (up to 95%) of silica. The frustule consists of two closely fitting halves, the **epitheca** and the **hypotheca** (figure 4.7). Planktonic diatoms usually have many small chloroplasts scattered throughout the cytoplasm, but in low light intensities, the chloroplasts may aggregate near the exposed cell ends.

Diatoms exist in an immense variety of shapes derived from two basic cell shapes. The frustules of most planktonic species appear radially symmetrical from an end view. Circular, triangular, and modified square shapes are common. These are known as centric diatoms. Other diatoms, especially benthic forms, display varying types of bilateral symmetry and are termed pennate diatoms. Only pennate diatoms are capable of locomotion. The mechanism for locomotion is not fully understood, but it is believed to involve a wavelike motion on the cytoplasmic surface that extends through a groove (the **raphe**) in the frustule. This flowing motion is accomplished only when the diatom is in contact with another surface. Diatoms capable of locomotion are generally restricted to shallow water sediments or to the surfaces of larger plants and animals.

The silicate frustules of diatoms exhibit large sculptured pits arranged irregularly or in striking geometric patterns (figure 4.8a). Each large pit penetrates a structural unit of the cell wall, usually hexagonal in shape,

Figure 4.6
This SEM illustrates the size difference between a typical centric diatom, *Thalassiosira,* and four coccolithophore cells, *Crenalithus;* both the diatom and the coccolithophore cells adhere to a pad of coccoliths on the underside of the diatom cell. The association between these two species is thought to be symbiotic, but its precise nature is still unresolved.
Courtesy F. Reid, Scripps Institution of Oceanography

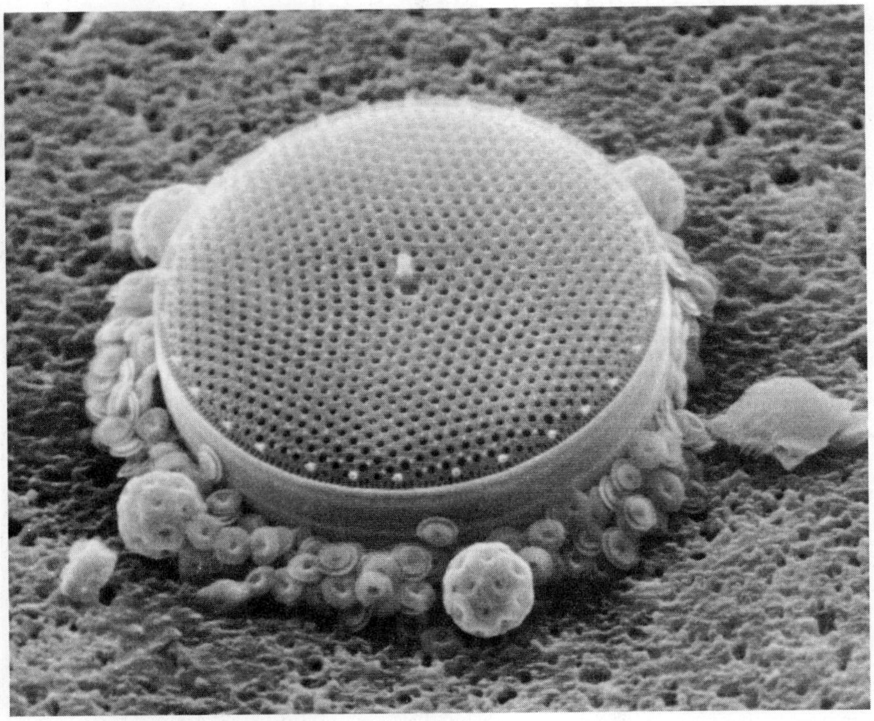

Figure 4.7
Another SEM view of *Thalassiosira,* a coastal diatom, clearly showing the epitheca, hypotheca, and a connecting girdle of cell wall material
Courtesy G. Fryxell

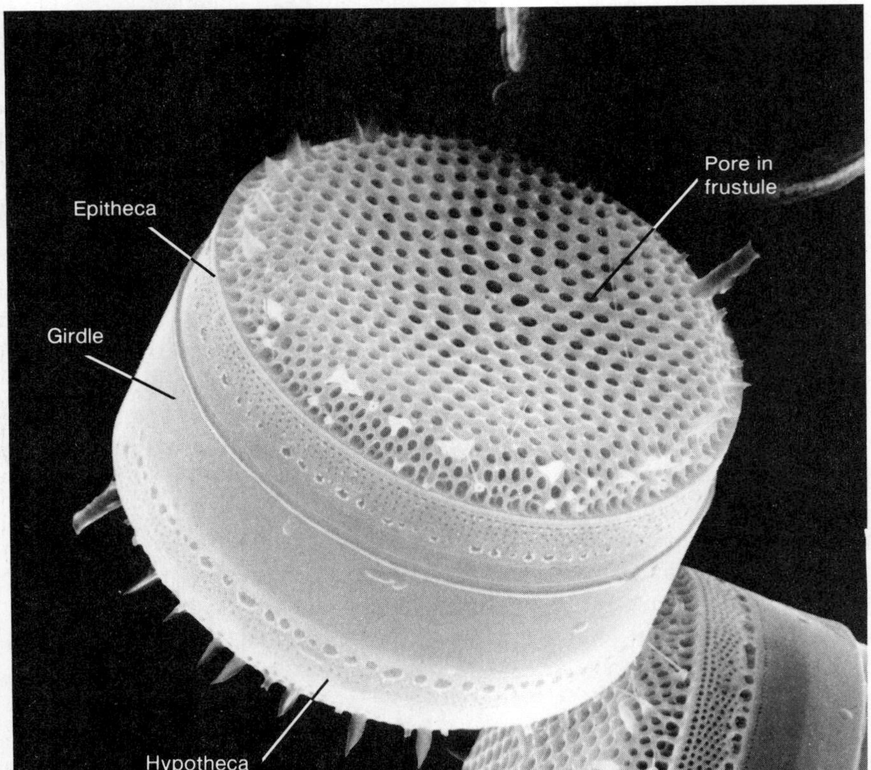

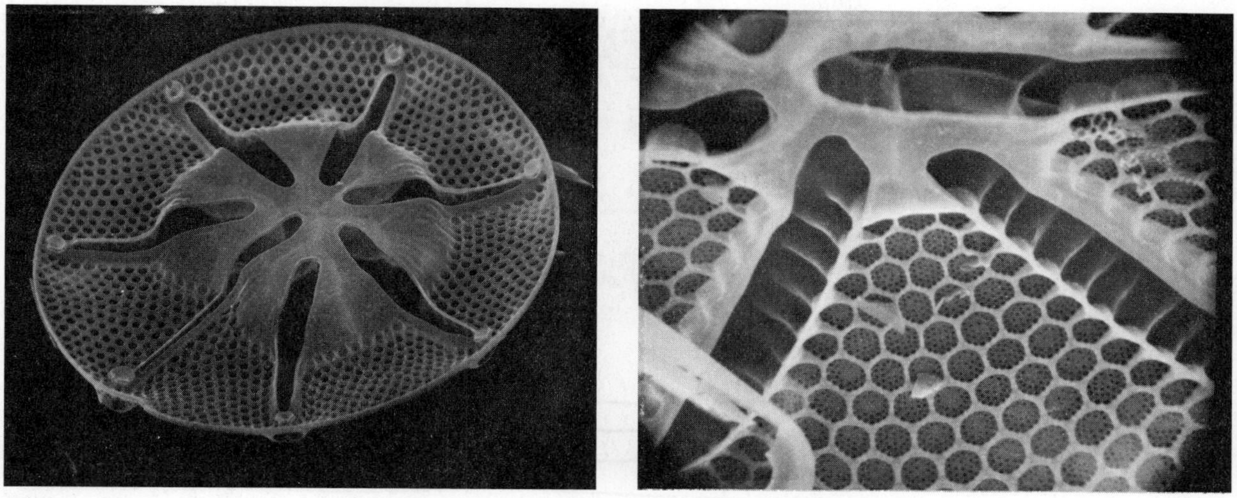

(a) (b)

Figure 4.8
SEMs of a centric diatom, *Asteromphalus heptacles.* (*a*) The entire cell (4700×); (*b*) a highly magnified portion of a similar cell showing the character of perforations through the frustule.
Courtesy E. Venrick, Scripps Institution of Oceanography

called the **areolus** (figure 4.8b). The large outer pit connects with fine inner pores to facilitate water, nutrient, and waste exchange between the diatom's cytoplasm and the external environment.

Diatoms and most other protists reproduce by simple cell division. An individual parent cell divides in half to produce two daughter cells (figure 4.9), and each daughter cell grows to repeat the process. This method of reproduction can yield a large number of diatoms in a short period of time. When conditions for growth are favorable, rates of cell division greater than once each day are not uncommon. By dividing every day, a single diatom requires less than three weeks to produce one million daughter cells. Populations of diatoms and other rapidly dividing unicellular plants thus have an exceptional capacity to respond rapidly to improved growth conditions.

Restrictions of size and shape imposed upon diatoms by the rigid frustule create a peculiar cellular reproduction problem (figure 4.10). During diatom cell division, two new frustule halves are formed inside the original frustule (b). One is the same size as the hypotheca of the parent cell (a) and is destined to become the hypotheca of the larger daughter cell (c). The other newly formed frustule half becomes the new hypotheca for the other daughter cell. Each daughter cell receives its epitheca from the original frustule of the parent cell. The daughter cells grow (c) and repeat the process (d, e). This method of cell division is efficient in the use of silica for new frustules, as the old frustules are not discarded. However, a slight decrease in the average cell size results with each successive cell division. Reduction of cell size may continue for many months, eventually reaching a minimum of about 25% of the original cell size. This size reduction is not observed in all natural diatom populations, suggesting that continual readjustment of cell diameter occurs in some species.

Figure 4.9
Cells in a chain of *Stephanopyxis* just after synchronized division was completed. The darker half of each cell is the newly formed hypotheca, still connected by a girdle of silicate.

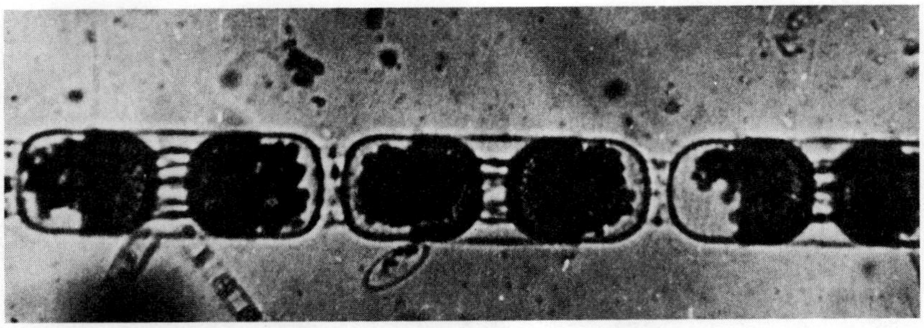

Figure 4.10
Diatom cell division and subsequent size reduction. Numerals represent distinct cell sizes.

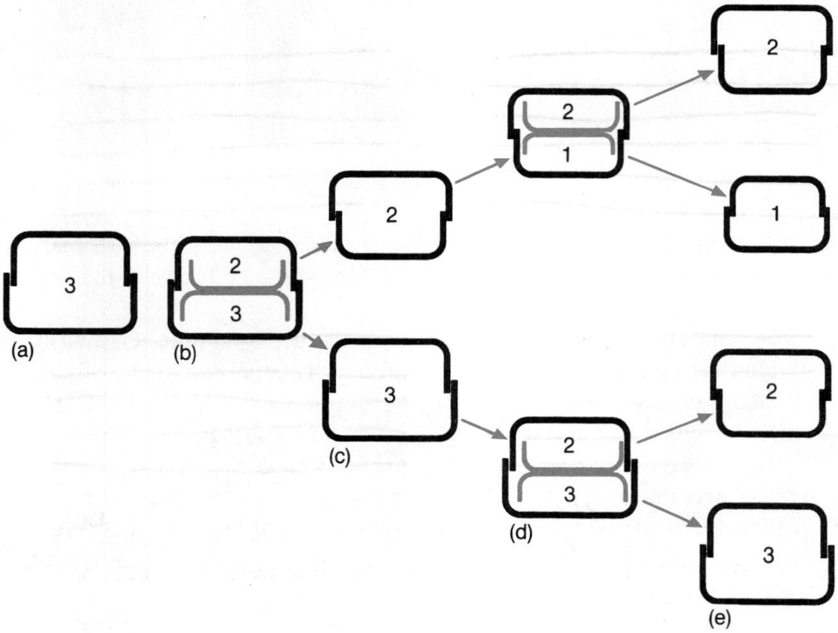

When the minimum cell size is reached, the small diatom sheds its enclosing frustule, and the naked cell, known as an **auxospore,** flows out. The auxospore enlarges to the original cell size, forms a new frustule, and begins dividing again to repeat the entire sequence.

The variety of planktonic diatom species existing in temperate waters is impressive. Figure 4.11 illustrates a few of the more common types.

Dinophyta

The division Dinophyta (also known as Pyrrophyta or dinoflagellates) includes a few species that are not photosynthetic; instead, they obtain energy from organic compounds dissolved in seawater or by ingesting particulate bits of food. However, most marine dinoflagellates are photosynthetic, and their share of the total marine plant production is significant; in warmer seas, it often surpasses that of diatoms.

Dinoflagellates (figure 4.12) are typically unicellular, with a large nucleus, two flagella, and several small chloroplasts containing photosynthetic pigments similar to those of diatoms. One broad, ribbonlike flagellum encircles the cell in a transverse groove. The other, a longitudinal flagellum, projects forward and pulls the cell, providing forward motion. Cell sizes range

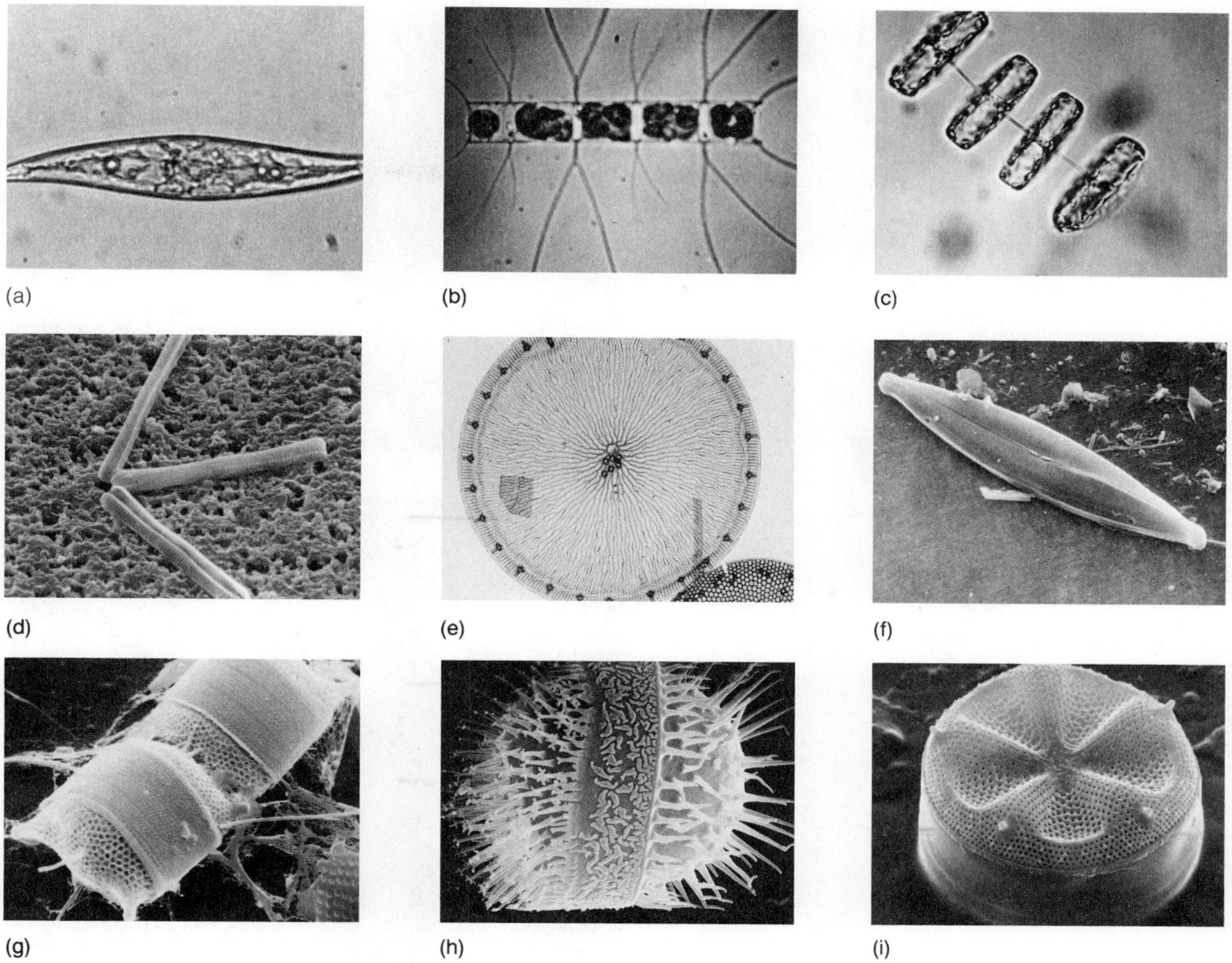

Figure 4.11
Light (*a–c*) and scanning electron (*d–i*) micrographs of several common types of temperate-water planktonic diatoms: (*a*) *Gyrosigma;* (*b*) *Chaetoceros;* (*c*) *Thalassiosira;* (*d*) *Thalassiothrix;* (*e*) *Coscinodiscus;* (*f*) *Nitzchia;* (*g*) *Biddulphia;* (*h*) *Chaetoceros,* resting spore; (*i*) *Actinoptychus*
Courtesy F. Reid and K. Lang, Scripps Institution of Oceanography

from 25 to 1,000 μm. In armored forms, the cell wall consists of articulating cellulose plates arranged irregularly over the cell surface. The plates may be perforated by many pores. Spines, wings, horns, or other ornamentations may also decorate the cell wall. Figure 4.13 illustrates a few common marine dinoflagellates.

Dinoflagellates reproduce asexually by longitudinal cell division. Each new daughter cell retains part of the old cell wall and quickly rebuilds the missing part after cell division. Intermittent sexual reproduction has been reported in a few species; it is rapid and usually occurs in the dark, making it difficult to observe in natural conditions. The rate of reproduction is extremely rapid and approaches that of diatoms. Under optimal growth conditions, dense concentrations of dinoflagellates are quickly produced. Cell concentrations in these **blooms** are often so dense that they color the water red, brown, or green.

At night, dense blooms of luminescent species (such as *Noctiluca* or *Ceratium*) become visible as a faint glow when disturbed by a ship's bow, a swimmer, or a wave breaking onshore. This luminescent glow is often highlighted by pinpoint flashes of larger crustaceans or ctenophores. This biological production of light, or **bioluminescence,** occurs in several species of dinoflagellates, some marine bacteria, and all major phyla of marine animals.

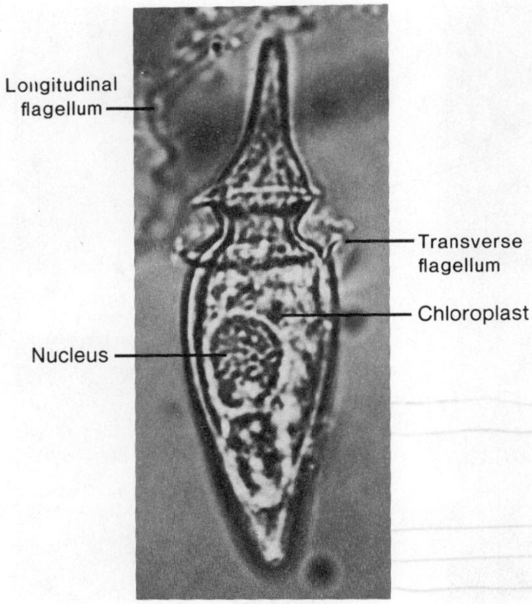

Figure 4.12

This light micrograph of a dinoflagellate, *Oxytoxum,* illustrates its major cellular features.

Courtesy F. Reid, Scripps Institution of Oceanography

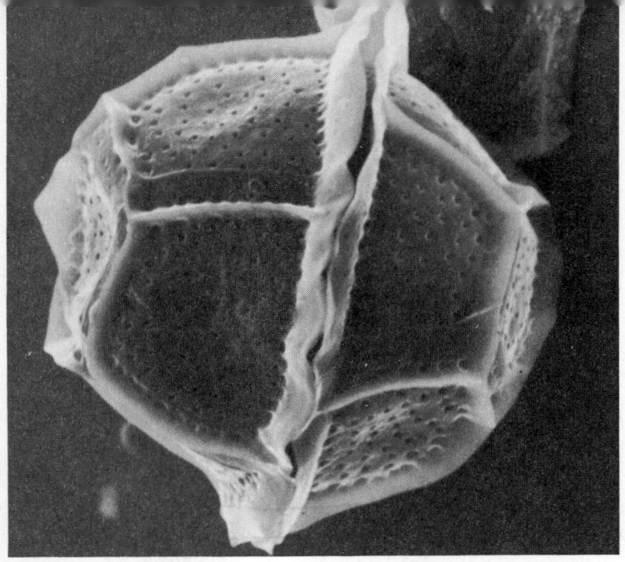

(a)

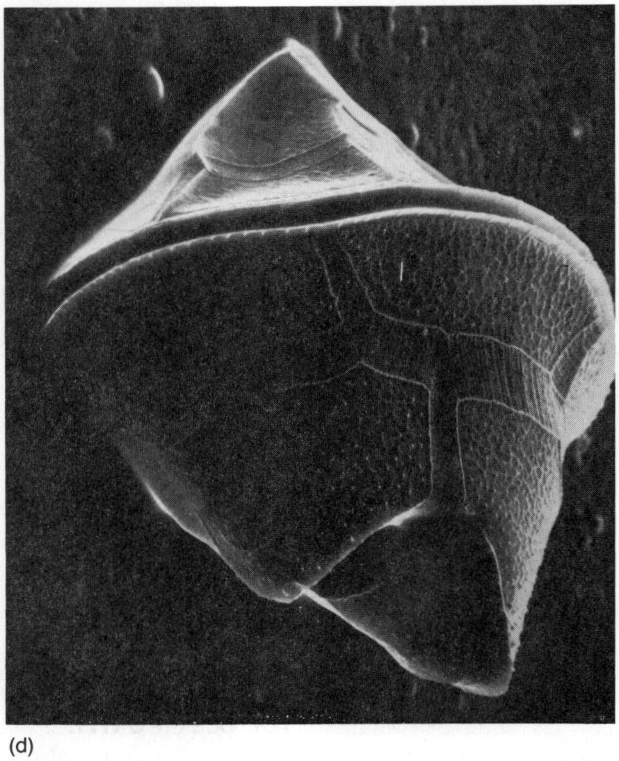

(d)

Light is produced when luciferin, a relatively simple organic compound, is oxidized in the presence of the enzyme luciferase. The glow reaction is a very efficient process, producing light but almost no heat. In some species of *Gonyaulax,* light production follows a circadian rhythm, with maximum light output occurring just after midnight.

Along the East and Gulf coasts of the United States, some species of nearshore dinoflagellates produce toxins that in bloom conditions are known as **red tides.** Red tides can cause high mortality in fish and other marine vertebrates. These dinoflagellate toxins either interfere with nerve functions, resulting in paralysis, or they irritate lung tissues of air-breathing vertebrates,

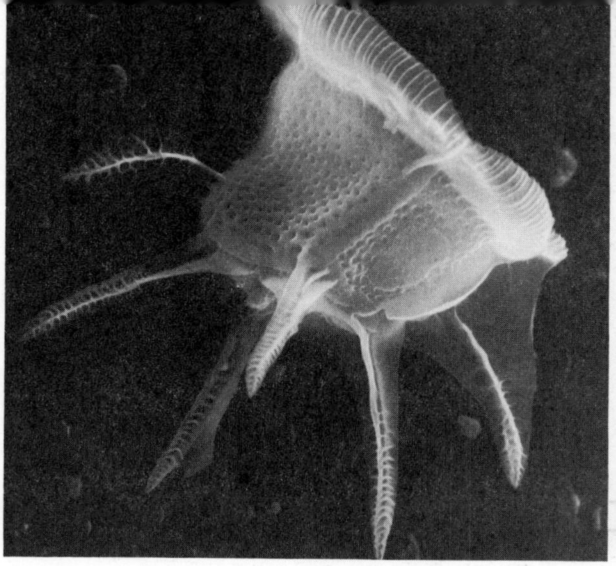

(b)

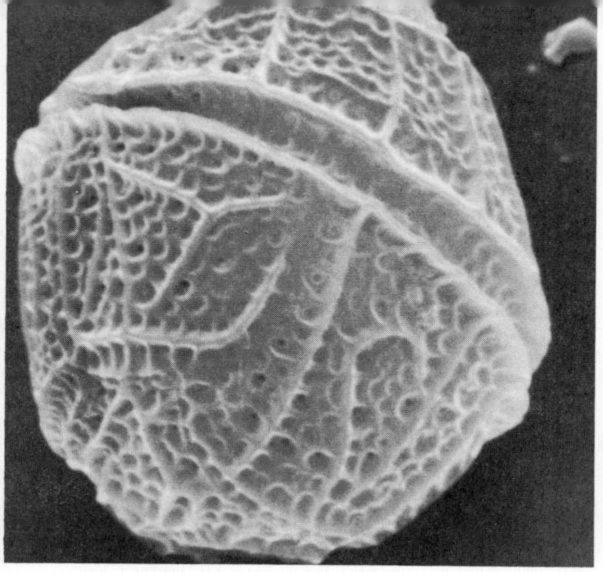

(c)

(e)

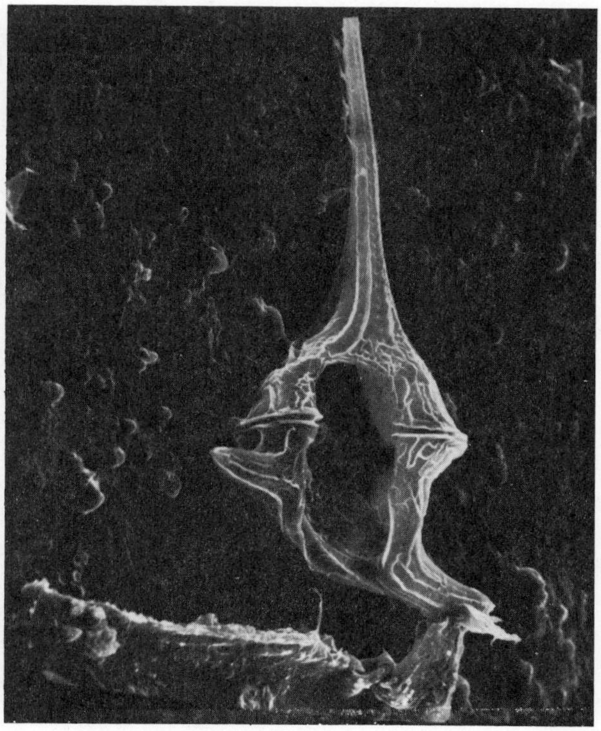

(f)

Figure 4.13
SEMs of some common marine dinoflagellates:
(*a*) *Heteroaulacus,*
(*b*) *Ceratocoup,*
(*c*) *Gonyaulax,*
(*d*) *Protoperidinium,*
(*e*) *Ceratium,* and
(*f*) Oxytoxum. All are 50–100 μm.
Courtesy F. Reid, E. Venrick and Scripps Institution of Oceanography

including humans. Widespread mortality of coastal fish populations sometimes occurs after particularly intense red tides, fouling beaches and near-shore waters with their decomposing bodies.

Other species of dinoflagellates produce toxins that accumulate in animals (particularly shellfish) and render their flesh toxic. For instance, people who eat butter clams (*Saxodomus*) during the summer months occasionally experience paralytic shellfish poisoning from **saxitoxin.** However, this toxin is actually produced by the dinoflagellate *Gonyaulax* and is ingested and concentrated in the tissue of *Saxodomus*. Saxitoxin is fifty times more lethal than two well-known terrestrial plant toxins, curare and strychnine.

Table 4.2
Size Ranges of the Major Groups of Marine Phytoplankton

	Cyanobacteria	Chrysophyta			Dinophyta	Chlorophyta
		Diatoms	*Silico-flagellates*	*Coccolith-ophores*		
Picoplankton	+	+	+	+		+
Ultraplankton	+	+	+	+		+
Nanoplankton		+	+	+	+	+
Microplankton		+			++	

Adapted from Platt and Li (eds). 1986.

Recent studies have cast doubt on the long-held assumption that the cyanobacterium *Lyngbya* is the source of the ciguatera toxin in tropical red snappers. In Hawaii, *Lyngbya* does cause an occasional contact dermatitis known as "swimmer's itch" during summer months, but its involvement in the production of ciguatera toxin has been seriously questioned. Another species of dinoflagellate, *Gambierdiscus,* seems to be a more likely candidate.

Other Phytoplankton

With sampling and microscopic techniques always improving, small phytoplankton from several other taxonomic groups are being recognized as important contributors to the trophic systems of many marine communities. Members of two additional classes of Chrysophyta and three unicellular classes of the division Chlorophyta are frequently found in filtered samples of coastal seawater. Chlorophytes are much more common in fresh water, and that is where most of the research on this group is concentrated. Since most of the identified marine unicellular chlorophytes have been obtained from estuaries and coastal waters, freshwater origins for many of the species found in seawater samples is likely.

Table 4.2 summarizes the size distribution of the major groups of marine phytoplankton. With so many extremely small groups, it is difficult to collect and evaluate the relative roles that the various groups of phytoplankton make to the total marine economy.

Special Adaptations for a Planktonic Existence

The evolutionary success of all phytoplankton hinges on their ability to obtain sufficient nutrients and light energy from the marine environment. Phytoplankton cells must be widely dispersed in their seawater medium to increase their utilization of dissolved nutrients, yet they must remain in the relatively restricted photic zone to absorb sufficient sunlight. These opposing conditions for successful planktonic existence have established some fundamental characteristics to which all phytoplankton and, indirectly, all other marine life have become adapted.

Size

One of the most characteristic features of all phytoplankton is their size. Almost without exception, they are microscopic, which suggests that a strong selective advantage accompanies smallness in phytoplankton. Why? In contrast to land plants, phytoplankton are constantly bathed in a medium that not only provides nutrients and water but also carries away waste products. Exchange of these materials in a fluid medium is accomplished by diffusion in either direction across the cell membrane of the plant.

The quantity of materials required by the cell is dependent on a number of factors such as the rate of photosynthesis and growth. But if these and other variables are held constant, the basic material requirements of the cell are nearly proportional to the size or, more accurately, to the volume of the cell. However, the ability of the cell to satisfy its material requirements is not a function of the volume but of the extent of cell surface across which the materials can diffuse. Thus, the ratio of cell surface area to cell volume becomes quite important. Those cells with higher surface-area-to-volume ratios achieve an advantage in the competition to enhance diffusive exchange between their internal and external fluid environments (figure 4.14).

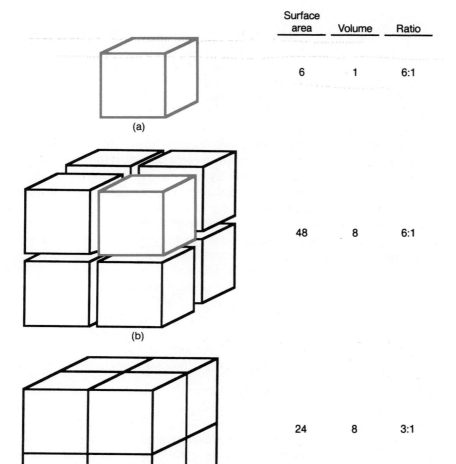

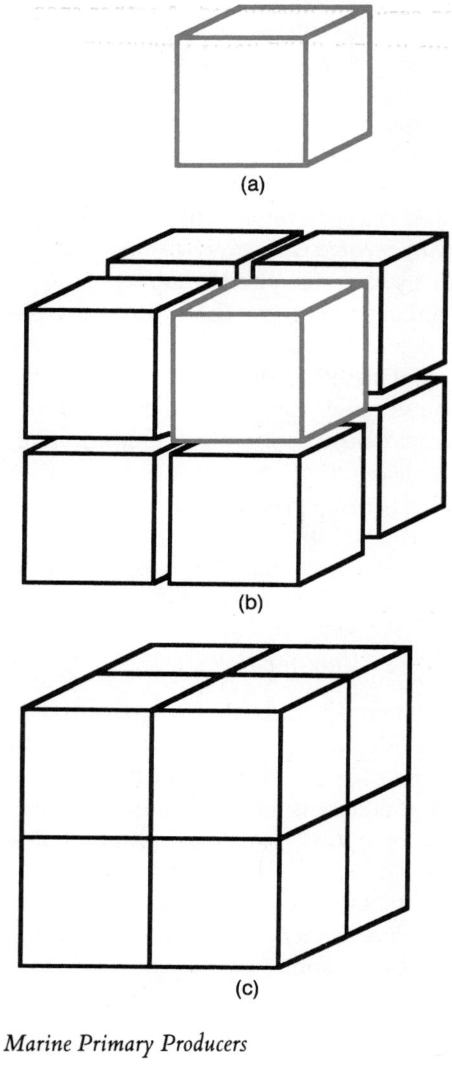

	Surface area	Volume	Ratio
(a)	6	1	6:1
(b)	48	8	6:1
(c)	24	8	3:1

Figure 4.14
With increasing size (*a* to *c*), the ratio of surface area to volume decreases unless the larger structure (*b*) remains subdivided so that the interior surfaces are exposed.

Reduction of cell size is an effective and widespread means of achieving high surface-area-to-volume ratios, but there are other means. Many phytoplankton cells have evolved complex shapes that increase the surface area while adding little or nothing to the volume. Cell shapes resembling ribbons, leaves, or long bars and cells with bristles or spines are all common mechanisms to increase the amount of surface area relative to volume and thus increase frictional resistance to sinking. Cell vacuoles filled with seawater are common in diatoms (refer to figure 4.7). These cells are large, but the actual volume of protoplasm requiring sustenance is only a fraction of the total volume of the cell.

Sinking

Phytoplankton, with their heavy cell walls, are generally a bit more dense than seawater and tend to sink away from surface waters and sunlight. The problem for phytoplankton is not to float, for that would create intolerable crowding at the sea surface. Instead, phytoplankton need to slow their sinking rates so that a small fraction of any reproducing cell line has a few members carried upward by turbulent mixing even as most continue their slow downward slide through the photic zone.

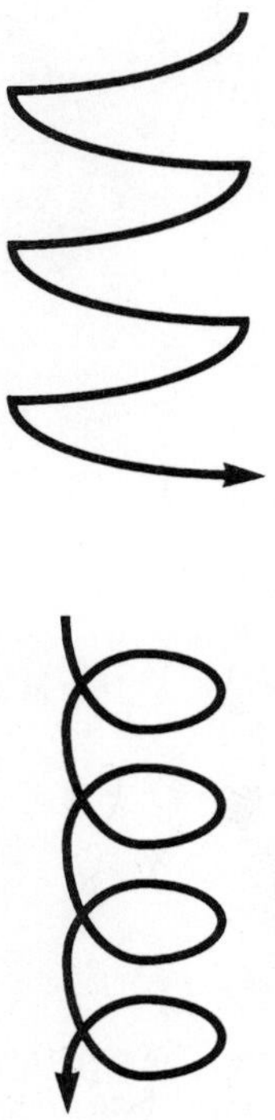

Figure 4.15
Sinking patterns of the elongate diatom, *Rhizosolenia* (top), and the spiral chain-forming diatom, *Asterionella* (bottom)

Phytoplankton exhibit many adaptations that slow the sinking rate and prolong their trip through the photic zone. One of the most effective adaptations is to increase the frictional resistance to their passage through water by increasing the surface-area-to-volume ratio. Reduced cell sizes accomplish this as do the production of horns, wings, or other cellular projections.

Other cells reduce their sinking rates with complex cell or chain shapes that trace zigzag or long spiral paths down through the water column. *Asterionella* and *Rhizosolenia,* shown in figure 4.15, demonstrate these adaptations. *Asterionella* forms long curved chains of cells that spiral slowly through the water. *Eucampia, Chaetoceros,* and many other diatoms form similar twisted chains of cells. The asymmetrically pointed ends of *Rhizosolenia* create a "falling-leaf" pattern that prolongs its stay in the photic zone.

Adaptations for reducing the sinking rate are not limited to structural variations. Mechanisms that reduce the average cell density by "lightening the load" are also evident in some phytoplankton. Planktonic diatoms generally produce thinner and lighter frustules than do benthic diatoms. *Ditylum,* for example, is capable of excluding higher density ions (calcium, magnesium, and sulphate) from its cell fluid and replacing them with less dense ions. In addition, the production and storage of low-density fats and oils also helps slow the rate of sinking.

Oscillatoria and some other planktonic cyanobacteria have evolved relatively sophisticated internal gas-filled vesicles to provide flotation. The walls of these vesicles are constructed of small protein units that can withstand outside water pressures experienced anywhere within the photic zone.

Adjustments to Unfavorable Environmental Conditions

Plankton have little or no capability of large-scale horizontal propulsion and must depend on the ocean's surface currents for dispersal. All of the adaptive features discussed above that extend the residence time of plankton in the horizontally moving surface currents also serve to increase their geographical distribution.

For protection, long spines and horns render phytoplankton less desirable to herbivorous grazers. There is some evidence to suggest that copepods, for instance, prefer nonspiny diatoms to spiny ones. Slimy gelatinous

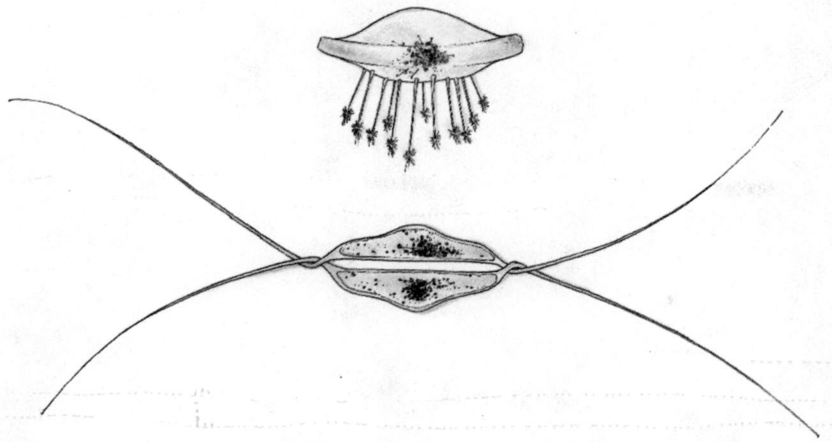

Figure 4.16
Inactive resistant stages of two species of *Chaetoceros.* (See fig. 4.11b for the active growth form.)

masses that sometimes surround large colonies of *Chaetoceros* and other diatoms also discourage grazers. Spines, cell chaining, and cell elongation all may be economical methods of increasing apparent cell size to reduce mortality.

The optimum growth period for phytoplankton in nonupwelling temperate and polar seas is restricted by reduced sunlight in winter and limited nutrient supplies in summer. Faced with the prospect of weeks or months with reduced photosynthesis, phytoplankton in these regions have limited options. Some move, some switch to other energy sources, or some simply hang on until conditions improve. The first choice does not generally apply to diatoms, but motility, limited as it is, is extremely important to flagellated cells. A swim of merely one or two cell lengths is often sufficient to place the cell away from its excreted wastes and into an improved nutrient supply. Toxins of dinophytes also serve to discourage predation by herbivores and sometimes inadvertently improve their own nutrient supply by causing extensive fish kills and thus accelerating the renewal of critical nutrients.

Strictly photosynthetic organisms must rely on stored lipids or carbohydrates for their short-term energy needs. When that source is depleted, some phytoplankton still have alternatives. Some species can improve their ability to harvest light by producing more chloroplasts that contain photosynthetic enzymes and pigments or by moving those chloroplasts closer to cell edges. Other species can absorb dilute but energy-rich dissolved organic material from surrounding seawater to tide them over. When these strategies have been exhausted, many diatoms produce dormant **cysts,** capsules which have reduced metabolic activity and increased resistance to environmental extremes (figure 4.16). It is likely that many near-shore species of dinoflagellates also produce dormant stages during periods of unfavorable growth conditions. With the return of improved growing conditions, these dormant cells germinate and commence photosynthesis and growth. At this point, the growing phytoplankton populations come under the regulatory influence of complex physical and biological factors considered in the next chapter.

Benthic Autotrophs

Benthic marine autotrophs are probably more familiar to seashore observers than are most phytoplankton. As most are members of the kingdom Plantae, they are more conspicuous because they are macroscopic, multicellular organisms usually large enough to pick up and examine. As with phytoplankton,

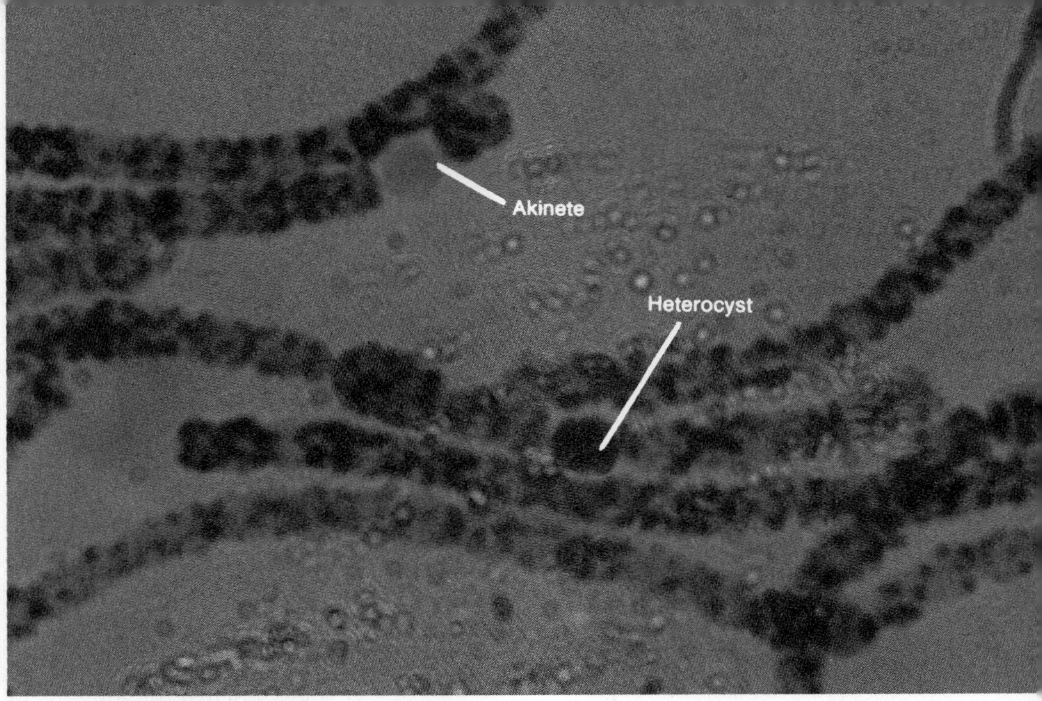

Figure 4.17
Micrograph of the cyanobacterium, *Anabaena,* showing spores (akinetes) and N_2-fixing heterocysts among vegetative cells

these organisms need sunlight for photosynthesis, and are confined to the photic zone. But the additional need for a solid sea bottom on which to attach limits the distribution of benthic autotrophs to that narrow fringe around the periphery of the oceans where the sea bottom is above the bottom of the photic zone (the inner shelf of figure 1.30). Some benthic autotrophs inhabit intertidal areas and must confront the many tide-induced stresses that affect their animal neighbors. (These will be discussed in Chapter 8.) Their restricted nearshore distribution limits the global importance of benthic autotrophs as primary producers in the marine environment. But within the nearshore communities in which they live, they play a major role as first trophic level organisms.

Unicellular Forms

Two groups briefly described here are unicellular forms and have already been introduced in the previous section on phytoplankton. Yet, a few species of cyanobacteria and diatoms are also abundant in many shallow benthic environments and merit mention here as contributors to the primary productivity of shallow sea bottoms.

Cyanobacteria

Benthic cyanobacteria can be found almost everywhere light and water are available. These organisms are individually microscopic and usually inconspicuous, but they may aggregate to produce macroscopic colonies. One abundant coral reef form, *Lyngbya,* develops long strands or hollow tubes of cells nearly a meter in length. Reproduction of cyanobacteria is usually accomplished by cell division. Occasionally the growing colony will fragment to disperse the cells. More complex modes of reproduction, involving motile or resistant stages, are also known.

On temperate seashores, some species of cyanobacteria (figure 4.17) appear as tarlike patches encrusting rocks in the intertidal or splash zones. Other species can be found in abundance on mudflats of coastal marshes, es-

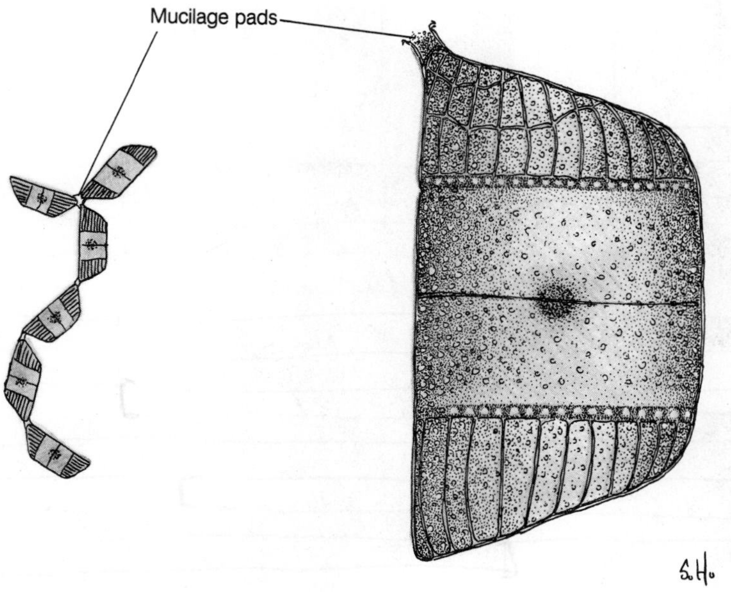

Figure 4.18
A benthic diatom, *Isthmia,* forming long, complex chains of cells. A close-up of a single cell is shown to the right.

tuaries, and in association with tropical coral reefs. One well-studied cyanobacterium, *Microcoleus,* is a major component of complexly laminated microbial mats found in stromatolites (figure 4.3).

Several species of cyanobacteria are capable of utilizing atmospheric nitrogen (N_2) to satisfy their metabolic nitrogen needs. The process of **nitrogen fixation** is poorly understood, but it is known to be limited to cyanobacteria and several types of bacteria. Field studies have shown that nitrogen-fixing cyanobacteria are fairly common in nearshore regions, often associated with large marine plants, but rare in oceanic waters. Apparently, even though most oceanic photosynthesizers are nitrogen-limited, few planktonic N_2-fixing cyanobacteria have evolved to take advantage of the situation.

Cyanobacteria exhibit a strong tendency to form symbiotic associations with other organisms. Various examples of symbiosis with animals are common. Two genera can even be found inhabiting marine planktonic diatoms, such as *Rhizosolenia.* Many cyanobacteria live as **epiphytes,** attached to larger plants. Some epiphytic cyanobacteria, for example those inhabiting turtle grass beds along the Gulf Coast of the United States, are also nitrogen-fixers. As such, they play an important role in the fertility and productivity of seagrass beds.

Benthic Diatoms

Bottom-living diatoms closely resemble their planktonic counterparts in cell structure, modes of reproduction, and other general characteristics. These organisms can be found on almost any solid substrate in shallow seawater: on mud surfaces, rocks, larger marine plants, manmade structures, and the hard shells of marine animals. One type, *Cocconeis,* even makes a home on the undersides of blue whales. Many of the benthic diatoms secrete a mucilage pad that connects adjacent cells into complex chains and branching forms (figure 4.18). In this manner, macroscopic diatom colonies a few cm long are formed.

(a)

(c)

(b)

Figure 4.19
(*a*) Calcareous red algae, *Jania,* in a small tide pool. (*b*) Intertidal rocks covered with the green alga, *Ulva.* (*c*) A brown alga, *Fucus,* in the middle intertidal.
(*a*) and (*b*) Courtesy G. Dudley; (*c*) Courtesy M. Frost

When compared to planktonic diatoms, the geographical distribution of benthic diatoms is severely restricted because of their need for light and for solid substrates. Still, benthic diatoms make a significant contribution to the total amount of plant production in estuaries, bays, and other localized shallow-water areas. Some species of these diatoms are also a key factor in the ecological succession of organisms that culminates in a rich growth of organisms on docks, boats, and other man-made structures (refer to figure 8.20). Several studies have indicated that marine bacteria are usually the first life forms to settle and grow on new or freshly denuded underwater structures. Development of a diatom film a few cells thick quickly follows and is succeeded by more complex populations of larger algae and invertebrate animals.

The Seaweeds

By far, the majority of large, conspicuous forms of attached marine plants are seaweeds. The term *seaweed* has sometimes been used to indicate a group of larger marine plants attached to the bottom in relatively shallow coastal waters. The term is used here in a more restrictive sense, referring only to macroscopic members of the plant divisions Chlorophyta (green algae), Phaeophyta (brown algae), and Rhodophyta (red algae). Table 4.1 includes a summary of some major characteristics of each division.

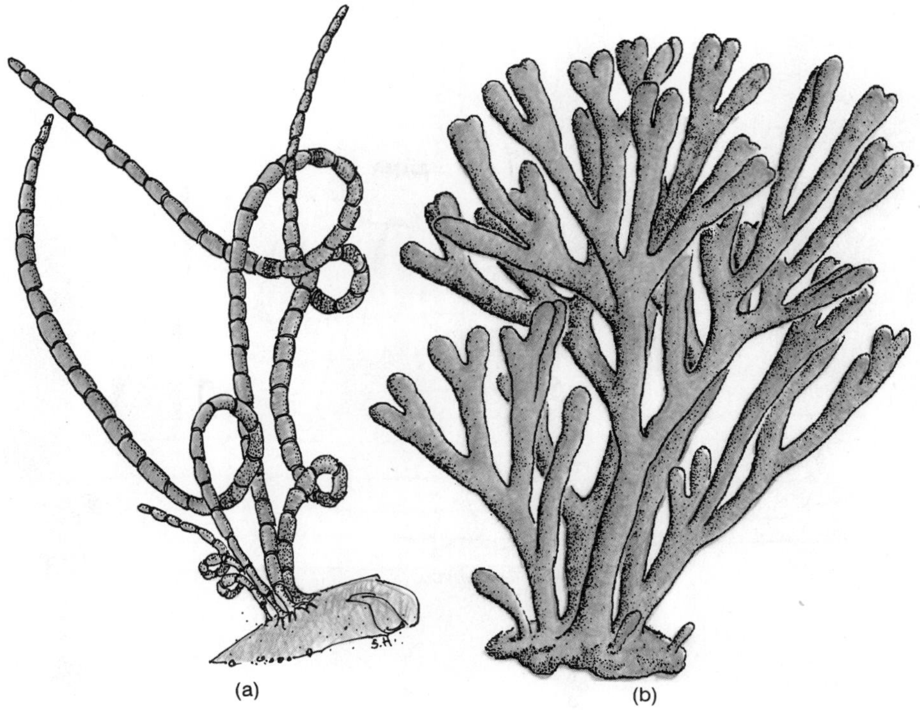

Figure 4.20
Two marine forms of green algae: (*a*) *Chaetomorpha* and (*b*) *Codium*

Seaweeds are abundant in intertidal zones and commonly extend to depths of 30 to 40 m. In clear tropical seas, some species of red algae thrive at depths as great as 200 m, and an unnamed species has been reported as deep as 268 m in the Bahamas. Many seaweeds tolerate extreme surf action on exposed rocky intertidal outcrops as long as they are securely fixed to the solid substrate. Where they are abundant, seaweeds greatly influence and modify existing environmental conditions for other types of shallow-water marine life by providing food, protection from waves, shade, and sometimes a substrate on which to attach.

Photosynthetic Pigments

Each seaweed division is characterized by specific combinations of photosynthetic pigments reflected in the color appearance (figure 4.19) and common name of each division (refer to table 4.1). The bright, grass-green color characteristic of green algae is due to the predominance of **chlorophylls** over other accessory pigments. Green algae vary in structure from simple filaments (figure 4.20a) to flat sheets and diverse complex branching forms (figure 4.20b). They are usually less than one-half m long, but one species of *Codium* from the Gulf of California occasionally grows to 8 m in length. When compared to brown and red algae, the Chlorophyta have fewer marine species. But in some locations their limited diversity is compensated with dense populations of individuals from one or two species.

The photosynthetic pigments of the Phaeophyta can sometimes be seen as a greenish hue. But more often the green of the chlorophyll is partially masked by the golden **xanthophyll** pigments, especially fucoxanthin, characteristic of this division. This blend of green and brown pigments usually results in a drab, olive-green color. Many of the larger and more familiar algae of

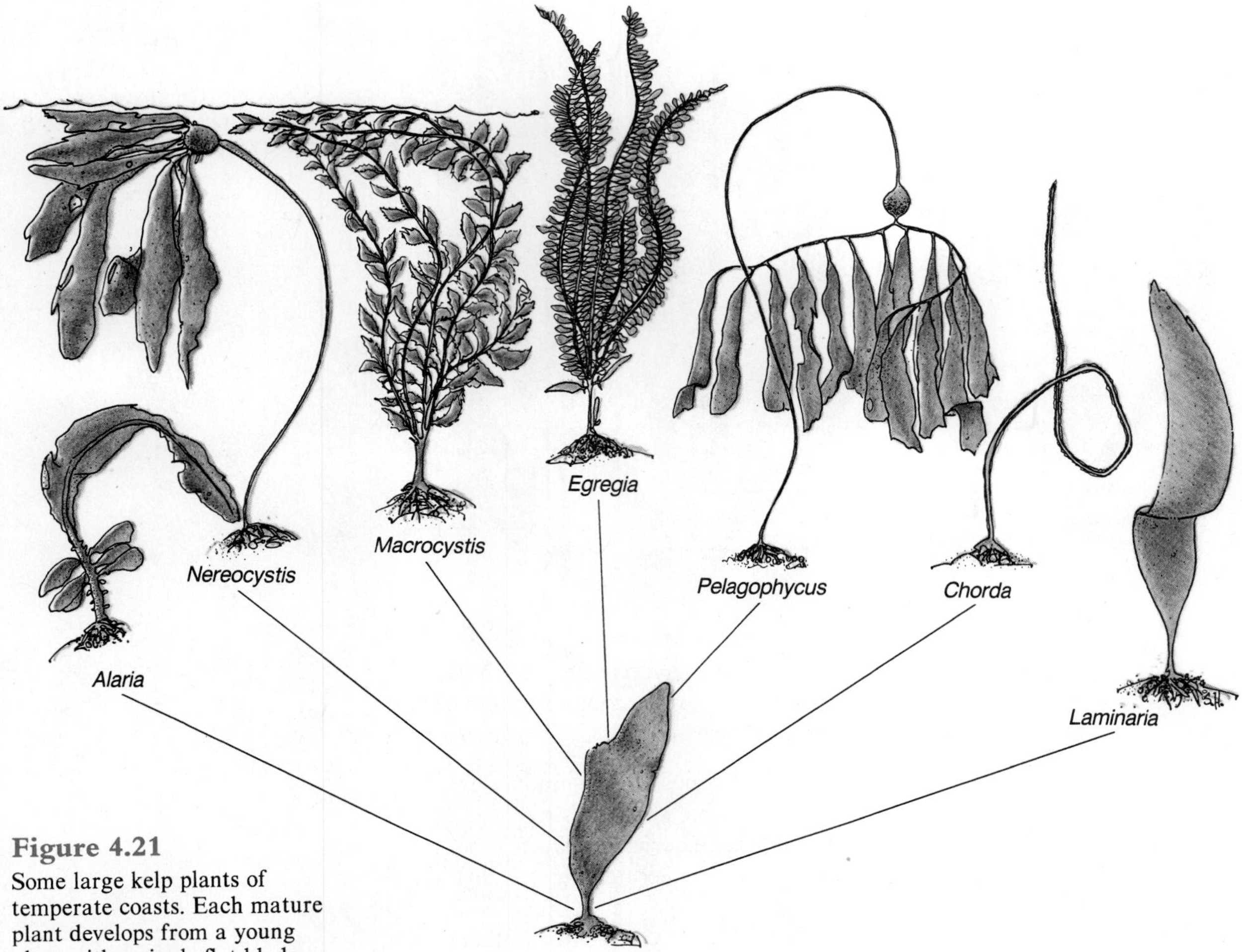

Figure 4.21
Some large kelp plants of temperate coasts. Each mature plant develops from a young plant with a single flat blade.

temperate seas belong to this division. A number of species are quite large and are sometimes collectively referred to as **kelp** (figure 4.21). In temperate and high latitudes, these species usually dominate the marine benthic vegetation. Numerous smaller, less obvious brown algae are also common in temperate and cold waters as well as in tropical areas.

Red algae, with red and blue **phycobilin** pigments as well as chlorophyll, exhibit a wide range of colors. Some are bright green and others are sometimes confused with brown algae. However, most red algae living below low tide range in color from soft pinks to various shades of red. Red algae are as diverse in structure and habitat as they are in coloration and they seldom exceed a meter in length.

Structural Features of Seaweeds

Seaweeds are not as complex as the flowering plants. Seaweeds lack roots, flowers, seeds, and true leaves. Yet within these structural limitations, seaweeds exhibit an unbridled diversity of shapes, sizes, and structural complexity. Microscopic filaments of green and brown algae can be found growing side by side with encrusting forms of red algae and flat sheetlike members of all three divisions. Many of the larger members of all three seaweed divisions develop into mature plants with similar general forms, each consisting of a blade, a stipe, and a holdfast.

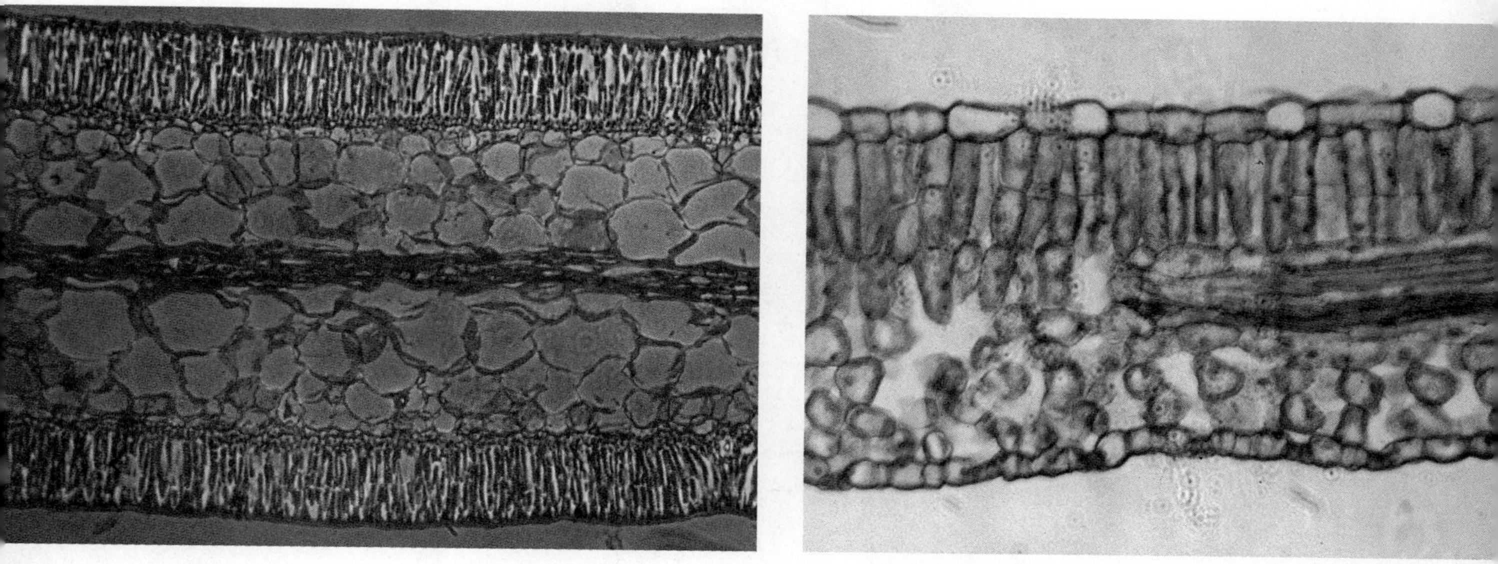
(a) (b)

Figure 4.22
Cross sections of (*a*) a blade of a typical marine alga, *Nereocystis,* and (*b*) a flowering plant leaf. Note the contrasting symmetry patterns.

The Blade The flattened, usually broad, leafy structures of seaweeds are known as **blades.** Seaweed blades often exhibit a complex level of branching and cellular arrangement. Large forms of brown algae produce distinctive blade shapes and blade arrangements (figure 4.21); yet each begins as a young plant with a single, unbranched, flat blade nearly identical to other young kelp plants.

The blades house photosynthetically active cells, but photosynthesis often occurs in the stipes and holdfasts as well. In cross section, seaweed blades (figure 4.22a) are structurally unlike the leaves of terrestrial plants (figure 4.22b). The cells nearer the surface of the blade are capable of absorbing more light and are photosynthetically more active than those cells near the center of the blade. "Veins" of conductive tissue and distinctions between the upper and lower surfaces are lacking in the blades of seaweeds. Since the flexible blades usually droop in the water or float erect, there is no permanent upper or lower surface. Each side of the seaweed blade is usually exposed equally to sunlight, nutrients, and water and is therefore equally capable of carrying out photosynthesis. Unlike seaweeds, the flowering plants (including sea grasses) exhibit an obvious asymmetry of leaf structure, with a dense concentration of photosynthetically active cells crowded near the upper surface (figure 4.22b). Below the upper surface is a spongy layer of cells separated by large spaces to enhance the exchange of CO_2, which is often 100 times *less* concentrated in air than in seawater.

Pneumatocysts Several of the large kelp plants have gas-filled floats, or **pneumatocysts,** to buoy up the blades near the more abundant sunlight of the surface. Again, there is a large diversity in size and structure. The largest pneumatocysts belong to *Pelagophycus,* the elkhorn kelp (figure 4.21). Each elkhorn kelp plant is equipped with a single pneumatocyst, sometimes as large as a basketball, to support six to eight immense drooping blades, each of which may be 1 to 2 m wide and 7 to 10 m long.

Sargassum produces numerous small pneumatocysts (figure 4.23). A few species of *Sargassum* lead a pelagic life afloat in the middle of the North Atlantic Ocean (the "Sargasso Sea"). In the Sargasso Sea, *Sargassum* produces large patches of floating plants that are the basis of a complex floating

Figure 4.23
A portion of the floating brown alga, *Sargassum,* with numerous small pneumatocysts
Courtesy D. Nelson

Sargassum community of crabs, fish, shrimp, and other animals uniquely adapted to living among the *Sargassum:* Large masses of this plant community sometimes float ashore on the United States East Coast, creating odor problems for beachgoers as the dying plants decompose. In the Sea of Japan, other species of attached intertidal *Sargassum* break off and also become free-floating for extended periods of time.

Pneumatocysts are filled with the gases most abundant in air: N_2, O_2, and CO_2. Surprisingly, the pneumatocysts of some kelp plants also contain relatively large concentrations (over 2%) of carbon monoxide, CO. The source of the CO is not known, but it is believed to be a by-product of metabolism.

The Stipe A flexible, stemlike **stipe** serves as a shock absorber between the wave-tossed upper parts of seaweeds and the securely anchored holdfast at the bottom. An excellent example is *Postelsia,* the sea palm (figure 4.24) that grows attached to rocks only in the most exposed, surf-swept portions of the intertidal zone. Its hollow, resilient stipe is remarkably well suited for yielding to the waves without breaking.

The blades of some seaweeds blend into the holdfast without forming a distinct stipe. In others, the stipe is very conspicuous and, occasionally, extremely long. The single long stipes of *Nereocystis* and *Pelagophycus* (figure 4.21) provide a kind of slack-line anchoring system and commonly exceed 30 m in length. The complex multiple stipes of *Macrocystis* (figure 4.21) are often even longer.

Special cells within the stipes of *Macrocystis* and a limited number of other brown and red algal species form conductive elements strikingly similar in form to those present in stems of terrestrial plants. Radioactive tracer studies have shown that these cells definitely transport the products of photosynthesis from the blades to other parts of the plant. In smaller seaweeds with photosynthetic stipes and holdfasts, the necessity for rapid, efficient transport through the stipe is minimal.

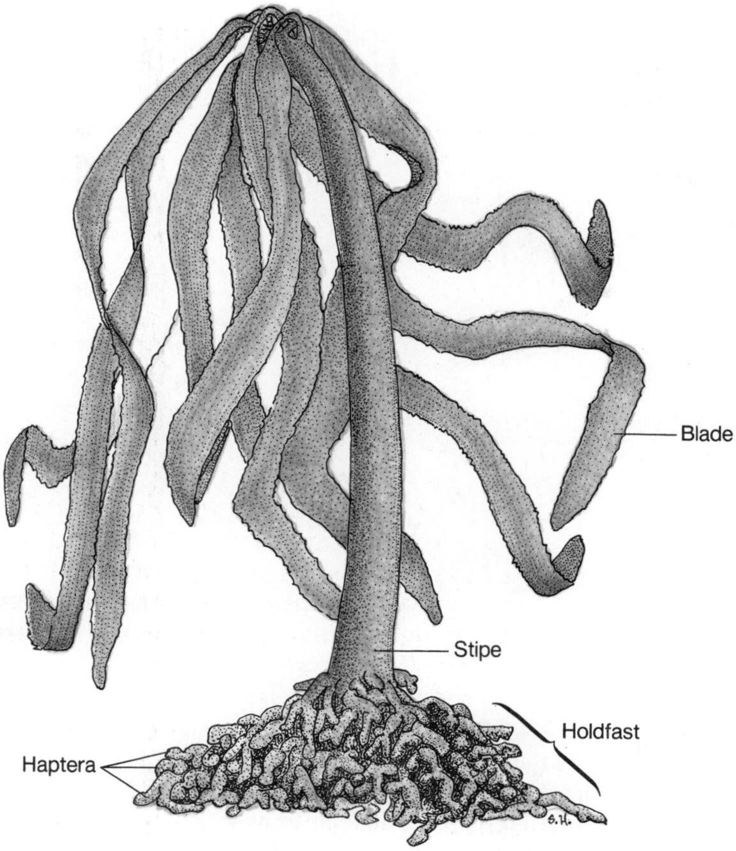

Figure 4.24
The northern sea palm *Postelsia* (Phaeophyta) is equipped with a relatively large stipe and a massive holdfast.

The Holdfast **Holdfasts** of the larger marine algae often superficially resemble root systems of terrestrial plants. However, the basic function of the holdfast is to attach the plant to the substrate. The holdfast seldom absorbs nutrients for the plant as do true roots. Holdfasts are well adapted for getting a grip on the substrate and resisting violent wave shock and the steady tug of tidal currents and wave surges. The holdfast of *Postelsia* (figure 4.24), composed of many short, sturdy, rootlike **haptera,** illustrates one of several types found on solid rock.

Other holdfasts are better suited for loose substrates. The holdfast of *Macrocystis* has a large, diffuse mass of haptera to penetrate sandy bottoms and stabilize a mass of sediment for anchorage. The holdfast *Penicillus* does the same thing on a much smaller scale, with many fine filaments embedded in sand or mud bottoms (figure 4.25).

Figure 4.25
Penicillus (Chlorophyta) with fine hairlike haptera for anchoring in loose sediments

A variety of small red algae are epiphytes and demonstrate special adaptations for attaching themselves to other marine plants. Figure 4.26 illustrates two common red algal epiphytes attached to strands of the surf grass, *Phyllospadix*. Using other marine plants as substrates for attachment is a common habit of many smaller forms of red algae.

Reproduction and Growth

Reproduction in seaweeds as well as in most other plants can be either sexual, involving the fusion of sperm and eggs, or asexual, a vegetative regrowth of new individuals (see figure 2.3). Some seaweeds reproduce both ways, but a

Figure 4.26
Two red algal epiphytes:
(*a*) *Smithora* and
(*b*) *Chondria* attached to a strand of *Phyllospadix*

few are limited to vegetative reproduction only. The pelagic species of *Sargassum,* for instance, maintain their populations by an irregular vegetative growth followed by fragmentation. The dispersed fragments of *Sargassum* are capable of continued growth and regeneration for decades. Sexual reproduction is lacking in the pelagic species of *Sargassum* but not in the attached benthic forms of the same genus.

Much of the structural variety observed in seaweeds is derived from complex patterns of sexual reproduction, patterns which define the life cycles of seaweeds. For our purposes, these complex life cycles can be simplified to three fundamental patterns. The sexual reproduction examples of the first two types described here are not meant to cover the entire spectrum of seaweed life cycles but are used to develop a basic pattern that underlies the complexity and variation involved in sexual reproduction of seaweeds.

In the life cycle of most of the larger seaweeds, an alternation of **sporophyte** and **gametophyte** generations occur. The green alga *Ulva* represents one of the simplest patterns of alternating generations (figure 4.27). This basic life cycle is unknown in animals but, with minor modifications, is common to many brown and green algae. The cells of the macroscopic sporophyte are diploid; that is, each cell contains two of each type of chromosome characteristic of that species. Some cells of the *Ulva* sporophyte undergo meiosis to produce single-celled, flagellated **spores.** As a result of meiosis, these spores contain only one chromosome of each pair present in the diploid sporophyte and are said to be haploid.

The spores are capable of limited swimming and then settle to the bottom. There they immediately germinate by a series of mitotic cell divisions to produce a large multicellular, still haploid, gametophyte. Cells of the gametophyte in turn produce flagellated, haploid gametes that are released into the water. When two gametes from different gametophytes meet, they fuse to produce a diploid, single-celled zygote. By repeated mitotic divisions, the zygote germinates and completes the cycle by producing a large sporophyte once again. In *Ulva,* the sporophyte and gametophyte generations are identical in ap-

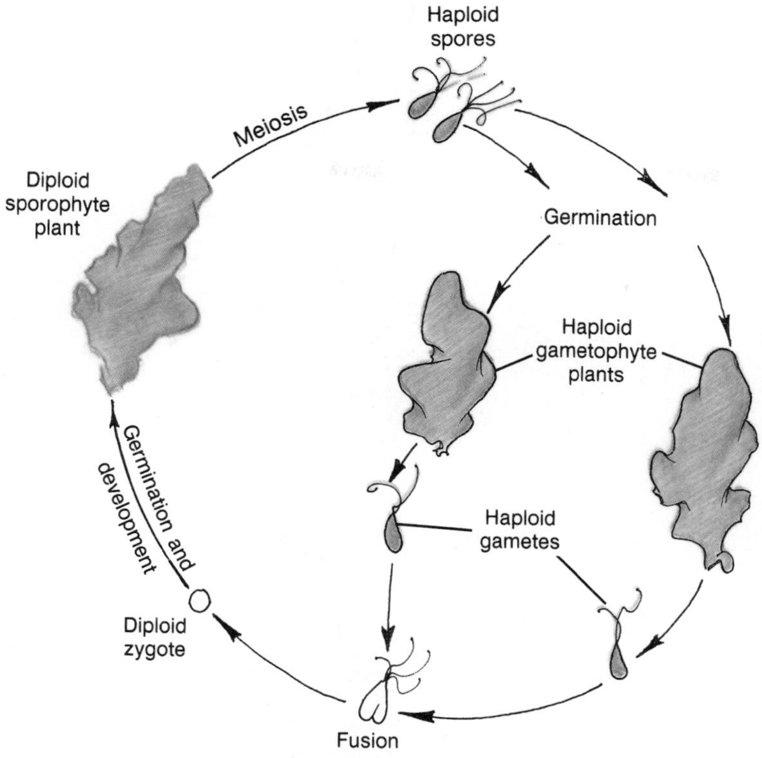

Figure 4.27
The life cycle of the green alga *Ulva,* alternating between diploid sporophyte and haploid gametophyte generations
Adapted from Dawson, 1966

pearance. The only structural difference between the two forms is the number of chromosomes in each cell; the diploid sporophyte has double the chromosomal complement of the haploid gametophyte cells.

The life cycles of numerous other seaweeds are characterized by a suppression of either the gametophyte or the sporophyte stages. In the green alga *Codium* and the brown alga *Fucus* the multicellular haploid generation is completely absent. The only haploid stages are the gametes. In other large brown algae, the gametophyte stage is reduced. The life cycle of *Laminaria* is similar to most other large kelp plants and serves as an excellent generalized example of seaweeds with a massive sporophyte that alternates with a diminutive, often unnoticed, gametophyte (figure 4.28). Special cells (called **sporangia**) on the blades of the diploid sporophyte undergo meiosis to produce several flagellated, microscopic spores. These haploid spores swim to the bottom and quickly attach themselves. They soon germinate into very small gametophytes composed of several cells. The female gametophyte produces large, nonflagellated eggs. The egg cells are fertilized in place on the female gametophyte by flagellated male gametes, the sperm cells produced by the male gametophyte. After fusion of the gametes, the resulting zygote germinates to form another large sporophyte.

The spores of green algae are characterized by four flagella; each gamete has two flagella that are equal in length and project from one end of the cell. The flagellated reproductive cells of brown algae always have two flagella of unequal lengths, and they insert on the sides of the cells rather than at the ends.

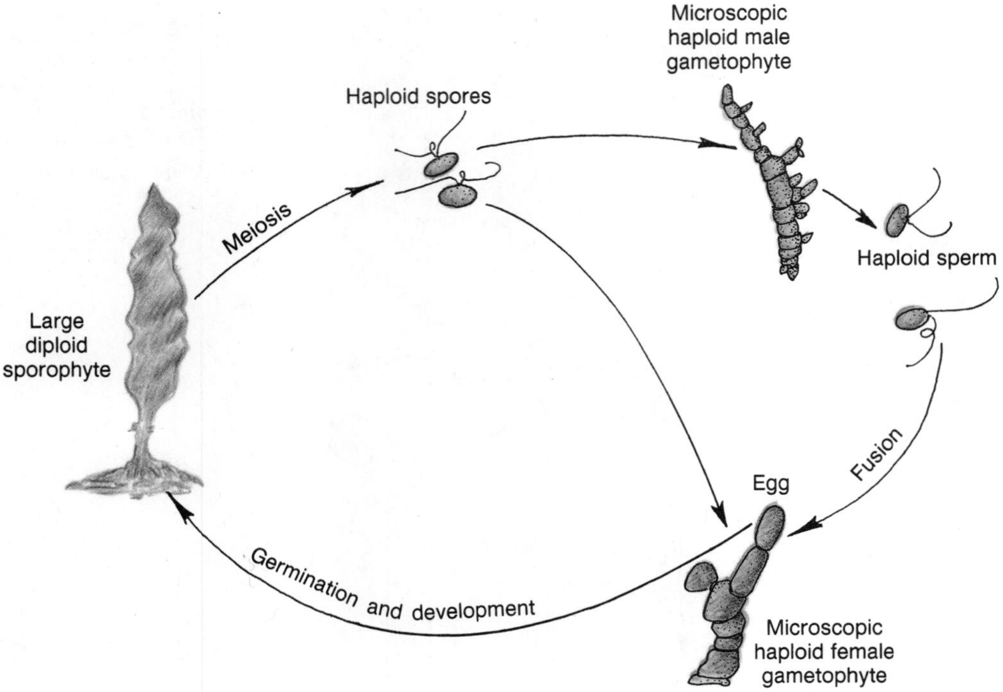

Figure 4.28
The life cycle of *Laminaria* (similar to the cycles of other large kelps) alternates between large diploid sporophyte and microscopic haploid gametophyte.

Red algae lack flagellated reproductive cells and are dependent on water currents to transport the male gametes to the female reproductive cells. The most common life cycle of red algae has three distinct generations, somewhat reminiscent of the reproductive cycle outlined for *Ulva* (figure 4.27). A diploid sporophyte produces haploid spores that germinate into haploid gametophytes. Instead of producing a new sporophyte, however, the gametes from the gametophytes fuse and develop into a third phase unique to the red algae, the **carposporophyte.** The carposporophyte then produces **carpospores** that develop into sporophytes, and the cycle is completed.

The development of a large multicellular seaweed from a single microscopic cell is essentially a process of repeated mitotic cell divisions. Subsequent growth and differentiation of these cells produce a complex plant with many types of cells, each specialized for particular functions. Once the plant is developed, additional cell division and growth occurs to replace tissue lost to animal grazing or wave erosion. However, such cell division is commonly restricted to a few specific sites within the plant that contain **meristematic** tissue with a capacity for further cell division. These meristems frequently occur at the upper growing tip of the plant. In kelp plants and some other seaweeds, additional meristems situated in the upper and lower portions of the stipe provide for elongation of the stipe and blades. The meristematic activity of a cell layer at or near the surface of some kelp stipes provides lateral growth to increase the thickness of the stipe. The stipes of a few perennial species of kelp, including *Pterygophora* and *Laminaria,* retain evidence of this secondary lateral growth as concentric rings that resemble the annual growth rings of trees.

In the spring months during periods of rapid growth, the rate of stipe elongation in *Nereocystis, Pelagophycus,* and *Macrocystis* often exceeds 30 cm per day. Growth rate estimates of some kelp plants on the east coast of

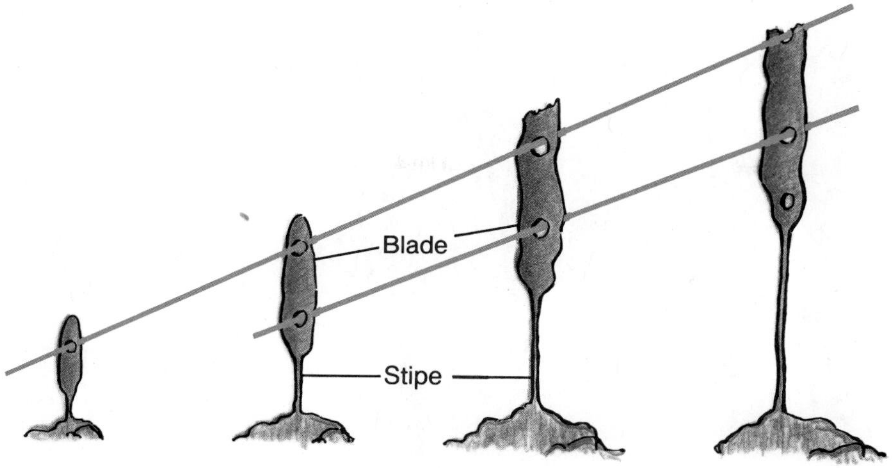

Figure 4.29

Generalized growth pattern of a kelp. Punched holes and blue lines indicate the pattern of blade elongation.

Adapted from Mann, 1973

Canada indicate that the kelp blades resemble moving belts of plant tissue (figure 4.29), growing at the base and eroding at the tips. At any one time, the plant itself (the standing crop) represents as little as 10% of the total plant material produced during a year.

Anthophyta

Marine flowering plants are abundant in localized areas along some seashores and in backwater bays and sloughs. Sea grasses often live completely submerged, whereas salt marsh plants and mangroves are emergent and seldom completely inundated by seawater. These plants represent a minor reinvasion of the marine environment by a few species of a predominantly terrestrial plant group—the flowering plants (division: Anthophyta).

Fourteen common genera, including about 45 species, of sea grasses are dispersed around coastal waters of the world. Most sea grasses are restricted to the tropics and subtropics and are seldom found deeper than 10 m. Three common genera in the United States are *Thalassia, Zostera,* and *Phyllospadix. Thalassia* or turtle grass (figure 4.30a), is common in quiet waters along most of the Gulf Coast from Florida to Texas. *Zostera marina,* or eel grass (figure 4.30b), is widely distributed along both the Atlantic and Pacific Coasts of North America. *Zostera* normally inhabits quiet shallow waters but is occasionally found as deep as 50 m. Less widespread in distribution is the surf grass, *Phyllospadix* (figure 4.30c), which is found on both sides of the North Pacific. Surf grass inhabits the lower intertidal and shallow subtidal rocks that are subjected to considerable wave and surge action.

Most sea grasses produce horizontal **rhizomes** that attach the plants in soft sediments or to rocks (figure 4.30). From the buried rhizomes, many erect grasslike shoots develop to form thick green masses of vegetation. These plants are a staple food for many near-shore marine animals and migratory birds. Densely matted rhizomes and leaves also accumulate nutrients and organic debris to further alter the living conditions of the area.

Many sea grasses reproduce vegetatively by sprouting additional vertical leaves from the lengthening horizontal rhizome or from seeds produced in incomplete flowers. The term "flowering plant," however, is not very descriptive for most sea grasses; only turtle grass produces brightly colored flowers

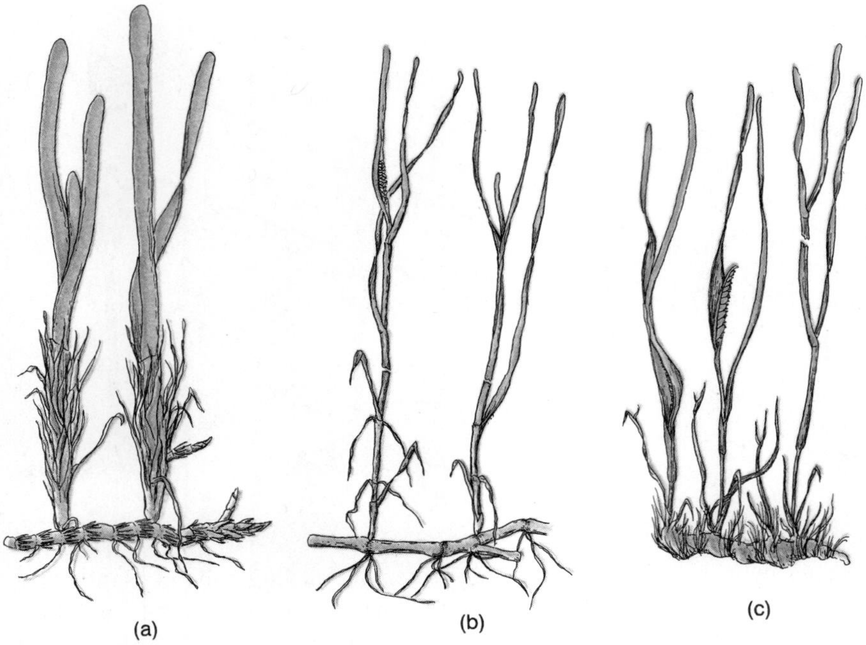

Figure 4.30
Three common seagrasses from different marine climatic regions: (*a*) turtle grass, *Thalassia;* (*b*) eel grass, *Zostera;* and (*c*) surf grass, *Phyllospadix*

on opening. The purpose of most showy flowers is to attract insects or birds so that **pollen** grains are transferred from one flower to another and cross-fertilization occurs. Pollen grains contain the plant's sperm cells, but submerged sea grasses cannot utilize animals or the wind to transport their pollen. In all sea grasses, pollination occurs underwater with water currents responsible for pollen transport.

Some sea grasses, including *Zostera,* produce threadlike pollen grains about 3 mm long (about 500 times longer than their cargo, the microscopically small chromosome-carrying sperm cells). After release, these elongated pollen grains become ensnared on the **stigma,** the pollen-receptive structure of the female portion of the flower, and fertilization occurs if there is a species match between the pollen grain and the stigma. The problem of achieving a species match is handled by turtle grass in a manner somewhat reminiscent of broadcast spawners (p. 200). The small round pollen grains of turtle grass are released in a thread of sticky slime. When the slime lands on the appropriate stigma (also covered with a surface film of slime), the two slime layers combine to produce a firm bond between the pollen grain and the stigma, and fertilization follows. This two-component adhesive acts like epoxy glue to produce a strong bond after the separate components are mixed. It also provides a mechanism for selecting between compatible and foreign types of pollen grains. Only on contact with pollen of the same species will the stigma-pollen bond be formed. Foreign pollen grains do not adhere and are washed away, possibly to try again on another plant.

The seeds of each type of sea grass are well suited to their environment. Eel grass seeds drop into the mud and take root near the parent plant. In contrast, the fruits of *Thalassia* may float for long distances before releasing their seeds in the surf. The fruits surrounding individual seeds of *Phyllospadix* are equipped with bristly projections. When shed into the surf, these bristles snag small branches of algae and the seeds germinate in place.

Figure 4.31
Dense mangal thicket lining a tidal channel

Several other species of flowering plants often exist partially submerged on bottom muds of quiet coastal salt marshes. These plants are usually situated so that their roots are periodically, but not constantly, exposed to tidal flooding. They are terrestrial plants that have evolved various degrees of tolerance to excess salts from sea spray and seawater. Some even have special structural adaptations for their semimarine existence. The cord grass, *Spartina,* for example, actively excretes excess salt through special two-celled salt glands on its leaves. Even so, several species of *Spartina* have higher experimental growth and survival rates in fresh water than in seawater. This strongly suggests that the salt marsh does not provide optimum growth conditions for *Spartina,* even though the salt marsh is its natural habitat. Competition with other land and freshwater plants may have forced *Spartina* and other salt-tolerant species into the restricted areas of the salt marshes.

Several species of shrubby to treelike plants, the mangroves, create dense thickets of tidal woodlands known as **mangals** (figure 4.31). Members of these mangal communities are supported on their muddy substrate by numerous prop roots that grow down from branches above the water.

Geographical Distribution

The interplay of a multitude of physical, chemical, and biological variables influences and controls the distribution of marine plants on a local scale. For instance, on an exposed rock in the lower intertidal zone on the Oregon coast, *Postelsia* may thrive; but 10 m away the conditions of light, temperature, nutrients, tides, surf action, and substrate may be such that *Postelsia* cannot survive. Yet on an ocean-wide scale, only a few factors seem to control the presence or absence of major groups of seaweeds. Significant among these are water and air temperature, tidal amplitude, and the quality and quantity of light.

With these factors in mind, a few generalizations can be made concerning the geographical distribution of benthic plants. In marked contrast to the impoverished seaweed flora of the Red Sea, the tropical western coast of

Africa, and the western side of Central America, seaweeds thrive in profusion along the coasts of southern Australia and South Africa, on both sides of the North Pacific, and in the Mediterranean Sea. The West Coast of the United States is somewhat richer in seaweed diversity than is the East Coast. From Cape Code northward, the East Coast is populated with subarctic seaweeds. South of Cape Cod, the effects of the warm Gulf Stream become more and more evident, until a completely tropical flora is encountered in southern Florida.

The red algae are not rare in cold-water regions but are more plentiful in the tropics and subtropics. Calcareous forms of red algae (and some brown and green as well) are characterized by extensive deposits of $CaCO_3$ within their cell walls (figure 4.19a). They are more abundant and conspicuous in the tropics. The use of calcium carbonate as a skeletal component by warm-water marine algae is apparently related to the decreased solubility of $CaCO_3$ in water at higher temperatures. In the tropics, plants expend less energy to extract $CaCO_3$ from the water, and here coralline algae contributes substantially to the formation and maintenance of coral reefs. Encrusting coralline algae grow over coral rubble, cementing and binding it into a mass that can resist the pounding of heavy surf. Some Indian Ocean "coral" reefs completely lack coral animals and are constructed and maintained entirely by coralline algae. The few calcareous forms of green algae that exist are also limited to warm water and play a large role in the production of $CaCO_3$ on some coral reefs.

The brown algae are a temperate-to-cold-water group, with few tropical representatives. Extensive kelp beds are seldom found nearer to the equator than 30° N or 30° S latitude. The large kelps are especially abundant in the North Pacific. Cord grass and other grassy salt marsh plants are also found generally outside warm tropical or subtropical regions. In tropical and subtropical protected mud-bottom habitats, salt marshes give way to extensive mangal thickets.

Plant-Dominated Marine Communities

Some of the larger forms of benthic marine plants flourish in such profusion that they dominate the general biological character of their communities. Such community domination, a common feature of land plants, is exceptional in the sea. Away from the near-shore habitats occupied by benthic plants, the microscopic phytoplankton prevail as the major primary producers. In the near-shore fringe, however, mangals, salt marshes and sea grass and kelp beds thrive where the appropriate bottom conditions, light, and nutrients exist.

Mangals and salt marshes are **emergent plant communities;** most of the plant growth occurs above the sea surface. Both occupy protected muddy habitats. Mangals form warm climate plant communities and seldom exist beyond 30° N and 30° S latitudes (figure 4.32). Because the leafy portions of these plants are above the water level, few animals graze directly on mangrove plants. Instead, leaves falling from these plants into the quiet waters surrounding their roots provide an important energy source for the detritus-based food chains of these communities.

In cooler climates, mangals are replaced by a variety of salt marsh plants that also contribute heavily to detritus production in their protected environments as well as in nearby bays and estuaries. (Salt marshes are discussed in chapter 6.) Some feature extensive stands containing several species

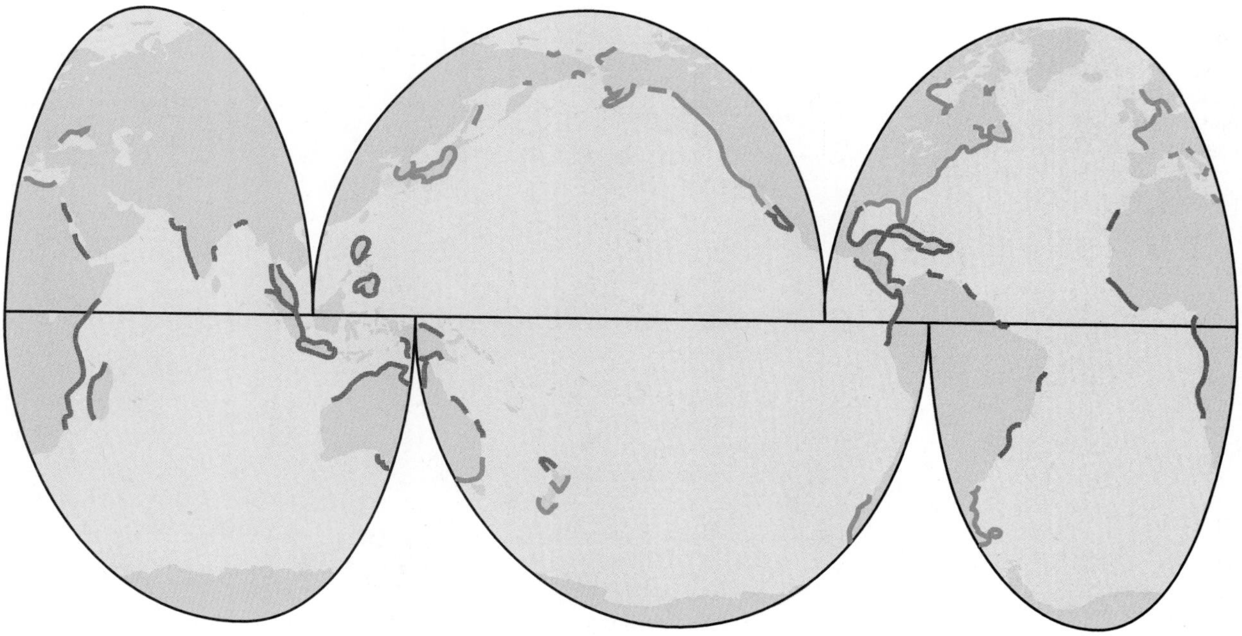

Figure 4.32
Distribution of salt marshes (teal blue) and mangals (gray)

of emergent grasses, particularly the various species of *Spartina.* At slightly higher elevations, these grasses give way to *Salicornia, Suaeda,* a variety of reeds and rushes, and the brush and smaller trees of the local area. These lush pastures are extremely productive and harbor a unique assemblage of organisms, including commercially important shellfish and finfish. Yet positioned as they often are near large urban centers, they have become popular sites for waste dumping, recreation, dredging and filling, and other detrimental uses. The degradation of salt marshes is a serious and worldwide problem that becomes more severe as human populations expand and place more pressure on these fragile habitats.

Well-developed sea grass and kelp beds seldom extend above the low tide line; they are **submergent plant communities.** Both sea grass and kelp beds abound with herbivores that graze directly on these plants and in turn become prey for higher trophic levels. The cooler water kelp plants form extensive layered forests of mixed species in both the Atlantic and Pacific oceans. The blades of the larger genera, *Macrocystis, Laminaria,* or *Nereocystis,* form the upper canopy and the basic structure of these plant communities. Shorter species of other brown algae and red algae provide secondary understory layers and create a complex, three-dimensional habitat with a large variety of available niches (figure 4.33). The maximum depth of these kelp beds, usually 20 to 30 m, is limited by the light available for the young growing sporophyte. The larger kelp plants, with their broad blades streaming at the sea surface, create substantial drag against currents and swells and are susceptible to storm damage by waves and surge. Cast on the shore, these decaying plants are a major food source for beach scavengers.

On both the Atlantic and Pacific coasts of the United States, kelp beds exist in a delicate balance with their major grazers, sea urchins. Since World War II, numerous kelp beds on both coasts have been devastated by dense aggregations of sea urchins grazing on the holdfasts, thereby freeing the remainder of the plant to wash onto the shore. These large urchin populations, capable of completely eliminating local kelp beds, seem free of the

Figure 4.33
Simplified cross section of a typical California kelp bed illustrating some of the complex, junglelike, vertical structures created by the kelp bed components

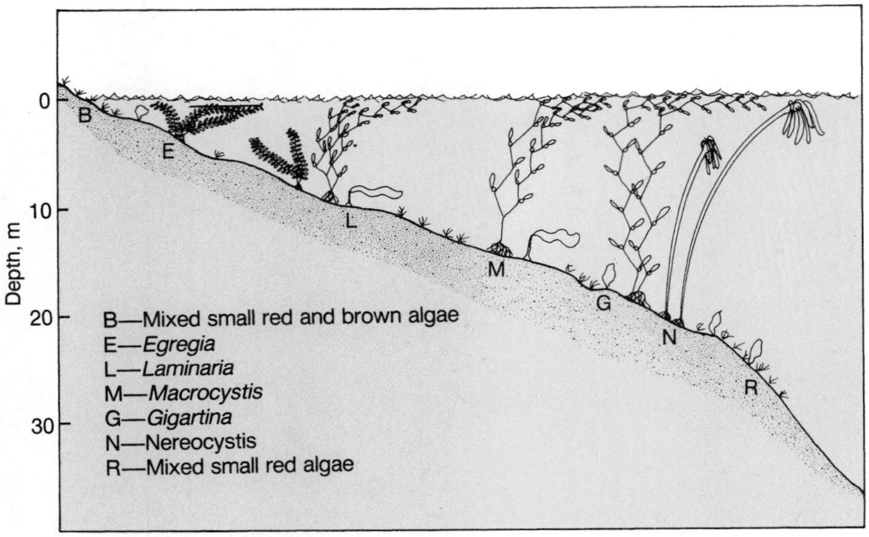

usual population regulatory mechanisms—predation and starvation. A major predator of West Coast kelp bed urchins is the sea otter (*Enhydra lutris,* figure 12.10). East Coast sea urchins are similarly preyed upon by the lobster (*Homarus americanus*). However, both of these predators have been subjected to intensive commercial harvesting and have experienced major population reductions in the past two centuries. Available evidence indicates that the effects of this reduced predation have been magnified by the increased concentrations of dissolved organic materials in coastal waters (mostly from urban sewage outfalls). These energy-rich substances apparently freed the urchin populations of the usual consequences that befall animal populations that seriously overgraze their plant food sources. These alternative sources of energy ensured that large numbers of urchins survived long enough after decimating one kelp bed to move to another. In central California kelp beds that sea otters have recolonized since 1950, urchin populations are now kept low. The kelp beds just off San Diego, however, have made a dramatic recovery since 1960 without sea otters. The recovery there is likely due to improved urban sewage treatment and the activities of other urchin predators, particularly sea stars and the sheephead fish.

Summary

Representatives of eleven divisions of primary producers live in seawater. Of these, five divisions are predominantly marine and seven divisions are reasonably common. Each group has a unique complement of photosynthetic pigments, storage products, cell wall characteristics, and habitats.

Cyanobacteria, coccolithophores, and silicoflagellates account for most of the smaller, less well-known phytoplankton (the pico- and ultra-plankton); diatoms and dinoflagellates comprise the larger and more familiar nano- and micro-plankton groups. All phytoplankton are microscopic and unicellular, and they generally exist throughout much of the photic zone. Members of both groups can reproduce rapidly by asexual cell division. Their small size and complex cell shapes promote high surface-area-to-volume ratios that accelerate exchange of nutrients and waste materials as well as increase the cells' frictional resistance to sinking.

Benthic marine plants are subject to quite different environmental limitations than are phytoplankton. Most are attached to the sea bottom or to other organisms, and several achieve large sizes. The dominant groups are green algae (Chlorophyta), brown algae (Phaeophyta), red algae (Rhodophyta), and flowering plants (Anthophyta). Benthic plants are limited to the very narrow periphery of the sea, and therefore they produce less plant material on a global scale than do phytoplankton.

Review Questions

1. Diatoms exhibit many adaptations that function to slow their sinking rate. Why is it critical for diatoms to decrease their sinking rates?
2. What adaptations do marine phytoplankton possess that permit them to decrease their sinking rate?
3. What adaptations do dinoflagellates possess that permit them to succeed in warm waters where diatoms do not thrive?
4. Summarize the selective advantages for extremely small size in some phytoplankton groups. Why don't these advantages hold true for seaweeds?

Questions for Further Discussion

1. How can you account for the relatively small contribution that seaweeds are thought to make to the total marine plant production system?
2. Why do thriving populations of phytoplankton tend to be dispersed throughout the photic zone rather than crowded together at the sea surface?

Suggestions for Further Reading

Books

Abbott, I. A. 1978. *How to know the seaweeds.* Dubuque, IA: Wm. C. Brown Publishers.

Boney, A. D. 1975. *Phytoplankton.* Baltimore: University Park Press.

Chapman, A. R. O. 1979. *Biology of seaweeds.* Baltimore: University Park Press.

Dawes, C. J. 1981. *Marine botany.* New York: John Wiley & Sons.

Dring, M. J. 1983. *The biology of marine plants.* Baltimore: University Park Press.

Round, F. E. 1973. *The biology of algae.* New York: St. Martins Press.

Teal, J., and M. Teal. 1975. *The Sargasso Sea.* Boston: Little, Brown.

Vinyard, W. C. 1980. *Diatoms of North America.* Eureka, CA: Mad River Press.

Werner, D., ed. 1977. *The biology of diatoms.* Berkeley: University of California Press.

Articles

Boatman, E. S., et al. 1987. Today's microscopy. *Bioscience* 37(6):384–94.

Dale, B., and C. M. Yentsch. 1978. Red tide and paralytic shellfish poisoning. *Oceanus* 21 (summer): 41–49.

Duffy, J. E., and M. E. Hay. 1990. Seaweed adaptations to herbivory. *Bioscience* 40(5):368–75.

Estes, J. A., and J. F. Palmisano. 1974. Sea otters: Their role in structuring nearshore communities. *Science* 185:1058–60.

Foster, M. S. 1975. Algal succession in a *Macrocystis pyrifera* forest. *Marine Biology* 32:313–29.

Fryxell, G. A. 1983. New evolutionary patterns in diatoms. *Bioscience* 33:92–98.

Hargraves, P. E., and F. W. French. 1983. Diatom resting spores: Significance and strategies. In: *Survival strategies of the algae* by G. A. Fryxell, ed., 49–68. New York: Cambridge University Press.

Krogmann, D. W. 1981. Cyanobacteria (blue-green algae)—their evolution and relation to other photosynthetic organisms. *Bioscience* 31:121–24.

Mann, K. H., and P. A. Breen. 1972. The relation between lobster abundance, sea urchins, and kelp beds. *Journal of the Fisheries Research Board of Canada* 29:603–9.

Margulis, L., D. Chase, and R. Guerrero. 1986. Microbial communities. *Bioscience* 36:160–70.

Marshall, H. G. 1976. Phytoplankton density along the eastern coast of U.S.A. *Mar. Biol.* 38:81–89.

Pettitt, J., S. Ducker, and B. Knox. 1981. Submarine pollination. *Scientific American* 244(3):134–43.

Philander, G. 1989. El Niño and La Niña. *American Scientist* 77(5):451–59.

Phillips, R. C. 1978. Sea grasses and the coastal environment. *Oceanus* 21(summer):30–40.

Pickett-Heaps, J. 1976. Cell division in eukaryotic algae. *Bioscience* 26:445–50.

Platt, T., and W. K. W. Li, eds. 1986. Photosynthetic picoplankton. *Can. Bull. Fish. Aquatic Sci.* 214:583.

Pomeroy, L. R. 1974. The ocean's food web, a changing paradigm. *Bioscience* 24:449–504.

Saffo, M. B. 1987. New light on seaweeds. *Bioscience* 37(9):654–64.

Smayda, T. J. 1970. The suspension and sinking of phytoplankton in the sea. *Oceanography and Marine Biology Annual Review* 8:353–414.

Smith, W. O. Jr., and D. M. Nelson. 1986. Importance of ice edge phytoplankton production in the southern ocean. *Bioscience* 36:251–57.

Steidinger, K. A., and K. Haddad. 1981. Biologic and hydrographic aspects of red tides. *Bioscience* 31(11):814–19.

Primary Production in the Sea

Chapter 5

Marine algae
Photo by T. Phillipp

The two major categories of autotrophs in the sea, the attached benthic plants and the pelagic phytoplankton, differ in more than their physical appearance. These differences reflect adaptations to the diverse physical and chemical terrains of the benthic and pelagic divisions of the marine environment. The narrow sunlit benthic fringe of the ocean is home to a variety of large, relatively long-lived, attached plants. Yet these plants account for only about 5 to 10% of the total amount of plant material produced in the ocean each year.

From our shore-based perspective, benthic plants gain immediate attention because of their high **standing crop** (the amount of plant material alive at any one time), but this is a poor indicator of the pattern of total primary production. The majority of marine primary production is accomplished by the small, dispersed pelagic phytoplankton. On an oceanic scale, the larger near-shore plants are minor players in the process of marine photosynthesis.

Primary production, a term interchangeable with photosynthesis, is the biological process of creating high-energy organic material from CO_2, H_2O, and other nutrients using solar energy. The organic material synthesized by the primary producers ultimately becomes transformed and is transferred to other trophic levels of the ecosystem.

Consider this example: A neatly trimmed lawn contains an easily measured amount of living plant material, its standing crop. If the lawn is maintained throughout a summer, it will be periodically mowed to maintain the same height, or in other words, the same standing crop. During that summer, the lawn clippings will total much more than the standing crop, but the lawn clippings are not part of the lawn. They represent the primary production that occurred during the summer. In an analogous sense, it is this rapidly consumed production by phytoplankton, with typically very low standing crops, that fuels the metabolic processes of most of the consumers living in the sea.

The total amount of organic material produced in the sea by photosynthesis represents the **gross primary production** of the marine ecosystem. Gross primary production is sometimes difficult to measure in nature; nonetheless, it is useful as a base of reference for understanding the production potential of the marine ecosystem. A portion of the organic material produced by photosynthesis is utilized in cellular respiration to sustain the life processes of the photosynthesizers. Any excess production is used for growth, reproduction, and losses due to death and is referred to as the **net primary production.** Net marine primary production represents the amount of organic material available to support the consumers, nonphotosynthetic protists, and decomposers of the sea. Different types of living material contain varying proportions of water, minerals, and energy-rich components. To minimize the problems of comparing different types of primary producers, standing crops are commonly reported in grams of organic carbon (gC). This unit represents approximately 10% of the live, or wet, weight of the standing crop. To compensate for differences in water content of different types of primary producers, production rates for phytoplankton are usually reported in units of grams of organic carbon fixed by photosynthesis under a square meter of sea surface per day or per year ($gC/m^2/day$ or $gC/m^2/year$).

The following discussion of some global aspects of marine primary production will emphasize production by phytoplankton, but the general concepts are also valid for the larger forms of attached plants.

In dark bottle (plant respiration)	In light bottle (net photosynthesis)	LB–DB (gross photosynthesis)	Photosynthesis (in arbitrary units)
−2.0	+4.0	6.0	
−1.9	+2.6	4.5	
−1.7	+1.6	3.3	
−1.6	+0.8	2.4	
−1.3	+0.3	1.6	
−1.1	−0.2	0.9	
−0.9	−0.5	0.4	
−0.7	−0.7	0.0	

Depth, m

Measured change in dissolved oxygen (in arbitrary units)

Net primary production
Plant respiration
Gross primary production
Critical depth
Bottom of photic zone
Respiration deficit

Measurements of Primary Production

Rates of primary production in the sea vary widely in time and space, and animals exploiting the autotrophs must adapt to the patterns. These production rates, and the ecological factors that affect them, have become clearer with the development of techniques for measuring primary production in the sea. Theoretically, the net photosynthetic rate of a phytoplankton population can be estimated by measuring the rate of change of some chemical component of the photosynthetic reaction (page 49) such as the rate of O_2 production or CO_2 consumption by the phytoplankton.

For the first half of this century, the light and dark bottle technique was used to study primary production in marine phytoplankton. With this method, measured changes in O_2 consumption and production are used to compute phytoplankton respiration and photosynthetic rates. Figure 5.1 describes how the technique works in its simplest form.

To begin, representative samples of phytoplankton and their surrounding water are collected at specific preselected depths and subsamples are placed in paired transparent (light) and opaque (dark) containers. Next, the containers are replaced at the depth from which each sample was obtained. After a few hours, the paired samples are retrieved, and the O_2 content of the water in each bottle is measured. Decreases in dissolved O_2 are used to estimate cellular respiration in the absence of light. In the light bottle, changes in O_2 concentration represent total (or gross) photosynthetic activity less the products of photosynthesis used in respiration. This is net photosynthesis, the excess of phytoplankton production over its respiration.

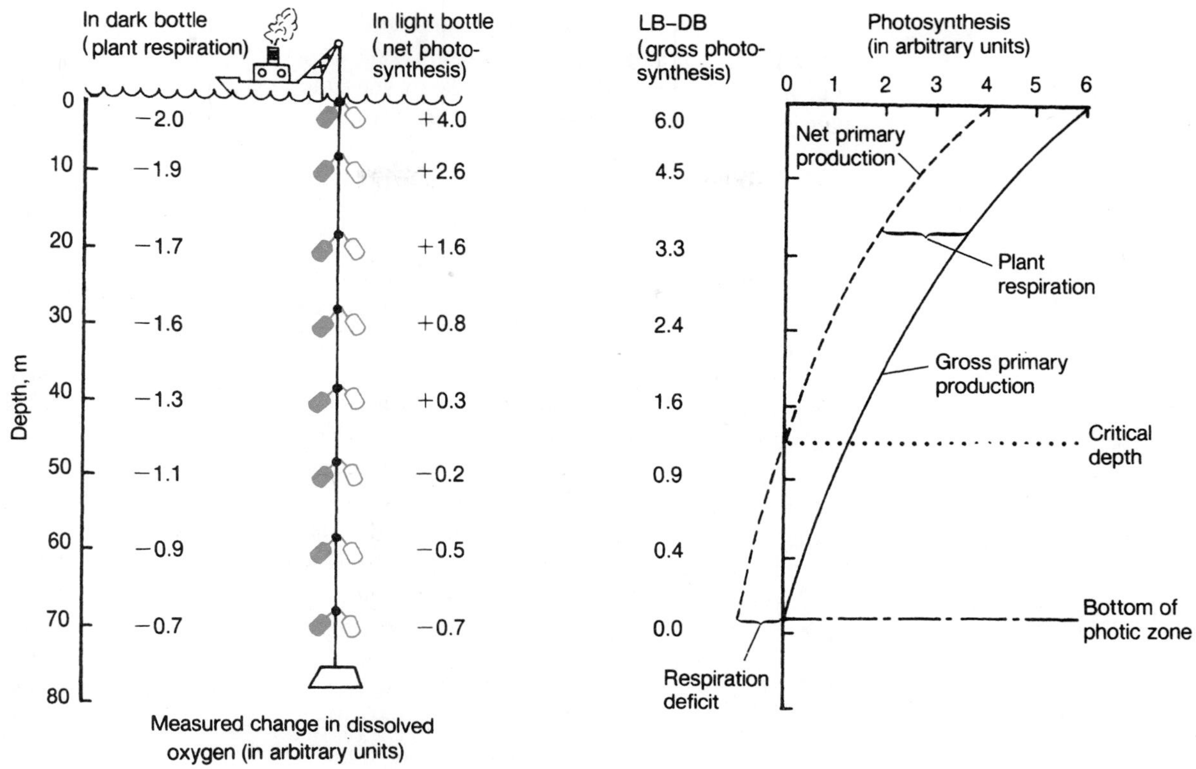

Figure 5.1

The results of a hypothetical light and dark bottle experiment. Water samples from 10 m depth increments are replaced at original depths in paired light and dark bottles. After a period of time, the bottles are retrieved and changes in O_2 are determined. Dark bottle (DB) values indicate O_2 decreases at each depth due to plant respiration without photosynthesis. Light bottle (LB) values represent O_2 changes from photosynthesis and respiration (net primary production) in the light. The difference between the two values (LB-DB) is the gross primary production. With these values, net and gross primary production curves can be drawn to represent the variation in photosynthesis because of depth.

The precision of the light and dark bottle technique hinges on the assumption that respiratory O_2 consumption in the dark bottle is the same as that in the light bottle. While this is an accurate assumption at optimum or below optimum light conditions, it is usually not true for phytoplankton in high light intensities. Some O_2 may be consumed by zooplankton or bacteria included in the light or dark bottles. Some of the problems inherent in productivity estimates based on O_2 changes in light and dark bottles can be avoided by determining rates of CO_2 uptake instead. In the early 1950s, Steemann Nielsen first employed a procedure that used radioactive carbon (C^{14}) as a tracer in photosynthesis. Improved C^{14} measurements are now the preferred method for marine primary production studies.

The C^{14} procedure is similar to the O_2 production technique, but it is more sensitive when productivity is very low. Paired light and dark bottles are used. Each bottle is injected with a known quantity of bicarbonate containing the labeled C^{14}. After a period of incubation at the proper depth, the samples are recovered. The phytoplankton of each sample are collected on membrane filters and dried. The amount of radioactive carbon assimilated by the phytoplankton in the bottles is measured with a radioactivity counting device. Net primary production is then computed using an appropriate conversion factor. The resulting error in estimating primary productivity is about $\pm 30\%$.

In photosynthetic plants, chlorophyll *a* is necessary to bring about photosynthetic reactions. One might assume, then, that the gross primary production in a volume of seawater is proportional to the amount of chlorophyll *a* contained in the living phytoplankton of the water sample. Such a relationship between gross primary production and chlorophyll *a* concentrations has been established, but only in an approximate fashion. Chlorophyll *a* concentration is a better indicator of the standing crop of phytoplankton. Standing crop sizes at any given moment are governed by a balance between crop increases (cell growth and division) and crop decreases (sinking and grazing). Most of the gross primary production of a healthy, actively growing phytoplankton population is not used in respiration but, instead, contributes to the existing standing crop. In contrast, old populations or healthy cells in poor growing conditions use a large portion of their gross production in respiration, and net production declines. If a net loss occurs, the population will eventually disappear.

The standing crop of a healthy phytoplankton population measured on successive days may demonstrate little or no increase, suggesting that no net production occurred from one day to the next. A more likely explanation is that significant net production did occur, but it replaced the portion of the crop lost to grazers and to sinking. Thus, the relationship between standing crop and productivity depends to a large degree on the **turnover rate** of newly created plant material.

The turnover rate of phytoplankton populations is extremely rapid. Many species of large phytoplankton divide once each day, and several of the smaller species divide even faster. The coccolithophore shown in figure 4.4, for instance, undergoes almost two divisions per day. Its population is completely replaced, or turned over, twice each day, so comparatively little plant material exists in the water at any one time. Even higher turnover rates are expected for the smaller pico- and ultra-plankton and in benthic algae.

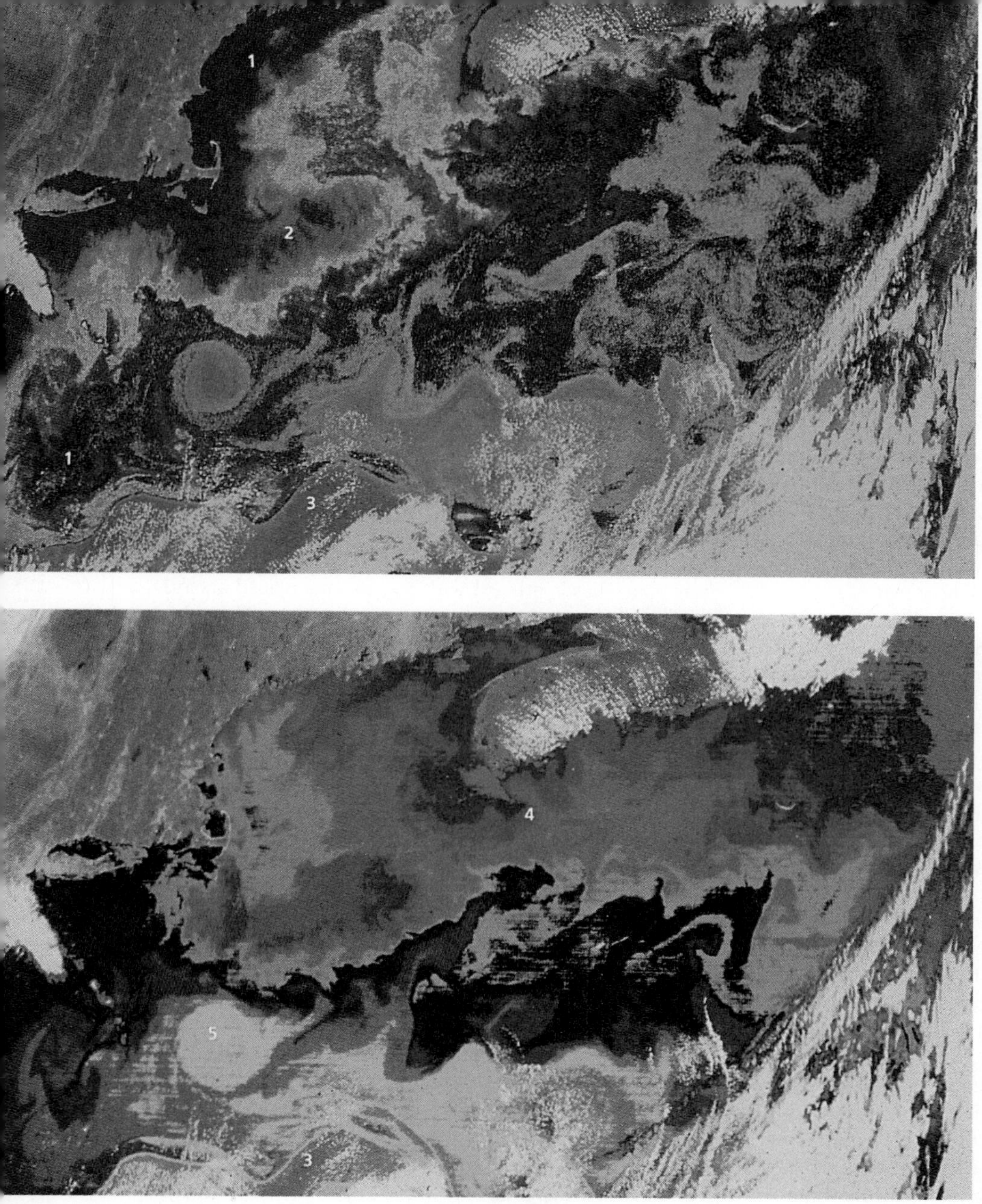

Figure 5.2
Composite satellite views of the North Atlantic Ocean. Top, phytoplankton concentrations, ranging from low (dark blue) to high (red). Bottom, sea surface temperature of the area shown at left, ranging from warm (red) to cold (dark blue).
Courtesy National Aeronautics and Space Administration

For decades, O_2 or C^{14}-based measurements of primary productivity and of standing crop have been made from ships at widely spaced sampling stations. Environmental changes that occurred as the ship steamed from one station to the next could not be measured, nor were the details between stations examined. It simply had to be assumed that the data collected at the sample stations could be averaged over the areas between stations and between sampling periods. The complexity and richness of small to moderate-scale spatial variations in phytoplankton abundance were missed, as were the day-to-day variations occurring at any sampling station.

In contrast to ship-based sampling, satellites can provide a general, and instantaneous, overview of a large portion of ocean (figure 5.2). Satellites cannot directly measure marine primary productivity. Instead, ocean surface color is measured with a coastal zone color scanner (CZCS) aboard the

Box 5 *Oceanography from Space*

Observations of ocean conditions at sea have been the basis for amassing the extensive store of information that underlies our present understanding of oceanic structures and their functions. Typically, this information has been collected from ships or unmanned instrument buoys. These approaches were (and still are) appropriate for studying such conditions as water temperature, waves and currents, salinity, and the change in marine organisms from the sea surface downward; however, they were less effective in providing detailed views of how the same features varied through time or were distributed across oceanic distances. So, until the middle of this century, long-time series of data collections were combined and averaged to provide a "typical" view of any of these features at large oceanic scales. It was not possible to obtain a synoptic, or instant snapshot, view of how any major component of the oceans was behaving at any particular time.

In 1959, the first of the TIROS series of weather satellites was placed in orbit. A remote eye-in-the-sky view of weather patterns over whole oceans has become standard (and expected) fare for television weather reports. The TIROS satellites have since been replaced with two newer series, NIMBUS and NOAA. Their capability to detect and track every hurricane on either side of North America has proved invaluable.

In the 1970s, the ERTS and LANDSAT series of satellites were launched to assess land-based resources. TRANSIT is a system of five satellites that provides global position-fixing capabilities anywhere on the globe. These position fixes are available every hour or two and are accurate within forty meters. Although none of these satellites were specifically designed for ocean observations, they have contributed to our understanding of the complex links between ocean conditions and weather, have given us our first detailed views of large-scale coastal features, and have provided oceanographers with a new and valuable ability to pinpoint the location of an experiment or a sample site at sea.

Since TIROS I, more than forty nondefense satellites capable of studying the oceans have been placed in orbit by the United States. Only one of these, SEASAT, was specifically designed for ocean research. It lasted three months before failing, but in that short time, it provided an extensive global view of the variation in altitude of the sea surface. The radar beams directed from SEASAT could measure the distance between the satellite and the sea surface to within 5 to 7 cm (2 to 3 in.). Useful information about the structure and composition of the sea floor was obtained by mapping the ocean surface from space. For example, the Gulf Stream varies about 100 cm in height across its width. Over seafloor trenches, the sea surface is as much as 60 m closer to the center of the earth, and a seamount causes the sea surface to bulge out about 5 m. SEASAT maps these variations in sea surface topography and the maps are used to construct a composite view of how the ocean floor and surface current patterns vary over time periods of a few weeks.

With the shutdown of SEASAT, oceanography from space has continued with instruments placed aboard satellites dedicated to other remote sensing tasks. The radar altimeter measurements initiated on SEASAT are being continued on the GEOS satellites. The Coastal Zone Color Scanner (CZCS) on NIMBUS 7 monitors chlorophyll concentrations in surface waters (figure 5.2 was obtained this way) and maps the large-scale distribution and abundance of marine phytoplankton, with a capability to repeat each observation every six days. Several satellites have radar, microwave, or infrared sensors that can measure sea surface temperature, rain rate, wind speed, sea surface roughness, and distribution of sea ice.

The use of satellite-based remote sensing devices has opened enormous possibilities for acquiring previously unattainable synoptic views of large expanses of the world ocean and has ushered in a new era of global oceanography. Presently, satellite remote sensing is the only method that can provide global scale information about variations of sea surface temperature, sea surface altitude, and phytoplankton productivity. A large problem accompanying this technology is associated with managing the acquired data. For example, the CZCS aboard NIMBUS 7 requires only four minutes to image an area of 1500 km^2. This single image is represented by 182 million bits of data that must be transmitted from the satellite to a ground station, stored, processed, and then made available to researchers at widely scattered locations. In spite of the information handling limitations, more ocean-oriented remote-sensing satellites are planned, ranging from sea surface temperature mapping to tracking individual whales. The information obtained cannot help but further our understanding of complex oceanic processes.

Box 5 *Oceanography from Space*

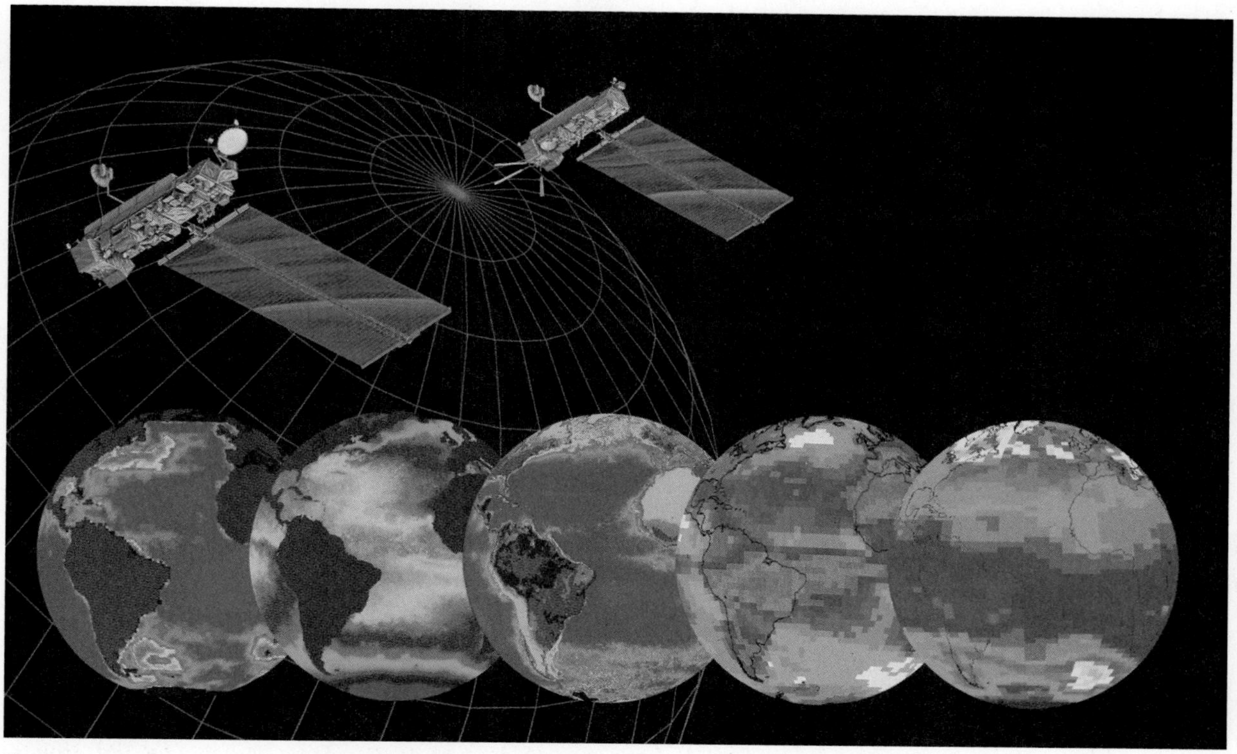

Courtesy National Aeronautics and Space Administration

NIMBUS 7 weather satellite (see box 5). The ocean color measurements are then used, with calibration from ship-based measurements, to estimate phytoplankton standing crops and growth rates and to extrapolate shipboard productivity measurements to large oceanic areas. Ultimately, it should be possible to use CZCS data alone to estimate primary production or growth rates.

Remote sensing of ocean color by satellite is the first technique to measure marine primary productivity on a global scale with enough resolution to permit analyses of phytoplankton changes over time scales of weeks or years. Since the CZCS was lofted into orbit in 1978, satellite imagery has revolutionized our view of primary productivity patterns in the ocean. As is apparent in figure 5.2, distribution patterns of phytoplankton are complex and show some similarities with sea surface temperature distributions. Patches and eddies of phytoplankton are common. In upwelling areas, plumes of phytoplankton-rich water (known as squirts) extend as much as 200 km offshore. A decade ago, these dominant features of marine phytoplankton distribution were completely unknown.

Figure 5.3
Patterns of population growth with and without limiting resources

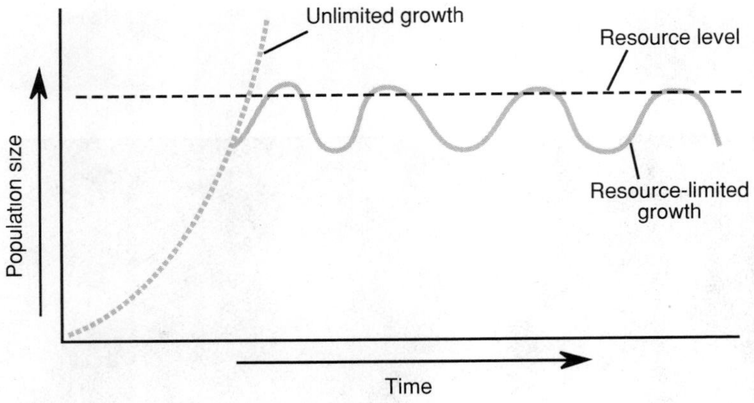

Factors That Affect Primary Production

The continued synthesis of organic material by marine phytoplankton depends on a set of interacting biotic (biological) and abiotic conditions. If nutrients, sunlight, space, and other parameters necessary for growth are unlimited, phytoplankton population sizes increase in an exponential fashion (figure 5.3).

In nature, phytoplankton populations do not continue to grow unchecked as figure 5.3 suggests. Rather, their sizes are controlled by their tolerance limits to certain environmental factors (including predators) or by the availability of substances for which there is a minimum need. Any condition that exceeds the limits of tolerance or does not satisfy the basic material needs of an organism establishes a check on further population growth and is said to be a **limiting factor.** Phytoplankton populations limited by one or a combination of these factors are forced to deviate from the exponential growth curve shown in figure 5.3. Important limiting factors for phytoplankton are light, nutrient availability, and herbivore grazing. In the ocean, each major group of phytoplankton responds differently to combinations of these factors. In general, diatoms and silicoflagellates thrive in lower light intensities and colder water than do dinoflagellates and coccolithophores. Consequently, conditions that promote the growth of either group tends to exclude the other. These factors will be examined, first alone, then in concert, in an attempt to convey the complex dynamic interactions that exist between these living communities and their immediate surroundings.

Light

The requirement for light imposes a fundamental limit on the distribution of all marine photosynthetic organisms. To live, these organisms must remain in the upper region of the ocean (the photic zone) where solar energy sufficient for photosynthesis will reach them. The depth of the photic zone is determined by the capacity of sunlight to penetrate seawater. This in turn is influenced by a variety of conditions: the atmospheric absorption of light, the angle between the sun and the sea surface, and water transparency.

The amount of energy reaching the sea surface depends on atmospheric conditions such as dust, clouds, and gases that absorb, reflect, and scatter a portion of the incoming solar radiation (figure 5.4). On an average day, about 65% of the incident radiation arriving at the outer edge of our at-

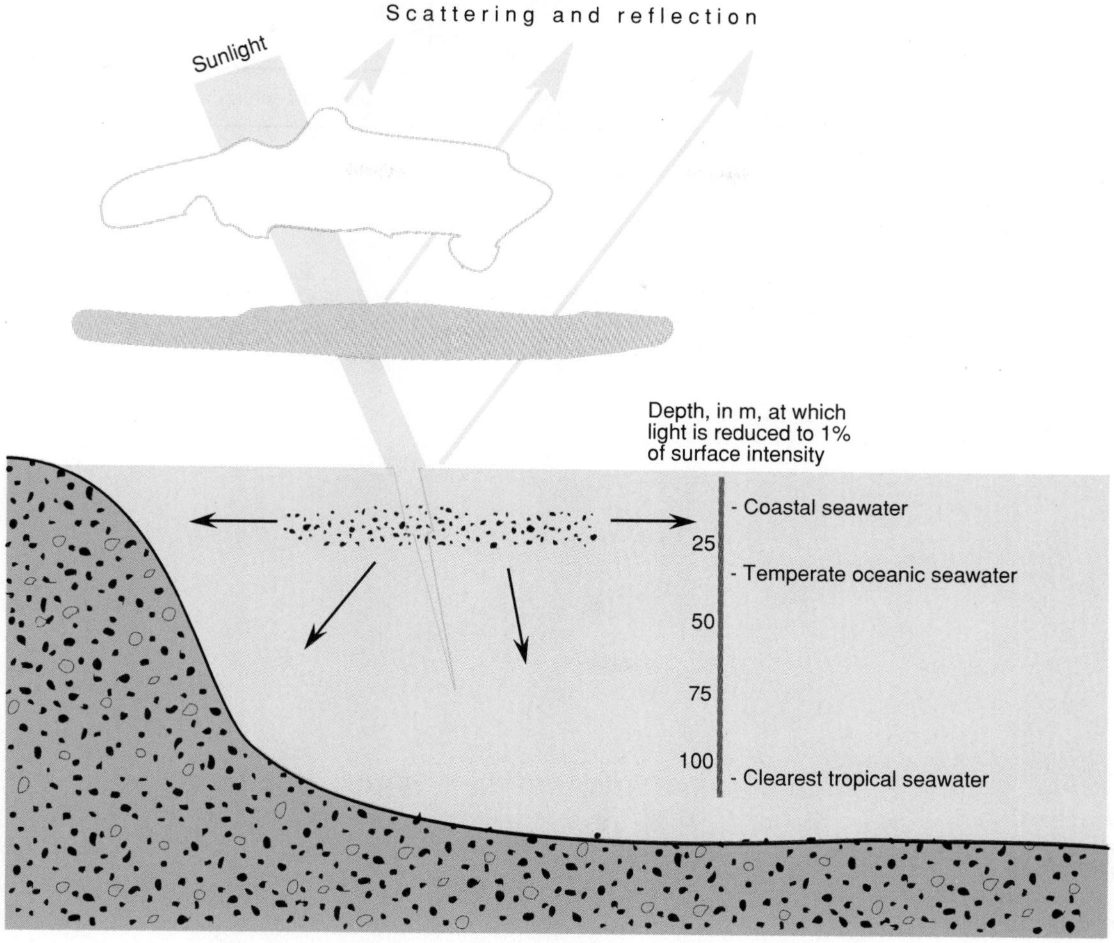

Figure 5.4
Fate of sunlight near the sea surface

mosphere reaches the earth's surface. The magnitude of incoming solar radiation is reduced when the angle of the sun is low, as in winter or at high latitudes.

A portion of the light that makes it through the atmosphere is reflected back into space by the sea surface itself. Below the sea surface, more light energy is lost through light absorption. Dissolved substances, suspended sediments, and plankton populations further diminish the amount of light available for photosynthetic activity and cause the depth of light penetration to differ dramatically between coastal and oceanic water (figure 5.4).

Sunlight, in its travels through our atmosphere and into the sea, is also changed qualitatively. Of the broad band of electromagnetic radiation that penetrates the atmosphere, we perceive only a very narrow band, the **visible spectrum.** Sunlight arriving at the sea surface includes all colors of the visible spectrum from violet through red (figure 5.5). Each color is characterized by a range of wavelengths measured in nanometers (nm). Photosynthetic pigments of autotrophs also respond to the same "visible" radiation, making it easier for us to understand what photosynthetic systems do with light energy.

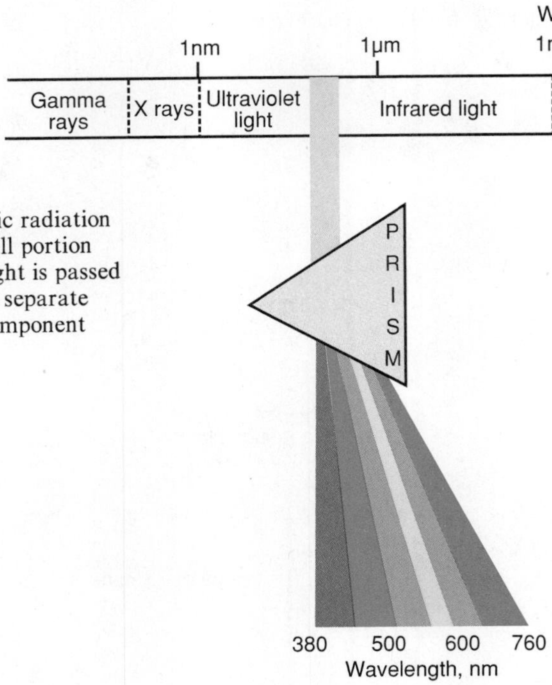

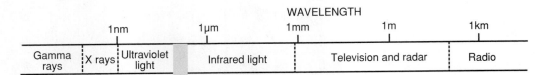

Figure 5.5
The electromagnetic radiation spectrum. The small portion known as visible light is passed through a prism to separate the light into its component colors.

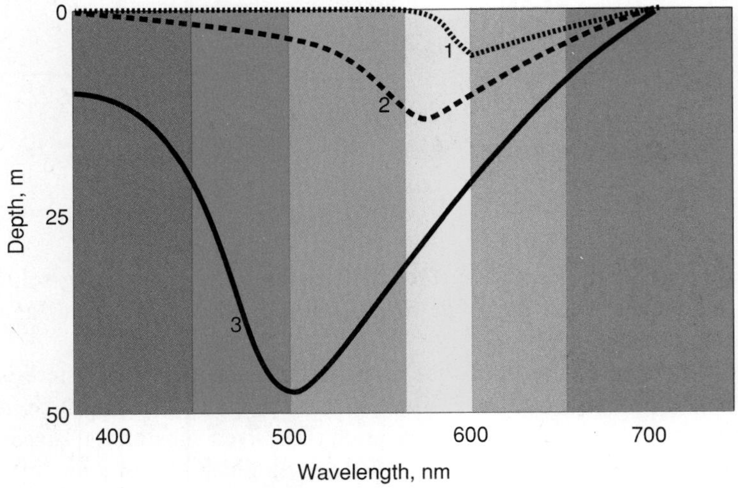

Figure 5.6
Penetration of various wavelengths of light in three different water types: (1) very turbid coastal water, (2) moderately turbid coastal water, and (3) clear tropical water. Note the shift to shorter wavelengths (bluer light) in clearer water.

Seawater quickly alters the color characteristics of light by differentially absorbing portions of the visible spectrum. Generally, the violet and the orange-red wavelengths of the spectrum are the first to be absorbed. Even in the clearest tropical waters, almost all of the red light is absorbed in the upper 10 m. Clear seawater is most transparent to the blue and green portions of the spectrum (450 to 550 nm); 10% of the blue light penetrates to 100 m. However, this light too is eventually absorbed or scattered (figure 5.6).

The greater penetration and eventual back-scattering of blue light account for the characteristic blue color of clear, tropical seawater. Coastal waters are commonly more turbid, with a greater load of suspended sediments

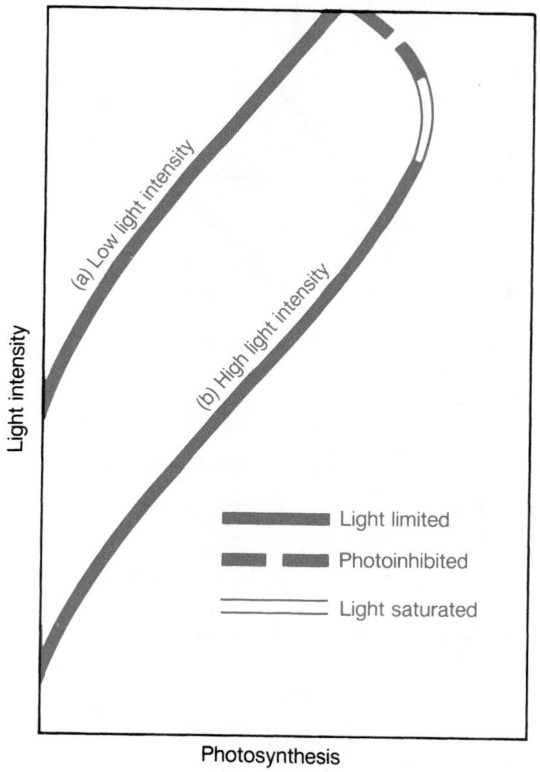

Figure 5.7
Relationship between photosynthesis and depth at low and high light intensities

and dissolved pigmented substances derived from land runoff. Here, there is a shift in the relative penetration of light energy, with green light penetrating deepest. In many coastal regions, green light is reduced to 1% of its surface intensity in less than 30 m. The cumulative effects of differential absorption and scattering of sunlight by seawater reduce the intensity and spectral width of the light available below the sea surface.

At some depth the light intensity is so faint that no photosynthesis will occur. This depth defines the bottom of the photic zone and varies from a few meters deep in coastal waters to over 200 m in clear tropical seas. At a depth somewhat above the bottom of the photic zone, the rate of photosynthesis is balanced by photorespiration. This depth of no net primary production is the **critical depth** (see figure 5.1). The critical depth is approximately equivalent to the depth at which the available light is reduced to 1% of its surface intensity (figure 5.4). In clear tropical waters, the critical depth often extends below 100 m throughout the year. In higher latitudes, it may reach 30 to 50 m in midsummer, but it nearly disappears during the winter months. (These are average critical depths for mixed phytoplankton assemblages composed of many different species; each species has its own peculiar critical depth.)

In moderate and low light intensities, photosynthesis by phytoplankton exhibits a direct relationship to light intensity (figure 5.7, curve a). At higher light intensities, photosynthesis ceases to follow the light intensity curve; it may stabilize or even decrease nearer the sea surface because of **photoinhibition** by strong light (figure 5.7, curve b). Between the light-limited and light-inhibited portions of the photosynthetic curve b in figure 5.7 is a zone of

Figure 5.8
A comparison of photosynthetic responses of two phytoplankton species to varying light intensities. The diatom *Planktonella* (curve *a*) shows marked photoinhibition at high light intensities; the photosynthetic rate of *Dinophysis*, a dinoflagellate (curve *b*), continues to increase even at high light intensities.
Adapted from Qasim *et al.*, 1972

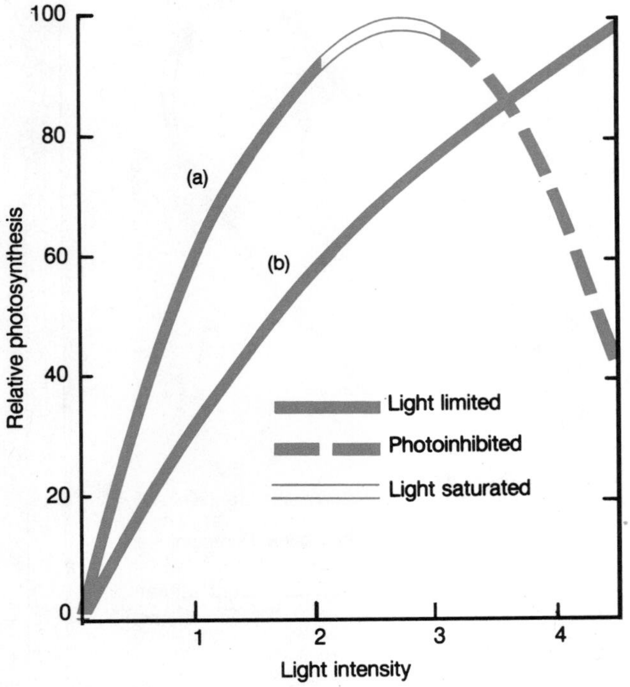

saturation light intensity. At this point, photosynthesis no longer increases in proportion to increasing light intensities. The photosynthetic machinery of phytoplankton cells is saturated with light, and higher light intensities nearer the sea surface fail to elicit proportionate increases in photosynthesis.

Phytoplankton from different environments exhibit some degree of photosynthetic adjustment to varying light intensities. Therefore, the saturation light intensity for any phytoplankton population changes with changing sets of environmental conditions. Variations in saturation light intensities are also found among major phytoplankton groups. Dinoflagellates seem to be better adapted than diatoms to intense light (figure 5.8). As a result, their relative contribution to the total marine primary production is much greater in tropical and subtropical regions.

Photosynthetic Pigments

The photosynthetic apparatus of all marine primary producers except cyanobacteria is located in the chloroplasts of actively photosynthesizing cells. It is in the chloroplasts (or the whole cells of bacteria and cyanobacteria) that the pigment systems containing chlorophyll and varying amounts of other photosynthetic pigments listed in table 4.1 are located. There they absorb light energy and convert it to forms of chemical energy that can be used by the plant and by other organisms.

Both cyanobacteria and eucaryotic autotrophs employ an elaborate two-part photosynthetic process involving complex pigment systems and two distinct sets of chemical reactions. In the first set, the **light reaction** portion of photosynthesis (figure 5.9), photons of light are absorbed by chlorophyll molecules located in two separate pigment systems. The photons energize electrons and pump them through a series of other enzymes whose function is to

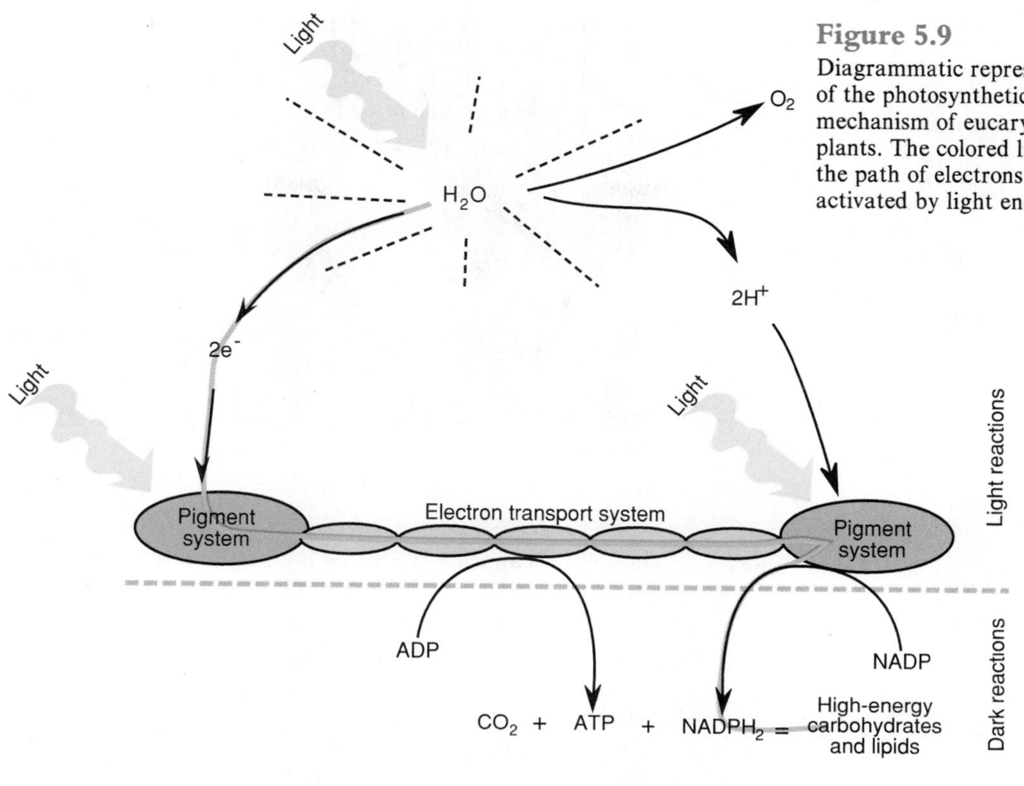

Figure 5.9
Diagrammatic representation of the photosynthetic mechanism of eucaryotic plants. The colored line traces the path of electrons initially activated by light energy.

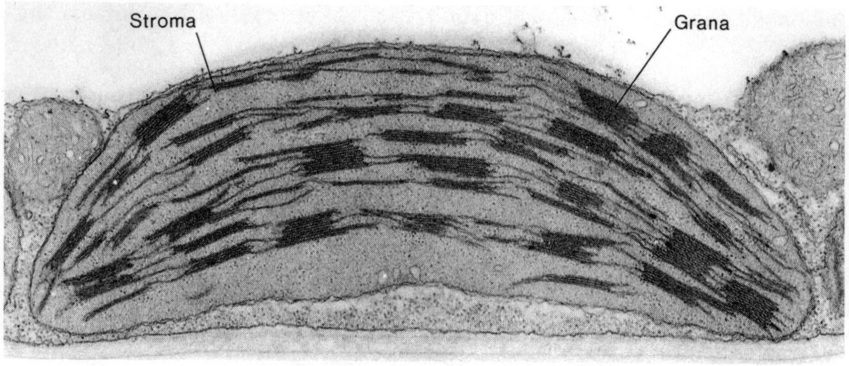

Figure 5.10
A TEM of a chloroplast with stacked sets of parallel membranes (narrow dark bands)
Courtesy Herbert W. Israel, Cornell University

manage some of that electron energy and transfer it to ATP and another high energy carrier molecule, $NADPH_2$. As the term implies, light is needed to drive the light reaction; without light, the reaction ceases.

The pigment systems and enzymes involved in the light reaction are housed within flattened sacs, which are stacked to form numerous **grana** within each chloroplast (figure 5.10). The **stroma** surrounds the grana and contains the enzymes needed for the next step of photosynthesis, the **dark reaction.** Light energy is not necessary to maintain the dark reaction, but the high-energy ATP and $NADPH_2$ produced by the light reaction are. Energy from these substances is used in the dark reaction to synthesize sugars and a variety of other organic compounds needed by the cell.

Figure 5.11
Patterns of light absorption for three photosynthetic pigments: phycoerythrin (an accessory pigment found in Rhodophyta and Cyanobacteria), fucoxanthin (an accessory pigment found in Phaeophyta, Chrysophyta, and Dinophyta), and chlorophyll *a*
Adapted from Sasso, 1987

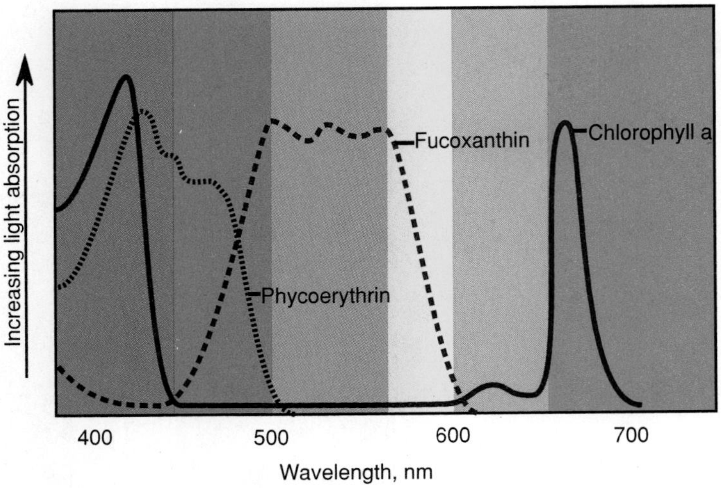

Chlorophyll appears green for the same reason coastal seawater appears green. Both absorb more of the available light energy from the violet and red ends of the spectrum, leaving the green light to be reflected back or to penetrate more deeply. Chlorophyll serves as the basic energy-absorbing pigment for land plants. However, a few meters of seawater absorbs much of the red and violet portions of the visible spectrum before it reaches the chloroplasts of most marine plants. Since chlorophyll best absorbs energy from red and violet light, its effectiveness is reduced in seawater.

The evolutionary response of most marine plant groups has been to supplement the light-absorption potential of chlorophyll with **accessory pigments** (figure 5.11). These pigments absorb light energy over a wide range of wavelengths and then transfer the energy to chlorophyll for introduction into the light reaction. Accessory pigments absorb light from spectral regions where chlorophyll cannot. Figure 5.11 illustrates the complementary effect of chlorophyll *a* and accessory pigments such as fucoxanthin, which is found in brown algae and diatoms. Fucoxanthin absorbs light primarily from the blue-green region of the spectrum, the region where chlorophyll absorbs least effectively. In combination, chlorophyll and fucoxanthin are capable of absorbing energy from most of the visible light spectrum. Another group of accessory pigments, the phycobilins, are found in red algae and cyanobacteria. These pigments have absorption spectra much like that of fucoxanthin. These and other accessory pigments listed in table 4.1 have enabled various groups of marine plants to adapt to the limited conditions of light availability in seawater.

The depth changes normally experienced by marine phytoplankton expose them to a wide variety of submarine light conditions. Their diverse pigments are capable of absorbing light energy at almost any depth within the photic zone. Patterns of vertical distribution of attached benthic plants are more complex. At first glance, it might appear that the green algae and sea grasses, with their preponderance of chlorophyll pigments, do not fare well at moderate depths because of their limited ability to absorb the deeper-penetrating green wavelengths. But plants can adapt to low or limited wavelength light conditions in other ways. For example, because some green algae have dense concentrations of chlorophyll that appear almost black, they are able to absorb light at essentially all visible wavelengths. In addition, most

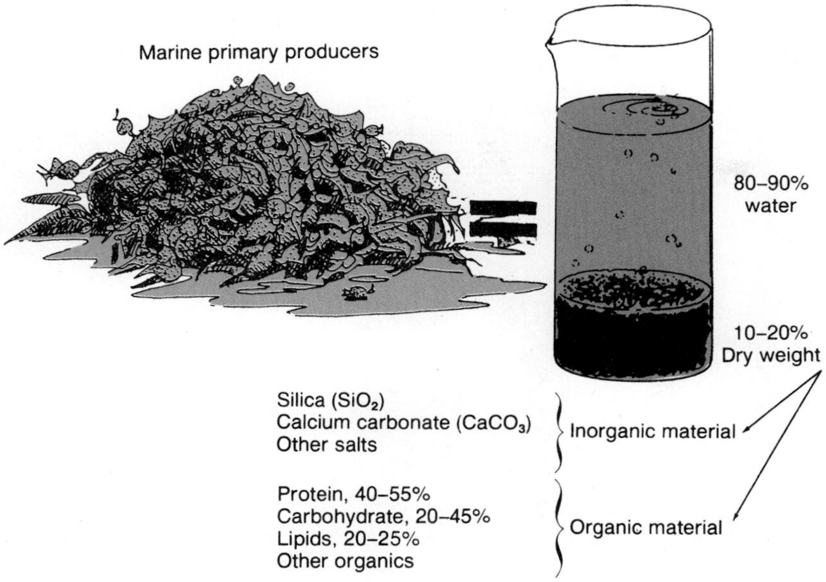

Figure 5.12
Chemical composition of typical marine autotrophs

green plants have chlorophyll b as well as chlorophyll a. Chlorophyll b has a strong light absorbing peak in the blue region of the visible spectrum (figure 5.11) and can collect a good fraction of the deep-penetrating blue light of tropical waters (see figure 5.6). Still, red and brown algae, with their abundant xanthophyll and phycobilin pigments working in concert with chlorophyll, appear to have a slight competitive advantage in occupying the deeper portions of the photic zone in turbid coastal waters and function at no disadvantage in shallow waters or intertidal zones.

Nutrient Requirements

The nutrients required by all primary producers are a bit more complex than might be indicated by the general photosynthetic equation presented on page 49:

$$6CO_2 + 6H_2O \rightarrow C_6H_{12}O_6 + 6O_2.$$

Proper growth and maintenance of cells depend on the availability of more than just water and carbon dioxide because plants are composed of compounds that cannot be assembled from C, H, and O alone.

These nutrient requirements can be best understood by determining the basic composition of the cell itself. Chemical analysis of a hypothetical "average" marine primary producer might yield the results shown in figure 5.12.

Generally, marine primary producers experience no difficulty in securing an adequate supply of water. Most are continuously and completely bathed by seawater, and few cells of any marine plant are seriously isolated from the external water environment. Some species living in the intertidal zone are subject to desiccation at low tide. These plants exhibit both resistance to and tolerance of water loss. Occasionally, a combination of low tides and dry winds from the land occur and seriously damage intertidal plants.

Figure 5.13

A simplified photosynthetic cell, illustrating the chemical requirements and products of several components of the cell

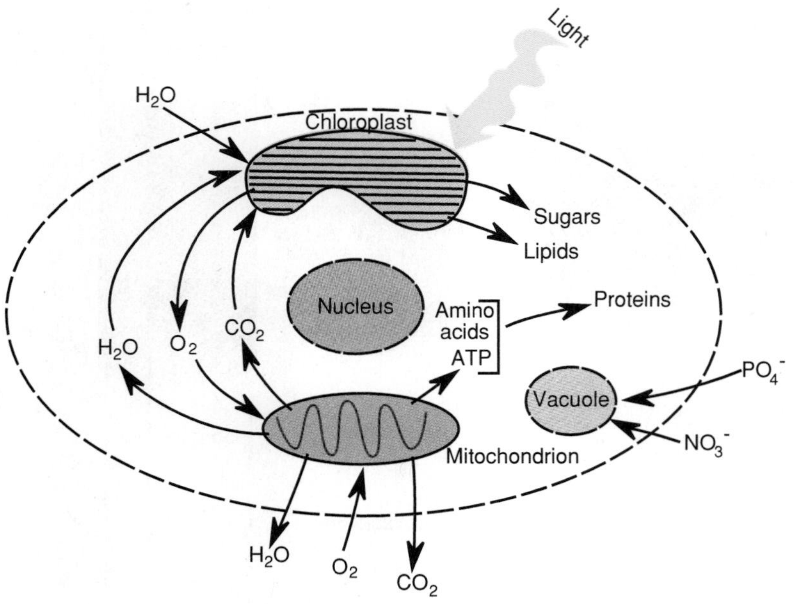

Coccolithophores and some seaweeds are equipped with cell walls or internal skeletons of calcium carbonate ($CaCO_3$). Carbon dioxide for carbonate formation and for photosynthesis exists in seawater as carbonic acid (H_2CO_3), bicarbonate (HCO_3^-), and carbonate (CO_3^{-2}). The abundance of these ions in seawater is influenced by photosynthesis, respiration, water depth, and pH balance (see page 24). However, the concentration of total CO_2 present in seawater is not low enough to inhibit photosynthesis or the formation of $CaCO_3$. Calcium ions (Ca^{+2}) necessary for calcium carbonate formation are also very abundant in seawater at all depths (see table 1.3). Silica (SiO_2) is required by silicoflagellates and diatoms, and concentrations of dissolved silica occasionally become so depleted that the growth and reproduction of these phytoplankton groups are inhibited.

Organic matter is a widely used term collectively applied to those biologically synthesized compounds that contain C, H, usually O, lesser amounts of N (nitrogen) and P (phosphorus), and traces of vitamins and other elements necessary to maintain life. Proteins, carbohydrates, and lipids are the most abundant types of organic compounds in living systems. Each contains carbon, hydrogen, and oxygen in varying ratios. Figure 5.13 summarizes the generalized nutrient needs of photosynthetic cells.

Primary producers require how much of each of these elements? Elemental analyses of phytoplankton whole-cell cultures grown under various light conditions provide an average atomic ratio of approximately 110C:230H:750:16N:1P. Carbon, hydrogen, and oxygen are abundantly available from carbonate (CO_3^{-2}) or bicarbonate ions (HCO_3^-) and water (H_2O). Nitrogen is much less plentiful but is present in seawater as nitrate (NO_3^{-2}), with lesser amounts of nitrite (NO_2^-), and ammonium (NH_4^+). High concentrations of molecular nitrogen (N_2), which constitute 78% of the earth's atmosphere, are also dissolved in seawater. However, most marine organisms are not metabolically equipped to utilize this latter source of N. They may, however, contribute a substantial portion of the total N used by the phytoplankton in nutrient-depleted seas. Phosphorus, present principally as phos-

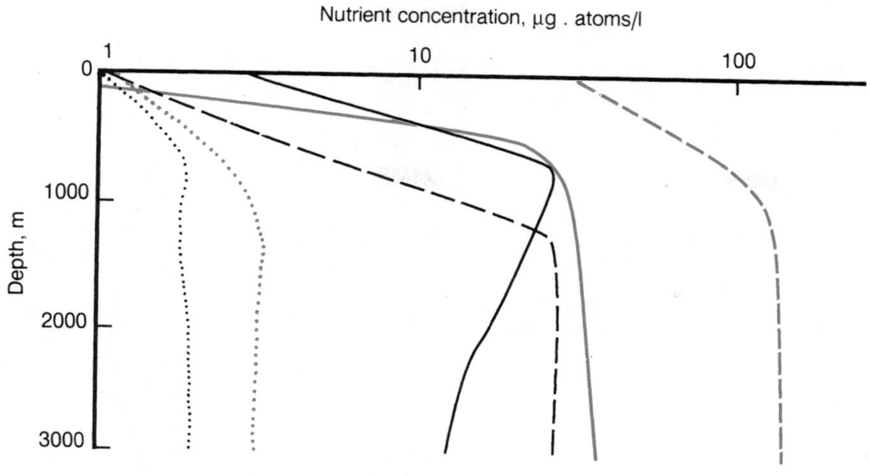

Figure 5.14
Distribution of dissolved silicate (dotted lines), nitrate (dashed lines), and phosphate (solid lines) from the surface to 3,000 m in the Atlantic (black) and Pacific (blue) oceans

Adapted from Sverdrup, Johnson, and Fleming, 1942

phate (PO_4^{-3}), is less abundant in seawater than is nitrate, but the biological demands on phosphate are also less but just as critical (for example, in the synthesis of ATP and cell membranes). The ratio of usable N and P in seawater is similar to the ratio of 16N:1P found in living cells of marine primary producers.

Figure 5.14 shows the vertical distribution patterns of silicate, nitrate, and phosphate in seawater. These nutrients are usually in short supply in the photic zone because of continual utilization by primary producers. In periods of rapid phytoplankton growth, needed quantities of one or more of these nutrients may not be available. In such circumstances, continued growth is limited by the rate of nutrient regeneration.

In addition to the nutrient elements just mentioned, marine autotrophs require several other elements in minute amounts. These **trace elements** include iron, manganese, cobalt, zinc, copper, and others. Depletion of iron in English Channel waters has been observed during spring diatom blooms, suggesting that iron availability may limit the size or composition of phytoplankton populations. But in most cases, it is not known whether natural concentrations of other trace elements dip to values sufficiently low to inhibit growth of marine primary producers.

Vitamins too are crucial for the proper growth and reproduction of primary producers. Some species of diatoms, for example, require more vitamin B_{12} during auxospore formation than at other times. Some can synthesize their own vitamins, while others must rely on free-living bacteria to provide this and other critical vitamins that they cannot synthesize for themselves.

Nutrient Regeneration

Most of the biomass produced by marine photosynthesis is eventually consumed by herbivores to be converted to more herbivore bodies or to be formed into fecal wastes. In either case, these compact particles quickly become colonized by bacteria and sink as "marine snow" to depths well below the photic zone. Other nutrients are excreted as N-containing urea and ammonia wastes and are taken up to the phytoplankton as quickly as they are excreted. Regeneration of the nutrients initially used to produce phytoplankton cells or

Figure 5.15
A simplified marine nutrient cycle
Adapted from Tett, 1982

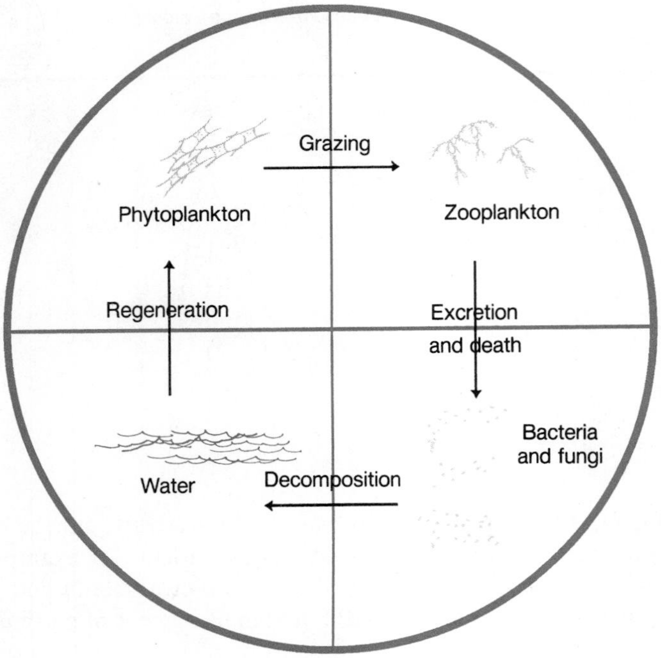

marine plants is dependent on respiration by consumers and on decomposition of organic material by bacteria and fungi living in the water column and on the sea bottom. Bacterial action decomposes organic material and returns phosphates, nitrates, and other nutrients to seawater in inorganic form for reuse by the primary producers (figure 5.15). Bacteria also absorb dissolved organic compounds from seawater and convert them to living cells that become an additional food source for many benthic and small planktonic animals.

Figure 5.14 indicates that major concentrations of limiting nutrients reside below the photic zone where they cannot be utilized by photosynthesizers. Their combined demands for light from the sea surface and nutrients from below impose severe restrictions on the rates of primary production. For much of the ocean, the sunlit photic zone is isolated from the nutrients of the deeper waters by a well-developed and permanent thermocline. Marine primary producers thrive only in those parts of the sea where active dynamic processes move colder nutrient laden waters upward into the photic zone. Molecular diffusion does not account for a very substantial return of nutrients to the photic zone. Much more significant to the rapid and continued growth of marine primary producers are large-scale mixing processes, including small scale turbulence and upwelling that rapidly transport nutrient-rich deep water upward.

Wind waves and tide create turbulence in near-surface waters and mix nutrients from deeper water upward. Turbulent mixing is most effective over continental shelves, where the shallow bottom prevents the escape of nutrients into deeper water. Tidal currents in the southern end of the North Sea and the eastern side of the English Channel, for example, are sufficient to mix the water almost completely from top to bottom. As a result, summer phytoplankton productivity there remains high as long as sunlight is sufficient to maintain photosynthesis.

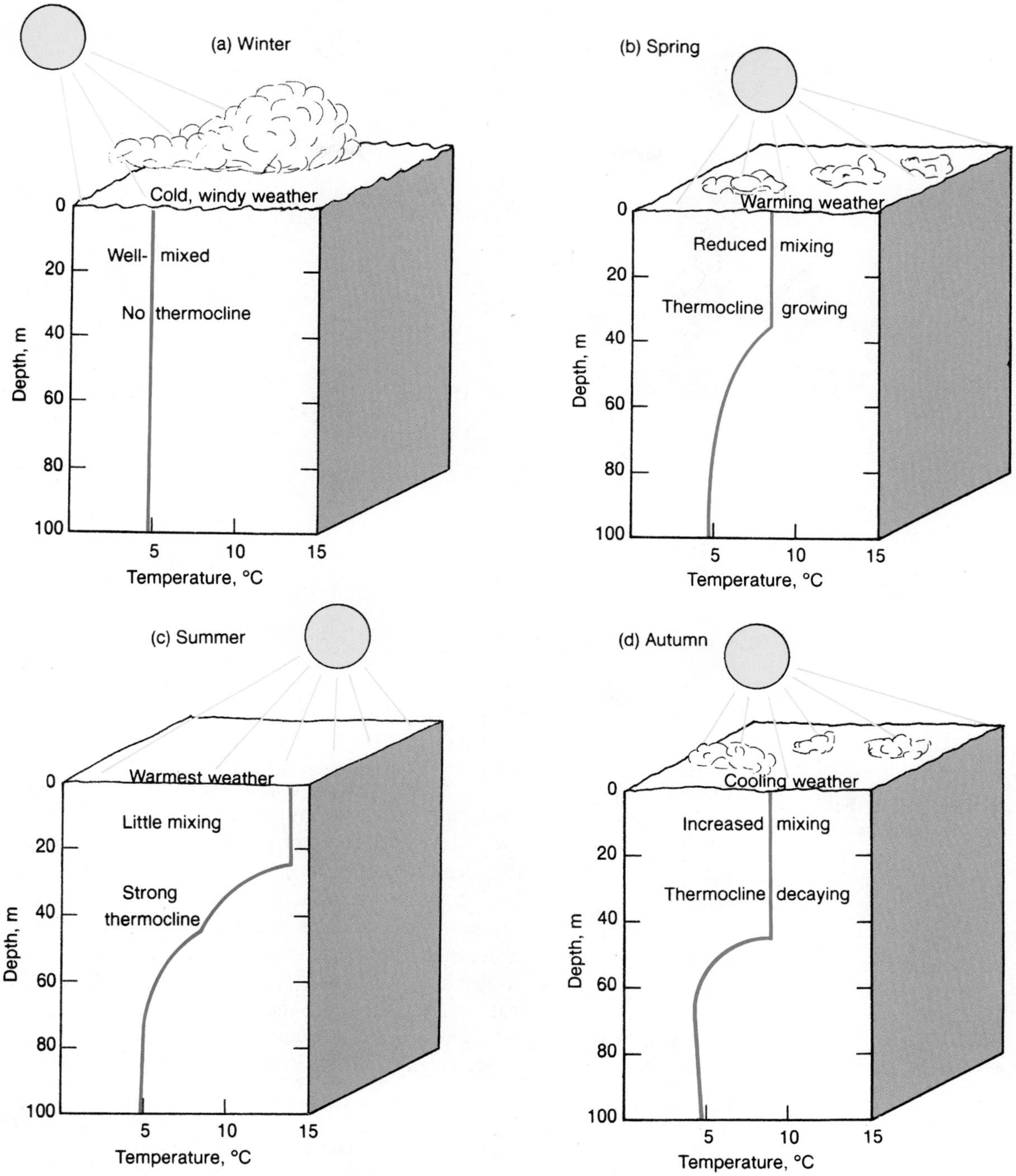

Figure 5.16
Growth and decline of the thermocline in temperate ocean waters.
Adapted from Dodimead *et al.*, 1963, for ocean station "P" off the west coast of North America at latitude 50° N, longitude 145° W.

In tropical and subtropical latitudes of most oceans, the strong year-round thermocline near the base of the photic zone acts as a strong barrier to inhibit upward mixing of deep nutrient-rich waters. Consequently, these regions have very low rates of primary production comparable to terrestrial deserts.

Thermoclines also develop in temperate waters to restrict the return of deep-water nutrients, but only on a seasonal basis (figure 5.16). During winter months, the surface water cools and sinks. The thermocline disappears

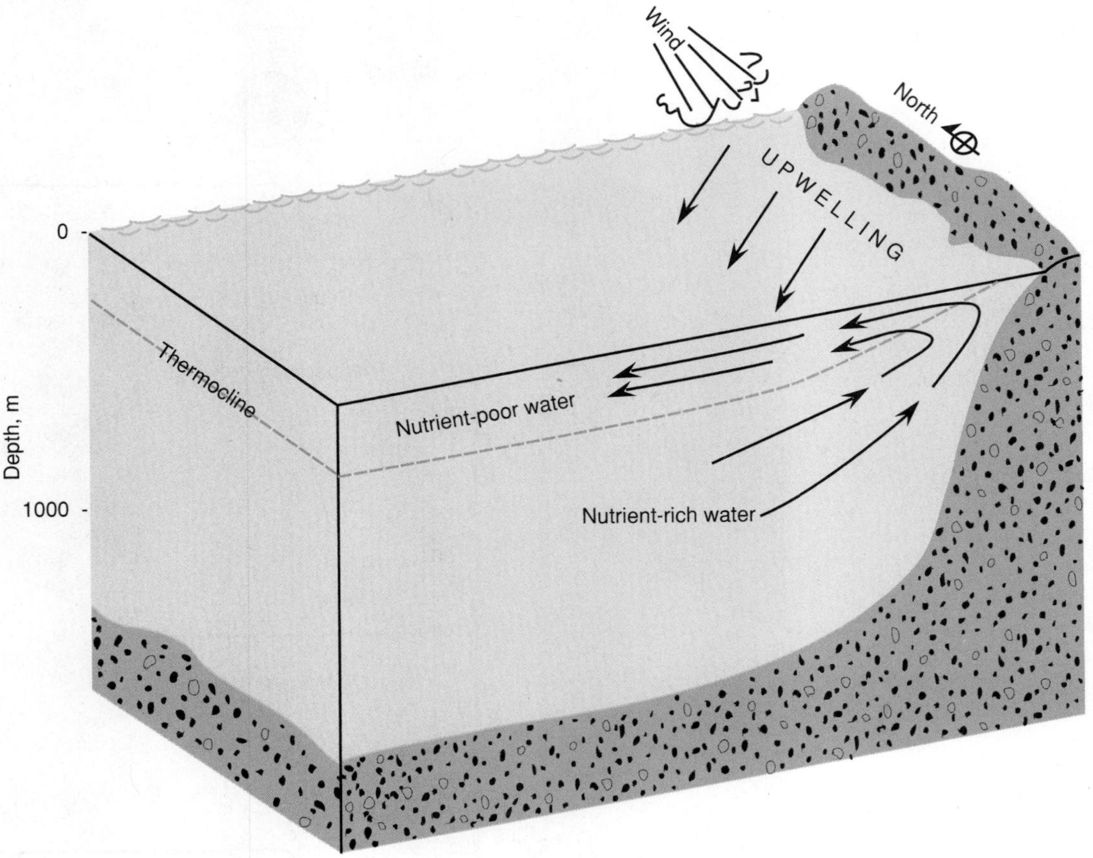

Figure 5.17
Coastal upwelling in the Northern Hemisphere

(a) and deeper nutrient-rich water is mixed with the surface water. As solar radiation increases in the spring, the surface water warms and the thermocline is reestablished (b). A well-developed summer thermocline (c) resembles the permanent thermocline of tropical and subtropical waters and creates an effective barrier blocking nutrient return to the photic zone. With shorter days and cooler weather in autumn (d), the thermocline weakens and then disappears in winter. This process of **convective mixing** is a seasonal phenomenon in temperate regions, continuing from late fall to early spring. But in high latitudes, continuous heat loss from the sea to the atmosphere and low amounts of solar radiation produces year-round convective mixing. Low light conditions rather than scarce nutrients usually limit the primary production in these polar regions.

Subsurface water is carried to the photic zone by several processes collectively termed **upwelling.** One type, coastal upwelling, is produced by winds blowing surface waters away from a coastline. The surface waters are replaced by deeper waters rising to the surface (figure 5.17). Near-shore currents, which veer away from the shoreline, produce the same result. Four major coastal upwelling areas occur in the California, Peru, Canary, and Benguela Currents, and lesser ones occur along the coasts of Somalia and western Australia. All of these currents are on eastern sides of subtropical current gyres (figure 5.18) and flow toward the equator. Figure 5.19 illustrates the influence of upwelling on nutrient availability in the photic zone. Note that the nitrate concentrations at a depth of about 50 m are 5 to 10 times higher in the upwelling systems than at similar depths in adjacent non-upwelled water.

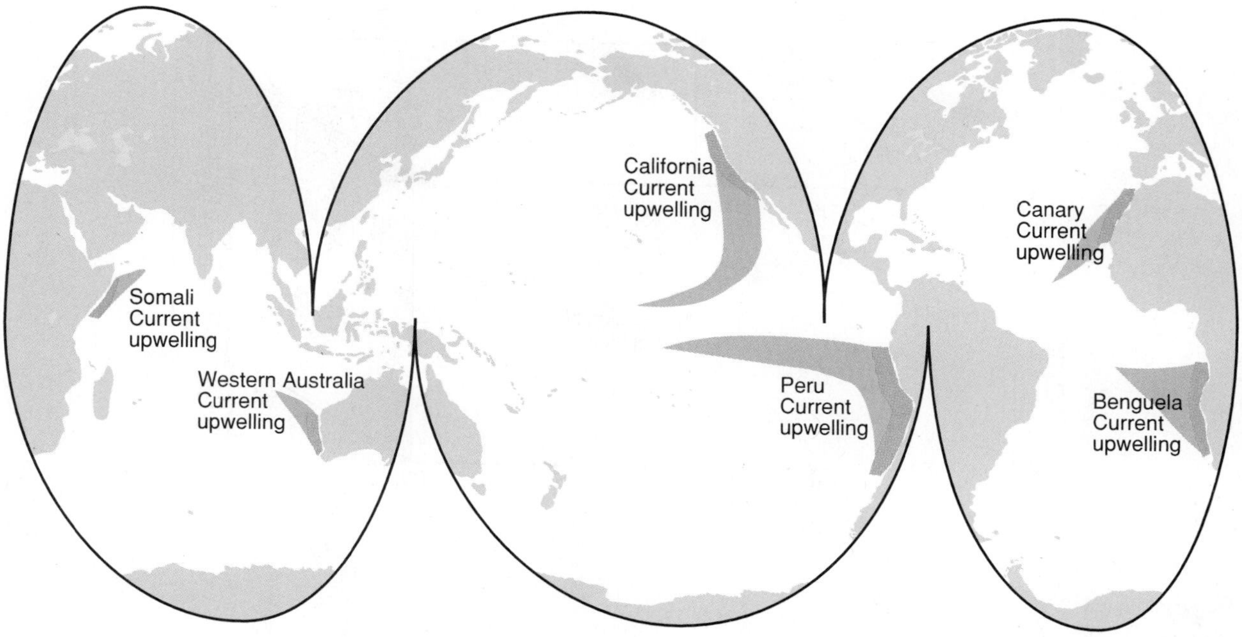

Figure 5.18
Principal regions of coastal upwelling (blue) and down-current areas of increased primary productivity (green)

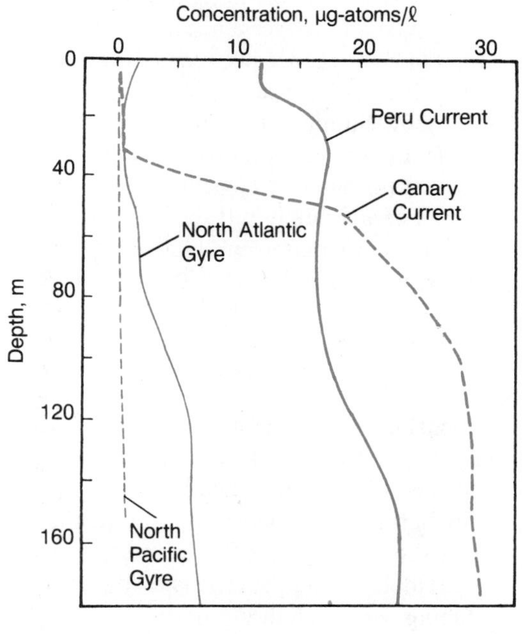

Figure 5.19
A comparison of the vertical distribution of nitrate in upwelling areas (heavy curves) and in adjacent nonupwelling central ocean regions (light curves)
Redrawn from Walsh, 1974

Another type of upwelling is more limited in extent and normally exists only in the central Pacific Ocean. The Pacific Equatorial Current flows westward straddling the equator. The Coriolis effect causes a slight displacement to the right for the portion of the current in the Northern Hemisphere and to the left for the portion of the current in the Southern Hemisphere. The resultant divergence of water away from the equator creates an upwelling of deeper water to replace the water that has moved away.

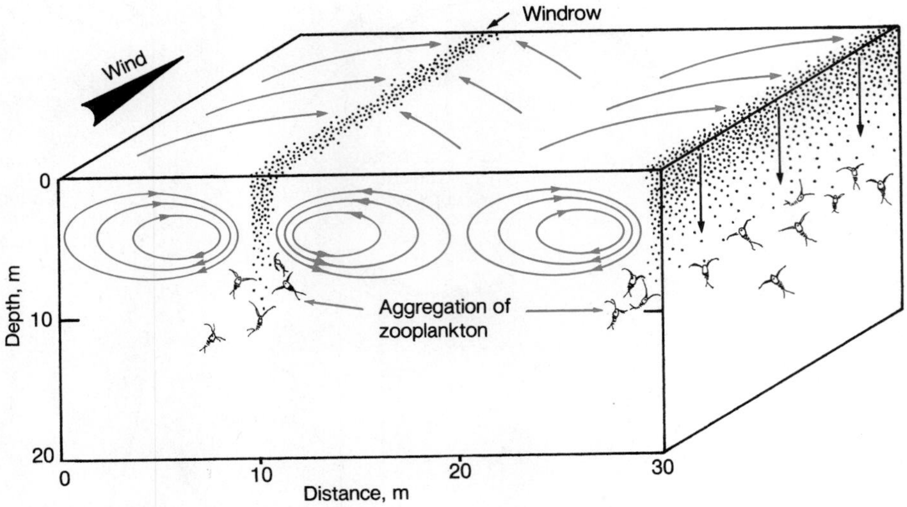

Figure 5.20
Circulation patterns of wind-driven Langmuir convection cells

Langmuir cells (named after Irving Langmuir, who first clarified their structure after he observed *Sargassum* in the North Atlantic floating in long rows parallel to the wind direction) are parallel pairs of small counter-rotating convection cells driven by surface winds. Langmuir convection cells set up alternating zones of divergence and convergence and sometimes sweep detritus and plankton to the lines of convergence between adjacent cells. This material is often evident at the surface as long parallel "slicks," foam lines, or rows of floating debris (figure 5.20). Similar accumulations may also be created by internal waves and other factors. Langmuir cells extend only a few meters deep and are not important for nutrient upwelling from deep water. However, these convection cells may create nutrient traps under the convergences. Phytoplankton and particulate debris that accumulate under the convergences attract grazing zooplankton in concentrations often 100 times more dense than those in adjacent areas.

Grazing

The trophic interrelationships of marine phytoplankton and small herbivores (mostly zooplankton and small fish) can be complex. Grazing may decrease the standing crop and sometimes the productivity of a phytoplankton population. The capacity of herbivorous zooplankton to quickly decimate a phytoplankton population is shown in figure 5.21. In an experimental setting, with initial conditions of a phytoplankton population having a density of one million cells/liter and reproducing once each day, a herbivore population density was adjusted to achieve a grazing rate that just held the phytoplankton population constant. When the zooplankton population density was doubled, the phytoplankton population was reduced to 27,000 cells in five days. At a density five times that necessary to hold the phytoplankton population constant, the zooplankton reduced the phytoplankton cell density to 24 cells/liter in three days, and the culture was essentially eliminated in five days.

Ideally, grazing rates should adjust to the magnitude of primary productivity to establish a balance between producer and consumer populations. Photosynthesis rates do limit the average size of the animal populations they

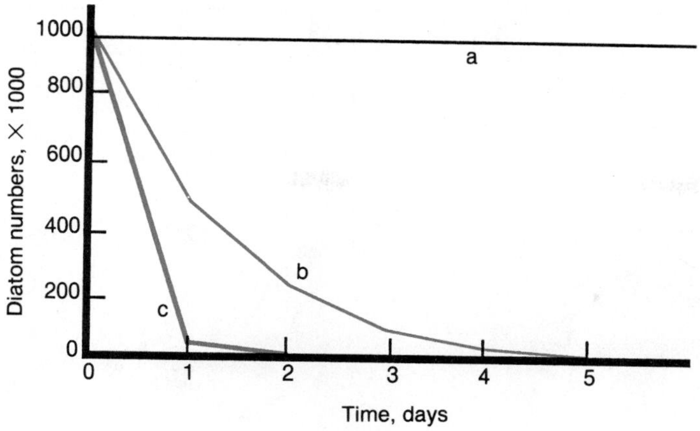

Figure 5.21
Changes in diatom population within the given time frame with (*a*) grazing rate equal to cell division rate, (*b*) grazing rate doubled, and (*c*) grazing rate increased five times
Adapted from Fleming, 1939

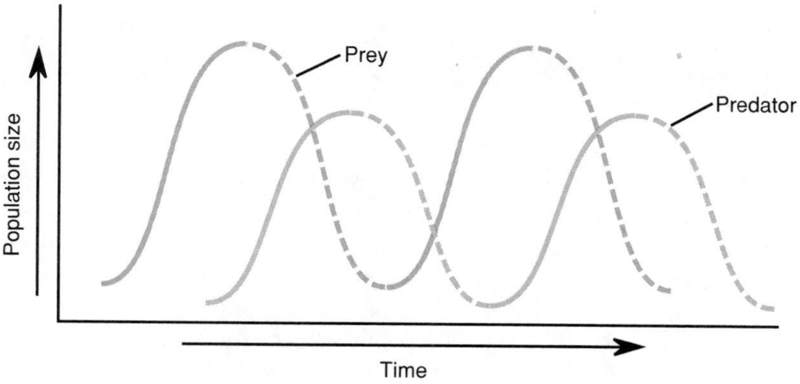

Figure 5.22
Generalized population changes of a prey species and its predator, oscillating between unlimited (solid lines) and limited (dashed lines) phases of population growth

support, yet short-term fluctuations of both phytoplankton and grazer populations often occur. The magnitude of these fluctuations tends to be moderated somewhat by stabilizing **feedback mechanisms** between all tropically related populations. An abundant food supply permits the grazers to reproduce and grow rapidly (figure 5.22). Eventually, however, they consume their prey more quickly than the prey can be replaced. Overgrazing reduces the phytoplankton population and its photosynthetic capacity, causing food shortages, starvation, and consequent reductions of the enlarged herbivore populations. When grazing intensity is reduced after herbivore population crash, the phytoplankton population may recover, increase in size, and again set the stage with an abundant food source to cause a repeat of the entire cycle. Such oscillations of population size may extend through many trophic levels of the food web.

In most cases, a delay exists between population peaks of the consumed and the consumer. The length of the time lag depends largely on the consumer's reproductive response to an increasing food supply. In favorable conditions, asexually reproducing phytoplankton can divide rapidly and can increase their population size more quickly than larger, sexually reproducing zooplankton. Phytoplankton, therefore, can achieve a greater population size before the zooplankton catch up and may experience larger population fluctuations than the more slowly breeding herbivores.

In addition to the large-scale geographical variations in phytoplankton density observed from satellites (figure 5.2), marine phytoplankton

Figure 5.23
A dynamic model for establishing and maintaining patches of marine phytoplankton and zooplankton
Adapted from Bainbridge, 1953

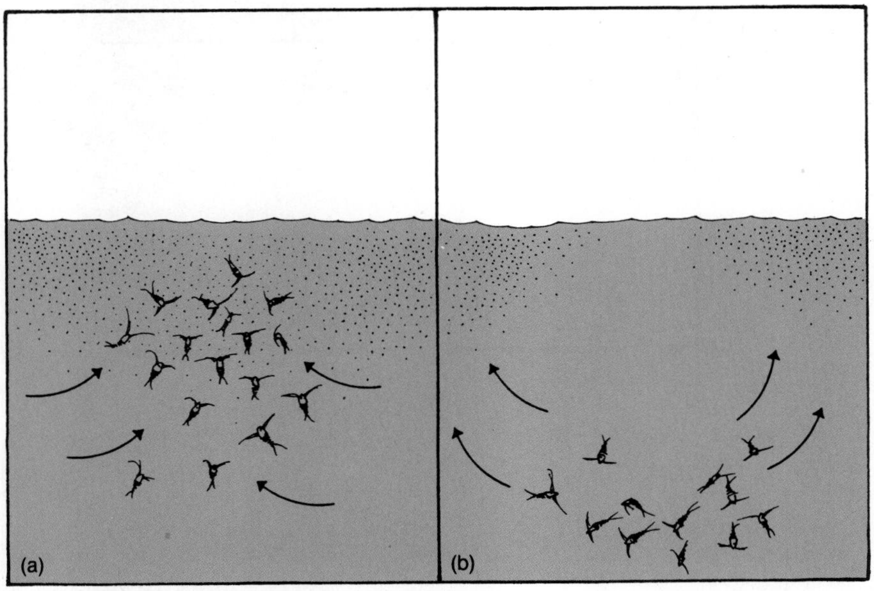

also exhibit much smaller scale localized patchiness. Dense patches of phytoplankton tend to alternate with concentrated patches of zooplankton. The inverse concentrations of phytoplankton and zooplankton densities stem in part from the effects of grazing and because of differences in their reproductive rates. A dynamic model of phytoplankton growth, grazing, and subsequent zooplankton migration that establishes and effectively maintains the alternating patchy distribution of marine phytoplankton and zooplankton is suggested in figure 5.23. This is but one of many models used to explain phytoplankton patchiness. Initially, a dense patch of phytoplankton provides favorable growth conditions for herbivores attracted from adjacent water into the phytoplankton patch (a). The grazing rate increases in the area of the patch and declines elsewhere. Production in the original patch soon decreases and increases in adjacent areas. Eventually, the original phytoplankton patch is eliminated by the dense concentration of grazers. The adjacent areas become the new phytoplankton patches (b) and attract herbivores from the recently overgrazed region, thus repeating the entire sequence.

Some species of zooplankton are attracted by particular phytoplankton species and repelled by others. External metabolites secreted by phytoplankton have been suggested as one cause for selective grazing. Detection of phytoplankton patches by the quality of light passing through them is another possibility. Some copepods, when exposed to predominantly red light, display a "red dance," with most of their movements oriented vertically. In light with a strong proportion of blue, the same copepods exhibit a "blue dance," with most of their movements oriented horizontally. The horizontal movements have been interpreted as hunting or searching. Horizontal motions eventually bring the copepods into or under a phytoplankton patch, where increased chlorophyll concentrations decrease the relative proportion of blue light. The copepods then shift to the vertical "red dance" that maintains their position within the phytoplankton patch.

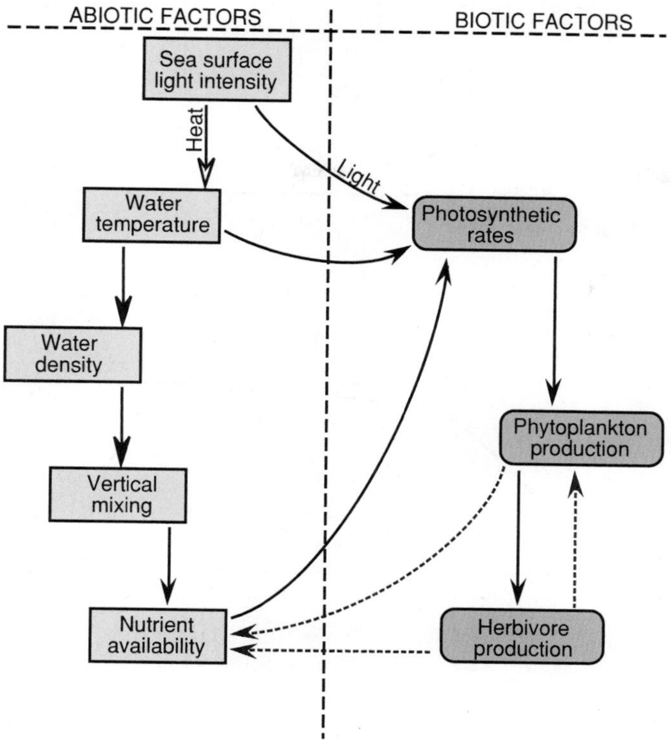

Figure 5.24
The seasonal variation of light intensity at the sea surface sets in motion a cascading series of changes in the photic zone. Eventually, these factors influence primary production, either directly (solid arrows) or through feedback links (dashed arrows).

Seasonal Patterns of Marine Primary Production

The spatial patchiness of phytoplankton is related on a large scale to areas of nutrient abundance and on much smaller scales to the local influences of grazers, near-surface turbulence, and nutrient patches. Seasonal phytoplankton variations, or patchiness in time, occurs in response to changes in light intensity, nutrient abundance, and grazing pressure. The underlying pulse for these time changes is the predictable seasonal variation in the intensity of sunlight reaching the sea surface. Figure 5.24 outlines the major links between factors involved in defining the actual pattern of phytoplankton production through time. With these in mind, the seasonal pattern of phytoplankton production for several marine production systems can be developed.

Temperate Seas

Figure 5.25 depicts a somewhat idealized graphical summary of major physical, chemical, and biological events in temperate areas well away from the effects of coastlines. A prominent feature in the production cycle of temperate seas is the spring diatom increase or diatom **bloom.** Diatom blooms are the result of combined seasonal variations of water temperature, light and nutrient availability, and grazing intensity. In early spring, water temperature and available light increase, nutrients are abundant in near-surface waters, and grazing pressure is diminished. Conditions are ideal for rapid and abundant growth of primary producers. If the bottom of the mixed layer extends below the critical depth (determined by light penetration), near-surface turbulence

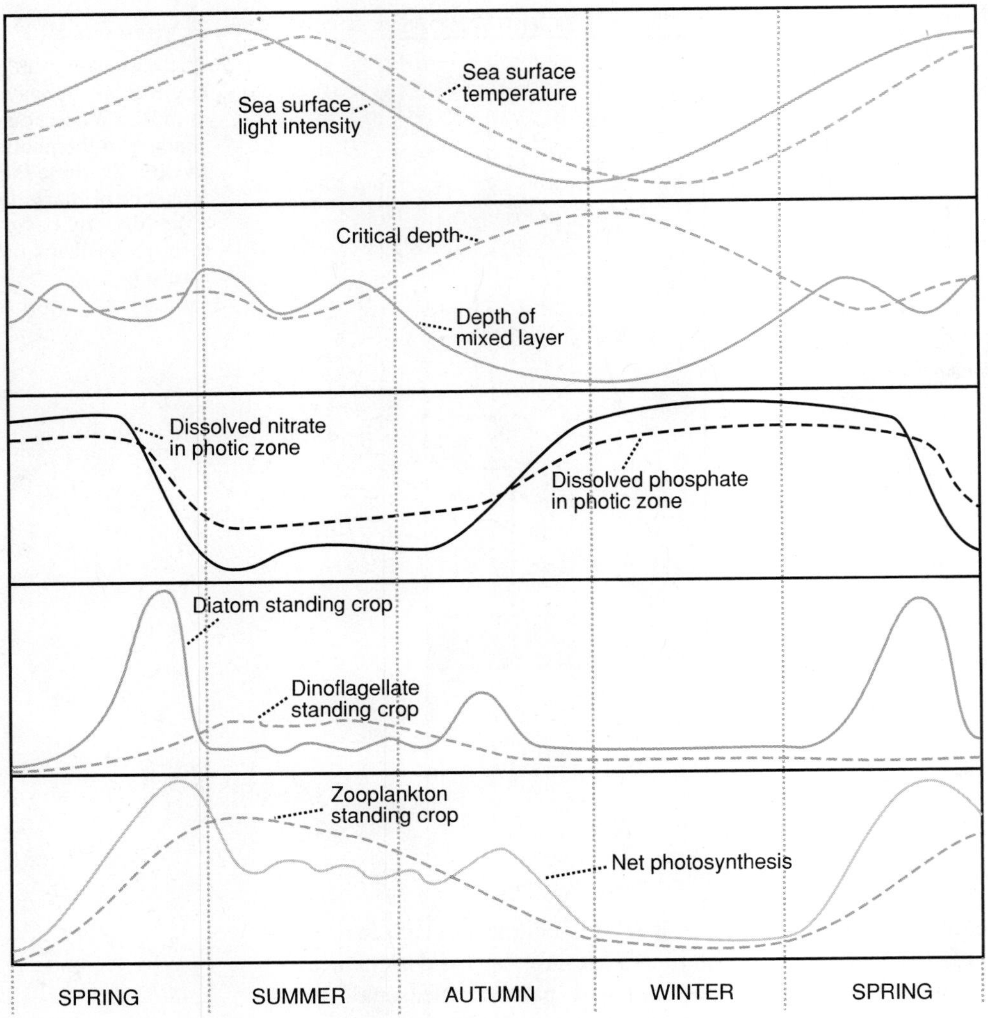

Figure 5.25
Seasonal fluctuations in the major features of a temperate water marine primary productivity system

will distribute the phytoplankton cells randomly throughout the mixed layer, and primary production will remain low. Cells in the deeper portions of the mixed layer will receive insufficient light, and no net production will occur. The spring bloom will commence only after the thermocline thins the mixed layer to a level above the critical depth. In general, bloom conditions in the open ocean occur as a broad band of primary production sweeping poleward with the onset of spring. The standing crop of diatoms increases quickly to the largest of the year and begins to deplete nutrient concentrations. The grazers respond to the additional forage by increasing their numbers.

As spring warms into summer, sunlight becomes more plentiful, but the now strongly developed seasonal thermocline effectively blocks nutrient return from deeper water. Coupled with increased grazing, the diatom population peaks and then declines and remains low throughout the summer. With food more scarce, the summer zooplankton population also drops off. Unlike diatoms, dinoflagellate populations increase slowly during the spring, remain healthy throughout the summer, and decline in autumn because of diminished light intensity. This replacement of diatoms by dinoflagellates is a form of seasonal succession resulting from some basic ecological differences between the two principal groups of phytoplankton. Recall that diatoms lack flagella, cannot swim, are more readily inhibited in high-light intensities, perform better in low-light intensities (figure 5.8), and have a nutrient need for silicate. These features give diatoms a competitive advantage in less well-lit, colder, denser, nutrient-rich waters and dinoflagellates an advantage in warmer, better-lit waters that may be deficient in silicate.

Cooler autumn air temperatures begin to break down the summer thermocline and allow convection to renew nutrients to the photic zone. The phytoplankton respond with another bloom, which, although not as remarkable as the spring bloom, is often sufficient to initiate another upswing of the zooplankton population. As winter approaches, the autumn bloom is cut short by decreasing light and reduced temperatures. As production goes down, resistant over-wintering stages of both phytoplankton and zooplankton become more abundant. Convective mixing continues to recharge the nutrient load of the surface waters in readiness for a repeat of the entire performance the following spring. It is now estimated that, on average, about 120 $gC/m^2/yr$ is produced in oceanic temperate and subpolar areas, with most of that total occurring during the spring diatom bloom.

Warm Seas

In temperate regions, the production characteristics of tropical and subtropical waters closely resemble those of continuous summer. Sunlight is available in abundance, yet production is low (about 40 $gC/m^2/yr$) due to a strong permanent thermocline that blocks vertical mixing of nutrients. The low rate of nutrient return is partially compensated for by a year-round growing season and a deep photic zone. Even so, production and standing crops are low, and dinoflagellates are usually more abundant than diatoms. Coral reefs and regions of equatorial upwelling are more productive (up to 1,000 $gC/m^2/yr$ for coral reefs), but both are very limited in areal extent.

Coastal Upwelling

Coastal upwelling in temperate seas alters the generalized picture presented in figure 5.24 by replenishing nutrients during the summer when they would otherwise be depleted. As long as light is sufficient and upwelling continues, high phytoplankton production occurs and is reflected in abundant local animal populations. In some areas, the duration and intensity of coastal upwelling fluctuate with variations in atmospheric circulation. Along the Washington and Oregon coasts, the variability of spring and summer wind patterns produces sporadic upwelling interspersed with short periods of no upwelling and lower primary productivity. In the Peru Current, upwelling is massive and is interrupted only by El Niño conditions (see box 6). In the absence of major disturbances like El Niño events, coastal upwelling zones have average productivity rates of about 300 $gC/m^2/yr$.

Polar Seas

Sea surface temperatures in polar regions are always low. The thermocline, if one exists at all, is poorly established and is not an effective barrier to nutrient return from deeper waters. Light, or more correctly the lack of it, is the major limiting factor for plant growth in polar seas. Sufficient light to sustain high

Box 6 *El Niño*

The cold and productive waters of the Peru Current flow in marked contrast to the dry and barren land of the adjacent coast. Each summer around Christmastime, a warm current from the north (called El Niño for the child Jesus) flows south, bringing rain and warmer temperatures. Occasionally though, this intrusion of warm tropical water penetrates much farther south, stays longer, and brings heavy rains to the coastal desert. These strong El Niño events bring an explosion of plant growth to the coastal land deserts; yet this same southerly flow of warm, less dense water blocks upwelling of nutrient-rich waters, and coastal marine populations decline. During severe El Niño years, some fish and dependent sea bird populations disappear altogether.

It was not until a few decades ago that oceanographers became aware that the seemingly isolated El Niño events of coastal Peru were linked by atmospheric conditions to dramatic weather changes all over the globe. In 1982–83, we experienced the most severe El Niño of this century, with a complete cessation of upwelling in the Peru Current, heavy flooding along the California coast, drought in Australia, and record-breaking cold in Europe.

It now seems clear that both the causes and effects of El Niño extend throughout the tropical Pacific Ocean as a fluctuation of atmospheric pressures, wind fields, surface ocean currents, and rainfall now called the Southern Oscillation. The term El Niño is now used to describe one-half of the Southern Oscillation, with weak trade winds, warm water temperatures in the eastern tropical Pacific, and small differences in surface air pressures across the tropical Pacific Ocean. The other phase of the Southern Oscillation, La Niña, is characterized by oceanographic and atmospheric conditions opposite those of El Niño. La Niña is generally described as the more benign or normal phase of the Southern Oscillation, but it is thought to be a contributor to the severe drought conditions of the central North American plains states in 1988. El Niño and La Niña are simply two contrasting expressions of the same global event, the Southern Oscillation. When the Pacific Coast was experiencing an intense El Niño in 1982–83, La Niña conditions prevailed over the Atlantic Ocean.

The detailed mechanics of the Southern Oscillation are far from understood, but we do know that it has an irregular time scale of a few years and that it is driven by large-scale changes in ocean surface winds and water temperatures of the tropical Pacific Ocean. The atmosphere over the tropical Pacific works like a convection engine to transport enormous loads of heat from the warm sea surface to the relative cold of the upper atmosphere 15 km above the sea surface. These zones of atmospheric convection normally shift back and forth across the equator with the sun each year. In El Niño years, the area of warm water drifts eastward along the equator, and the zone of convection follows. The trade winds relax, causing the Equatorial Currents to slow and the Equatorial Countercurrents to increase their flow of warm surface water eastward. The eastern tropical Pacific experiences warmer sea surface temperatures (right figure), blocked upwelling, and increased rainfall. Eventually, the area of warm tropical water contracts westward, and El Niño conditions are replaced by the typical La Niña features of cooler eastern tropical Pacific surface temperatures (left figure), low rainfall, and well-developed coastal upwelling along Peru and northern Chile.

---

phytoplankton growth rates lasts for only a few months during the summer. Even so, photosynthesis can continue around the clock during those few months to quickly produce huge phytoplankton populations. As the light intensity and day length decline, the short summer diatom bloom declines rapidly. Winter conditions closely resemble those of temperate regions except that in polar seas the conditions endure much longer. There the complete cycle of production consists of a single short period of plant growth, equivalent to a typical spring bloom immediately followed by an autumn bloom and decline that alternates with an extended winter of reduced net production.

In both the Arctic Ocean and around the Antarctic continent, the formation and melting of sea ice plays a central role in shaping patterns of primary productivity. As ice melts in the spring, the low salinity meltwater forms a low density layer near the sea surface. This increases vertical stability, which encourages phytoplankton to grow near the sunlit surface. The melting ice also releases temporarily frozen phytoplankton cells into the water to ini-

Box 6 *El Niño*

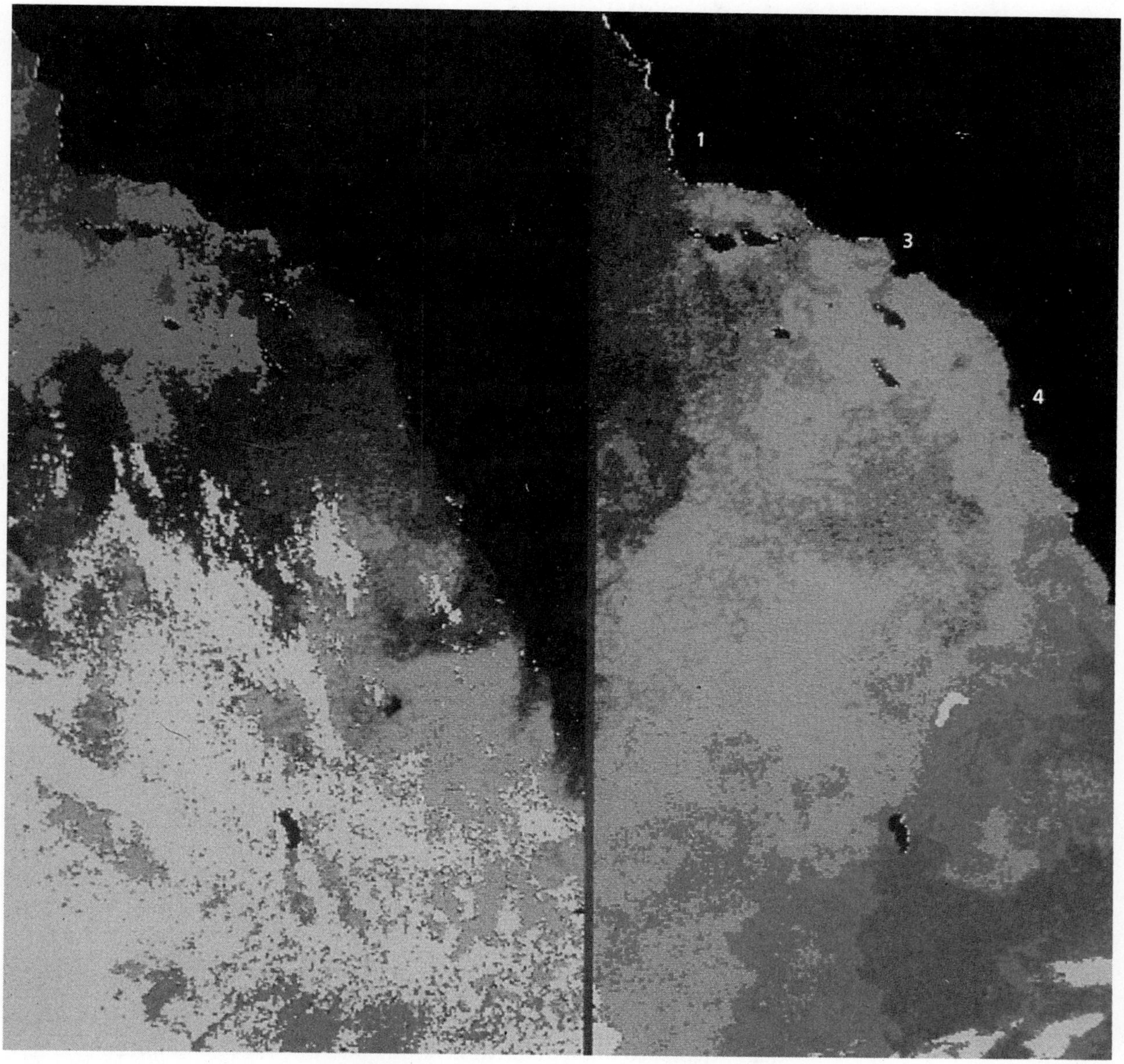

Courtesy National Aeronautics and Space Administration

tiate the bloom. As the sea ice continues to melt in early summer, the zone of high phytoplankton productivity follows, creating a very productive, seasonal, migrating ice edge community of diatoms, krill, birds, seals, fish, and whales. Animals that do exploit this production system must be prepared to endure long winter months of little primary production. The annual average productivity rates for polar seas are low (about 25 $gC/m^2/yr$) because so much of the year passes in darkness with almost no plant growth.

Major upwelling areas also occur around the Antarctic continent. In these regions, water that sinks in the Northern Hemisphere and flows south at mid-depth surfaces between 50° and 60° S latitude (see figure 1.28), bringing with it a thousand-year accumulation of dissolved nutrients. The extraordinary fertility of the Antarctic seas stands in sharp contrast to the barrenness of the adjacent continent. Consequently, almost all Antarctic life, whether terrestrial or marine, depends on marine food webs supported by this massive upwelling.

Predictive Modeling

The cause-and-effect interactions between organisms and their environment suggest that a **predictive model** of primary production in the marine ecosystem can be devised if those interactions can be measured and studied. In itself, the ability to make accurate predictions is a useful tool for analyzing and wisely using natural resources. Moreover, the ability to design an accurate predictive model is a good measure of our understanding of how the system works. These models are not meant to be exact duplicates of nature. Instead, they remain as crude simplifications of the real world, but in their simplicity they reveal some fundamental processes of the system. Information regarding only a relatively small number of variables is frequently a sufficient basis for a workable model because many times only a few key factors control or dominate a significant part of the action.

Several attempts have been made to reduce to relatively simple mathematical expressions the multiplicity of environmental factors that affect the rate of primary production in the sea. The pioneering work of Riley serves as an example of the general applicability of predictive models for marine production systems. Over four decades ago, Riley presented a rather rigorous mathematical equation for computing a theoretical seasonal growth curve for phytoplankton. His equation included expressions for phytoplankton population size, average surface light intensity, extinction of light in seawater, photic zone depth, rate of nutrient depletion, phytoplankton respiration rate, water temperature, and herbivore grazing rate. Using this model, Riley calculated the expected changes in the phytoplankton population of Georges Bank for a full year.

In recent years, Riley's early models have been superseded by more refined computerized attempts to model larger segments of pelagic ecosystems (for example, Steele's recent attempt to model the time course of the dynamic interactions between phytoplankton and their herbivorous grazers in the North Sea or Walsh's spatial model of the Peru upwelling ecosystem). But rather than attempt to evaluate them here, the interested reader is directed to references at the end of this chapter. The point to be made is that in spite of some untested assumptions and sparse data, the predicted productivity values are generally within ±25% of the actual measured values. And as our understanding of the processes that govern the dynamics of marine populations continues to expand, these models are improving all the time.

Global Marine Primary Production

High latitudes, shallow regions, and zones of upwelling generally support large populations of marine primary producers, but most of this production is ac-

Table 5.1
Rates of Net Marine Plant Production for Several Ocean Regions

Region	Area 10^6 km	% of Ocean	Average $gC/m^2/yr$	Total net 10^9 Tons of C
Open Ocean				
Tropics and Subtropics	190	51	40	7.6
Temperate and Subpolar	100	27	120	12.0
Polar	52	14	25	1.3
Continental Shelf				
Nonupwelling	26.6	7.2	200	5.3
Coastal Upwelling	0.4	0.1	300	.1
Estuaries and Salt Marshes	1.8	0.05	800	1.4
Coral Reefs	0.1	—	1000	.1
Seaweed Beds	0.02	—	1000	.02
				27.8

Data from Falkowski 1980, Walsh 1984, Smith and Nelson 1986, and Tett 1984

complished during the warm summer months when light is not a growth-limiting factor. Open ocean regions, especially in the tropics and subtropics where a strong thermocline is a permanent feature and in polar seas where light is limited through much of the year, have low (<50 $gC/m^2/yr$) rates of primary production.

Table 5.1 lists and compares several marine production zones. Figure 5.26 presents a more general picture of marine primary production. Published values included in syntheses such as this vary somewhat, depending on the sets of assumptions used to make productivity estimates for poorly studied regions of the globe, but most published values are within 20% of each other. Since 1970, the estimates of marine primary production have slowly crept upward, and further revisions are expected. Seventy-two percent of the total primary production occurs in the open ocean, spread thinly over 92% of the ocean's area. The more productive regions are very limited in geographic extent. Collectively, they account for about one-fourth of the total, with estuaries, coastal upwelling regions, and coral reefs producing only about one billion tons of carbon each year.

The productivity numbers of table 5.1 indicate that nearly 28 billion tons of carbon, or 250–300 billion tons of photosynthetically produced material, are generated each year in the world ocean. For comparison, the entire human population of the earth requires five billion tons of food annually to sustain itself. And many members of that population are hungrily eyeing the bounty of the sea. But for several reasons to be discussed in chapter 13, this abundant profusion of plant material will probably never be utilized on a scale sufficient to alleviate the serious nutritional problems already rampant in much of our population. Instead, this vast amount of organic material will continue to fuel the metabolic machinery of the animal members of marine trophic organizations.

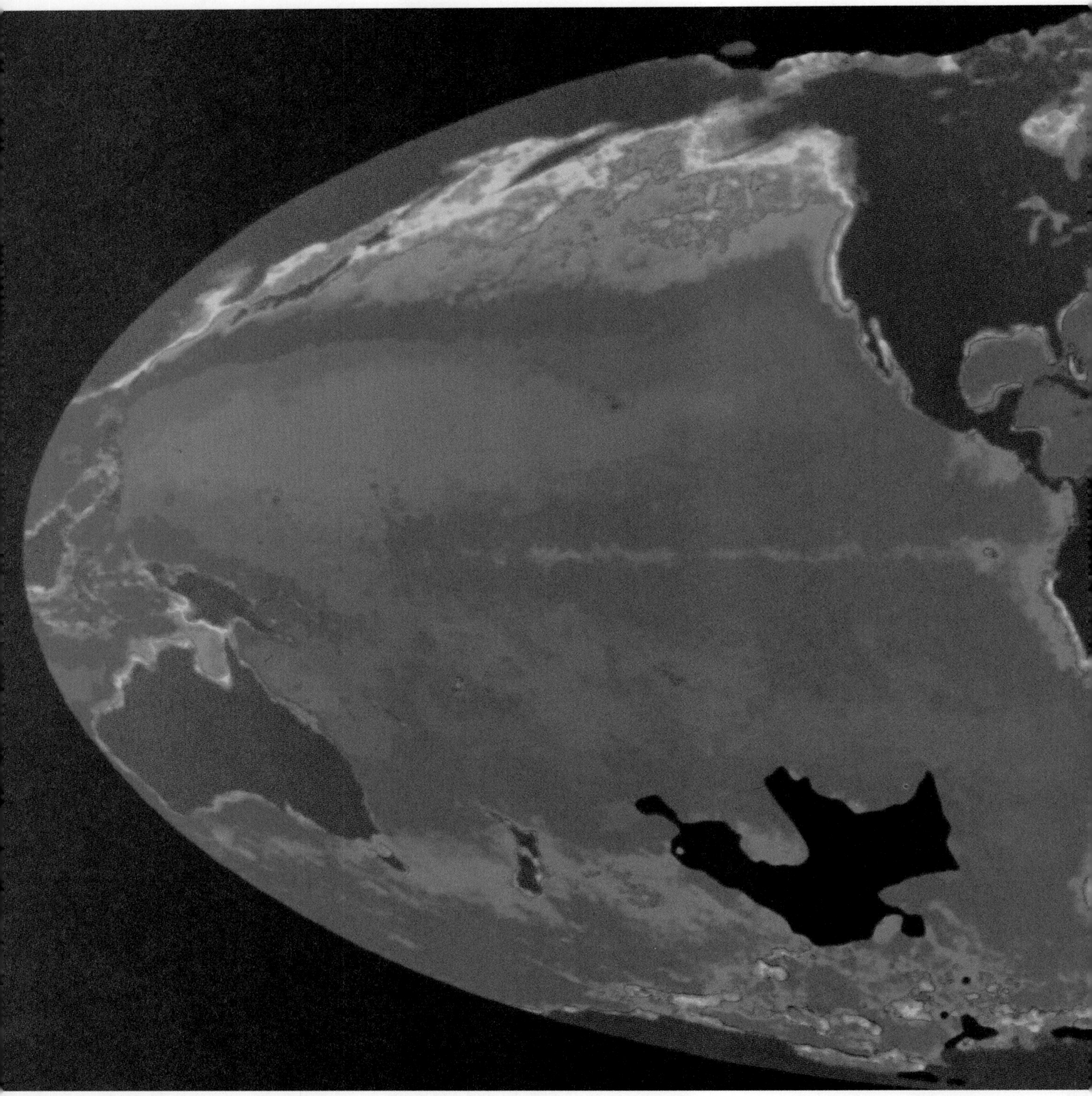

Figure 5.26

The geographic variation of marine primary production, compiled from over three years of observations by the satellite-borne Coastal Zone Color Scanner. Primary production is low (less than 50 gC/m2/year) in the central gyres (magenta to deep blue), moderate (50-100 gC/m2/year) in the light blue to green areas, and high (greater than 100 gC/m2/year) in coastal zones and upwelling areas (yellow, orange, and red).

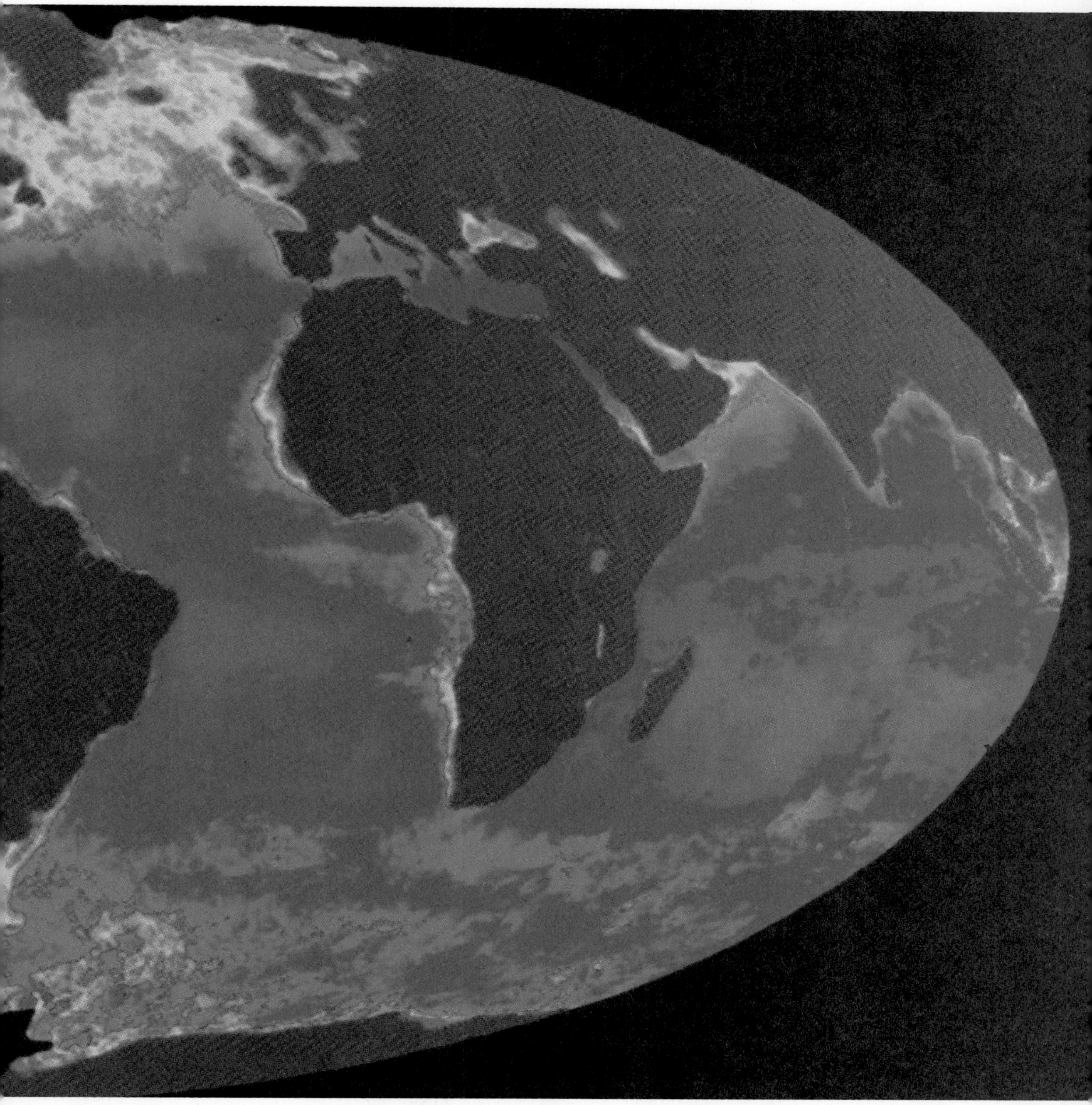

Photo by Gene Felderman/NASA/GSFC Space Data
Computing Div., Greenbelt, MD

Summary

Rates of photosynthesis by marine autotrophs (gross primary production) and rates of net primary production are measured with light and dark bottle O_2 evolution techniques or radioactive C^{14} techniques. With these techniques, the effect of several environmental factors on the rates of primary production in the sea can be studied. Significant among these factors are light intensity and quality, nutrient availability, and grazing pressure.

Several groups of marine autotrophs complement the light-absorbing capabilities of chlorophyll with various accessory pigments that give them their characteristic coloration. The light and nutrient requirements of primary producers are usually spatially separated in the sea; light is available at the sea surface, yet great stores of dissolved nutrients are concentrated in waters below the photic zone. Only in areas where upwelling and mixing return the deep-water nutrients to the photic zone do marine primary producers thrive.

The cumulative effects of cyclic grazing pressures and varying light intensity and nutrient availability create a complex pattern of seasonally and geographically variable primary production. Taken as a single production system, the marine environment generates 250–300 billion tons of photosynthetically produced material each year.

Review Questions

1. Name three ocean current regions characterized by coastal upwelling.
2. List three obvious, specific, and different adaptations of diatoms that function to slow their sinking rates.
3. For each of the following processes of returning nutrients to the photic zone, list the general geographical regions where the named process exerts the major influence on the rate of nutrient return: diffusion, coastal upwelling, and convective mixing.
4. List and describe the physical and chemical factors that initiate the spring and fall diatom blooms in temperate ocean waters.
5. Describe the absorption spectra of seawater, chlorophyll *a,* and an accessory pigment; explain why large attached marine plants have large concentrations of accessory pigments and relate this to their general depth distribution.

Questions for Further Discussion

1. In areas of upwelling, the rate of marine primary productivity may often be comparable to good farmland, although the phytoplankton population sizes may be very low. Using phytoplankton standing crop and turnover rates, explain why this is true.
2. What advantage does the radioactive carbon method for measuring primary productivity have over the oxygen evolution method used earlier? Of satellite-borne sea surface color scanners over the C^{14} method?

Suggestions for Further Reading

Books

Bougis, P. 1976. *Marine plankton ecology.* New York: Elsevier.

Falkowski, P. G., ed. 1980. *Primary productivity in the sea.* New York: Plenum Press.

Lembi, C. A., and J. R. Waaland, eds. 1988. *Algae and human affairs.* New York: Cambridge University Press.

Lobban, C. S., and M. J. Winne, eds. 1982. *The biology of seaweeds.* Berkeley, CA: University of California Press.

Steele, J. H. 1974. *The structure of marine ecosystems.* Cambridge: Harvard University Press.

Steeman Nielsen, E. 1975. *Marine photosynthesis.* New York: Elsevier.

Articles

Baker, J. D., and W. S. Wilson. 1986. Spaceborne observations in support of earth science. *Oceanus* 29(4):76–85.

Brown, O. B., et al. 1985. Phytoplankton blooming off the U.S. east coast: A satellite description. *Science* 229:163–67.

Correll, D. L. 1978. Estuarine productivity. *Bioscience* 28:646–50.

King, R. J., and W. Schramm. 1976. Photosynthetic rates of benthic marine algae in relation to light intensity and seasonal variations. *Marine Biology* 37:215–22.

Landry, M. R. 1976. The structure of marine ecosystems: An alternative. *Marine Biology* 35:1–7.

Levine, R. P. 1969. The mechanism of photosynthesis. *Scientific American* 221 (December):58–70.

Mcpeak, R. H., and D. A. Glantz. 1984. Harvesting California's kelp forests. *Oceanus* 27(1):19–26.

Malone, T. C. 1971. The relative importance of nannoplankton and netplankton as primary producers in tropical oceanic and neritic phytoplankton communities. *Limnology and Oceanography* 16:633–39.

Mann, K. H. 1973. Seaweeds: Their productivity and strategy for growth. *Science* 182:975–81.

Perry, M. J. 1986. Assessing marine primary productivity from space. *Bioscience* 36:461–67.

Smith, W. O. Jr., and D. M. Nelson. 1986. Importance of ice edge phytoplankton production in the southern ocean. *Bioscience* 36:251–57.

Walsh, J. J. 1975. A spatial simulation model of the Peru upwelling ecosystem. *Deep Sea Research* 22:201–36.

———. 1984. The role of ocean biota in accelerated ecological cycles: A temporal view. *Bioscience* 34:499–507.

Estuaries

Chapter 6

Mangrove leaves

Introduction

Estuaries are semienclosed coastal embayments where freshwater rivers meet the sea. Here fresh water and seawater mix, creating a unique and complex ecosystem. In addition, estuaries are molded on local scales by inputs of suspended particles and by tide and current patterns. As such, they provide important transitional habitats between freshwater rivers and the open sea. These relatively small coastal features embody most of the processes that shape the abundance and distribution of marine life in larger oceanic systems and can provide us with easily accessible systems with which to begin our study of marine communities.

Estuaries are unstable ecosystems that constantly change due to many physical, geological, chemical, and biological factors important to the ecology of specific estuaries. The change from fresh water to salt water occurs over an area that differs for each estuary. The estuaries of large rivers like the Columbia River may extend many miles inland whereas the estuaries of small streams may only be a few hundred meters in extent. The water of an estuary may be well-mixed, stratified, or partially-mixed. The location of estuaries varies from areas such as steep-sided coastal fjords to shallow and flat bays and sloughs. No two estuaries are identical.

The size and shape of estuaries are influenced by the amount of fresh water entering the estuary and by the geological history of the area. Geological movement of the earth's crust has elevated and lowered coastal areas. The resulting changes in sea level alter the size and shape of estuaries by altering the water depth and the extent of submerged coastal features.

Physical forces at work also influence the chemistry of an estuary. When fresh water draining from a coastal watershed mixes with the ocean tides, the fate of sediments and pollutants being carried downstream becomes complicated. Saline water pushes upstream during high tides and encounters suspended river sediments, causing much of the sediment load to be deposited near the mouth of the estuary. Since many pollutants are transported downstream in the river water or adsorbed onto sediments, unique estuarine conditions can also influence the fate and availability of pollutants to the inhabitants of the ecosystem.

Estuaries are some of the most biologically productive ecosystems on earth. These special habitats are created by the combination of turbulent mixing, daily fluctuating tidal cycles, and the downstream flow of inland fresh water that usually changes seasonally in velocity and volume. When these forces meet in an estuary, they exert considerable and complicated effects on the system, creating diverse terrestrial and aquatic habitats atypical of either the river or the sea. More than two-thirds of commercial and recreational fish catches depend on estuaries for feeding or as nursery areas. Estuaries also provide habitat for thousands of species of terrestrial and aquatic life, including many threatened, endangered, and rare species.

Since the study of estuaries was not a vital part of their specialty, estuaries were largely disregarded by both freshwater ecologists and oceanographers for many years. During that time, the overall role of estuaries in coastal primary productivity was seriously underestimated. Recently, however, attitudes about estuaries have changed considerably; there is a growing recognition that estuaries and their surrounding wetlands are fragile environments that have been heavily used and disturbed. Estuaries have become an

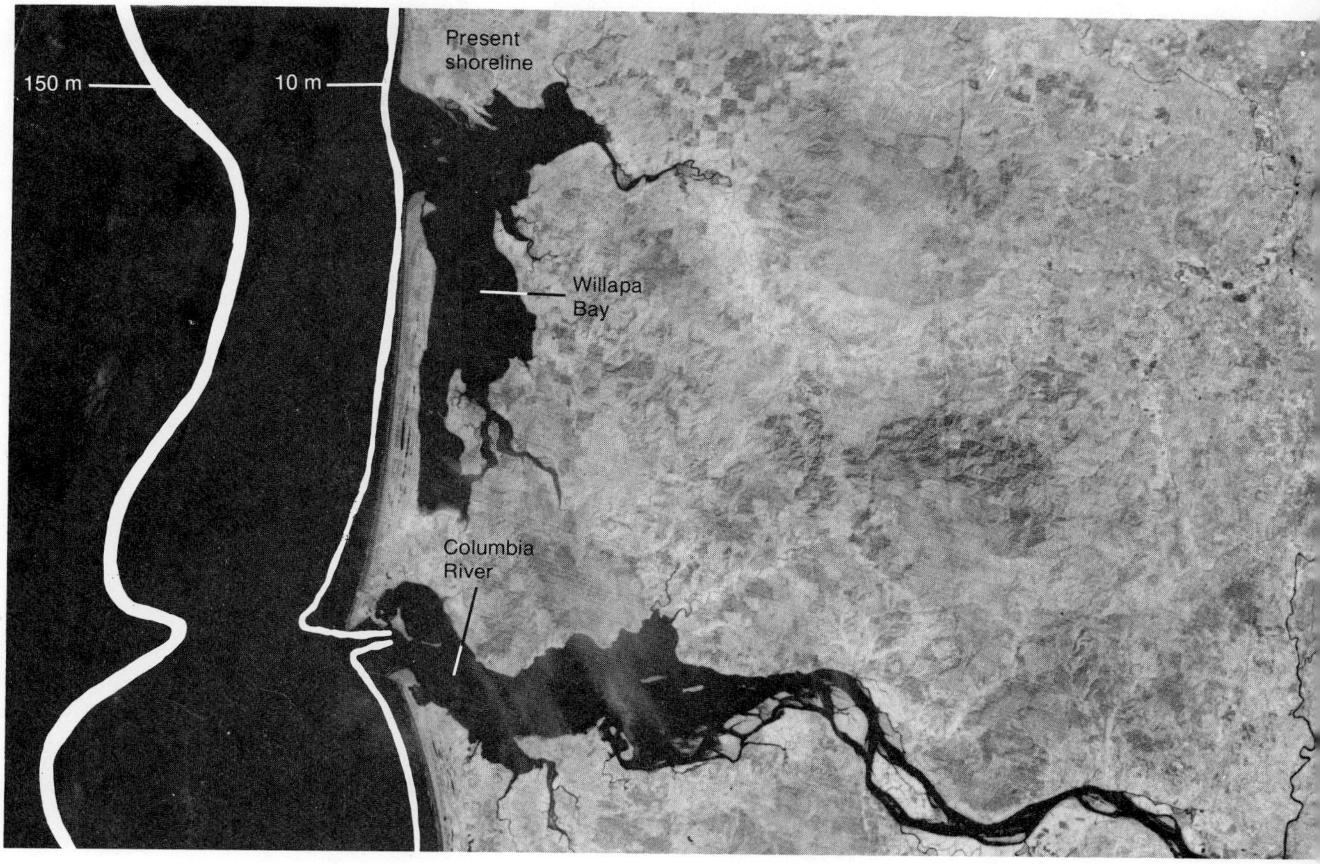

Figure 6.1
Columbia River estuary and Willapa Bay, with shorelines at present, and at 10 m (light line) and 150 m (heavy line) below the present shoreline
Courtesy Earth Resources Technology Program

endangered type of natural habitat. Many estuaries that used to be rich sources of fish, game, and shellfish have become stagnant and unproductive as a result of unregulated economic exploitation and pollution. Dredging navigation channels in estuarine ports, filling unique estuarine wetlands for development, disposing wastewaters from coastal communities, diverting rivers for irrigation purposes, and allowing pesticide contaminated rainwater to run into coastal watersheds have changed the character of estuaries and threatened their ecological integrity. Restoration and enhancement efforts are underway to reverse some of the environmental degradation and biological devastation of many of the world's major estuaries.

Types of Estuaries

The local character of individual estuaries depends largely on their recent geological history. Most owe some of their present configuration to ancient patterns of river or glacial erosion that occurred during the LGM (last glacial maximum), when sea level worldwide was about 150 m lower than at present. These scoured river or glacial channels assumed their present configuration when the great continental ice sheets melted and gradually flooded them. Many estuaries remain very sensitive to slight changes in sea level; increases of only a few meters could drown small estuaries, and comparable decreases could shrink others back to their present sizes (figure 6.1).

Figure 6.2
(*a*) Satellite photograph of the Chesapeake and Delaware bays, two coastal plain estuaries; (*b*) satellite photograph of bar-built estuaries of the south Texas coast, and (*c*) steep-sided fjord in southern British Columbia.

(*a*) Courtesy National Oceanic and Atmospheric Administration
(*b*) courtesy Earth Resources Technology Satellite Program

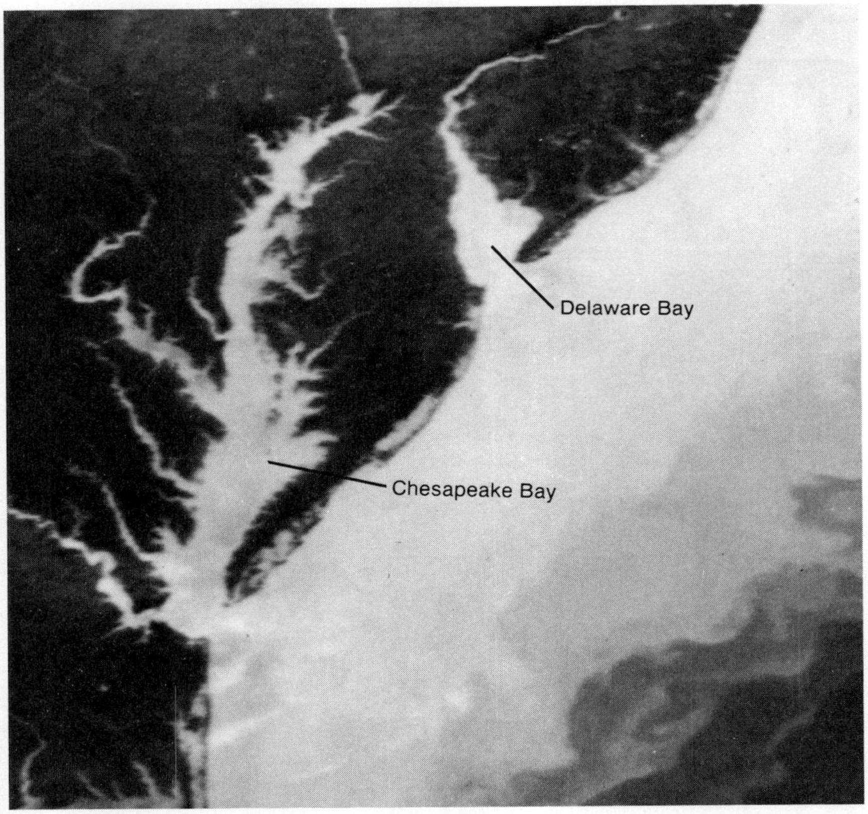

(a)

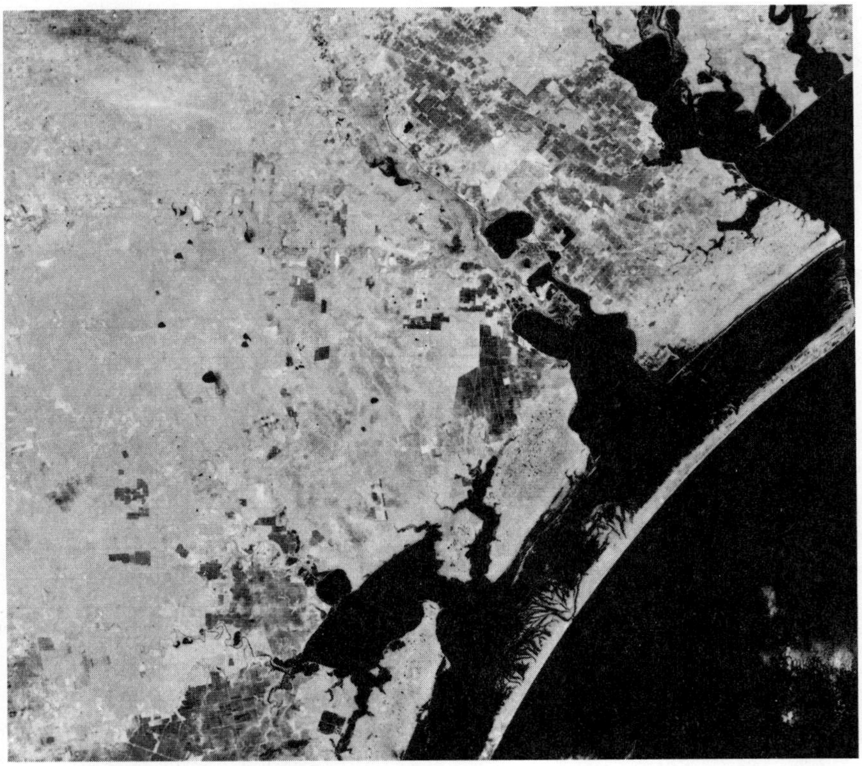

(b)

(c)

Estuaries are found in some form along most coastlines of the world, but most are evident in wetter climates of temperate and tropical latitudes. In such areas, land drainage provides the necessary freshwater input at the head of the estuary to keep salinities below those of adjacent open ocean waters. In North America, excellent examples of all major types of estuaries exist. **Coastal plain estuaries** (figure 6.2a) lie along the north and central Atlantic coast, the Canadian Maritime region, and many areas of the West Coast of North America. These estuaries are broad, shallow embayments formed from deeper V-shaped channels as the sea level rose and flooded river mouths following the last episode of continental glaciation. Sea level was lower because polar ice caps were larger then, and more of the world's water was trapped in the ice caps. Changes in climate after the LGM melted ice caps and caused sea level to rise to its current level.

The rising sea level flooded valleys of coastal drainage basins, forming the **drowned river valley** type of estuary. The extent to which the sea invaded these coastal river valleys is determined by the steepness and size of the valley, its rate of river discharge, and the range and force of the tides of the adjacent sea. This type of estuary continues to be gradually modified as wave erosion cuts away some existing shorelines and siltation creates others by building mudflats.

Bar-built estuaries are common along the south Atlantic coast, the Gulf of Mexico (figure 6.2b) in North America, and along the coastal lowlands of northwestern Europe. These estuaries are formed as near-shore sand

and mud are moved by coastal wave action to build an obstruction, or bar, in front of a coastal area fed by one or more coastal streams or rivers. Usually these small coastal rivers and streams have little freshwater flow so the estuary may be partially or completely blocked by sand deposited by ocean waves. During rainy seasons, however, the increased runoff often temporarily reopens the estuary mouth.

Not all estuaries have restricted mouths. Some estuaries have broad, poorly defined fan-shaped mouths called **deltas.** The Mississippi River delta and other similar delta estuaries are created as very heavy loads of sediments eroded from the upstream watersheds are deposited at the river mouth. Different still are tectonic estuaries such as San Francisco Bay, created when the underlying land sank in response to crustal movements of the earth. As coastal depressions created by these movements sank below sea level, they filled with water from the sea and also became natural land drainage channels, directing the flow of land runoff into the new estuary basin.

From the central West Coast northward, estuaries become more deeply incised into coastal landforms and gradually merge into the deep, glacially carved **fjords** of British Columbia, southeastern Alaska (figure 6.2c), Norway, and southern Chile. In cross section, fjords resemble the Black Sea (see figure 1.29). In general, fjords are deeper than other types of estuaries, and the deepest regions of fjords are in the upstream reaches. The shallow sills at their mouths partially block the inflow of sea water and lead to stagnant conditions near the bottoms of deeper fjords.

Estuarine Circulation

In addition to their structural differences, estuaries also exhibit differing patterns of freshwater and seawater mixing within the basin. The upstream-to-downstream variations in salinity, water temperature, turbidity, and current action are complex and change markedly during a tidal cycle and in response to seasonal changes in the volume of freshwater stream discharge. Salinity values typically increase from the surface downward (figure 6.3) and downstream from the estuary head. As tides change sea level in a typical estuary, higher density seawater moves in and out along the estuary bottom and is gradually mixed upward into the outflowing low-salinity surface water. Because of this mixing, there is an inward flow of nutrient-rich water along the bottom of the estuary and a net outward flow at the surface. This upward mixing generates, on a localized scale, a process of estuarine upwelling that replenishes nutrients and promotes growth of estuarine primary producers.

Mixing occurs in many ways in estuaries, resulting in complex patterns of salinity gradients. The shape of an estuary's basin is a major factor in determining its mixing pattern. A triangular estuary with a wide, deep mouth allows sea water to move farther upstream. The currents are usually strong and the water is well-mixed, so salinity is nearly the same from top to bottom. In narrow-mouthed estuaries, circulation is decreased, creating more pronounced horizontal and vertical salinity gradients. These narrow-mouthed estuaries are usually well-stratified. They have a pronounced seawater wedge under the less dense fresh water on the surface (figure 6.3), with an abrupt salinity change where seawater and fresh water meet. By analyzing water samples taken at fixed depths throughout a tidal cycle and connecting points

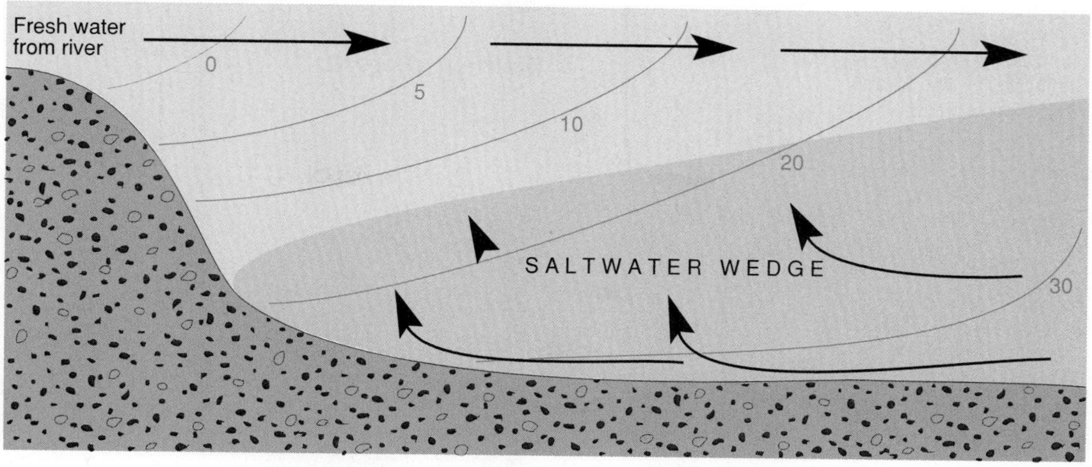

Figure 6.3
A cross section of circulation (black arrows) and resulting salinity distribution (color) of a typical coastal plain estuary. Salinity values are in ‰.

with the same salinity values, lines of equal salinity, or **isohalines,** can be plotted. The shape of the isohalines is useful in classifying types of estuaries and in understanding the distribution of estuarine organisms.

In addition to the more predictable effects of tides and river discharge, circulation in estuaries often changes rapidly and less predictably in response to short-term influences of heavy rainfall or changing winds. The Coriolis effect also exercises its influence (see figure 1.24) on circulation patterns within estuaries by forcing seawater farther upstream on the left sides (when looking downstream) of estuaries in the Northern Hemisphere and on the right side of estuaries in the Southern Hemisphere.

The time necessary for water in an estuary to be moved out to sea is called the **flushing time.** Complete flushing, which replaces all of an estuary's water volume, may take from days to years depending on the combination of tides, river flow, wind, and salinity gradients. The importance of flushing time in an estuary will be examined in more detail in connection with the discussion of the fate of pollutants in estuaries.

Salinity Adaptations

To survive in most estuarine conditions, benthic organisms must be able to tolerate frequent changes in salinity and internal osmotic pressure. Species diversity in estuaries is constantly influenced by the continual migration of estuaries up and down continental edges as continental glaciers grow and recede through geological time.

A small fraction of animal species that live in estuaries, especially insect larvae, a few snails, and polychaete worms, have their closest relatives in fresh water; however, the great majority are derived from marine forms (figure 6.4) and include some of the same species found on nearby beaches and nonestuarine mudflats. Some animal species have poorly developed osmoregulatory capabilities and avoid osmotic problems by not venturing too far into estuaries. Others employ a number of adaptive strategies to overcome the osmotic problems of recurring exposure to low and variable salinities of estuarine waters. Some of these adaptations are modifications of structural or

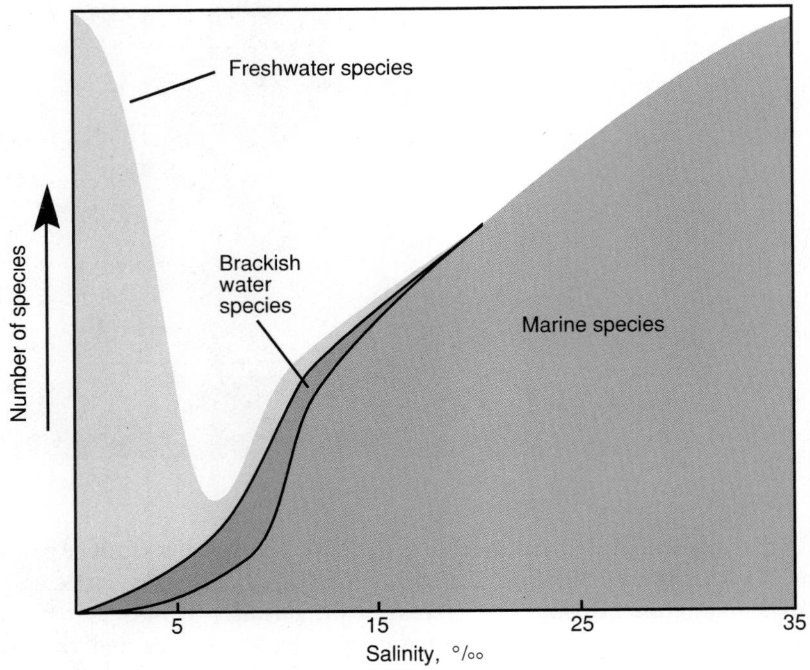

Figure 6.4
Relative contributions of freshwater, brackish water, and marine species to estuarine fauna
Redrawn from Remane, 1934

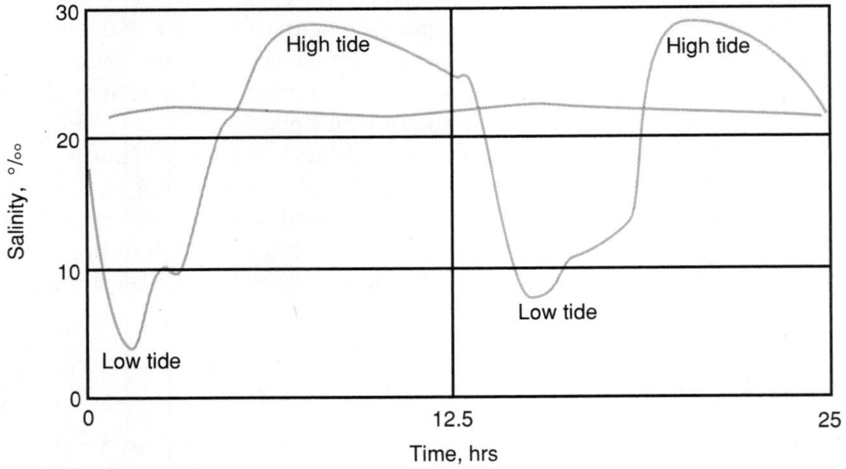

Figure 6.5
Comparison of salinity variations through a typical tidal cycle of interstitial water (tan) with that of the overlying water (blue) in Pocasset Estuary, Massachusetts
Adapted from Mangelsdorf, 1967

physical systems already imperative for survival on exposed intertidal shorelines. Oysters and other bivalve mollusks, for instance, simply stop feeding and close their shells when subjected to the osmotic stresses of low salinity water. Isolated within their shells, they switch to anaerobic respiration and await high tide, when water higher in salinity and O_2 will return. Other animal species retreat into mud burrows, where salinity fluctuations due to tidal cycles are usually much less severe (figure 6.5).

Tunicates, anemones, and several other soft-bodied estuarine epifauna are **osmotic conformers.** Osmotic conformers are unable to control the osmotic flooding of their tissues when subjected to low salinities, so their body fluids fluctuate and remain isotonic with the water around them (figure 6.6); in addition, they tolerate large variations of internal ionic concentrations without serious damage.

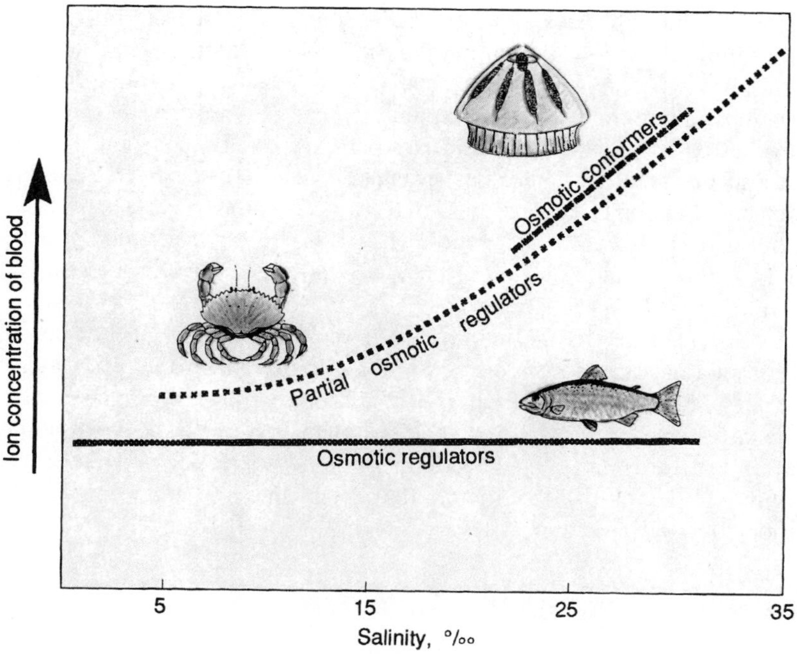

Figure 6.6
Variations in ion concentrations of body fluids or blood with changing external water salinities for osmotic conformers, partial osmotic regulators, and osmotic regulators

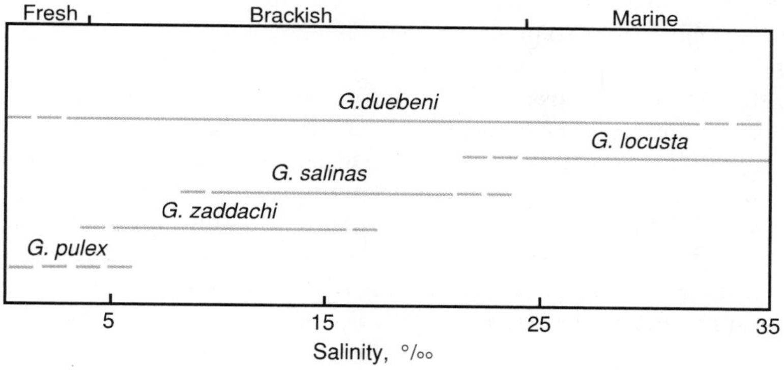

Figure 6.7
Differing salinity tolerances of five species of amphipods (*Gammarus*). Of these, only *G. duebeni* is euryhaline.
Adapted from Nicol, 1967

The most successful and abundant groups of estuarine animals have evolved mechanisms to stabilize the water and ion concentrations of their body fluids in spite of external variations. These mechanisms are as varied as the organisms themselves, yet all involve systems that acquire essential ions from the external medium and excrete excess water as it diffuses into their bodies.

The body fluids of estuarine crabs remain nearly isotonic with their external medium in normal seawater but become progressively hypertonic as the seawater becomes more dilute. When these partial osmotic regulators are subjected to reduced salinities, additional ions are actively absorbed by their gills to compensate for the ions lost in their urine (figure 6.6). Thus, these and most other estuarine crustaceans are osmotic conformers at or near normal seawater salinities and **osmoregulators** in dilute seawater.

Most estuarine animals are **stenohaline;** they tolerate exposure to limited salinity ranges and therefore occupy only a limited portion of the entire range of salinity regimes available within an estuary (figure 6.7). Only a few species of estuarine organisms are **euryhaline,** capable of withstanding a wide range of salinities. These species can be found throughout the range of estuarine salinities, with a limited number of euryhaline species also found in high salinity lagoons that fringe some of the world's arid coastlines. Lagoons such as those along the coast of Texas and both sides of northern Mexico have shallow bottoms, high summer temperatures, excessive evaporation, and high salinities. The osmotic problems experienced by animal species in these high salinity lagoon populations are similar to those encountered by bony fish in seawater and are so severe that reproduction is seldom successful. Continued immigration of euryhaline species from nearby estuaries sustains these lagoon populations.

Species diversity and numbers of individuals usually decline considerably from a maximum near the ocean to a minimum near the headwater of an estuary. The distributional patterns of estuarine animals are governed by salinity variations, patterns of food and sediment preferences, current action, water temperature variations, and competition between species. It is the collective interaction of all these factors that establishes and maintains the distribution of estuarine organisms.

Sediment Transport: Creating Habitats

Sediments are transported into estuaries from rivers that drain coastal watersheds and from coastal areas outside the estuary mouth. River sediment particles range in size from gravels and coarse sands to fine silts, clays, and organic detritus. They are derived from erosion of river banks denuded of their natural plant cover and from the scouring of meandering river channels. Fast-moving rivers carry large amounts of particles, but as the rivers widen and slow in coastal flood plains, they begin to meander and their sediments settle to the bottom. Estuaries thus serve as effective catch basins for much of the fine suspended sediments washed off the land. The current speed necessary to keep the sediment load suspended diminishes in the protected and quiet waters of estuaries and the water slows to a point where only the finest silts and clays remain suspended in the water.

Storms and nearshore currents of the open ocean can also move coastal sand and detritus materials into the mouth of an estuary and add to the complex mix of estuarine sediments. Typically, these deposits show a characteristic distribution of different sediment types, with coarse particles at the heads of estuaries and finer particles nearer the mouth. These graded and sorted sediment deposits transported down from rivers and in from the sea provide a rich and varying substrate to support the estuarine communities.

Estuarine Habitats and Communities

Estuarine communities include wetlands, mudflats, and channels. The areas of highest elevation are the **wetlands;** they are periodically covered by estuarine water at high tides and consist of dense plant communities that tolerate contact with seawater. **Mudflats,** or tideflats, are lower in elevation than the wetlands and are alternately submerged and exposed by changing tides. **Channels,** those areas that are under water even at the lowest tides, are prevented from filling with sediments by the scouring action of tides or river flow.

Figure 6.8
A dense stand of salt grass, *Spartina*
Courtesy P. Flannigan

Temperate Wetlands: Salt Marshes

Wetlands are wet grasslands, or **salt marshes,** that grow along estuarine shores. The dominant members of these marshes are **halophytes,** a few species of plants that are tolerant to saline waters (figure 6.8). Salt marshes develop in the muddy deposits around the edges of temperate and subpolar estuaries, creating a transition zone between land and estuarine plant communities. Salt marshes may be inhabited by several plant species, each with its own specific set of mud, water, and exposure requirements. The lowest parts of a marsh, submerged for longer periods of time, may be dominated by pickleweed, which stores excess salt in its fleshy leaves, and salt grass, which has special glands that enable it to rid itself of excess salt. In higher marsh zones, grasses and sedges that cannot tolerate prolonged submersion by the tides dominate the landscape.

Salt marshes form an important part of the base of estuarine food webs. Some of the plants in the estuary are eaten directly by marsh herbivores, but most of the vegetation decays and enters the food web as detritus. The flooding and ebbing of the tides transport the detritus from the marsh into the estuary and surrounding tidal creeks, where the detritus sinks and decomposes further. There it becomes the target of decomposing bacteria. The microbial activities of the bacteria further break down the plant matter, convert some of it to bacterial cells, and release dissolved organic materials and inorganic nutrients to be reused by other plants into the estuary.

Figure 6.9
Food particle production and utilization in a typical estuary
Adapted from Correll, 1978

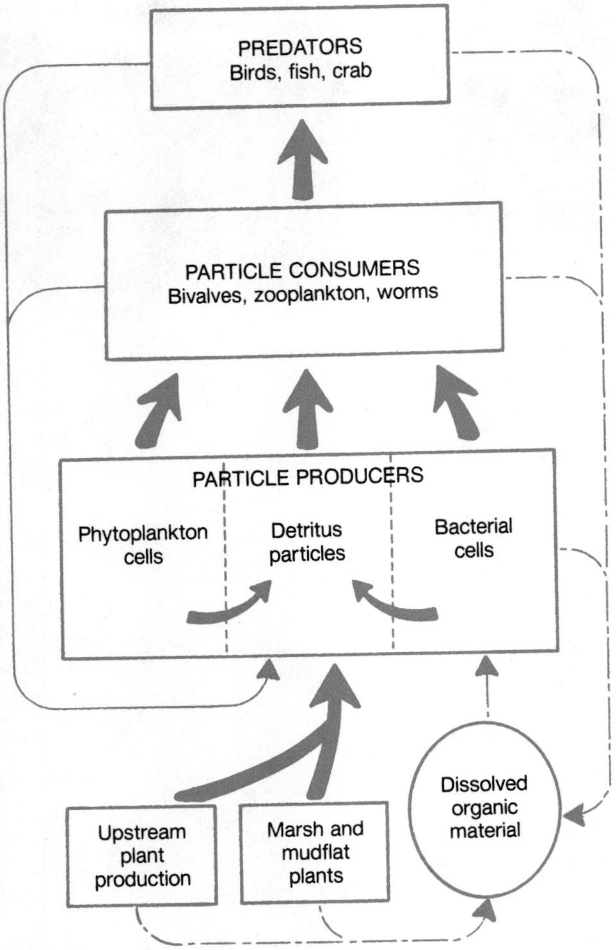

Thus bacteria, as well as the phytoplankton of the overlying waters, contribute heavily to the production of small, energy-rich detrital food particles. These microorganisms then become a major source of food for large populations of estuarine particle consumers (figure 6.9). The particle consumers themselves produce still more food particles in the form of feces and rejected food items. These particles are eventually recolonized by bacteria and recycled into the particle pool of the estuary. In this manner, estuarine bacteria and other microorganisms play a central role in transforming the productivity of the estuary margins into small detrital food particles available to numerous other species of estuarine animals.

Tropical Wetlands: Mangals

Dominating large expanses of rich estuarine muds in warmer climates are excellent examples of both emergent and submergent plant-based communities. Several species of mangroves (see figure 4.31) inhabit the shores of protected coastal lagoons and estuaries in tropical and subtropical latitudes. **Mangroves** are small shrubby trees that are tolerant to seawater and capable of establishing their peculiar prop roots in black anaerobic muds. Collectively, mangrove plants, the major component of **mangal** communities, line about

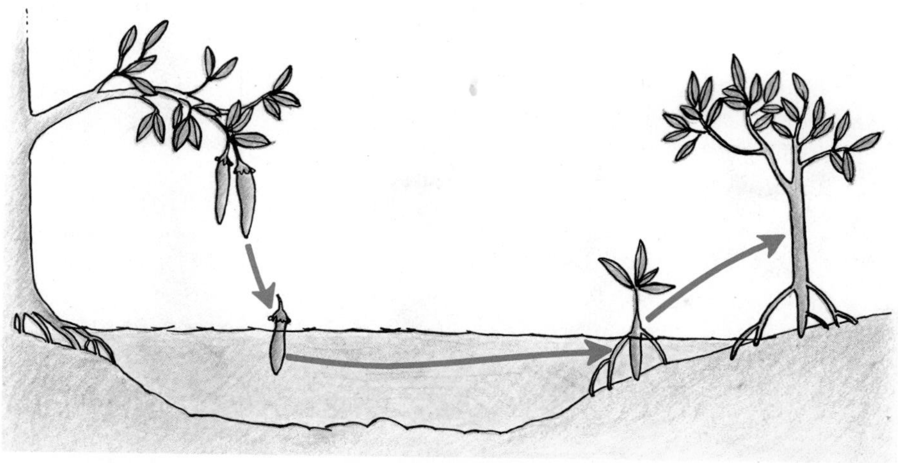

Figure 6.10
Germination cycle of a mangrove seed

two-thirds of the tropical coastlines of the world. In the United States, the distribution of mangals reflects their need for warm waters protected from wave action; they are found only along portions of the Gulf of Mexico and the Atlantic Coast of Florida.

Mangroves are seed plants, and their pattern of development illustrates well a series of adaptations needed to exist on muddy tropical shores (figure 6.10). Red mangroves (*Rhizophora*) produce seeds that germinate while still hanging from the branches of the parent tree. As the seedlings develop and grow longer, their bottom ends become heavier. When the seedlings eventually drop from the parent plant into the surrounding water, they float upright at the water's surface, are dispersed by winds or tides, and finally settle in shallow water on muddy shoreline. There, the seedlings promptly develop small roots to anchor themselves and continue to mature. The resulting tangle of roots traps additional sediments and increases the structural complexity of mangal communities. Birds, insects, snails, and other terrestrial animals occupy the upper leafy canopy of the mangroves and a variety of fish, crustaceans, and mollusks live on or among the root complex growing down into the mud.

Mudflats

Mudflats are large estuarine expanses composed primarily of rich muds that are exposed at low tide. Where marine waters and rivers mix and the salinity gradients are large, dissolved ions interact with the sediments and **flocculate** (bind together to form larger particles), and add to the accumulating richness of the bottom muds. These unstable soft mud deposits serve as the principal structural foundation of soft bottom communities that thrive in estuaries. In many ways, these conditions of fine anaerobic muds and abundant bacteria resemble environmental conditions on muddy shores (see chapter 8).

A sometimes all-too-obvious feature of mud flats is the anaerobic condition that exists just below the surface. There, oxygen-depleted muds serve as an important habitat for many species of anaerobic bacteria. Some of these species produce hydrogen sulfide, the gas responsible for the rotten egg smell so characteristic of exposed mudflats. Other types of sediment dwellers, such as clams and mud shrimp, burrow in the muds to be protected from predators, to be sheltered from the drying effects of the sun at low tide, and to be in an environment where the salinity of the mud is more constant than that of the overlying water (figures 6.5 and 6.11).

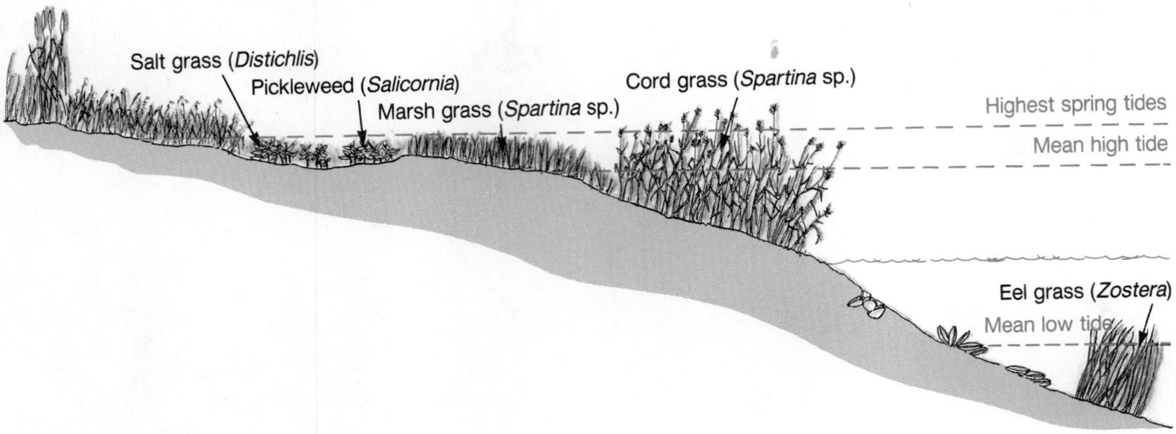

Figure 6.11
Plant-dominated salt marsh, mud flat, and channel habitats of Chesapeake Bay and other East Coast estuaries; their vertical position relative to high tide is indicated.

Animals living in the mudflats have developed a variety of feeding habits to cope with the environment. Most of the burrowing infauna are suspension feeders, gleaning small food particles from water currents above their burrows. Deposit feeders, such as lug worms, digest the bacterial and organic coatings from sediment particles passing through their digestive system. Other types of burrowing animals, such as the arrow goby, leave their burrows at high tide and forage for food over the mud flat.

Three major groups of primary producers are found on mudflats: diatoms, larger algae, and eelgrass. Microscopic benthic algae, including abundant diatoms, coat the muds with a golden brown film. These photosynthesizers are a rich and important food source for benthic invertebrates. Green mats of macroscopic algae, such as sea lettuce, commonly cover rocks, shells, and pieces of wood debris on mudflats. These are important food sources for herbivores, especially certain worms, amphipods and crabs.

Seagrasses, found at lower levels of the intertidal region, grow on substrates that range from clean sands to muds. Eelgrass and a few other sea grasses comprise one of the few types of flowering plants that can survive completely submerged in saltwater (figure 6.12). Eelgrass gets its name from the long, thin, straplike leaves (that can grow up to two meters in length) that weave back and forth in the currents like eels. Eelgrass production contributes greatly to the pool of detrital particles within an estuary. As a source of detritus, it is a valuable food source and is fed upon by some species of ducks (such as widgeon and brandt), invertebrates, fish, and insect larval stages. Algae and diatoms grow on its leaves, as do many types of hydroids, clam larvae and crustaceans. In addition to its role in the detritus food web, eelgrass is usually the first rooted plant to take hold in shallow water. Its roots and long leaves trap fine particulate materials and produce an ideal, food-rich, protected habitat. Finally, it also serves as a nutrient pump by taking nutrients from the sediment for growth and later releasing them to the water when it dies at the end of the growing season.

Channels

A **channel** is that area of the estuary where water is always present under all tidal conditions (figure 6.11). It may be as broad as the entire estuary or it may be restricted to a narrow creeklike channel between mudflats. Most of

Figure 6.12
A bed of eelgrass, *Zostera,* at low tide
Courtesy P. Flannigan

the organisms that inhabit the channel are planktonic and rely on the action of currents to move them around. Larval stages of marine fish and invertebrates are also abundant in channels during certain times of the year. Permanent adult fish populations consist of species such as starry flounders or sculpins.

Channel areas are also used as spawning and nursery areas for many animals. Herring and sole are ocean fish that move into the protected areas of the estuary to spawn and to allow the juveniles to feed on the large amounts of available food. Crabs also use the estuaries as nursery areas. Anadromous fish such as salmon use the estuary to get from the ocean to their spawning areas in freshwater streams, and then they return to the sea. Before continuing their migration upstream, they may linger for a time in the estuary to feed while adjusting to the seawater conditions.

Economic Uses of Estuaries

Estuaries on both coasts of North America and in other areas of the world are ecologically critical areas that support a wide variety of biological communities and serve as vital resting and feeding stops within the migratory paths of ducks, geese, bald eagles and many species of shorebirds. Salt marshes, in particular, serve as important natural filters, trapping pollutants and converting them to less harmful substances. They also play a role in moderating flooding and sedimentation processes.

Most salt marshes and virtually all estuaries have been altered to some extent by human activity. These modifications have affected estuarine productivity, species diversity, and water quality. The environmental quality of

Figure 6.13
Common sources of pollutants entering estuaries

estuaries depends on the types and intensity of human activities throughout the coastal drainage basin. The effects of development and industrialization in an estuary, combined with effects from pollutants carried downstream from the upper watershed, create conditions that have contributed to worldwide environmental degradation. Since estuaries have always been important economic resources for coastal communities, balancing the many conflicting uses and managing pollution sources is critical to protecting the economic values and natural resources of estuaries.

Estuarine shorelands are used for a wide variety of commercial and recreational industries (figure 6.13): agricultural and forest production; residential, commercial, industrial, and shipping facilities; and disposal sites for dredged materials. Most of the world's major seaports are situated in estuaries, so they become centers for industrialization and extensive population growth. Commercial and industrial activities lead to modification of estuaries. To facilitate shipping, estuary channels are often dredged to maintain proper depth for large ships. Docks, pilings, piers, and jetties alter the flushing and circulation patterns of the estuary. To facilitate development, many wetlands have been dredged and filled to create additional flat acreage. This disturbs the bottom, reduces the number of species that live in the estuary, and affects the primary productivity of the estuarine ecosystem. Over 75% of the estuarine wetlands in the United States have been lost due to draining and diking to create agricultural lands or areas for commercial development.

Estuaries have also been used extensively as disposal sumps for municipal and industrial wastes generated by activities associated with coastal developments. Since one third of the population in the United States lives near estuaries, this is a serious pollution load, especially in estuaries with long flushing times. Solids dumped into the estuaries often smother benthic communities. Toxic chemicals from wastewaters accumulate in water, sediments and animal tissues; excessive amounts of conventional pollutants such as organic materials or fertilizers create a high biochemical oxygen demand (BOD) and can reduce the estuary of life-supporting oxygen. Human encroachment into estuaries reduces their water quality and productivity.

In addition to sources of pollutants that discharge directly into estuaries, pollutants from upstream sources in the watershed can wash long distances downstream and accumulate in estuaries. These substances may change in toxicity after their first, intended use because of the complex physical and chemical processes at work in estuaries. Pesticides such as DDT and contaminants such as PCBs and dioxin have all been found in high concentrations in estuarine sediments and in several fish and wildlife species (see box 7). Water quality in estuaries directly affects the quality and size of sport and commercial harvests of shellfish and finfish. Oysters, salmon, and other food species must be grown in waters free of pathogens, toxic contamination, and excessive suspended sediments. Dredging, harbor development, and discharge of untreated pollutants from agriculture runoff or waste discharges can seriously degrade habitats for these species, damage industries based on their harvesting, and threaten human health.

Although multiple shoreland uses are an integral part of all coastal economies, they contribute contaminants to the coastal river and estuary systems that can cause habitat loss and a change in the ecological integrity that cumulatively affects public health, fish and wildlife habitat, and recreational resources. Despite past regulatory and management efforts, the water quality and habitat within estuaries has been seriously degraded around the world, and it continues to decline. To better understand some of the conflicts which surround the use of estuarine resources, we will examine in detail one major and well-known estuary, the Chesapeake Bay system on the east coast of the United States.

The Chesapeake Bay System

The variety of estuary types that exist in North America makes the task of characterizing even the major estuaries difficult. Therefore, the focus of the remainder of this chapter will be one of the world's largest estuaries, Chesapeake Bay. This system exemplifies the physical, chemical, and biological features of estuaries as well as the substantial problems generated by conflicts between natural estuarine processes and the many additional uses imposed on these coastal habitats by humans.

The Chesapeake Bay system is a cascading series of five major and numerous smaller estuaries (figure 6.14). These estuaries were linked together when the ancestral Susquehanna River valley flooded after the LGM. The bed of the ancient Susquehanna is deep, but most of the Bay is sufficiently shallow to allow sunlight to penetrate to the bottom.

Chesapeake Bay drains a heavily populated and agriculturally rich land area of the central Atlantic coastal plain. Human activities have imposed some serious stresses on the Bay in the form of increasing loads of heavy metals, fertilizers, pesticides, and incompletely treated sewage. Reduced O_2 levels in the waters of the Bay is only one of several complications resulting from this input. Yet, Chesapeake Bay has been referred to as a protein factory. Millions

Box 7 *Estuaries and Eagles: The Columbia River*

The Columbia River drains the second largest watershed in the United States. It starts in the ice fields of British Columbia and flows through a drainage basin that extends over parts of five states and two provinces. It is rich in natural resources, supporting some of the largest salmon runs in the world and providing special habitat for sensitive, rare, and endangered species. One of these is our national symbol, the bald eagle.

The Columbia River also supports a diverse economy and serves as a major transportation route for world commerce. It provides a fairly typical example of the conflict that often exists between utilization and conservation of estuarine natural resources. The Columbia River drainage basin, home to over 8 million people, receives heavy waste loads associated with all populated and industrially developed areas. Industrial discharges from pulp and paper mills and aluminum plants, wastewater from cities, and runoff from agricultural fields, forest harvest areas, and city streets all contribute fertilizers, pesticides, petroleum products, heavy metals, oxygen-consuming organic materials, silt, and soil bacteria to the Columbia River's drainage.

The estuary of the Columbia River extends from the river mouth upstream over 200 km to Bonneville Dam, located between the states of Oregon and Washington. Most pollutants that run off the land into the river or are discharged through pipes directly into the river eventually move downstream and end up in the estuary. Recent studies have shown that the introduction of two toxic pollutants, PCB and DDE (a degradation product of DDT), and the loss of critical habitat have had an adverse effect on bald eagles.

Refrigerants, wastes from plastics manufacture, and leaking electrical generators and transformers are common sources of PCB in the environment. The insecticide DDT was banned in 1972 (see chapter 14), but its metabolite DDE is still biologically available. The sources of DDE and DDT are not known, but it is thought that they enter the river in storm runoff carrying sediments contaminated with agricultural pesticides or in sediments disturbed during river dredging operations. Both compounds are stable, are slow to chemically degrade, and are biologically persistent, thus enhancing their ability to reenter the river and become magnified in food chains of the estuary.

The Columbia River Estuary is also home to twenty-four pairs of breeding bald eagles, and as many as 150 that visit seasonally. The Oregon Cooperative Wildlife Research Unit at Oregon State University recently completed a study on the effects of DDE and PCB on bald eagles in the Columbia River Estuary. The study revealed high concentrations of DDE (4 to 16 ppm) and PCB (4.8 to 26.7 ppm) in bald eagle eggs and carcasses found in the estuary.

Bald eagle
Courtesy R. Zahn, U.S. Fish and Wildlife Service

Associated with these high concentrations of DDE and PCB was significant thinning of eggshells (mean eggshell thickness was 14% thinner than the shells of normal eggs) and consequent high reproductive failure. Only about 40% of the healthy eagle pairs around the Columbia River Estuary successfully raised chicks each year, the lowest reproductive success of any breeding bald eagle population in the Pacific Northwest. Detectable levels of DDE and PCB were also found in the blood of nestlings, and elevated blood levels of both DDE and PCB were common in subadults and adults.

Many contaminants are suspected of being biologically available to the eagles through estuarine food chains. This assumption is supported by recent studies of the United States Fish and Wildlife Service that found elevated levels of DDE and PCBs in harbor seals, river otters, and various fish species in the Columbia River Estuary. All of these species (as well as bald eagles and humans) feed on fish and are susceptible to accumulating these contaminants in their tissues.

The bald eagle is listed as a threatened species in the lower forty-eight states. Both pollution-related reproductive failure and significant loss of appropriate habitat have contributed to that threatened status. The new Pacific Bald Eagle Recovery Plan of the United States Fish and Wildlife Service requires that for bald eagles to be removed from their present threatened status, breeding populations must have an average reproductive rate of one young per nest site, with an average success rate of not less than 65

Box 7 *Estuaries and Eagles: The Columbia River*

percent throughout the occupied nesting territory. Bald eagle productivity in the Pacific Northwest is reaching these values. The eagles of the Columbia River Estuary are far from that goal.

The environmental and economic stability of a broad region around this estuary depend on our ability to wisely manage the Columbia River Estuary in ways that will support commercial opportunities while still protecting its natural resources. In order to begin assessing the levels of contaminants present and their impact on estuarine populations such as bald eagles, the state governments of Oregon and Washington have joined together to design and implement an interstate water quality study which will obtain crucial information about the health of the estuary and the types and amounts of contaminants present. Diverse governmental agencies and public interest groups, along with Indian tribes and industries that depend on the Columbia River Estuary for their livelihood, will also participate in this study. For a long-term Columbia River Estuary program to be successful, the affected public must care enough to be involved in supporting such studies and finding solutions to the problems they uncover.

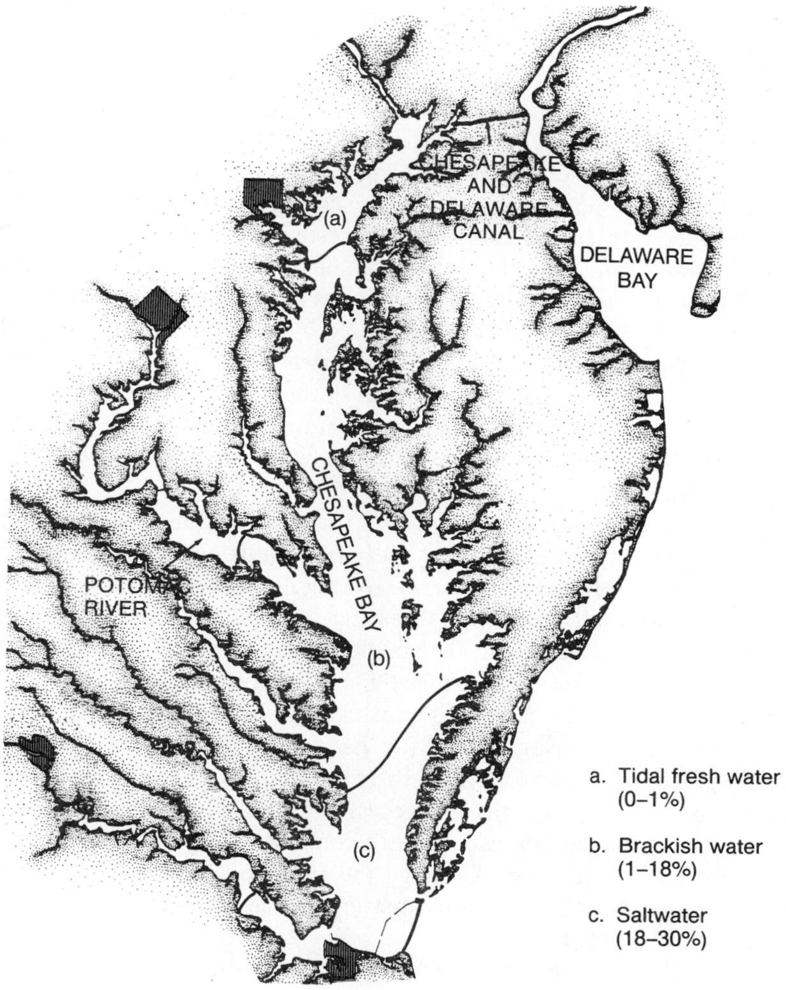

Figure 6.14
Chesapeake Bay and its numerous smaller side estuaries, showing mean surface salinity zones

of blue crabs, oysters, striped bass, and other finfish are harvested from these Chesapeake Bay waters each year. In 1980, fisheries had a one billion dollar impact on the economies of Maryland and Virginia. When the recreational, military, shipping, and other uses of Chesapeake Bay are added to the mix of conflicting uses, we have in microcosm a picture of some of the same problems confronting the larger world ocean.

In Chesapeake Bay, the existing salinity gradient creates an up-Bay low salinity zone, a mid-Bay brackish zone, and a lower-Bay marine zone (figure 6.14). Although the tides in Chesapeake Bay have an average vertical range of only 1 to 2 m, they are the major short-term mixing influence in the Bay. On longer time scales, seasonal flooding and storms have dramatic effects on the salinity distribution patterns in the Bay.

For animals capable of tolerating the dynamic fluctuations of Chesapeake Bay and other estuaries, these habitats offer nearly ideal nursery conditions for their young. Estuaries provide some protection against the physical stresses of nearby open coasts, and there is an abundance of food available in a large range of particle sizes. The majority of fish species commercially exploited along the Atlantic and Gulf coasts of the United States use estuaries as spawning or juvenile feeding areas. Some species occupy estuaries throughout their lives; others occupy estuaries for only a particularly crucial stage of their development. Figure 6.15 illustrates this range of utilization patterns with a sampling of a few commercially important or otherwise notable Chesapeake Bay species.

At one extreme are oysters (*Crassostrea*), which typically spawn, mature, and die within the confines of the Bay (although some larvae occasionally may be transported to other nearby estuaries). Oysters are broadcast spawners, with fertilization and a two-week larval development period occurring in the moving water above the benthic habitat of the adults. The double-layered circulation pattern of the Bay is used by oyster larvae to avoid being washed out of the estuary. During ebb tides, when most of the tidal outflow is in the surface layers, the larvae remain in the deeper inflowing saltwater. During slack or incoming tides, the larvae venture into the shallower portions of the larger Bay or its smaller side estuaries, where high levels of larval settling and retention occur.

Horseshoe crabs, menhaden, and turtles are all marine species that use Chesapeake Bay for early life stages only. Adult horseshoe crabs (*Limulus*) move into the Bay only to spawn. During high tides in the spring, these animals crawl into salt marshes at the water's edge. There the female digs a depression to deposit her eggs. The smaller male, who hitches a ride on the female's back, sheds sperm to fertilize the newly deposited eggs. The eggs are then covered to await hatching two weeks later, when they are again flooded by the next series of spring tides. After hatching, the larvae swim and feed near the surface while currents carry them out to sea where development continues through as many as thirteen successive larval stages.

The menhaden (*Brevoortia*) is a commercially valuable fish species of the middle Atlantic coast. Although the adults live and spawn in coastal waters, menhaden larvae drift into estuaries such as Chesapeake Bay to continue their development.

For blue crabs (*Callinectes*), the pattern of Bay utilization is nearly reversed from that of menhaden. Adults live in estuaries along most of the United States Atlantic and Gulf coasts. After mating, females seek higher

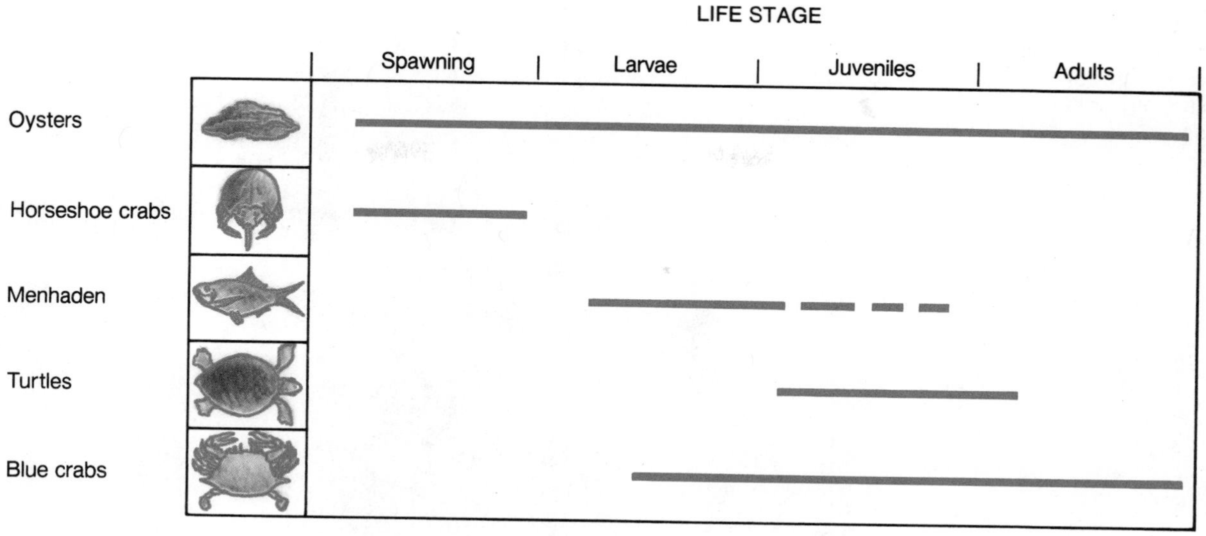

Figure 6.15
Utilization of estuaries by differing life stages of five common inhabitants of Chesapeake Bay

salinities in the open sea before releasing their larvae (figure 6.16). Larval development continues in coastal waters outside the Bay, where winds and coastal currents combine to keep blue crab larvae close to shore until they return to the Bay as young crabs. It is at this time that exchange of individuals between neighboring estuaries sometimes occurs, preventing genetic isolation of the crabs that occupy any one estuary. Within the estuary, young blue crabs seek eel grass beds and salt marshes as winter nursery areas for food and protection until they grow sufficiently to exploit other estuarine habitats.

Juvenile marine turtles (loggerheads and Atlantic ridleys are the most common) also graze on the slowly shrinking beds of eel grass found along the Bay edges. The 200 to 300 Atlantic ridleys seen each year in Chesapeake Bay may represent nearly all the existing juveniles of this seriously endangered species.

Through their roles as nursery areas and feeding grounds, the value of estuaries such as Chesapeake Bay extends far beyond the bounds of the estuary itself. Yet, the very health of Chesapeake Bay, as well as that of most of the earth's other major estuaries, has gradually, but seriously, deteriorated in the past few decades. Since 1960, submerged vegetation in the Bay, especially eel grass beds, has declined in size and abundance. Most of the decline has been in the upper and western parts of the Bay, but the problem is moving down the Bay as well. Dissolved nutrient loads draining into the Bay have increased, causing changes in the species composition of the water. In the upper reaches of Chesapeake Bay, concentrations of cyanobacteria and dinoflagellates have increased 250-fold since 1950. During the same time period, submerged eel grass and marsh grass beds have declined dramatically. These changes in patterns of primary productivity have resulted in extremely high concentrations of algae, which die and sink to the bottom. Such sinking of algal cells is part of the normal cycle of estuarine processes. However, when it occurs in such high densities, bacterial decomposers of this algal detritus consume O_2 that is also needed by other members of estuarine communities. Presently, most of the Bay water deeper than 13 m (downstream from near

Figure 6.16
Spawning migration of adult female blue crabs and return routes of planktonic larval stages

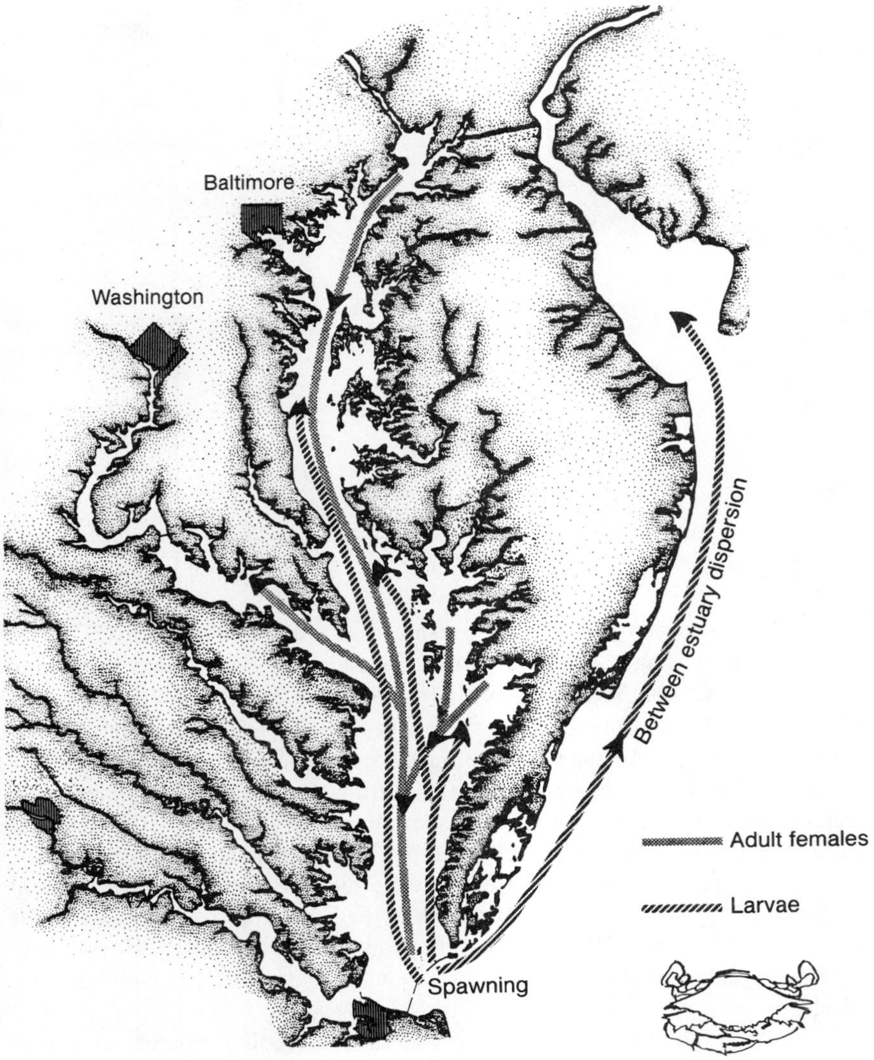

the mouth to the Rappahannock River) has little or no dissolved O_2. As a consequence of these biological changes, recent catches of alewives, shad, striped bass, and oysters have declined dramatically.

Serious and sustained efforts on the part of cooperating federal and state regulatory agencies are required to stem these adverse changes and reduce the nutrient and toxic substance loads presently carried into the Bay. Only when these efforts are successful can we be assured of the continuing health of this hardy and beautiful estuary system that is Chesapeake Bay.

Summary

Estuaries are partially enclosed coastal embayments where fresh water and seawater meet. A large variety of estuary types exist, but most owe their present configuration to river or glacial erosion since the Last Glacial Maximum. General patterns of water circulation in estuaries result from interactions between the outward flow of low density fresh water over a higher density layer of seawater beneath. Tides, winds, and the Coriolis effect add additional complexity to the circulation patterns and salinity gradients within the estuaries.

Estuarine inhabitants exhibit varied adaptations to deal with the range of salinities found in most estuaries. Osmotic conformers are unable to regulate their internal fluid environments. Other inhabitants actively regulate the exchange of dissolved ions and water across their body tissue surfaces. Both approaches result in some species that are stenohaline, tolerating only narrow salinity ranges, and other species that are euryhaline, tolerating wider salinity ranges.

Tides and river flow transport a mix of sediment particles that are sorted and deposited within estuaries, creating varied and changing substrates on which estuarine communities eventually develop. Salt marshes become established along the edges of many temperate latitude estuaries, creating transition zones between land and marine communities. Nearer the equator, estuarine fringes are occupied by mangals, which are composed principally of low-growing mangrove trees. Salt marsh grasses, mangroves, and sea grasses of mudflats and deeper channels are the macroscopic primary producers in these estuaries. Much of their production is decomposed to detritus by bacteria and, with contributions from phytoplankton and additional detritus carried into estuaries by tides, they maintain a rich pool of small food particles for estuarine deposit and suspension feeders.

Alteration of estuaries and their upstream watersheds have led to a reduction in size and a degradation in the water quality of most of the world's estuaries. The conversion of estuarine marshland to agricultural or industrial uses, in addition to contaminating estuarine waters with commercial, residential, and agricultural wastes, has contributed to sometimes dramatic alterations of existing estuarine community structures and serious reductions in fish and shellfish harvests.

In North America, the Chesapeake Bay system is the largest and most productive estuary. Because of its long history of use, it exemplifies the problems created when resource use and habitat protection come into conflict with each other.

Review Questions

1. Describe the pattern of water circulation in a typical estuary during periods of high river runoff. Of low river runoff.
2. Describe the resulting general vertical distribution of salinity values from the estuary mouth upstream to its head.
3. Draw a food web of Chesapeake Bay.
4. Compare the selective advantages and disadvantages of being an osmotic conformer in a typical estuary.

Questions for Further Discussion

1. Why is it critical to nonestuarine animals, such as migratory ducks and geese, that some estuaries remain relatively undisturbed by human activities?

2. Describe how you imagine the Chesapeake Bay appeared during the Last Glacial Maximum.

Suggestions for Further Reading

Books

Barnes, R. S. K. 1974. *Estuarine biology.* Baltimore, MD: University Park Press.

Britton, J. C. 1989. *Shore ecology of the Gulf of Mexico.* Dallas, TX: Texas Press.

Cloern, J., and F. Nichols. 1985. *Temporal dynamics of an estuary.* Boston, MA: Kluwer Academic.

Lippson, A. J., and R. L. Lippson. 1984. *Life in the Chesapeake Bay.* Baltimore, MD: The Johns Hopkins University Press.

McRoy, C. P., and C. Helfferich. 1977. *Seagrass ecosystems.* New York: Marcel Dekker, Inc.

National Wildlife Foundation. 1989. *A citizen's guide to protecting wetlands.* Washington, D.C.: National Wildlife Foundation.

Siry, V. 1984. *Marshes of the ocean shore.* Austin: Texas A & M University Press.

Teal, J., and M. Teal. 1983. *Life and death of the salt marsh.* Boston, MA: Little, Brown, and Co.

Warner, W. W. 1976. *Beautiful swimmers.* Boston, MA: Little, Brown, and Co.

Articles

Botton, M. L., and H. H. Haskin. 1984. Distribution and feeding of the horseshoe crab, *Limulus polyphemus,* on the continental shelf off New Jersey. *Fishery Bulletin* 82:383–89.

Coutant, C. C. 1986. Thermal niches of striped bass. *Scientific American* 255:98–104.

Durbin, A., and E. Durbin. 1974. Grazing rates of the Atlantic menhaden (*Brevoortia tyrannus*) as a function of particle size concentration. *Marine Biology* 33:265–77.

Heinle, D. R., R. P. Harris, J. F. Ustach, and D. A. Flemer. 1977. Detritus as food for estuarine copepods. *Marine Biology* 40:341–53.

Johnson, D. R. 1985. Wind-forced dispersion of blue crab larvae in the Middle Atlantic Bight. *Continental Shelf Research* 3:425–38.

Marshall, H. G. 1980. Seasonal phytoplankton composition in the lower Chesapeake Bay and Old Plantation Creek, Cape Charles, Virginia. *Estuaries* 3:207–16.

Miller, J. M., and M. L. Dunn. 1980. Feeding strategies and patterns of movement in juvenile estuarine fishes. In: *Estuarine Perspectives* by V. S. Kennedy, ed. New York: Academic Press.

Milliman, J. 1989. Sea levels: Past, present, and future. *Oceanus* 32(2):40–43.

Nichols, F., et al. Temporal dynamics of an estuary: San Francisco Bay. *Science* 231(4738):567–73.

Phillps, R. C. 1978. Seagrasses and the coastal marine environment. *Oceanus* 21:3–40.

Valiela, I., and J. Teal. 1979. The nitrogen budget of a salt marsh ecosystem. *Nature* 280:652–56.

Zedler, J., T. Winfield, and D. Mauriello. 1978. Primary productivity in a southern California estuary. *Coastal Zone* 3:649–62.

Benthic Communities

Chapter 7

Heart urchin
Photo by T. Phillipp

Over 90% of the animal species found in the ocean and nearly all of the larger marine plants live in close association with the sea bottom. These organisms form the benthos. Benthic primary producers exist only in the shallow, near-shore fringe where the sea bottom coincides with the photic zone, introduced in chapter 5. Benthic animals range from high intertidal zones to cold, perpetually dark trenches more than 10,000 m deep.

Benthic organisms occupy the interface between the sea bottom and the overlying water. The characteristics of the sea bottom and the overlying water, the exchange of substances between the sediments and the overlying water, and conditions established by the other living members of their communities define the environmental demands benthic organisms must meet for survival.

This chapter will examine the general conditions of life on the seafloor, with emphasis placed on subtidal benthic communities. The following two chapters will focus on two well-known but very different types of shallow marine benthic communities: temperate climate intertidal shorelines and warm-water coral reefs.

Living Conditions on the Bottom

Benthic animals that crawl about on the surface of the sea bottom or sit firmly attached to it are referred to as the epifauna. Epifauna are associated with rocky outcrops or the surface of firm sediment deposits. Other benthic animals, the infauna, find food or protection within the substrate forming the bottom. Figure 7.1 shows the relative abundance of epifauna and infauna at different marine climatic zones. Note that epifauna seem to be more sensitive than infauna to climatic differences.

Infaunal clams, worms, and crabs are macroscopic and are familiar to anyone who has spent a few moments digging in a sandy beach or mudflat. These **macrofauna** either swallow or displace the sediment particles around themselves as they move. Less obvious, but no less important, are **microfauna,** microscopic infauna less than 50 μm in size. Intermediate in size between the macrofauna and microfauna is the **meiofauna,** a very interesting and abundant group of animals. The meiofauna are also referred to as **interstitial animals,** because they occupy the spaces (the interstices) between sediment particles.

Seafloor Characteristics

The sea bottom supports the weight of many organisms considerably more dense than seawater. Some animals excavate burrows or construct tubes of soft sediments. On hard bottoms, animals and plants secure a firm attachment in order to resist the tug of waves and currents. Benthic organisms are adapted for life on or in particular bottom types; and the character of life there, to a large extent, is dependent on the properties of the bottom material, which varies from solid rock surfaces to very soft, loose deposits.

The sea bottom also functions to accumulate plankton, waste material, and other detritus sinking from the sunlit waters above. In some regions, fallout of organic detritus from the photic zone is the only source of food for the inhabitants on the bottom. A variety of worms, mollusks, echinoderms, and crustaceans obtain their nourishment by ingesting accumulated detritus and digesting its organic material.

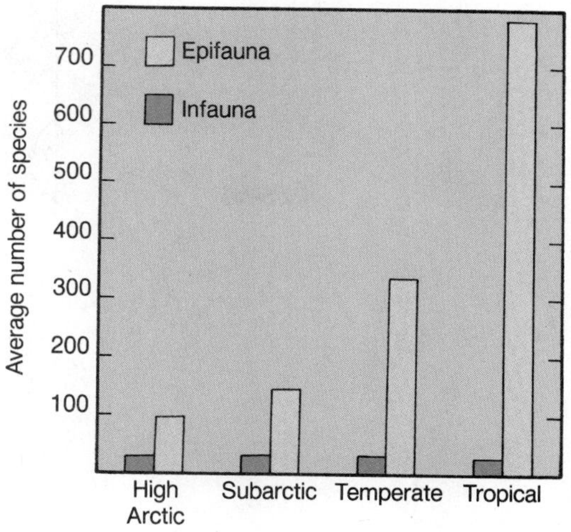

Figure 7.1
Variations in the average number of species of several bottom invertebrate groups from equal-sized coastal areas in different latitudes
Adapted from Thorson, 1957

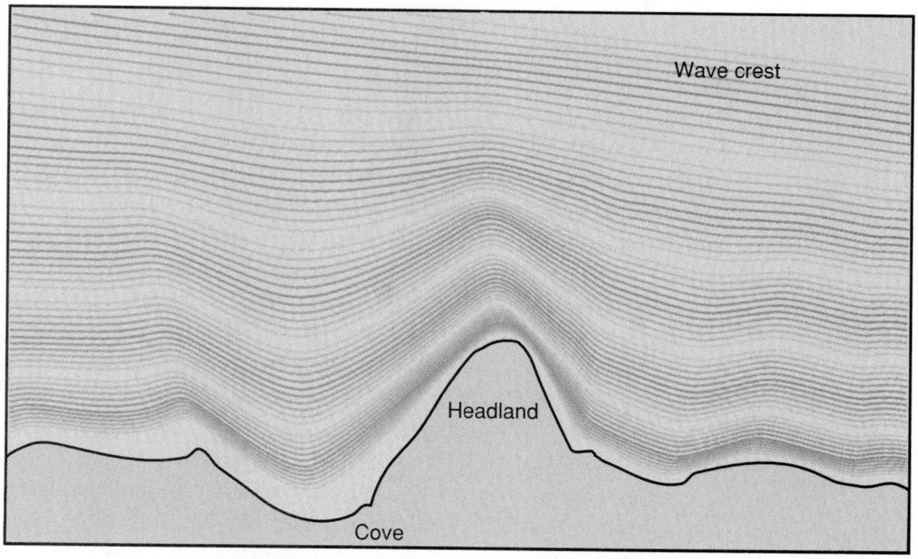

Figure 7.2
In coves and bays, refraction of advancing ocean waves spreads out the wave crests (and their energies) and concentrates them on headlands and other projecting coastal features.

The composition of the sea bottom is determined by its constituent materials and, in shallow water, by the amount of energy available in the wind-driven waves and currents at the sea surface. Chapter 1 explained that the energy of the waves (and their ability to move particles) decreases from the sea surface downward (figure 1.23) and disappears at depths equal to one-half the wavelength. The coastline shape also strongly influences the amount of energy expended on the shore when waves break. Wavefronts approaching shore start to slow down just as they begin interacting with shallow reefs and bars. As a result, the wavefronts lag behind the rest of the wave as it approaches shore and changes shape to approximately match the curvature of an irregular coastline (figure 7.2). This process redistributes the energy in the breaking waves, concentrating wave energy on headlands while spreading out and diminishing the energy of waves entering bays, coves, and other coastal indentations. Taken together, the overall behavior of wind waves causes large

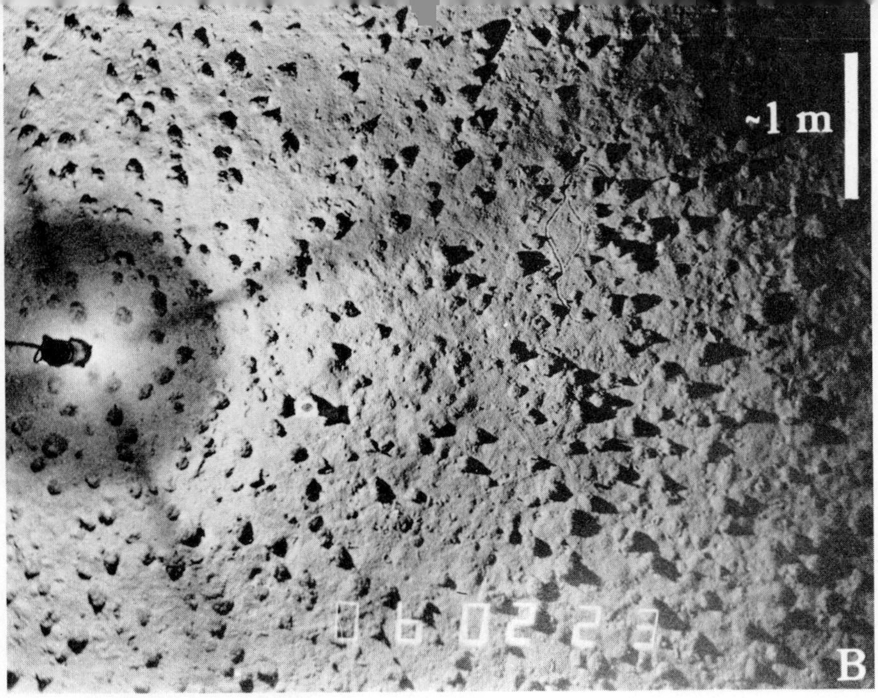

Figure 7.3
Manganese nodules scattered on the surface of the seafloor in the Pacific Ocean
Courtesy Scripps Institution of Oceanography

amounts of energy to be expended on headlands in shallow waters (shallower than one-half the wavelength of the waves) and lesser amounts of energy to be expended in coastal indentations and in deeper waters. On exposed headlands, erosion is the principal result of breaking waves. These high-energy environments are continuously swept clean of fine sediment particles, detritus, and anything not securely attached to the bottom. This debris is washed offshore into deeper water or alongshore into bays or low-energy coastal features where it settles to the bottom and adds to the growing deposits already there.

On an oceanic scale, rocky bottoms are scattered around the edges of the ocean basins where erosional processes dominate. Rocky outcrops also occur in association with deep-sea ridges, rises, and volcanoes, but the outcrops are comparatively small and geographically isolated.

Most of the sea bottom is covered with small sediment particles and other debris that have settled from the surface. Marine sediments are derived from several sources. A few minerals precipitate from their dissolved state in seawater to produce irregular deposits on the seafloor. Manganese nodules (figure 7.3) are a well-known example of this type of deposit. Such deposits may eventually have some commercial importance as a source of minerals, but they also may have an important influence on the structure of some benthic communities.

Marine sediments nearshore and on the continental shelves are largely the products of erosion on land and subsequent transport by rivers (and, to a lesser extent, winds) to the sea (figure 7.4). Once in the ocean, suspended sediment particles are carried and sorted by current and wave action according to their size and density. Larger, dense sand grains quickly settle to the bottom near shore. Very fine clay particles are often carried several hundred km out to sea before settling.

Much of the sedimentary material found in the deep ocean basins away from continental margins is composed of the mineralized skeletal remains of planktonic organisms. These deposits, known as oozes, are characterized by their chemical composition. Siliceous oozes contain cell walls of

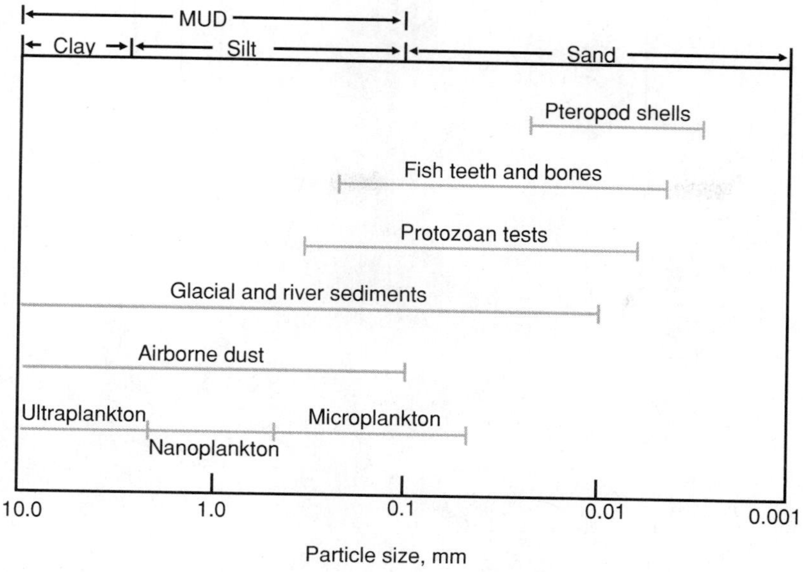

Figure 7.4
Particle size ranges for some common sources of marine sediments. Biogenic particles are shown in blue, terrigenous particles in tan.

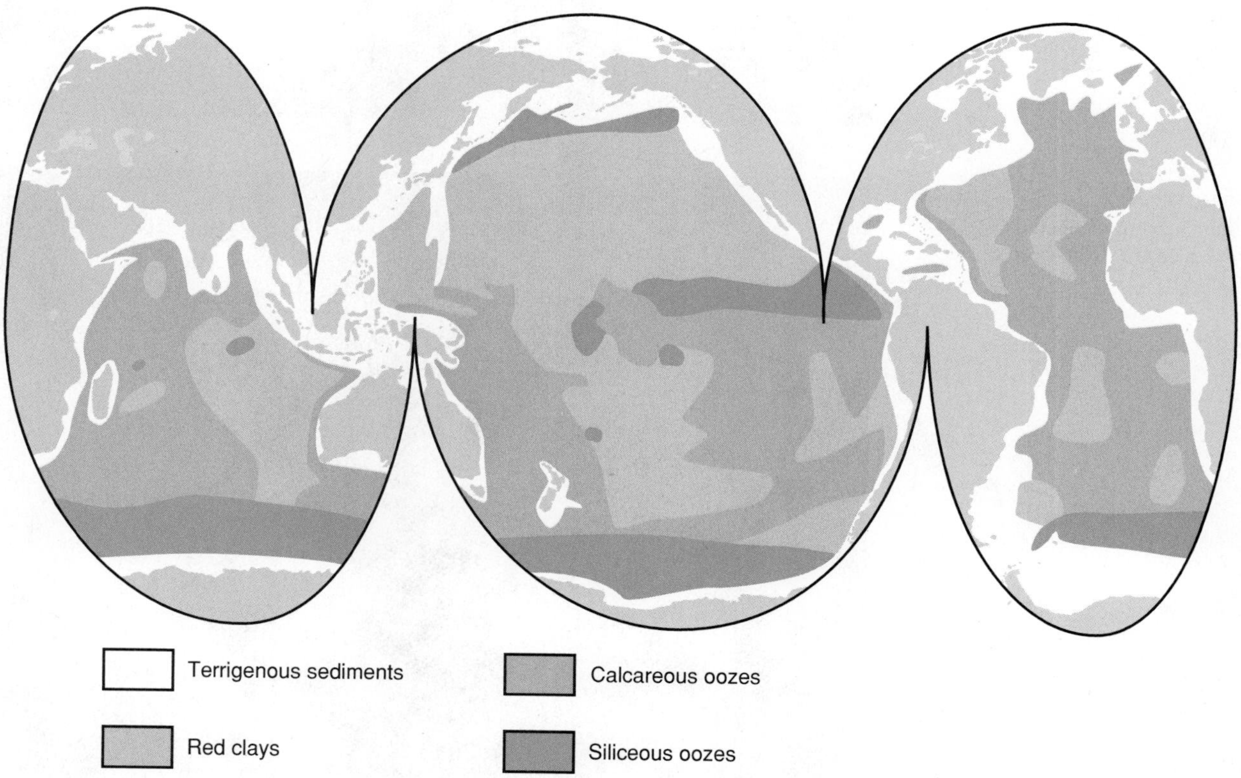

Figure 7.5
Distribution of ocean bottom sediment deposits
Adapted from Tait, 1968, and Sverdrup, Johnson, and Fleming, 1942

diatoms and the internal silicate skeletons of planktonic radiolarians (see figure 3.4). The skeletons of other planktonic protozoans, the foraminiferans, constitute most of the extensive calcareous oozes found on the ocean floor. These oceanic oozes accumulate very slowly, approximately 1 cm of new sediment every 1,000 years. In the deep sea, oceanic oozes exhibit distributional patterns that reflect the surface abundance of their plant and animal sources. These patterns are shown in figure 7.5.

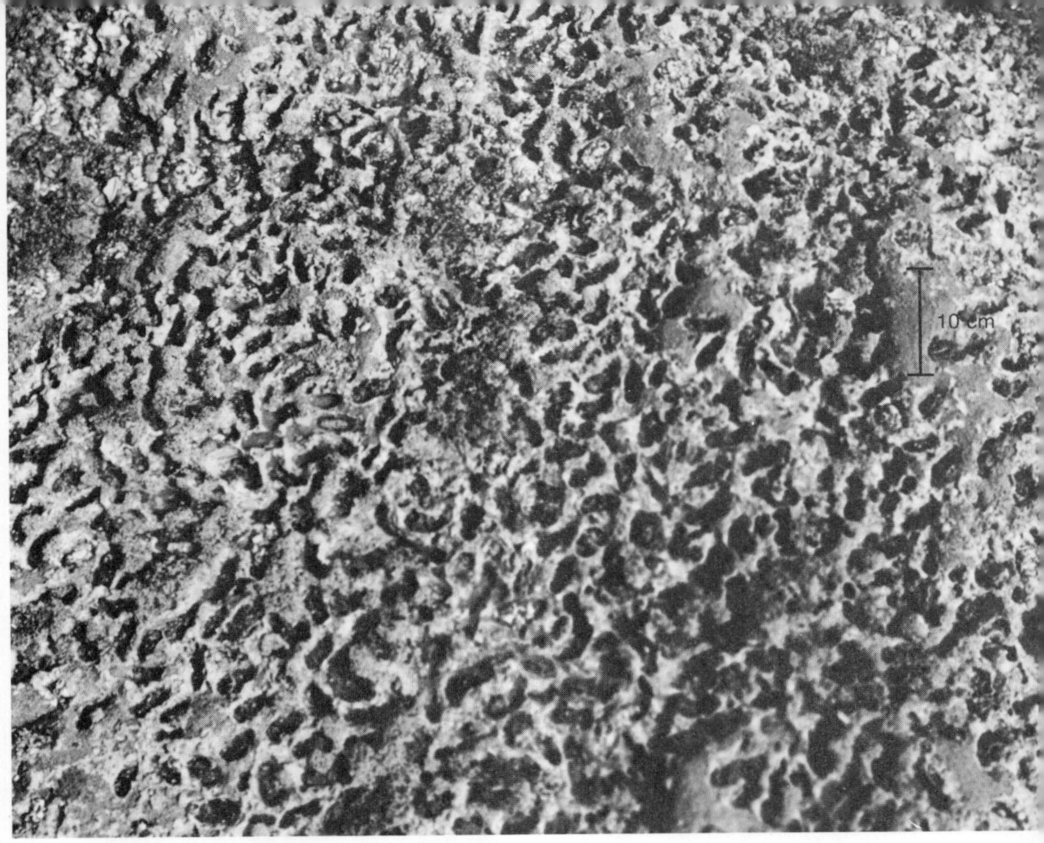

Figure 7.6
Sandstone erosion pits created by the rasping actions of small chitons

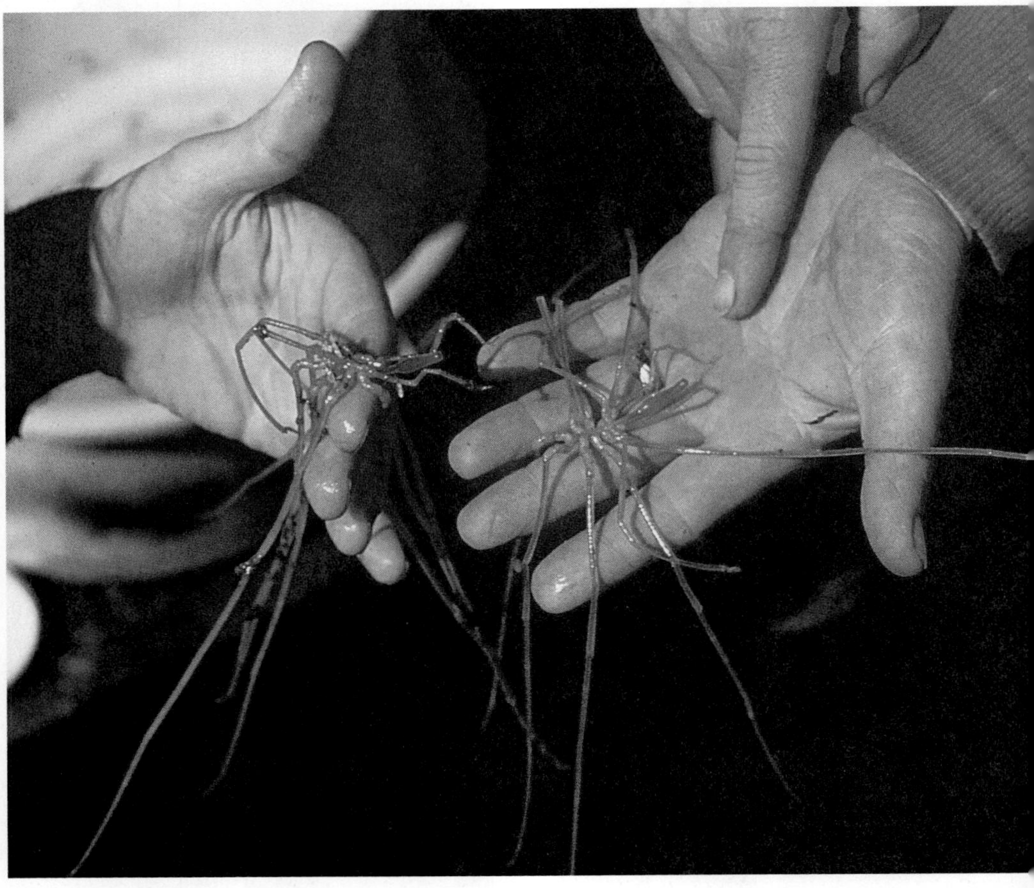

Figure 7.7
Two large pycnogonids dredged from the deep sea bottom

Figure 7.8
Barnacles, *Balanus,* attached to a snail shell with their feathery filtering appendages extended.
Photo by T. Phillipp

Animal-Sediment Relationships

Benthic animals mix and sort the sediments through their burrowing and feeding activities. Oxygen and water from sediment surface circulate down into the sediment through these tubes and burrows. Further modification of sedimentary characteristics is accomplished when particles are cemented together to form tubes and when sediments are compacted to form fecal pellets and castings. On rocky bottoms, the grazing activities of chitons, gastropods, and sea urchins aid the erosive processes of waves by scraping away rock particles as well as food (figure 7.6). There are even a few benthic animals, such as pholad clams, that are especially adapted for boring into solid rock.

The distributional patterns of benthic plants and animals are strongly influenced by the firmness, texture, and stability of their substrate. These features govern the effectiveness of locomotion or, for nonmotile species, the persistence of their attachment to the bottom. Epifauna are most frequently associated with firm or solid bottom material. When found on softer muds, some display elongated, stiltlike legs or fins that extend into or along the sediment for better support and traction (figure 7.7).

The particle size and organic content of the bottom material limit the versatility and distribution of specialized feeding habits. **Suspension feeders** depend on small plankton or detritus for nutrition. Filtering devices (figure 7.8) or sticky mucus nets or sheets collect minute suspended food particles from the water. Suspension feeders generally require clean water to avoid clogging their filters with indigestible particles. Therefore, they are usually found on rocks or are associated with coarse sediments.

Figure 7.9
A godwit probing for food in the lower intertidal zone

In deep-ocean basins, mudflats, and other soft-bottom areas, **deposit feeding** is common. Deposit feeders engulf sediments and process them through their digestive tracts. They extract nourishment from the organic material in the sediment in much the same manner as earthworms do. Some deposit feeders indiscriminately ingest any available sediments; others select organically rich substrates for consumption.

Several animal species are capable of extracting sufficient nourishment from sediments by conducting digestive processes outside their bodies. These animals absorb the products of digestion either through specialized organs or across the general body wall. Deep-sea pogonophorans, small worms related to the large tube worms recently discovered in association with deep-sea hot springs (figure 7.22), depend on this type of **absorptive feeding,** as do numerous echinoderms. Sea stars are usually carnivorous, but a few species are quite opportunistic. When feeding on bottom sediments, *Patiria,* the bat star, extrudes its stomach outside its body and then digests and absorbs organic matter from the sediments. The omni-present bacteria also depend on extracellular digestion. As they absorb nutrients and their population grows, they in turn become a significant source of particulate food for deposit feeders.

The benthic environment abounds with **predators** and **scavengers** who feed on the residents of the bottom or on their remains. Most bottom predators and scavengers are permanent members of the benthos and are eventually eaten by other benthic consumers. However, fish often make serious inroads into intertidal animal populations during high tides, and shore birds replace them as predators at low tide (figure 7.9).

Regardless of the feeding habit employed by benthic animals, the ultimate source of food is the primary producers of the photic zone. Intertidal and shallow-water benthic plants provide direct sources of nutrition for the abundant herbivorous **algal grazers.** Some algal grazers nibble away bits of the larger seaweeds (figure 7.10). Most, however, rasp filmy growths of diatoms, cyanobacteria, and small encrusting plants from rocky substrates. Sea

Figure 7.10
A large snail, *Norrisia,* grazing on a kelp stipe
Photo by T. Phillipp

urchins use their five-toothed Aristotle's lantern to remove algal growths. Herbivorous gastropods and chitons accomplish similar results with their filelike radula.

Larval Dispersal

A sluggish benthic life-style does not limit sedentary bottom creatures to narrow geographic ranges. One-fifth of the common shallow-water animal species found at San Diego, California, for example, can also be found along the entire west coast of the United States and in British Columbia. Several other benthic species are even more widely dispersed, often in similar ecological conditions on opposite sides of the same ocean basin. *Mytilus edulis,* variously known as the bay mussel, blue mussel, or edible mussel, is common to temperate coasts of both sides of the Pacific and Atlantic oceans.

A few animals, including a small percentage of barnacles, often hitch rides on floating debris, on the hulls of ships, or in the ballast water of ships to cross transoceanic distances. An Australian barnacle, *Elminius modestus,* was apparently introduced to England on or inside the hulls of supply ships during World War II. It has since colonized the coasts of Ireland, France, Belgium, the Netherlands, Germany, and Denmark. In many sheltered reaches of these coastlines, *E. modestus* is competing with and replacing native barnacle populations.

A far more common adaptation for extending the geographical limits of temperate- and warm-water benthic species involves the production of temporary planktonic larval stages (known collectively as **meroplankton**). These

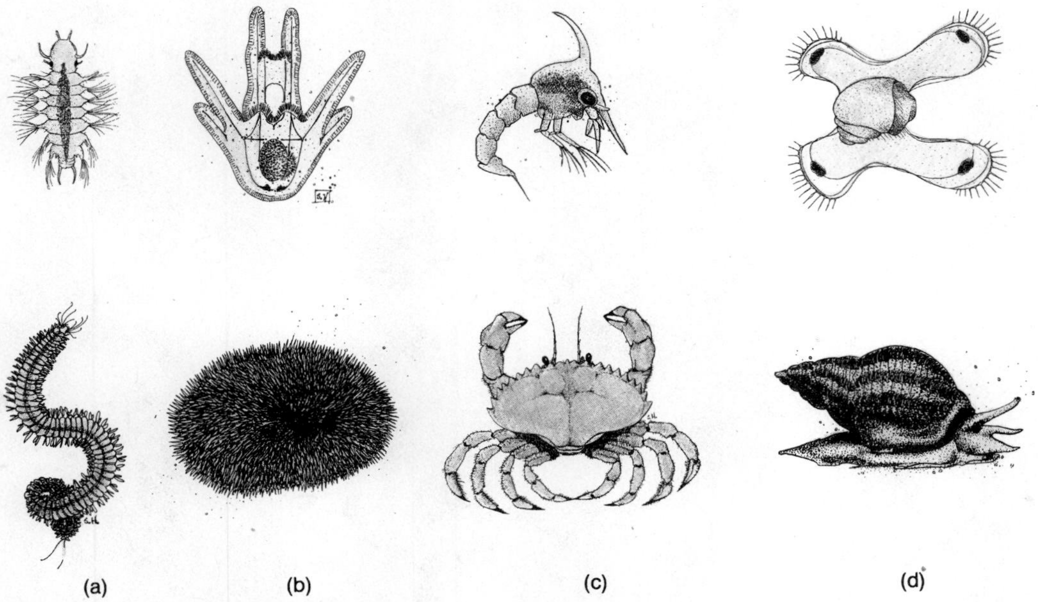

Figure 7.11
Planktonic larval forms (above) and adult forms (below) of some common benthic animals: (*a*) polychaete worm, (*b*) sea urchin, (*c*) crab, and (*d*) snail

small, feeble swimmers, bearing little resemblance to their parents (figure 7.11), drift with the ocean's surface currents for some time before they metamorphose and assume their benthic life-styles.

It has been estimated that about 75% of shallow-water benthic invertebrate species produce larvae that remain planktonic for two to four weeks. Over 5% of the species examined had planktonic larval stages exceeding three months, with a few as long as six months in duration (figure 7.12). Our understanding of ocean currents suggests that none but the most prolonged larval stages can make direct transoceanic trips before settling to the bottom. For each extra day the larvae remain in the plankton, they are exposed to additional threats of predation, increased pressures of finding food, and greater possibilities of being carried by the currents to areas where survival is unlikely. Yet the perils of a planktonic existence provide several advantages to offset the enormous mortality experienced by these larvae.

Even in very slow ocean currents, drifting planktonic forms may spread far beyond the geographical limits of the adult population. Many are swept into unfavorable areas and perish. But any survivors may expand their parents' original range or settle into and mix with other populations and reduce their genetic isolation.

During their planktonic existence, many types of larvae react positively to sunlight and remain near the sea surface and their food supply, the phytoplankton. As their planktonic life draws to a close and they seek their permanent homes on the bottom, some larvae remain near the sea surface and ride into intertidal shorelines on waves and tides. Other larvae shun the light and swim near the bottom. Most enter a swimming-crawling phase and settle to the bottom, investigate it, and if it is not suitable, swim up to be carried elsewhere.

Just how larvae know when a suitable substrate is encountered is an important, but as yet unanswered, question. Chemical attractants, current speeds, types and textures of bottom material, and the effects of light are only partial answers to the question. Specific bottom types, such as sand or hard

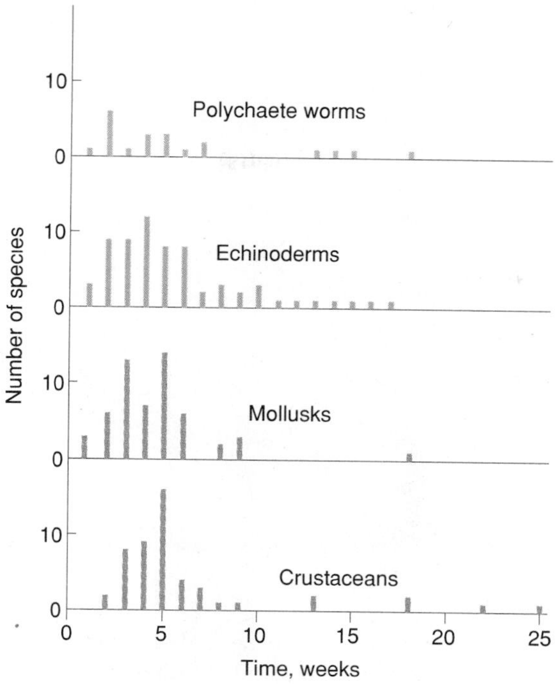

Figure 7.12

Typical duration of planktonic existence for four common groups of marine benthic invertebrates

Adapted from Thorson, 1961

rock, do not attract larvae from a distance. Once the appropriate bottom type is encountered, larvae may be induced to remain and quickly **metamorphose** into a young bottom stage. In contrast, chemical substances diffusing from established populations of some attached animals, including oysters and barnacles, attract larvae of their own species. This may be beneficial for oyster and barnacle larvae, for the presence of adults in the settling site ensures that physical conditions are appropriate for survival. Also, the larvae's eventual reproductive success may be enhanced if they are in the proximity of several other members of their species. However, for many other larvae, settling among their adults is catastrophic. Older, established individuals generally have relatively lower demands for food and oxygen, have more stored energy, and in general, can effectively compete for resources with the newly settled young. In times of shortages, the younger or smaller individuals are usually the first to suffer. Figure 7.13 illustrates the more obvious environmental features that may guide and influence larval settling.

Until they settle to the bottom, planktonic larvae are not in competition for food or space with the adults of their species. Even so, competition for food among plankton is often rigorous. About 10% of the species with long larval phases produce large yolky eggs that provide larvae with most or all of their nutritional supply. However, most species hatch from small eggs with little stored food and must begin feeding and competing with each other almost immediately.

Some benthic species, especially those in the tropics and the deep sea, spawn all year long; others have short and well-defined spawning seasons. In the latter group, the timing of reproduction or spawning is geared to produce young at times most advantageous to their survival. For many species of benthic animals, the spawning periods are timed to place their larvae in the plankton community when phytoplankton is abundant and readily accessible. In shallow waters, temperature and day-length provide two of the more obvious cues for

Figure 7.13
Several major environmental factors that influence the selection of suitable bottom types by planktonic larvae

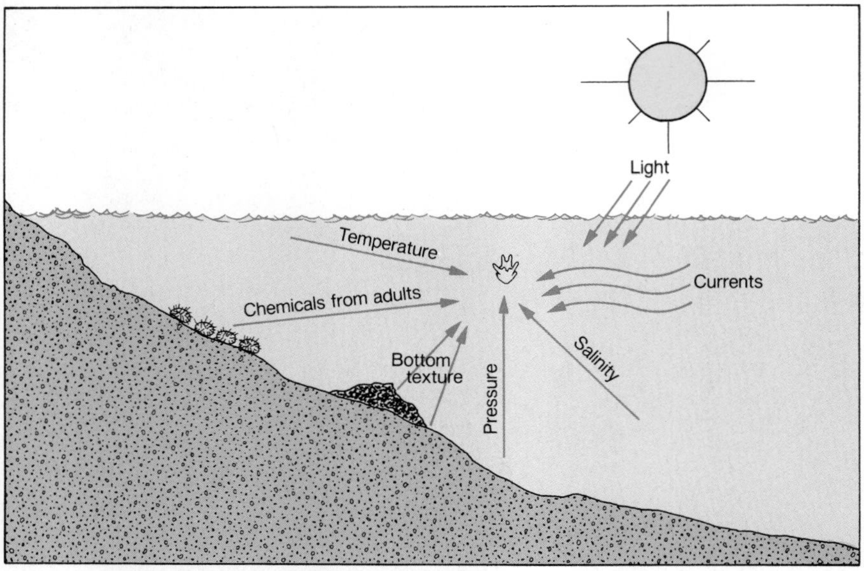

timing reproduction. The gonads of spring and summer spawners develop in response to rising water temperatures and lengthening days. Oysters, for instance, refrain from spawning until a particular water temperature is reached.

Regardless of how many eggs are produced, the reproductive success or fitness of an individual requires that its **fecundity** (the production of eggs or offspring) exceed its offspring **mortality** (the rate at which individuals are lost). Any population whose mortality consistently exceeds its fecundity will shrink and eventually disappear. Adaptations that increase fecundity and/or reduce mortality improve the chances for successful reproduction.

The fecundity of some shallow-water benthic animals is truly inspiring. The females of many of these species each produce over ten million eggs annually. A sea slug *(Aplysia)* weighing a few kg produced an estimated 478 million eggs during five months of laboratory observations. Such excessive reproduction enthusiasm would quickly place any shoreline knee-deep in sea slugs if the spawning efforts of only a few adults were all to survive.

Obviously, egg and larval mortality in these species are extremely high. Of the millions of potential offspring produced, very few attain sexual maturity. In some benthic animals, internal fertilization is accomplished before the eggs are released into the water. Some species of snails, crabs, sea stars, and other invertebrates retain their larvae internally or in special brood pouches until the larvae are at reasonably advanced stages of development. For some of these invertebrates, brooding may be an adaptive consequence of small adult size. Smaller species of benthic invertebrates, with correspondingly smaller gonads, are less likely to produce sufficient planktonic larvae to equal their larger competitors. Consequently, they employ internal fertilization and larval incubation to reduce offspring mortality to some extent.

Many of the abundant and familiar seashore animals are **broadcast spawners;** they spew great quantities of eggs and sperm into the surrounding water and fertilization occurs. These numerous eggs are necessarily small and hatch quickly into planktonic larval forms ready to experience the benefits and

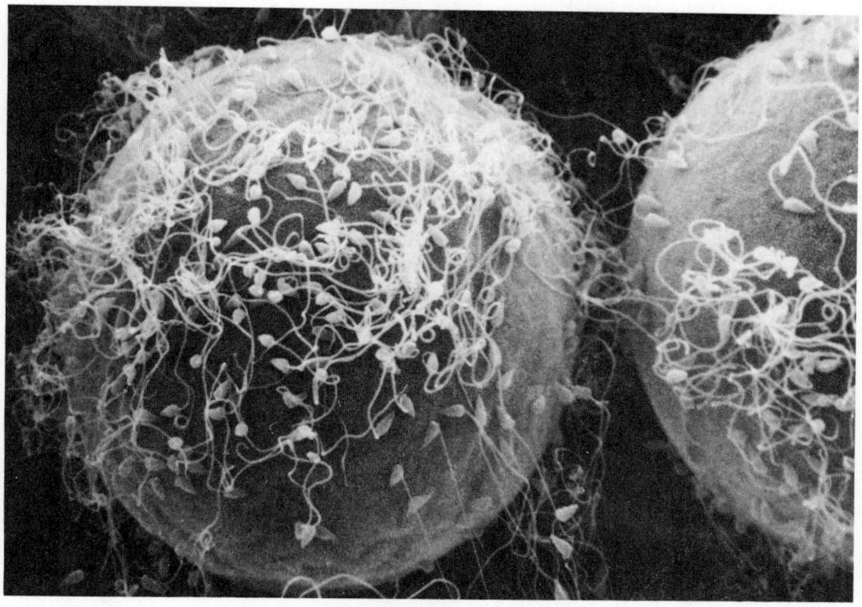

Figure 7.14
A SEM of a sea urchin egg covered with sperm cells
Courtesy M. Tegner, Scripps Institution of Oceanography

perils of a temporarily pelagic life-style. Each larva, then, is a relatively low-cost genetic insurance policy for spawning adults, there to insure that the genes of the parents survive another generation.

Fertilization in these broadcast spawners is not as haphazard as it may seem. Chemical substances (referred to as **pheromones**) are present in the egg or sperm secretions of sea urchins, oysters, and many other marine invertebrates. When shed into seawater, these pheromones induce other nearby members of the population to spawn, and they in turn stimulate still others to spawn until much of the population is spawning simultaneously. As you might guess, spawning pheromones are quite specific. For instance, the sperm secretions of one sea urchin induce members of the same species to spawn, but the secretions have no effect on oysters or other species of sea urchins. A structural protein, contained in the heads of sea urchin sperm cells, only unites with other proteins on the surface coat of sea urchin eggs (figure 7.14). Together with pheromones, these substances regulate the timing of spawning, the specificity of sperm for eggs of the same species, and ultimately the overall prospects for successful fertilization by broadcast spawners.

It is distressing to note that, for many years, smashing sea urchins has been a popular and sporting method of removing these "pests" from the kelp beds on which they feed. Diving clubs frequently organized competitions, with prizes going to the club killing the most urchins in a specific time. The impact of these eradication programs on sea urchin populations is questionable, for a smashed sea urchin (if it was ready to spawn) releases not only its own eggs or sperm but also pheromones that cause its neighbors to do likewise. Thus a Sunday afternoon's efforts to eliminate a few thousand urchins may, in fact, trigger a mass-spawning of billions of sea urchin eggs (enough to replace the animals destroyed with more than a few left over). Worse yet, such activities promote the attitude that humans are capable of interfering with and correctly altering the character of natural systems to fit their own needs without first understanding the basic features of those systems.

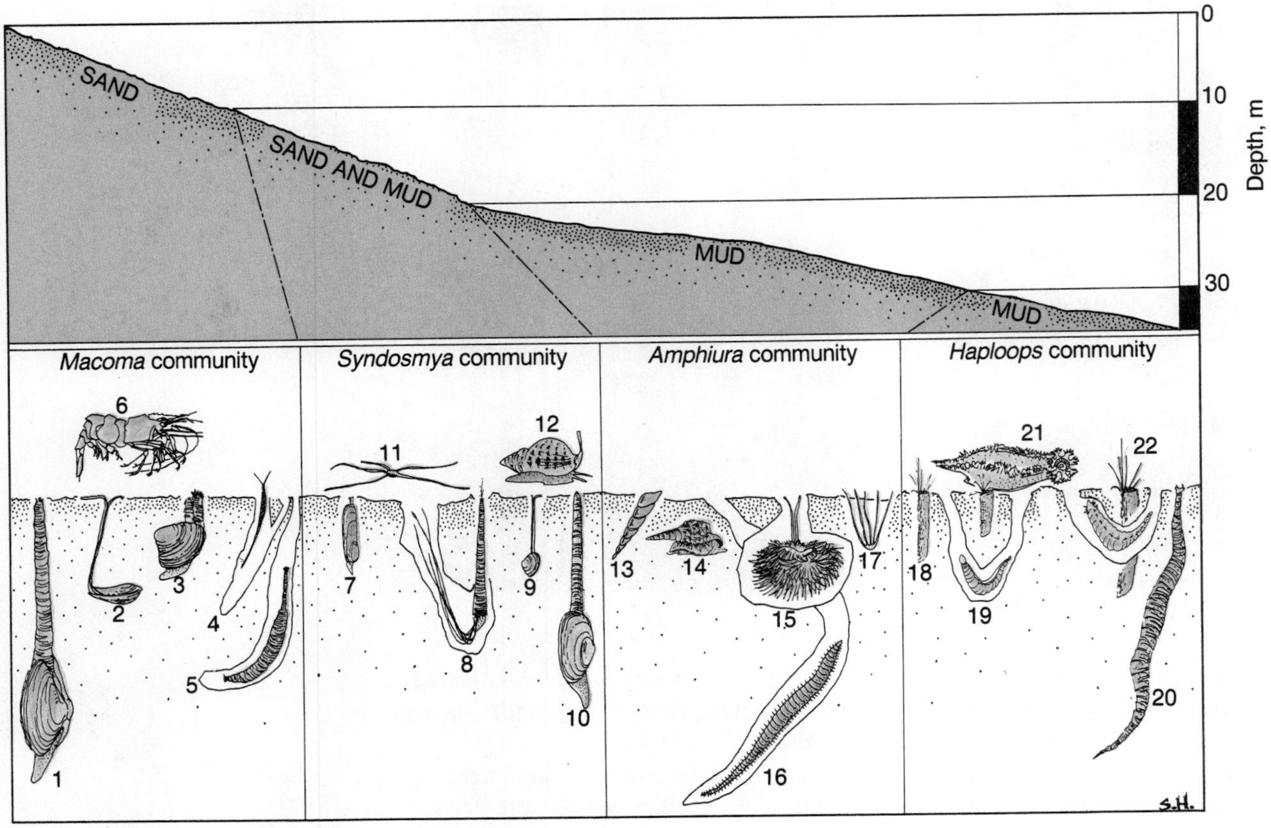

Figure 7.15
A series of soft-bottom benthic communities in the Danish seas, including bivalve mollusks (1, 2, 3, 7, 9, 10), gastropod mollusks (12, 13, 14), crustaceans (4, 6, 18, 22), polychaete worms (5, 8, 16, 19, 20), and echinoderms (11, 15, 17, 21)
Adapted from Thorson, 1968

Subtidal Communities

Living conditions on the sea bottom change gradually as wave action, light intensity, and water temperature diminish with increasing depth. Sand and mud deposits become more extensive and dominate the seafloor below the low tide line. The soft bottoms of the continental shelves are comparatively level and are characterized by a uniformity and simplicity of environmental conditions not found along the intertidal shoreline. Benthic plants are largely restricted to occasional small reefs, rocky outcrops, and kelp forests on the inner shelf. Nearly all the bottom fauna are dependent on the slow rain of plankton and detritus from the sunlit photic zone above. Filter-feeders, deposit-feeders, and their predators are well established.

Shallow Muddy Bottoms

Extensive studies of the life in shallow-water soft bottoms were initiated by the Danish biologist, C. G. J. Petersen, in the early part of the twentieth century. His intent was to evaluate the quantity of food available for flounders and other commercially useful bottom fish. After sorting and analyzing thousands of bottom samples from Danish seas, Petersen concluded that large areas of the level sea bottom are inhabited by recurring associations, or communities, of infaunal species (figure 7.15). Each community has a few very conspicuous or abundant macrofauna as well as several less obvious forms. On other bottom types, distinct communities of other species can be found. When

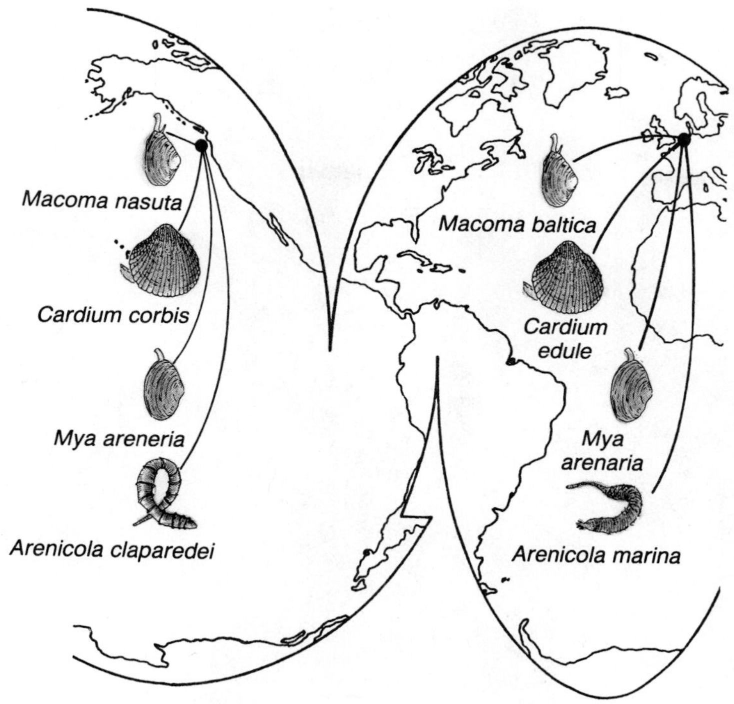

Figure 7.16
Diagram showing the close similarity in composition of soft-bottom communities in the northeast Pacific and the northeast Atlantic
Adapted from Thorson, 1957

exposed to similar combinations of environmental conditions, widely separated shallow-bottom communities in temperate waters closely resemble each other in structure and species composition (figure 7.16). Although Peterson considered his communities statistical units only, these recurring and predictable links between certain animal species and particular environmental features led G. Thorson to argue for the recognition of Petersen's communities as biological realities.

Since Petersen's time, a prime objective of many benthic ecologists has been to describe the manner in which the benthos is distributed on the seafloor and to explain how this distribution is related to the sediments, the overlying water, and the influence of community members on each other. Using diving gear for direct observations in shallow water and an assortment of dredges, trawls, and grabs to obtain bottom samples in deeper water, benthic ecologists have found parallel shallow-water communities in much of the cold and temperate regions of the world ocean. This parallel community concept has been extended beyond obvious animal associations to include bottom type, depth, and water temperature as additional key factors in shaping benthic community structures. However, Petersen's concept of parallel communities breaks down in tropical and subtropical waters. Here, large numbers of species exist, and seldom does a single species dominate a community.

The Abyss

Beyond the continental shelves, the sea bottom descends sharply to the stygian depths of the deep-sea floor. Three-quarters of the ocean bottom (the abyssal and hadal zones of figure 1.30) lie at depths below 3,000 m. Studies of deep-sea life have been fragmentary, slowed by the cost of sampling the ocean's

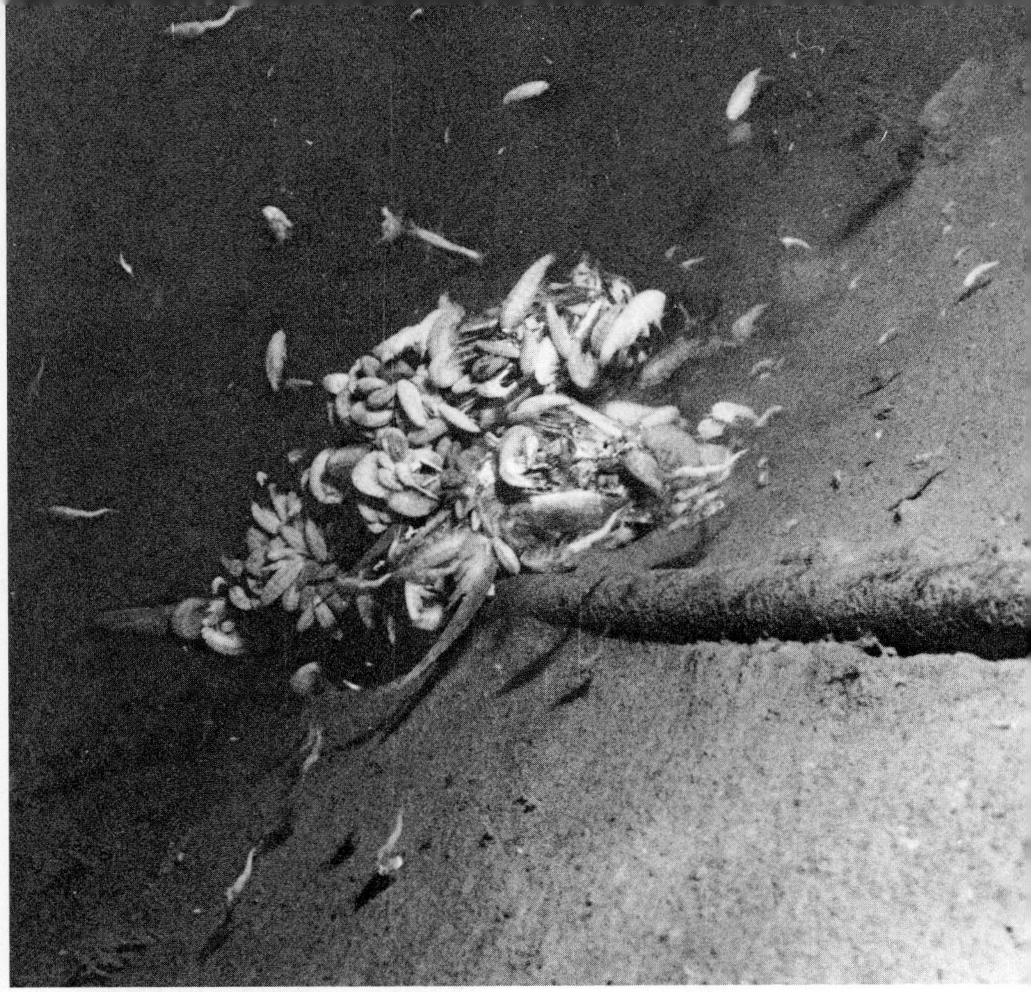

Figure 7.17

A group of large crustacean amphipods feeding on bait in the Peru-Chile Trench at a depth of 7,000 m. For scale, the cable at right is just over 6 cm in diameter.

Courtesy Scripps Institution of Oceanography, Marine Life Research Group

bottom and by the difficulties of bringing healthy deep-sea animals to the surface for observations. Captured animals encounter extreme temperature and pressure changes when hauled from the bottom. By the time they reach the surface, they are usually dead or seriously damaged.

The deep sea is one of the most rigorous and constant environments on earth. Because there is no sunlight, there are no primary producers. The bottom, with very few exceptions, is composed of soft, fine-grained clays and accumulated skeletal remains of near-surface plankton. The water is cold, averaging 2° C and dipping slightly below 0° C in polar regions. Pressures created by the overlying water are tremendous; pressures vary between 300 and 600 **atmospheres (atm)** on the abyssal seafloor and exceed 1,000 atm in the deepest trenches. (Each 10 m of water depth adds another atmosphere of pressure.) Laboratory studies have confirmed that metabolic rates of deep-sea bacteria are lower at pressures normally experienced on the seafloor than they are at sea surface pressures. Less is known about the response of multicellular organisms to high pressures, but a few studies suggest pressure-induced reductions in metabolic rates lead to lowered growth and reproductive rates and increased life spans in the deep sea. It has been suggested that the occasional gigantism found in some deep-sea species is due to the metabolic adjustments to the extreme pressures. Because the effects of extreme pressures on growth rates and maximum sizes of deep-sea animals are not yet known, such speculation may be premature (figure 7.17).

The inhabitants of the deep-sea floor are a distinctive group even though few exhibit structural adaptations that make them appear notably different from their shallow-water relatives. Instead, a shift in dominant taxonomic groups occurs in deeper water. Echinoderms (especially sea cucumbers and crinoids), polychaete worms, pycnogonids, and isopod and amphipod crustaceans become abundant whereas bivalves and other mollusks and sea stars decline in number. Some taxonomic groups are virtually absent until relatively great depths are reached. Most species of pogonophorans, for instance, are found below 3,000 m, and 30% of them are restricted to trenches below 5,000 m.

It is not possible to establish a precise global depth boundary between the animals of the deep sea and the shallow-water fauna of the continental shelves. Generally, the boundary exists as a vague region of transition on the continental slopes bordering the deep-sea basin. However, animals of the "deep sea" commonly extend into shallower water in polar seas and, on occasion, even extend to the inner portions of continental shelves.

In the physically stable environment of the deep sea, patterns of reproduction are thought to differ appreciably from the reproduction patterns of shallow-water benthic animals. Very few deep-water benthic species produce planktonic larvae because the larvae's chances of reaching the food-rich photic zone several km above and successfully returning to the ocean floor for permanent settlement are extremely remote. To compensate for the absence of a dependable external food supply, larger eggs are produced. The larvae are supplied with adequate yolks so they can develop to fairly advanced stages prior to hatching. Brood pouches and other similar adaptations further enhance the chances of survival by protecting the eggs until they hatch. Consequently, the larvae have a reasonable chance of completing their development in one of the most severe environments on earth.

Low temperatures, high pressures, and a limited food supply led to an early and widespread belief that the rigorous and specialized climate of the deep sea would not support a highly diversified assemblage of animals. It was assumed that only a few highly adapted animals could succeed in the abyss. But because of recent improvements in sampling equipment, deep-sea communities have been found to contain a variety of species comparable to or even exceeding soft-bottom communities in shallow inshore waters. To explain the unexpected diversity of deep-sea life, researchers hypothesize that the number of deep-sea species has gradually increased as the species adjusted to each other and assumed narrower, more specialized niches within their stable environment. This may leave underused resources open to exploitation by other narrowly specialized species.

A critical and variable resource in the deep sea is food. In the open ocean, food for deep-sea benthic communities, by necessity, comes from above; but little is known of the food's condition when it arrives at the bottom. After being repeatedly consumed by pelagic scavengers and bacteria, small plankton particles may be of little nutritive value by the time they settle to the bottom. However, before leaving the photic zone, much of the near-surface plankton production is aggregated into large compacted fecal pellets of zooplankton, which settle more rapidly to the bottom. This fallout of fecal particles accelerates the transport of organic material to the abyss, falling from the surface waters in a few days rather than the weeks or months of settling time necessary for smaller plankton particles.

Figure 7.18

Macurid fish scavenging around a bait can (center) lowered 5.850 m to the sea bottom north of Hawaii

Courtesy Scripps Institution of Oceanography, Marine Life Research Group

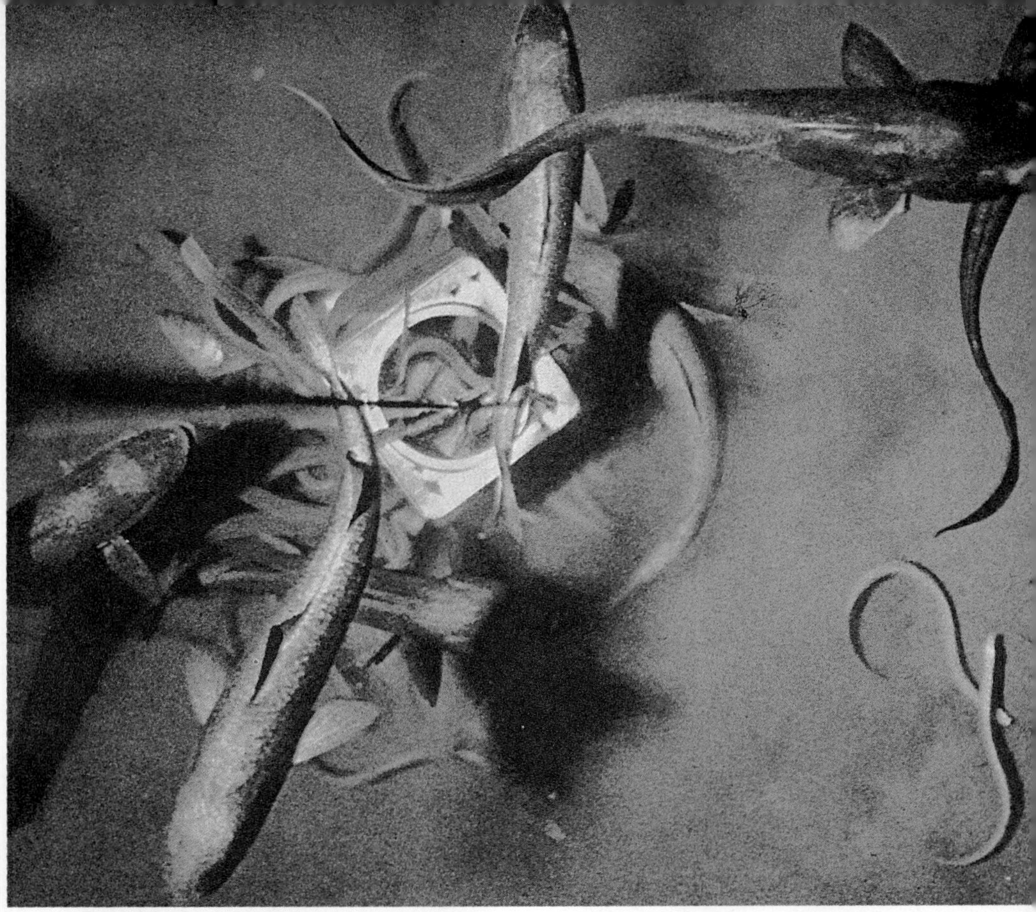

Large, rapidly sinking particles, including dead squids, fish, and an occasional whale, may provide a significant, although unpredictable supply of food to the deep-sea floor inhabitants. If large food parcels do contribute significantly to the energy budget of the deep sea, they are rapidly consumed by various wide-ranging scavenger-predators (figure 7.18). Most scavenger-predators seem swift enough to evade bottom trawls and are best known from photographs taken by underwater cameras baited with food. They seem to be food generalists, capable of rapidly locating and dispatching large food items as they arrive on the bottom. Some of the food is eventually dispersed as detritus and fecal wastes to the remainder of the bottom community.

A portion of the smaller particles of organic material settling to the bottom is immediately claimed by suspension feeders. However, the majority of benthic animals in the deep sea are infaunal deposit feeders. Analyses of their stomach contents indicate that they indiscriminately engulf sediments containing smaller infauna and bacteria as well as dead organic material. Claude Zobell estimated that 30 to 40% of the organic material available at the bottom is first absorbed by benthic bacteria, which in turn are consumed by larger animals. An important component of the organic material is the chitinous exoskeletons shed by crustaceans; it cannot be digested by most animals but is decomposed and utilized by bacteria.

Dayton and Hessler have proposed the general term **"cropper"** for deep-sea animals that have merged the roles of predator and deposit feeder (figure 7.19). They suggest that these croppers, by preying heavily on populations of smaller deposit feeders, are responsible for reducing competition for

Figure 7.19
An aggregation of deep-sea cucumbers, *Scotoplanes,* feeding on bottom deposits at a depth of approximately 1,000 m
Courtesy E. Barham, National Marine Fisheries Service

food and for permitting coexistence between species sharing the same food resource. Thus, even though a deep-sea community as a whole is food-limited, populations within the community need not be as long as they are heavily preyed upon. With competition for food reduced by cropping, fewer species are pushed to extinction (on a local scale) and the diversity of the community remains high. The disruptive effects of large croppers on smaller ones can be compared to predators, ice, or logs, as disturbance mechanisms in rocky intertidal communities. By nonselectively reducing competition, they lessen the possibility of a species being excluded from a community, or from existence, by resource competition.

Deep-Sea Hot Springs

Tectonic spreading centers along seafloor ridge and rise systems are sites of active vulcanism. Several remarkable discoveries associated with these centers have been made in the past two decades. These discoveries are radically changing our understanding of life in the deep sea and are clarifying how metal-rich mineral deposits are formed from chemical interaction between seawater and the earth's crust. At seafloor ridge and rise axes, crustal plates are spreading apart (see figure 1.5), and molten magma is rising to fill the gap. The molten magma cools, solidifies, and creates a new oceanic crust. This oceanic crust is basalt, a black volcanic rock. It was predicted that hot springs like those found in Yellowstone National Park also occur in the deep sea at areas of comparable volcanic activity.

Figure 7.20
Locations of deep-sea vent communities on the axis of the East Pacific Rise. Other vent communities have been discovered on the Mid-Atlantic Ridge and at a nonridge site in the South Pacific Ocean.
Courtesy National Geophysical Data Center

Deep-sea hot springs were first directly observed in 1977 when a team of geologists studying the Galapagos Rift Zone west of Equador discovered several remarkable assemblages of living animals nearly 3 km deep. Dense aggregations of large mussels, clams, giant tube worms, and crabs were found clustered in small areas of shimmering warm water pouring from the seafloor.

The Galapagos Rift Zone is a site of active seafloor spreading, with extensive lava flows so young that very little sediment has had a chance to accumulate. In the few years since this discovery, enough other vent communities have been found along the axes of both the Mid-Atlantic Ridge and the East Pacific Rise to suggest that such communities may be a normal feature of hot, actively spreading rift zones in other oceans as well (figure 7.20).

Water temperature sometimes exceeds 100° C at the hot spring sites, in sharp contrast to the near-uniform 2° C abyssal water just a few meters away. These hot springs are the end product of seawater circulating through the many cracks and fissures of the new crust as it forms along the axes of the rise system. It has been estimated that a volume of water equivalent to the volume of all the earth's oceans circulates through these ridge crack systems approximately every 8 million years.

As seawater percolates through these cracks, it is heated to about 350° C, and some complex chemistry occurs between the circulating seawater and the hot basaltic rock of the ocean crust. Sulfate (SO_4^{-2}) is the third most abundant ion dissolved in seawater. When heated, sulfate reacts with water to form hydrogen sulfide (H_2S). H_2S, in spite of being toxic to most animals, then plays a central role in subsequent processes as the heated water emerges from the seafloor vent as a hot spring.

Some of the H_2S reacts with iron and other metal ions within the crust to form metal sulfides in concentrations several million times greater than those found in average seawater. At the vent opening, this super-enriched metal sulfide solution quickly mixes with cold surrounding seawater, and a dense black "smoke" of iron sulfide particles is produced (figure 7.21). These particles either settle immediately around the vent or are oxidized by dissolved oxygen to produce thick deposits of metal oxides in the vicinity of the hot spring.

The massive quantities of H_2S spewing from the chimneys atop these hot springs (known as "black smokers," figure 7.22) are utilized as a primary energy source by perpetual dense blooms of bacteria. Bacteria use dissolved O_2 from the surrounding water to oxidize the abundant H_2S back to SO_4^{-2}, releasing energy in the process. These bacteria are the primary producers of the hot spring communities, relying on **chemosynthesis** rather than photosynthesis to fuel their metabolic requirements. The bacteria in turn are consumed by dense populations of clams and mussels that are found nowhere else in the sea.

The clams and mussels are suspension feeders well-adapted to remove the extremely small bacterial cells from the water. The red-plumed giant vestimentiferid worm, *Riftia* (figure 7.23), however, completely lacks a digestive tract. Instead, it maintains internal bacterial symbionts that oxidize H_2S within a specialized organ, the **trophosome.** Major blood vessels link the trophosome to the bright red **obturacular plume,** where gas exchange occurs. The blood of *Riftia* contains two proteins to deal with the high concentrations of dissolved H_2S and small amounts of dissolved O_2 in the deep-sea hot spring environment. The first protein is a rare sulfide binding protein used to transport large

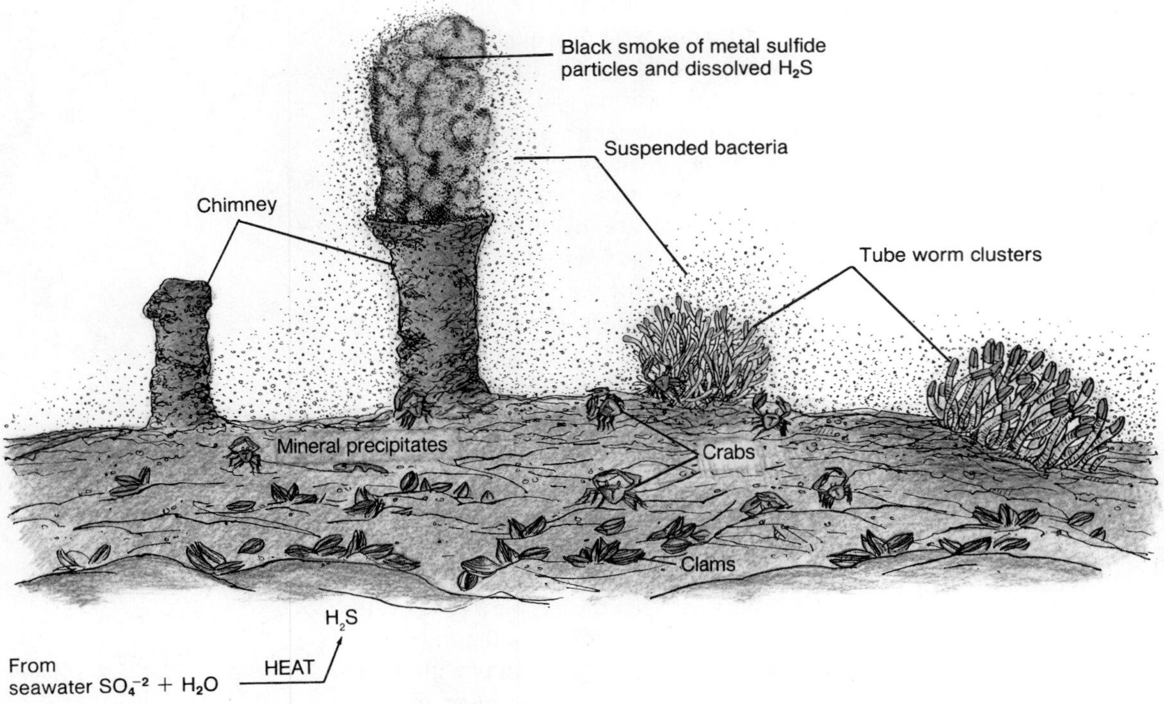

Figure 7.21
A simplified drawing of a deep-sea hot spring community. Some of the organisms shown here can also be seen in figure 7.23.

quantities of H_2S from the obturacular plume, where it is absorbed, to the trophosome, where it is used by bacterial symbionts. **Hemoglobin,** the other blood protein, is used to bind and transport O_2 within these animals.

In these deep-sea hot spring communities, bacterial use of O_2 from the water in the immediate vicinity of the vents is extensive. To compete effectively with bacteria for the limited available O_2, larger animals need some type of blood pigment with a strong affinity for O_2. Hemoglobin is abundant in *Riftia* and in large bivalve mollusks, including the giant white clam *(Calyptogena)*. In the crabs most commonly found in deep-sea hot spring communities *(Bythograea),* the blue pigment **hemocyanin** is used instead. The blood pigments of these hot spring animals are typically quite insensitive to changing temperatures. Such temperature insensitivity is unusual and likely has evolved to accommodate the extremely wide range of water temperatures experienced over very short distances around vents. These pigments thus assist the larger deep-sea hot spring animals to extract the little O_2 left over by the abundant bacteria. With these adaptations, these populations of benthic animals have tapped into an unusual energy source—the heat and chemicals of the earth's crust—and have achieved a nutritional emancipation from the fall-out products of the photic zone above.

How these hot springs are initially colonized is still a puzzle. The distances between hot spring communities are often a thousand km or more, and several "bridging" mechanisms to explain the presence of the same species at different hot springs have been proposed. An intriguing one is the outgrowth of a modest observation made off the California coast in 1987 from the deep-sea research submersible *Alvin.* A decomposing, but still identifiable,

Figure 7.22
A black smoker on the Galápagos Rift Zone
Photo by D. Foster

Figure 7.23
Red-plumed tube worms, *Riftia,* with a few other members of this unusual deep-sea community.
Courtesy Scripps Institution of Oceanography

whale carcass on the sea floor was surrounded by numerous clams of two species previously seen only at hot spring sites. Dense mats of sulfide bacteria were also found. This suggests that hot spring community members "hop" from carcass to carcass, eventually moving long distances along the sea bottom. It is now yet known if such 'whalefalls' occur frequently enough to provide the larval-hopping network of food-rich material necessary to bridge the distances which exist between these remarkable deep-sea communities.

Summary

The sea bottom is one of the most varied and, in places, rigorous habitats on earth. The variety of benthic life forms attests to the diverse range of niches available on the bottom. The seafloor, the water just above the bottom, and other living plants and animals all shape the environmental conditions faced by the benthos. Feeding, locomotion, and reproduction are all strongly influenced by characteristics of the sea bottom.

Dispersal of many shallow-water benthic species is accomplished with planktonic larval forms that are usually quite different in appearance from their parents. During their planktonic existence, these larvae experience environmental pressures often unknown to their bottom-dwelling adults.

The benthic animals of the abyss are not well known. They experience little in the way of fluctuations in their physical environment and are limited by the absence of a constant and abundant food supply. Most are thought to have very generalized feeding habits and to function either as wide-ranging predator-scavengers or as sedentary croppers.

Deep-sea hot springs, recently discovered along the axis of the East Pacific Rise, support unique communities of deep-sea animals. Dissolved H_2S emerging from seafloor cracks is used as an energy source by chemosynthetic bacteria. The bacteria in turn are the source of nutrition for dense animal populations clustered around these springs.

Review Questions

1. List two specific advantages and two disadvantages of broadcast spawning by shallow-water benthic animals.
2. List the various feeding methods of benthic animals and relate those methods to the type of substrate the animals occupy.
3. List and discuss the ecological and survival advantages of planktonic larval stages for benthic animals living in shallow water.
4. Why are planktonic larval forms not equally advantageous for the benthic animals of the abyss?

Questions for Further Discussion

1. Where in the Atlantic Ocean would you predict that additional deep-sea hot springs and their associated communities might be found? Why?

Suggestions for Further Reading

Books

Ernst, W. G., and J. G. Morin, eds. 1982. *The environment of the deep sea.* Englewood Cliffs, NJ: Prentice-Hall, Inc.

Higgins, R. P., and H. Thiel, eds. 1988. *Introduction to the study of meiofauna.* Washington, D.C.: Smithsonian Institution Press.

Articles

Arp, A. J., and J. J. Childress. 1983. Sulfide binding by the blood of the hydrothermal vent tube worm *Riftia pachyptila. Science* 219:295–97.

Childress, J., H. Felback, and G. Somero. 1987. Symbiosis in the deep sea. *Scientific American* 256(5):114–20.

Corliss, J. B., and R. D. Ballard. 1977. Oases of life in the cold abyss. *National Geographic* 152:441–53.

Edmond, J. M., and K. Von Damm. 1983. Hot springs on the ocean floor. *Scientific American,* April:78–93.

Hollister, C. D., A. R. M. Nowell, and P. A. Jumars. 1984. The dynamic abyss. *Scientific American,* March:42–53.

Jannasch, H. W., and C. O. Wirsen. 1977. Microbial life in the deep sea. *Scientific American,* 236 (June):42–52.

Rex, M. A. 1973. Deep-sea species diversity: Decreased gastropod diversity at abyssal depths. *Science* 181:1051–53.

Schener, P. J. 1977. Chemical communication of marine invertebrates. *Bioscience* 27:644–68.

Sebens, K. P. 1985. The ecology of the rocky subtidal zone. *American Scientist* 73:548–57.

Intertidal Communities

Chapter 8

Intertidal rocks

The coastal strip where land meets the sea is home to some of the richest and best studied marine communities found anywhere. Although this coastal strip is narrow, its influence is enhanced by the wealth of marine organisms present. Typically, the total biomass in a square meter at the low tide line is at least ten times higher than that of a comparable area on the bottom at 200 m and is several thousand times higher than that found in most abyssal areas.

The periodic rise and fall of the tides have a dramatic effect on a portion of the coastal zone known as the intertidal, or **littoral,** zone. In the littoral zone, the sea, the land, and the air all play important roles in establishing the complex physical and chemical conditions to which all intertidal plants and animals must adapt. Before proceeding to a detailed study of intertidal communities, we will examine the mechanics and resulting patterns of ocean tides.

T*ides*

Tides are ocean surface phenomena familiar to anyone who has spent time on a seashore. They are very long period waves that are usually imperceptible in the open ocean and become noticeable only against coastlines where they can be observed as a periodic rise and fall of the sea surface. (Compare these waves to other ocean waves in figure 1.22.) The maximum elevation of the tide, known as **high tide,** is followed by a fall in sea level to a minimum elevation, the **low tide.** On most coastlines, two high tides and two low tides occur each day. The vertical difference between consecutive high tides and low tides is the **tidal range,** which varies from a few centimeters in the Mediterranean Sea to over 15 m in the long, narrow Bay of Fundy between Nova Scotia and New Brunswick.

In 1687, in his *Principia Mathematica,* Sir Isaac Newton explained ocean tides as the consequence of the gravitational attraction of the moon and sun on the oceans of the earth. Newton's law of universal gravitation states that the gravitational attraction between two bodies is directly proportional to their masses and inversely proportional to the square of the distance between the bodies. The mass of the sun is about 27,000,000 times greater than that of the moon. Yet the moon exercises twice as much influence on the earth's tides because the earth-moon distance is 1/400th of the earth-sun distance.

The moon completes one orbit around the earth each lunar month (27.5 days). To maintain that orbit, the gravitational attraction between the earth and moon must exactly balance the centrifugal force holding the bodies apart. In concert, these two opposing forces create two tide-producing forces at the earth's surface.

Hypothetically, if the earth were completely covered with water, two bulges of water, or lunar tides, would pile up; one on the side of the earth facing the moon and the other on the opposite side of the globe (figure 8.1). As the earth makes a complete rotation every 24 hours, a point on the earth's surface (indicated by the marker in figure 8.1) would first experience a high tide (a), then a low tide (b), another high tide (c), another low tide (d), and finally another high tide (e). During that rotation, however, the moon advances in its own orbit so that an additional 50 minutes of the earth's rotation is required to bring that point directly in line with the moon again. Thus the reference point experiences only two equal high and two equal low tides every 24 hours and 50 minutes (a lunar day).

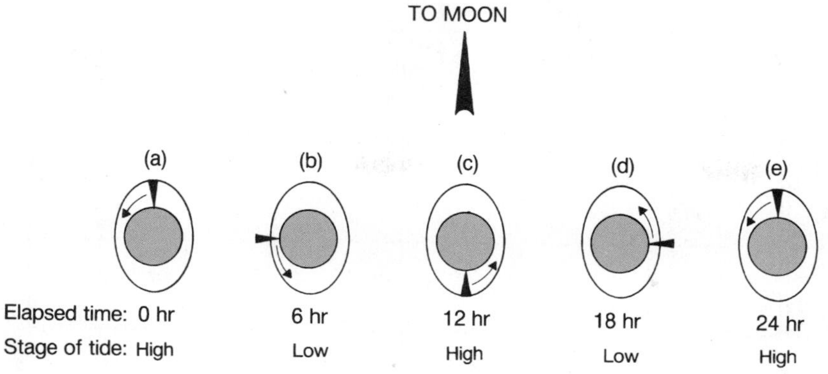

Figure 8.1
Each day as the earth rotates, a point on its surface (indicated by the marker) experiences high tides when under tidal bulges and low tides when at right angles to tidal bulges.

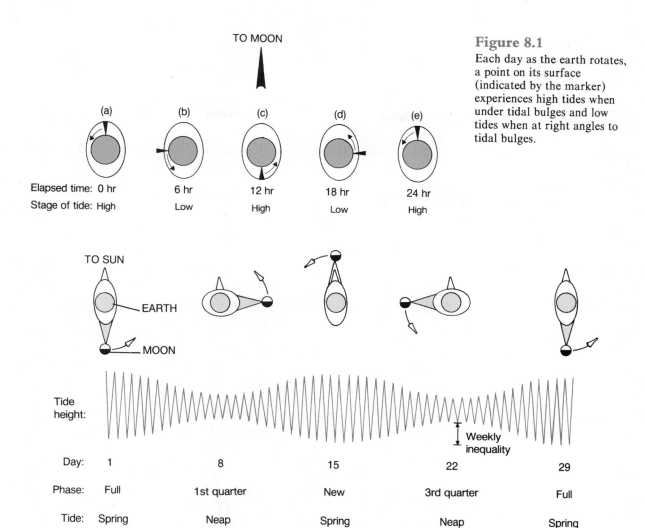

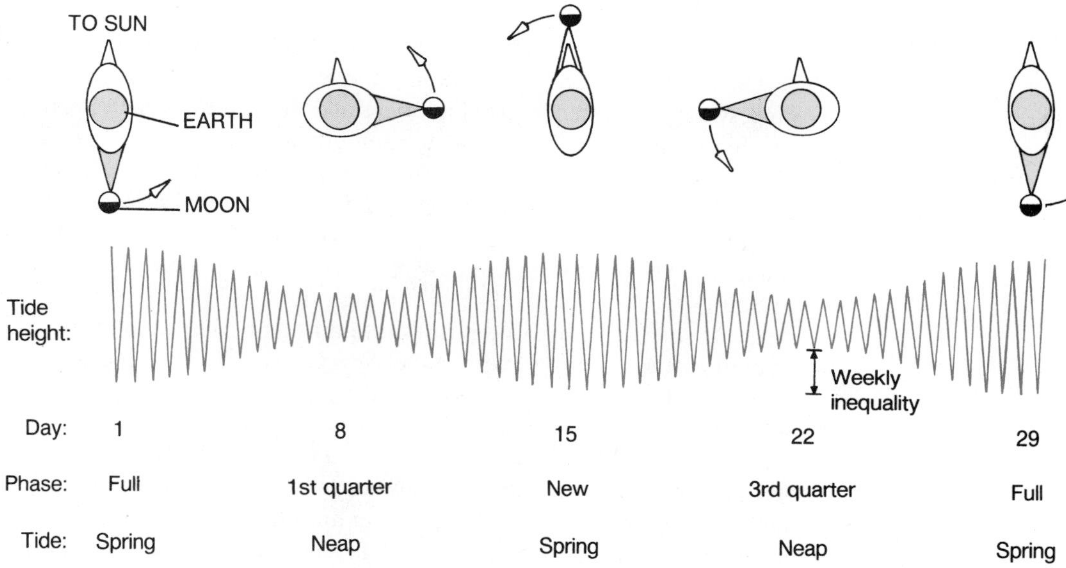

Figure 8.2
Weekly tidal variations caused by changes in the relative positions of the earth, moon, and sun

In a similar manner, the sun-earth system also generates tide-producing forces that yield a solar tide about one-half as large as the lunar tide. The solar tide is expressed as a variation on the basic lunar tidal pattern, not as a separate set of tides. When the sun, moon, and earth are in alignment (at the time of the new and full moon, figure 8.2), the solar tide has an additive effect on the lunar tide, creating extra-high high tides and very-low low tides (**spring tides**). One week later, when the sun and moon are at right angles to each other, the solar tide partially cancels the lunar tide to produce moderate tides known as **neap tides.** During each lunar month, two sets of spring tides and two sets of neap tides occur.

So far, we have considered only the effects of tide-producing forces in a not very realistic ocean covering a hypothetical planet without continents. What happens when continental landmasses are taken into consideration? The continents act to block the westward passage of the tidal bulges as the earth rotates under them. Unable to move freely around the globe, these tidal impulses establish complex patterns within each ocean basin that often differ markedly from the tidal patterns of adjacent ocean basins or other regions of the same ocean basin.

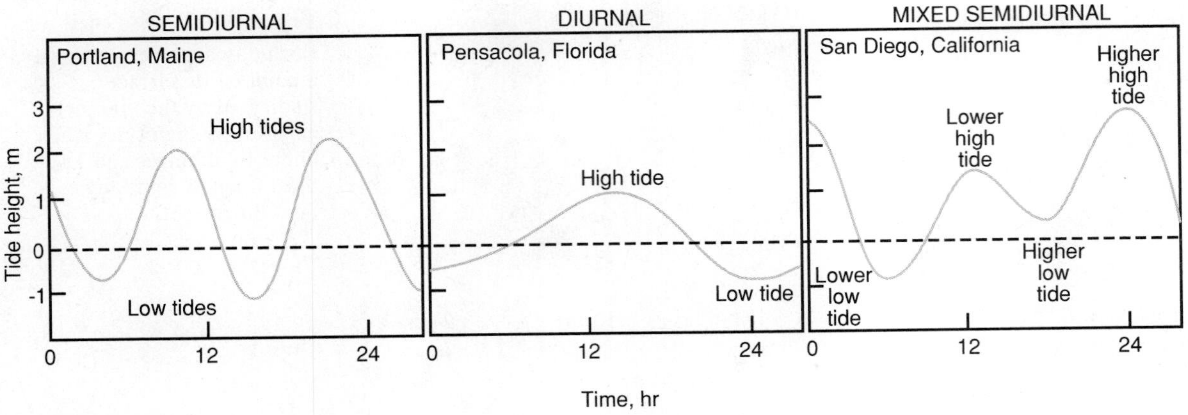

Figure 8.3
Three common types of tides

Figure 8.3 shows some regional variations in the daily tidal configuration at three stations along the east and west coasts of North America. Portland, Maine, experiences two high tides and two low tides each lunar day. The two high tides are quite similar to each other, as are the two low tides. Such tidal patterns, referred to as **semidiurnal** (semidaily) tides, are characteristic of much of the East Coast of the United States. The tidal pattern at Pensacola, Florida, on the Gulf Coast, consists of one high tide and one low tide each lunar day. This is a **diurnal,** or daily, tide. Different yet is the daily tidal pattern at San Diego, California. There, two high tides and two low tides occur each day, but successive high tides are quite different from each other. This type of tidal pattern, characteristic of the West Coast of North America, is a **mixed semidiurnal** tide. Figure 8.4 outlines the geographical occurrence of diurnal, semidiurnal, and mixed semidiurnal tides.

Tidal conditions for any day on a selected coastline can be predicted because the periodic nature of tides is easily observed and recorded. For the most part, prediction of the timing and amplitude of future tides is based on historical observations of past tidal occurrences at tide-recording stations along coastlines and in harbors around the world. The National Ocean Survey of the United States Department of Commerce uses information from these records to compile and publish annual "Tide Tables of High and Low Water Predictions" for principal ports along most coastlines of the world.

Intertidal Communities

Tidal fluctuations of sea level often expose intertidal plants and animals to severe environmental extremes, alternating between complete submergence in seawater and nearly dry terrestrial conditions. Local characteristics of the tides, including their vertical range and frequency, determine the amount of time intertidal plants and animals are out of water and exposed to air. Still, regardless of their locations, most intertidal regions have exposure curves that resemble figure 8.5.

For most intertidal plants and animals, low tide is a time of physiological stress. When the tide is out, exposed organisms are subjected to wide variations of atmospheric conditions. The air may dry and overheat their tissues in hot weather or freeze them during cold weather. Rainfall and freshwater runoff create osmotic problems as well. Predatory land animals, such as birds, rats, and raccoons, also make their presence felt in the intertidal zone

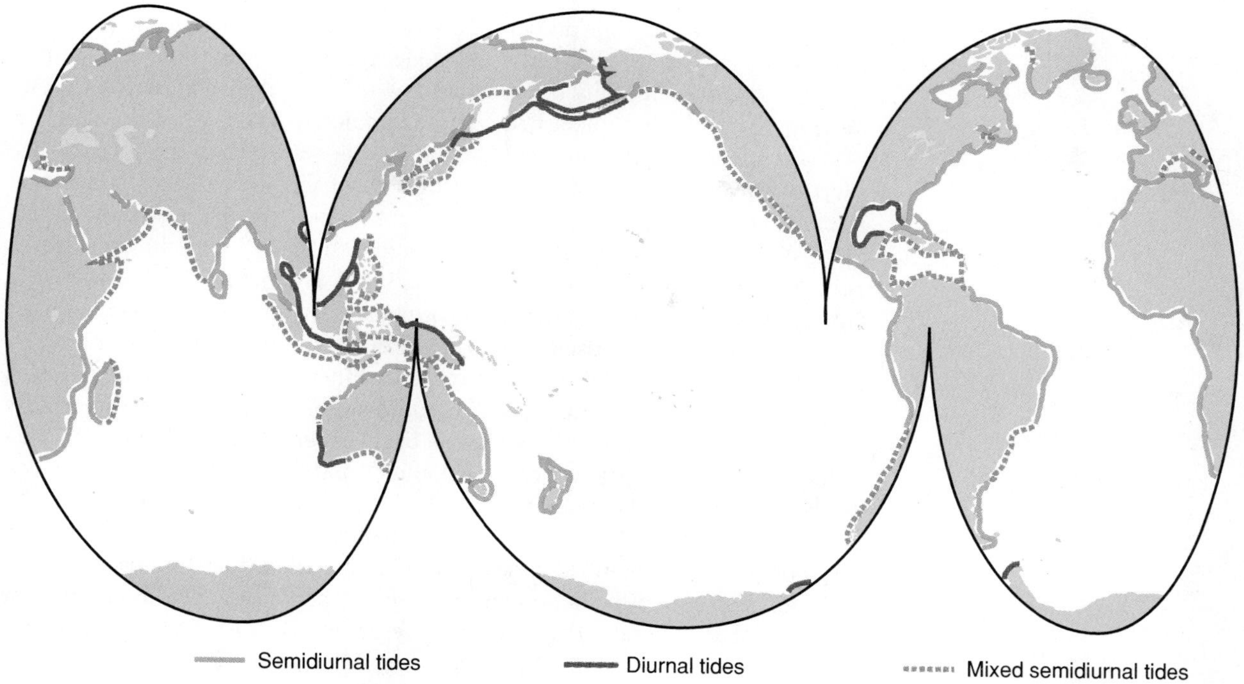

Figure 8.4
The geographical occurrence of the three types of tides described in figure 8.3

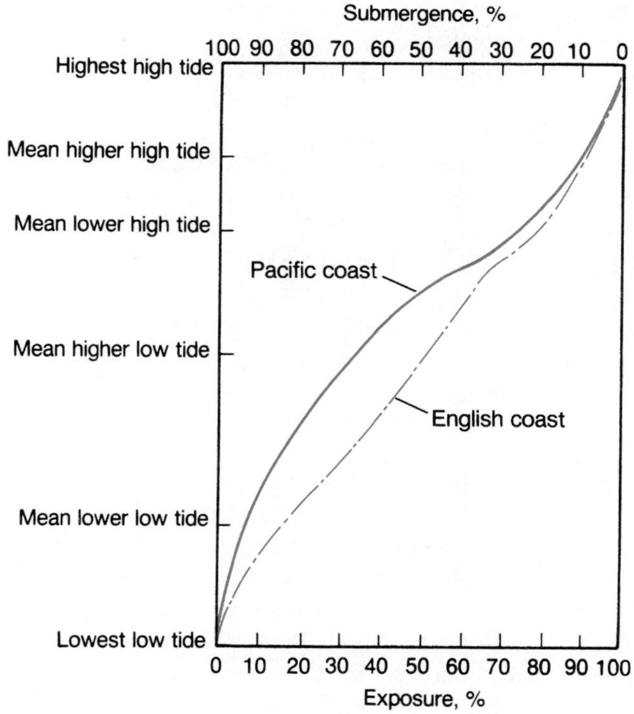

Figure 8.5
Exposure curves for the Pacific coast of the United States and the Atlantic coast of England
Adapted from Ricketts and Calvin, 1968, and Lewis, 1964

at low tide. Only at high tide are truly marine conditions restored to the intertidal zone. The returning waters moderate the temperature and salinity fluctuations brought on by the previous low tide. Needed food, nutrients, and dissolved oxygen are replenished, and accumulated wastes are washed away.

Accompanying the beneficial effects of seawater is the physical assault of waves and surf. The influence of wave shock on the distribution of intertidal plants and animals is apparent on all exposed coastlines of the world. Surf, storm waves, and surface ocean currents shift and sort sediments, transport suspended food, and disperse reproductive products. Much of the wave energy expended on the shore and the organisms living there eventually serves to shape and alter the essential character of the shoreline itself. Continually modified by the power of ocean waves, shorelines assume a variety of forms (figure 8.6). Rocky shorelines are constantly swept clean of finer sediments by heavy surf or strong currents. Waves on beaches remove fine silt and clay particles but leave sand grains behind. The finer materials are washed out to sea or are deposited in the quiet, protected waters of bays and lagoons.

The variety of tidal conditions, bottom types, and wave intensities along the shore create a boundless assortment of living conditions for coastal plants and animals. It is difficult to characterize the prevailing conditions on long stretches of shoreline without risking overgeneralization. The west coast of North America, for instance, has many rugged rocky cliffs exposed to the full force of wave action. Yet interspersed between these cliffs and headlands are numerous sandy beaches and quiet mud-bottom bays and estuaries. On the East Coast, conditions vary from the spectacular rugged coastline of northern New England and the Canadian Maritime Provinces to extensive sandy beaches in the mid-Atlantic states. From Chesapeake Bay south to Florida, numerous coastal marshes are protected from extensive wave action by long, low barrier islands that parallel the mainland. Similar conditions with smaller tidal ranges exist along much of the Gulf Coast (see figure 6.2b).

The southern tip of Florida is the only shoreline on the continental United States to experience tropical conditions. Tropical shorelines are typically marked by large coral reefs (see chapter 9) or by extensive swampy woodlands of mangroves. The coral reef system off the Florida Keys, fairly typical for the Caribbean, is unlike any other part of the continental United States. Mangroves grow in profusion along Florida's southern coast and recently have become established along the extreme southern Texas coast. Included among these mangroves are several types of shrubby and treelike plants that grow together to form impenetrable thickets. Their branching prop roots trap sediments and detritus to extend existing shorelines or to form new low-lying islands.

Within a particular type of coastal environment, the interrelated influences of tidal exposure, bottom type, and intensity of wave shock produce an infinitely varied set of vertically arranged habitats. The vertical distribution of coastal plants and animals reflects the vertical changes in the shoreline's environmental conditions. Different species tend to occupy different levels or zones within the intertidal shoreline. Quite often, each zone is sharply demarcated from adjacent zones by the color, texture, and general appearance of the species living there. The result is a well-defined vertical series of horizontal life zones, sometimes extending for substantial horizontal distances along a coastline.

Figure 8.6
An aerial photograph of a portion of the Oregon coast with protected coves, exposed headlands, sandy beaches, and offshore rocky reefs. Note the complex pattern of wave refraction around the offshore reefs.
Courtesy U.S. Geological Survey

Figure 8.7
The relative force of breaking waves over a range of wave heights for several different intertidal animals
Adapted from Denny, 1985

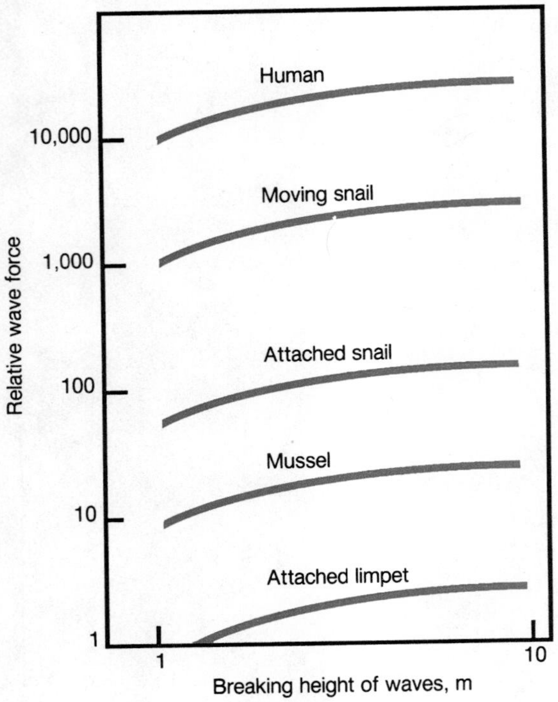

The vertical distribution of intertidal plants and animals is governed by a complex set of environmental conditions that vary along gradients above and below the sea surface. Temperature, wave shock, light intensity, and wetness are some of the more important physical factors that vary along such gradients. Breaking waves can impose very large forces on intertidal organisms (figure 8.7). These organisms in turn demonstrate a remarkable variety of adaptations to deal with those forces. Several biological factors, including predation and competition for food and space, are superimposed on the physical gradients to further delineate the life zones of the shoreline. The combination of physical and biological factors frames and limits the range of an organism's existence. It, as well as the biological role the organism plays in its habitat, defines the organism's **niche.** The complex interplay of physical and biological conditions and the variety of shore life itself create an abundance of niches for intertidal organisms.

As the tides advance and recede over the intertidal portions of the shoreline, so too do the vertically graded changes in temperature, light intensity, degree of predation, and other environmental factors. Ocean tides are not the sole cause of vertical zonation within the intertidal shoreline. They do, however, modify and compress the pattern of zonation to make it more pronounced. (Vertically arranged sequences of plant and animal populations also can be found on mountainsides, in the sea beneath low tide, and in tideless lakes and ponds.)

For years, marine biologists have wrestled with the intricate problems of defining and identifying specific subzones within the intertidal shoreline. However, the multiplicity of factors influencing intertidal zonation have seriously compounded the task. As a result, each of the major subzones are frequently subdivided on the basis of locally abundant plant or animal populations. The makeup of intertidal populations may vary from place to place, causing the patterns of zonation to change; yet vertical zonation remains a visible unifying feature on all shorelines. It therefore seems a logical and appropriate basis on which to compare and describe the marine life of a few selected shores.

Rocky Shores

Chapter 2 emphasized that ecosystems have two complementary pathways for energy transfer: a grazing food chain and a detritus food chain. The grazing food chain routes energy and nutrient material from the primary producers through the grazers and predators. Detritus eaters utilize the bits and pieces of dead and decaying matter available within the ecosystem. Within the coastal zone, neither rocky shores nor sandy beaches appear to be complete ecosystems by themselves. The trophic relations within rocky shore communities exhibit well-developed and complicated grazing food chains but very little in the way of detritus food chains. The erosional nature of rocky shores simply prohibits the accumulation of detritus and the existence of those animals dependent on it for food.

In rocky intertidal communities, patterns of distribution and abundance, as well as trophic relationships, are complex and sometimes change dramatically over short distances and from season to season. A shaded northern exposure may harbor several species absent from nearby sunny slopes. Tide pools contain an assemblage of plants and animals quite different from that surrounding well-drained platforms. The variety of life on one side of a boulder may differ markedly from life on the other side. And if you look under the boulder, still other species may be found.

With such a bewildering array of niches available on a small stretch of shoreline, it might seem improbable to find recurring themes of vertical zonation on widely separated shorelines. Yet similar patterns of zonation do exist on temperate rocky shores, whether in New England, Australia, British Columbia, or South Africa. Vertical zonation is such a compelling feature of life on rocky shores that considerable effort has been expended in devising schemes to identify and describe distinct intertidal subzones and their inhabitants. If you desire a detailed account of life on intertidal rocky shores, several works with regional emphasis are listed at the end of this chapter.

The following discussion examines some of the more conspicuous intertidal plants and animals and the adaptations that permit them to remain conspicuous. Three rather ill-defined zones, the upper, middle, and lower intertidal zones, are used for reference. Because the boundaries separating these zones are artificial, they are frequently violated by their residents. You are likely to see species that dominate one zone scattered throughout other zones as well.

The Upper Intertidal

In the upper intertidal, living conditions are sometimes nearly as terrestrial as they are marine. Often only a vague demarcation separates land and marine vegetation.The area is wetted infrequently by extremely high tides and splash from breaking waves and is sparsely inhabited by marine organisms. Dark mats of the cyanobacterium *Calothrix* or the lichen *Verrucaria* frequently form a band or series of tarlike patches to mark the uppermost part of the rocky intertidal. Small tufts of *Ulothrix,* a filamentous green algae, may also extend into the highest parts of the intertidal. These plants are tolerant to large temperature changes and are adapted for resisting desiccation. The small, tangled filaments of *Calothrix* are embedded in a gelatinous mass to maintain

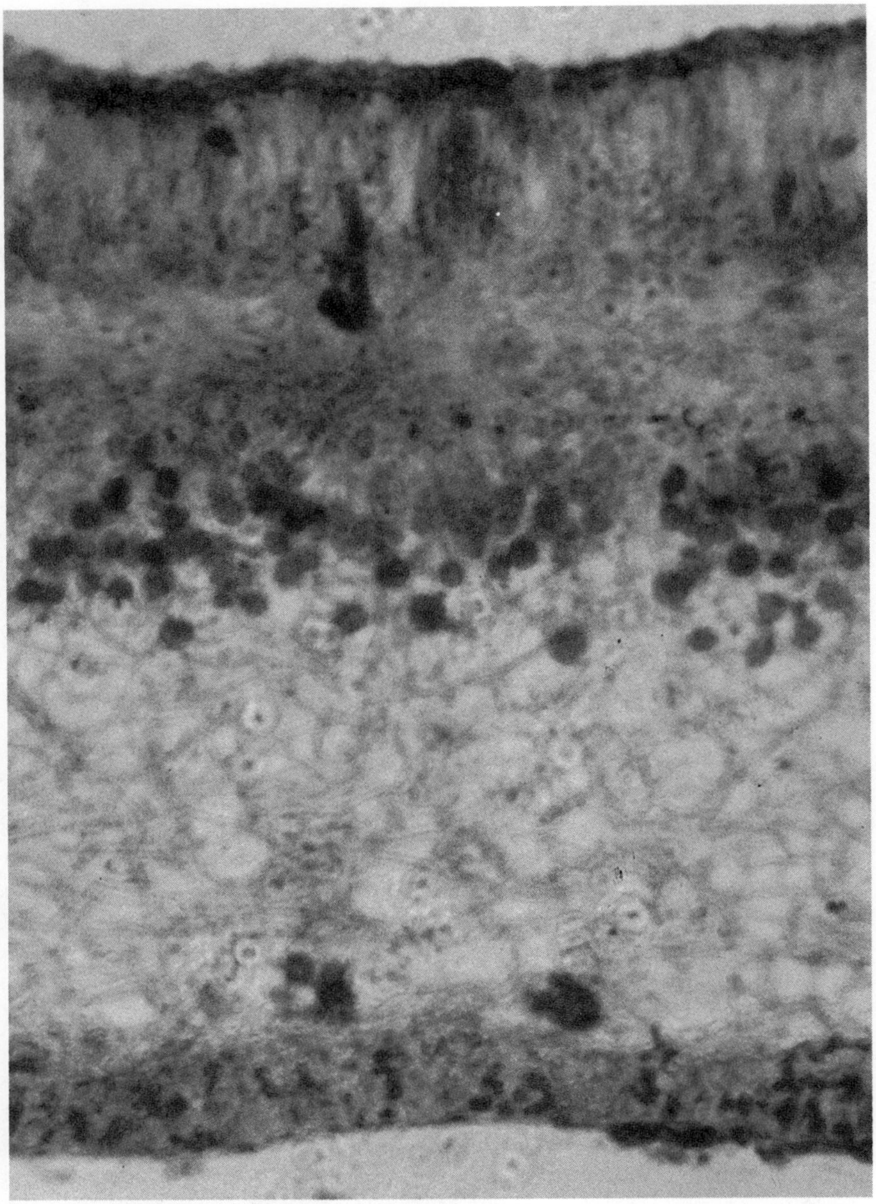

Figure 8.8

Magnified cross section of a lichen with algae cells (dark spots) embedded in fungal filaments (light strands). The cup-shaped feature is an ascocarp, a reproductive structure.

Courtesy Carolina Biological Supply Company

their store of water and to reduce evaporation. Lichens, such as *Verrucaria,* are symbiotic associations of a fungus and a unicellular alga (figure 8.8). In the case of *Verrucaria,* the fungal part absorbs and holds several times its weight of water, water used by the fungus as well as by the photosynthetic algal cells that produce food for the entire lichen complex.

Only a few species of snails, limpets, and occasional crustaceans graze on the sparse and scattered vegetation of the upper intertidal (figure 8.9). Unlike its other close marine relatives, the small littorine snail, *Littorina,* is an air-breather. *Littorina* use a highly vascularized mantle cavity in much the same manner as land snails do for gas exchange. Some species of littorine snails are so well-adapted to an air-breathing existence that they drown if forced to remain underwater. Like littorines, limpets of the upper intertidal

Figure 8.9
Two members of a sparsely populated rocky upper intertidal: the shore crab, *Pachygrapsus,* and the periwinkle snail, *Littorina*

(especially *Acmaea*) are amazingly tolerant to temperature changes. Both littorines and limpets can seal the edges of their shell openings against rock surfaces to anchor themselves and to retain moisture. They are algal grazers and use their filelike radulae (figure 8.10) to scrape the small algae and lichens from the rocks.

A conspicuous zone of small barnacles frequently appears just below the lichens and blue-green algae (figure 8.11). Barnacles are filter-feeders, but in the high intertidal, they are able to feed only when wetted by high spring tides a few hours each month. While submerged, their feathery feeding appendages extend from their volcano-shaped shell and sweep the water for minute plankton. Between high tides, a set of hinged calcareous plates blocks the entrance to the shell and the seals in the remainder of the animal.

Figure 8.10
SEM view of the radula of a gastropod mollusk
Courtesy Dr. Carole S. Hickman

Most barnacles are **hermaphroditic;** they contain gonads of both sexes. Yet most generally refrain from fertilizing their own eggs. During mating, a long tubular penis is extended into a neighboring barnacle, and the sperm are transferred to fertilize the neighbor's eggs. The eggs develop and hatch within the barnacle's shell and are released as microscopic free-swimming planktonic organisms known as **nauplii** (figure 8.12a). After several molts of its exoskeleton, the nauplius develops into a **cypris larva** (figure 8.12b). The cypris eventually settles to the bottom, selects a permanent settling site, and then cements itself to the bottom with a secretion from its antennae. Cypris larvae are attracted by the presence of other barnacles, thus insuring settlement in areas suitable for barnacle survival and for obtaining future mates. Soon after settling, the cypris turns over, loses its larval appearance, and begins to surround itself with a wall of calcareous plates (figure 8.12c).

Connell's work on two species of Atlantic intertidal barnacles provides a clear example of how the interplay of physical and biological factors influences the eventual vertical distribution of adult barnacles. In England, the larvae of one barnacle, *Chthamalus,* settle principally in the upper half of the intertidal, while the larvae of the other barnacle, *Balanus,* settle throughout the entire intertidal range (figure 8.13). Desiccation in the upper

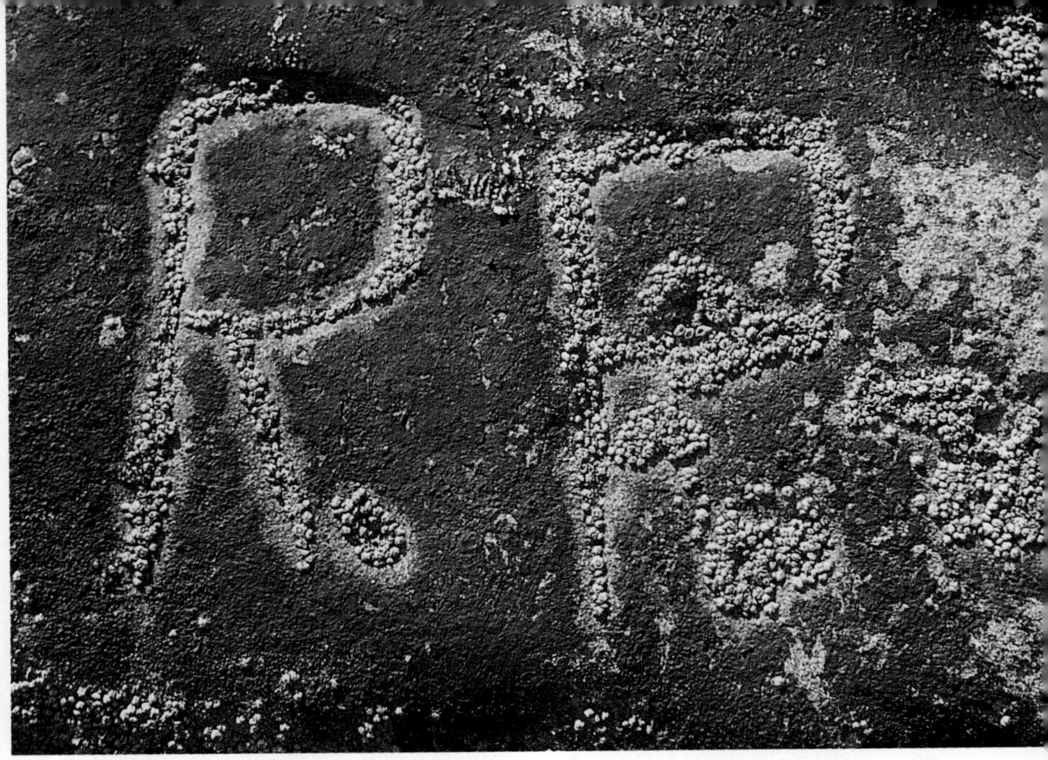

Figure 8.11
Stunted acorn barnacles, *Chthamalus,* survive in the shallow depression of carved letters.

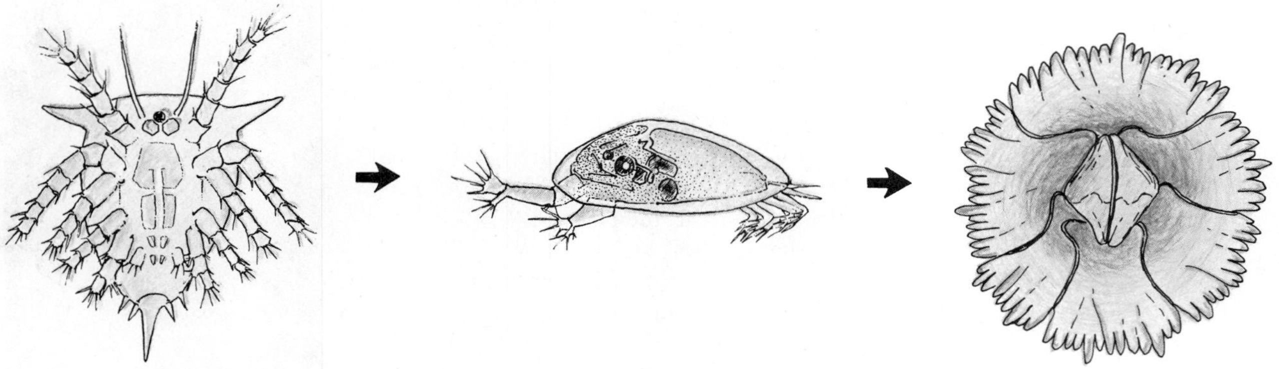

(a) (b) (c)

Figure 8.12
Planktonic and early benthic stages of the barnacle *Balanus:* (*a*) nauplius stage, (*b*) cypris stage, and (*c*) early benthic stage

extremes of the intertidal rapidly eliminates a good number of the settled *Balanus* but has little effect on *Chthamalus* at the same levels. Below the level of significant desiccation effects, however, *Balanus* is clearly the better competitor for space, overgrowing and undercutting *Chthamalus* wherever the two species overlap. The resulting distribution of adult forms of both species provides a useful generalization applicable to other attached animals living in space-limited intertidal situations: The upper limit of species distribution is restricted by the species' ability to cope with environmental stresses and other physical factors, such as temperature or desiccation, whereas a species' lower vertical range is limited by biological factors, especially competition with superior species.

The Middle Intertidal

The middle intertidal is occupied by greater numbers of individuals and species than is the upper intertidal zone. This zone, sufficiently inundated by tides and waves, provides an abundance of plant nutrients, O_2, and plankton food

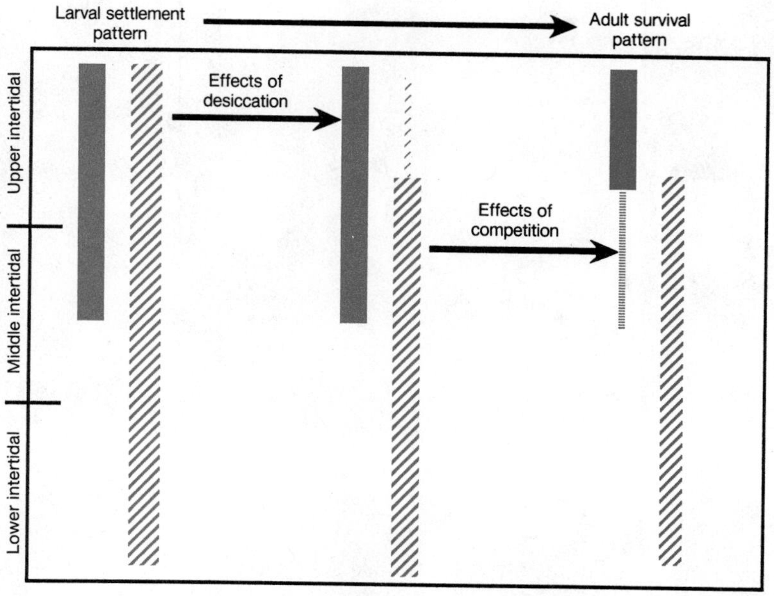

Figure 8.13
The limiting effects of desiccation and competition on the vertical distribution of two species of intertidal barnacles, *Chthamalus* (solid bars) and *Balanus* (hatched bars)
Adapted from Connell, 1961

for filter-feeding animals. The lush growths of green, red, and brown algae also furnish a bountiful supply of locally produced food for grazers.

Occasional small, water-filled, tide pools protect hermit crabs, snails, nudibranchs, anemones, and a few small fish species from exposure and the physical assault of the surf. The upper range of anemones is usually determined by their tolerance to desiccation. Aggregate anemones of the Pacific Coast *(Anthopleura elegantissima)* are known to withstand internal temperatures as great as 13° C above the surrounding air temperature. Yet serious water loss will destroy them. These anemones combat extreme desiccation and temperature fluctuations by retracting their tentacles and attaching bits of light-colored stone and shell to themselves, presumably to reflect light and heat.

The clumped mats characteristic of the aggregate anemone (figure 8.14) are the result of a peculiar mode of asexual reproduction. To divide, these anemones pull themselves apart by simultaneously creeping in opposite directions. Each half quickly regenerates its missing portion, producing two new individuals to replace the original. All the members of a clump resulting from this asexual fission are **clones,** or genetically identical individuals, with the same sex and color patterns. The clonal clumps of anemones are uniformly spaced and are separated from adjacent clones by bare zones about the width of a single anemone. These anemones also have separate sexes and can reproduce sexually by releasing eggs and sperm into the water.

These bare zones between anemones result from the subtle warfare between dissimilar individuals from adjacent clones. They are armed with special tentacles, or **acrorhagi,** that can inflict serious damage to anemones of opposing clones but that have no effect on individuals of the same clump. In these border wars, anemone clumps rely on a mechanism of self-recognition so that the aggressive response is directed only to members of genetically dissimilar clones.

The dominant and conspicuous members of the middle intertidal zone (figure 8.15) are mussels *(Mytilus),* barnacles (usually *Balanus*), some chitons and limpets, and several species of brown algae (especially *Fucus* or *Pelvetia*).

Figure 8.14
The aggregate sea anemone, *Anthopleura*. Individuals above the waterline have retracted their tentacles and covered themselves with light-reflecting shell fragments.

Figure 8.15
Close-up view of mussels, *Mytilus*, acorn barnacles, *Balanus*, and gooseneck barnacles, *Polinices*, of the middle intertidal

These animals securely anchor themselves to the substrate and generally present low, rounded profiles to minimize resistance to breaking waves (see figure 8.7). The plants are secured by strong holdfasts and usually have sturdy but flexible stipes to absorb much of the wave shock. *Fucus* and *Pelvetia* have thickened cell walls to resist water loss during low tide (figure 8.16).

In the densely populated middle intertidal zone, mussels, barnacles, brown algae, and other sessile creatures are limited by two commonly shared resources: the solid substrate on which they live and the water which provides their dissolved nutrients and suspended food. Mussels, barnacles, and algae compete for these critical resources in different ways. In regions where physical factors permit each to survive, these three competing groups interact by dominating the available attachment space or by overgrowing their competitors and monopolizing the resources available from the water (figure 8.17).

Figure 8.16
Fucus, a brown alga, thrives next to small, black mussels (*Mytilus*) on a Maine intertidal rock

Figure 8.17
A bed of acorn barnacles (*Balanus*) severely deformed because of crowding. Because the barnacles were inhibited from expanding laterally by their neighbors, they grew upward instead.

Available space on the rock surfaces of the middle intertidal is crucial for survival, yet it is seldom fully utilized. A number of interacting biological and physical processes occasionally create patches of open space. Sea stars and predatory snails continually remove small areas of barnacles and mussels. Seasonal die-offs of algae, and even battering by heavy surf and drifting logs, also clear patches for future settlement and competition.

Chance events and their relationship to seasonal patterns of reproduction wield appreciable influence in settlement patterns. Most of the middle intertidal animals have free-swimming larval stages and are capable of settling almost anywhere within the intertidal zone. Algal spores and barnacle larvae simultaneously settling on bare rock eventually grow and compete for available space. Because of the space limitations that may exist on exposed coasts, the algae are usually squeezed out as the barnacles increase in diameter and dislodge or overgrow them. On some sheltered rocky coasts, though, recruitment of barnacle larvae is prevented by sweeping action of wave-tossed algal blades. Only in this manner can *Fucus* achieve and maintain spatial dominance over barnacles. If the barnacles are not removed before they are securely cemented into place, they escape the adverse effects of algal blades because of growth and may eventually force *Fucus* off the rocks.

Barnacles are not necessarily safe once they have outgrown or overgrown their algal competitor. They are consumed in prodigious numbers by sea stars, carnivorous snails, and certain fish. Even herbivorous limpets have a detrimental, and sometimes severe, impact on barnacle populations. Young barnacles are eaten or dislodged by limpets as limpets bulldoze their way through their grazing activities. Limpets seem to have less effect on the small crack-inhabiting *Chthamalus* than on larger more exposed *Balanus.* Thus in the presence of limpet disturbance, *Chthamalus* gains a slight competitive advantage over the otherwise dominant *Balanus.*

The larval stages of mussels do not require bare rock exposures; they will settle on algae and barnacles and among aggregates of adult mussels. After settling, the young mussels crawl over the bottom, seeking improved conditions before they attach themselves to the substrate with several strong elastic **byssal threads.** Byssal threads are formed from a fluid secreted by an internal byssal gland. The fluid flows down a groove in the small tongue-shaped foot and onto the substrate. On contact with seawater, the fluid quickly toughens to form an attachment plate and a thread. Then the foot is moved slightly and additional plates and threads are formed.

If left undisturbed, mussels eventually overgrow barnacles and algae. Seldom, however, do rocky intertidal conditions remain undisturbed for long. Mussels are extensively preyed on by sea stars (such as *Pisaster* on the Pacific Coast and *Asterias* on the Atlantic Coast). These sea stars are quite sensitive to desiccation, and are limited to sites that remain underwater. Consequently, their impact on mussel populations is much more severe in the lower portions of the mussels' intertidal range. Young mussels are also devoured by *Nucella* and other predatory snails. Some mussels survive those predatory onslaughts by numerically swamping an area with more individuals than the local predators can consume. In time, the mussels, too, may escape through growth, becoming so large that snails are incapable of drilling through their shells to consume the soft flesh within.

As patches of mussels are cleared out by predators or broken off by waves, they are temporarily replaced by algae or barnacles; but gradually the mussels regain their ascendancy. In this way, diversity of species is main-

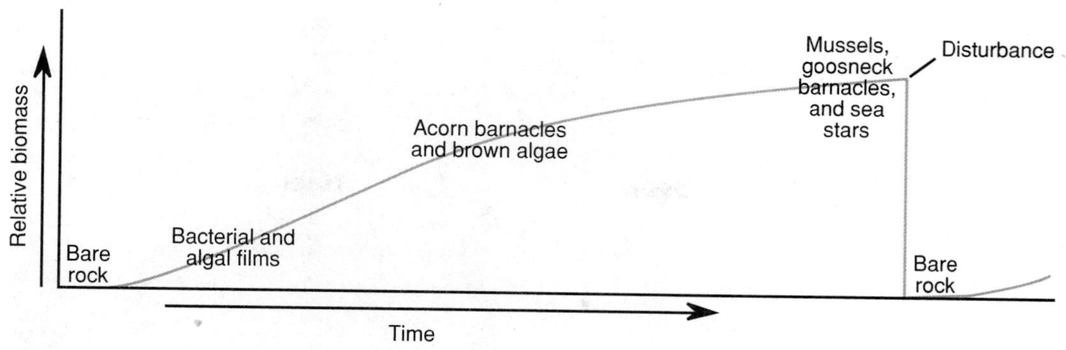

Figure 8.18
General pattern of succession through time on temperate rocky shores. Blue curve indicates relative biomass.

tained. It is ultimately the dynamic balance resulting from competition between these dominant organisms and the patterns of disturbance that affect their survival that shapes the biological character of the middle intertidal. These organisms, in turn, influence the distribution and abundance of other plant and animal species.

A cursory examination of mussel beds often reveals two other conspicuous animal species, filter-feeding gooseneck barnacles and predatory sea stars. But living on the mussel shells or among the thick masses of byssal threads underneath is an extremely complex community of more fragile and often unseen animals. This submussel habitat protects several common species of clams, worms, shrimps, crabs, hydroids, and many types of algae. Many of these species utilize mussel shells as available substrate for attachment. Others exist because they are unable to survive in the same area without the protection afforded by the canopy of mussels overhead.

This complex association of organisms is wholly dependent on the existence of thick masses of well-anchored mussels. This is the culmination, the **climax** stage, of a long succession of plant and animal populations that begins on bare rock and progresses through a sequence of population changes (figure 8.18). Eventually, this process of **biological succession** may reach the stable climax stage: in this case, the mussel bed-gooseneck barnacle-sea star community. When natural disturbances remove the mussels and disrupt the stability of the community, the mussels are quickly replaced by a predictable succession of nonmussel populations (see figure 8.18). Thus the structure of communities such as those dominated by mussels are seldom stable for long; rather, they achieve a state of dynamic equilibrium between the stabilizing effect of succession and the many disruptive factors that reduce that stability.

The Lower Intertidal

The biological character of lower intertidal rocky coasts differs markedly from the zones above it. It is difficult for some species and impossible for others to tolerate the exposed conditions found in the upper and middle intertidal zones. The few species that do are often present in vast numbers. In the lower intertidal, the emphasis changes to a community with a high diversity of species, often without the conspicuous dominant types so characteristic of the middle and upper intertidal.

The lower intertidal usually abounds with seaweeds. Brown, red, and even a few species of green algae of moderate size spread a protective canopy of wet blades over much of the zone (figure 8.19a). In other places, extensive beds of seagrasses achieve a similar effect (figure 8.19b). Tufts of small filamentous brown and red algae carpet many of the rocks. Calcareous red algae

Figure 8.19
(*a*) A brown algal canopy in the lower intertidal. (*b*) Surf grasses interspersed with calcareous red algae in the same lower intertidal.

(a)

(b)

Figure 8.20
The green anemone *Anthopleura*

become especially prolific at these levels. The pinkish hue of *Lithothamnion* encrusting rocks and lining the sides of tide pools is a common sight.

The animals of the lower intertidal include a few species from all the major and several minor phyla. It is here that there is the diversity, complexity, and sheer beauty of intertidal marine life. On the East Coast, a large white anemone, *Metridium,* occurs in tide pools and on exposed portions of the lower intertidal. *Anthopleura,* a beautiful green anemone (figure 8.20) occupies a similar habitat on the West Coast. Securely anchored by discs at their bases, anemones are active predators of planktonic animals and small fish. They capture prey by discharging many microscopic nematocysts from special cells in their tentacles. When touched with a finger, nematocysts produce a slight tingling, sticky sensation.

The batteries of nematocysts found on anemone tentacles effectively discourage the hostile intentions of most predators, but they do not guarantee complete immunity against predation. A few snails and sea spiders penetrate the sides of anemones and feed on the unprotected tissues. Eolid nudibranchs also commonly graze on anemones and the closely related hydroids. These nudibranchs possess mechanisms, not yet completely understood, that block the discharge of the toxic nematocysts. During digestion, the undischarged nematocysts are preserved and passed to special storage sacs in the rows of fingerlike **cerata** along the back (figure 8.21). There the nematocysts possibly serve as defensive mechanisms against predators.

The echinoderms are another familiar group of animals in the lower intertidal. Sea stars, sea urchins, brittle stars, and sea cucumbers are all quite sensitive to desiccation and salinity changes and are seldom seen in abundance above the lower intertidal zone. Although slow-moving, sea stars are voracious predators of mussels, barnacles, snails, an occasional anemone, and even other echinoderms.

Sea stars continuously liberate substances that initiate alarm reactions in their prey; actual contact usually leads to even more vigorous escape movements. Prey species apparently recognize and identify their sea star predators by the substances they exude. They react violently to the touch or presence of sea stars that usually prey on them, but they seldom respond to those

Figure 8.21
A nudibranch, *Hermissenda,* with long fingerlike cerata projecting from its upper surface. The white mass is a string of microscopic eggs.

Figure 8.22
A swimming anemone, *Actinostola,* evading a predatory sea star. The anemone has detached itself from the bottom and is somersaulting away.
Photo by C. Birkland, courtesy P. Dayton, Scripps Institution of Oceanography

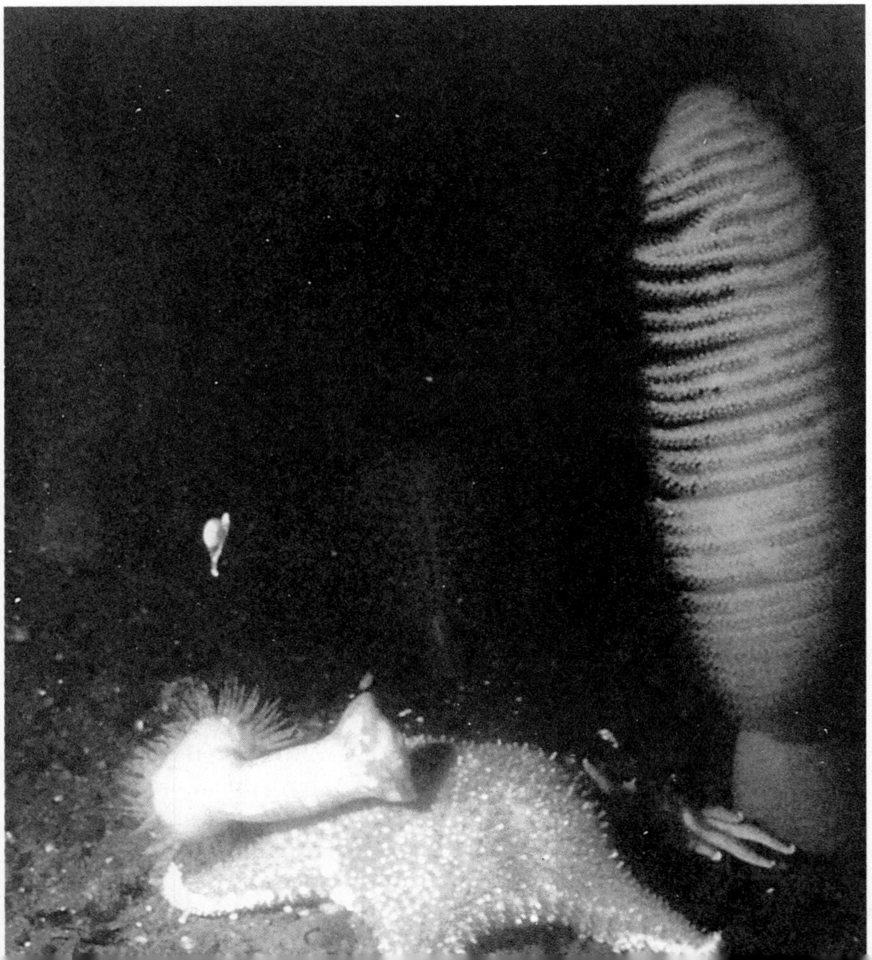

Figure 8.23
Vertical zonation patterns on a 3 m high rock on the British Columbia coast

not encountered in their normal habitat. When approached by some species of sea stars, many normally sessile species execute remarkable escape responses. Scallops swim jerkily away, clams and cockles leap clear of the sea star, and sea urchins and limpets rapidly crawl away. Some sea anemones detach themselves and somersault or roll aside when touched by certain sea stars (figure 8.22).

In summary, rocky intertidal zones of temperate shores have a dynamic pattern of organization dominated by physical forces at the upper extreme that diminish in influence downward and are gradually replaced by competition, predation, and other biological interactions. Figure 8.23 shows the general pattern of vertical zonation of intertidal plants and animals on temperate rocky shores.

At the low tide line, the lower intertidal merges with the uppermost part of the inner shelf zone. Where rocky bottoms extend below the low tide line and are not covered by sediments, the transition from intertidal to subtidal is gradual. Many plant and animal species common to the lower intertidal also are abundant in neighboring shallow subtidal regions. However, rocky substrates eventually give way to soft sediments. In protected stretches of coastlines or below the sea surface, wave action is diminished and loose sediments and detritus begin to accumulate. Organisms of the rocky shore disappear and are replaced by those typical of sand or mud bottoms.

Sandy Beaches and Muddy Shores

Beaches and mudflats, the ecological complement to rocky shores are the depositional features of the coastal zone and are best developed along sinking (or subsiding) coastlines. They are unstable and tend to shift and conform to conditions imposed by waves and currents. Large plants find the shifting nature of soft sediments difficult to cope with, and few exist there. The few plants that have managed to adapt support even fewer grazers. Detritus food chains dominate on these depositional shores. Bits of organic material washed off adjacent rocky shores and the surrounding land or drifted in from kelp beds further offshore sustain the detritus eaters of sandy and muddy shores.

Beaches are made of whatever loose material is available. Quartz grains, black volcanic sand, or pulverized carbonate plant and animal skeletons are most common. Beaches occur where waves are sufficiently gentle to allow sand to accumulate but still strong enough to wash the finer silts and clays away. A good portion of the sand on many beaches is eroded away by large winter waves and deposited as underwater sandbars offshore. Smaller waves the following summer move the sand back on shore. Longshore currents also slowly move beach sands parallel to the shore. In response, populations of beach inhabitants may fluctuate widely from season to season and from one year to the next.

Mudflats are somewhat more stable than beach sands, but they too may be altered by seasonal variations in current patterns and wave activity. Intertidal mudflats are usually found in estuaries or quiet reaches of bays and lagoons. Only in these protected coastal environments can significant amounts of finer silt and clay particles settle out. Mudflats contain some sand, but the sand is mixed with varying amounts of finer silt and clay particles to produce mud. The terms sand, silt, and clay have widely accepted general meanings, but each also refers to a specific range of sediment particle sizes (see figure 7.5).

Several properties of marine sediments are established by the size and shape of sediment particles. The size of spaces between sediment particles (the interstitial spaces) decreases with finer sediments. Interstitial space size, in turn, regulates the porosity and permeability of sediments to water. In coarse sands, water flows freely between sand grains, recharging the supply of dissolved O_2 and flushing away wastes. Beaches, on the other hand, are usually steeper than mudflats, so they drain and dry out more quickly. In fine-grained muds, sediment particles are packed so tightly that little water can percolate through. With the exchange of interstitial water restricted, O_2 used by mud dwellers is not rapidly replenished and their wastes are not quickly removed.

Fine-grained muds with small interstitial spaces are effective traps for particles of organic debris. Much of the accumulated organic material is found in a thin, brownish, oxygenated surface layer about one cm thick. Below this layer, the organic content of the muds usually decreases as animals and decomposing bacteria and fungi consume it. Respiration by the inhabitants of the muds also reduces the available dissolved O_2 supply of the interstitial waters. The lower limit of O_2 penetration in organic-rich sediments is usually apparent as a color change, from a light color in the oxygenated surface layer to a dark or even black color in the anaerobic zone below. The anaerobic conditions of deeper muds inhibit, but do not halt, decomposition of the organic material.

Bacteria and fungi are the major groups of marine organisms capable of utilizing the rich organic accumulations in the anaerobic portion of muddy sediments. Without O_2, these anaerobic decomposers must use other available elements for their respiratory processes. Sulphate, an abundant ion in seawater, is commonly reduced to H_2S in a process much the reverse of the che-

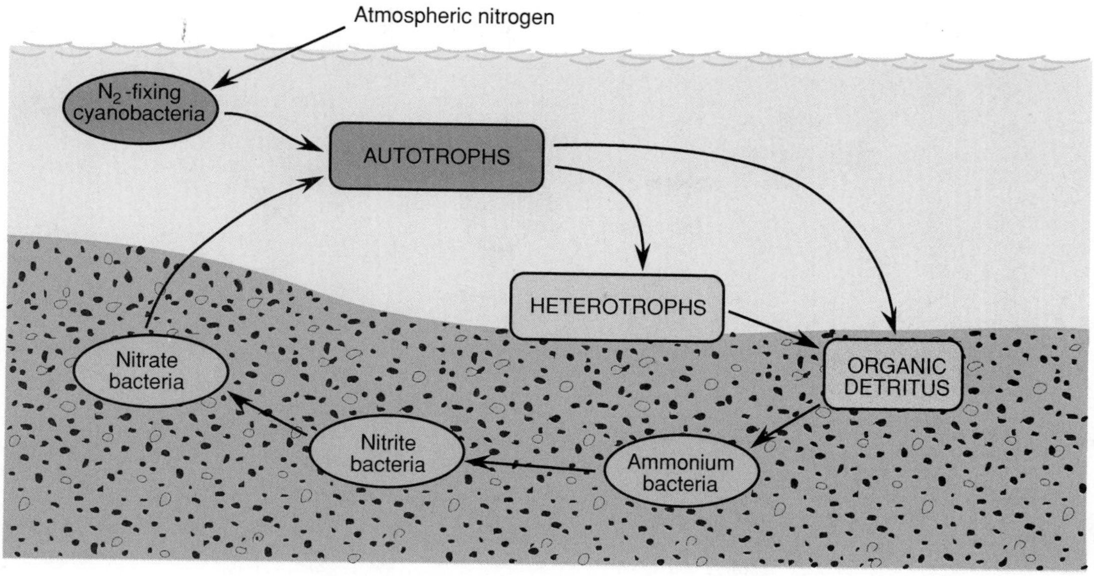

Figure 8.24
Nitrogen cycle of a soft bottom marine community. Several types of bacteria sequentially reduce and excrete nitrogen compounds for reuse by marine autotrophs.

mosynthetic pathways used by deep-sea hot spring bacteria (page 209). The H_2S is responsible for the memorable rotten-egg odor and black color so characteristic of anaerobic marine muds.

Not all benthic bacteria and fungi are anaerobic, however. Aerobic decomposers dominate the surface oxygenated layer of mud, but their numbers decline rapidly with depth. Beneath the oxygenated layer, the anaerobes are active down to 40 to 60 cm, where their numbers also dwindle rapidly: The overwhelming abundance of both aerobic and anaerobic decomposers is responsible for most of the chemical changes that occur in marine sediments. The results of these chemical reactions include the decomposition of organic material, consumption of dissolved O_2 near the bottom, and the recycling of critical plant nutrients back to the water (figure 8.24).

When compared to the teeming populations of the rocky intertidal, beaches appear to be quite desolate. Macroscopic algae, and large, obvious epifauna are rare. Shifting, unstable sands are unsuitable platforms for surface anchorage, and nearly all the permanent residents of the beach dwell underground. Patterns of zonation are more difficult to demonstrate, yet under the sand, there are distinguishable life zones comparable to those on rocky shores (figure 8.25).

The upper portions of sandy beaches along temperate coasts are occupied by a few species of amphipods, particularly *Talitrus* or *Orchestoidea*. The common name of "beach hopper" reflects the unusual bounding mode of locomotion these small crustaceans use. Beach hoppers prefer to burrow a few cm into the sand during the day, but are most active at night. Occasionally, they make excursions down the beach face as the tide recedes.

In the upper parts of tropical beaches, talitrid amphipods are replaced by ghost crabs. Like the talitrids, ghost crabs are nocturnal scavengers. They live in burrows and return infrequently to water to dampen their gills. Like the nearly terrestrial littorine snails of the upper rocky intertidal zone, ghost crabs are well-adapted for long stays on the upper beach without contact with water.

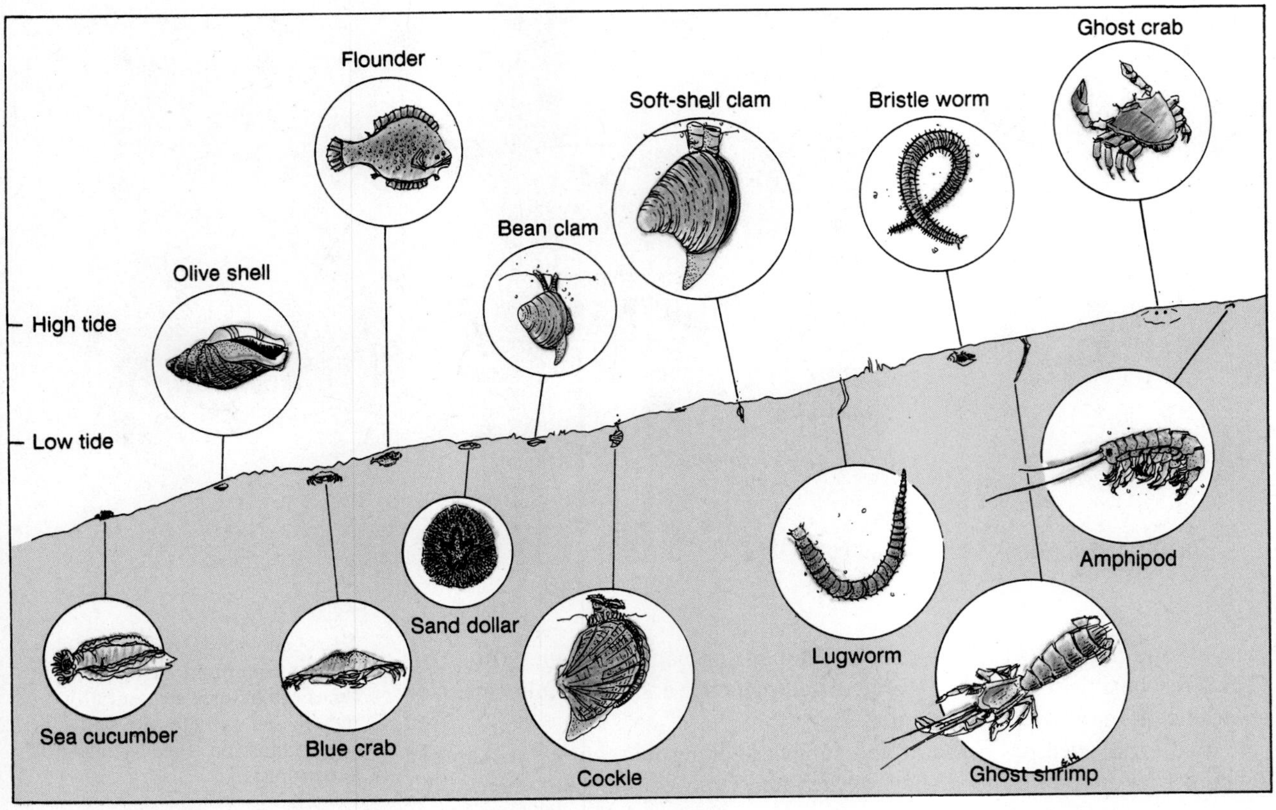

Figure 8.25
Sandy beach zonation along the East Coast of the United States. The species change rapidly from the portion permanently under water at left to the dry part of the beach above high tide at right.

The middle beach is frequently populated by a variety of other amphipods, lugworms *(Arenicola),* dense concentrations of isopod crustaceans, and the sand crab, *Emerita.* These amphipods demonstrate the fundamental feeding methods employed by the larger members of the beach community. *Arenicola* occupies a U-shaped burrow with its head usually buried just below a sand-filled surface depression. The burrows are more or less permanent, for waves stir up and move sediment and detritus to the head region where they are consumed. Mounds of coiled castings indicate the location of the other end of this sediment ingester.

Small isopods are usually less than 1 cm long. They actively prey on smaller interstitial animals that inhabit the pore spaces between sand grains. Many animal phyla are represented in the interstitial fauna of beaches, and a few groups such as harpacticoid copepods and gastrotrichs are practically confined to the interstices of beach sands. In spite of their divergent backgrounds, most interstitial animals exhibit the basic adaptations needed for life between sand grains. They are elongated, small (no more than a few mm), and move with a sliding motion between sand grains without displacing them. Examples of interstitial animals from different phyla are shown in figure 8.26. Some interstitial animals are carnivorous, others feed on detritus deposits and material in suspension. A specialized feeding habit, unique to interstitial animals, is sand-licking. Individual sand grains are manipulated by the animals' mouth parts to remove minute bacterial growths and thin films of diatoms.

The sand crab illustrates a third feeding mode common to many beach macrofauna. When feeding, *Emerita* burrows tail first in the sand and faces down the beach (figure 8.27). Only its eyes and a pair of large feathery an-

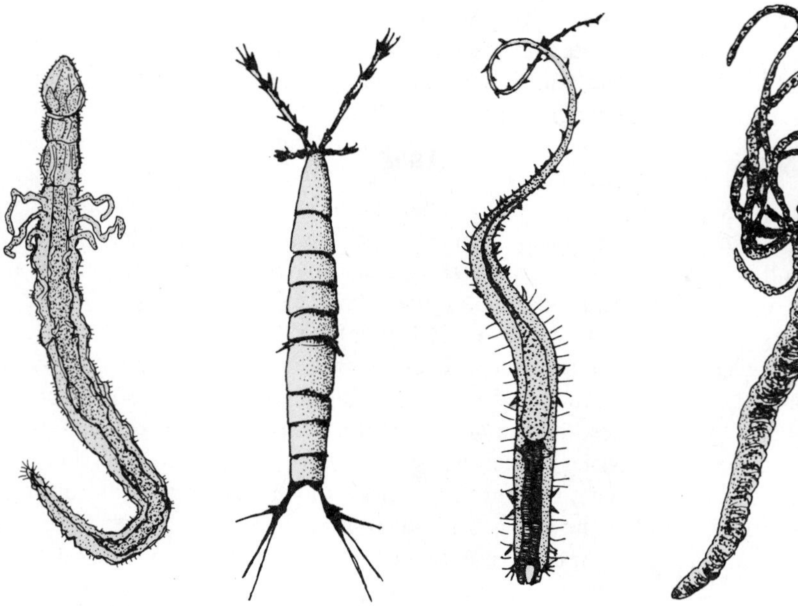

Figure 8.26
A few examples of the interstitial fauna of sandy beaches. Each is of a different phylum, yet all exhibit the small size and worm-shaped body characteristic of interstitial fauna: (*a*) a polychaete, *Psammodrilus,* (*b*) a copepod, *Cylindropsyllis,* (*c*) a gastrotrich, *Urodasys,* and (*d*) a hydra, *Halammohydra.*
Redrawn in part from Eltringham, 1972

Figure 8.27
The sand crab, *Emerita,* with feeding antennae extended
Courtesy A. Wenner

tennae protrude above the sand. When a wave breaks over the crab and begins to recede, the antennae are extended against the rush of water. Entrapped phytoplankton (and possibly even large bacteria) are swept from the filtering antennae and moved to the mouth by other feeding appendages.

In the lower portion of intertidal beaches, the variety of life increases. Polychaete worms, still other amphipods, and an assortment of clams and cockles appear. Many of these lower beach inhabitants, such as soft-shelled clams and cockles *(Cardium)* of the Atlantic coast, represent the upper fringes of much larger subtidal populations. The small wedge-shaped bean clam, *Donax,* of the Atlantic and Gulf coasts (but not the Pacific coast species) migrates up and down the beach with the tides; yet it is usually considered an inhabitant of the lower beach. *Donax* responds to the agitation of incoming waves of rising tides by emerging from the sand to feed. After the wave carries the clam up the beach, it digs in to await the next wave and another ride. During ebb tides, the behavior is reversed. *Donax* emerges only after a wave breaks and begins to wash back down the beach. So, with little energy expenditure of its own, this small clam capitalizes on the abundance of available wave energy to carry it up and down the beach face.

Donax is one of many sandy beach inhabitants to exhibit a rhythmic behavior that corresponds to the tidal cycle. Fiddler crabs *(Uca)* quietly sit out submergence by high tides, then emerge from their burrows at low tide to feed or engage in social activities. When fiddler crabs are removed to the laboratory, their activity rhythms remain in concert with the changing tidal cycle for some time in spite of the absence of tidal cues.

Most organisms, and possibly all of them, have an innate time sense, a **"biological clock."** Rhythmic cycles of body temperatures, activity levels, O_2 consumption, and a host of other physiological variations occur independently of changes in the external environment. The internal "mechanism" of the clock is not known, but its existence has been demonstrated in a wide variety of organisms ranging from single-celled diatoms to humans.

The tide-related cycle of activity exhibited by the fiddler crab is known as a **circalunadian rhythm;** tidal cycles repeat every lunar day (24.8 hours). The coloration of fiddler crabs depends on **circadian rhythms** (based on a solar day of 24 hours). They are light-colored at night but darken during the day.

Clean sandy beaches commonly grade into intermediate muddy sand and eventually to the muddy shores of bays, estuaries, and other sheltered coastal environments. The concepts of vertical zonation as they were applied to the sloping faces of beaches and rocky shores become inappropriate on these nearly level expanses of mudflats. The epifauna of mudflats are dominated by mobile species of gastropod mollusks, crustaceans, and polychaete worms. These organisms sometimes range over wide areas of the mudflat and demonstrate only blurred, weakly established patterns of lateral zonation.

Mud-dwelling organisms, however, do occupy vertically arranged zones in the sediment. A few cm below the mud surface, the interstitial water is generally devoid of available O_2, and the infauna must obtain their O_2 from the water just above the mud or to do without. The numerous openings of tubes and burrows on the surfaces of estuarine mudflats (figure 8.28) attest to an unseen wealth of animal life underneath. Bivalve mollusks extend tubular siphons through the anaerobic mud to the oxygenated water above. The depth to which these animals can seek protection in the mud is limited largely by the lengths of their siphons and thus, indirectly, by their ages. Other infauna utilize the sticky consistency of fine-grained organically rich muds to construct permanent burrows with connections to the surface (figure 8.25).

During high tides, the submerged portions of intertidal beaches and mudflats are visited by shore crabs, shrimps, fish, and other transients from deeper water. Some come to forage for food; others find the protected waters ideal for spawning. Their forays are only temporary, however, for they leave with the ebbing tide and surrender the intertidal to shorebirds and coastal mammals. During low water, the long-billed curlews and whimbrels probe for

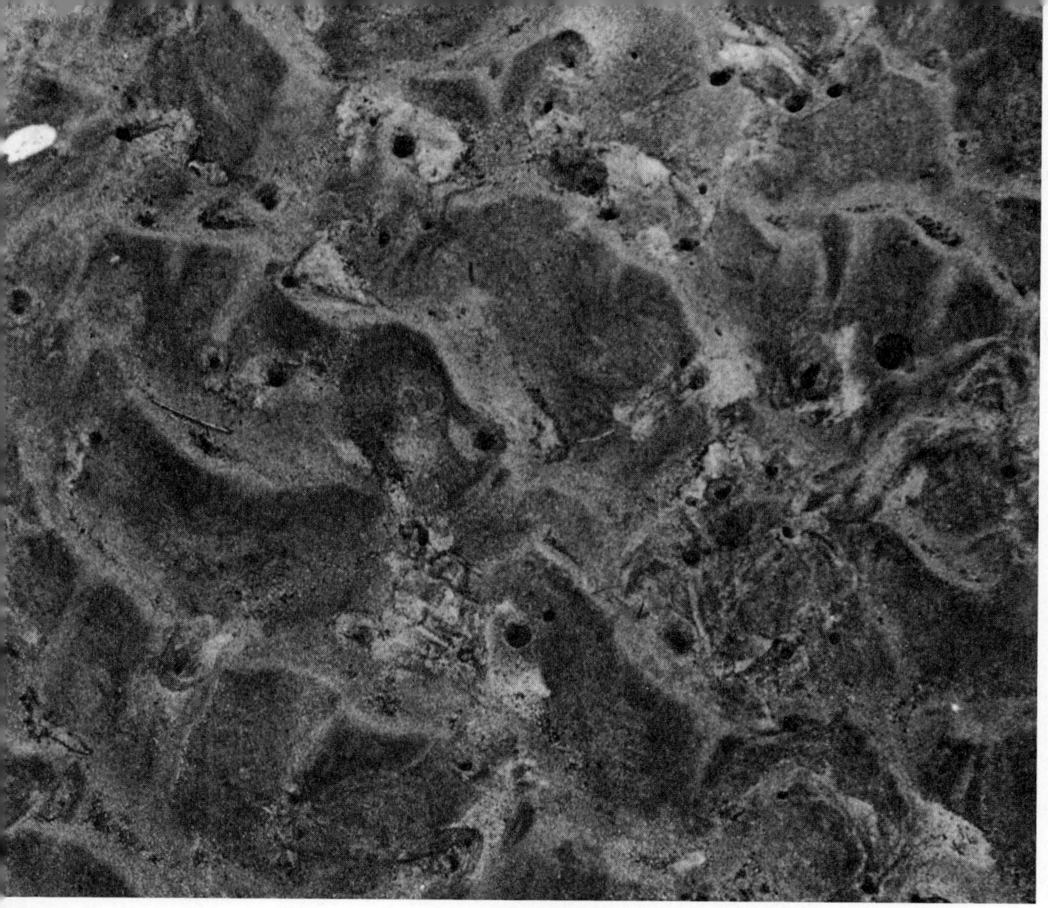

Figure 8.28
Barren surface of a mudflat, with tubes, openings, burrows, and other evidence of abundant animal life beneath the surface

the deeper infauna, while sandpipers and other short-billed shorebirds concentrate on the shallow infauna and small epifauna. Bats, rats, raccoons, and coyotes also patrol the shore at night during low tides.

When the tide is out, the infauna of muddy shores must also cope with an absence of available O_2 and with changing air temperatures. Some switch from aerobic to anaerobic respiration. In doing so, many encounter a dilemma in trying to match the relative inefficiency of anaerobic respiration as an energy-yielding process with the increased metabolic rates forced by increasing tissue temperatures. Larger infauna exist anaerobically only temporarily and revert to aerobic respiration as soon as they are covered by the tides. But for many of their smaller burrowing neighbors with no direct access to the oxygen-laden waters above, anaerobic respiration is a permanent feature of their infaunal existence in intertidal muds.

Summary

The periodic rise and fall of the tides along coastlines adds to the environmental complexity of the intertidal sea bottom. Organisms on the sea bottom must deal with the effects of exposure to the atmosphere. This exposure, in concert with other physical and biological factors, produces graded sets of life zones. In the upper intertidal, desiccation and an intermittent food supply are major problems. The organisms of the more densely populated middle intertidal experience a much less restrictive physical environment but encounter increased interspecific competition. In the lower intertidal, the emphasis on a few well-adapted and dominant species is replaced by a much more diversified assemblage of plants and animals.

Sandy beaches and muddy shores are depositional environments characterized by deposits of loose sediments and organic detritus. Patterns of vertical zonation do occur, but they are as apparent within the sediment as along its surface.

Review Questions

1. What are the major factors that influence the vertical distribution of intertidal plant and animal species? How are these factors affected by tidal variations on a shoreline?
2. Discuss the ecological relationships between mussels, barnacles, *Fucus*, and sea stars on a temperate intertidal coast.
3. Why are benthic epifauna and attached plants seldom found on sandy beaches exposed to wave action?
4. Draw and label a tidal curve representing a typical lunar day on your local coastline.

Questions for Further Discussion

1. Discuss the advantages of living on solid bottom substrates rather than on mud or sand.
2. Compare the species diversity of the middle and lower intertidal zones on rocky shores. On sandy beaches. What accounts for these differences?

Suggestions for Further Reading

Books

Brafield, A. E. 1978. *Life in sandy shores.* Studies in biology no. 89. London: Edward Arnold.

Carson, R. L. 1979. *The edge of the sea.* Boston, MA: Houghton Mifflin Company.

Eltringham, S. K. 1972. *Life in mud and sand.* New York: Crane, Russak & Co.

Lewis, J. H. 1964. *The ecology of rocky shores.* London: English Universities Press.

McLusky, D. S. 1971. *Ecology of estuaries.* London: Heinemann Educational Books.

Moore, P. G., and R. Seed. 1986. *The ecology of rock coasts.* New York: Columbia University Press.

Newell, R. C. 1979. *Biology of intertidal animals.* Faversham, Kent, U.K: Ecological Surveys Ltd.

Reise, K. 1985. *Tidal flat ecology.* New York: Springer-Verlag.

Ricketts, E. F., J. Calvin, and J. W. Hedgpeth. 1986. *Between Pacific tides.* 4th ed. Revised by D. W. Phillips. Standford, CA: Stanford University Press.

Stephenson, T. A., and A. Stephenson. 1972. *Life between tidemarks on rocky shores.* San Francisco: W. H. Freeman.

Articles

Abele, L. G., and K. Walters. 1979. Marine benthic diversity: A critique and alternative explanation. *Journal of Biogeography* 6:115–26.

Armstrong, R. A., and R. McGehee. 1980. Competitive exclusion. *American Naturalist* 115:151–70.

Connell, J. H. 1961. The influence of interspecific competition and other factors on the distribution of the barnacle *Chthamalus stellatus*. *Ecology* 42:710–23.

Dayton, P. 1971. Competition, disturbance and community organization: The provision and subsequent utilization of space in a rocky intertidal community. *Ecological Monographs* 41:351–89.

Denny, M. W. 1985. Wave forces on intertidal organisms: A case study. *Limnology and Oceanography* 30(6):1171–87.

Feder, H. M. 1972. Escape responses in marine invertebrates. *Scientific American* 227(July):92–100.

Harger, J. R. E. 1972. Competitive coexistence among intertidal invertebrates. *American Scientist* 60:600–7.

Koehl, M. A. R. 1982. The interaction of moving water and sessile organisms. *Scientific American* 247 (December):124–34.

Lubchenco, J. 1978. Plant species diversity in a marine intertidal community: Importance of herbivore food preference and algal competitive abilities. *American Naturalist* 112:23–39.

Menge, B. A. 1975. Brood or broadcast? The adaptive significance of different reproductive strategies in the two intertidal sea stars *Leptasterias hexactis* and *Pisaster ochraceus*. *Marine Biology* 31:87–100.

Palmer, J. D. 1975. Biological clocks of the tidal zone. *Scientific American* 232(February):70–79.

Schneider, D. C. 1978. Equalization of prey numbers by migratory shorebirds. *Nature* 271:353–54.

Whitlatch, R. B. 1981. Patterns of resource utilization and coexistence in marine intertidal deposit-feeding communities. *Journal of Marine Research* 38:743–65.

Coral Reefs

Chapter 9

Gorgonians
Photo by T. Phillipp

Figure 9.1
(*a*) Extended polyps of a coral colony. (*b*) Cleaned corallite skeletal bases of a hard coral, with obvious septa.
(*a*)Photo by T. Phillipp

For many people, visions of tropical islands conjure up a special type of marine ecosystem, the coral reef. Unlike the intertidal communities discussed in the previous chapter, reef-forming corals serve dual roles as important members of their communities and as major producers of the reef substrate on which other community members thrive. Since the reef itself is alive and cannot survive for long out of water, it rarely extends upward above the low tide line. Below the sea surface, in the warm, shallow waters around oceanic islands, these massive $CaCO_3$ reef structures have created the basis for extremely diverse marine communities.

Reef-Forming Corals

Corals, like sea anemones, are cnidarians. Both corals and anemones are radially symmetrical, capture prey with nematocyst-armed tentacles, and are permanently attached to a solid substrate. A major difference between corals and anemones is the nature of their substrates. Coral polyps sit in calcareous skeletal cups, or **corallites,** of their own making (figure 9.1). Several bladelike

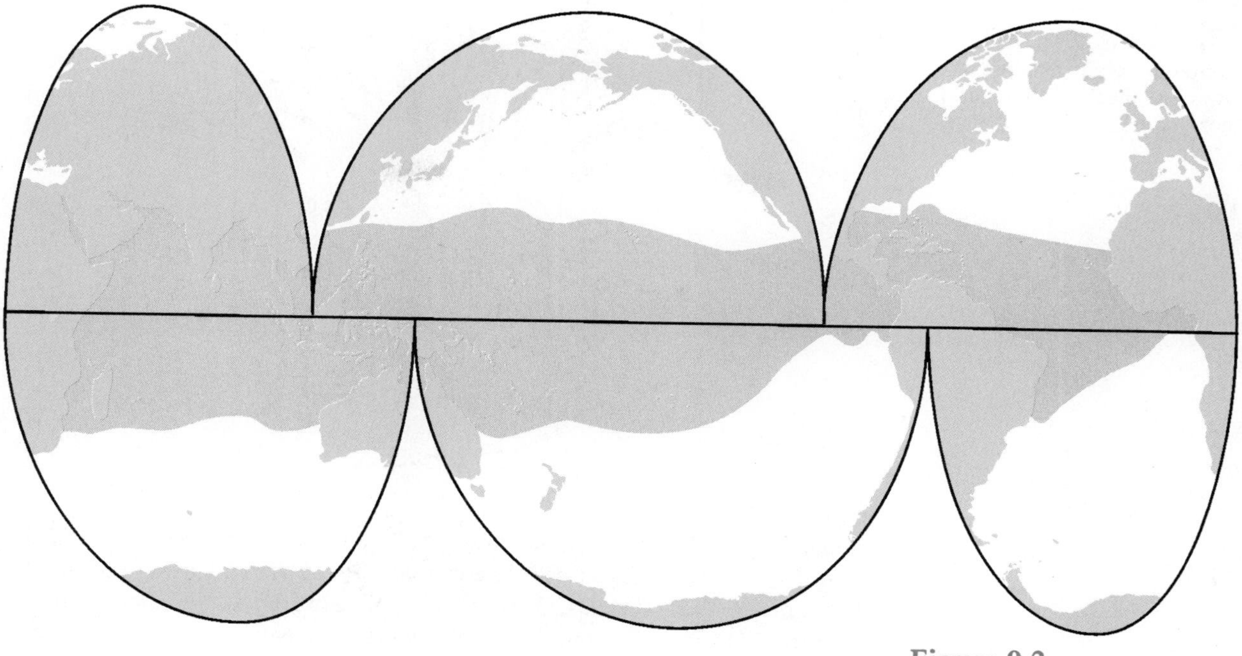

Figure 9.2
Distribution of reef-forming corals (peach) based on cool water temperatures of 18° C

septa radiate from the center of each corallite. Periodically, the coral polyp withdraws its soft parts from the bottom portion of the corallite and secretes a partition. The partition provides a new elevated bottom on the corallite. As the coral polyp grows, it may bud off new polyps asexually or produce planktonic larvae by sexual reproduction.

Like anemones, corals are ubiquitous. They can be found in the deep sea as well as on temperate and tropical shores. However, reef-forming corals are restricted to tropical and subtropical regions where the water temperature never dips below 18° C (figure 9.2). Reef corals are most abundant and diverse in the Indian and Pacific oceans (about 700 species) than in the Atlantic Ocean (about 35 species).

Vigorously growing reef corals require clean water, a firm sea bottom, moderately high salinities, and plenty of sunlight. Consequently, corals do not thrive near river mouths because of their discharges of fresh water and suspended sediments. Many corals are quite adept at cleaning their surfaces of suspended sediments, but they may be growth-limited in turbid waters because they cannot find a suitable foundation on the muddy seafloor. Corals require clear water for still another reason. Living in the surface tissues of all reef-building corals are masses of symbiotic **zooxanthellae.** Zooxanthellae are unicellular dinophytes that, like all other photosynthetic organisms, require light. They occur in concentrations of up to one million cells per cm^2 of coral surface and often provide most of the color seen in corals.

Both zooxanthellae and coral derive several benefits from each other. Corals provide the zooxanthellae with a constant, protected environment and an abundance of nutrients (CO_2 and nitrogenous and phosphate wastes from cellular respiration of the coral). In return, the corals gain O_2, avoid the necessity of excreting some of their cellular wastes, and receive photosynthetic products from the symbiotic algae (figure 9.3). Thus, this relationship is considered a mutualistic one (see figure 2.13). Some controversy does exist concerning the role zooxanthellae play in the nutrition of their hosts. Corals are

Figure 9.3
Material exchange between zooxanthellae and their coral host

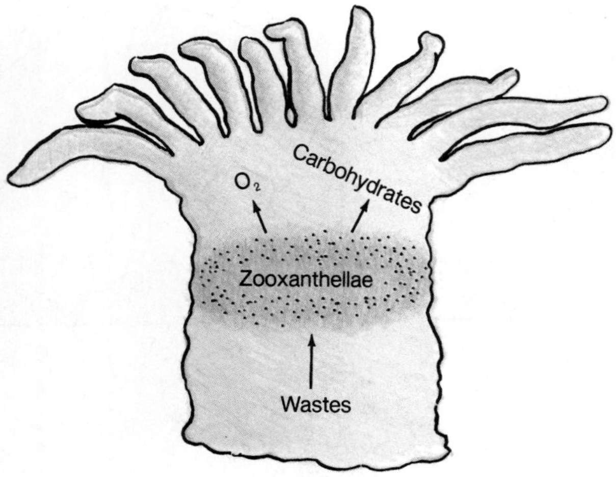

apparently unable to consume zooxanthellae directly because they lack the enzymes needed to digest cellulose cell walls. Experiments using radioactive C^{14} indicate that labeled CO_2 is taken from seawater by the photosynthetic zooxanthellae and is eventually transferred as carbohydrates to the coral tissue. In living corals, then, the zooxanthellae themselves are not digested, but sometimes as much as 90% of the organic material they manufacture photosynthetically is transferred to the host coral tissue. This is sufficient to satisfy the daily energy needs of several species of corals. On many reefs, the total contribution of symbiotic zooxanthellae to the energy budget of the reef is several times higher than phytoplankton production occurring in the waters above the reef.

In spite of the nutritional contribution of zooxanthellae, coral polyps remain superbly equipped to utilize external sources of food, and few, if any, depend solely on zooxanthellae. Corals with large polyps and tentacles, such as *Favia* or *Mussa,* feed exclusively on small fish and larger zooplankton. Species with smaller polyps use ciliary currents to collect small plankton and detritus particles. Most coral polyps may be capable of harvesting organic particles as small as suspended bacteria, bits of drifting fish slime, and organic substances dissolved in seawater.

Sunlight and water temperature restrict the development of coral reefs to shallow tropical waters. Only in warm waters can the high rates of $CaCO_3$ deposition needed for reef building be achieved. Zooxanthellae may also be critical in facilitating the addition of new $CaCO_3$ to the coral's evergrowing reef surface, although their role in this process is not understood.

Coral reefs occur as three general types: **fringing reefs, barrier reefs,** and **atolls.** Fringing reefs form borders along the shoreline. Some of the Hawaiian reefs and other relatively young reefs are of this type. Barrier reefs are further offshore and are separated from the shore by a lagoon. The Great Barrier Reef of Australia is by far the largest single biological feature on earth, bordering some 2,000 km of Australia's northeast coast. Smaller barrier reefs are common in the Caribbean Sea. Atolls are generally ring-shaped reefs from which a few low islands project above the sea surface (figure 9.4).

While serving as a naturalist aboard the H.M.S. *Beagle* in the 1830s, Charles Darwin studied the reef forms of several oceanic islands. He proposed that essentially all oceanic coral reefs were supported by volcanic mountains

Figure 9.4
Kayangel Atoll, capped with four small low-lying islands, in the Belau Islands, Micronesia

beneath the surface. Fringing reefs, barrier reefs, and atolls, he suggested, were related stages in the sequence of island reef development. Within the tropics, he argued, newly formed volcanic islands and submerged volcanoes that almost reach the sea surface are eventually populated by planktonic coral larvae from other nearby coral islands. The coral larvae settle and grow near the surface close to the shore, forming a fringing reef (figure 9.5*a*). The most rapid growth occurs on the outer sides of the reef where food and oxygen-rich waters are more abundant. Waves break loose pieces of the reef and move them down the slopes of the volcano. More corals establish themselves on this debris and grow toward the surface.

The weight of the expanding reef and the immense burden of the volcano itself depress the ocean floor, and the island slowly sinks. If the upward growth of the reef keeps pace with the sinking island, the coral maintains its position in the sunlit surface waters. If the upward growth of the reef does not keep pace with the sinking island, the reef sinks into the cold darkness of the depths and expires. As the island sinks away from the growing reef, many of the massive corals left in the quiet waters behind the reef die. The corals are

Figure 9.5
The developmental sequence of coral reefs, from young fringing reefs (*a*) to barrier reefs (*b*), and finally to atolls (*c*). In the cross sections, volcanic island material is dark brown and reef formations are tan.

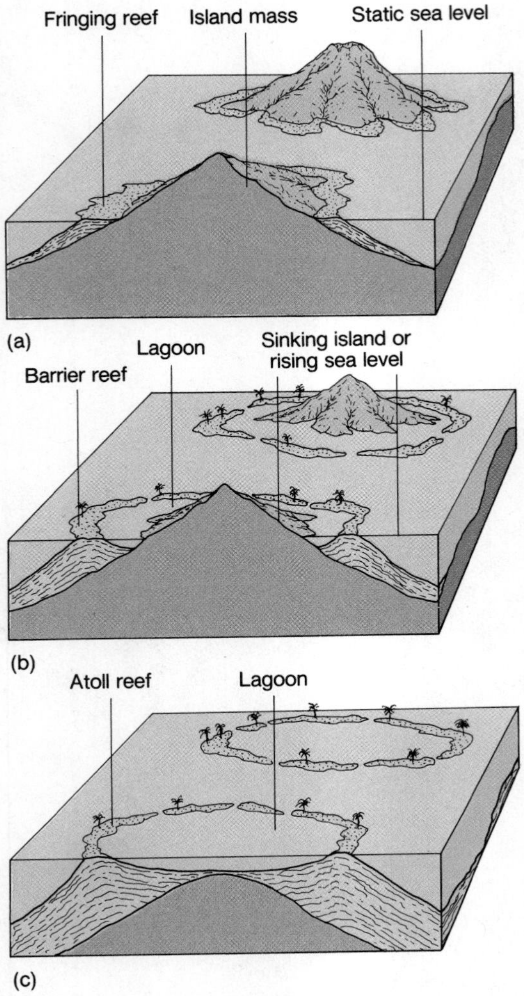

soon covered with reef debris and form a shallow lagoon. Delicate coral forms survive in the lagoon, protected from the waves by what is now a barrier reef (figure 9.5*b*). With further sinking, the volcanic core of the island may disappear completely beneath the reef cap and leave behind a chain of low-lying atoll islands supported on a platform of coral debris (figure 9.5*c*).

Darwin's concept of coral reef formation is, with a few modifications, widely accepted today. Test drilling on several atolls has revealed, as Darwin predicted, thick caps of carbonate reef material overlying submerged volcanoes. Two test holes drilled on Enewetak Atoll (the site of United States H-bomb tests in the 1950s) penetrated over 1,000 m of shallow-water reef deposits before reaching the basalt rock of the volcano. For the past 30 million years, Enewetak apparently has been slowly subsiding as the reef grew around it.

For the past several hundred thousand years, the formation and melting of vast continental glaciers have produced extensive worldwide fluctuations in sea level. Darwin was unaware of these fluctuations and had no means of predicting their effects on coral reef development. Seventeen thousand years ago during the LGM (last glacial maximum), average sea level was about 150 m below its present level. As the ice melted, the sea level grad-

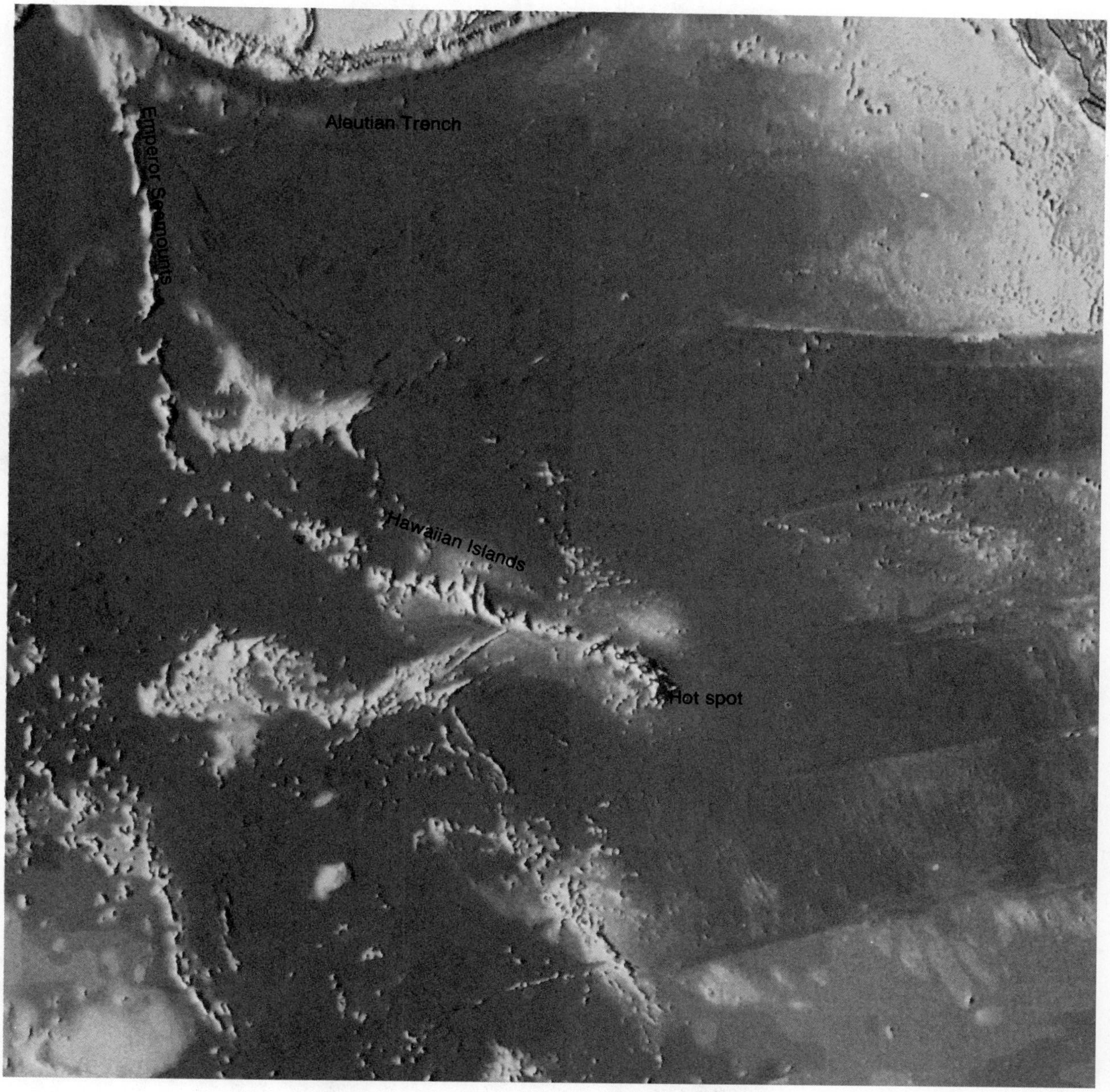

Figure 9.6
The Hawaiian Island-Emperor Seamount chains of volcanoes are carried, in a conveyor-belt fashion, north into deeper water by the movement of the Pacific Plate. Each volcano was formed over the "hot spot," a continuous source of new molten material presently under Hawaii, and is carried to its eventual destruction in the Aleutian Trench.
Courtesy National Geophysical Data Center

ually rose (about 1 cm each year) until it reached its present level nearly 6,000 years ago. Many coral reefs did not grow upward quickly enough and perished. Those that did keep up with the rising sea are the living reefs we see today.

Coral reefs have also been subjected to the effects of global plate tectonics. The Hawaiian Islands and the reefs they support have been transported to the northwest by the movement of the Pacific Plate. Atolls at the northern end of the chain appear to have drowned as they reached the "Darwin Point," a threshold beyond which coral atoll growth cannot keep pace with recent changes in sea level (figure 9.6). At the Darwin Point, only about 20% of the necessary $CaCO_3$ production is contributed by corals. Several types of encrusting and segmented calcareous red (and a few species of green) algae,

Figure 9.7
Spawning corals; (*a*) female staghorn coral releasing eggs, (*b*) male mushroom coral releasing sperm.
Courtesy Animals Animals/OSF Photos by P. Harrison

(a)

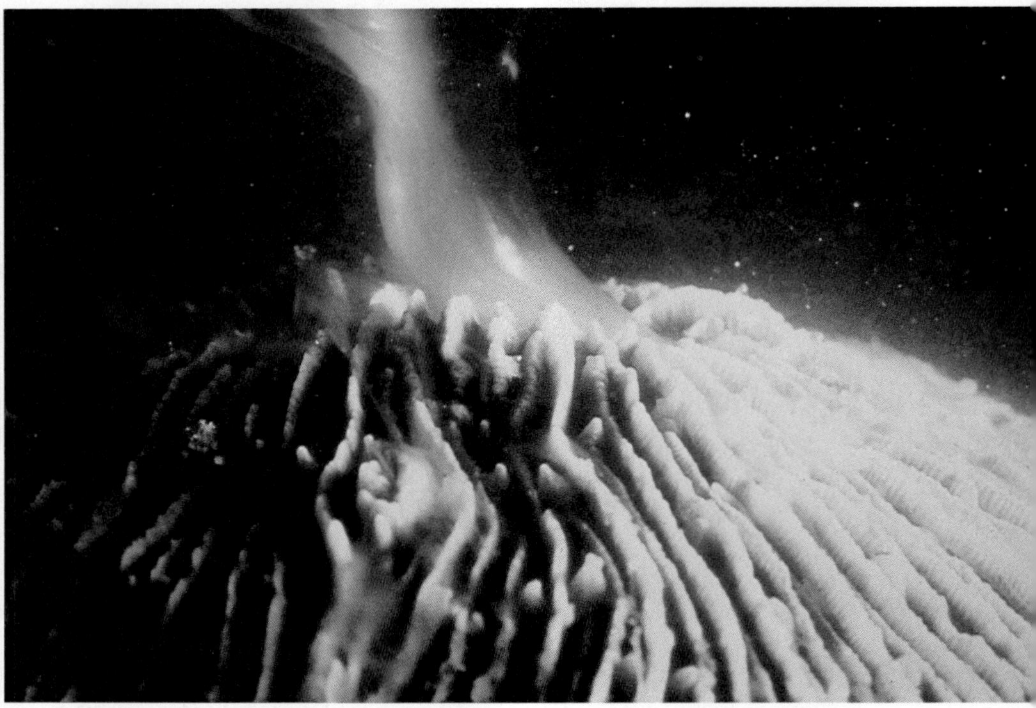

(b)

calcareous colonial hydrozoans, skeletons of single-celled foraminiferans, mollusk shells, sea urchin tests and spines, and the calcareous remains of other reef inhabitants also contribute to the structure of coral reefs. From this encrusted, integrated base of skeletal remains, coral reef ecosystems have evolved as the most complex of all benthic associations.

The living richness of coral reefs stands in obvious contrast to the generally unproductive nature of surrounding tropical oceans. The precise trophic relationships between producers and consumers on the reef are still

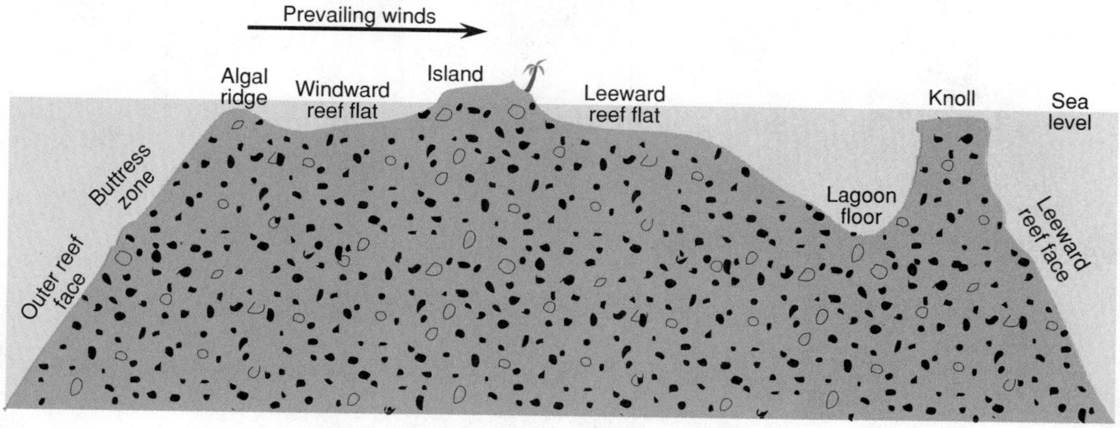

Figure 9.8
Major life zones across a typical Indo-Pacific coral reef

largely unknown. Coral colonies seem to function as highly efficient trophic systems, each with its own photosynthetic, herbivorous, and carnivorous aspects. Critical nutrients are rapidly recycled between the producer and consumer components of the coral colony. Because much of the nutrient cycling is accomplished within the coral tissues, little opportunity exists for the nutrients to escape from the coral production system. Coral colonies, therefore, are able to rapidly recycle their limited supply of nutrients between internal producer and consumer components and keep productivity in coral reef communities high.

Reproduction in Corals

About 65% of reef-forming coral species are broadcast spawners. On the Great Barrier Reef of Australia, coral spawning is a spectacular sight. More than 100 of the 340 species of corals found there spawn on only one, and the same, spring night each year (figure 9.7). This is not a universal behavior of reef corals; in the northern Red Sea, none of the major species of coral reproduce at the same time as any of the other major species.

A few days after spawning, a drifting, swimming **planula** larva develops. These larvae, each with its own supply of zooxanthellae, settle and thrive only if they encounter their preferred water and bottom conditions. From these planula larvae, new coral colonies develop. During their planktonic phase, these larvae are capable of settling new volcanic islands some distance from their island of origin. When they do, the reef form they eventually create depends on existing environmental conditions and the prior developmental history of the reef.

Zonation on Coral Reefs

Environmental conditions that favor some coral reef inhabitants over others in a particular habitat depend a great deal on wave force, water depth, temperature, salinity, and a host of biological factors. These conditions vary greatly across a reef and provide for both horizontal and vertical zonation of the coral and algal species that form the reef. Parallel zonation of other animals also occurs. Figure 9.8, a cross section of an idealized Indo-Pacific coral reef, includes the major features and zones of the reef.

Figure 9.9
Leaf coral, *Montipora,* surrounded by various growth forms of *Acropora* (Palau Island)
Courtesy M. Weeks

The living base of a coral reef begins as deeply as 150 m below sea level. Between 150 and 50 m on outer reef slopes, a few small, fragile species, such as *Leptoseris,* exist. Despite the fact that little sunlight penetrates at these depths. Above 50 m, and extending up to the base of vigorous wave action (approximately 20 m), is a transition zone between deep and shallow water associations. In this zone, the corals and algae receive adequate sunlight yet are sufficiently deep to avoid the adverse effects of surface waves. Several of the delicately-branched species commonly found in the protected lagoon waters also occur in this transition zone (figure 9.9).

From a depth of about 20 m to just below the low tide line is a rugged zone of spurs, or **buttresses,** radiating out from the reef. Interspersed between the buttresses are grooves that slope down the reef face. These grooves drain debris and sediment off the reef and into deeper water. Continual heavy surf has limited detailed studies of the buttress zone, but it is known to be dominated by massive coral growths (such as *Acropora*) and by several species of encrusting coralline algae. The massive corals thrive in this zone of breaking waves, intense sunlight, and abundant oxygen. Small fish seem to be in every hole and crevice on the reef, and many of the larger fish of the reef—sharks, jacks, barracudas, and tunas—patrol the buttresses and grooves in search of food.

Figure 9.10
Echinometra, a common tropical sea urchin
Courtesy T. Ebert

A large portion of the geographical range of coral reefs is swept by the broad reaches of the trade winds. The waves generated by these winds crash as thundering breakers on the windward sides of reefs. Windward reefs are usually characterized by a low, jagged **algal ridge.** The algal ridge suffers the full fury of incoming waves. In this severe habitat, a few species of calcareous red algae, especially *Porolithon* and *Lithothamnion,* flourish and produce the ridge, producing new reef material as rapidly as the waves erode it. A few snails, limpets, and urchins (figure 9.10) can also be found wedged into surface irregularities. Slicing across the algal ridge are surge channels that flush bits and fragments of reef material off the reef and down the seaward slope.

Extending behind the algal ridge to the island (or, if the island is absent, to the lagoon) is a **reef flat,** a nearly level surface barely covered by water at low tide. The reef flat may be narrow or very wide, consists of several subzones, and has an immense variety of coral species and growth forms. In places where the water deepens to a meter or so, small raised **microatolls** occur. Microatolls are produced by a half-dozen different genera of corals and, with other coral growth forms, provide the framework for the richest and most varied habitat on the reef. Burrowing sea urchins are common, and calcareous green algae and several species of large foraminiferans thrive and add their skeletons to the sand-sized deposits on the reef flat. The sand, in turn, provides shelter for other urchins, sea cucumbers, and burrowing worms and mollusks.

Possibly the most spectacular animal of the reef flat is the giant clam, *Tridacna.* The largest species of this genus occasionally exceeds a meter in length and weighs over 100 kg. Some tridacnids sit exposed atop the reef platform; others rock slowly to work themselves into the growing coral structure beneath (figure 9.11). Like corals and many other invertebrates, tridacnids house dense concentrations of zooxanthellae in specialized tissues, particularly

Figure 9.11
Red, branching gorgonian, *Melithaea,* with a giant clam *Tridacna* below (Palau Island).
Courtesy M. Weeks

the enlarged mantle that lines the edges of its shell. When the shell is open, the pigmented mantle tissues with their zooxanthellae are fully exposed to the energy of the tropical sun.

Tridacnid clams were long thought to "farm" their zooxanthellae in blood sinuses within the mantle and then transport them to the digestive glands where they were digested by single-celled **amebocytes.** Using elaborate staining and electron microscope techniques, Fankboner demonstrated that the digestive amebocytes of *Tridacna* selectively cull and destroy old or degenerate zooxanthellae. Healthy zooxanthellae are maintained to provide photosynthetic products to their hosts in dissolved rather than cellular form.

The tranquil waters of the lagoon protect two general life zones: the lagoon reef and the lagoon floor. The lagoon reef forms the shallow margin of the lagoon proper. It is a leeward reef, free of severe wave action. It lacks the algal ridge characteristic of the windward reef and, in its place, has a more

Figure 9.12
Mixed species of fish on the outside reef (Palau Island).
Courtesy M. Weeks

luxuriant stand of corals. Other algae, some specialized to burrow into coral, and uncountable species of crustaceans, echinoderms, mollusks, anemones, gorgonians, and representatives of many other animal phyla flourish in the lagoon reef. In this gentle, protected environment, single coral colonies of *Porites* and *Acropora* may achieve gigantic proportions. Branching bush and treelike forms extend several meters from their bases. The plating, branching, and overtopping structures common in the protected lagoon are most likely structural adaptations evolved in response to competition for particles of food and sunlight, two resources vital to the survival of reef-forming corals.

Associated with the reef and lagoon, but with the mobility to escape the limitations of a benthic existence, are thousands of species of reef fish (figure 9.12). These fish find protection on the reef, prey on the plants and animals living there, and sometimes nibble at the reef itself. Several groups are common to all the major regions characterized by coral reefs. These include moray eels, porcupine fish, butterfly fish, squirrel fish, groupers, trigger fish, gobies, wrasses, surgeonfish, sea horses, and occasional sharks, skates, and rays. Many of these fish are thought to be major importers of important limiting nutrients to local reef systems. By feeding on pelagic prey during the day, then defecating at night while resting on the reef, the results of these fishes predation are converted through detritus food chains to dissolved nutrients usable by plants, phytoplankton, and the coral-based zooxanthellae.

Symbiotic Relationships in Coral Reef Fish

Excellent examples of all three types of symbiosis (refer to fig. 2.13) can be found in many of the abundant animal groups of the coral reef. Our discussion will be limited to some of the better-known symbiotic relationships involving coral reef fish. The relationships span the entire range, from very casual commensal associations to highly evolved parasitic relationships.

Small schools of the pilot fish (*Naucrates*) form loose commensal associations with large predatory sharks. The pilot fish swim below and in front of their hosts and scavenge bits of food from the shark's meal. Neither the pilot fish nor the shark show any structural specialization for this relationship.

Figure 9.13
Two remoras, *Remora,* with modified dorsal fins visible
Courtesy M. Weeks

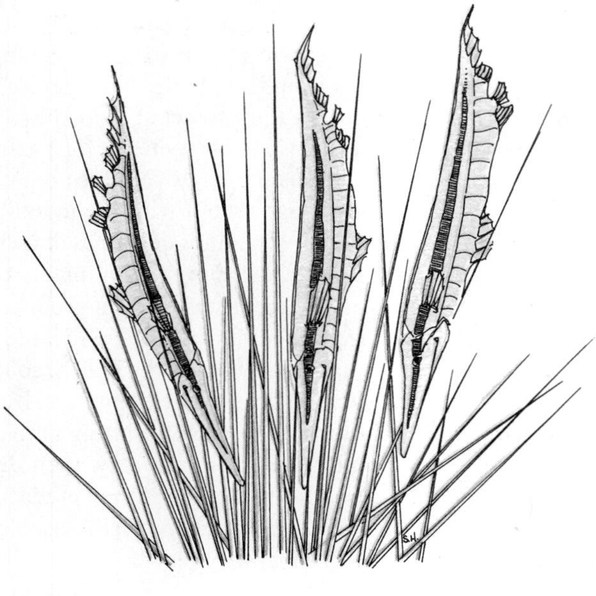

Figure 9.14
Shrimpfish, *Aeloiscus,* seeking shelter amid the spines of a sea urchin

The remoras (figure 9.13) also associate with large sharks and occasionally even with whales and turtles. The remora's first dorsal fin is modified as a sucking disc and is used to attach itself to its host. From its attached position, it feeds on scraps from the host and often cleans the host of external parasites.

The small shrimpfish often swim head down among the long sharp spines of sea urchins (figure 9.14). The shrimpfish acquire protection from the sea urchins without altering the urchins' behavior. A similar association exists between small man-of-war fish (*Nomeus*) and the Portuguese man-of-war (*Physalia*). The *Physalia's* long venomous tentacles provide a protected retreat for the small fish.

Figure 9.15
Clown fish, *Amphiprion,* hovering near their host anemone
Photo by T. Phillipp

The brightly colored anemonefish finds equally effective shelter by nestling among the stinging tentacles of several species of sea anemones (figure 9.15). This relationship, somewhat more complex than those just described, is probably a mutualistic one. In return for the protection they obtain, anemonefish assume the role of "bait" and lure other fish within reach of the anemone. They occasionally collect morsels of food and, in at least one instance, catch other fish and feed them to the host anemone. In addition, clown fish chase away fish predators of the anemone. Anemonefish, however, are not immune to the venomous nematocysts of the host. Still, they mouth and nibble at the anemone's tentacles. This nibbling transfers mucus from the anemone tentacles to the fish, and substances contained in the mucus provide the mechanism to inhibit nematocyst discharge.

The increased popularity of skin diving and scuba diving has revealed some remarkable cleaning associations involving a surprising number of animals. **Cleaning symbiosis** is a form of mutualism; one partner picks external parasites and damaged tissue from the other. The first partner gets the parasites to eat; the other partner has an irritation removed.

The behavioral and structural adaptations of cleaners are well developed in a half dozen species of shrimps and several groups of small fish. Tropical cleaning fish include the butterfly fish, young stages of angelfish, gobies, and several wrasses, including all known species of *Labroides* (figure 9.16). All tropical cleaning fish are brightly marked, are equipped with pointed pincerlike snouts and beaks, and occupy a cleaning station around an obvious rock outcrop or coral head. Most are solitary; a few species, however, live in pairs or larger breeding groups.

Host fish approach cleaning stations, frequently queuing up and jockeying for position near the cleaner. Often, they assume unnatural and awkward poses similar to courtship displays. As the cleaner fish moves toward the host, it inspects the host's fins, skin, mouth, and gill chambers and then picks away parasites, slime, and infected tissue.

Figure 9.16
The small wrasse, *Labroides*, cleaning external parasites from a turkey fish
Courtesy C. Farwell, Scripps Institution of Oceanography

In the Bahamas, Limbaugh tested the cleaner's role in subduing parasites and the infections of other reef fishes. Two weeks after removing all known cleaners from two small reefs, the areas were vacated by nearly all but territorial fish species. Those species that remained had an overall ratty appearance and showed signs of increased parasitism, frayed fins, and ulcerated skin. Limbaugh concluded that symbiotic cleaners were essential in maintaining healthy fish populations in his study area.

Similar studies by Losey were conducted on a Hawaiian reef. In this situation, the small cleaning wrasse, *Labroides phthirophagus* (the major cleaner on the reef) was excluded from the study site for more than six months. During that time, no increase in the level of parasite infestation was observed. This suggests that for some cleaner-host associations the role of the cleaner is not crucial. The cleaner may be dependent on the host for food, but the host's need for the cleaner seems to be variable.

The fine line separating mutualistic cleaning of external parasites and actual parasitism of the host fish is occasionally crossed by cleaning fish such as *Labroides*. In addition to unwanted parasites and diseased tissue, some cleaning fish take a little extra healthy tissue or scales or grazing on the skin mucus secreted by the host. Thus, the total range of associations displayed by cleaning fishes encompasses mutualism, commensalism, and parasitism.

Since parasitism is such a widespread way of life in the sea, few fish avoid contact with parasites at some time in their lives. The groups notorious for creating parasitic problems in humans—viruses, bacteria, flatworms, roundworms, and leeches—also plague marine fish.

In spite of the bewildering array of parasites that infest fish, very few fish become full-time parasites themselves. One remarkable exception is the small pearl fish (*Carapus*). It finds refuge in the intestinal tracts of sea cu-

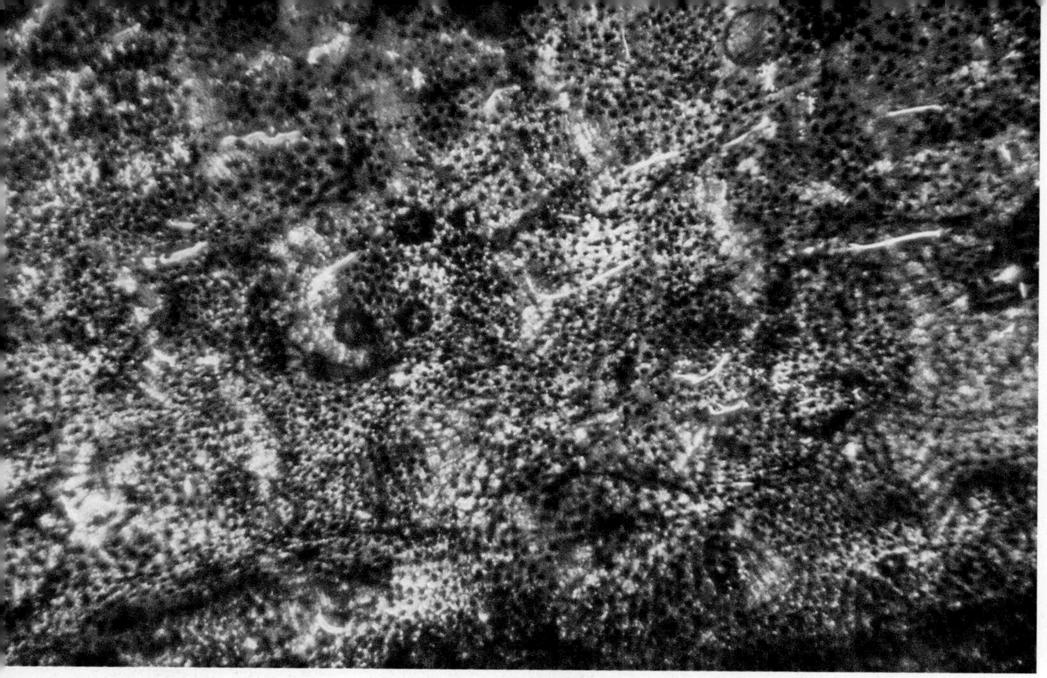

Figure 9.17
Magnified chromatophores from a section of fish skin. The black and brown pigments of some are expanded and diffused; others are densely concentrated in small spots.
Courtesy C. Stepien, Scripps Institution of Oceanography

cumbers and the stomachs of certain sea stars. When seeking a host, pearl fish detect a chemical substance from the cucumber and then orient themselves toward the respiratory current coming from the cucumber's anus. (Sea cucumbers draw in and expel water through their anuses for gas exchange.) The fish enters the digestive track tail-first via the anus. The hosts are not willing participants in this relationship. They are sometimes seen ejecting their digestive and respiratory organs in an attempt to rid themselves of the symbiont. But once this association is established, the pearl fish assume a parasitic existence, feeding on and seriously damaging the host's respiratory structures and gonads.

Coloration in Coral Reef Fish

Against the colorful background of their coral environment, reef fish have evolved equally brilliant hues and color patterns. The colors are derived from skin or internal pigments and from iridescent surface features (like those of a bird's feathers) with optical properties that produce color effects. Most fish form accurate visual color images of what they see. Like humans, they too are susceptible to misleading visual images and camouflage.

Our interpretation of the adaptive significance of color in fish falls into three general categories: concealment, disguise, and advertisement. Some seemingly conspicuous fish resemble their coral environment so well that they are nearly invisible when in their natural setting. Extensive color changes often supplement their basic camouflage when they are moving to different surroundings. These rapid color changes are accomplished by expanding and contracting the colored granules of pigmented cells (**chromatophores**) in the skin and are governed by the direct action of light on the skin, by hormones, and by nerves connected to each chromatophore. As the chromatophore pigments disperse, the color changes become more obvious (figure 9.17). When contracted, the pigment retreats to the center of the cell and little of it is visible. Other cells, called **iridocytes,** contain reflecting crystals of guanine. Iridocytes can produce an entire spectrum of colors within a few seconds.

Figure 9.18
Disruptive coloration patterns of a butterfly fish, *Chaetodon*
Courtesy C. Farwell, Scripps Institution of Oceanography

Several distinctive fish conceal themselves with color displays reminiscent of disruptive coloration, or dazzle camouflage. Bold, contrasting lines, blotches, and bands tend to disrupt the fish's image and draw attention away from recognizable features such as eyes. Since eyes are common targets for attack by predators, a disguised eye is a protected eye. One common strategy masks the eye with a dark band across the black staring pupil so it appears continuous with some other part of the body (figure 9.18). To carry the deception even further, masks around the real eyes are sometimes accompanied by fake eyespots on other parts of the body or fins. Eyespots, intended as visual attention getters, are usually set off by concentric rings to form a bull's-eye. Presumably, predators are drawn away from the eyes and head and drawn to less vital parts of the body.

The flashy color patterns of cleaning fish serve different functions. If the fish are to attract any business, they must be conspicuous. So they advertise themselves and their location with bright startling color combinations. These bold advertisement displays are also useful for sexual recognition. In certain species, one or both sexes assume bright color patterns during the breeding period. The colors play a prominent role in the courtship displays, which lead to spawning. During this period, the positive value gained from sexual displays must offset the adverse impact of attracting hungry predators. Between breeding periods, these fish usually assume a drab, less conspicuous appearance.

Advertisement displays are also employed to warn potential predators that their prey carry sharp or venomous spines, poisonous flesh, or other features that would be painful or dangerous if eaten. Predatory fish recognize the color patterns of unpalatable fish and learn to avoid them.

Occasionally, a species capitalizes on the advertisement displays of another fish by closely mimicking its appearance. The cleaner wrasse (*Labroides,* the small fish in figure 9.16) is nearly immune to predation because of the cleaning role it performs for its potential predators. Over much of its range, *Labroides* lives in close proximity to a small blenny (*Aspidenotus*). The

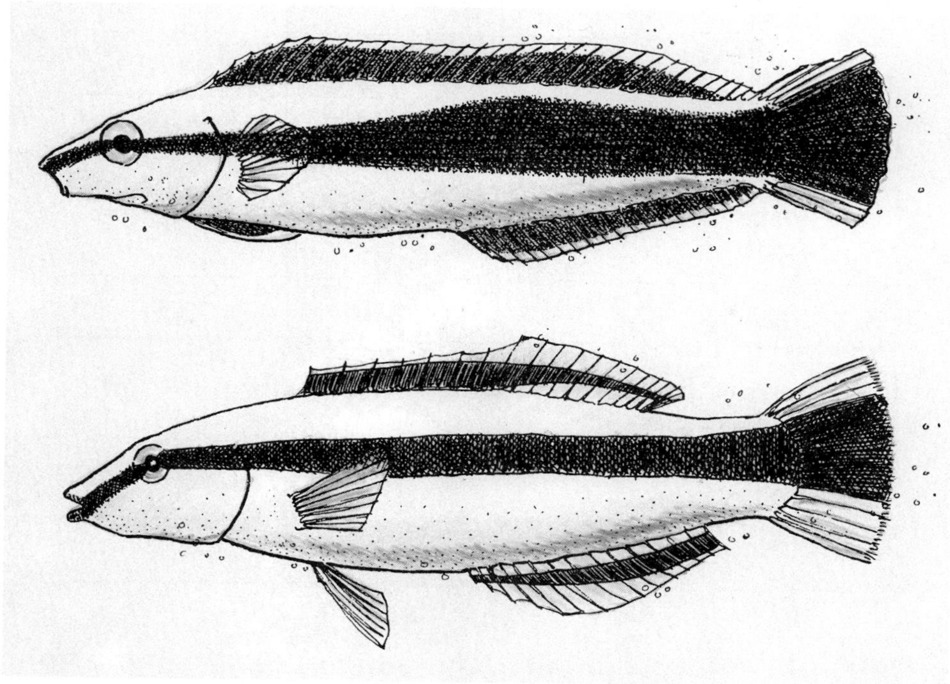

Figure 9.19
The small cleaner *Labroides,* (above) and its mimic, *Aspidenotus* (below)

blenny so closely resembles *Labroides* in size, shape, and coloration (figure 9.19) that it fools many of the predatory fish that approach the wrasse's cleaning station. Not content to share *Labroides* immunity to predation, the blenny also uses its disguise to prey on fish that mistakenly approach it for cleaning. This ability to disguise and thereby be protected is known as mimicry.

Only in the clear waters of the tropics and subtropics does color play such a significant role in the lives of shallow-water animals. In the more productive and turbid waters of temperate and colder latitudes, light does not penetrate as deeply nor is the range of colors available. In coastal waters and kelp beds, monotony and drabness of appearance, not brilliance, is the key to camouflage. In the deep ocean, color is even less important. Without light to illuminate their pigments, it matters little whether deep-water organisms appear red, blue, black, or chartreuse when viewed at the surface. In the abyss, they would all assume the uniform blackness of their surroundings were it not for bioluminescence (discussed in chapter 5).

Summary

Reef-forming corals are colonial cnidarians whose growth is limited to the photic zone of tropical and warm subtropical coasts where clean, hard substrates are available. Reef-forming corals contain photosynthetic zooxanthellae that nourish the coral polyps and dramatically increase the productivity of the reef. These corals form the structural foundation for very complex shallow-water communities. Symbiotic associations are common, and numerous examples of commensalism, mutualism, and parasitism exist. The brightly colored patterns of coral reef fish illustrate the advertisement, disguise, and concealment roles of brilliant coloration in a color reef environment.

Review Questions

1. List, in sequence, the names of the three stages of coral reef development around a new volcanic island.
2. List two specific functions of bright coloration in coral reef fish.

Questions for Further Discussion

1. Coral reefs give the appearance of highly productive ecosystems, yet they exist in oceanic regions with very low production rates and standing crops. Why do coral reefs appear to be so productive?

Suggestions for Further Reading

Books

Darwin, C., [1842] 1962. *The structure and distribution of coral reefs.* Berkeley, CA.: University of California Press.

Endean, R. 1983. *Australia's Great Barrier Reef.* New York: The University of Queensland Press.

Fox, D. L. 1979. *Biochromy: Natural coloration of living things.* Berkeley, CA.: University of California Press.

Halstead, B. W., P. S. Auerbach, and D. R. Campbell. 1990. *A colour atlas of dangerous marine animals.* Boca Raton, FL: CRC Press.

Kaplan, E. H. 1988. *A field guide to coral reefs of the Caribbean and Florida including Bermuda and the Bahamas.* Boston, MA.: Houghton Mifflin Co.

Thresher, R. E. 1984. *Reproduction in reef fishes.* Neptune City, NJ: T.H.F. Publications.

Articles

Birkeland, C. 1989. The Faustian traits of the crown of thorns starfish. *American Scientist* 77(2):154–63.

Chamberlain, J. A. 1978. Mechanical properties of coral skeleton: Compressive strength and its adaptive significance. *Paleobiology* 4:419–35.

Goreau, T. F., N. L. Goreau, and C. M. Yonge. 1971. Reef corals: Autotrophs or heterotrophs? *Biological Bulletin* 141:247–60.

Jackson, J. B. C., and T. P. Hughes. 1985. Adaptative strategies of coral-reef invertebrates. *American Scientist* 73:265–74.

Muscatine, L., and J. W. Porter. 1977. Reef corals: Mutualistic symbiosis adapted to nutrient-poor environments. *Bioscience* 27:454–60.

Schener, P. J. 1977. Chemical communication of marine invertebrates. *Bioscience* 27:644–68.

Scott, R. D., and H. R. Jitts. 1977. Photosynthesis of phytoplankton and zooxanthellae on a coral reef. *Marine Biology* 41:307–15.

Stoddart, D. R. 1973. Coral reefs: The last two million years. *Geography* 58:313–23.

Zooplankton

Chapter 10

Salp
Photo by R. Brusca

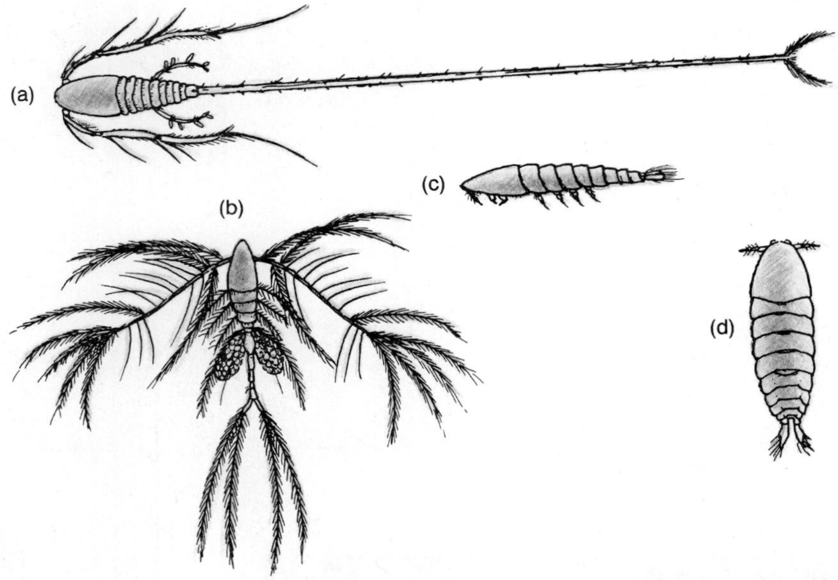

Figure 10.1
Some planktonic copepods exhibiting structural adaptions for flotation: (*a*) *Aegisthus,* (*b*) *Oithona,* (*c*) side and (*d*) top views of *Sapphirina*
Redrawn from Sverdrup, Johnson, and Fleming, 1942

Life in the pelagic division of the marine environment exists in a three-dimensional, nutritionally dilute medium. Microscopic protists and the major groups of small herbivores and many of their larger predators live in near-surface waters. The distribution of pelagic animals reflects their nutritional dependency on the primary producers of the sea. Like primary producers, pelagic animals concentrate in regions of upwelling, over continental shelves and other shallows, and elsewhere in or near the photic zone. The upper few hundred meters of the sea teem with animal life. At greater depths, population densities diminish rapidly but never completely disappear.

The animals of the pelagic division include the zooplankton and nekton. Most nektonic animals begin life as members of the zooplankton community. As the zooplankton grow and improve their swimming capabilities, they eventually graduate to the status of nekton. This chapter examines some general aspects of the biology of zooplankton; chapter 11 considers the nekton.

Zooplankton Groups

Zooplankton are represented by temporary planktonic larval stages of shallow-water invertebrates and fish (the meroplankton), and a variety of permanent planktonic forms (the holoplankton). The meroplankton, like their parents, are concentrated in near-shore neritic provinces over continental shelves and near shallow banks, reefs, and estuaries. Their abundance is related to the seasonal productivity cycles of local phytoplankton communities.

Over 5,000 species of holoplankton have been described, recruited from numerous phyla in two kingdoms. Prominent among these are unicellular forms, cnidarians, ctenophores, mollusks, chaetognaths, crustacean arthropods, and invertebrate chordates (the tunicates). The microscopic tintinnids, flagellates, and other protists seldom move far under their own power. Because of their very small cell sizes, they have great difficulty trying to overcome the viscous forces between water molecules by swimming. As a result, there is almost no

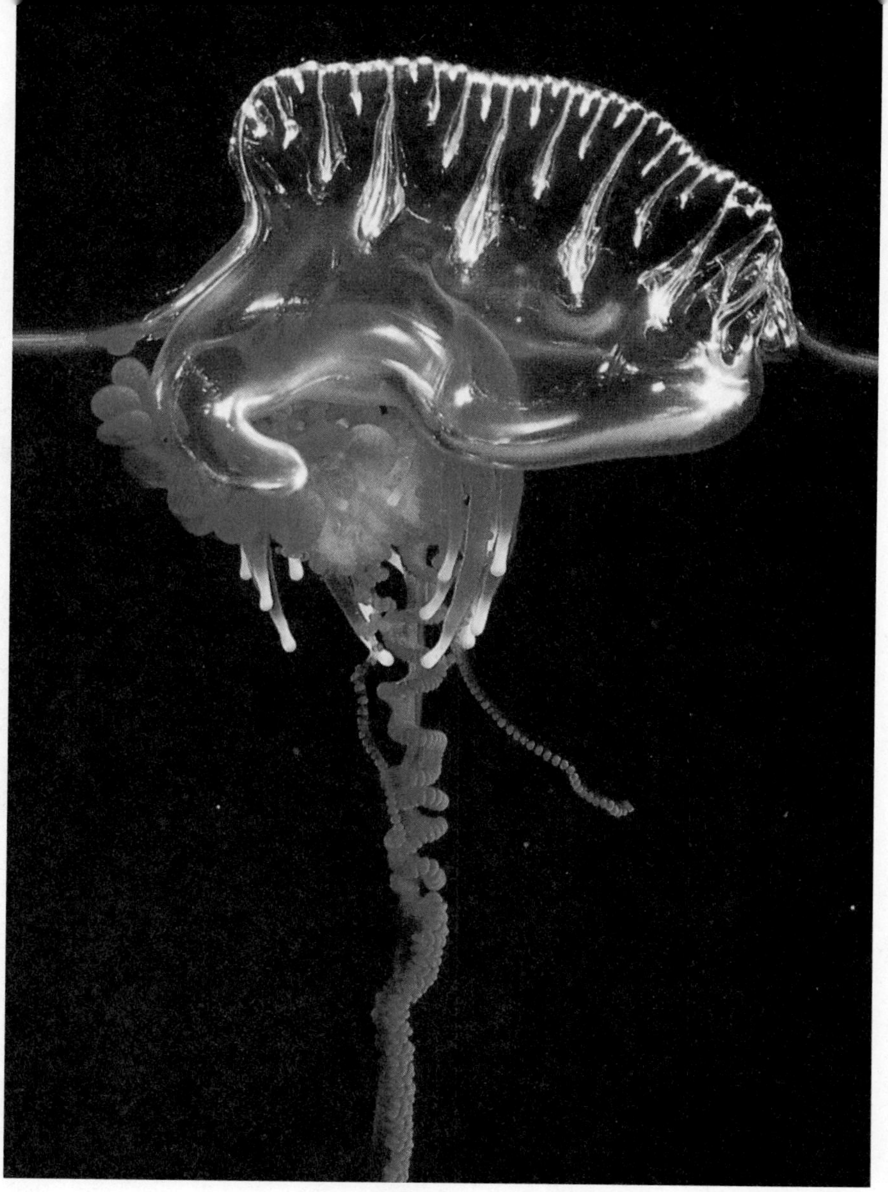

Figure 10.2
The Portuguese man-of-war, *Physalia,* floating at the sea surface. The trailing tentacles may reach 50 m in length.
Courtesy J. Trent, Scripps Institution of Oceanography

glide in this microscopic world. A cell must swim continuously in order to move. When it stops working, it stops swimming. They employ flotation and buoyancy devices similar to those found in phytoplankton. Since most holoplankton are characteristically small, they increase their frictional resistance to the water by having high surface areas to body volumes ratio. A profusion of spines, hairs, wings, and other surface extensions also increases frictional resistance to sinking (figure 10.1).

A few genera of siphonophores (a type of colonial cnidarian) maintain neutral or even positive buoyancy by secreting gases into a float, or **pneumatophore.** *Velella* (sometimes called by-the-wind sailor, Jack-by-the-wind, or simply, purple sail) and the larger Portuguese man-of-war, *Physalia* (figure 10.2) have large pneumatophores and float at the sea surface. The pneumatophore, acting as a sail, catches surface breezes and transports the colony long distances. Both *Velella* and *Physalia,* with only one species in each genus, have worldwide distributions.

Figure 10.3

A mid-water siphonophore with a small gas-filled pneumatophore at the upper end

Courtesy A. Alldridge

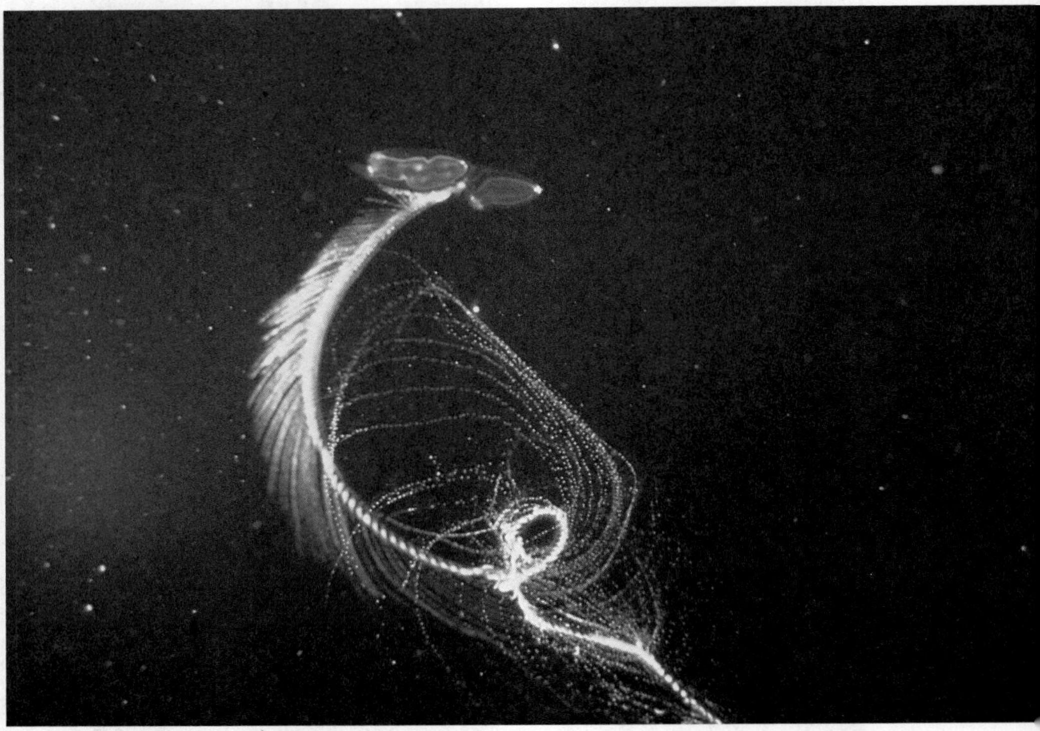

Other siphonophores with gas floats are neutrally buoyant and can easily change their vertical position in the water column by swimming (figure 10.3). A gas gland within the pneumatophore secretes gas into the float. Excess gases are vented through a small pore that is opened and closed by a sphincter muscle, and the siphonophore's buoyancy is adjusted accordingly.

Gas is also used for buoyancy by a small planktonic snail, *Glaucus*. It produces and stores intestinal gases to offset the weight of its shell. Another planktonic snail, *Ianthina,* forms a cluster of bubbles at the surface and clings to it. This adaptation is apparently related to the snail's preference for feeding on the soft parts of *Velella* (which also floats at the surface). These and other zooplankton adapted to live at the air-seawater interface are known as **neuston.** (Another example of a neuston is the water strider shown in figure 1.12.)

A large variety of gelatinous zooplankton exists, including numerous medusae (or jellyfish), siphonophores, pelagic mollusks (figure 10.4*a*), ctenophores (figure 10.4*b*), and tunicates. The tunicates include barrel-shaped salps, with life cycles alternating between solitary individuals and colonial clones (figure 10.4*c*); as well as the smaller appendicularians. Since the bodies of all these gelatinous species contain at least 95% water and their body densities are very close to that of seawater, buoyancy is not a problem. Their small proportion of organic material accounts for their low metabolic rates and for their body sizes, which range from about one mm to several m. Their relatively large sizes (in comparison to other zooplankton) and nearly transparent appearance in water confer some protection from larger pelagic predators.

Crustaceans are the most numerous and widespread species of holoplankton. Copepods, euphausiids, amphipods, decapods, and ostracods (figures 10.1 and 3.26) all contribute greatly to near-surface plankton communities.

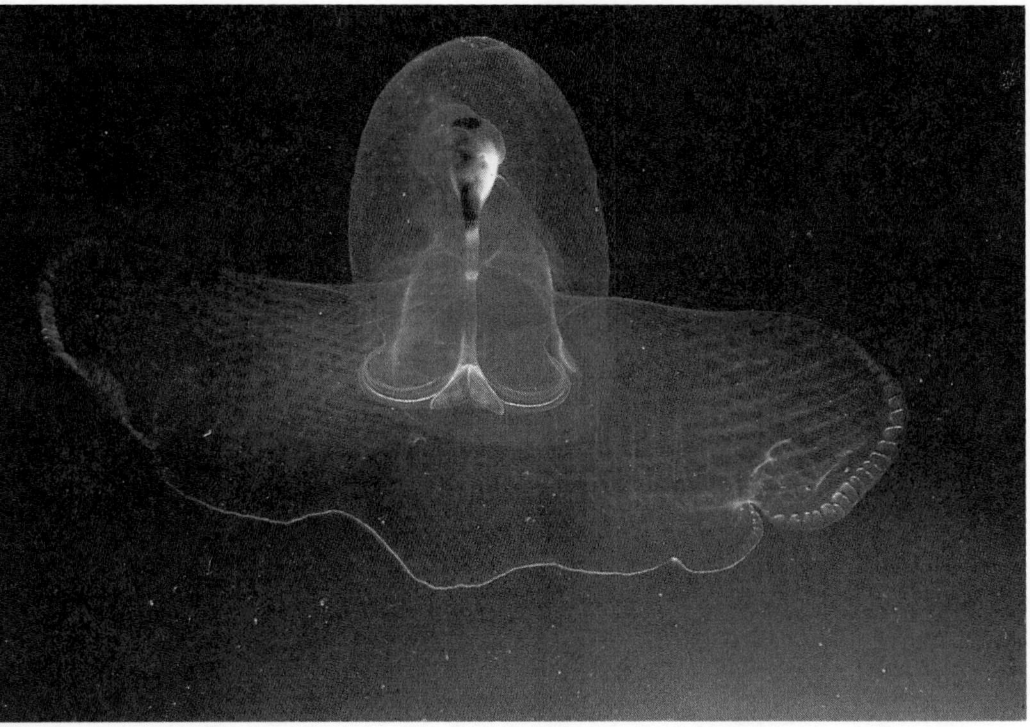

(a)

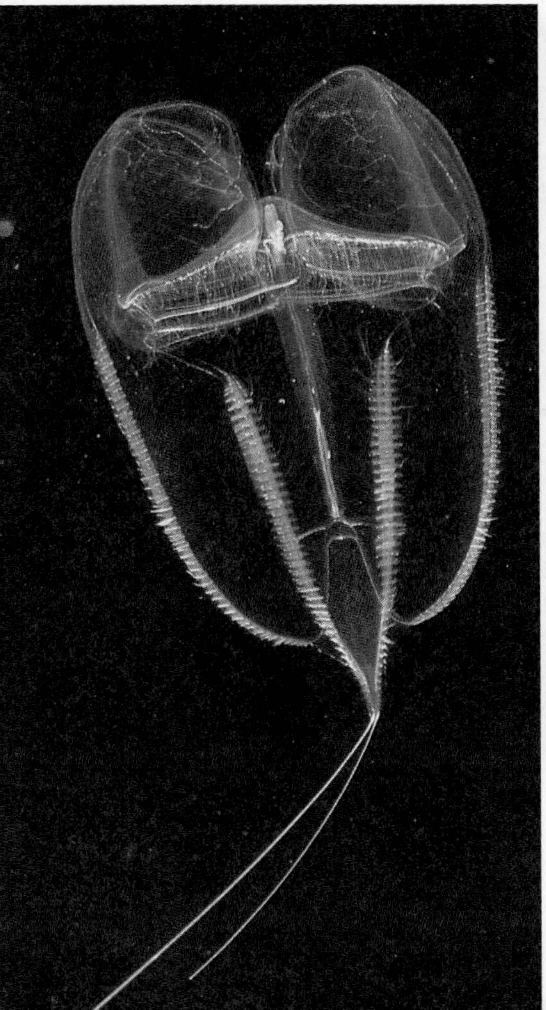

(b)

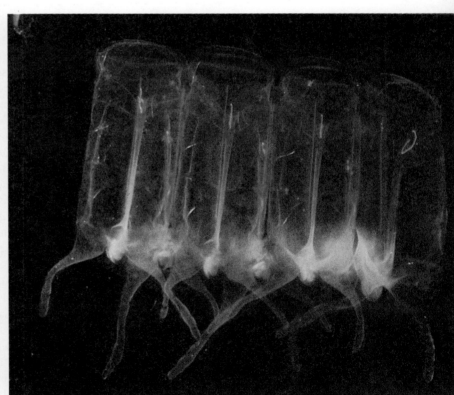

(c)

Figure 10.4
Some large gelatinous zooplankton. (*a*) A pelagic mollusk, *Corolla.* (*b*) A ctenophore, *Eurhamphea,* swimming with eight rows of ciliated combs. (*c*) A short chain of seven salps (*Pegea*) cloned from a single parent. All photos approximately life-size.

Courtesy J. Trent, Scripps Institution of Oceanography

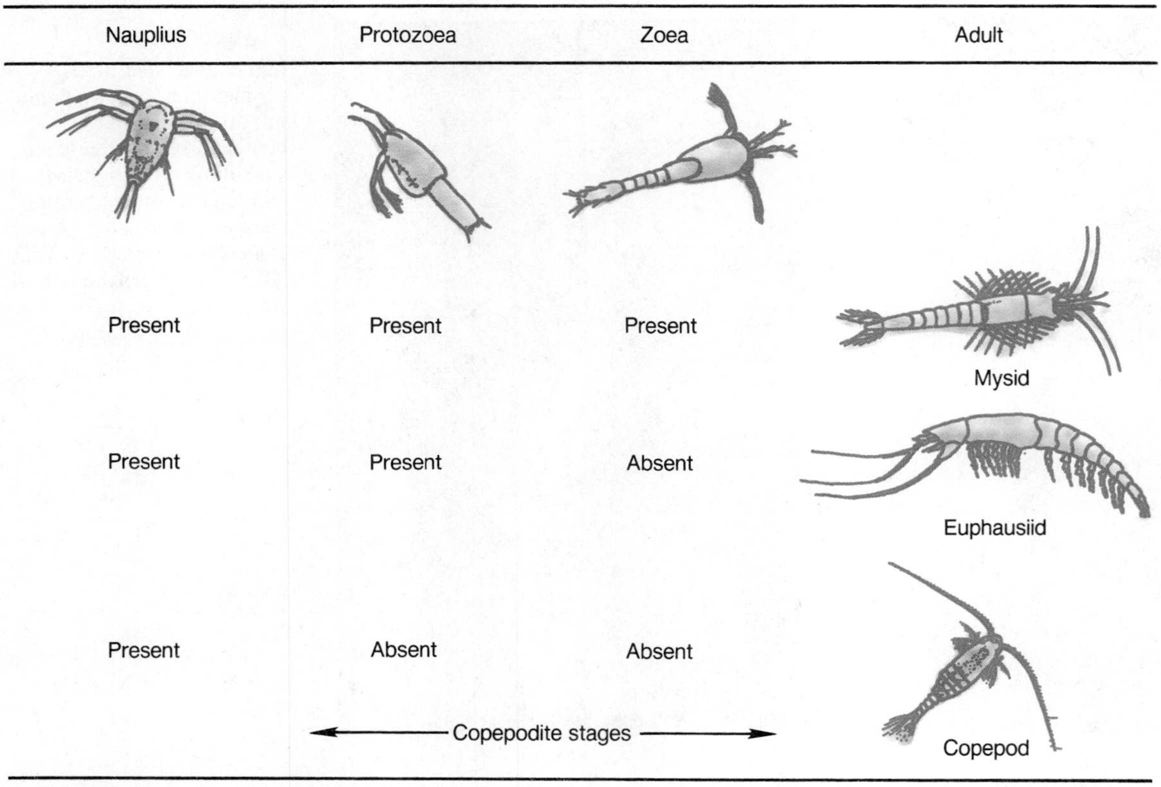

Figure 10.5
Developmental stages of three groups of planktonic crustaceans

Calanoid copepods, such as *Calanus* and *Acartia,* account for the bulk of herbivorous zooplankton in the 1 to 5 mm size range. Euphausiids, the giants of the planktonic crustaceans, seldom exceed 5 cm.

Life cycles in planktonic crustaceans involve several definable stages, each punctuated by one or more molts of the exoskeleton and some accompanied by structural metamorphosis. Planktonic mysids exhibit a fairly generalized crustacean life cycle, which includes four distinct stages: the **nauplius, protozoea, zoea,** and adult (figure 10.5). These stages are seen in the development of many other crustaceans, including crabs, shrimps, and euphausiids (figure 10.5, middle). Planktonic copepods have life cycles (figure 10.5, bottom) that differ somewhat from mysids and euphausiids. Their eggs hatch into nauplius larvae that move with their antennae. After six molts, the larvae enter the copepodite stage, a sexually immature form resembling adults. Five more molts lead to the adult stage; thereafter no more molts occur. The yearly growth and reproductive cycles for a copepod are shown in figure 10.6.

The Pelagic Environment

The pelagic division of the world ocean is a realm that presents few obvious ecological niches for its inhabitants. With little local variation in temperature and chemical characteristics smoothed out by turbulent mixing and diffusive processes, patterns of light intensity, water temperature, and food availability change only on horizontal scales of several km.

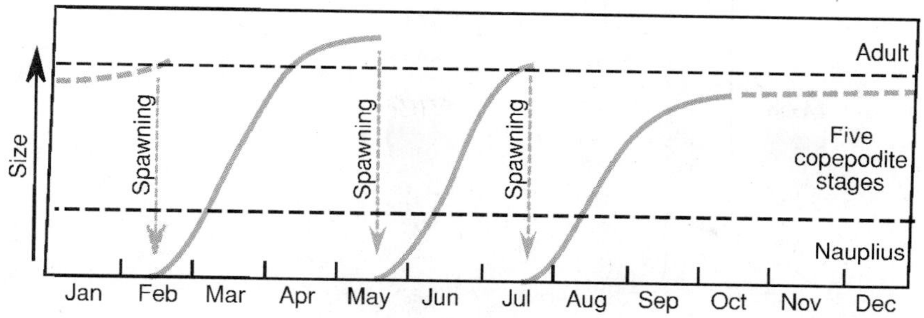

Figure 10.6
Growth and reproductive cycles of a North Atlantic copepod (*Calanus finmarchicus*). The adults of each brood produce eggs for the next brood (arrows). Dashed lines indicate overwintering of copepodites in deep water that experiences little growth.
Adapted from Russell, 1935

Away from the influences of continental borders, zooplankton in the upper 200 m of the world ocean slowly drift along in large, semienclosed current gyres. This upper layer of the oceanic province, the **epipelagic zone,** is approximately coincident to the photic zone. In marked contrast to the numerous life zones available to animals on the sea bottom, the epipelagic zone can be partitioned into only a few major habitats, each broadly defined by its own unique combination of temperature and salinity characteristics. These major epipelagic habitats reflect the major marine climatic zones shown in figure 1.18. Each habitat is occupied by a suite of zooplankton species that, over a long period of time, have adapted to a special set of environmental conditions.

Figure 10.7 maps the distribution patterns of six species of planktonic euphausiids. These patterns resemble the general large-scale distribution of many other epipelagic animal species. As noted in figure 10.7, there is a tendency for each species to be distributed in a broad latitudinal band across one or more oceans. Well-defined patterns of tropical (*Euphausia diomediae*); subtropical (*E. brevis*), and south polar (*E. superba*) distribution are evident. Some species, such as *E. diomediae* and *E. brevis,* are broadly tolerant to their environmental regimes and occupy wide latitudinal bands. Other species, (*E. longirostris, Thysanoessa gregaria,* and *E. superba*) occupy narrower latitudinal ranges. Similar regimes in both the Northern and Southern Hemispheres are frequently inhabited by the same species. The subtropical *E. brevis* and the temperate water *T. gregaria* exhibit this **biantitropical distribution.** Often these lower latitude species extend into all three major ocean basins (*E. brevis* and *T. gregaria*), but occasionally they do not (*E. diomediae* is conspicuously absent from the tropical Atlantic). The distribution of *E. diomediae* suggests that although comparable latitudes in the Atlantic, Pacific, and Indian Oceans provide similar environmental conditions, each ocean still retains significant individual differences.

High latitude species in the Southern Hemisphere (*E. longirostris* and *E. superba*) also extend around the globe, aided by extensive oceanic connections between Antarctica and the other southern continents. Similar circumglobal distributions are less common in the higher latitudes of the Northern Hemisphere (*T. longipes* is restricted to the North Pacific).

The boundaries of these zones overlap slightly; but analyses of the distribution patterns of numerous other species of zooplankton and nekton confirm that these boundaries define, in a very real way, the major epipelagic habitats of the oceanic province. However, smaller scale variations of environmental features do exist and do influence the structure of pelagic communities by contributing additional texture to the physical-chemical terrain

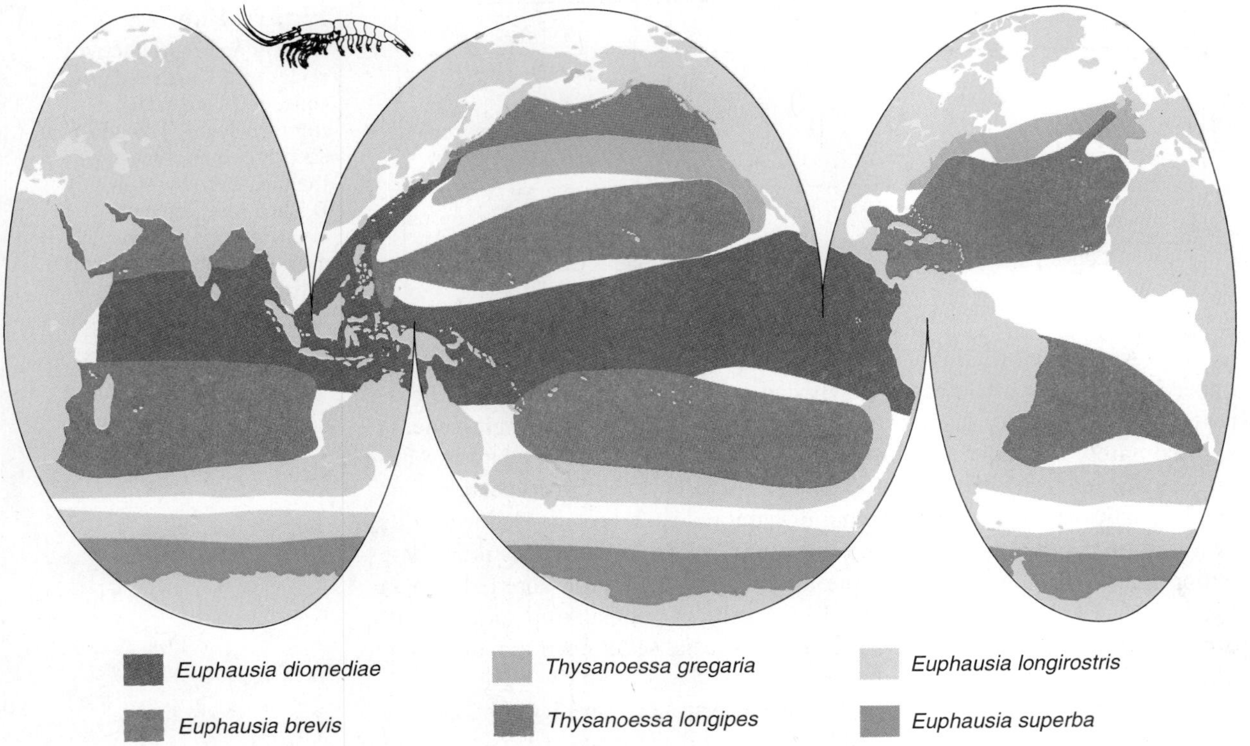

Figure 10.7
The global distribution of six species of epipelagic euphausiids

and by creating potential niches for occupation. Zooplankton, like phytoplankton, have patchy distributions at virtually all levels of sampling, from several km down to microscopic distances. Some of this patchiness develops from the local effects of grazing or predation, some from responses to chemical and physical gradients, and some from the social responses of planktonic species (such as aggregation or avoidance).

Even finer scale patchiness develops around macroscopic particles. Such particles are produced in epipelagic waters by two associated processes that package extremely small, abundant particles into a few larger particles. One of these processes is the production of fecal pellets by herbivorous grazers (figure 10.8). The other process is the incorporation of living and dead material into variously shaped organic aggregates sometimes known as "marine snow." These aggregates, ranging from one mm to several mm in size, occur in concentrations up to 30,000/m^3 in neritic waters and are composed of living and dead phytoplankton cells, abundant bacteria, exoskeletons shed by crustaceans, and detrital material. (Sometimes these aggregates also include fecal pellets, so the distinction between the two types of particles blurs somewhat.) Both types of particles serve as sites of additional aggregation by other members of the plankton community. Bacteria inoculate the particles and initiate processes of decomposition. Dinoflagellates exploit the nutrients released by the activity of the bacteria; and grazing herbivores are attracted by the concentration of energy-rich organic material, both living and dead.

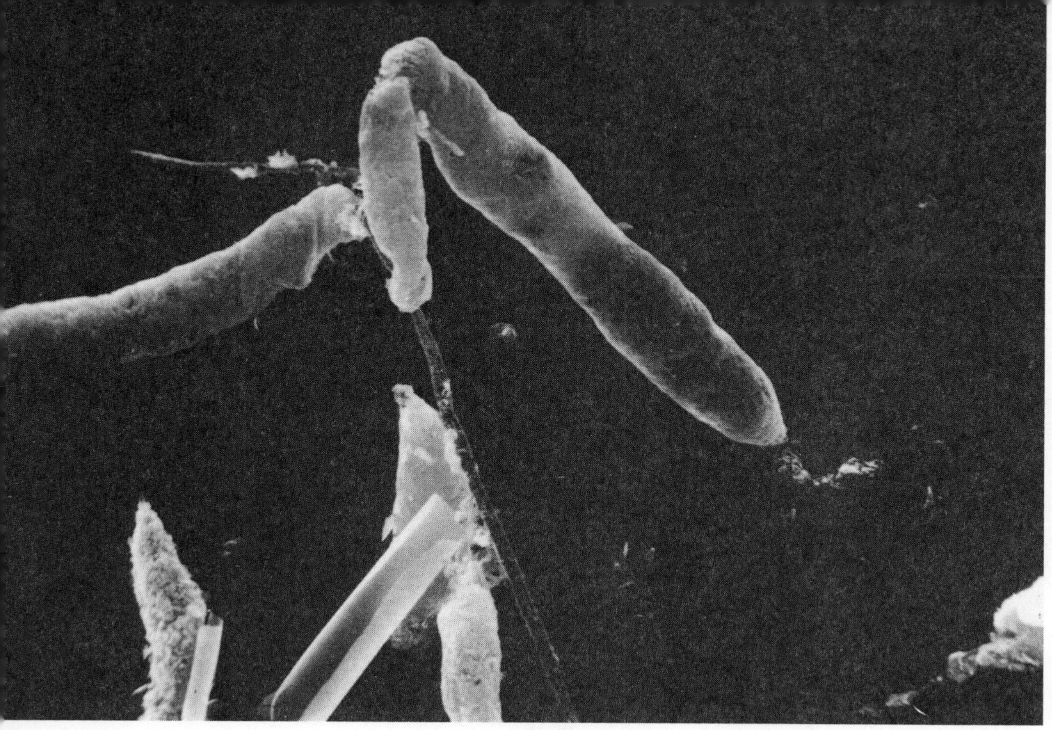

Figure 10.8
An SEM of a copepod fecal pellet containing fragments of phytoplankton cells
Courtesy P. Azam, Scripps Institution of Oceanography

Vertical Migration

Zooplankton, by definition, cannot make directed, long-distance horizontal movements. They can, however, experience major environmental changes by vertically moving modest distances (a few tens of meters). Water temperature, light intensity, pressure, and food availability all change markedly as the distance from the sea surface increases.

Below the sunlit waters of the epipelagic zone lies the **mesopelagic zone,** a world where animals live in very dim light and depend on the rain of living and dead debris from the photic zone above for food. The mesopelagic zone extends from the bottom of the epipelagic zone down to about 1,000 m. The permanent members of the mesopelagic zone rely totally on the flux of particles from above for food. This downward transport is accelerated by the conversion of dispersed microscopic cells to fecal pellets and organic aggregates. The fecal pellets of calanoid copepods, for instance, sink about ten times faster than do the individual phytoplankton cells constituting the pellet.

The mesopelagic zone offers some distinct advantages when compared to life nearer the sea surface. Predators find it more difficult to see their prey in the dim light. Decreased water temperatures at mid-depths lower the metabolic rates and the food and O_2 requirements of mesopelagic animals. The cold water, with its increased density and viscosity, also slows the sinking rates of food particles.

Large numbers of mesopelagic animals (including many fish species) periodically migrate upward to feed in near-surface waters. The most common pattern of vertical migration occurs on a daily cycle. At dusk, these mid-water animals ascend to the photic zone and feed throughout the night. Before daybreak, they begin migrating to deeper, darker waters to spend the day. The following evening, the pattern is repeated. In the productive Antarctic, the

Figure 10.9
A generalized kite diagram of net collections of adult female copepods, *Calanus finmarchicus,* during a complete one-day vertical migration cycle. Night hours are shaded.

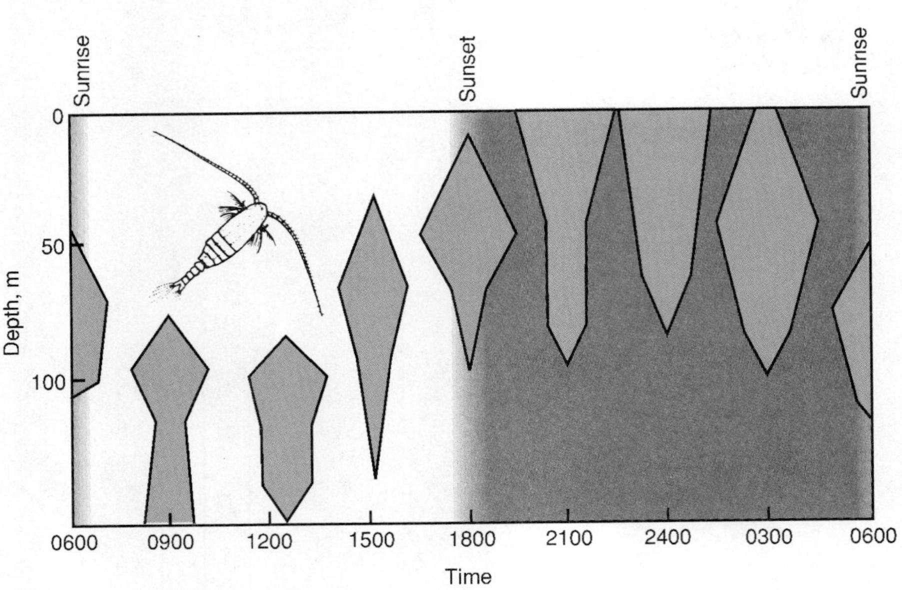

daily pattern of vertical migration often breaks down; the animals generally remain in the photic zone during the summer and in deeper waters during the winter.

The general pattern of daily, or diurnal, **vertical migration** has been deduced from numerous sources of information. Net collections of animals from several depths at different times throughout the day have shown that more animals are near the surface at night (figure 10.9). Direct observations from submersible vehicles support these conclusions.

Underwater sound pulses from ship-mounted echo sounders have also been used extensively to study the behavior of vertically migrating animals. The pulses are partially reflected by concentrations or layers of mid-water animals. These sound-reflecting, **deep scattering layers** (DSL) ascend nearly to the surface at dusk and then break up (figure 10.10). At daybreak, the layers reform and descend to their usual daytime depths (200–600 m). Often three or more distinct layers are discernible over broad oceanic areas.

The composition of the DSL is still an unsettled question. Most inhabitants of the mesopelagic zone are too small or too sparsely distributed to strongly reflect sound signals. Net tows and observations from manned submersibles suggest that there are three groups of animals that cause the deep scattering layers: euphausiids, small fish (primarily lantern fish, figure 10.11), and siphonophores (figure 10.3). Euphauiids and small fish are often abundant members at depths where the DSL occur. The strong echoes of sound pulses may be due, in part, to the resonating qualities of the gas-filled swim bladders of lantern fish and air floats of siphonophore. Relatively few swim bladders or air floats are necessary to produce strong echoes at certain sound frequencies.

Whatever the composition of the DSL, they are merely sound-reflecting indicators of a much more extensive vertically migrating assemblage of animals not detected by echolocation. Undoubtedly, members of the DSL graze on smaller vertical migrators and are, in turn, preyed upon by larger fish and squid.

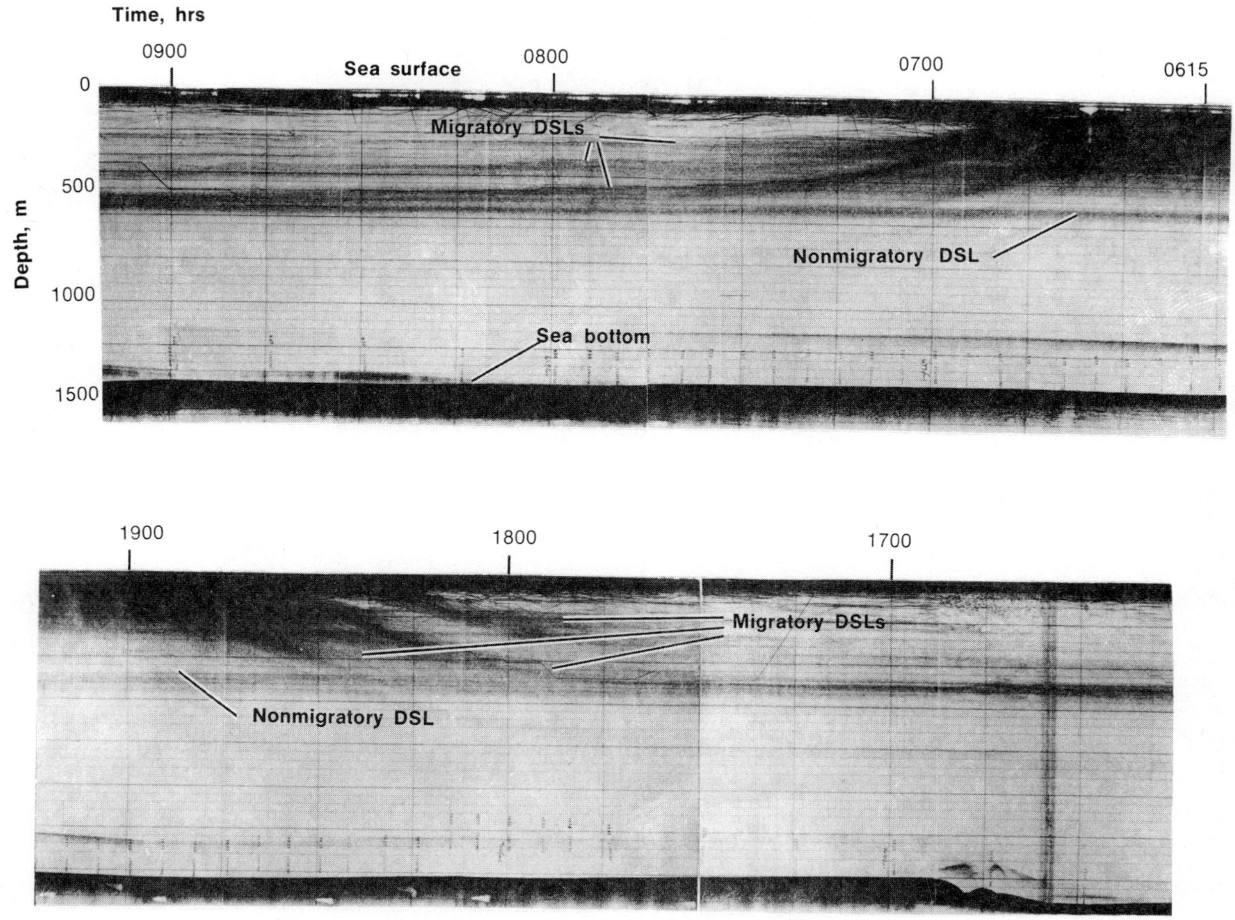

Figure 10.10
A SONAR record of several distinct sound scattering layers at a station near the Canary Islands. Except for slight drift corrections, the recording ship remained stationary. The time scale reads from right to left. Multiple layers begin migrating downward at daylight (0700 hrs.), remain near 500 m throughout the day, then migrate upward in the evening (1800–1900 hrs).
Courtesy E. Kampa, Scripps Institution of Oceanography and the National Institute of Oceanography

These vertical migrations, only a few hundred meters in extent, occur in a short period of time. The copepod, *Calanus,* for example, is only a few mm long, yet it swims upward at 15 m/hr and descends at 50 m/hr. Larger euphausiids (2 cm long) move in excess of 100 m/hr. If diurnal vertical migrations are foraging trips from below into the productive photic zone, why do these animals descend after feeding? Why don't they remain in the photic zone? Many explanations for the adaptive value of vertical migration have been offered.

One possible explanation is that diurnal vertical migration allows animals to capitalize on the more abundant food resources of the photic zone in the dark of night and to escape visual detection by predators in the refuge of the dimly lit mesopelagic zone during the day. But vertical migration is useful in other ways. Lower water temperatures at the deeper depths reduce an animal's metabolic rate and its energy requirements. The energy conserved may be sufficient to offset the lack of food during the day and the slight energy expenditures incurred during the actual migration. Each of these explanations offers plausible mechanisms favoring the selection of individuals possessing the genetic information required to accomplish vertical migration.

Figure 10.11

A midwater lantern fish, *Bolinichthys.* Small black dots are light-producing photophores.

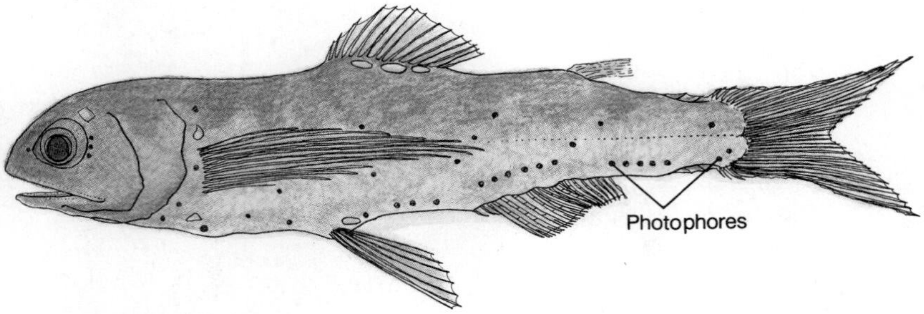

Figure 10.12

The upward migration of a scattering layer (colored portions of the graph) at sunset, November 4, near the Canary Islands. Note the very close correspondence between the isolume and the top of the scattering layer, with both rising as the surface light intensity diminishes.

Redrawn from Boden and Kampa, 1967

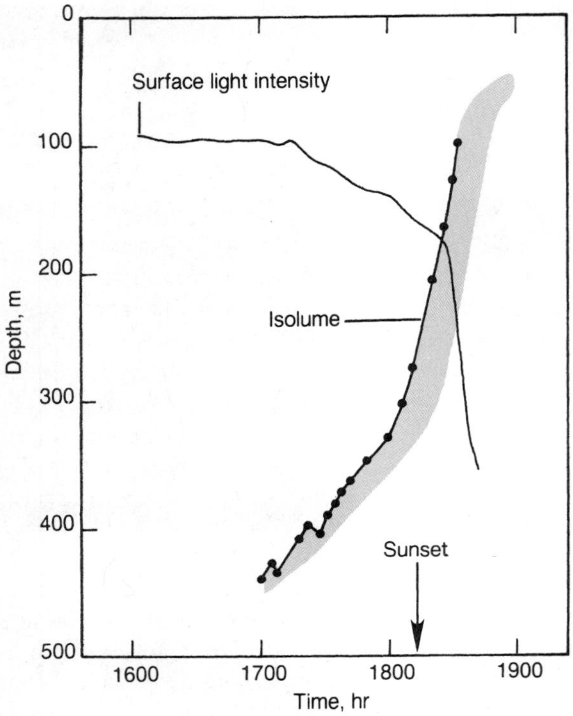

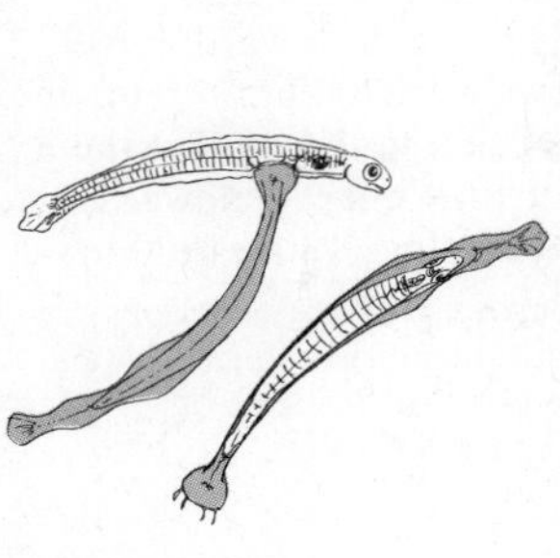

Figure 10.13

A small chaetognath, *Sagitta* (color), capturing and consuming a fish larva its own size

Vertical migrations of zooplankton and small nekton can also occur on seasonal time scales. While in the late copepodite stage, the *Calanus finmarchicus* spends the winter months of low productivity in the North Atlantic at depths near 1,000 m. When the spring diatom bloom develops, they molt to the adult form and begin to rise into the photic zone. In polar seas, diurnal vertical migration is often completely suppressed during summer months of continuous daylight and high plant productivity. Major herbivores, such as *Euphausia superba,* rise from winter depths of 250–500 m to the surface in late spring. In autumn, they descend once more to their wintertime depths.

Daily or seasonal changes in light intensity seem to be the most likely stimulus for vertical migrations. Large-scale experiments with mixed coastal zooplankton populations have demonstrated that, under constant light and temperature conditions, some species of copepods maintained their diurnal migratory behavior as a circadian rhythm for several days without relying on external cues such as light intensity. Other species did not migrate and ap-

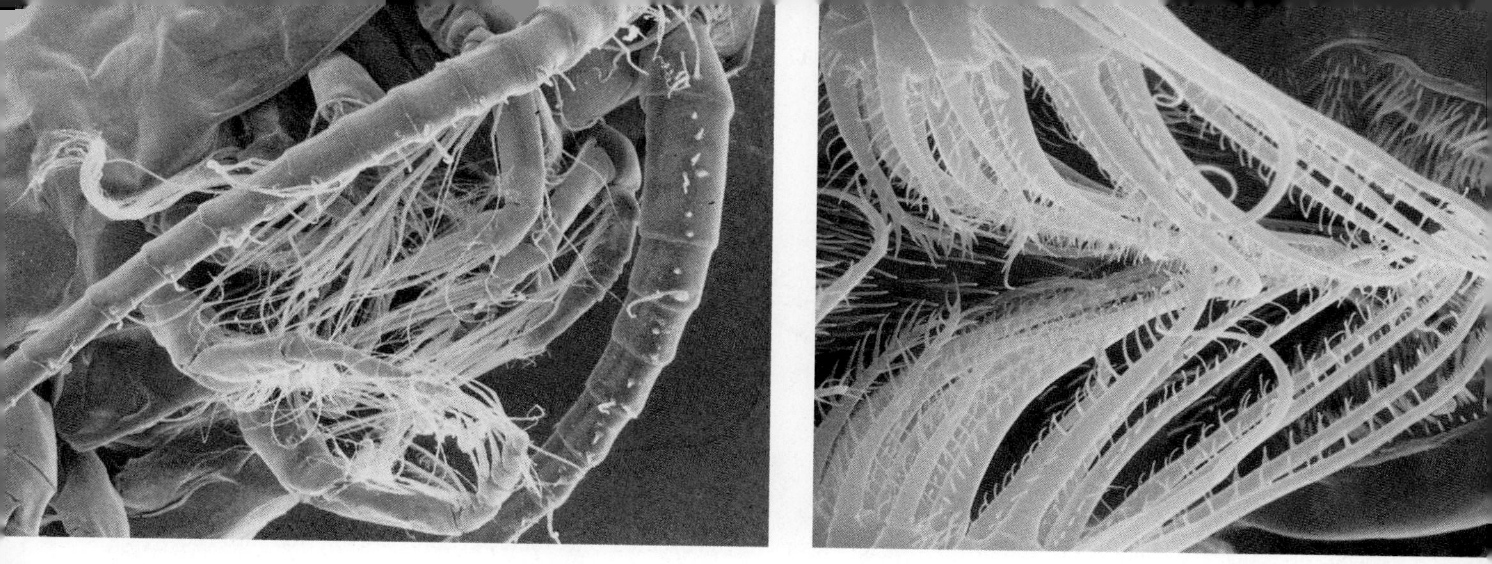

Figure 10.14
(left) An SEM of the thorax and filtering mechanism of *Calanus*, shown in side view. (right) Higher magnification of *Calanus*, showing the ventral view of the two mandibles (far left) and the filtering basket formed by the second maxillae.
Courtesy J. R. Strickler

parently required light or another external stimulus to induce vertical migration. Electric lights lowered into the water at night and bright moonlight have actually driven the DSL downward from 60 m to 300 m. Solar eclipses cause the opposite to occur; vertical migrators move toward the surface during an eclipse, even at midday.

These responses demonstrate a sensitivity to light intensity by natural populations of vertical migrators. Each DSL follows an isolume (a constant light intensity) characteristic of the top of the layer at its normal daytime depth (figure 10.12). As the sunlight intensity decreases in late afternoon, the isolume moves toward the sea surface and the DSL follows with a precision seldom seen in natural populations.

Feeding

Zooplankton employ all conceivable methods of capturing food, from suspension feeding of bacteria and phytoplankton to the direct predation on other zooplankton and small nekton. The small, soft-bodied chaetognaths, a minor phylum with about sixty species, are voracious predators of other zooplankton. They are found throughout the world ocean in numbers sufficient to decimate whole broods of young fish (figure 10.13). In addition to their significant role in pelagic food chains, some species of chaetognaths are well-known biological indicators of distinctive types of surface ocean water.

Copepods are common prey of chaetognaths. All adult calanoid copepods species are similar in body form and general feeding behavior, suggesting a very successful functional form. Copepods and other small pelagic particle grazers are typically exposed to a wide spectrum of food particle sizes. Food particles range from abundant minute bacteria through the common types of phytoplankton to organic aggregates and large centric diatoms. This size spectrum presents an opportunity for small, versatile particle grazers to adopt a feeding strategy that involves selectivity of optimum-sized food items.

Although copepods prey on large phytoplankton cells when they are available, calanoid species can capture the smaller, more abundant microplankton with a basketlike filtering mechanism derived from their complex feathery head appendages (figure 10.14). The hairlike setae on the appendages of *Calanus* are fine enough to retain food particles larger than 10 μm.

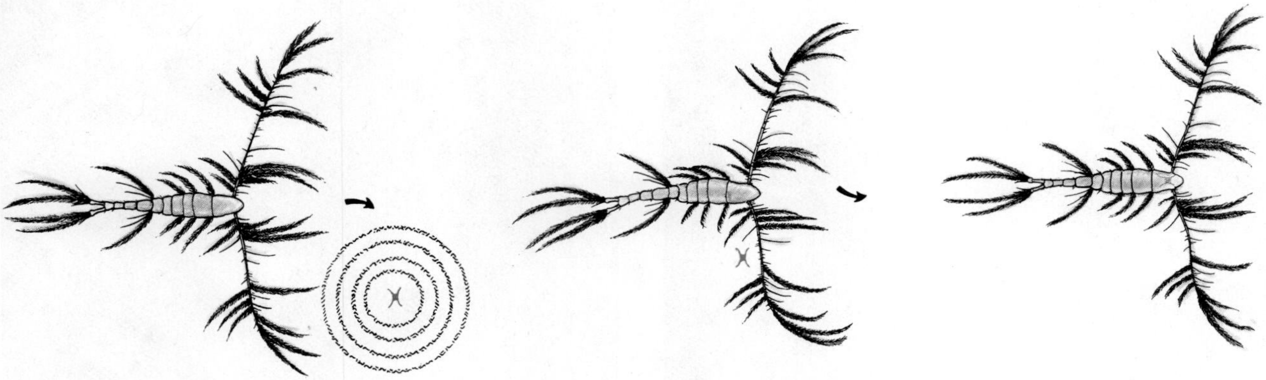

Figure 10.15
Copepod detection and capture behavior of individual diatoms (green). Sensory cells arranged in arrays on large antennae provide information to detect prey and guide the response until the capture is made (right).

Laboratory observations have revealed that food particles are carried into the filter basket by currents generated by the feeding appendages and the five posteriorly-positioned pairs of thoracic swimming legs. Special long setae on the feeding appendages remove the trapped particles and direct them to the mouth. With this filtering mechanism, *Calanus* is capable of exploiting a wide size range of food particles.

Even though *Calanus* and similar copepods can shift rapidly from one food particle size to the other, they prefer larger food particles to smaller ones. Recent studies, using high-speed microphotography techniques, have shown that calanoid copepods efficiently capture sparsely scattered single large food items such as protozoans, small fish eggs, and large diatoms. As the copepods feeding actions drive them forward in the water, their antennae extend laterally to function as an array of flow sensors that detect minute disturbances surrounding larger food items (figure 10.15). If the food particle is detected near the end of an antenna, the animal quickly adjusts its swimming direction to bring the particle within reach of an extended feeding appendage. The mouthparts then seize and manipulate the particles before eating them. Because filtering and large-particle seizure cannot operate simultaneously, this mode of feeding is interrupted when the copepods are filtering small particles.

Such particle-size selectivity by copepods is likely an important factor in stabilizing phytoplankton populations. When phytoplankton populations of a particular cell size become more abundant through growth and reproduction, they attract increased grazing pressures as more copepods shift feeding strategies to concentrate on them. It is unlikely, however, that the phytoplankton population would be grazed to extinction. Several species exhibit ingestion rates that are dependent on the concentration of phytoplankton cells (figure 10.16). For a certain food particle size, ingestion rates increase with increasing particle density to some critical maximum. Beyond the maximum particle density, some aspect of the copepod's food-processing system appears to become saturated, and no further increase in ingestion rates occurs. Conversely, ingestion rates decrease with decreasing phytoplankton densities; copepods most likely shift to another nearly optimum concentration of food particles before the first population is completely decimated.

In contrast to the rigid filter devices of crustaceans, many gelatinous herbivores rely on nets or webs of mucus to ensnare food particles. One highly evolved example is *Gleba,* a planktonic pteropod mollusk. When feeding, *Gleba* secretes a mucous web that often exceeds 2 m in diameter. The free-floating web spreads horizontally as it is produced, maintaining a single point of attachment at the mouth. As the animal and web slowly sink, small plankton

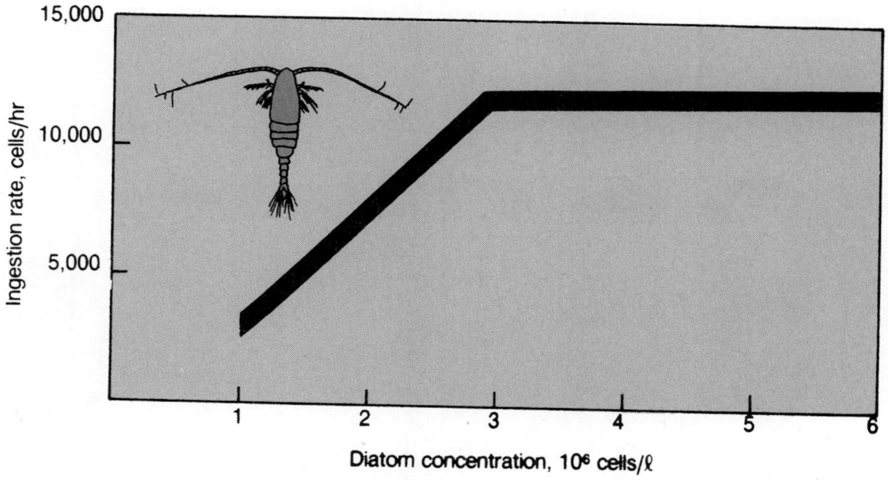

Figure 10.16
The ingestion rate of a copepod, *Calanus,* as a function of the concentration of its food (in this case, the diatom *Thalassiosira,* shown in figure 4.6). The ingestion rate peaks near 3,000 diatom cells per ml, and no further increase is seen even at much higher concentrations.
Redrawn from Frost, 1972

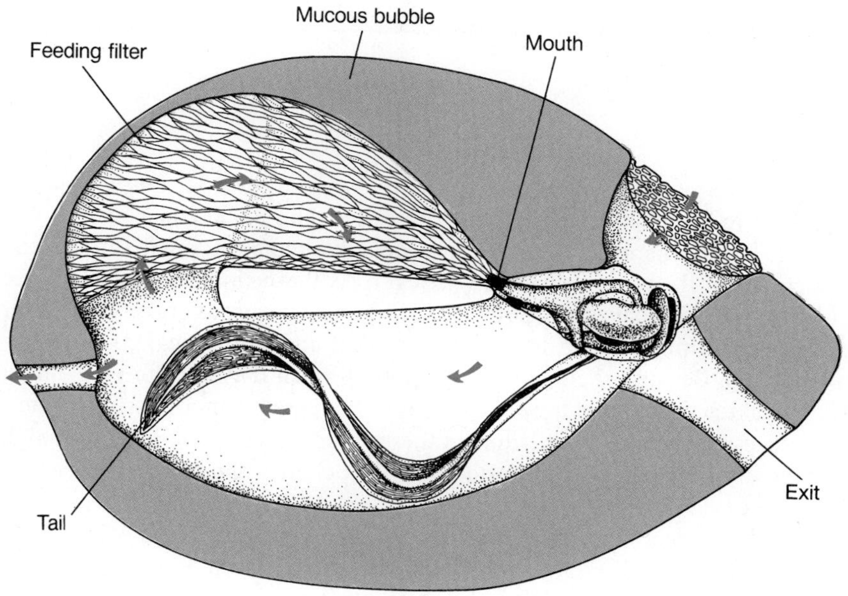

Figure 10.17
The appendicularian, *Oikopleura,* within its mucous bubble. Arrows indicate path of water flow.

and other particles become trapped in the mucus. The web, with its load of food, is then formed into a mucous string, directed to the mouth, and ingested. *Gleba* then swims upward to repeat the behavior.

Another elaborate mucous feeding system is found in appendicularians, small, tadpole-shaped invertebrate chordates. Most appendicularians live enclosed within delicate, transparent mucous bubbles (figure 10.17). Food-laden water, pumped by the tail beat of the occupant, enters the bubble through openings at one end. These openings are screened with fine-meshed grills to exclude large phytoplankton cells. Smaller cells enter the bubble and are trapped on a complex internal mucous feeding filter. Every few seconds, the animal sucks the particles off the filter and into its mouth. When the incurrent filter becomes clogged or the interior is fouled with feces, the entire bubble is abandoned and a new one is constructed, sometimes in as little as ten minutes.

With this feeding mechanism, bacterial-sized particles can be harvested with high efficiency, for these animals achieve filtering rates several times higher than those of calanoid copepods. The larger salps are even better;

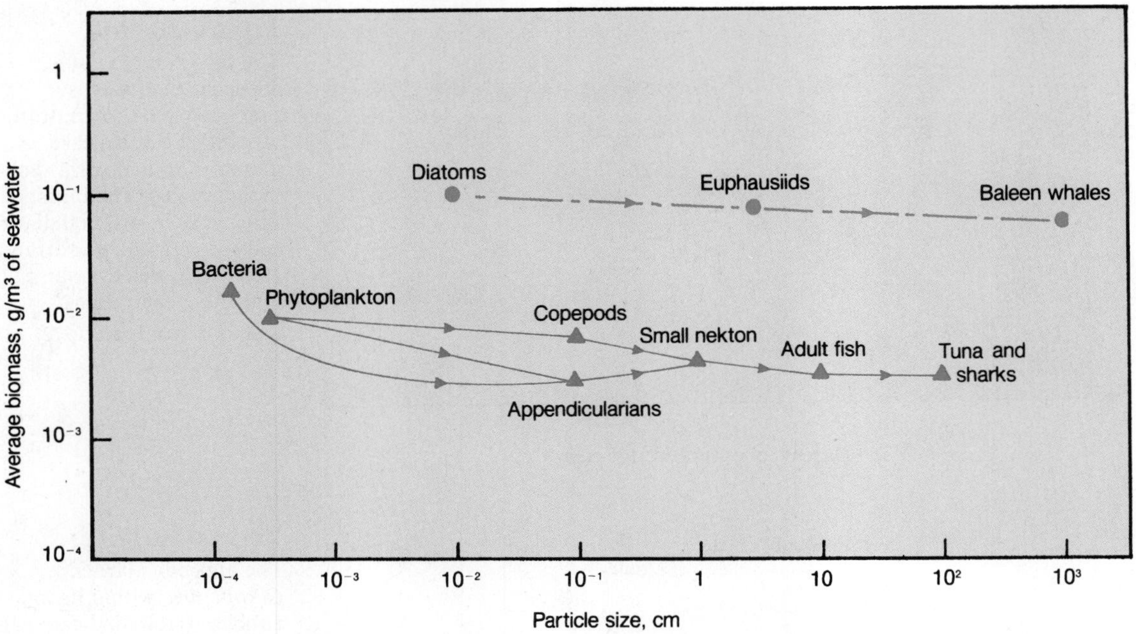

Figure 10.18
The relationship between food particle size and biomass in two pelagic food chains. Note that the biomass in the Antarctic (dashed lines) is about ten times higher at all trophic levels than those in subtropical gyres (solid lines) and that the biomass of each food chain is approximately the same at all trophic levels.
Redrawn from Steele, 1980

a small chain of colonial salps (such as the seven shown in figure 10.4*c*) is estimated to be capable of filtering more water than 3,000 copepods.

The mechanisms employed by zooplankton to glean small, diffuse food particles from the water reflect the critical roles these animals play in pelagic food chains. Planktonic tunicates are the largest herbivorous grazers to exploit the very small phytoplankton found in tropical and subtropical areas of low productivity. Because their filters clog quickly when they encounter the high phytoplankton densities of upwelling areas or temperate climate spring blooms, they are less successful competitors in these areas. It is in these regions of high productivity that planktonic crustaceans, particularly the calanoid copepods and euphausiids, thrive.

Two generalized food chains are shown in figure 10.18 to illustrate some fundamental differences in trophic linkages between oceanic regions of high and low productivity. Food chains of subtropical waters are low in biomass, begin with very small phytoplankton, and include several trophic levels; leading to tuna-sized predators. The Antarctic up-welling system, in contrast, is characterized by relatively large (though still microscopic) primary producers, larger filter-feeding herbivores, and fewer trophic levels; this system produces carnivores of immense size.

In the productive waters of the Antarctic (which correspond to the area occupied by *Euphausia superba* in figure 10.7), the average biomass at all trophic levels is approximately ten times greater than that in subtropical gyres. Within each region, the biomass is about the same at each trophic level. In other words, during summer months, a km^2 of Antarctic ocean surface includes as much diatom material as it does baleen whale biomass. The difference in life span from hours in diatoms to decades in whales permits the whales to compensate for their relatively small population with very large individual body size. These animals of higher trophic levels are the subjects of the remainder of this text.

Summary

Permanent members of zooplankton communities are drawn from several animal phyla. Small crustaceans are the most abundant phyla, with fewer species of medusae, tunicates, and other gelatinous forms. All live in a vast fluid environment characterized by latitudinally defined geographical life zones. Vertically, conditions of light intensity, water temperature, and food availability decrease markedly below the epipelagic zone. Herbivorous zooplankton, like the phytoplankton they consume, are characterized by large- and small-scale patchy distribution patterns.

Many zooplankton and small nekton make daily roundtrip vertical migrations between the productive waters near the surface and the darker, cooler waters below the photic zone. Feeding mechanisms employed by zooplankton are varied, but the most common mechanisms utilize filters or mucous nets to collect small, dispersed food particles. The zooplankton's ability to collect very small food particles and package them into larger ones place zooplankton in critical positions in marine food chains.

Review Questions

1. Describe mechanisms that establish and maintain patchy distributions of zooplankton.
2. Describe the role of the deep scattering layer in the exchange of nutrients and energy between the epipelagic zone and deeper water masses.
3. List three types of animals commonly found in the deep scattering layer (DSL).
4. Describe two plausible benefits of daily vertical migration for members of the DSL.

Questions for Further Discussion

1. Describe how temperature and light intensity change along the sea surface from the equator poleward. From the sea surface at the equator downward to 1,000 m.
2. Discuss what competitive advantages gelatinous bodies might confer on zooplankton like medusae and tunicates.

Suggestions for Further Reading

Books

Briggs, J. C. 1974. *Marine zoogeography.* New York: McGraw-Hill.

Hardy, A. 1971. *The open sea: Its natural history. Part I: The world of plankton.* Boston: Houghton Mifflin.

Kerfoot, W. C., ed. 1981. *Evolution and ecology of zooplankton communities.* Halstead, NH: University Press of New England.

Marshall, S. M., and A. P. Orr. 1972. *The biology of a marine copepod.* New York: Springer-Verlag.

Steele, J. S., ed. 1978. *Spatial pattern in plankton communities.* New York: Plenum Press.

Wickstead, J. H. 1976. *Marine zooplankton.* London: E. Arnold.

Articles

Allan, J. D. 1976. Life history patterns in zooplankton. *American Naturalist* 110:165–80.

Alldredge, A. 1976. Appendicularians. *Scientific American* 235 (July):94–102.

Alldredge, A. L., and L. P. Madin. 1982. Pelagic tunicates: Unique herbivores in the marine plankton. *Bioscience* 32:655–63.

Benson, A. A., and R. F. Lee. 1975. The role of wax in oceanic food chains. *Scientific American* 232 (March):76–86.

Boyd, C. M. 1976. Selection of particles sizes by filter-feeding copepods: A plea for reason. *Limnology and Oceanography* 21:175–79.

Dietz, R. S. 1962. The sea's deep scattering layers. *Scientific American* 207 (August):44–50.

Isaacs, J. D. 1977. The life of the open sea. *Nature* 267:778–85.

Lam, R. K., and B. W. Frost. 1976. Model of copepod filtering response to changes in size and concentration of food. *Limnology and Oceanography* 21:490–500.

Porter, K. G., and J. W. Porter. 1979. Bioluminescence in marine plankton: A coevolved antipredation system. *American Naturalist* 114:458–61.

Rubenstein, D. I., and M. A. R. Koehl. 1977. The mechanisms of filter feeding: Some theoretical considerations. *American Naturalist* 111:981–94.

Sheldon, R. W., A. Prakash, and W. H. Sutcliffe, Jr. 1972. The size distribution of particles in the ocean. *Limnology and Oceanography* 17:327–40.

Silver, M. W., A. L. Shanks, and J. D. Trent. 1978. Marine snow: Microplankton habitat and source of small-scale patchiness in pelagic populations. *Science* 201:371–73.

Steele, J. 1980. Patterns in plankton. *Oceanus* 25 (summer):3–8.

Turner, J. T., P. A. Tester, and W. F. Hettler. 1985. Zooplankton feeding ecology. *Marine Biology* 90:1–8.

Zaret, T. M., and J. S. Suffern. 1976. Vertical migration in zooplankton as a predator avoidance mechanism. *Limnology and Oceanography* 21:804–13.

The Nekton

Chapter 11

Schooling anchovies
Photo by T. Phillipp

More than five thousand species of nektonic animals roam the pelagic province of the world ocean. These animals represent some of the taxonomic groups that have achieved the larger body sizes and greater swimming powers needed to exploit the pelagic realm of the world ocean. Absolute body size is crucial; once a well-muscled animal exceeds a few cm in body length, the viscous forces of water that limit continuous swimming by zooplankton begin to diminish, and more efficient patterns of swimming are possible.

Of the numerous groups of marine invertebrates, only the squids and a few species of shrimps are truly nektonic. In some regions, vast numbers of small squids (less than one m in length) form important intermediate links in epipelagic food chains. The giant squid *(Architeuthis)* lives at greater depths. These large animals reach at least 18 m in length and weigh half a ton. Various parts of the body are scaled proportionally, with tentacles approximately 10 m long and eyes as large as soccer balls.

Most nektonic animals are vertebrates, and most vertebrates are fish. Thus, this chapter is, to a large extent, a chapter about fish.

The Vertebrates

All fish are vertebrates and are members of the phylum Chordata. The family tree of vertebrates goes back over 400 million years (figure 11.1). Fish is a term used to designate vertebrates that grow or live in water, that use gills to extract oxygen from the water surrounding them, and that swim with fins for propulsion and control. Early fish, the armor-plated ostracoderms and placoderms, probably evolved from free-swimming invertebrate chordate ancestors. Of the three existing classes of fish, only two are comparatively abundant: the sharks (class Chondrichthyes) and bony fish (class Osteichthyes). The class Agnatha is represented by two small groups of jawless fish, the lampreys and hagfish.

As a group, sharks and the less numerous skates and rays came very close to extinction about 350 million years ago, but they seem to be secure now, with about 650 species scattered throughout all oceans. About 200 species belong to the order that includes the hammerhead and requiem sharks. Sharks are very distinctive in their external appearance, and their conservative body profiles are easily identified. Besides general appearance, sharks also differ from bony fish by their skeletons of cartilage (rather than bone) and by the absence of a swim bladder.

The bony fish are a more recent group, but their success has been spectacular. There are now as many species of bony fish as there are of all other vertebrate groups combined. Bony fish, with their more complex osmoregulating gills and kidneys, are widespread in freshwater and estuarine habitats (refer to figure 2.5), as well as the ocean. In no other class of vertebrates can we see better examples of adaptive radiation into such a diversity of aquatic habitats.

The other group of marine vertebrates is the tetrapods—the reptiles, birds, and mammals (figure 11.1). Although their origins are terrestrial and they have peculiar restraints placed on their ability to adapt to a nektonic existence, some tetrapod groups have reoccupied the sea with notable success. Tetrapods characteristically have two pairs of appendages for locomotion and breathe air with lungs. Because marine tetrapods are important components of many nekton communities, they are introduced in this chapter. The next

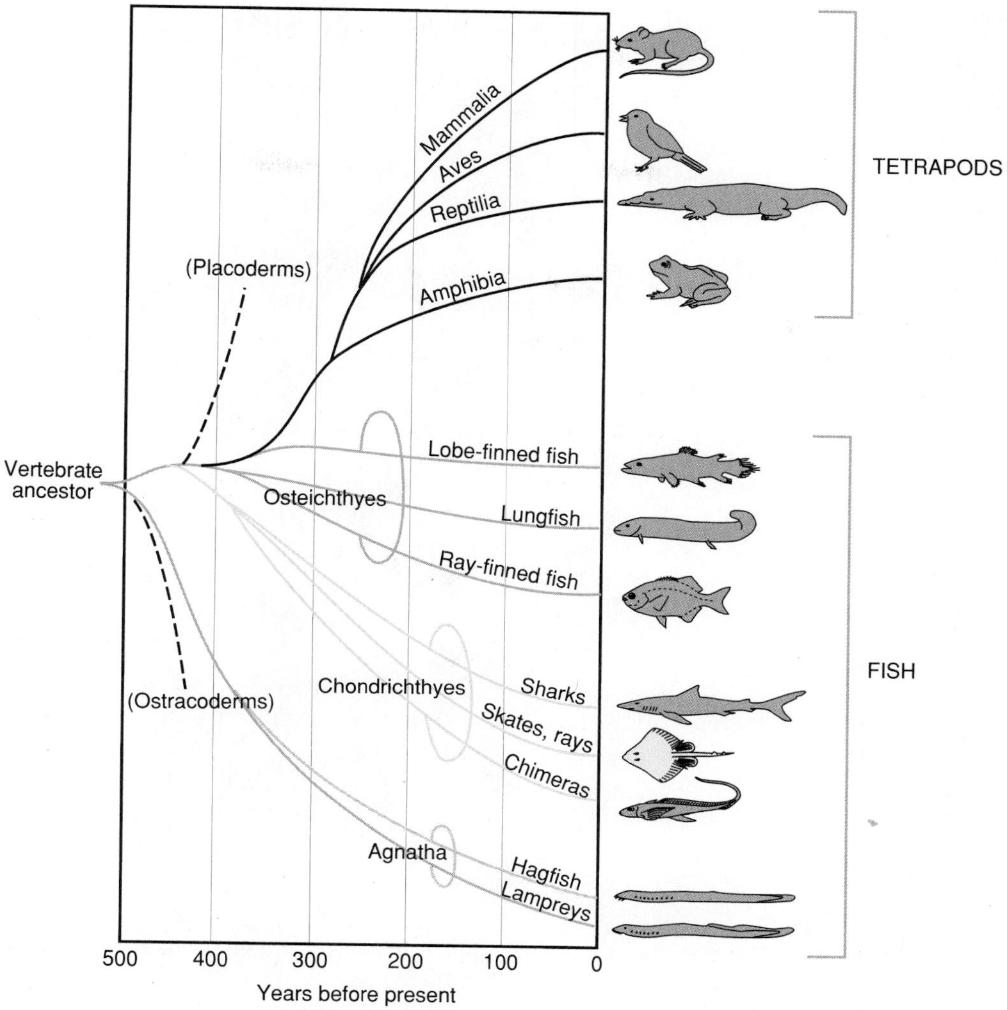

Figure 11.1
Phylogenetic relationships of vertebrates, with emphasis on fish. Extinct groups are in parentheses.

chapter will examine the special adaptations that these air-breathing vertebrates need to succeed in the sea.

Vertical Distribution of Nekton

Even though two thirds of the ocean's volume lies below the epipelagic and mesopelagic zones, the majority of nektonic species are found in those zones. Considerably less is known about the biology of mesopelagic animals than about those animals living in the epipelagic zone, and less still is known about animals living below 1,000 m. Most epipelagic nekton are carnivorous predators of the higher trophic levels of pelagic food chains. They are typically large in size when compared to zooplankton, are effective swimmers, and have a variety of well-developed sensory capabilities for prey detection, orientation, and navigation. Some accomplish impressive feats of migration to locate food or to improve their chances of successful reproduction.

Epipelagic animals of the open ocean seldom exhibit the bright coloration so common in coral reef fish and invertebrates. Instead, **countershading** is a common pattern of coloration. Many abundant fish, whales, and squids have dark, often green or blue, pigmentation on their dorsal surfaces, and have silvery or white pigmentation on their ventral surfaces. When viewed from

Figure 11.2
Some mesopelagic fish:
(*a*) *Aristostomias;*
(*b*) *Opistoproctus;* and
(*c*) *Argyropelecus*. All are less than 5 cm in length.

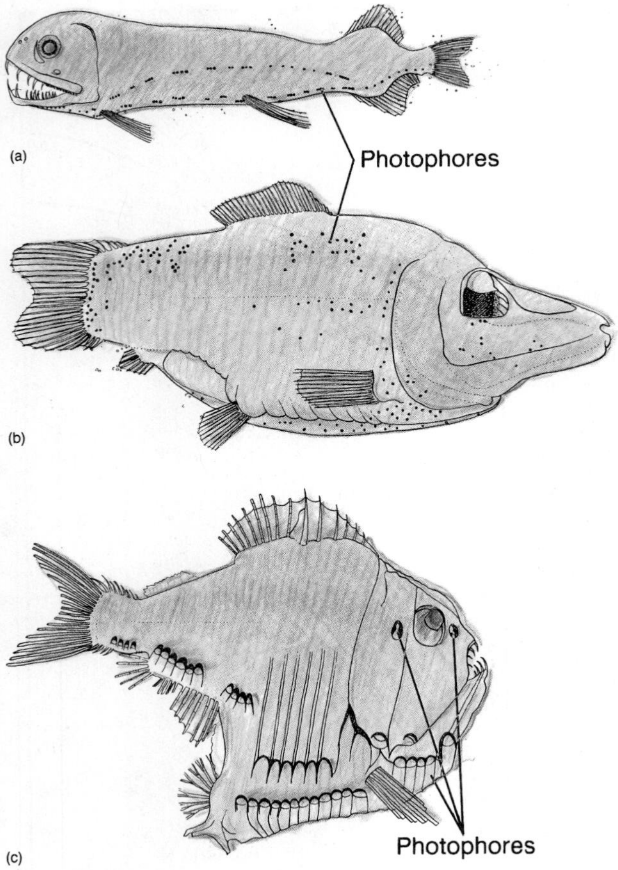

above, the pigmented upper surfaces of counter-shaded fish blend with the darker background below. From beneath, the silvery undersides are difficult to distinguish from the ambient light coming from the sea surface. From either view, these fish tend to visually blend into rather than stand out against their watery background. Not only does countershading protect animals against predators, but the flashing of silvery bellies or dark backs during abrupt turns may alert individuals in the school to the maneuvers of their immediate neighbors.

Fish living in the mesopelagic zone are typically much smaller than fish of the epipelagic zone. This group includes lantern fish (figure 10.11) and many other vertical migrators. Mesopelagic fish seldom exceed 10 cm in length and most are equipped with well-developed teeth and large mouths (figure 11.2*a*). Since only dim light penetrates from above, many species have evolved large, light-sensitive eyes (figure 11.2*b*) to detect prey and predators alike. Regardless of their color at the sea surface, they appear uniformly black at these depths.

Correlated with large eyes is the presence of **photophores,** light-producing organs most commonly arranged on the ventral surface of the body (figure 11.2c). The position and arrangement of photophores suggest two likely functions. The light produced by the ventral photophores approximates the

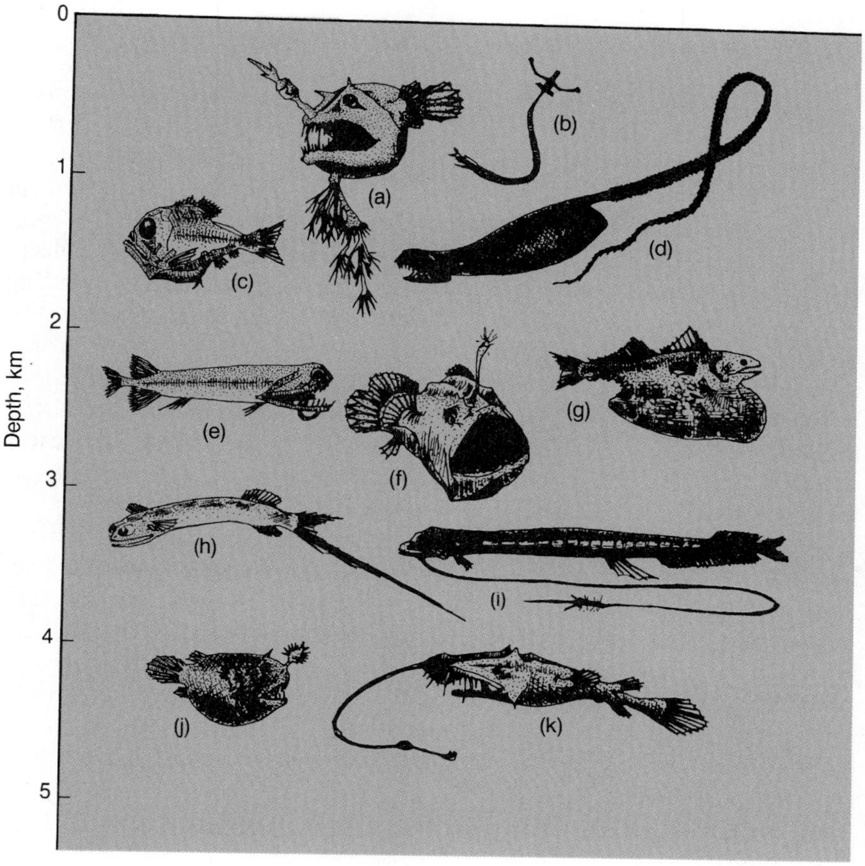

Figure 11.3
A few fish of the deep sea, shown at their usual depths. Most have reduced bodies, large mouths, and lures to attract prey. (*a*) An angler, *Linophyrne,* (*b*) young *Idiacanthus* with eyes on stalks, (*c*) a hatchetfish, *Argyropelecus,* (*d*) a gulper, *Saccopharynx,* (*e*) a widemouth, *Malocosteus,* (*f*) another angler, *Melanocetus,* (*g*) the "great swallower," *Chiasmodus,* with a larger fish in its stomach, (*h*) a giant tail *Gigantura,* and three more anglers, (*i*) *Eustomias,* (*j*) *Borophyrne,* and (*k*) *Lasiognathus.*

intensity of the background light found at the normal day-time depths of these fish. The light from the photophores may disrupt the visual silhouette of the fish when observed from below and causes the fish's silhouette to visually blend with the background light from above. The effect of the photophores is similar to countershading in near-surface fish. Elaborate arrangements of photophores are unique to single species and suggests that photophores are also used for species identification. With little to be seen at these depths except the pattern of photophores, appropriate mate selection may depend on the existence of species-specific patterns of photophores.

Below the mesopelagic zone, light from the surface is so dim it cannot be detected with human eyes and it does not stimulate the visual systems of deep-sea fish. The light seen at depths below 1,000 m comes largely from photophores. At these depths, photophores are employed as lures for prey, as species recognition signals, and possibly even as lanterns to illuminate small patches of the surrounding blackness. Most fish found at these depths are not vertical migrators. Instead, they depend on the unpredictable sinking of food particles from the more heavily populated waters above. These fish are typically small and have flabby, soft, nearly transparent flesh supported by very weak bones (figure 11.3). Their bodies serve as little more than appendages to feebly move their oversized mouths from one victim to the next.

Buoyancy

Living in the water, free from the solid bottom, presents some buoyancy problems for most pelagic marine animals because most of the tissues of these animals are more dense than seawater (which has a specific gravity of 1.02–1.03). The specific gravity of muscle is near 1.05; of bone, scale, and shell, 2.0; of cartilage, 1.1; and of fat, wax, and oil, 0.8–0.9.

Like many of the planktonic animals already mentioned, some deep-water nekton offset the weight of heavy bone and muscle tissue by reducing body fluid densities and by storing fats or oils. The giant squid, *Architeuthis,* excludes divalent ions from its body fluids and replaces them with less dense ammonium ions derived from metabolic wastes. Another squid, *Chiroteuthis,* has one of its four pairs of arms filled with low density body fluids. These arms, which have less muscle than the other arms and appear swollen, are located on the ventral side of the animal. Because these arms are lighter than seawater, they may cause *Chiroteuthis* to swim and float upside down.

Stored fats and oils, which are less dense than water, are also common buoyancy devices in pelagic marine animals. Whales, elephant seals, and other large marine animals maintain thick blubber layers just under the skin. The average blue whale is about 18% blubber. Approximately 80% of that blubber is fat and the remainder is connective tissue and blood vessels. Blubber also streamlines these animals and insulates them against heat loss. Many sharks and a variety of bony fish store great quantities of oils in their livers and muscle tissues. In fact, in some species of sharks, the liver accounts for more than one-quarter of the body weight.

Gas Inclusions

Fats, oils, and body fluids of reduced densities, although widely employed for buoyancy, are still only slightly less dense than seawater. This poses a serious problem for many small but active nektonic species. They cannot energetically afford to pack around a huge oily liver or a thick blubber layer nor can they sacrifice muscle and bone to lighten the load. This problem is solved for many marine animals with an internal gas-filled flotation organ. At sea level, air is only about 0.1% as dense as seawater. Thus, a small gas volume provides a relatively large amount of lift.

The amount of lift derived from a volume of gas depends on the volume of seawater the gas displaces. Unlike water, gases are compressible; they occupy different volumes at different pressures and depths. At sea level, the pressure created by the earth's envelope of air is about 1 kg/cm^2 or 15 lb/in^2 or 1 atmosphere (atm). Below the sea surface, the water pressure increases about 1 atm for each 10 m increase in depth. Thus, the total pressure experienced by a fish at 5,000 m is 501 atm (more than 3.5 $tons/in^2$).

The gas-filled buoyancy organs of some marine animals are rigid and strong and can structurally resist the increased water pressures found at great depths. Other organs maintain their buoyancy in flexible, compressible containers.

Rigid Gas Containers

Rigid-walled gas containers are found only in a few types of cephalopods. All cephalopods are believed to have evolved from an ancestral stock that had an external shell (figure 11.4). *Nautilus* is the only living cephalopod that has retained its external shell. The shells of other living cephalopods are either

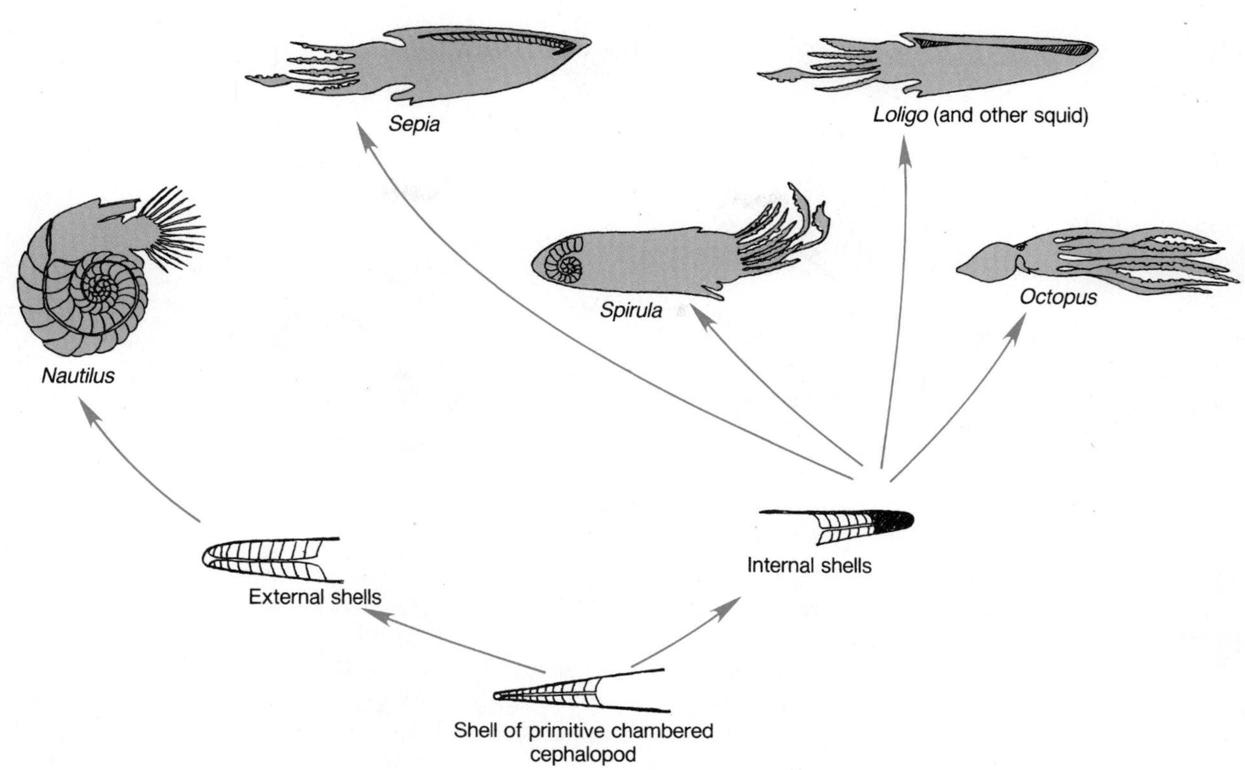

Figure 11.4
The probable evolutionary relationships of living and extinct cephalopods, with the shape and structure of the chambered shells emphasized. Darkened areas represent structural support.

reduced to an internal chambered structure, as in the cuttlefish *(Sepia)* and *Spirula* (a deep-water squid) or are absent entirely, as in *Octopus*. In squids other than *Spirula*, a thin chitinous structure (the **pen**) extends the length of the mantle tissue and represents the last vestige of what was once an internal shell.

Nautilus, Sepia, and *Spirula* all have numerous hard transverse **septa,** partitions that separate adjacent chambers of the shell. In *Nautilus*, only the last and largest chamber is occupied by the animal. As *Nautilus* grows, it moves forward in its shell and adds a new chamber by secreting another transverse septum across the area it just vacated. The chambers are connected by a central tubelike tissue, the **siphuncle.** The siphuncle of *Nautilus* removes salts from the fluids left behind when a new chamber is formed. Water within the chamber then diffuses into the siphuncle because of the osmotic gradient maintained by the siphuncle. As water leaves, it is replaced by gases (mostly N_2) from tissue fluids. The gases are allowed to diffuse in and the total pressure of the gases dissolved within the chambers never exceeds 1 atm. The lift obtained from the gas inclusion offsets the weight of the shell in water, and *Nautilus* becomes neutrally buoyant. *Sepia* and presumably *Spirula* evacuate fluids from their chambered shells in a similar manner.

These chambered cephalopods are confronted with the same depth-limiting factor that plagues submarines. Their depth ranges are limited by the resistance of their shells to increased water pressure. Each species has a critical implosion depth where the external water pressure becomes too great for the design and strength of its shell and the shell collapses. The implosion depth of *Nautilus* shells, for example, is somewhat below 500 m, yet this animal does not normally live below 240 m.

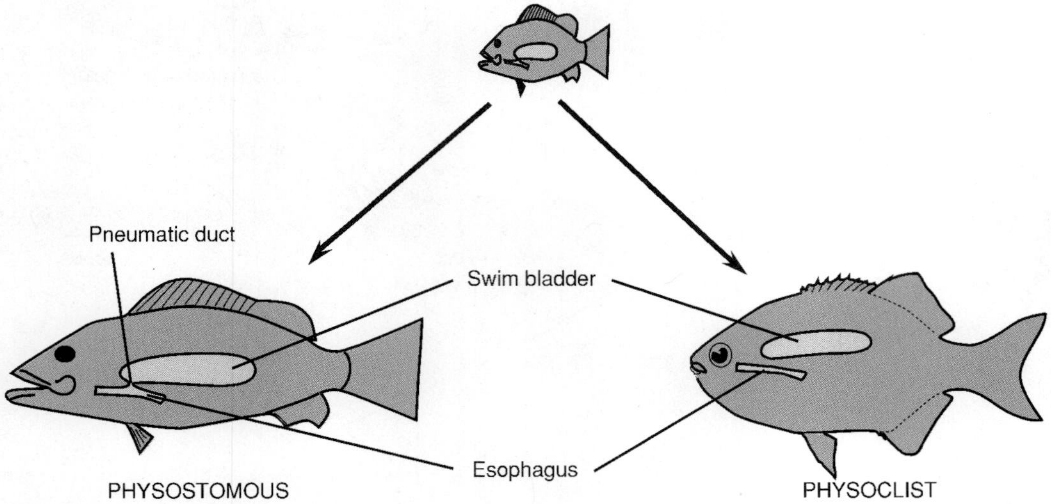

Figure 11.5
The development and relative positions of physostomous and physoclist swim bladders

Nonrigid Gas Inclusions

Many bony fish, especially active species with extensive muscle and skeletal tissue, have body densities about 5% greater than that of seawater. To achieve neutral buoyancy, many of these fish have an internal swim bladder filled with gases (mostly N_2 and O_2). The swim bladders of modern bony fish develop embryonically from an out-pouching of the esophagus (figure 11.5). The densely woven fibers that make up the bladder wall are embedded with a layer of tiny overlapping crystals of guanine to make the bladder wall nearly impermeable to O_2 and N_2 gases.

The connection between the esophagus and swim bladder, called the **pneumatic duct,** is present during the larval or juvenile stages of all bony fish. In some species, the pneumatic duct remains unchanged in the adult. (This is known as a **physostomous** condition.) In other primarily marine species, the duct disappears as the fish matures. (This is a **physoclist** swim bladder, figure 11.5.) Nearly half of the more than 20,000 species of bony fish, however, lose not only the pneumatic duct but also the swim bladder when they mature. Swim bladders are notably lacking in bottom fish and in active, continuously swimming fish such as tuna.

Swim bladders are not rigid structures. As such, the volume of water they displace is subject to changing water pressures at different depths. To maintain neutral buoyancy at different depths, a fish's swim bladder volume must remain constant. A fish that swims downward experiences greater external water pressures, which compresses its swim bladder and reduces the bladder's volume. The quantity of gas in the bladder must then be increased to compensate for the pressure change. Conversely, an ascending fish must get rid of swim bladder gases as rapidly as they expand. Some shallow-water physostomous fish fill their swim bladders simply by gulping air at the sea surface. Excess gases from physostomous swim bladders are also expelled through the pneumatic duct and eventually out the mouth or gills. Lacking a pneumatic duct, a fish with a physoclist swim bladder must reabsorb excess gases into the bloodstream. Physoclist swim bladders have a specialized region, the oval body (figure 11.6), that is richly supplied with blood vessels for resorption of gases. The oval body is isolated from the remainder of the swim bladder by a muscle ring, or sphincter, that restricts access of the bladder gases to the oval body.

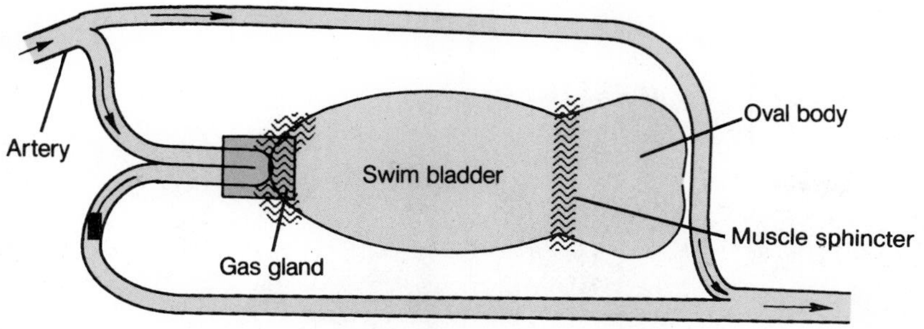

Figure 11.6
A physoclist swim bladder. Arrows indicate the direction of blood flow. Note the lack of any connection between the bladder and the esophagus. The area within the rectangle is diagrammed in greater detail in figure 11.10.

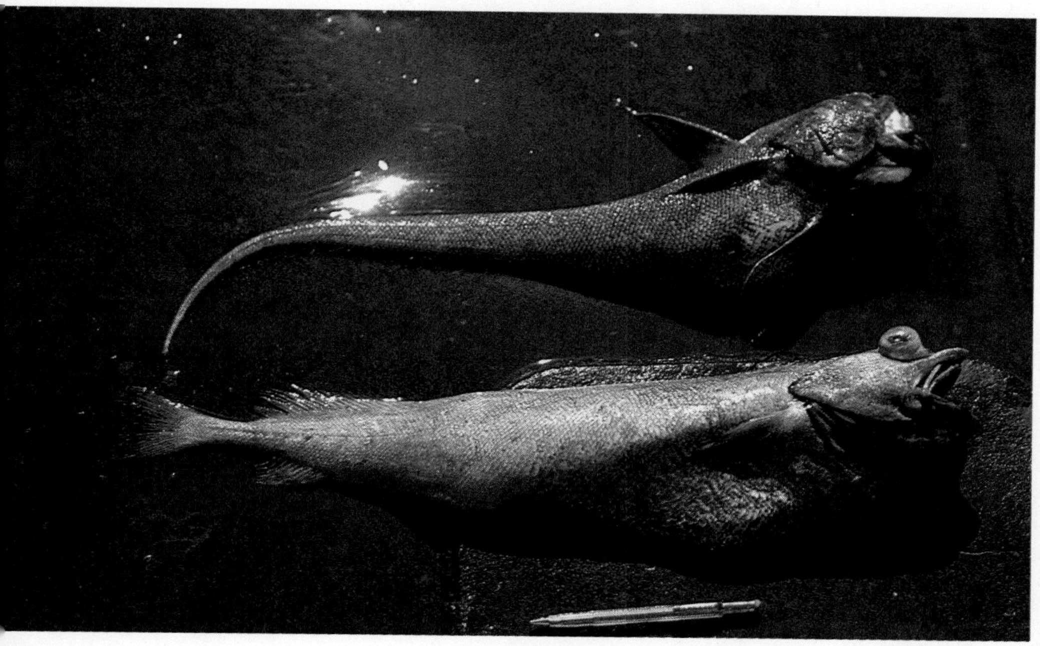

Figure 11.7
Two deep-sea fish on the deck of a ship after being hauled up from a depth of 800 m. Both fish were seriously damaged and distorted by the rapid expansion of gases in their swim bladders as they were brought to the surface.

In most cases, both types of swim bladders have a gas gland that secretes gas from the blood into the bladder when these fish have no access to air. But again there are exceptions. Herring, for example, lack gas glands and are restricted to reasonably shallow waters. The capacity of fish with physoclist swim bladders to quickly add or remove bladder gases to compensate for a rapid depth change is limited. If a deep-water fish rapidly ascends, the decreased water pressure allows the gases within the somewhat elastic swim bladder to expand and reduce the overall density of the fish. The density decrease may be so great that the fish is unable to descend for some time. This fact is well illustrated by the appearance of many fish brought to the surface (unwillingly, of course) from deep water on fishing lines or in trawls. It is not unusual for the swim bladders of such fish to expand (figure 11.7), causing severe internal organ damage.

In shallow water, the gas composition of swim bladders resembles the gas composition of air, about 20% O_2 and 80% N_2. At greater depths, the pressure of both gases increases to match the increasing water pressure. Fish with gas-filled swim bladders have been taken from depths as great as 7,000 m.

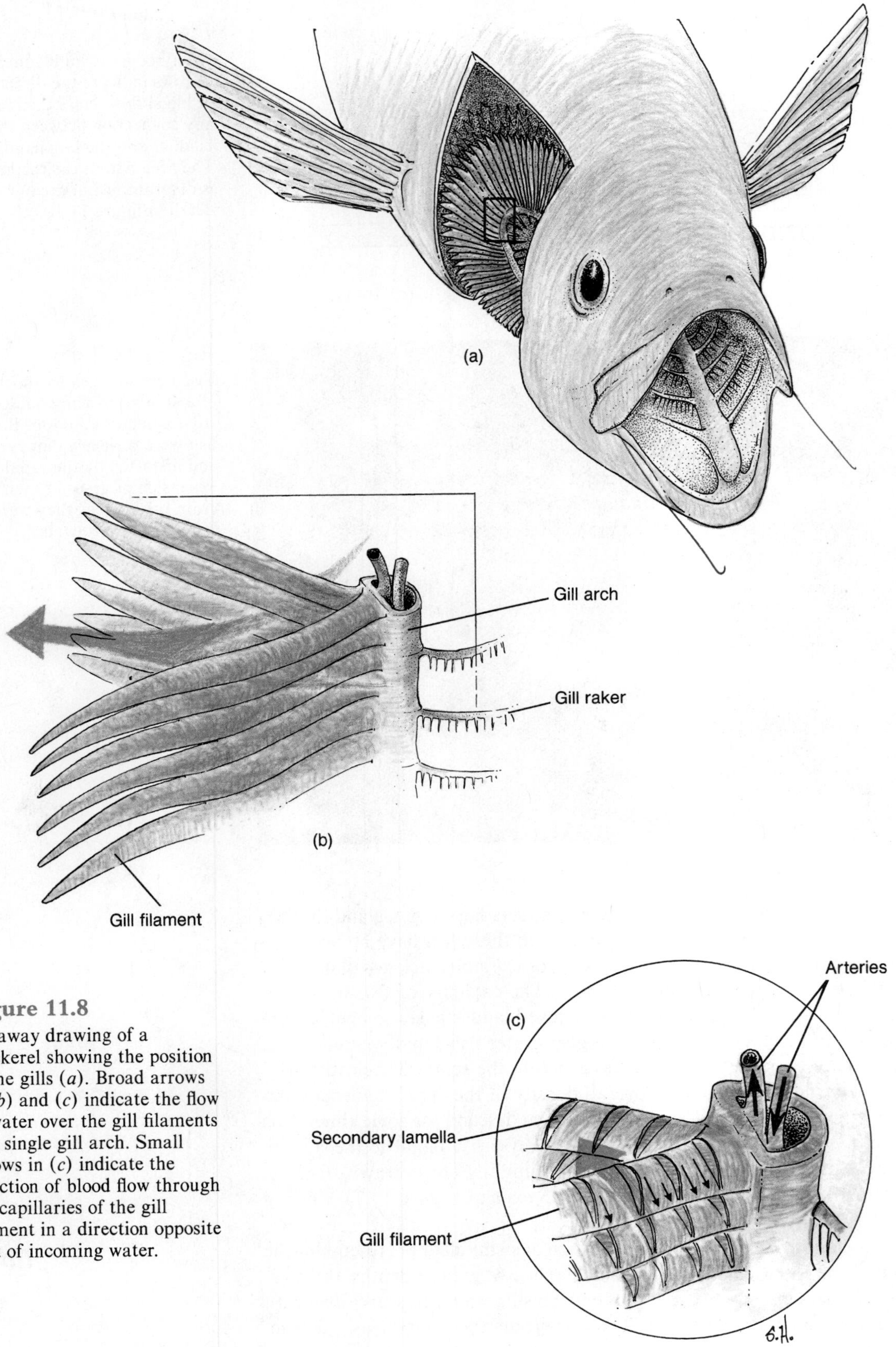

Figure 11.8
Cutaway drawing of a mackerel showing the position of the gills (*a*). Broad arrows in (*b*) and (*c*) indicate the flow of water over the gill filaments of a single gill arch. Small arrows in (*c*) indicate the direction of blood flow through the capillaries of the gill filament in a direction opposite that of incoming water.

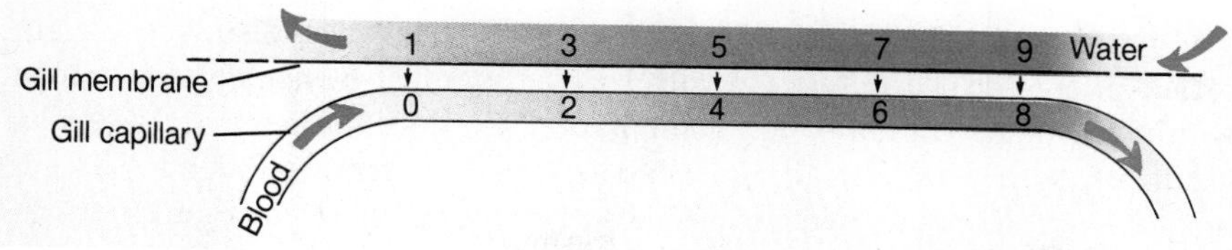

Figure 11.9

A countercurrent gas exchange system of fish gills. Nearly all the O_2 from water flowing right to left diffuses across the gill membrane into the blood flowing in the opposite direction. Numbers represent arbitrary O_2 units.

The gas pressure needed within the swim bladder to balance the water pressure at that depth (5 tons/in^2) is about 700 atm. Such extreme gas pressures are achieved by a dramatic increase in the O_2 concentration of the bladder gases. Oxygen commonly accounts for more than 50%, and occasionally exceeds 90%, of the gas mixture of the swim bladders of deep-ocean fish.

The general picture of swim bladder gas composition poses two intriguing questions concerning the mechanism for filling the swim bladder in deep water. First, how are O_2 and N_2, which are dissolved in seawater at pressures no greater than 1 atm, concentrated in swim bladders at pressures as great as 700 atm? Second, why is O_2 so much more abundant than N_2 within swim bladders at great depths when N_2 is more abundant than O_2 in seawater? In some instances, O_2 is at least 1,000 times as concentrated within the swim bladders of deep-water fish as in the water in which they are swimming. Nitrogen is generally concentrated by no more than 10–20 times.

Deep-water fish fill their swim bladders with N_2, O_2, and traces of other gases absorbed from seawater by their gills. These gases are transported in the blood to the gas gland of the swim bladder, then secreted into the bladder at pressures equal to external water pressures. An explanation of this process requires a brief digression.

Fish take water and dissolved gases into their mouths and pump them over their gills. Each **gill arch** supports a double row of bladelike **gill filaments** (figure 11.8). Each flat filament bears numerous smaller **secondary lamellae** to further increase the gill surface available for gas exchange. Active fish, like mackerel, may have up to 10 times as much gill surface as body surface. The gill surfaces of sedentary bottom fish, on the other hand, are not as extensive because their O_2 requirements are not as great.

Microscopic capillaries circulate blood very near the inner surface of the secondary lamellae. As long as the O_2 concentration of the blood is less than that of the water passing over the gills, O_2 continues to diffuse across the very thin walls of the lamellae and into the bloodstream. In fish gills, the efficiency of O_2 absorption into the blood is enhanced by the direction of water flow over the gill lamellae (arrows, figure 11.8), a direction reverse that of the blood flow within the lamellae. Oxygen-rich water moving opposite to the flow of O_2-depleted blood establishes a very effective **countercurrent system** for gas exchange (figure 11.9). Blood returning from the body with a low concentration of O_2 enters the lamellae adjacent to water that has already given up much of its O_2 to blood in other parts of the lamellae. As the blood moves across the lamellae, it continually encounters water with greater O_2 concentrations; as a result, the blood picks up more O_2 as it goes. Thus, O_2 continually diffuses from the water into the blood along the entire length of the capillary bed within the lamellae. With such a countercurrent O_2 exchanger, some fish are capable of extracting up to 85% of the dissolved O_2 present in the water passing over the gills. In contrast, air-breathing vertebrates, such as humans, generally use less than 25% of the O_2 that enters their lungs.

Oxygen is transported in vertebrate blood not as dissolved O_2 but rather in chemical combination with the red pigment **hemoglobin** contained within red blood cells. In such combination, O_2 does not generate diffusion gradients, so it is osmotically invisible as long as it remains bound with hemoglobin. Although nitrogen is also absorbed by the gills, much less is transported because it remains dissolved in the fluids of the blood. Hemoglobin functions by combining with O_2 at the high levels found at the gills (or lungs in other vertebrates) and by releasing O_2 to the body tissues at low O_2 concentrations. The quantity of O_2 carried by hemoglobin depends on the O_2 concentration of the water flowing over the gills and on the demands made by the tissues where it is used. Antarctic ice fish and a few types of eel larvae are among the very few fish that lack hemoglobin.

Now, back to the swim bladder. When hemoglobin loaded with O_2 reaches the gas gland of the swim bladder (see figure 11.6), the O_2 must be induced to leave the hemoglobin and diffuse into the swim bladder, often in the face of high O_2 pressures within the bladder. The role of the gas gland in this process is simple, but critical. As oxygenated blood enters the gas gland, lactic acid is produced. The lactic acid diffuses into the blood vessels and lowers the pH of the blood. Lower pH conditions reduce the O_2-carrying capacity of hemoglobin and induce it to dump part of its O_2 load. The unloaded O_2, which has not yet left the blood, is now no longer associated with the hemoglobin. Additional lactic acid production creates lower blood pH conditions and may cause hemoglobin to release up to 50% of its O_2 load. The total effects of lactic acid on hemoglobin are sufficient to produce about two atm of O_2 pressure at the gas gland of the swim bladder.

Eventually, the O_2 will diffuse into the swim bladder if the O_2 pressure there is not greater than 2 atm. This mechanism alone, however, is not capable of producing the very high gas pressures found in the swim bladders of deep-water fish. All deep-water fish with gas-filled swim bladders have an extensive network of capillaries, a **rete mirabile** (wonderful net), leading to and going away from the gas gland (figures 11.6 and 11.10). The capillaries that approach the gas gland carrying O_2-rich hemoglobin are situated adjacent to and parallel with capillaries leaving the gas gland. A rete system may contain a few hundred or as many as 200,000 such capillary channels, depending on the species. These complex rete systems form another countercurrent exchange system that operates on the same principle as that described for the gills, but here the exchange system acts as a countercurrent multiplier.

Large amounts of O_2 forced to dissociate from hemoglobin by lactic acid at the gas gland may be blocked from diffusing into the swim bladder because of the higher gas pressures there. If the O_2 leaves the region of the gas gland via a capillary of the rete system, it diffuses across the capillary walls and back into the incoming blood of adjacent capillaries. The O_2 forced off the hemoglobin is thus trapped in this recycling system as it leaves the gas gland. Eventually, the pressure of O_2 in the capillaries surpasses even the very high pressures of the swim bladder, and O_2 diffuses from the gas gland into the bladder.

As one might expect, a longer rete is capable of concentrating more O_2 at the gas gland. Still the rete need not be unmanageably long. It has been estimated that a rete only 1 cm long could secrete O_2 at pressures up to 2,000 atm, well in excess of the swim bladder pressures needed in the deepest parts

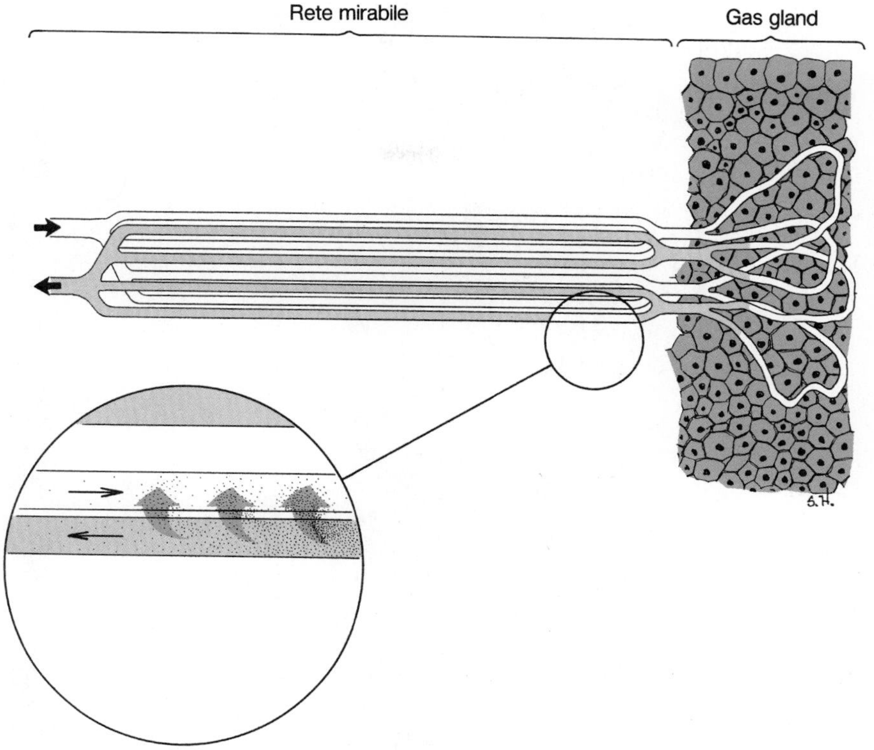

Figure 11.10
A simplified diagram of the rete mirabile and gas gland associated with the swim bladders of many bony fish. Inset illustrates the countercurrent arrangement of blood flow (small arrows) and the diffusion of O_2 from outgoing to incoming blood vessels (broad arrows).
Adapted from Hoar, 1966

of the sea. The rete mirabile concentrates N_2 as well as O_2. The lack of a specialized transport system for N_2 (as hemoglobin is for O_2), however, relegates N_2 to the role of a minor gas in swim bladders at great depths.

As the pressure of gases inside swim bladders increases, so do their densities. At 7,000 m, the gas within a swim bladder is so compressed that its specific gravity is about 0.7, or similar to that of fat. For some fish at great depths, the constant energy costs necessary to maintain a full swim bladder become unrealistic. At these depths, many fish have fat-filled swim bladders. Fat-filled swim bladders provide almost as much buoyancy as gases do at 7,000 m but have few of the attendant maintenance problems. Fat-filled swim bladders are also found in vertically migrating fish species, such as lantern fish (figure 11.9), that face the problems of moving through pressure changes of 10 to 40 atm twice daily.

Locomotion

Animals move to improve their conditions for survival. Such movements are made to reproduce, migrate, find food, avoid predators, obtain lift, aerate the gills, and for a host of other reasons. Structural or behavioral adaptations that permit animals to swim with reduced energy expenditures mean that more energy can be diverted to increased growth and reproduction and contribute to the potential success of an individual.

Different marine organisms swim in varying ways. While most are generalists (like the surfperch in figure 11.11), others are specialized for one

Figure 11.11
Examples of body shape specialization for three different swimming modes
Adapted from Webb, 1984

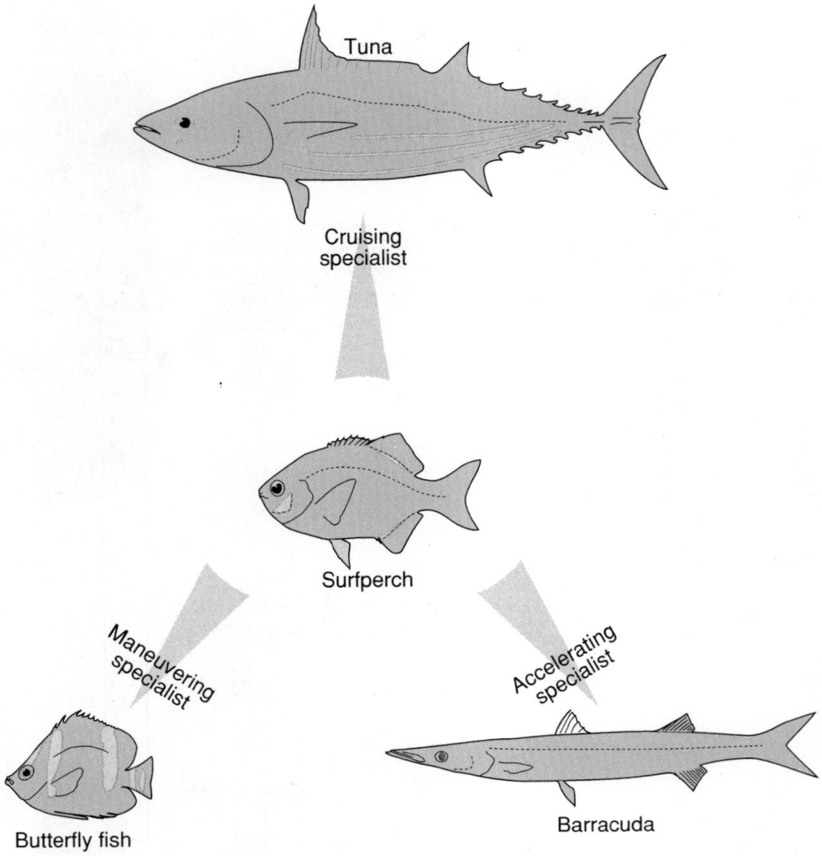

of three modes of swimming: sprinting (barracuda), fine maneuvering (butterfly fish), or nearly continuous high-speed cruising (tunas). These specialized approaches to swimming, with appropriate adaptations of body shape, fins, and muscle, reflect the variety of ecological niches available to nekton.

Body Shape

Some fish live in situations, especially near the ocean bottom or in coral reefs or kelp beds, where speed is not critical for survival, but camouflage is. In these situations, body shape is often quite variable (figures 11.2 and 11.3).

The streamlined shape of most fast nekton is actually a compromise between various possible body forms that allows the animal to slip through the water with as little resistance, or drag, as possible. **Frictional drag** results from the interaction of the animal's surface with the water surrounding its body. If frictional drag alone is to be reduced, the ideal shape would be a sphere, which has a minimal surface area for the animal's volume (figure 11.12*a*). However, an animal swimming through water must overcome more than just frictional resistance. As it swims forward, an amount of water equal to the size of the animal's largest cross-sectional area (from a head-on view) must be displaced to permit the animal to progress. **Form drag,** by itself, can be minimized with a shape that has a small cross-sectional area, a body shaped like a long, thin cylinder (figure 11.12*b*). The actual shape of a fast swimmer like a tuna or porpoise is neither spherical nor cylindrical; it is a compromise form (figure 11.12*c*). One additional drag factor, **turbulence,** must also be con-

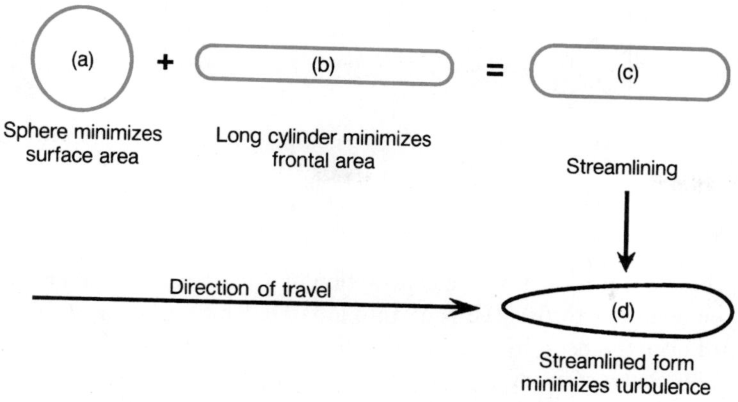

Figure 11.12
The combination of shapes needed to minimize frictional, form, and turbulent resistance to a body moving through a fluid results in the streamlined shape

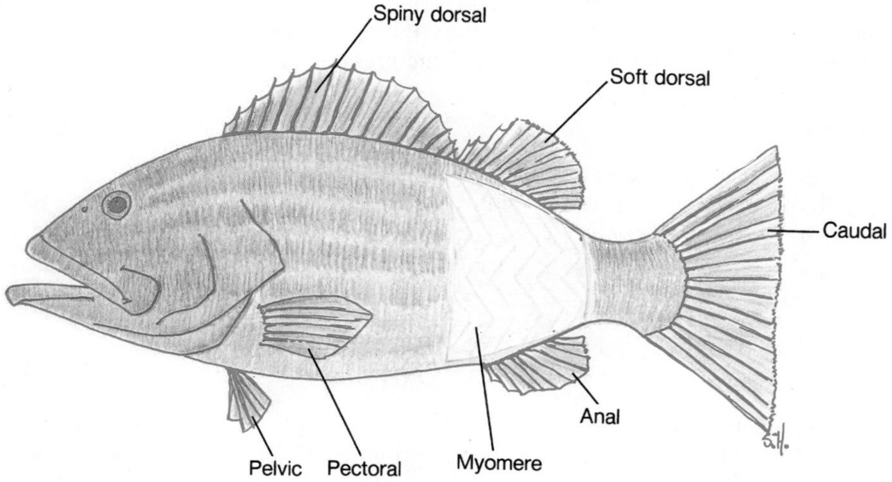

Figure 11.13
Position and name of fish fins. A portion of the musculature has been exposed to show the arrangement of myomeres.

sidered. Wind tunnel tests have demonstrated that the ideal shape of a high-speed body in a fluid medium, be it fish, missile, or torpedo, is one that has a length about 4.5 times its greatest diameter. Additionally, it should be roundly blunt at the front end, tapered to a point in the rear, and round in cross-section (figure 11.12*d*). The form shown in figure 11.12*d* is the optimum overall shape to minimize the total drag resulting from friction (a function of surface area), form (a function of cross-sectional area), and turbulence (a function of streamlining). Most fast marine animals, excluding their fins, closely approximate this ideal shape.

In contrast, rapidly accelerating fish, such as barracudas, tend to have thinner, more elongated bodies, possibly to reduce their chances of being seen and recognized as they rush their prey. On the other hand, maneuverers such as butterfly fish are tall and elliptical in cross-section, with large fins extending even greater distances from the body. The increased amount of body surface, while adding to the overall drag, produces additional thrust and also serves as a control surface for making fine position adjustments.

Fins

The push, or thrust, needed for swimming generally comes from the sides and fins of the animal's body (figure 11.13). The bending motion of the anterior

Figure 11.14
Examples of shapes and aspect ratios for caudal fins

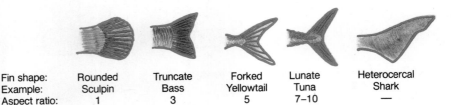

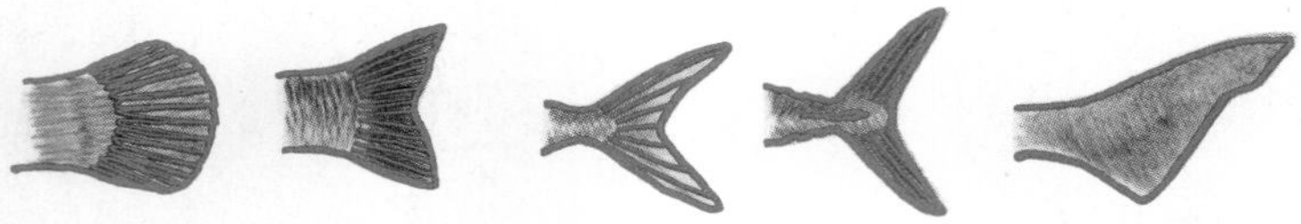

part of the body, initiated by the contraction of a few muscle segments (**myomeres**) on one side, throws the body into a curve. This curve, or wave, passes backward over the body by sequential contraction and relaxation of the myomeres. The contraction of each myomere in succession reinforces the wave form as it passes toward the tail. Immediately after one wave has passed, another starts near the head on the opposite side of the body, and the entire sequence is repeated in rapid succession. Forward thrust is developed almost entirely by the backward component of the pressure of the animal's body and fins against the water.

Fin shape: Rounded Truncate Forked Lunate Heterocercal
Example: Sculpin Bass Yellowtail Tuna Shark
Aspect ratio: 1 3 5 7–10 —

Caudal Fins

Caudal fins typically flare dorsally and ventrally to provide additional surface area to develop thrust. Increased fin size increases the total frictional drag of the fish. The ratio of thrust to drag changes with the shape of the caudal fin. One index of the propulsive efficiency of the fin, based on its shape, is the **aspect ratio:**

$$\text{Aspect ratio} = \frac{(\text{fin height})^2}{\text{fin area}}$$

The caudal fins of most pelagic fish fit into five profile categories: rounded, truncate, forked, lunate, and heterocercal (figure 11.14). Each has a different aspect ratio.

The angelfish has a rounded caudal fin that is soft and flexible and has a low aspect ratio. When the fin moves laterally, it bends and allows water to "slosh" past it. This flexibility permits the caudal fin to be used effectively for accelerating and maneuvering. Truncate and forked fins have intermediate aspect ratios, produce less drag, and are generally found on faster fish. These fins are also flexible for maneuverability.

The lunate caudal fin characteristic of tuna, sailfish, marlin, and swordfish has a high aspect ratio (up to 10 in swordfish) for reduced drag at high speeds. The shape closely resembles the swept-wing design of high-speed aircraft. These fish are among the fastest marine animals. The caudal fin is quite rigid for high propulsive efficiency but is poorly adapted for slow speeds and maneuvering. Fish with high aspect ratio caudal fins (especially forked and lunate types) are capable of long-distance, continuous swimming.

The heterocercal tail (figure 11.14) characteristic of sharks has a shape very different from that of most bony fish (which are homocercal, or symmetrical about the long axis of the body). The heterocercal tail is asymmetrical. When the caudal fin is moved from side to side, a forward thrust develops. Because of the angle of the trailing edge of the tail, however, it produces some lift as well (figure 11.15*a*). The caudal fin asymmetry (and the lift it produces) is reduced in several species of fast-swimming pelagic sharks; at higher speeds a smaller fraction of their total swimming power output is needed to create lift. The paired pectoral fins of sharks are flat and large and extend

Figure 11.15
A pelagic great white shark, *Carcharhinus.* Lift is obtained from its herterocercal tail and the large pectorals extending from the flattened underside of the body.
Courtesy M. Snyderman

horizontally from the body like wings of an aircraft (figure 11.15*b*). The ventral side is nearly flat in front and, with the flat extended pectoral fins, produces a large hydrofoil surface. This hydrofoil meets the water at an angle and produces lift for the front part of the body to balance the lift produced by the tail. Pelagic sharks and other cartilaginous fish lack swim bladders and need this lift to maintain their position in the water column. This mechanism for achieving lift, however, does have its disadvantages. These fish cannot stop or hover in midwater. To do so would cause them to settle to the bottom, a bottom that may be some distance away in the open ocean. Maneuverability is also reduced; the large and rigid paired fins that function as hydrofoils are not well suited for making fine position adjustments.

Paired Fins

Unlike sharks, bony fish equipped with swim bladders have their pectoral and pelvic fins free for other uses. In most bony fish, the paired fins are used solely for turning, braking, balancing, or other fine maneuvers. When the fish are swimming rapidly, these fins are folded back against their bodies. Wrasses and sculpins, however, swim with a jerky, fanning motion of their pectorals and hold the remainder of their bodies straight. Some skates and rays swim by gracefully undulating the edges of their flattened pectoral fins, or in the cases of manta and eagle rays, by flapping their pectorals like large wings.

The greatly enlarged pectoral fins of the flying fish in figure 11.16 do not allow this animal to actually fly; it merely glides for long distances. Flying fish build up considerable speed while just under the sea surface and then leap

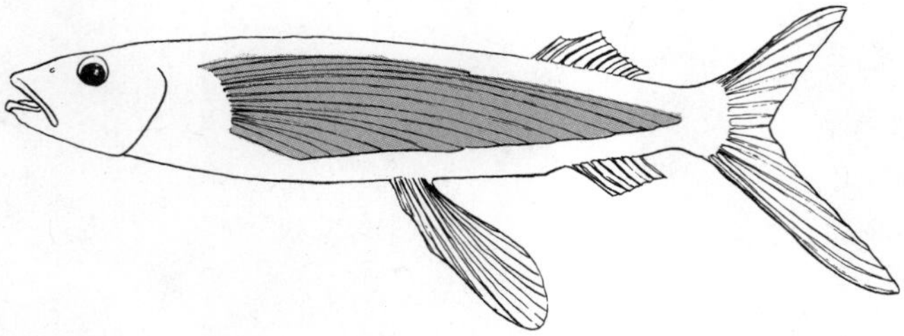

Figure 11.16
A flying fish, *Exocoetus,* uses enlarged pectoral fins for gliding.

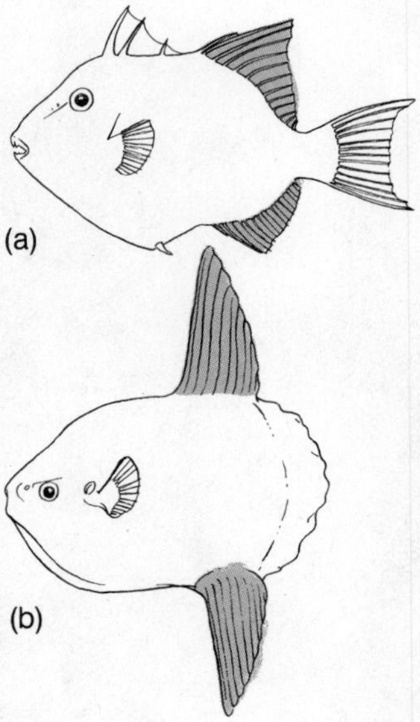

Figure 11.17
Two fish that use their dorsal and anal fins for propulsion: (*a*) triggerfish, *Balistes,* and (*b*) ocean sunfish, *Mola*

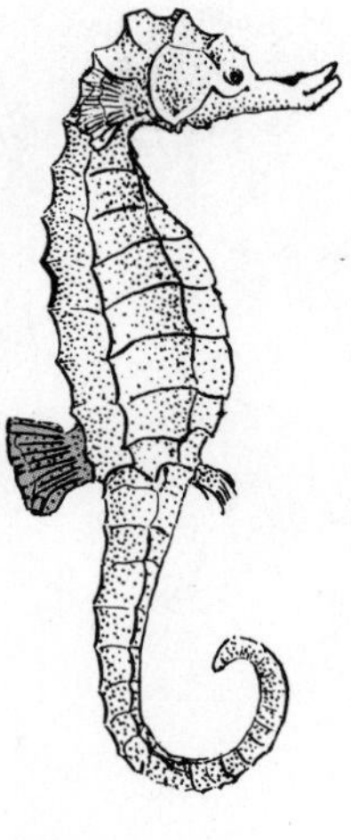

Figure 11.18
The sea horse, *Hippocampus,* swims vertically, using its dorsal fin for propulsion

upward with their pectorals extended. The pectorals do not flap during flight, so the length of the glide is dependent on wind conditions and the initial speed of the fish as it leaves the water. These "flights" are apparently a means of escaping predators; glides up to 400 m have been reported.

Anal and Dorsal Fins

Triggerfish (*Balistes*) and ocean sunfish (*Mola*) swim by undulating their anal and dorsal fins (figure 11.17). These fins extend along much of the triggerfish's body (a). The large sunfish (b), which reaches lengths of nearly 3 m and attains weights up to a ton, is a sluggish fish and is often seen "sunning" at the surface. The little swimming it does is accomplished by the long dorsal and anal fins and the foreshortened caudal fin.

The sea horse usually swims vertically with its head at right angles to the rest of its body (figure 11.18). The prehensile tail tapers to a point and is used to cling to coral branches and similar objects. Sea horses and the closely related pipefish rapidly vibrate their dorsal and pectoral fins to achieve propulsion.

Propulsion by Other Nekton

Examples of fish counterparts can be found in the swimming patterns of several types of nonfish vertebrates, from sea snakes to whales; and generalizations made concerning fish swimming patterns apply equally well here. Other nekton lack midline fins for propulsion, yet are nonetheless effective swimmers. Most marine invertebrates are not well known for their speed, but a few are fast and can maneuver well enough to be successful nekton. Shrimps and prawns use their abdominal paired appendages (**pleopods**) and their tail fan for swimming. Squids and other cephalopods take water into their mantle cavities and then expel it at high speeds through a nozzlelike **siphon.** The siphon can be aimed in any direction for rapid course corrections and for maneuvering purposes. Squids and cuttlefishes also use their undulating lateral fins in much the same manner as skates and rays.

Speed

Several species of nekton have recently become subjects of much research because of their amazing swimming speeds. *Stenella,* an oceanic porpoise, has been clocked in controlled tank situations at better than 40 km/hr (approximately 25 mi/hr). Top speeds of killer whales are estimated to be 40 to 55 km/hr. A barracuda only 1 m long has been clocked at 40 km/hr. For a comparison, consider that human Olympic-class swimmers achieve sprint speeds of only 4 to 5 km/hr. To clock fish that can easily outdistance a speeding ship, specially designed fishing poles have been developed to measure the speed at which the fishing line is stripped from the reel. When a fish takes the bait and

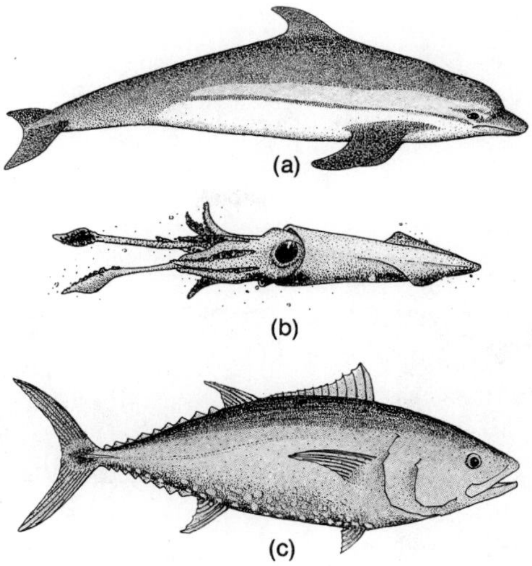

Figure 11.19
Three swift pelagic animals with streamlined body forms: (*a*) bottle-nosed dolphin, *Tursiops;* (*b*) squid, *Loligo;* and (*c*) tuna, *Thunnus*

flees, its speed is measured and recorded. In this manner, investigators clocked a yellowfin tuna (*Thunnus albacares*) less than 1 m long at a maximum speed of 74.6 km/hr (45 mi/hr) for 0.19 second. A tunalike wahoo (*Acanthocybium*) slightly more than 1 m in length was clocked at 77 km/hr for about 0.1 second. It has been suggested that large tuna are capable of speeds in excess of 110 km/hr (70 mi/hr). This may not be as farfetched as it seems since some species of tuna achieve lengths of 4 m and presumably would be much faster than a fish only 1 m long. This 110 km/hr speed estimate has yet to be confirmed.

What enables tuna to swim so fast? Most fast marine animals exhibit nearly optimum streamlined body shapes (figure 11.19). Yet the exceptional swimming abilities of tuna and tunalike fish go beyond simply having a streamlined body form and an efficient caudal fin. The streamlined body form is complemented by other friction-reducing features. The first dorsal fin can be retracted into a slot and out of the path of water flow when not needed for maneuvering. Tuna scales are small and minimize friction with the water. Their eyes do not bulge beyond the profile of their head and are covered with adipose eyelids to further reduce turbulence. Numerous small median **finlets** on the dorsal and ventral sides of the rear part of the body function to reduce turbulence in that region. Their body is quite rigid and provides little of the forward thrust.

Most of the caudal flexing is localized in the region of the **caudal peduncle,** the region where the caudal fin joins the rest of the body. The caudal peduncle, flattened in cross section, produces little resistance to lateral movements. Several small finlets just anterior to the peduncle guide the water posteriorly toward the caudal fin rather than allowing it to slosh over the peduncle. The rigid caudal fin is lunate in shape and has a high aspect ratio (usually greater than 7). The tail beats rapidly with relatively short strokes. This type of caudal fin creates little drag but also provides very little maneuverability.

Nearly 75% of the total body weight of a tuna is comprised of swimming muscles. In tuna, each myomere overlaps several body segments and is anchored securely to the vertebral column. Tendons extend from the myomeres across the caudal peduncle and attach directly to the caudal fin.

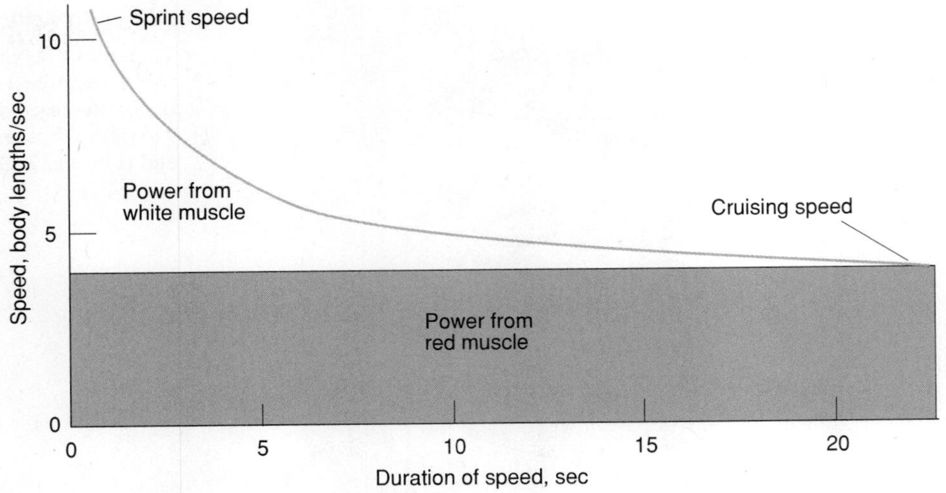

Figure 11.20
Duration of swimming speeds for white and red muscles. White muscle is used for short bursts at flank speed and fatigues rapidly; red muscle maintains continuous cruising speeds.
From Bainbridge, 1960

Fish muscle consists of segregated masses of red and white muscle fibers. Structurally, red muscle fibers are much smaller in diameter (25 to 45 μm) than white muscle fibers (135 μm) and are rich in **myoglobin** (a red pigment with a strong chemical affinity for O_2 similar to that of hemoglobin). The small size of the red muscle cells provides additional surface area that, in conjunction with myoglobin, greatly facilitates O_2 transfer to the red muscle cells. Physiologically, red muscle cells respire aerobically and white muscle cells respire anaerobically, converting glycogen to lactic acid.

The metabolic rate (and power output) of tuna red muscle, and probably of red muscle in other fish, is about six times as great as that of white muscle. The relative amount of red and white muscle a fish has is related to the general level of activity the fish experiences. A slow-moving grouper has almost no red muscle but its large mass of white muscle fibers can power short, fast lunges to capture prey or elude predators. At the other extreme are tuna, with over 50% of their swimming muscles composed of red muscle fibers. The red muscles of sculpins, which operate their pectoral fins, and of puffers, which swim by fanning their anal and dorsal fins, are concentrated at the bases of their swimming fins.

Electrodes have been inserted into red and white muscle tissue of small sharks and some tuna to measure muscle activity. At slow, normal cruising speeds, only red muscles contract. White muscles come into play only at above normal speeds. Top speeds of about ten body lengths/second can be maintained for about one second, but cruising speeds of 2 to 4 body lengths/second can be maintained indefinitely (figure 11.20). Apparently, the power for continuous swimming comes from the red muscle, with white muscle being held in reserve for peak power demands. White muscle does not require an immediate O_2 supply; it can operate anaerobically and accumulate lactic acid during stress situations. The lactic acid can be converted back into glycogen or some other substance when the demand for O_2 has diminished. Tuna, with a greater proportion of red muscle, are able to indefinitely maintain a faster cruising speed that most other fish.

Fish are generally thought to be poikilothermic animals. The heat generated by metabolic processes within the body may elevate the body temperature slightly above the ambient water temperature, but the heat gain is

Table 11.1
Elevation of Red Muscle Temperatures above Seawater Temperatures for Some Marine Fish

Fish with Slightly Elevated Temperatures		Fish with Dramatically Elevated Temperatures	
Yellowtail *(Seriola)*	+ 1.4° C	Mackerel shark *(Lamna)*	+ 7.8° C
Mackerel *(Scomber)*	+ 1.3° C	Mako shark *(Isurus)*	+ 4.5° C
Bonito *(Sarda)*	+ 1.8° C	Tuna *(Thunnus)*	+ 5 to + 13° C
			occasionally to + 23° C

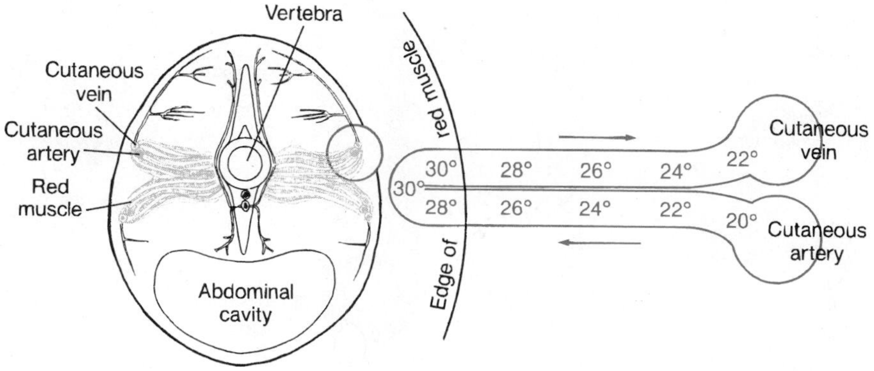

Figure 11.21
Cross section of a tuna showing the position of the red muscles (shaded) and the countercurrent system of small arteries and veins serving the red muscles. The numbers in the blood vessels represent temperatures within an enlarged portion of the countercurrent system.
From Carey, 1973

quickly lost to the surrounding seawater (table 11.1, left column). A few exceptionally fast fish, however, have red muscle masses that are much warmer than the surrounding water (table 11.1, right column). The magnitude of muscle temperature elevation above the water temperature is usually consistent for each species. The one well-studied exception is the bluefin tuna (*Thunnus thynnus*), which has a consistently high red muscle temperature regardless of water temperature. In water of 25° C, for example, the core muscle temperature of the bluefin tuna is near 32° C and declines only slightly to 30° C when the animal is moved to seawater with a temperature of 7° C.

Within certain limits, metabolic processes, including muscle contractions, occur more rapidly at higher temperatures. Consequently, the power output of a warm muscle can be greater than that of a cold muscle. Tuna and mackerel sharks exhibit some behavioral characteristics that elevate and control their internal temperatures to some extent. These fish are most abundant in tropical and subtropical regions where differences between body and water temperatures are not great. More important, though, are their heat-conserving anatomical features. In most bony fish, the swimming muscles receive blood from the dorsal aorta just under the vertebral column. The major blood source for the red muscle masses of mackerel sharks and most tuna is a cutaneous artery under the skin on either side of the body (figure 11.21). The blood flows from the cutaneous artery to the red muscle and then returns to the cutaneous

Table 11.2
Functional Comparison of Some Features that Influence the Swimming Speeds of a Noncruising Fish (Rockfish) and a Specialized Cruiser (Tuna)

Characteristic	Rockfish	Tuna
Body Features		
Shape Front view		
Rigidity	Flexible body	Rigid body
Scales	Abundant large scales	Small scales
Eyes	Bulging eyes	Nonprotuding eyes covered with adipose lid
% of thrust by body	50%	Almost none
Dorsal fin	Broad-based and high	Small, fits into slot
Caudal Peduncle		
Form	Broad	Restricted
Cross-sectional shape		
Keels	Absent	Present
Finlets	Absent	Present
Caudal Fin		
Aspect ratio	Low, 3	High, 7–10
Rigidity	Flexible	Rigid
Maneuverability	Good	Poor
Tail beat frequency	Low	High
Tail beat amplitude	Large	Small
Swimming Muscles		
% of body weight	50–65%	75%
% red muscle	20%	50% or more
Body temperature	Ambient	Elevated

Modified from Fierstine and Walters 1968

vein. Between the cutaneous vessels and the red muscles are extensive countercurrent heat exchangers that facilitate heat retention within the red muscle. Cold blood enters the countercurrent system and is warmed by the blood leaving the warm red muscle. As a result, little of the heat generated in the red muscles is lost.

All the previously described features collectively function to provide tuna and other similar fish with the capability of cruising continually at moderate speeds and with the opportunity to be the efficient pelagic predators they are. Table 11.2 summarizes these features and compares tuna to a normally noncruising fish (a rockfish) that typically lies in wait for its prey.

Schooling

The successful use of filter-feeding techniques by large whales, numerous fish, and even a few birds and seals is dependent on the presence of abundant and dense aggregations of smaller animals. In addition to the patchiness of zooplankton described in the previous chapter, hundreds of species of smaller fish

Figure 11.22
A skipjack (*Katsuwonus*) in a school of baitfish
Courtesy Honolulu Laboratory, National Marine Fisheries Service, NOAA, Department of Commerce

and a few types of squids and larger crustaceans create well-defined social organizations called **schools.** Fish schools vary in size from a few fish to enormous populations extending over several square km. Schools usually consist of a single species with all members similar in size or age. Larger fish swim faster than smaller ones, and mixed populations quickly sort themselves out according to their size. The spatial organization of individuals within a school remains remarkably constant as the school moves or changes direction. Individual fish line up parallel to each other, swim in the same direction, and maintain fixed spacings between individuals. When the school turns, it turns abruptly and the animals on the flank assume the lead. The spatial arrangement within schools seems to be maintained with the use of visual or vibration cues.

Why do small fish band together to be so conveniently eaten by larger predators (as shown in figure 11.22)? Ironically, part of the answer seems to be that for small animals with no other means of individual defense, schooling behavior provides a degree of protection.

Our present understanding of the survival value of schooling behavior is based on conjecture because experiments with natural populations are exceedingly difficult to conduct and evaluate. Predatory fish have less chance of encountering prey if the prey are members of a school because the individuals of the prey species are concentrated in compact units rather than dispersed over a much larger area. Large numbers of fish in a school may achieve additional survival advantages by confusing predators with continually shifting and changing positions; they might even discourage hungry predators with the illusion of an impressively large and formidable opponent. Finally, schooling may act as a drag-reducing behavior and allow closely spaced individuals to capitalize on the turbulence generated by their neighbors.

Laboratory studies with fish that instinctively school also indicate that if these fish are isolated at an early age and prevented from schooling, they learn more slowly, begin feeding later, grow more slowly, and are more prone to predation than are their siblings who are allowed to school. It is also thought that schooling serves as a mechanism to keep reproductively active members of a population together. Schooling species typically reproduce by broadcast spawning. Dense concentrations of mature individuals spawning simultaneously ensure a high proportion of egg fertilization and probably greater larval survival (for the same reasons that large numbers of their parents survived to produce them).

Migration

Many species of larger marine animals take part in well-defined migratory movements larger in both time and space scales than the patterns of vertical migration described in the previous chapter. For some migrators, the distances are oceanic in scale. In general, these migrations are adaptations to encourage exploitation of a greater range of resources needed for successful reproduction or feeding. For example, the food available in spawning areas may be appropriate for larval and juvenile stages, but it might not support the mature members of the population. So the adults congregate in rich feeding areas that may be unsuitable for the survival of the younger stages. This behavior likely reduces competition for food between adults and their offspring. The actual migratory routes link the feeding areas with regions used for reproduction. Other migrations occur as animals follow advancing fronts of primary productivity.

Migratory patterns of marine animals often exhibit a strong similarity to patterns of ocean surface currents. Some migration routes are in the same direction as the currents; others oppose the current direction. Juvenile stages of some species are commonly carried long distances from spawning and hatching areas by ocean currents. Although adults may utilize currents for a free ride, many types of larvae and juvenile fish are absolutely dependent on current drift for their migratory movements. The downstream drift of these young may require the adults to make an active, compensatory return migration upstream against the current flow to return to the spawning grounds.

Seldom can these migrations of oceanic animals be observed directly. These oceanic animals often move below the sea surface and well away from the coast. Most of the understanding of oceanic migrations has been inferred from tagging studies and from distributional patterns of eggs and subsequent developmental stages. Tagged animals yield valuable information about their migratory routes and speeds, but only if the tags are recovered. The application of tagging programs is thus limited to animals that can be recaptured in large numbers, usually commercially important species. Recently, new techniques, such as tracking individual animals fitted with radio or sound transmitters, have added to our store of knowledge concerning oceanic migrations.

Migratory patterns may also be determined by analyzing the distribution of eggs, larvae, young individuals, and adults of a species. When a gen-

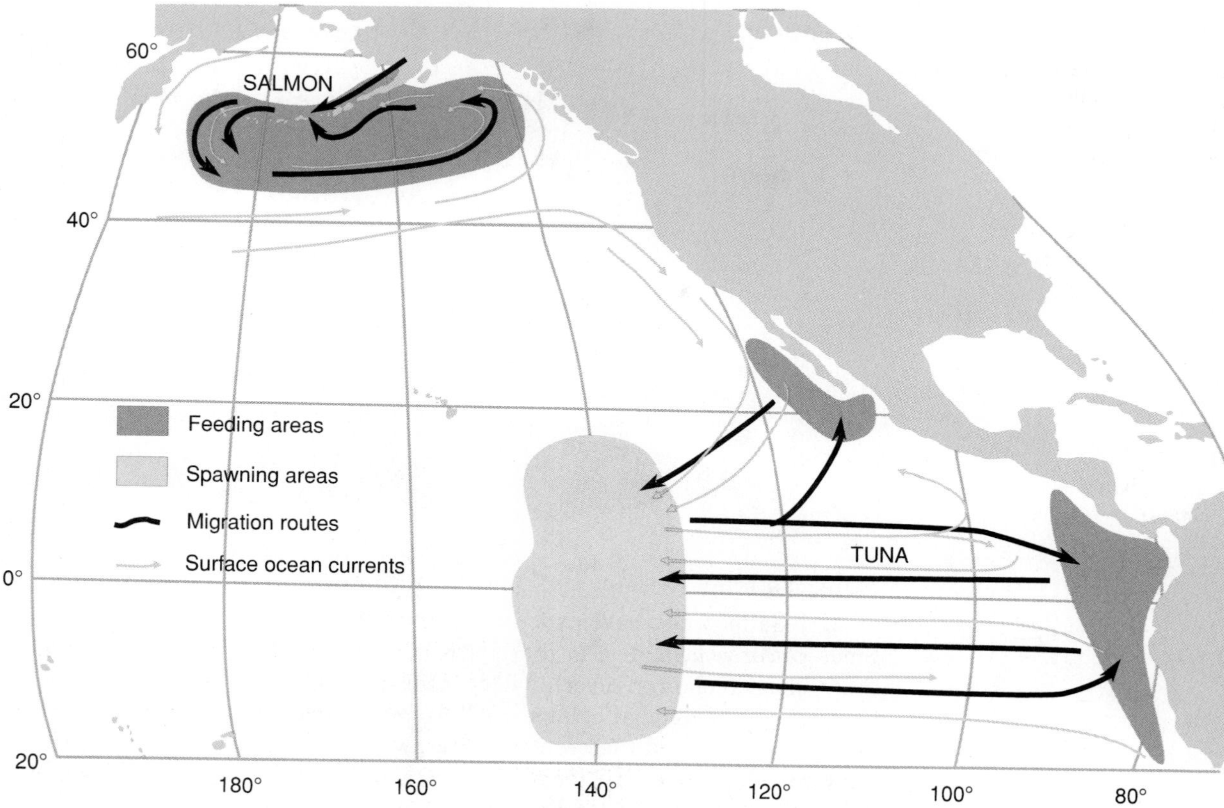

Figure 11.23
The general oceanic migratory patterns of the eastern Pacific skipjack tuna and the Bristol Bay sockeye salmon. Note the apparent relationship between these migratory patterns and surface ocean currents. These currents are identified in figure 1.25.

Adapted from Royce, Smith, and Hartt, 1968, and Williams, 1972

eral progression of developmental stages from egg to adult can be found extending from one oceanic area to another, a migratory route between those areas may be inferred.

Some Examples of Extensive Oceanic Migrations

The skipjack tuna is widely distributed in the warm waters of the world ocean. Several genetically distinct populations probably exist, but we will examine only the eastern Pacific population.

Skipjack tuna spawn during the summer in surface equatorial waters west of 130° W longitude (figure 11.23). For several months, the young fish remain in the central Pacific spawning grounds. After reaching lengths of approximately 30 cm, they either actively migrate or are passively carried to the east in the North and South Equatorial Countercurrents. These adolescent fish remain in the eastern Pacific for about one year while they mature. Two feeding grounds, one off Baja California and another off Central America and Ecuador, are the major centers of skipjack concentrations in the eastern Pacific.

As the skipjack approach sexual maturity, they leave the Mexican and Central-South American feeding grounds and follow the west-flowing Equatorial Currents back to the spawning area. After spawning, the adults follow the Equatorial Countercurrents they followed as adolescents. However, the feeding adults are seldom found as far to the east. Subsequent returns to the spawning area follow the general pattern established by the first spawning migration.

Figure 11.24
Variation in vertebral counts of anguillid eels collected in America and in Europe
Redrawn from Cushing, 1968

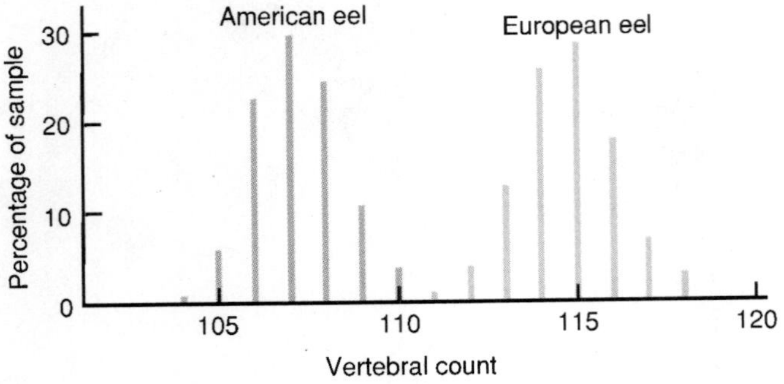

Figure 11.25
A leptocephalus larva of the eel *Anguilla*

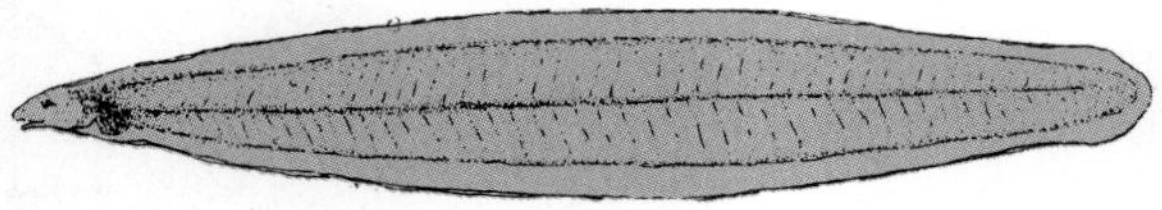

Salmon also have extensive migrations. Six species of salmon in the genus *Oncorhynchus* live in the North Pacific. They are the sockeye, pink, chum, masu, coho (or silver), and chinook salmon (also known as the king, tyee, spring, or quinnat salmon). All are **anadromous;** they spend much of their lives at sea and then return to freshwater streams and lakes to spawn. They deposit their eggs in beds of gravel and the eggs remain there through the winter. After spawning, the adult salmon die.

Because the migratory patterns of the various types of salmon are similar, only the patterns of the sockeye salmon will be described here. After hatching in the spring, the young sockeye remain in freshwater streams and lakes for about two years as they develop to a stage known as **smolts.** The smolts then migrate downstream and into the sea and enter a period of heavy feeding and rapid growth.

Accumulating evidence indicates that the sockeye, as well as other salmon, follow well-defined migratory routes, usually 10 to 20 m deep, during the oceanic phase of their migrations. These migrations closely follow the surface current pattern in the North Pacific (figure 11.23), but the sockeye move faster than the currents. After several years at sea, the sockeye approach sexual maturity, move toward the coast, and seek out freshwater streams. Strong evidence supports a home-stream hypothesis that each salmon returns to precisely the same stream and tributary in which it was spawned. There it spawns for its only time and then dies.

The Atlantic eel (*Anguilla*) exhibits a migratory pattern just the reverse of the Pacific salmon. This eel also migrates between fresh and salt water. But, in complete contrast to salmon, Atlantic eels are **catadromous.** They hatch at sea and then migrate into lakes and streams where they grow to maturity.

It is thought that two species of the Atlantic eel exist—the European eel (*A. anguilla*) and the American eel (*A. rostrata*). The distinction between the species is based on geographical distribution and the anatomical and biochemical differences of the adults (figure 11.24). Both species spawn deep beneath the Sargasso Sea region of the North Atlantic. Their eggs hatch in the spring to produce a leaf-shaped, transparent **leptocephalus larva** about

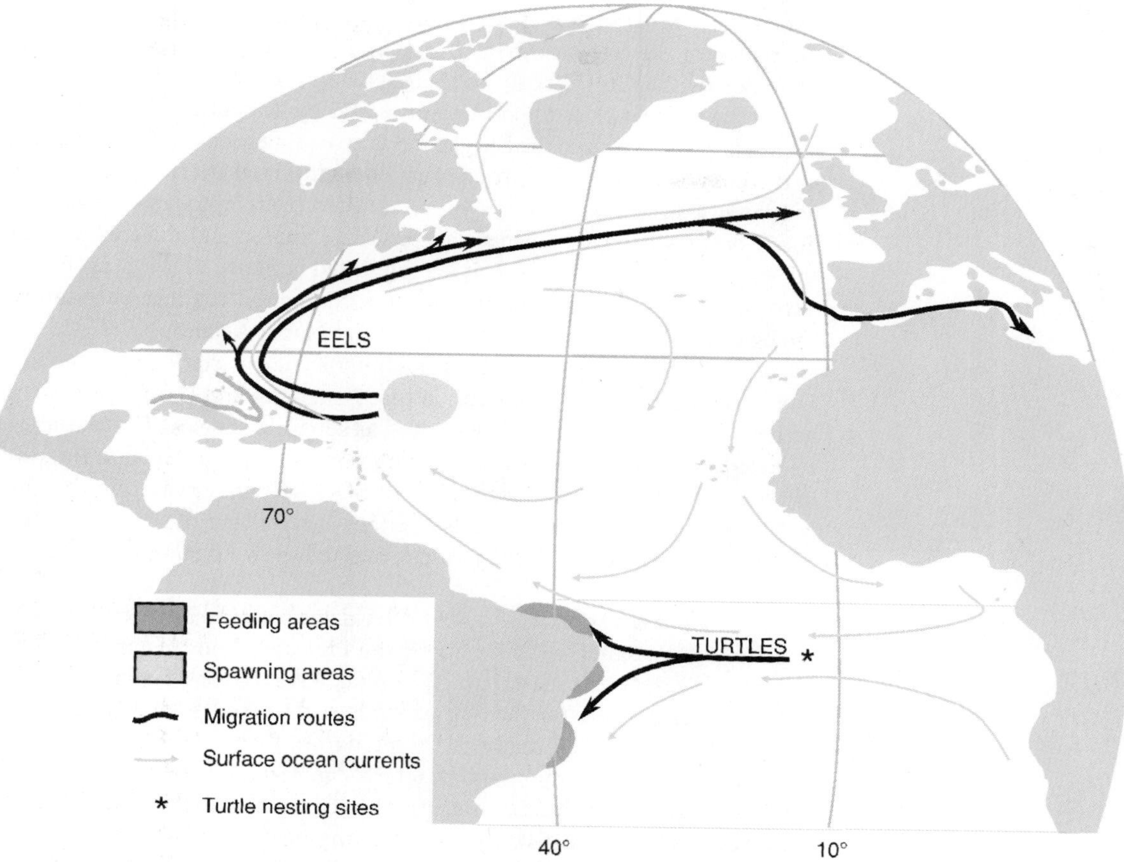

Figure 11.26
Migratory routes of the larvae and young of anguillid eels and green turtles. The return migrations of the respective adults have been omitted for clarity.

Adapted from Carr, 1965 and FAO, 1972

5 mm long (figure 11.25). The leptocephalus larvae, drifting near the surface, float out of the Sargasso Sea and move to the north and east in the Gulf Stream. After one year of drifting, American eel larvae metamorphose into young **elvers** that move into rivers along the eastern coast of North America. The European eel larvae continue to drift for another year across the North Atlantic to the European coast (figure 11.26). There, most enter rivers and move upstream. The remainder of the European population requires still another year to cross the Mediterranean Sea before entering fresh water.

After several years (sometimes as many as ten) in fresh water, the mature eels (now called yellow eels) undergo physical and physiological changes in preparation for their return to the sea as silver eels. Their eyes enlarge and they assume a silvery and dark countershaded pattern characteristic of mid-water marine fish. Then they migrate downstream and, presumably, return to the Sargasso Sea where they spawn and die.

Very few adult silver eels have been captured in the open sea, and none have been taken from the spawning area itself. Thus, the spawning migration back to the Sargasso Sea is still a matter for supposition. The European eels may backtrack the path they followed as leptocephalus larvae. However, in order to swim against the substantial current of the Gulf Stream, increased energy expenditures would be required. A more likely route would take the eels into the south-flowing Canary Current after leaving European rivers, then west in the North Atlantic Equatorial Current, and eventually to the region of the Sargasso Sea (figure 11.26). The American eels apparently swim across the Gulf Stream to their spawning area.

An alternative hypothesis proposed by Tucker suggested that European eels never return to the Sargasso Sea spawning grounds, but instead perish in the coastal waters off Europe. Tucker maintained that both the European and American *Anguilla* stocks were recruited from leptocephalus larvae produced only by spawning American eels. The anatomical differences between the American and European eels, as suggested in figure 11.24, must be caused, according to Tucker, by the different environmental regimes encountered by the eggs and larvae as they drift across the North Atlantic.

However, more recent studies of molecular variation in mitochondrial DNA support the earlier contention that American and European eels are genetically isolated and should be treated as separate species. These studies also revealed a hybrid population of eels inhabiting streams in Iceland. But, in spite of repeated attempts with sophisticated SONAR, underwater video cameras, and high-speed nets, no adult eels of either species (nor of their hybrids) have yet been observed or captured in the presumed spawning areas of the Sargasso Sea.

South of the Sargasso Sea, several species of sea turtles lay their eggs in nests dug in sandy beaches above the high tide lines of tropical and subtropical shores. Green sea turtles, *Chelonia,* have a strong tendency to migrate for nesting from coastal feeding grounds to remote, isolated islands. These islands apparently lack many of the predators that would harass the turtles and raid their nests on mainland beaches. The best documented feats of island-finding by green turtles are migrations between the east coast of Brazil and Ascension Island. Ascension Island is a tiny piece of land only 8 km wide in the Atlantic Ocean midway between Brazil and Africa (figure 11.26).

These turtles lay their eggs in the warm, sandy beaches along the north and west coasts of Ascension Island. Immediately after hatching, the young turtles instinctively dig themselves out of the sand, scurry into the water, and head directly out to sea. During this very short period, they are heavily preyed upon by seabirds and large fish. Once they are beyond the hazards of shoreline and surf, they presumably are picked up by the South Atlantic Equatorial Current and are carried toward Brazil at speeds of 1 to 2 km/hr. Less than two months is needed to passively drift to Brazil, yet nothing is known of the young turtles' whereabouts or activities during their first year.

As they mature, the turtles congregate along the mainland coast of Brazil where they graze on turtle grass and other sea grasses in shallow flats. Features of the nesting migration back to Ascension Island are not well known, but the adult turtles do show up there in great numbers during the nesting season.

Mating apparently occurs only near the nesting ground. Either the males accompany the females on their migration from Brazil to Ascension, or they make a precisely timed, but independent, trip on their own. Either way, the males get to the nesting area and can be seen just outside the surf zone splashing and fighting for the attentions of the females.

The females go ashore several times during the nesting season and deposit about one hundred eggs each time. This provides the only opportunity researchers have to capture and tag large numbers of green turtles at their nesting sites. (Because males do not leave the water, almost nothing is known about their migratory behavior.) The tagging results indicate that the females

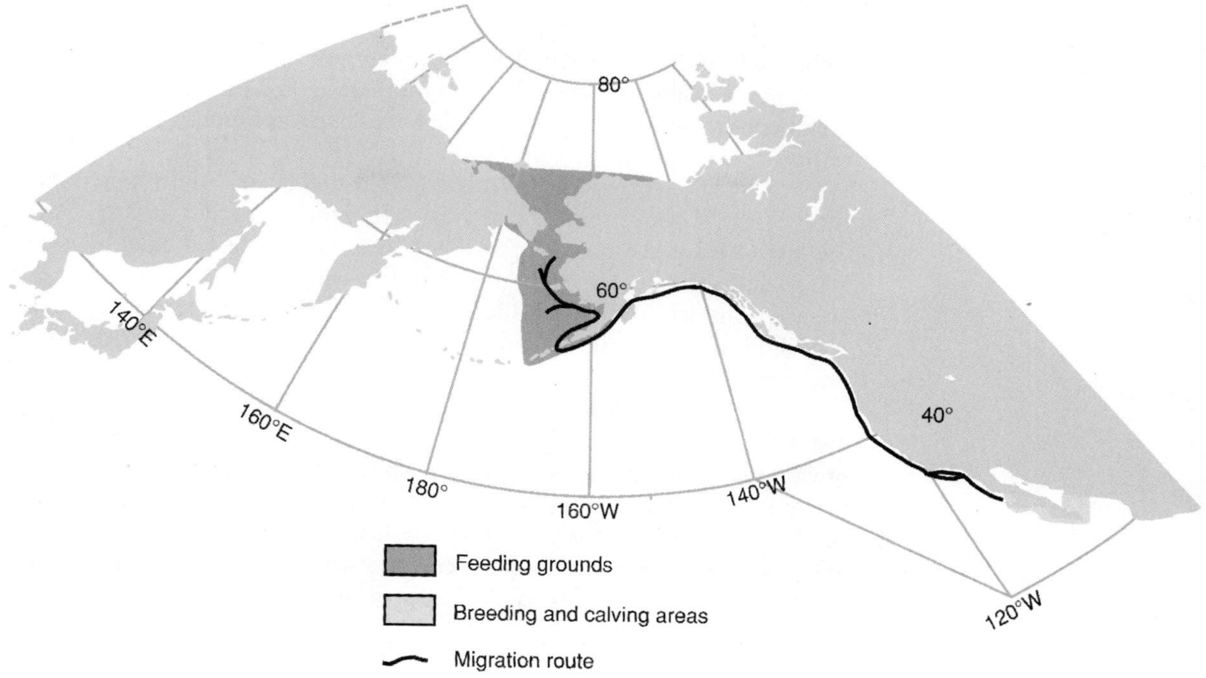

Figure 11.27
The migratory route of the California gray whale

leave Ascension Island after laying the eggs and return to the Brazilian coast. Two or three years later, they return to the tiny island of Ascension again to mate and lay their eggs.

Like marine turtles, several of the larger marine mammals undertake impressive seasonal migrations. The large whales alternate between cold-water summer feeding grounds and warm-water winter breeding and calving grounds. The annual migration of the California gray whale has been extensively studied and is the best known of the large whale migrations. These whales migrate an impressive 18,000 km (11,000 mi) round-trip each year. Most gray whales spend the summer months in the Bering Sea and adjacent areas of the Arctic Ocean as far north as the edge of the pack ice. Their habit of feeding on bottom invertebrates and their limited capacity to hold their breath (4 to 5 minutes) restrict their feeding activities to the shallow portions of these seas (usually less than 70 m).

The southward migration is initiated in autumn possibly in response to shortening days or to the formation of sea ice in Arctic waters. The migration is a procession of gray whales segregated according to age and sex. Pregnant females leave first and are followed by nonpregnant females, immature females, adult males, and finally immature males. Recent observations have shown that, after they pass through the Aleutian Islands, gray whales follow the long, curving shoreline of Alaska (figure 11.27).

South of British Columbia, the whales can be observed traveling reasonably close to the shoreline (in water usually less than 200 m deep). However, a few travel well offshore in water over 1,000 m deep. The average speed of southbound gray whales is 8 km/hr, or 200 km/day. At that speed, most of the whales reach the warm protected coastal lagoons of Baja California, by late January.

It is in these lagoons that the pregnant females give birth and the males and nonpregnant females mate. The new mothers remain with their calves in the lagoons for about two months. During that time, the nursing calves rapidly put on weight to face the rigors of a long migration back to the chilly waters of the Bering Sea.

In early spring, the northward migration begins, and is much the reverse of the previous southbound trip, with nursing females and their calves the last to leave the lagoons. Traveling at a more leisurely pace than when going south, the whales reach their Arctic feeding grounds in the late spring or early summer. They spend the summer rapidly restoring their depleted fat and blubber reserves in preparation for their next migratory performance a few months later.

A few generalizations can be made from these examples of long-distance migrations of marine animals. For many migrating species, timing or precise routes are simply not known. In spite of these gaps in our information, we do know that numerous species of marine animals do undertake and successfully accomplish long and sometimes complex migrations. Generally, the migrations link areas that ensure reproductive success with other areas that provide an abundance of food. And quite often, these migratory paths follow ocean current patterns.

Orientation

One aspect of migration that has not yet been considered is how it is done. How do migratory species know where they are and where they are going? Before an animal can successfully accomplish a directed movement from one place to another, it must orient itself both in time and in space.

Biological clocks operating on circadian and longer period rhythms (see chapter 7) are important factors in the orientation process. A variety of environmental factors serve as cues to adjust or reset the timing of these rhythms. Well-known among these timing factors is the day length that changes with predictable regularity through the seasons. Day length, water temperature, and food availability might serve as useful cues for following the passage of the seasons. These and other factors have been suggested as cues that trigger the seasonal migrations of gray whales and other marine animals.

Orientation in space is somewhat more complex than time orientation. Terrestrial animals and birds are known to use recognizable landmarks to orient themselves. Much of the gray whale migration occurs within sight of land. These whales frequently thrust their heads vertically out of the water; it has been suggested that this behavior is a means of getting visual bearings on coastal headlands and other recognizable landmarks. Because they usually stay inside the 200 m depth contour, gray whales might also follow ocean bottom contours of the continental shelf.

Several species of birds are capable of accurately navigating over completely unfamiliar terrain. Studies by Keeton found evidence that homing pigeons somehow sense the direction of the earth's magnetic field. When Keeton attached small magnets to the birds' necks to disrupt the earth's magnetic field around the birds' heads, they lost their homing ability. Control birds with nonmagnetic bars on their necks homed correctly under the same conditions. Sharks, skates, and rays also have a demonstrated ability to sense and respond to the earth's magnetic field. Whether they use this capability to orient themselves in the sea is not known.

Some species of birds are known to navigate at night using only a few stars for guidance. Directional information derived from the apparent position of the sun, moon, and stars might also be useful to migrating marine animals, but only if they can see the sky. Whales and turtles are frequently at the surface to breathe and might get their bearings and make course corrections using celestial cues. However, present evidence indicates that these air-breathing marine tetrapods have quite myopic vision in air and, thus, may have difficulty seeing stars or coastline clearly.

It has been hypothesized that adult green turtles may use a straightforward navigation system using the sun on their spawning migration back to their Ascension Island nesting sites. Ascension Island lies due east of Brazil at 8° S latitude. The adult turtles could conceivably utilize the height of the noonday sun to judge latitude, swim to the east at 8° S latitude, and eventually make landfall on Ascension Island. Though still hypothetical, this system would allow the turtles to make course corrections if they wander or drift to the north or south of the 8° S latitude line. Island-finding by the turtles might be improved if, once they were within about 50 km of Ascension Island on the down-current side, they detected a characteristic chemical given off by the island. No one is sure how well green turtles can use celestial cues (if at all), or how well they can smell and taste. Until these aspects of turtle biology are studied further, the guidance system of green turtles must remain hypothetical.

It is known that eels, salmon, sharks, and many other fish have extremely keen senses of smell. In the past twenty years, an impressive body of evidence has been gathered to support the idea that salmon use olfactory cues to guide them to their home stream. Rather than assuming that each stream and tributary has its own characteristic odor detectable some distance out to sea, Hardin-Jones has postulated a slightly different sequential odor hypothesis for migrating salmon. He suggests that young salmon smolt are imprinted with a sequence of stream odors during their downstream trip to the ocean. When returning as adults, the remembered cues are played back in reverse. Hardin-Jones also suggests that the odors in the river are not "homed" on as they are encountered, but rather they act as a sequence of **sign stimuli** that release a positive response to swim upstream.

The chemical nature of the characteristic odors in stream water are still unidentified. However, these or similar odors are not likely to be concentrated sufficiently in the open ocean to guide the oceanic phase of the salmon's migration. What then are the guideposts available to marine fish migrating across huge expanses of open ocean well below the sea surface?

Currents are among the most stable regional features of the oceans. The migratory patterns of many fish and other marine animals seem closely related to surface current patterns. But how can a fish detect the direction or speed of an ocean current if it can see neither the surface nor the bottom? The sharp temperature and salinity gradients sometimes found at the edges of ocean currents might be detected by some fish, but only if the fish leaves the current. Available evidence suggests, however, that salmon, tuna, and possibly adult eels migrate within currents and not along their edges.

Current speeds and directions are difficult to detect from the surface if the observer is being carried by the current. But fish below the surface may be able to detect ocean surface currents by visually observing the speeds and direction of horizontally moving debris and plankton (figure 11.28). In the

Figure 11.28
Possible speed and direction cues for fish in an ocean current. To a drifting fish above an accumulation of debris and plankton (shaded region), the debris appears to move backward. From below, the debris appears to be carried forward in the direction of the current.

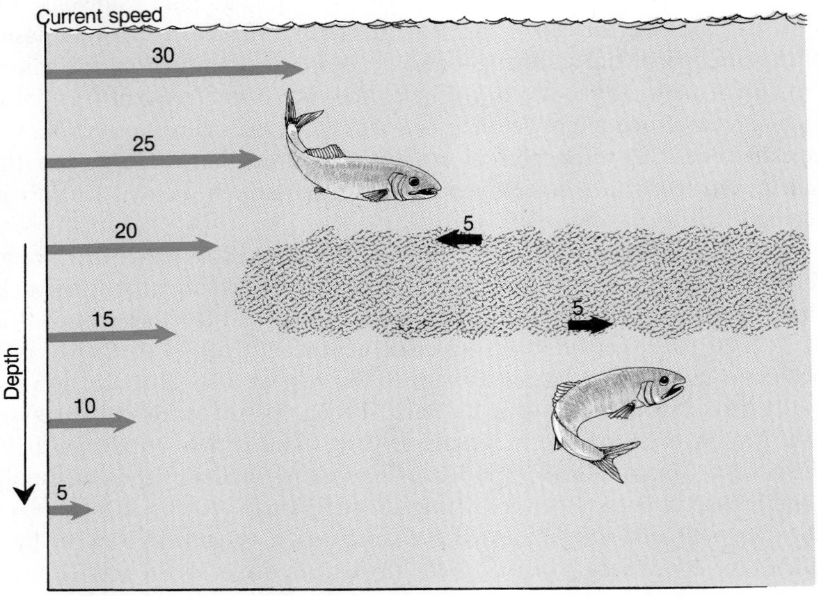

ocean, the water velocity generally decreases with depth. Fish near the bottom of the current should see particles above them moving in the direction of the current. Slower-moving particles below the fish would appear to move backward as the fish was carried forward by the current. In this manner, the fish could determine the current direction and orient its swimming motions either in the same direction or directly against it.

When electrically charged ions of seawater are moved by the ocean's currents through the magnetic field of the earth, a weak electric potential is generated. (A process that is similar to the operation of an electrical generator.) These ocean current potentials have been measured with ship-towed electrodes and are used to compute current speeds. Some preliminary laboratory evidence suggests that both the Atlantic eels (*Anguilla*) and Atlantic salmon (*Salmo*) are sensitive to electrical potentials of the same magnitude as those generated by ocean currents. In addition, they are most sensitive to the electrical potential when the long axes of their bodies are aligned with the direction of the current. If fish can detect these potentials in the ocean, some, at least, have an extremely accurate system for locating and responding to the directionality of ocean currents.

Sensory Reception

To participate successfully in migration, feeding, mating, or any other important life events, animals must be able to evaluate their immediate surroundings and to update those evaluations repeatedly. This is accomplished by employing a variety of sensory devices that serve to connect their internal nervous systems with chemical, mechanical, or electromagnetic stimuli from their external world. These sensory devices are receptor cells or organs specialized to convert stimuli into a nerve impulse; the nerve impulse is then conducted to the brain where perception of the stimulus occurs and a response is initiated. This section will focus on the more obvious or important sensory devices of nekton, and most of that attention will be directed to fish. The equally important internal visceral sensory systems used to maintain homeostatic conditions by monitoring internal states such as temperature, blood pressure or pH, and skeletal muscle tension will be excluded from the discussion.

To begin, the concept that vertebrates possess five basic sensory capabilities (taste, smell, touch, vision, and hearing) is outdated. As mentioned in the previous section, some vertebrates exhibit electroreceptive and magnetoreceptive abilities that have no known counterparts in most terrestrial vertebrates, including humans. In addition, when animals submerged in sea water are considered, even comfortable human notions like the differences between taste and smell become confusing. Our ability to smell depends on tens of millions of ciliated sensory cells located in the nose that detect thousands of different chemicals carried to us by air. Taste, on the other hand, responds to a limited range of substances (sugars, acids, and salts) that must be dissolved in water and delivered to a few hundred taste buds on the tongue, mouth, and lips. How are these distinctions of taste and smell to be applied to invertebrates lacking noses and tongues or to vertebrates that live constantly underwater?

Chemoreception

Both taste and smell are chemoreceptive senses. For nekton, they are used to detect and identify chemical substances dissolved in sea water. For marine fish swimming in an aquatic medium of near-uniform salinity, with a buffered pH, and a nearly complete absence of sugar, an ability comparable to human taste may be of limited use. But **olfaction,** the detection with olfactory sensory cells of chemicals dissolved in water, is highly evolved in fish. Salmon and some species of large, predatory sharks respond to very low concentrations of odor molecules. Just a few parts per billion of chemicals in the water of their olfactory sacs (see figure 11.33) are sufficient for recognition. With such olfactory capabilities, it is possible for predatory sharks to locate odor sources using very dilute chemical trails left by injured prey or for a migrating salmon to locate and identify the stream of its birth.

Vision

Most animals rely on ambient light from the sun, moon, or stars to illuminate their visual fields and provide the energy needed to stimulate their photoreceptor cells. (A few animals, especially mid- and deep-water fish, have light-producing photophores to illuminate their own very small visual fields.) Although sunlight travels several km through our atmosphere with little loss in intensity, an additional few hundred m through the clearest ocean water so reduces the intensity that photosynthesis is impossible, and vision is very limited. As light intensity is reduced, visual fields shrink to a few meters and the range of colors available narrows to the green and blue portions of the visible spectrum. (See the section on light in the sea in chapter 5.)

Marine vertebrate groups, and all cephalopods except *Nautilus,* obtain visual images of their surroundings with a remarkable organ, the camera eye (figure 11.29). The basic structure is similar to a human's eye, with light focused by a lens through a light-tight and nearly spherical eye cavity to the light-sensitive receptor cells of the retina at the back of the eye. In contrast to eyes fit for vision in air, fish and squid eyes must accommodate the higher

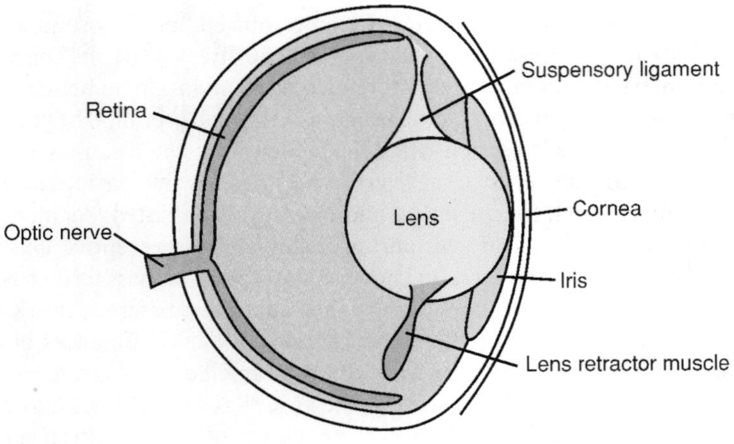

Figure 11.29
Cross section of a fish eye. Note the solid, round lens that is focused by being moved near to or away from the retina by the retractor muscle.

refractive power of water. Fish and squid eyes are typically flattened in front and are fitted with a round and rigid lens that focuses by moving nearer to or away from the retina rather than by changing shape.

Rods, in vertebrates, are a type of light-sensitive retinal cell specialized for low-intensity light detection. They can be triggered with lower light energies than can **cones,** the other light-sensitive retinal cells. Typically, cones serve as high-light and color receptors, and rods serve as low-light receptors. Fish living below the photic zone usually have fewer cones than rods, and deep-sea fish often lack cones. For all fish with only one type of cone (or no cone cells at all), vision is limited to detecting variations in light intensity; they see their world in varying shades of gray. Many fish species nearer the surface and in better-illuminated marine environments such as coral reefs, are capable of varying degrees of color vision. The retinas of these fish contain either two or three different types of cone cells, each type sensitive to a particular and different range of wavelengths. In bright light and clear water, those fish with three types of cones apparently possess a color acuity that rivals humans.

Equilibrium

A critical aspect of orientation in space is knowing which way is up or down. For human divers away from surface light or diving at night, the absence of clear notions of up and down can be very disorienting. The equilibrium organs of a range of marine animals from jellyfish to whales detect the tug of gravity. From that, they obtain enough information to sense and control their orientation in space. The equilibrium organs are small fluid-filled structures called **statocysts;** they contain a calcareous particle (the statolith) suspended by cilia extending from sensory cells (figure 11.30) lining the statocyst. Statocysts respond only to the pull of gravity.

It is useful for actively moving animals to also know their rate of speed, and any changes in their direction. With this information, body positions and orientations can be updated repeatedly. To do this, almost all nekton have two types of receptors within their organs of equilibrium; one detects gravity, and the other detects acceleration forces.

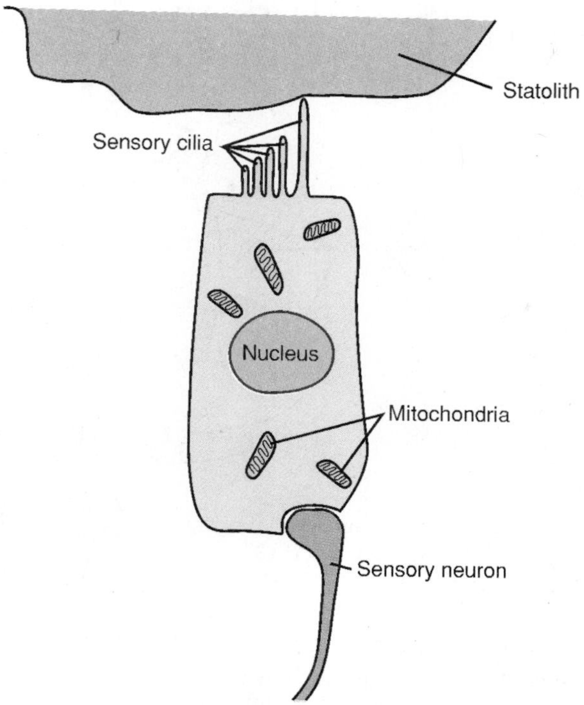

Figure 11.30
General structure of a mechanosensory hair cell. When the sensory cilia of the hair cell are bent, a nerve impulse is initiated and passed to the associated sensory neuron.

In squids and cuttlefish, the organs of equilibrium are embedded in the capsule surrounding the brain. Each organ contains extensive plates of sensory hair cells (like those shown in figure 11.30) to detect the movement of the statolith or the surrounding fluid.

Vertebrates use the basic sensory hair cell design in the form of a **neuromast** to serve a variety of mechanoreceptive chores. Fish and other vertebrates have an equilibrium organ similar in both structure and function to that of squids. It is the **labyrinth organ,** located on either side of the head (figure 11.31). Each labyrinth organ consists of three semicircular canals and two smaller sac-shaped chambers. These sac-shaped chambers are the gravity detectors, with small stony secretions suspended by neuromast cells. The canals are the acceleration detectors. Each canal is filled with endolymph and has an enlarged ampulla that is lined with hair cells supporting a cupola. Acceleration in any direction moves the endolymph against the cupola and stimulates the neuromasts of at least one canal.

Sound Reception

Sound is transmitted through air or water as spreading patterns of vibrational energy. This energy travels at 1500m/s in water, about five times faster than in air. Although the sea may at times seem suprisingly silent to human divers, animals with sensory organs attuned to that medium must find it a somewhat noisy place. Swimming animals produce unintentional noises as they move, feed, and bend their bodies. Others make intentional grunts, groans, chirps, and other noises. Add those to surface wave noises and vocalizations from whales, and the ocean has a cacophony of sounds within, below, and well above the range of human hearing.

Figure 11.31
Anatomical location (left) and general structure (right) of a labyrinth/otolith organ of a bony fish

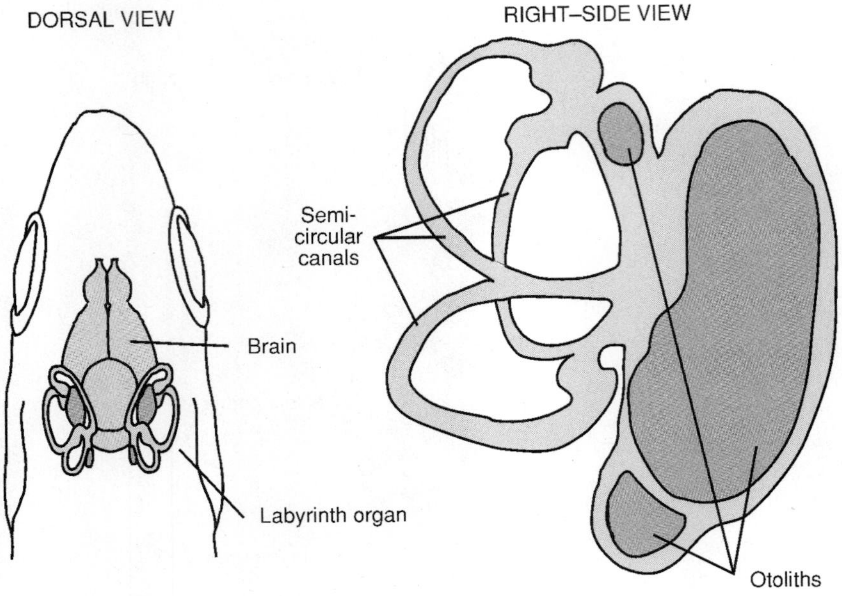

Fish detect sounds with mechanoreceptive sensory hair cells nearly identical to those in their organs of equilibrium. The organs associated with sound detection in fish are the otoliths (figure 11.31) and, possibly, the lateral line systems. Otoliths are small calcareous stones embedded in and associated with part of the labyrinth organ. Together they constitute the inner ear. On each side of the head, two or three otoliths are suspended in fluid-filled sacs where they contact neuromasts. Arriving sound waves move the fish very slightly, and the more dense otoliths lag behind, bending the neuromast cilia and stimulating a nerve impulse. Neuromasts with different orientations relative to the otoliths may provide some directional information about the sound source.

The lateral line system of fish consists of canals contained in scales and extending along each flank and in complex patterns over their heads (figure 11.32). Within the canals are numerous grouped bundles of neuromasts. The cilia of the neuromast cells are stimulated by water movement and by pressure differences at the fish's body surface, communicated to the lateral line canals through pores in the skin surface. In this way, lateral lines function to detect disturbances caused by prey or by predators, by swimming movements of nearby schooling companions, and sometimes by sound vibrations.

Electroreception and Magnetoreception

Humans are totally oblivious to the weak electric and nonvisible electromagnetic energy fields generated by contractions of muscles in swimming animals, by water currents moving past inanimate objects, and even by the earth's own magnetic field. Yet organisms as small as bacteria and as large as sharks detect and respond to some of these signals. These specialized senses are known or suspected to exist in several classes of vertebrates, but the best studied examples are the cartilaginous fish. Sharks, skates, and rays all exhibit an extensive network of tiny pores or pits arranged on the top of their heads (figure 11.33). Each pit connects, via a short jelly-filled canal, to a flask-shaped **ampulla of Lorenzini.** These ampullae are associated with the lateral line system

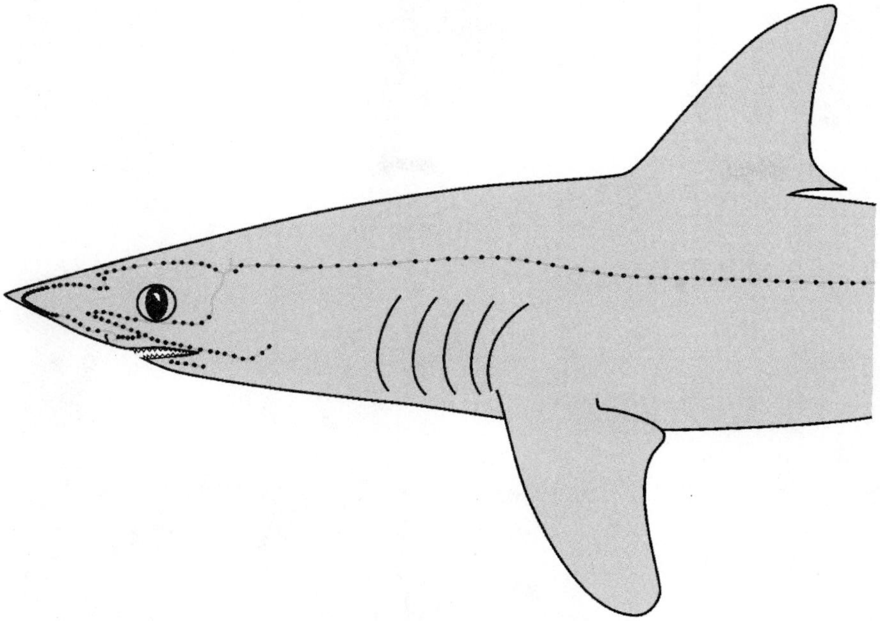

Figure 11.32
The major branches of the left lateral line system (blue) of a shark

Figure 11.33
External pores of the numerous ampullae of Lorenzini of a great white shark
Courtesy M. Snyderman

of cartilaginous fish and at least one marine bony fish, the marine catfish. Electroreception is accomplished by sensory cells, possibly evolved from the basic lateral-line sensory hair cell located at the bottom of each ampulla. With this sensory system, some sharks and skates are able to detect (at distances of a meter or so) bioelectric fields equivalent to those generated by the muscle contractions of typical prey species of fish. Similar electric fields are also produced by some metal objects in sea water. The seemingly erratic responses by some sharks to these objects may be explained as the sharks' normal response to electric fields mimicking those produced by their usual prey.

Figure 11.34
Grunion, *Leuresthes,* spawning in the sands of a southern California beach

The study of geomagnetic reception in animals is still in its infancy. It is confirmed or suspected in cartilaginous fish, some bony fish such as tuna and salmon, some birds, and possibly some whales. The ampullae of Lorenzini are thought to be the organs of detection in sharks, skates, and rays; in other vertebrate groups, the organs of detection have not yet been identified.

Reproduction

Reproduction in pelagic animals usually proceeds as in most other animal groups. The eggs of the female are fertilized by the male in the water or within the female's reproductive tract, and embryonic development leads to a new generation. Breeding, spawning, and other reproductive activities are generally periodic and are most often associated with higher water temperatures or the greater primary production of spring and summer months.

Nonseasonal Reproduction

Those species in which reproductive cycles deviate from annual cycles do so for a couple of reasons. Deep-water species experience little seasonal change in their environment and may breed or spawn irregularly. Still, little is known about the reproductive features of most deep-ocean pelagic animals.

Other species vary from seasonal reproductive patterns because small size permits them to reproduce more frequently or because their very large size prohibits them from meeting an annual reproductive schedule. At one extreme are the large whales that, after reaching maturity, breed only every second or third year. Their **gestation period** (the time between fertilization and birth) is slightly over one year, and the energy demands that a year of pregnancy followed by six months of nursing make on the mother are enormous. Consequently, most of the larger species of whales include at least a year of rest and recovery between pregnancies.

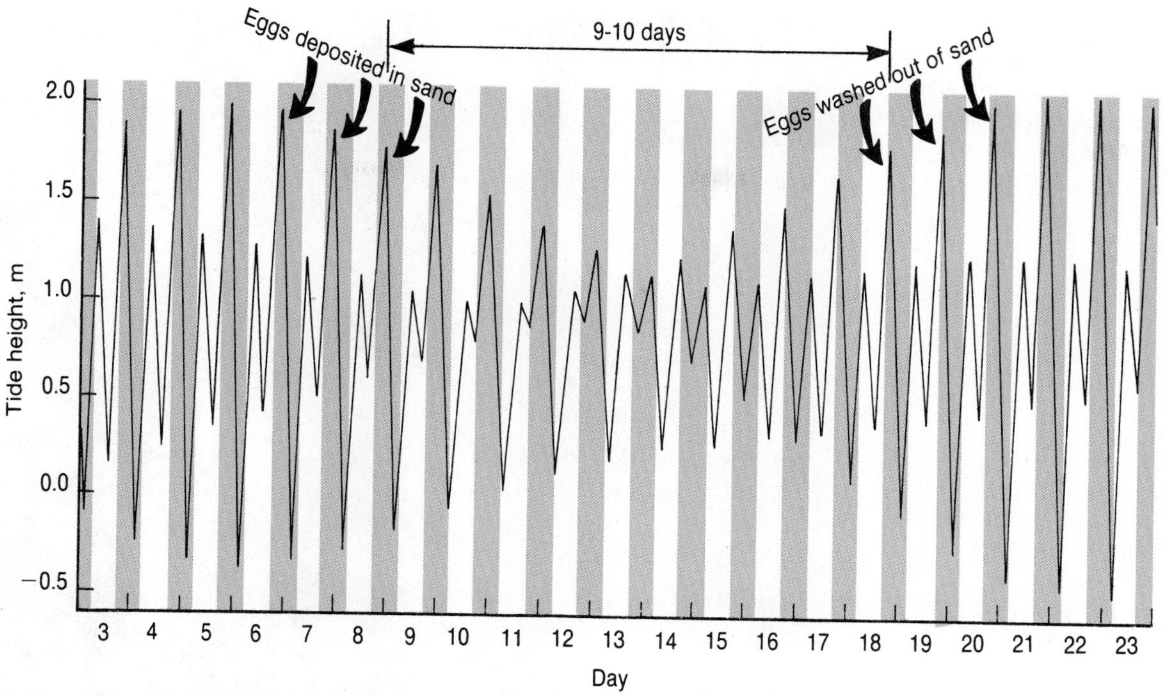

Figure 11.35
Predicted tide heights for a three-week period at San Diego, California. Spring tides appropriate for grunion spawning occur on days 6, 7, and 8 (arrows at left). Nine to ten days later, the next set of spring tides (arrows at right) wash the eggs from the sand and the eggs hatch. Shaded portions indicate night hours.

The grunion *(Leuresthes tenuis)*, a small fish found in coastal waters of southern California, exhibits a curious and unusual spawning behavior (figure 11.34). On the second, third, and fourth nights after each full or new moon of the spring and summer spawning season, the grunion move up on the beach by the thousands to deposit their eggs in the sand and away from water. Even more remarkable is their precise timing; they spawn only during the first three hours immediately following the highest part of the highest spring tides. During the spring and summer months, these tides occur only at night.

As the highest spring tides occur at the time of full and new moons, the grunion spawn immediately after high tides, but they spawn on successively lower tides each night (figure 11.35). Thus, the eggs are buried by sand tossed up on the beach by the succeeding lower tides, and they are not washed out of the sand until the next series of spring tides. Nine or ten days after the last spawning, tides of increasing height reach the area where the lowest eggs were buried (figure 11.35). Wave action erodes the sand away and bathes the eggs with seawater. Almost immediately after being agitated and wetted by the waves, the eggs hatch and the young grunion swim out to deeper water. There they feed and grow, reaching sexual maturity about one year later.

From Yolk Sac to Placenta

The act of giving birth to live young (a process labeled **viviparity**) is often considered a trait characteristic of mammals. Fish, on the other hand, are generally thought to be egg layers (**oviparity**). Many fish are, and some are quite prolific at it. A mature female cod may lay as many as 15 million eggs in a single season. These eggs are small and hatch into meroplanktonic larval stages that experience very high mortality rates. In contrast, skates, rays, and benthic sharks usually produce only a few larger eggs (figure 11.36). A single egg of a whale shark can measure 30 cm in length. The developing embryos

Figure 11.36
Developing swell shark embryo, *Cephaloscyllium ventriosum,* enclosed in a tough, protective egg case
Courtesy R. E. Williams

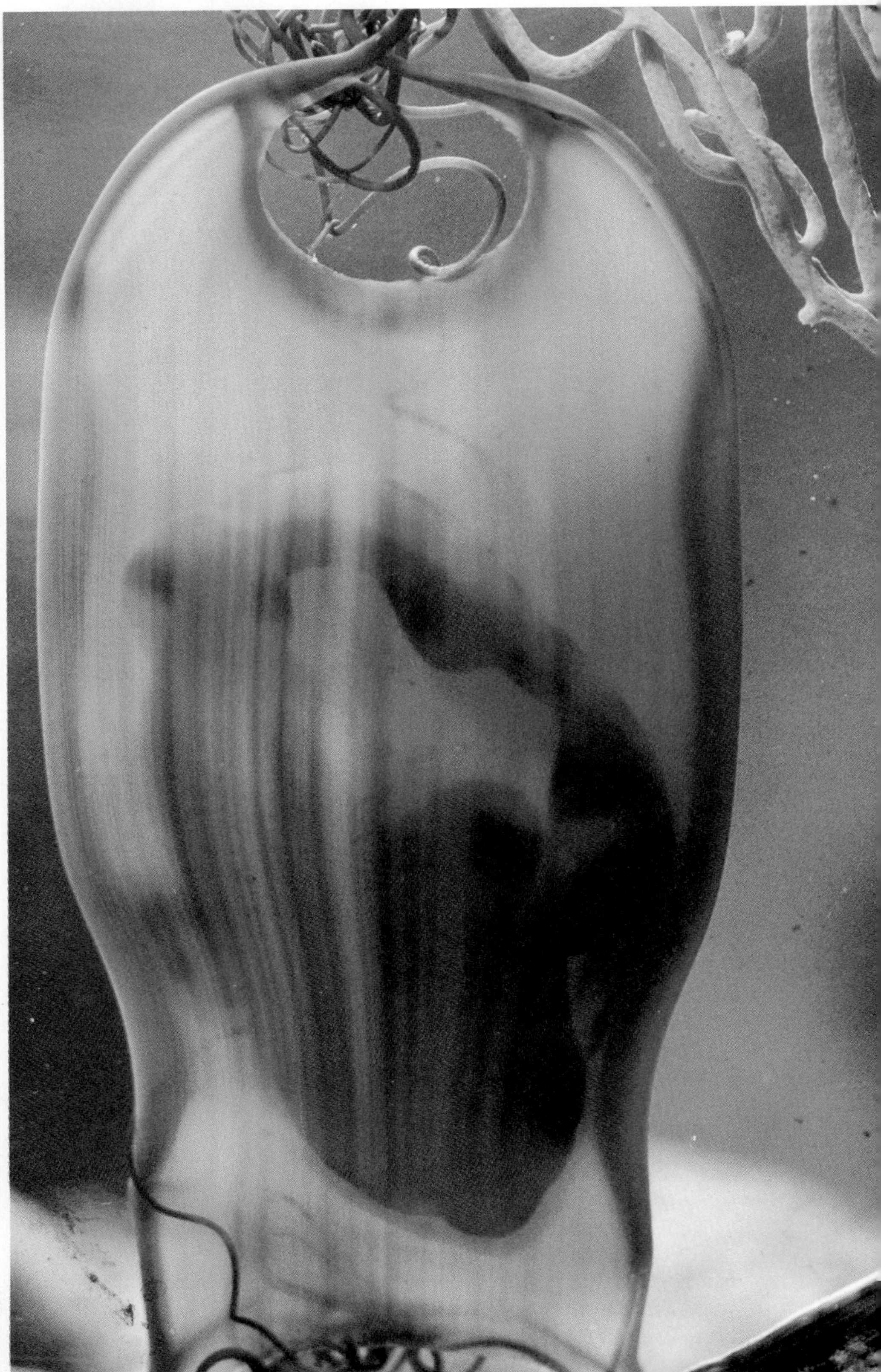

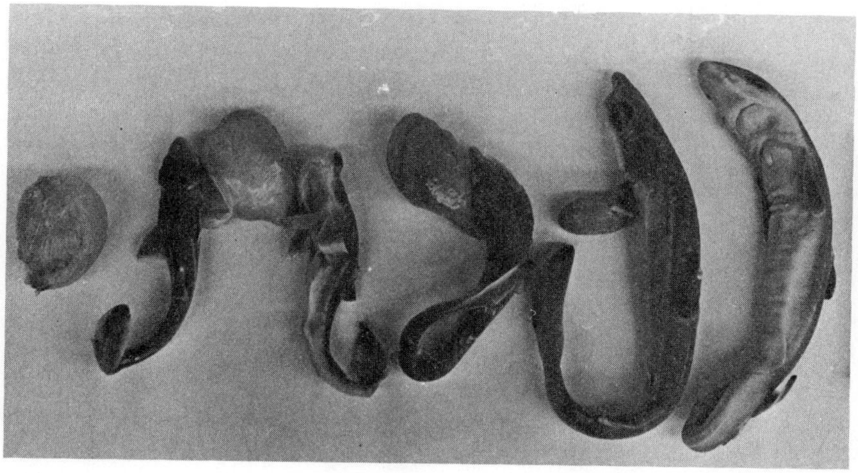

Figure 11.37
A developmental series of the dogfish shark, *Squalus,* from an egg (left) to a completely formed embryo ready for birth (right). Note the twins (second from left) joined to a common yolk.

are protected by a durable outer case and are nourished by the abundant yolk inside. When the sharks' eggs hatch (sometimes several months after laying), the young fish are well-developed and quite capable of surviving on their own.

Other sharks and a few bony fish produce eggs that are maintained within the reproductive tract of the female until they hatch. They are thus delivered alive into the world, but the developing embryos obtain all of their nourishment from the yolk of their own eggs, which was produced by the ovaries prior to fertilization. In the dogfish shark (figure 11.37), gestation requires 20 to 22 months. This intermediate condition between viviparity (live birth) and oviparity (egg-laying) is known as **ovoviviparity.** Ovoviviparity, a method for incubating the eggs internally, differs little functionally from the pouch-brooding habit of seas horses and pipefish. Only it is the male sea horse and pipefish that are equipped with abdominal brood pouches. The eggs are deposited in these pouches by the females and remain for the eight- to ten-day incubation period.

Extending the practice of internal security for developing embryos are several species of ovoviviparous fish that provide embryonic nutrition in addition to the nutrition contained in the yolk. The oviducts and uterus of some pelagic sharks and rays are lined with numerous small projections called **villi.** The villi secrete a highly nutritive uterine milk for the embryos. In one stingray (*Pteroplatea*), the secreting villi of the uterus extend down into the esophagus of the embryo. Thus nourished, the young of *Pteroplatea* at birth are fifty times larger than the initial size of their yolk sacs. Other fish, such as the white-tip shark (*Carcharhinus*) and the hammerhead (*Sphyrna*), absorb nutrients through a placenta-like connection between the yolk sac and the uterine wall. The embryos of surfperches are equipped with large, vascularized fins to absorb additional nutrients from the mothers' uterine walls.

Between the ovoviviparous fish (such as *Squalus*) and those fish that are obviously viviparous exists a continuum of reproductive conditions, some of which are rather exotic and do not fit neatly into either category. The embryos of the mackerel shark, *Lamna,* for instance, have no structures with which to absorb nutrients from the reproductive tract of the female. When the oldest embryo within a female *Lamna* has used its own yolk, it simply turns on the other eggs within the oviduct and consumes them. With the nutrition gained from its potential siblings, the single embryo is developmentally much better prepared for a pelagic existence before leaving the protective confines of its mother.

An extension of the strategy employed by *Lamna* is that of the sand tiger shark found off the United States east coast. The single enormous ovary found in females of this species produces large numbers of pea-sized eggs. After the two surviving embryos, one in each of the two uterine horns, have consumed their developing siblings, they remain in the uterus and consume thousands of additional eggs released by the ovary. This process may continue for a year, producing two shark pups each about one meter long (a notable feat for a mother only 2.5 m in length).

Some Alternatives to Conventional Sex Ratios

Most species of sexually reproducing animals include approximately equal numbers of females and males. The maleness or femaleness of many animals is determined by their complement of **sex chromosomes.** In humans, the nucleus of each cell houses twenty-three pairs of chromosomes; one pair is the sex chromosomes, the other twenty-two pairs are **autosomes** not directly involved in sex determination. A human female has two large, similar sex chromosomes (an XX condition), human males have one large X and one small Y chromosome. The same is true for all other mammals. Sex in birds is also established by a pair of sex chromosomes, but the pattern is opposite that of mammals. Male birds have two similar sex chromosomes and male birds have chromosomes that differ in size and shape.

The influence of sex chromosomes on the gender of fish is less straightforward and, in fact, is quite variable. Some guppies, for instance, reflect the mammalian pattern of sex chromosomes; XX is female and XY is male. Occasionally, though, an XX guppy occurs as a sexually functional male, and an XY individual occurs as a sexually functional female. The sex chromosomes of bony fish lack the absolute control over gender determination found in birds and mammals. The genes involved in gender determination of fish are, unlike mammals and birds, also carried on the autosomes. In some fish, these autosomal sex genes apparently influence and even regulate the production of sex hormones, especially **androgen,** a male hormone, and **estrogen,** a female hormone. These hormones, in turn, influence the expression of several sexual characteristics and the determination of gender. Fishery scientists have found that a high percentage of salmon eggs treated with estrogen will hatch as females and that most salmon eggs treated with androgen will hatch as males.

The fluid and unfixed nature of gender determination in bony fish has been effectively exploited through the evolution of a broad range of sex ratios and reproductive habits not common in other vetebrate groups. Part of this sexual diversity is due to the separation of sexes. Separate sexes housed in different individuals eliminates the possibility of self-fertilization and its accompanying reduction in genetic variation. Even in hermaphroditic fish such as the seas basses, *Serranus* and *Serranelus,* behavioral interactions with others of the same species ensure that cross-fertilization will occur. Some deep-sea fish also function simultaneously as both males and females (simultaneous hermaphrodites). Because the paths of these fish cross infrequently in the deep sea, encounters between two hermaphrodites will be successful, whereas similar meetings between individuals belonging to the same gender will not.

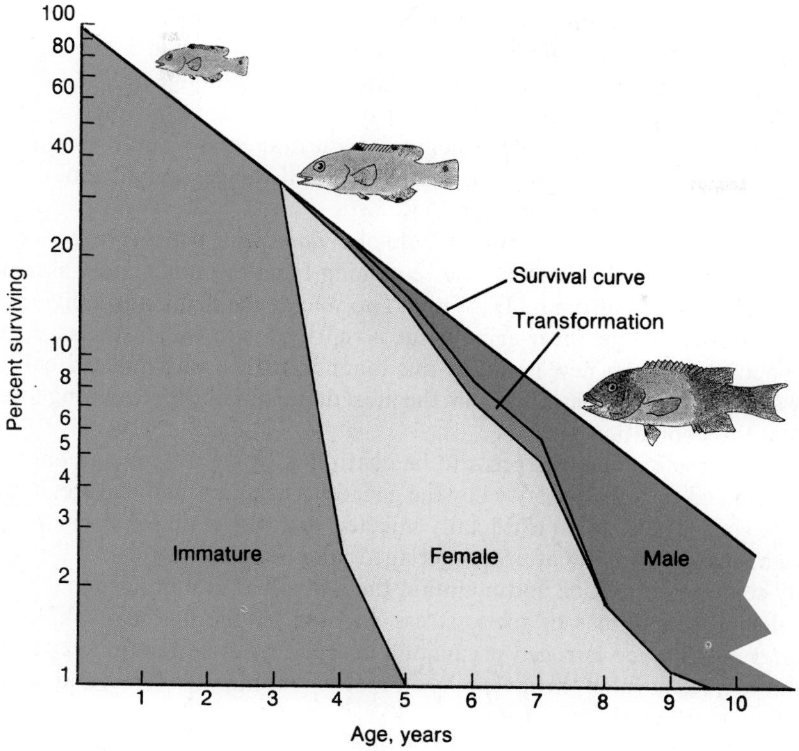

Figure 11.38
Distribution of sexes according to age of the Catalina Island sheepshead population. The survival curve is based on an assumed 30% annual mortality rate. The ages of sexual maturity and sexual transformation determine the relative numbers of females and males in the population at any one time.
Adapted from Warner, 1973

As males of many species are capable of fertilizing the eggs of several females, fewer males than females are needed to accomplish reproduction. Thus, in a reproductive sense, the males of some fish populations are sexual excesses, and the reproductive potential of the individual would be better served were it a female instead.

A few fish species are exceptions to the 1:1 sex ratio. These species produce offspring that all clearly show the functional characteristics of one sex as they mature; then, at some point in their lives, some or all of them undergo a complete and functional transformation to the opposite sex. These fish are hermaphroditic, but, unlike *Serranus,* they are **sequential hermaphrodites.** The entire gonad functions for one sex when it first matures, and then changes to the opposite sex. In the California sheephead, the fish become sexually mature as females at about four years of age. Those that survive to seven or eight years of age undergo sex transformation, become functional males, and mate with the younger females. The actual ratio of females to males depends on the survival curve of the population (figure 11.38) and the age at which sex transformation occurs. For the sheephead, it is approximately five females to one male. In *Labrus* (belonging to the same family, Labridae, as the sheephead), sex transformation is size dependent. All *Labrus* mature as females and remain so until they reach a length of about 27 cm. Beyond that size about 50% of the surviving individuals change to males. A few species of sea basses do the reverse; they begin life as males and then they change to females.

The ultimate example of manipulating the sex ratio for increased reproductive potential is found in the tropical cleaner fish, *Labroides* (also in the family Labridae). This inhabitant of the Great Barrier Reef of Australia occurs in small social groups of about ten individuals. Each group consists of one dominant functional male and several females existing in a hierarchical social group. The single male accommodates the reproductive needs of all the females. This type of social and breeding organization is termed **polygyny.** In polygynous populations, only the dominant, most aggressive individual functions as the male and, by himself, contributes half the genetic information to be passed on to the next generation.

In the event the dominant male of a *Labriodes* population dies or is removed, the most dominant of the remaining females immediately assumes the behavioral role of the male. Within two weeks, the dominant individual's color patterns change, the ovarian tissue is replaced with testicular tissue, and the population has a new male. In this manner, males are produced only as they are needed, and then only from the most dominant of the remaining members of the population.

These sex changes seem to be controlled by the relative amounts of androgen and estrogen produced by the gonads as fish grow and mature. Young female sheepheads, when artificially injected with the male sex hormone androgen, change to males at a younger age than normal. Injections of estrogen delay sex transformation and maintain the individual in a prolonged state of femaleness. Conditions of social stress imposed by the dominant male *Labriodes* may induce estrogen production in the females and inhibit sex transformation. Removal of the male may eliminate that imposed stress and permit the dominant female to transform.

These examples are but a few of the vast array of reproductive patterns occurring in marine fish. In the course of evolution, the selective advantage of each is being continually tested and retested. Whether the reproductive strategy of a particular species relies on millions of small eggs or a few large ones, oviparity or viviparity, separate sexes or hermaphroditism, each in its own way contributes to the biological success of that species.

Summary

The nekton of the world ocean are comprised principally of two groups of vertebrates, the sharks and bony fish, although tetrapod vertebrates and a few species of swimming invertebrates are also included. Most nekton are found in or just below the epipelagic zone. Those living in deeper waters exhibit adaptations to sparse food supplies, less variable environmental conditions, and low-light intensities.

Fat or oil deposits, gas-filled flotation devices, or lift from swimming movements provide buoyancy for those animals with tissues more dense than seawater. Air-filled floats are reasonably simple devices for animals that do not change depths or that have rigid gas containers. However, air and other gas mixtures are compressible, and if the container is also compressible (as are swim bladders in bony fish), some pressure-compensating mechanism is needed. The gas gland and associated countercurrent *retia mirabile* of some bony fish are capable at high pressures of concentrating gases from the blood into their swim bladders.

With their buoyancy problems solved, nekton have evolved a large variety of swimming patterns and associated body forms and fin shapes. These are forms and shapes related to some combination of specializations for fine maneuvering, rapid sprinting, or prolonged cruising.

Many species of large nekton make long distance migrations to optimize conditions for survival. These migrations generally link reproductive areas with the feeding areas of adults. These are often thousands of km apart. Several factors, from coastal landmarks and ocean currents to stars and the sun, may be employed as navigational cues by the animals that undertake these migrations.

To find food and mates or to migrate in the ocean, nekton must be able to sense conditions and changes in their immediate surroundings. Fish exhibit several sophisticated sensory receptors to monitor dissolved chemicals, sound vibrations, light intensity, color, their own body orientations, and weak electric and magnetic fields in the water.

Reproductive patterns vary immensely in pelagic animals. Some spawn frequently and produce large numbers of eggs. Others reproduce infrequently and conservatively. Some are oviparous, some ovoviviparous, others viviparous. A few even undergo sex transformation. Regardless of the different reproductive strategies, the goal is the same: to produce offspring that will achieve maturity and eventually reproduce.

Review Questions

1. Match the vertebrate classes listed in question 1 below with the following features:
   a. homeothermic
   b. poikilothermic tetrapod
   c. lacks paired appendages
   d. has swim bladder
   e. has paired fins and internal fertilization
2. List two anatomical locations in adult tuna where countercurrent blood vessel systems are found.
3. List and discuss the adaptive advantages of sequential hermaphroditism in polygynous fish.
4. How do fish achieve extremely high concentrations of gases in their swim bladders? At great depths, why is nitrogen, the most abundant gas in air, of relatively minor importance in swim bladders?
5. Explain the structural and physiological adaptations that account for the high swimming speeds achieved by tuna and similar fish. Compare these high-speed fish to a typical lunger, such as a bass or a grouper.
6. Describe the structural and physiological differences that allow a greater work output from the red muscle of fish than from a similar amount of white muscle.

Questions for Further Discussion

1. Arrange the following classes of the phylum Chordata in order of increasing evolutionary advancement or complexity: Osteichthyes, Chondrichthyes, Mammalia, Reptilia, Agnatha.
2. Discuss the adaptive advantages of schooling by fish.
3. Discuss and compare the life cycles and migratory patterns of European eels and sockeye salmon.

4. Suggest a relationship between the evolution of the swim bladder in bony fish and their high species diversity and widespread distribution.

Suggestions for Further Reading

Books

Alexander, R. McN. 1970. *Functional design in fishes.* London: Hutchinson.

———. 1988. *Elastic mechanisms in animal movement.* New York: Cambridge University Press.

Blake, R. W. 1983. *Fish locomotion.* New York: Cambridge University Press.

Bond, C. E. 1979. *Biology of fishes.* Philadelphia: W. B. Saunders Co.

Compagno, L. J. V. 1988. *Sharks of the order Carcharhinoformes.* Princeton, NJ: Princeton University Press.

Greenwood, P. H., and J. R. Norman. 1976. *A history of fishes.* New York: Halsted Press.

Keenleyside, M. H. A. 1979. *Diversity and adaptation in fish behaviour.* Springer-Verlag: New York.

Nicol, J. A. C. 1989. *The eyes of fishes.* New York: Oxford University Press.

Smith, R. J. F. 1985. *The control of fish migration.* New York: Springer-Verlag.

Articles

Blaxter, J. H. S. 1980. Fish hearing. *Oceanus* 23(3):27–33.

Carey, F. G., et al. 1971. Warm-bodied fish. *American Zoologist* 11:137–45.

Eastman, J. T., and A. L. DeVries. 1986. Antarctic fishes. *Scientific American* 255 (November):106–14.

Kalmijn, A. J. 1977. The electric and magnetic sense of sharks, skates, and rays. *Oceanus* 20:45–52.

O'brien, W. J., H. I. Browman, and B. I. Evans. 1990. Search strategies in foraging animals. *American Scientist* 78:152–60.

Oceanus. 1980. Special issue on sensory reception in marine organisms. 23(3).

Oceanus. 1982. Special issue on sharks. 25(4).

Partridge, B. L. 1982. The structure and function of fish schools. *Scientific American* 246:114–23.

Pennisi, E. 1989. Much ado about eels. *Bioscience* 39:594–98.

Perutz, M. F. 1978. Hemoglobin structure and respiratory transport. *Scientific American* 239 (December):92–125.

Robertson, D. R. 1972. Social control of sex reversal in a coral-reef fish. *Science* 177:1007–09.

Scholander, P. F. 1957. The wonderful net. *Scientific American,* 196 (April):96–107.

Shapiro, D. Y. 1987. Differentiation and evolution of sex change in fishes. *Bioscience* 37(7):490–97.

Shaw, E. 1962. The schooling of fishes. *Scientific American,* 206 (June):128–36.

Warner, R. R. 1984. Mating behavior and hermaphroditism in coral-reef fishes. *American Scientist* 72:128–36.

Webb, P. W. 1984. Form and function in fish swimming. *Scientific American* 251:72–82.

Marine Tetrapods

Chapter 12

Humpback whale lunge feeding

Courtesy C. D'Vincent

10 mult. choice
18 T/F
6 matching - order/class

Table 12.1
Classes and Orders of Marine Tetrapods

Class	Order	Common Names	Number of Marine Species
Reptilia (reptiles)	Squamata	snakes, iguanas	21
	Crocodilia	crocodiles, caymens	6
	Testudines	turtles	6
Aves (birds)	Podicipediformes	grebes	18
	Sphenisciformes	penguins	17
	Procellariiformes	albatrosses, petrels, shearwaters, fulmars	95
	Pelecaniformes	tropic birds, cormorants, boobies, gannets, pelicans, frigate birds	53
	Anseriformes	ducks, geese	?
	Ciconiiformes	herons	66
	Falconiformes	osprey, eagles	2
	Gruiformes	rails, coots	138
	Charadriiformes	stilts, avocets, plovers, sandpipers, turnstones, phalaropes, skuas, jaegers, gulls, terns, skimmers, auks, murres, puffins	204
Mammalia (mammals)	Carnivora	seals, sea lions, walrus, sea otters, polar bears	30
	Cetacea	whales, dolphins, porpoises	79
	Sirenia	manatees, dugongs	4

Sharing the pelagic realm with the numerous fish are three of the four existing classes of air-breathing tetrapods (figure 11.1): the reptiles, the birds, and the mammals. Within each class, various groups have evolved a marine existence independently of each other, yet each has a four-footed terrestrial predecessor somewhere in its distant evolutionary past.

Marine tetrapods are a diverse lot, ranging from sea snakes and turtles to birds and to abundant and widespread mammals (table 12.1). Each of these groups depends on the sea for food and spends a good portion of time in the sea. In spite of the obvious specializations of each of the three classes, these groups still share several important adaptations. They are all air breathers in an environment where air is available only at the sea surface. Many successfully prey on other active animals even though they have no sense of smell underwater and have only limited vision. All tetrapods have body fluids that are hypotonic to seawater—they lose water to the environment by osmosis. Because fresh water is not readily available away from shore, food must satisfy all water needs of completely marine tetrapods. It seems a paradox that, with these limitations imposed by their terrestrial ancestry, several groups of tetrapods have invaded the sea and have done so very successfully.

(a) (b)

Figure 12.1
(*a*) Emperor penguins on an Antarctic ice ridge. (*b*) A mixed flock of shorebirds, including godwits, plovers, terns, and a gull.

(*a*) Courtesy Sea World, Inc., San Diego

Marine Birds and Reptiles

There is a greater diversity of marine birds (table 12.1) than of either reptiles or mammals, and their impact on marine communities can be considerable. The term marine has a variety of meanings for birds. A few birds, like penguins (figure 12.1*a*), spend most of their lives at sea, going ashore only to breed and raise their young. Ducks, geese, grebes, and coots are common in inland ponds and lakes and are hardly marine at all, but some species do move into coastal waters to feed. Herons, stilts, sandpipers, turnstones, and other shorebirds (figure 12.1*b*) venture into shallow coastal waters only to feed on benthic animals. Others, including albatrosses, petrels, gannets, pelicans, gulls, terns and murres, are more pelagic and forage extensively at sea and often rest on the sea surface rather than returning to land to roost.

Pelagic birds, from pelicans to penguins, prey extensively on animals living in neritic waters. Their patterns of pursuit differ greatly (figure 12.2). Cormorants and penguins pursue their prey underwater and use either their feet or their wings, respectively, for propulsion. Pelicans, gannets, and boobies

Figure 12.2
Pursuit patterns of some marine birds. From left to right: cormorant (*Phalocrocorax*), pelican (*Pelecanus*), whale bird (*Pachyptila*), and penguin (*Pygoscelis*).

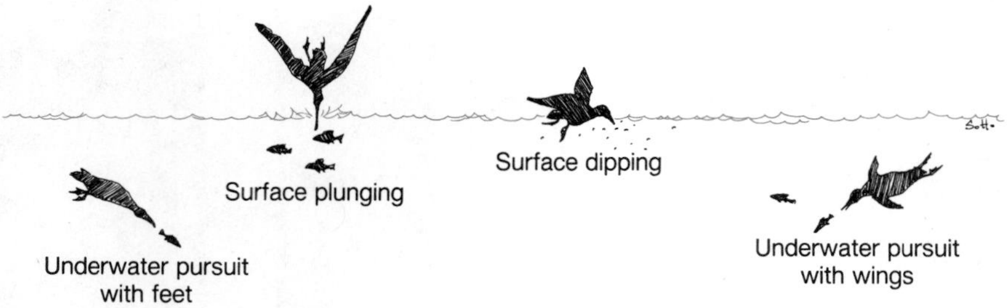

Figure 12.3
A lesser albatross with prominent nasal openings for salt excretion
Photo by J. Harvey

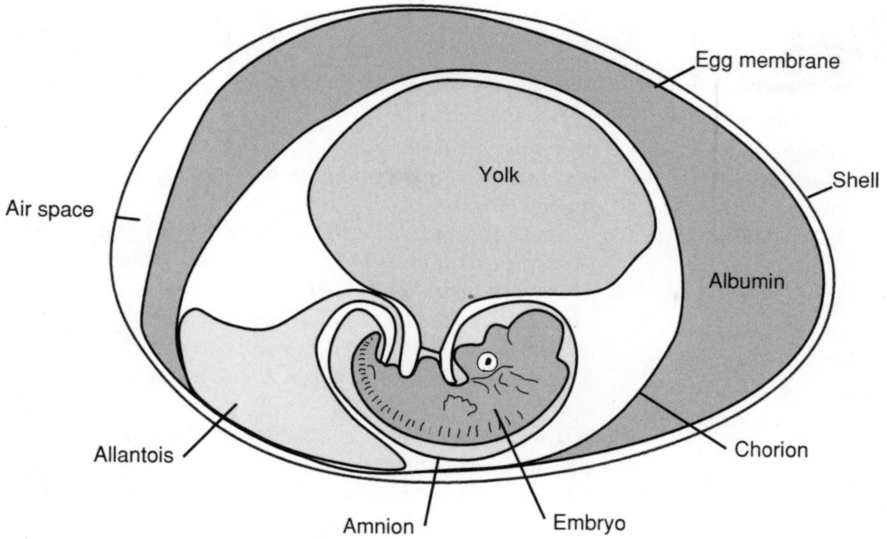

Figure 12.4
Cross section of a typical amniotic egg, showing the major internal membranes. The amnion, for which this type of egg is named, surrounds and protects the developing embryo.

plunge from several meters above the surface to snare their food. The filter-feeding whalebirds of Antarctic waters paddle at the sea surface, dipping their heads to scoop up crustaceans with their baleen-like bills.

Marine reptiles and birds have evolved a double-barreled solution to deal with the shortage of fresh water and with the extra salt loads associated with feeding at sea: special nasal glands and kidneys. Both birds and reptiles have complex salt-excreting glands (figure 12.3), one above each eye, that can concentrate salt to twice the concentration of seawater. After concentration, this salty solution drips down or is blown out the nasal passages. The kidneys of both birds and reptiles convert toxic nitrogen wastes from body metabolism to **uric acid** rather than to urea as the kidneys of mammals and many fish do. Uric acid is a nearly nontoxic substance that requires only about two grams of water for each gram of uric acid excreted. The white uric acid paste is mixed with feces for elimination, so urine production (and its associated water loss) as we know it in mammals does not occur in either birds or reptiles.

The ability to produce uric acid is related to another major evolutionary advancement of birds and reptiles, the shelled egg, or **amniotic egg** (figure 12.4). Although a few sea snakes are ovoviviparous, most reptiles and all birds lay large shelled eggs that require some period of incubation prior to hatching. During this incubation period, the enclosed developing embryo floats in its own water-filled sac, the **amnion,** while its nitrogen wastes are stored as concentrated uric acid in the **allantois** because waste cannot be eliminated across the protective outer eggshell. Gas exchange occurs freely during development across a third membrane, the **chorion.** When the egg hatches, the shell, inner membranes, and uric acid are abandoned (figure 12.5).

Fertilization of shelled eggs must occur before the protective shell is in place. All birds and reptiles have some form of copulatory organ for internal fertilization of eggs. Yet shelled eggs, uric acid excretion, and even internal fertilization were early adaptations for life out of water. For birds and reptiles that have returned to the sea, laying and incubating their eggs ashore is still the norm.

Box 8 *Cetacean Intelligence*

The actions of cetaceans (like those of many other animals) often seem purposeful and intelligent, as the following description of care-giving behavior directed to a captive Pacific common dolphin during birth demonstrates.

On December 13, 1963, a female Pacific common dolphin, Delphinus bairdi *Dall, arrived in Marineland . . . . The common dolphin is difficult to maintain in a captive environment. This species appears to be peculiarly emotional and particularly sensitive to the competitive feeding behavior normally demonstrated by larger, more aggressive forms. This specimen, however, appeared to adapt rapidly to an enclosure shared with delphinids of four other genera. Dolphins in the latter stages of pregnancy normally display a pronounced distention of the inguino-abdominal region. The small common dolphin failed to show these signs. It was, therefore, a surprise when, at approximately 11:50* A.M. *on February 15, observers saw a small tail protruding from her birth canal. The birth progressed very rapidly and by 12:05* P.M. *the entire posterior portion of the fetus had been expelled. The umbilical cord, which seemed stretched and taut, was clearly visible. The striped dolphins and false killer whale followed the laboring female. The dolphins showed particular interest and nosed the female's abdominal region on several occasions.*

The dorsal fin of the calf appeared to obstruct its further passage. In normal births, the dorsal fin folds at its base either to the right or left, but in this case it remained erect and caught internally at the apex of the vaginal introitus.

At 12:15 P.M., *one of the striped dolphins grasped the fetal tail flukes in its mouth and withdrew the infant from the parental birth canal. A discharge of amniotic fluid and a little blood followed the delivery. The infant was stillborn, and delayed expulsion at a critical phase of parturition was no doubt incriminated in this fetal death . . . .*

Our common dolphin, attended by the striped dolphins, carried her dead infant's body to the surface. These efforts were, however, terminated by the male pilot whale, who seized the body by its head. The pilot whale devoured the small cadaver, entire, after carrying it to and from the surface for 38 minutes.

The common dolphin at first seemed little affected by the intervention of the pilot whale but appeared greatly distressed by its ingestion of the cadaver. Whistling constantly, she moved rapidly around the tank, swimming in an erratic manner, apparently searching for her calf. The animal quickly resumed a more normal swimming pattern, in the company of the striped dolphins, but she continued to vocalize intermittently for several hours.

Since 1:00 P.M., *continuous uterine contractions had caused a three-inch length of the umbilical cord to move in and out of the female's urogenital opening. At 4:06* P.M., *the common dolphin sought the company of the*

Figure 12.5
Marine turtle hatchling emerging from its egg
Photo by Scott A. Eckert

female false killer whale. She was observed at this time to deliberately avoid the company of the striped dolphins and begin to swim on the west side of the tank quite close to the surface.

The false killer whale swam to the little dolphin and, after an apparent deliberate examination of her genital area, gently grasped the umbilical remnant in her mouth and with a lateral movement of her head withdrew this tissue some six inches from the common dolphin's body. The dolphin rolled on her back and broke away from the larger animal but then returned and again waited for the false killer whale. Once more, the whale seized the placenta and repeated the behavior previously described and withdrew the membrane another three inches. The common dolphin during these periods was observed to actively flex her body and appeared to try to assist the false killer whale in its attempts to remove the afterbirth. At the third attempt, the female false killer whale was successful and withdrew the entire placental membrane from the smaller animal. This was released and immediately both animals resumed normal activity in the tank.[1]

The interpretation of such behavior as intentional or intelligent acts to provide assistance to another animal in distress, appealing though the concept is, is not presently supported by behavioral evidence.

The widespread belief that cetaceans are intelligent seems linked with an equally widespread assumption that cetaceans have large brains. When brain size is expressed as a ratio of brain size to body size, the smaller toothed whales compare well (many dolphins have brain/body ratios slightly greater than those of humans), but the larger baleen whales have ratios smaller than those of cows or rabbits. Numerous studies have rejected proposed relationships between such a simple index and intelligence. In several respects, the associative structures of the cetacean brain cortex have remained quite primitive while the absolute size of the entire brain has grown.

Then why the large brains? Two researchers, Crick and Mitchison, suggest that most mammals use a process of reverse learning during REM sleep (rapid-eye-movement sleep, a sleep associated with dreaming) to erase useless memories and free neural networks for more useful interactions. So far, the two types of mammals shown to lack REM sleep, toothed whales and spiny anteaters (primitive egg-laying mammals), have brain/body ratios comparable to those of primates. Toothed whales and spiny anteaters may have large brains, not because they are intelligent, but because they are incapable of clearing out old and useless memories. If cetacean intelligence actually is on a level with that of dogs or parrots, we need to understand that, for they may not be intelligent enough to protect themselves in interactions with those "brainy" mammals known as humans.

1. Brown, D. H., D. K. Caldwell, and M. C. Caldwell. 1966. By permission of Los Angeles County Museum of Natural History, *Contributions in Science,* pp. 7–12.

Marine Mammals

Of all the tetrapod classes, only the mammals are characterized by viviparity, or live birth. They have freed themselves of the need to return to land to reproduce. Some, like the pinnipeds (seals, walrus, and sea lions), still reproduce on land; but the whales and sirenians are completely divorced from land, and their streamlined body forms demonstrate their structural commitment to a life in the sea.

The marine mammal orders listed in table 12.1 have experienced varying degrees of adaptation and modification in their evolutionary transition from life on land to life in the sea. Sea otters differ little from their nonmarine

Figure 12.6

A 70-day embryo of a gray whale. Note the definite rear limb buds (arrow).

From Rice and Wolman 1971. *The Life History and Ecology of the Gray Whale (Eschrichtius robustus).* Spec. Publ. No. 3, American Society of Mammalogists. Courtesy D. Rice.

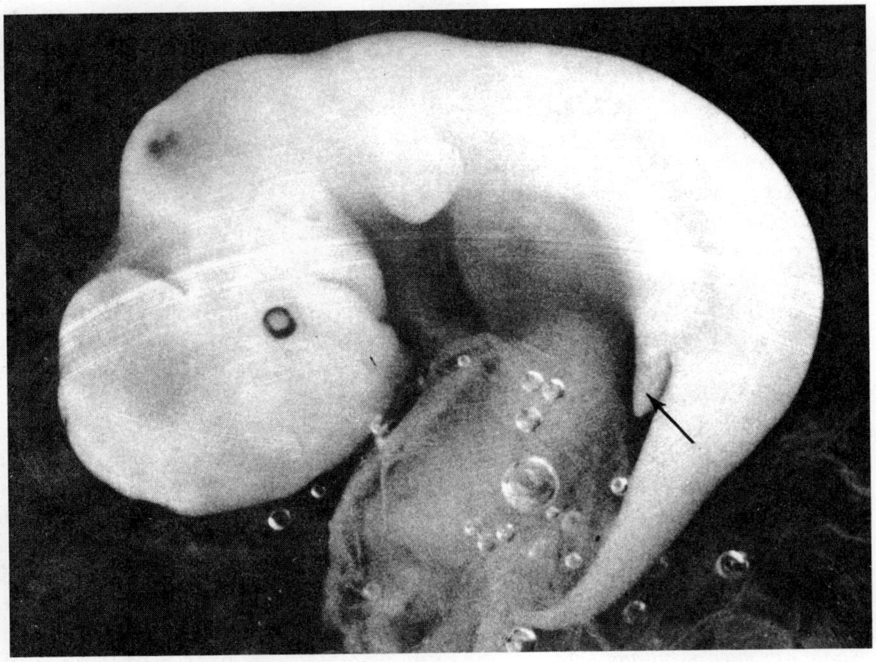

relatives. At the other extreme are the cetaceans. Their evolution from terrestrial ancestors to a totally marine existence has culminated in a remarkable assemblage of structural, physiological, and behavioral changes. In contrast to typical mammals, cetaceans lack pelvic appendages and body hair. (Some whales retain short, scattered bristles that may serve a sensory function.) They breathe through a dorsal blowhole, are streamlined, and propel themselves with broad, horizontal tail flukes. Convincing evidence of the tetrapod ancestry of whales can be seen during embryonic development. Rear limb buds develop (figure 12.6) and then disappear prior to birth, leaving only a vestigial internal remnant of pelvic appendages. Large size, streamlined bodies, blubber layers, and systems of echolocation (a biological sonar used to perceive surroundings in dark or murky waters) have evolved independently in several marine mammal groups.

Marine mammals derive from three different orders: Carnivora, Sirenia, and Cetacea. Members of the last two orders are completely aquatic. The order Carnivora includes many common land predators such as cats, bears, weasels, and dogs. It also includes sea otters (figure 12.10) and polar bears (*Ursus*). For the past several decades, it has been generally accepted that pinnipeds had a dual origin, with seals more closely allied with catlike ancestors than with sea lions and walrus (figure 12.7). Recent studies comparing molecular structures of blood and eye lens proteins and of DNA from seals, walrus, and sea lions, however, indicate that pinnipeds do, in fact, have a common evolutionary origin. They are a group distinct from other members of the order Carnivora, and the use of the formal name Pinnipedia for this suborder of mammals is justified based on presently available evidence.

Figure 12.7
Weddell seal, *Leptonychotes.*
Courtesy G. Kooyman, Scripps Institution of Oceanography

Figure 12.8
Walrus, *Odobenus*
Courtesy Scripps Institution of Oceanography

Pinnipeds evolved from terrestrial carnivores and, in the sea, have maintained their predaceous habits. Only one species of walrus (*Odobenus,* figure 12.8) survives today. Walrus, found in shallow Arctic waters of the Pacific and Atlantic oceans, feed on benthic mollusks. Seals and sea lions (figure 12.9) are not as easily distinguished from each other as they are from the walrus. Like walrus, sea lions and eared seals have large front flippers and can rotate their rear flippers beneath their bodies to provide a clumsy walking gait when on land. In the water, sea lions swim using a slow, underwater "flying" motion of their front flippers. Earless seals, as their name implies, lack external ears. They also have smaller front flippers, and when out of water, their rear flippers trail uselessly behind. When swimming, seals propel themselves with side-to-side movements of their rear flippers.

Sea otters (figure 12.10) have retained a strong resemblance to their fish-eating relatives of freshwater lakes and streams. Sea otters prefer to eat benthic invertebrates they find along the shallow edges of the North Pacific.

Figure 12.9
Steller sea lions, *Eumatopia*
Courtesy B. Mate, Oregon State University

Figure 12.10
A sea otter, *Enhydra*
© Pat and Tom Leeson/Photo Researchers, Inc.

At some point in their evolutionary past, sea otters entered a tool-using stone age of their own. Using rocks carried to the surface with their food, they float on their backs and crack open the hard shells of sea urchins, crabs, abalones, and mussels to get at the soft insides.

Manatees, dugongs, and sea cows (order Sirenia, figure 12.11) are large, ungainly creatures with paddlelike tails and no rear limbs. They are docile, herbivorous animals and are now completely restricted to shallow tropical and subtropical coastal waters where they can secure an abundance of large marine and freshwater vegetation. They inhabit coastal regions along both sides of Africa, across southern Asia and the Indo-Pacific, and across the western Atlantic from South America to Florida. At one time, the Steller's sea cow occupied parts of the Bering Sea and the Aleutian Islands. It took hunters and whalers less than thirty years, from the time the explorer Bering discovered these slow, quiet animals in 1741, to exterminate the species.

Figure 12.11
Manatee cow and calf (*Trichechus*)
Courtesy Sirenia Project, U.S. Fish and Wildlife Service

Figure 12.12
An adult gray whale in its winter breeding lagoon. The baleen plates attached to the upper jaw of its open mouth are evident.
Courtesy B. Reitherman

The modern whales (order Cetacea) are of two distinct types. The filter-feeding baleen whales (suborder: Mysticeti) lack teeth and, in their place, rows of comblike **baleen** project from the outer edges of their upper jaws (figure 12.12). All except the gray whale feed on planktonic crustaceans or small shoaling fish. The character of the baleen, as well as the size and shape of the head, mouth, and body, differ markedly between species of baleen whales (figure 12.13). Bowhead whales (*Balaena* spp.) have very fine, long baleen well adapted to collect *Calanus* and other small copepods less than 1 cm in size. Most of the rorquals (*Balaenoptera* spp.) and the humpback whales (*Megaptera novaengliae*) have coarser baleen fibers and greatly distensible throats. They feed by engulfing entire shoals of euphausiids, sand lances, or capelin. The gray whale has the coarsest and shortest baleen of all mysticetes.

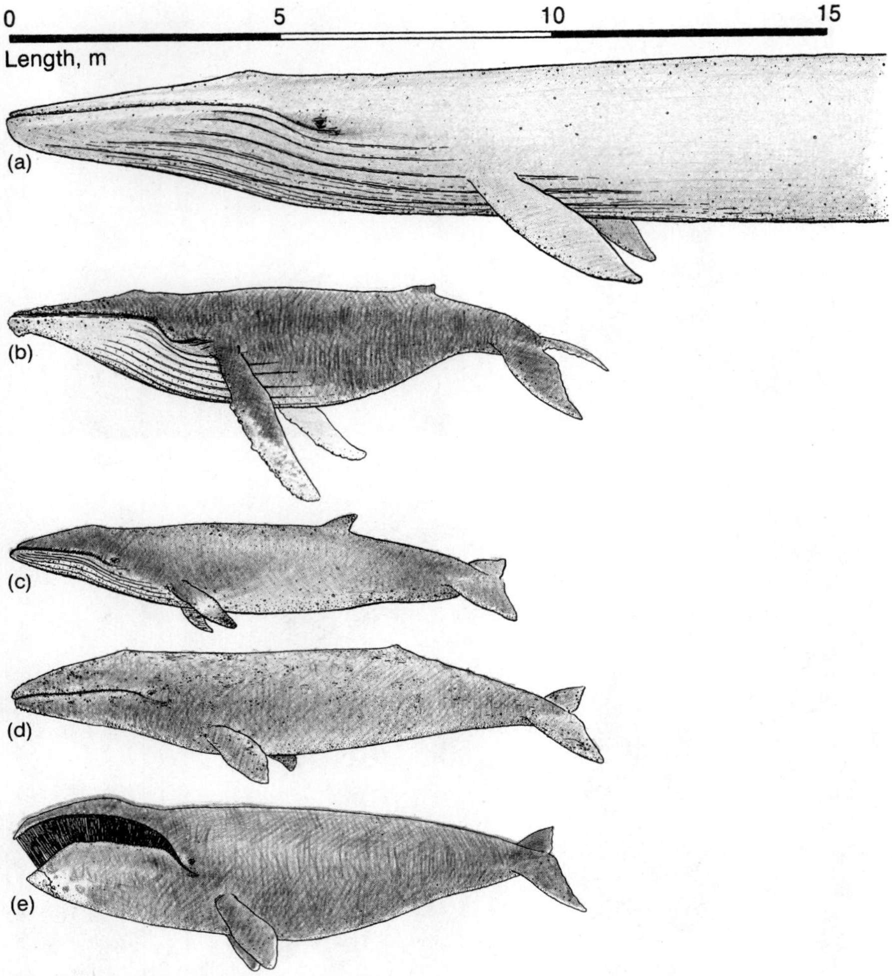

Figure 12.13
A few species of cetaceans, showing the immense range of body sizes at maturity. Baleen whales are on the left, toothed whales on the right: (*a*) blue whale, *Balaenoptera musculus;* (*b*) humpback whale, *Megaptera novaeangliae;* (*c*) southern minke whale, *Balaenoptera bonaerensis;* (*d*) gray whale, *Eschrichtius robustus;* (*e*) bowhead whale, *Balaena mysticetus;* (*f*) pilot whale, *Globicephala macrorhynchus;* (*g*) bottlenosed dolphin, *Tursiops truncatus;* (*h*) sperm whale, *Physeter catodon;* (*i*) orca, *Orcinus orca;* (*j*) beluga whale, *Delphinapterus leucas.*

Several distinct types of feeding behaviors have been described for baleen whales, depending on the type of whale as well as on its prey. The large, slow right whales and bowhead whales use their very long and fine baleen plates to trap copepods and other small planktonic crustaceans (figure 12.14). The larger and faster blue whales and fin whales are equipped with 70 to 80 throat pleats that permit the floor of their mouths to expand enormously. These whales engulf tens of tons of water with the contained zooplankton in each mouthful. Their gigantic muscular tongues act as huge pistons (sometimes in concert with surfacing behavior) to force the water out through the baleen and to assist in swallowing trapped zooplankton. Humpback whales frequently lunge open-mouthed into shoals of prey. When prey are too dispersed for lunge-feeding, humpback whales sometimes produce a curtain or net of ascending bubbles to concentrate the prey into tight food balls for more efficient feeding (figure 12.14).

These distinctive feeding patterns are best observed in the Northern Hemisphere, where competition for food encourages specializations for and partitioning of available food resources. In the Southern Hemisphere, all of the large baleen whale species exploit a single prey, the enormously abundant krill, *Euphausia superba,* of the Antarctic upwelling region.

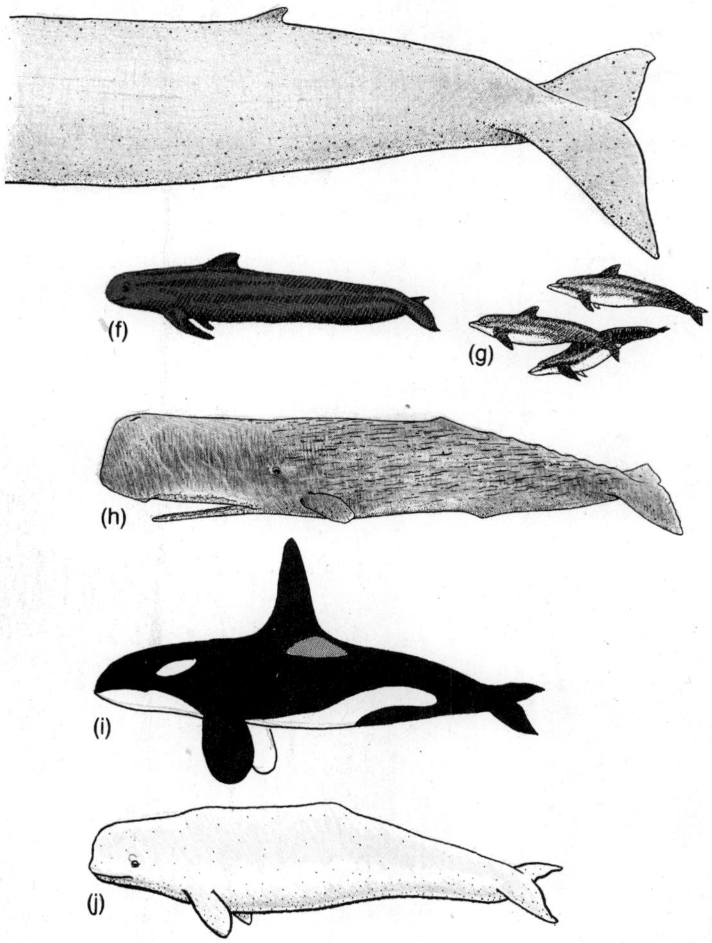

Gray whales exhibit the most unusual feeding behavior of all mysticetes. In their shallow summer feeding grounds of the Bering and Arctic seas, these medium-sized whales feed on bottom invertebrates, especially amphipod crustaceans. It was thought that gray whales fed by dredging up mouthfuls of soft sediment and the resident invertebrates, flushing the mud out through the coarse baleen. But recent direct observations on the feeding behavior of gray whales demonstrate that these animals roll to one side and suck their prey into the side of the mouth and expel water out the other side (figure 12.14).

All other living whales (including porpoises and dolphins) are toothed whales (suborder: Odontoceti). They lack baleen, are generally smaller than mysticetes, and are well equipped to catch fish, squid, and other slippery morsels of food. The stomach contents of one 15 m sperm whale yielded an intact giant squid 10.5 m in length. A study of sperm whale stomach contents, however, indicated that squid ingested by sperm whales averaged about 1m in length. The slightly smaller killer whales have gained a reputation as voracious predators, particularly of other marine mammals. In a study by Rice, stomachs of ten killer whales taken off the west coast of the United States

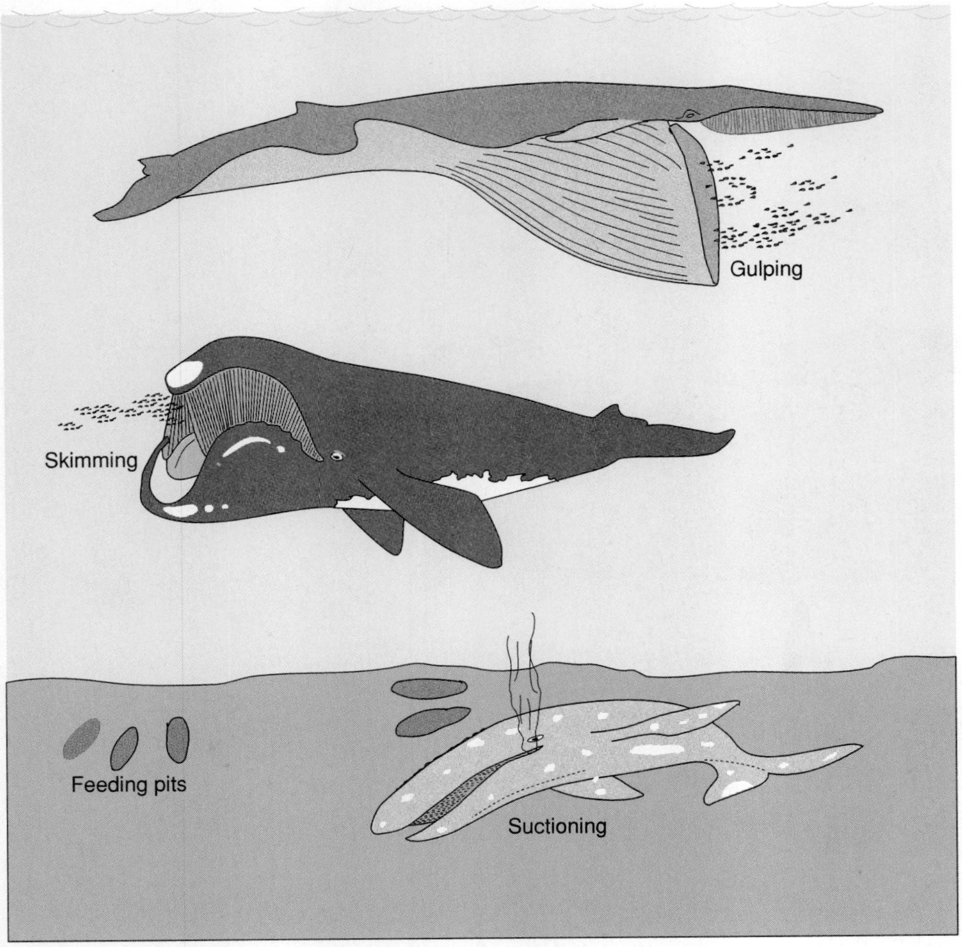

Figure 12.14
Three different feeding styles of baleen whales. Top, fin whale; middle, right whale; bottom, gray whale. Benthic feeding pits are created by the feeding activities of gray whales.
Adapted from Pivorunas, 1979, and Nerini, 1984

were examined. They contained the remains of one minke whale, seven sea lions, seven elephant seals, four porpoises, two sharks, a squid, and assorted large fish. The larger seals and sea lions had been dismembered, but smaller ones were swallowed whole.

The smaller odontocetes, especially, are very social and are thought by many to be highly intelligent animals (See box 8). Ongoing studies evaluating cetacean intelligence and communication capabilities remain highly visible aspects of marine mammal research. These studies are necessarily biased toward smaller species that are easily maintained in captivity and are complemented by information derived from animals killed in commercial harvests, from examination of singly or mass stranded animals (figure 12.15), and from research programs conducted in the animal's natural habitat. It is the combined results of all these efforts that underlie our present understanding of the biology of marine mammals.

Echolocation

Vision in most tetrapod species is well-developed. Yet several groups function well in conditions where the lack of light renders vision nearly useless. About 20% of all mammal (and even a few bird) species have overcome the problems

of orienting themselves and locating objects in the dark by producing sharp sounds and listening for reflected echoes as the sounds bounce off objects. Bats are well-known echolocators, but so too are some shrews, golden hamsters, flying lemurs, and many marine mammals.

Figure 12.15
Some of the forty-one sperm whales stranded on the Oregon coast in June 1979. None survived; the cause of the stranding was not established.

Soon after the first microphone was lowered into the sea, it became apparent that whales and pinnipeds could generate a tremendous repertoire of underwater vocalizations. Many of the moans, squeals, and wails are evidently for communication. Bottle-nosed dolphins (*Tursiops*) also produce a large variety of whistlelike sounds, and captive individuals have been shown to understand complex linguistic subtleties. Other sounds, especially those of the humpback whale (*Megaptera*), have a fascinating musical quality. The songs of each humpback whale population are identifiably different from the songs of other populations, are probably produced exclusively by breeding males, and are culturally transmitted from one individual to another within each population. Each song is composed of numerous phrases, some of which are repeated several times. During each breeding season, the songs evolve; some phrases are modified and others are added or deleted.

The sounds most useful for echolocation are neither squeals nor songs but are trains or pulses of clicks of very short duration. Much more is known about the echolocating capabilities of the smaller whales, such as *Tursiops,* for they are easily and frequently maintained in captivity. *Tursiops* uses clicks consisting of sound frequencies audible to man as well as higher-frequency clicks well beyond the upper range of human hearing. Each click lasts only a fraction of a millisecond and is repeated as often as 800 times each second. Click repetition rates are adjusted to allow the click echo to return to the animal during the very short lull between outgoing clicks. As each click strikes a target, a portion of it is reflected back to the source (figure 12.16). The time required

Figure 12.16

Pattern of click production for echolocation. Outgoing clicks (solid blue areas) are spaced so that echoes returning from the target (stippled blue areas) can be received with little interference.

Figure 12.17

A pod of dolphins at sea

for a click to travel from an animal to the reflecting target and back again is a measure of the distance to the target. As that distance varies, so will the time necessary for the echo to return. Continued evaluation of returning echoes from a moving target can indicate the target's speed and direction of travel.

Low-frequency clicks usually serve as orientation or scanning clicks for surveying an animal's general surroundings. Higher-frequency clicks always occur in situations where fine discriminations must be made. Relying solely on their echolocating abilities, blindfolded bottle-nosed dolphins have repeatedly demonstrated an aptitude for discriminating between objects of a similar nature: two fish of the same general size and shape, plates of different metals, and pieces of metal differing only slightly in thickness. In the wild, these animals must acoustically survey their surroundings, while simultaneously distinguishing their own echolocation clicks from the cacophony of other sounds so frequently present in large herds of wild dolphins (figure 12.17).

How do whales produce the sounds involved in echolocation, and how do they receive and process the echoes? The larynx of toothed whales is well-muscled and complicated in structure, yet it lacks vocal cords. The elongated

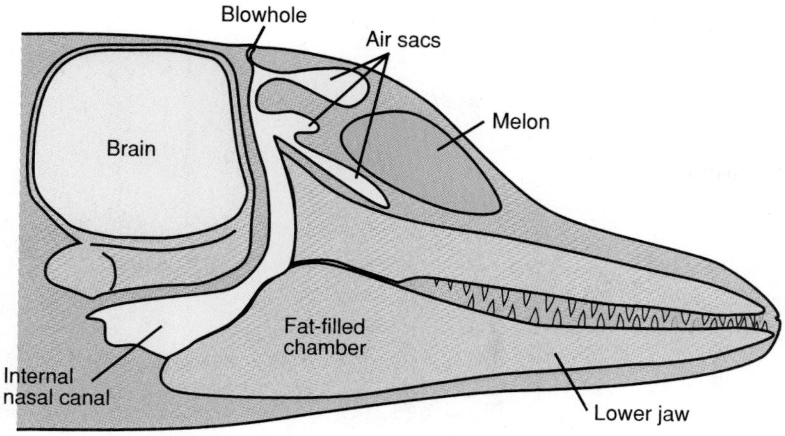

Figure 12.18
Midsection of a dolphin head, showing the bones of the head, the air passages, and the structures associated with sound production

Figure 12.19
A bottle-nosed dolphin (*Tursiops*) with a prominent melon

tip of the larynx extends across the esophagus into a common tube leading to the blowhole at the top of the head. This arrangement completely separates the pathways for food and air; consequently, underwater feeding and sound production can occur simultaneously.

At the blowhole are a pair of heavily muscled valves, the **nasal plugs.** These plugs, with an associated complex of **air sacs** branching from the nasal passage, are the sites of click production in the smaller toothed whales (figure 12.18). High intensities of emitted clicks measured over the surface of the head tend to be centered above the margins of the upper jaw and suggest a sound production site somewhere in the vestibular sac region. Clicks produced here are directed forward by the concave front of the skull and then focused by the fatty lens-shaped **melon** (the rounded forehead structure so characteristic of toothed whales, (figure 12.19) to concentrate the clicks into a narrow, directional beam. Recent research indicates that some species of toothed whales may also stun fish prey with intense blasts of sound energy, presumably using the same sound production system used for echolocation.

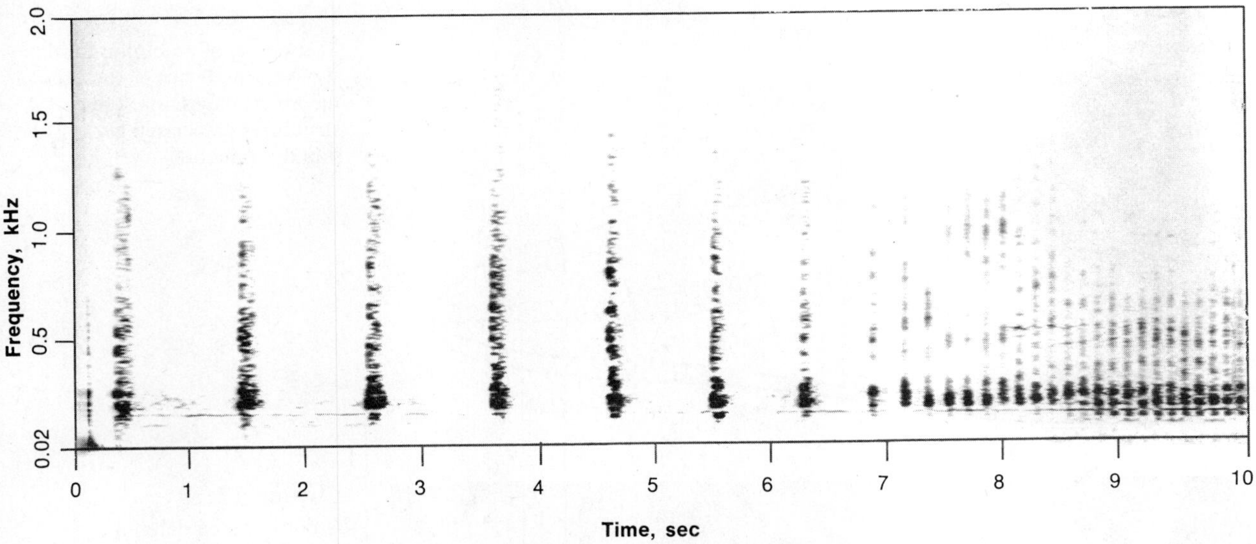

Figure 12.20

A sonogram of the echolocation click pulses of a sperm whale approaching a recording hydrophone. Each pulse shown (starting about 1 sec apart) consists of several separate clicks not resolved in this illustration. Note the accelerating pulse repetition rate.

Courtesy J. Fish, Naval Undersea Center, San Diego

The echolocation clicks of the much larger sperm whales are lower in frequency and generally have a slower repetition rate. They can be quite powerful and may carry for several kilometers in the sea. Each click lasts about 24 milliseconds and is composed of a pulse or burst of up to nine separate clicks. Figure 12.20 is a sonogram of a portion of a train or sequence of click pulses emitted by a sperm whale at sea. The boat from which the recording hydrophone was suspended was apparently the target of the whale's echolocation efforts. As the whale swam toward the boat to investigate, the time required for successive pulses to travel from the whale to the boat and back to the whale decreased. The whale compensated by increasing the repetition rate of click pulses (middle of figure 12.20) to keep the echoes returning between the outgoing sound pulses. Near the boat the click pulses were being emitted very rapidly and then abruptly ceased as the whale passed beneath the boat and presumably came within visual range.

The powerful, long-range echolocation systems of sperm whales may partially explain their success as efficient predators of the larger squid of mid-water depths. Visualize these whales cruising along at the sea surface with all the air they need, periodically scanning the unseen depths below with a short burst of echolocation click pulses. Only when a target worthy of pursuit is detected and its location pinpointed does the whale depart from its air supply and go after its meal. In addition to their likely function in echolocation, there is some evidence to suggest that the click trains of sperm whales also serve as a means of communication between individual whales during dives. These sounds travel well underwater, and the patterns of clicks produced serve as recognition codes for individual whales so that they can keep track of other pod members while diving.

A complex sound production system has been proposed for the compound click pulses of sperm whales. These whales are noted for their massive and very distinctive foreheads. Inside the forehead is a highly specialized melon, the **spermaceti organ,** that may occupy 40% of the whale's total length and 20% of its weight. This organ is filled with waxy spermaceti oil, a fine-quality liquid once prized by whalers for candlemaking and for burning in lanterns.

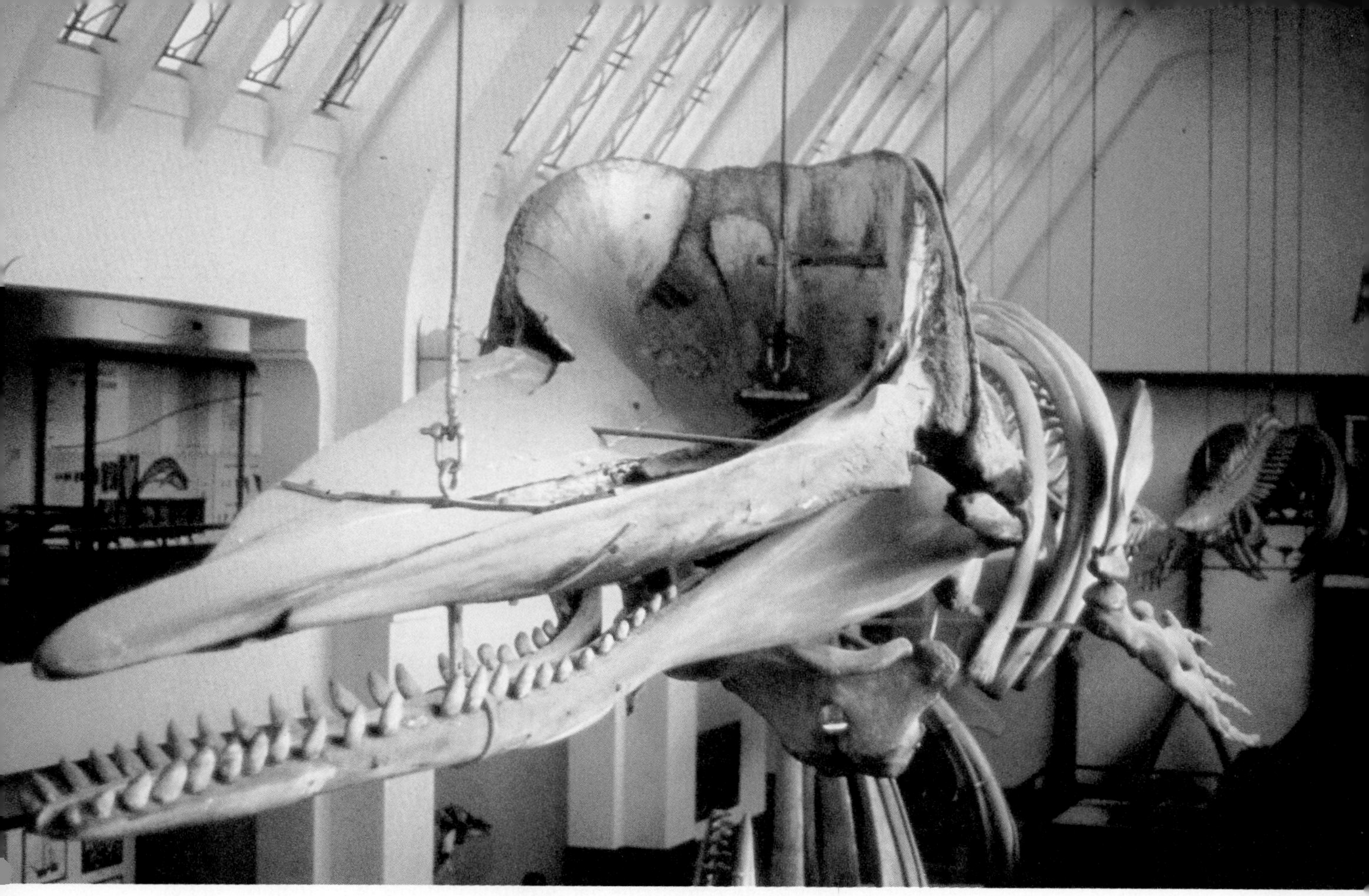

Figure 12.21
A sperm whale skeleton. Note the concave shape of the skull, which in life is filled by the spermaceti organ.
Courtesy J. Harvey

The spermaceti organ is encased within a wall of extremely tough ligaments, and the entire structure sits in the hollow of the rostrum and the amphitheater-like front of the skull (figure 12.21).

At either end of the spermaceti organ are two large flattened air sacs. These sacs are connected to each other and to the remainder of the respiratory system by the **left** and **right nasal passages** (figure 12.22). The large left nasal passage penetrates the spermaceti organ and leads directly to the blowhole at the tip of the snout. One branch of the much smaller right nasal passage extends to the **frontal air sac** at the posterior end of the spermaceti organ; the other branch is directed anteriorly along the base of the spermaceti organ and ends at the **monkey's muzzle.** The monkey's muzzle is a structure that consists of a pair of hard, well-matched, and tightly compressed lips. In front of these lips, the **distal air sac** continues upward to the blowhole, connects with the left nasal passage, and completes the loop of air passages associated with the spermaceti organ.

Norris and Harvey propose that these structures are responsible for the production of the multiple-click pulses of sperm whales. They suggest that clicks are produced as air is forced between the hard lips of the monkey's muzzle; the hard lips part and abruptly snap back together to create a sharp report or click. A portion of this sound signal is emitted directly into the water ahead of the whale and probably represents the first click of each click pulse. Subsequent clicks of declining intensity within a click pulse may be derived

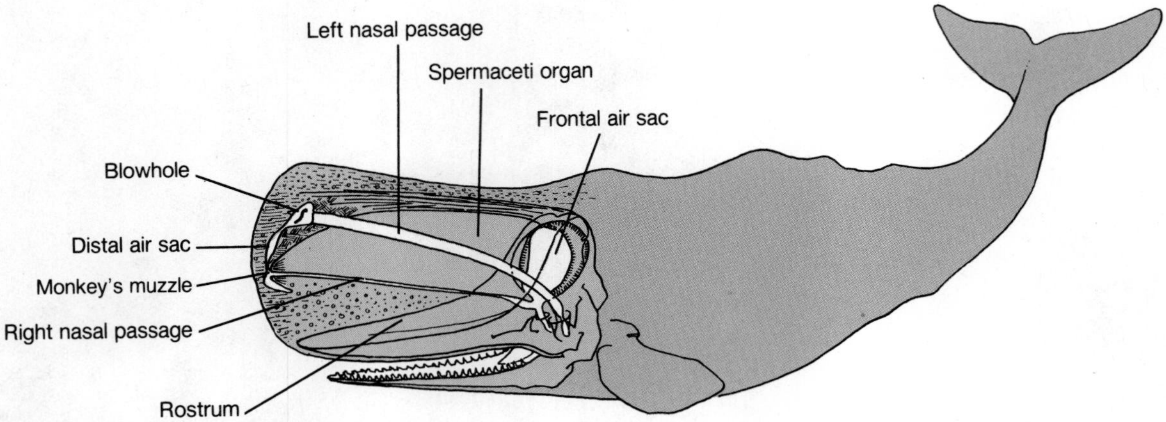

Figure 12.22
A cutaway view of the complex melon structure of the sperm whale
Adapted from Norris and Harvey, 1972

from reverberations of that initial signal as it bounces between two sound mirrors, the distal and frontal air sacs, at each end of the spermaceti organ. All of these rapidly reverberated clicks together produce one of the click pulses shown in figure 12.20. The spermaceti organ itself may function as an effective sound channel to guide the reflected click between the two air sacs. The air used to activate the lips of the monkey's muzzle can be recycled back through the left nasal passage and can be used repeatedly without loss during a dive.

Behavioral studies suggest that all marine mammals have good hearing. Experimental evidence, however, is largely restricted to studies of captive small toothed whales. Humans are sensitive to sound frequencies ranging from 16 to 20,000 vibrations per second (1 vibration/s = 1 Hertz [Hz]). The bottle-nosed dolphin, and presumably some other toothed whales, respond to sound frequencies in excess of 150,000 Hz. Their sound-detection systems must be attuned to very weak echoes of their own clicks but must simultaneously withstand the powerful blast of outgoing clicks generated in adjacent regions of the head. The sound-processing structures of the middle ear are enclosed in a bony case, the **tympanic bulla.** In toothed whales, the bulla is separated from adjacent bones of the skull by air sinuses filled with an insulating emulsion of mucus, oil, and air. The bulla is suspended in this emulsion, supported only by a few wisps of connective tissue. Thus, each middle ear functions as a separate sound receiver to pinpoint sound sources better.

The **external auditory canal** is the usual mammalian sound channel connecting the external and middle ears. The auditory canal of mysticetes is commonly blocked by a plug of earwax; in toothed whales, the canal is reduced to a tiny pore or is completely covered by skin. Mapping of acoustically sensitive areas of dolphins' heads have shown the external auditory canal to be about six times less sensitive to sound than the lower jaw. These results support the hypothesis of a very unique sound reception system in toothed whales. The bones of the lower jaw are flared toward the rear and are extremely thin. Within each half of the lower jaw is a fat body (or, in some cases, liquid oil) that directly connects with the wall of the bulla of the middle ear. The fat or oil bodies, like the oil of the sperm whale's spermaceti organ, act as a sound channel to transfer sounds from the flared portions of the lower jaw directly to the middle ear. An area on either side of the forehead is nearly as sensitive as the lower jaw, providing multiple hearing channels with four very sensitive centers for sound reception.

How common is echolocation in marine mammals? Presently, it is uncertain because it is difficult to establish whether wild populations are indeed using echolocation-like clicks for the purposes of orientation and location. If judgments can be made from the types of sounds produced, then echolocation should be suspected in all toothed whales, some pinnipeds (the Weddell seal, California sea lion, and possibly the walrus), and at least a few baleen whales. Click trains have been recorded in the presence of gray whales in the North Pacific and blue whales and minke whales in the North Atlantic. It is not unreasonable to assume that these animals use these sounds, as well as any other sensory means they possess, to find food, locate the bottom, and evaluate the nonvisible portion of their surroundings.

Respiratory and Circulatory Adjustments to Diving

Aristotle recognized over 20 centuries ago that dolphins were air-breathing mammals. Yet, it was not until the classic studies conducted by Irving and Scholander nearly halfway into the twentieth century that the physiological basis for the deep and prolonged breath-holding dives by marine mammals was defined. The diving capabilities of marine mammals vary immensely. Some are little better than the Ama pearl divers of Japan who, without the aid of supplementary air supplies, repeatedly dive to 30 m and remain underwater for 30 to 60 seconds. The maximal free-diving depth for humans is about 60 m; breath-holds lasting as long as 6 minutes have been independently achieved, although not while diving. But even the best efforts of humans pale in comparison to the spectacular dives of some whales and pinnipeds (table 12.2). With dive times often exceeding 30 minutes, these exceptional divers are no longer closely tied to the surface by their need for air.

When diving, marine tetrapods experience a triad of worsening physiological conditions: Stored O_2 is diminished while CO_2 and lactic acid become more concentrated at the very time that activity is increasing.

Several respiratory adjustments are necessary to achieve prolonged dives such as those listed in table 12.2. As the last column of the table indicates, breathing rates of marine mammals are decidedly less than those of humans and other terrestrial mammals. The pattern of breathing is also quite different. Generally, marine mammals exhale and inhale very rapidly, even when resting at the sea surface, then hold their breaths for prolonged periods before exhaling again. Smaller porpoises, for instance, exhale and inhale in a fraction of a second, then hold their breaths for 20 to 30 seconds before repeating the pattern. Even the larger baleen whales can empty their lungs of 1,500 liters of air and refill them in as little as two seconds. In the larger species of whales, dives of several minutes' duration are commonly followed by several blows 20 to 30 seconds apart before another prolonged dive is attempted. This **apneustic breathing** pattern (figure 12.23) is also exhibited by pinnipeds both in and out of the water.

Extensive elastic tissue in the lungs and diaphragms of these animals (figure 12.24) is stretched during inspiration and recoils during expiration to rapidly and nearly completely empty the lungs. Apneustic breathing provides time for the lungs to extract additional O_2 from the air held in the lungs. Dolphins can remove nearly 90% of the O_2 contained in each breath. (Humans use only about 20% of the O_2 inspired.) Oxygen uptake within the **alveoli** (air

Table 12.2
Diving and Breath-Holding Capabilities of Humans and a Few Marine Mammals

Animal	Maximal Depth (m)	Maximal Time of Breath-Hold (min)	Resting Breathing Rate (breaths/min)
Human (*Homo*)	66.5	6	15
Dolphin (*Tursiops*)	305	6	2–3
Sea lion (*Zalophus*)	168	30	6
Fin whale (*Balaenoptera*)	500	30	1–2
Weddell seal (*Leptonychotes*)	600	75	?
Elephant seal (*Mirounga*)			
female	1250	62	?
male	1530	77	?
Sperm whale (*Physeter*)	2,250	90	?

Compiled from Kooyman and Andersen, in Andersen, 1969; Norris and Harvey 1972; Kooyman et al. 1981; Delong, unpubl.

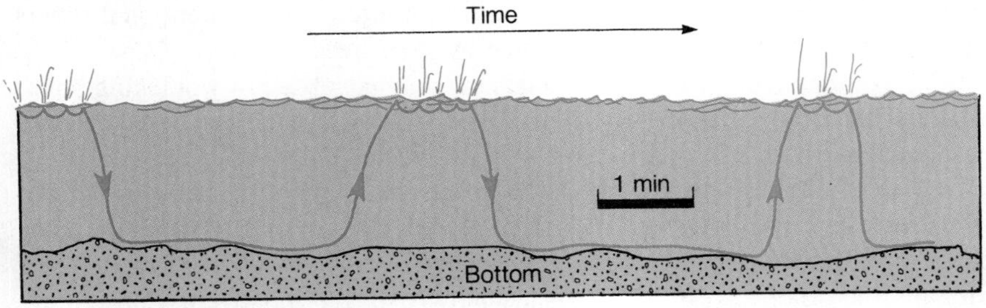

Figure 12.23
Apneustic breathing pattern of a gray whale, observed while feeding. Blows at the surface represent individual breaths.

sacs) of the lungs may be enhanced as lung air is moved into contact with the walls of the alveoli by the kneading action of small muscles scattered throughout the lungs. In some species, an extra capillary bed surrounds each alveolus and may also contribute to the exceptionally high uptake of O_2.

Each of these features may seem insignificant by itself, but taken together they represent a style of breathing that permits marine mammals increased freedom to explore and exploit their environment some distance from the sea surface. Still, apneustic breathing alone cannot explain how some seals and whales are capable of achieving extremely long dive times.

Cetaceans typically dive with full lungs, while pinnipeds often expire prior to diving. These differences suggest that the volume of lung air at the beginning of a dive is adjusted to achieve neutral buoyancy and is of little value in supplying O_2 during a dive. Moreover, the lungs and their protective rib cage are sufficiently resilient to allow the lungs to collapse as the water pressure increases with depth (figure 12.25). For a dive from the sea surface

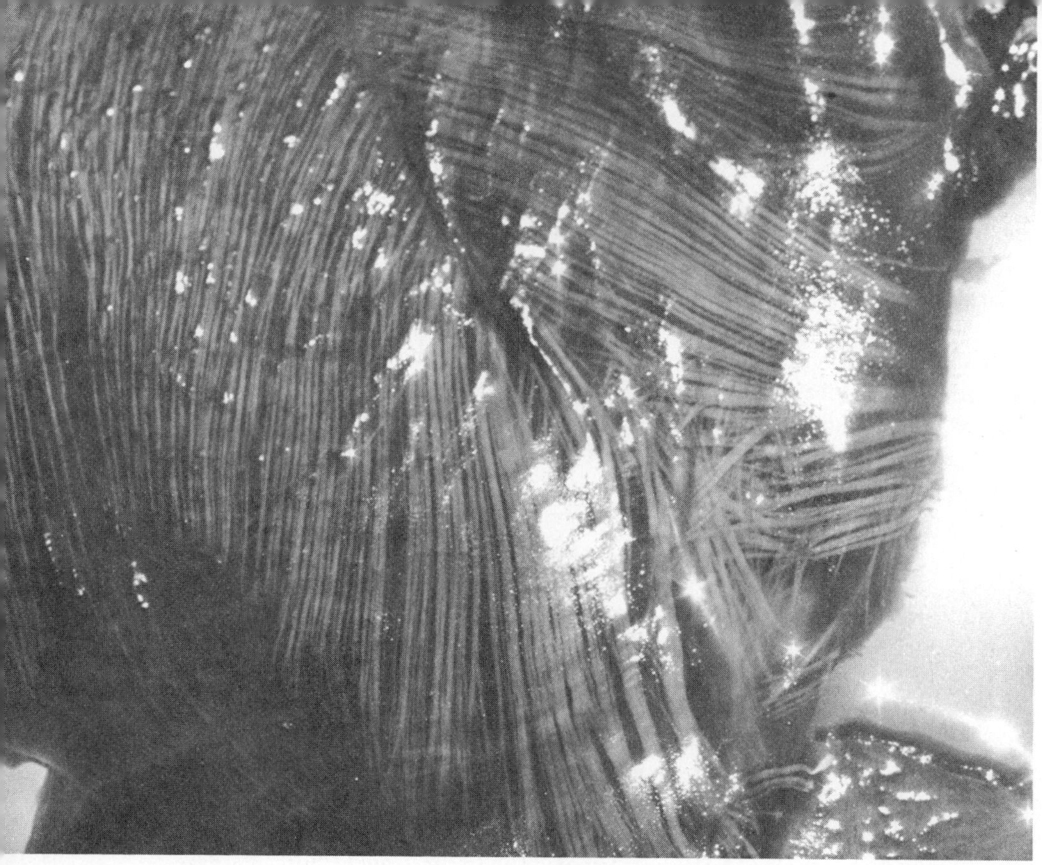

Figure 12.24

Elastic fibers within the diaphragm of a small dolphin, *Stenella*

Figure 12.25

A self-portrait of Tuffy, a bottle-nosed dolphin, taken at a depth of 300 m. The water pressure at that depth caused the thoracic collapse apparent behind the left flipper.

From Ridgway, Sam H., *Mammals of the Sea, Biology and Medicine,* 1972. Courtesy of S. Ridgway.

to 10 m, the external pressure is doubled, causing the air volume of the lungs to be compressed by half and the air pressure within the lungs to double. Complete lung collapse probably occurs in the upper 100 m; any air remaining in the lungs below that depth is squeezed by increasing water pressure out of the alveoli and into the larger air passages (the **bronchi** and **trachea,** or windpipe). Even the trachea is flexible and undergoes partial collapse during deep dives.

By tolerating complete lung collapse, these animals sidestep the need for respiratory structures capable of resisting the extreme water pressures experienced during deep dives (over 200 atm for a sperm whale at 2250 m). And they receive an additional bonus. As the air is forced out of their collapsing alveoli during a dive, the compressed air still within the larger air passages is blocked from contact with the walls of the alveoli. Consequently, little of these compressed gases are absorbed by the blood, and marine mammals avoid the serious diving problems (**decompression sickness** and **nitrogen narcosis**) sometimes experienced by humans when they breathe compressed air at moderate depths while underwater. After prolonged breathing of air under pressure (with hard hat or scuba gear), large quantities of compressed lung gases (particularly N_2) are absorbed by the blood and distributed to the body. As the external water pressure decreases during rapid ascents to the surface, these excess gases are frequently not discharged quickly enough by the lungs. Instead, they form bubbles in the body tissues and blood, causing excruciating pain, paralysis, or even death. Excess N_2 dissolved in the blood also has a narcotic effect on human divers and seriously restricts the time within which they can function effectively at depth. Deep-diving marine mammals avoid both of these problems simply because the air within their lungs is forced away from the walls of the alveoli as the lungs collapse during a dive, thereby preventing excess N_2 from diffusing into the blood.

Since the collapsed lungs of deep-diving marine mammals are not effective stores for O_2, it must be stored elsewhere in the body or its use must be seriously curtailed during a prolonged dive. Both options are exercised by diving mammals. Additional stores of O_2 are maintained in chemical combination with hemoglobin of the blood or with myoglogin in muscle cells. Red blood cells (which contain the hemoglobin) are about the same size in diving mammals and nondiving mammals; however, there are more red blood cells in diving mammals and each cell tends to be somewhat inflated by its extra load of hemoglobin. The blood volume of diving mammals is also significantly higher than in nondiving mammals. About 21% of the total body weight of sperm whales, for instance, is blood. Much of the additional blood volume is accommodated in numerous *retia mirabilia,* such as the extensive retia found along the dorsal side of the thoracic cavity (figure 12.26). Other retia, functioning as heat exchangers, are located on either side of the vertebral column and can be found in the flukes, in the dorsal fin and flippers, and around the brain, the optic nerves, and in the air spaces surrounding the middle ear. Some blood is also stored in enlarged blood vessels. The **vena cava** (the major vein returning blood to the heart) in some species is baglike and elastic. In the elephant seal, it alone can accommodate 20% of the animal's total blood volume. These features all contribute to the total reserve of stored O_2 for use during a dive.

The muscles of marine mammals are exceedingly rich in myoglobin, giving them a deep, dark red appearance. About half the total store of O_2 for a dive is bound by the myoglobin of the swimming muscles (O_2 on hemoglobin in the blood accounts for the remainder). These muscles are quite capable of

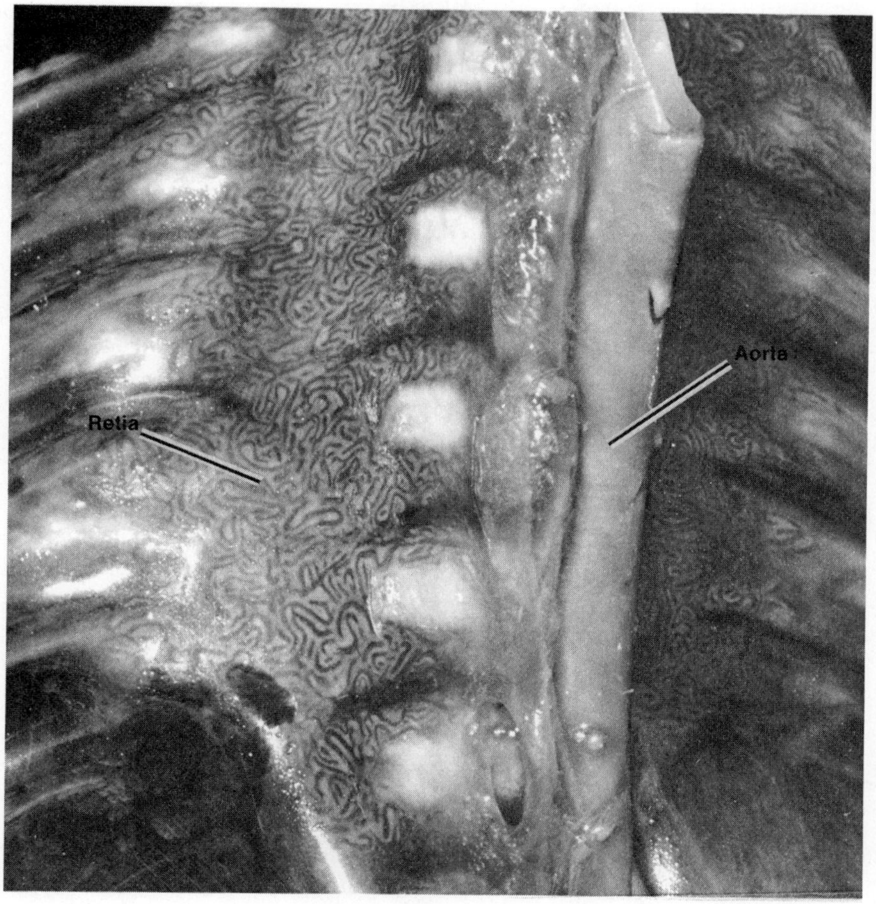

Figure 12.26
The right thoracic retia mirabilia of a small dolphin, *Stenella*

functioning either aerobically or anaerobically. They are also extremely tolerant to accumulations of lactic acid, a metabolic product of anaerobic respiration. These muscles begin dives with a ready supply of O_2. When that supply is depleted, they switch to anaerobic respiration and continue working for some time before their O_2 reserves need to be replenished.

The swimming muscles of marine mammals are highly tolerant to anaerobic conditions during a dive, so they and other nonessential organs (such as the kidneys and digestive tract) may be deprived of the reserve O_2 stored in the blood. The arteries leading to these peripheral muscles and organs constrict, and most of the circulating blood is shunted to a few vital organs, primarily the heart and brain. Simultaneously, the heartbeat rate slows dramatically to accommodate pressure changes in a much-reduced circulatory system comprised of the heart, the brain, and connecting blood vessels. Other circulatory structures also help to smooth out and moderate fluctuations in the pressure of blood going to the brain. An elastic bulbous "natural aneurism" in the **aorta** (the large artery leaving the heart) and a rete in the smaller arteries at the base of the brain both help to dampen blood pressure surges each time the heart beats.

Bradycardia (the marked slowing of the heartbeat rate that accompanies a dive) probably occurs in all diving vertebrates, including birds, reptiles, and mammals. Even grunion (see figure 11.34) experience bradycardia

Table 12.3
A Summary of Dive Responses in Weddell Seals

1. Cessation of breathing
2. Variable bradycardia depending on dive duration
3. Variable peripheral and central vasoconstriction
4. Reduced aerobic metabolism in most organs
5. Rapid depletion of muscle O_2
6. Lactic acid accumulation in muscles after 20 minutes
7. Variety of blood chemistry changes during and immediately following dive, depending on dive duration
8. Voluntary reduction of core body temperature

when they come out of the water to spawn and are deprived of a continuous supply of O_2. The intensity of bradycardia varies widely between marine mammal groups. During experimental dives in laboratory conditions, heartbeat rates of restrained cetaceans are reduced to 20 to 50% of their predive rates. Many seals in similar conditions drop their resting heartbeat rates of 100 to 150 beats/min to 10 beats/min when diving. The triggering mechanism for bradycardia is not completely understood, but is seems to involve sensors in the face and possibly in the respiratory system. The combined response of bradycardia and peripheral circulation shutdown has been referred to as the **diving reflex**.

Recent studies of Weddell seals in Antarctic waters suggest a very different picture of diving responses in unrestrained mammals in their natural habitat. Kooyman equipped numerous seals with instrument packages to record dive time, depth, heartbeat rate, and other physiological responses. He monitored lactic acid buildup by taking blood samples before and immediately after the dive. Weddell seals were ideal subjects for this type of study since they breathe by surfacing at holes maintained in the fast sea ice. To breathe, each seal must return to its own hole after a dive. The instrument pack can then be retrieved.

Kooyman and his associates found that Weddell seals can perform breath-holding dives of about 25 minutes in length without turning on any of the mechanisms previously described. Only during dives lasting longer than 25 minutes are peripheral circulation shutdown and bradycardia apparent. These results suggest that Weddell seals have enough stored O_2 at the initiation of a dive to last about 25 minutes. If the dive is to be shorter, none of the O_2 conserving mechanisms are employed. For longer dives, the magnitude of the diving reflex is a function of the length of the dive. It appears that these animals know as they start a dive how long it will last, and they make appropriate circulatory adjustments prior to leaving the sea surface. Together, these responses (summarized in table 12.3) allow Weddell seals to accomplish some of the longest breath holds known for mammals.

Although not as well studied, elephant seals may surpass Weddell seals in their breath-holding ability. Elephant seals spend months at sea foraging for squid and fish at depths between 300 and 1500 m (see table 12.2). Their feeding dives are typically 20 to 25 minutes long, with females usually going to depths of about 400 m and males to depths of 750 to 800 m. Both sexes dive night and day for weeks on end without sleeping and usually spend only 2 to

4 minutes at the surface between dives. These short surface times between long, deep dives suggests that these are not unusual dives but are the norm for this species. Further studies may show that the dive responses of Weddell seals, as outlined in table 12.3, are essentially what all breath-holding vertebrate divers do to varying degrees; the concept of a dive reflex to explain long breath holds may have to be abandoned completely.

Temperature Regulation

For most of their lives, marine mammals exist in direct contact with seawater much colder than their body temperatures. Most live in the food-rich waters of the Arctic and Antarctic where water temperatures always hover near the freezing point. But even in more temperate latitudes, the high heat capacity of water (about 25 times as high as air of the same temperature) is a major heat sink and makes serious inroads into the heat budgets of these mammals.

Marine mammals exhibit several adaptations that reduce their body heat losses to tolerable levels. Apneustic breathing lessens heat loss because warm air is exhaled from the lungs less frequently. The reduction of peripheral circulation that accompanies bradycardia during a dive also limits heat loss by restricting the flow of warm blood from the core of the body to the cooler skin. This feature is especially useful during deep dives, when an animal usually experiences water temperatures several degrees cooler than those at the surface. To further decrease heat losses, Weddell seals, at least, can apparently voluntarily depress their core body temperatures about 2° C before beginning a series of dives and rapidly elevate their body temperatures to normal levels immediately after their last dive.

Marine mammals are large and, for the most part, streamlined. Both of these features tend to reduce the extent of body surface in contact with seawater and the amount of heat transferred to the water. The major muscles of propulsion (which generate considerable heat) are positioned within the animal's trunk rather than on the exposed parts of the much reduced limbs. Finally, the body is wrapped in and further streamlined by an insulating layer of blubber or dense fur.

Internally, the extensive *retia mirable* described earlier serve to maintain locally high temperatures as well as to supply oxygenated blood to a few strategic locations, namely the eyes, inner and middle ears, brain, and thoracic cavity. Other heat-conserving mechanisms are associated with the retia of the flippers and, in cetaceans, the dorsal fin and flukes (figure 12.27). These retia are arranged in a countercurrent heat-exchange fashion reminiscent of those found along the flanks of tuna and other warm-bodied fish (figure 11.23). Arteries penetrating these appendages are surrounded by several veins carrying blood in the opposite direction. Heat from the warm blood of the central artery is absorbed by the cooler blood in the surrounding veins and carried back to the warm core of the body before much of it can be lost to the skin.

These adaptations are not solely to conserve body heat. Actively swimming animals or those marine mammals in tropical waters can become overheated. In these situations, the blood flow to the skin and appendages is increased. The central artery of the countercurrent rete shown in figure 12.27 dilates to transport more blood to the skin and restrict its return through the surrounding veins. The blood must then find alternate return routes through other veins nearer the skin.

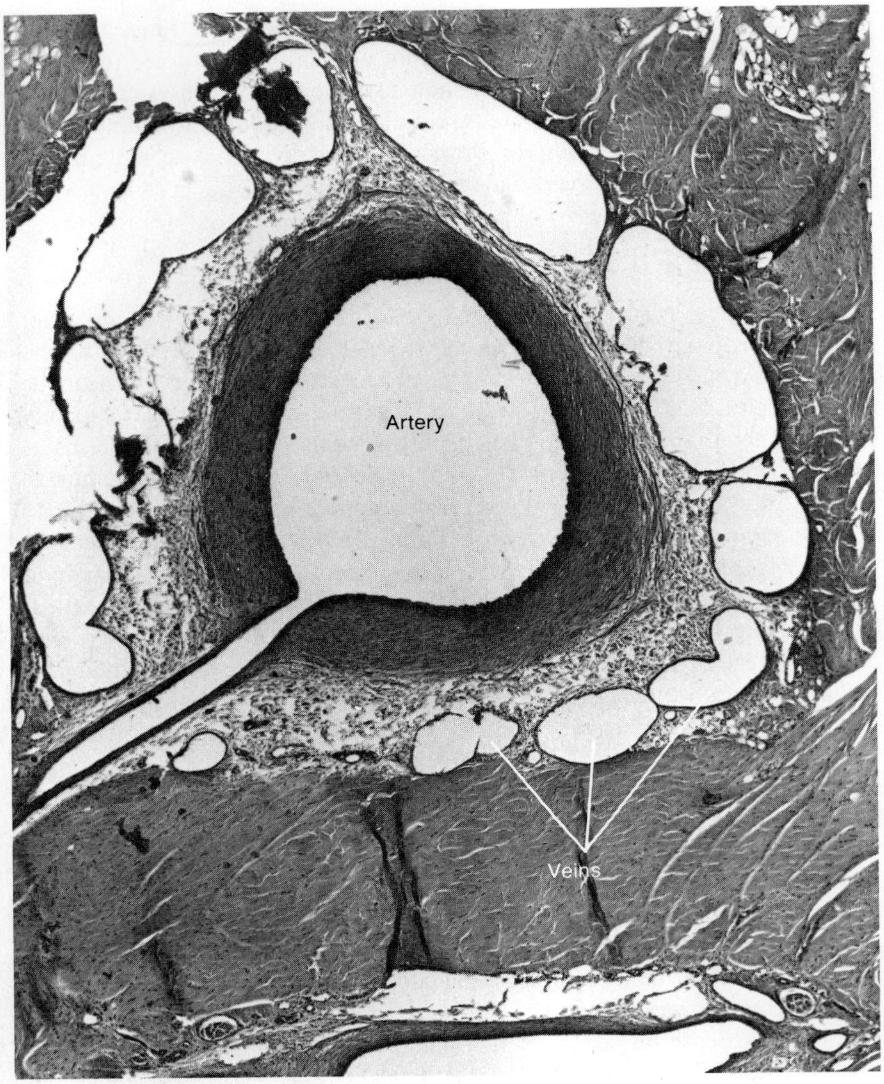

Figure 12.27

A cross section of a small artery from the tail fluke of a bottle-nosed dolphin. The muscular artery in the center is surrounded by several thin-walled veins carrying blood in the opposite direction.

From Ridgway, Sam H., *Mammals of the Sea, Biology and Medicine,* 1972. Courtesy of Charles C. Thomas, Publisher, Springfield, Illinois.

Reproduction

Most of our knowledge concerning the reproductive patterns of marine mammals has been gleaned from observations of captive animals in oceanariums, from carcasses on board whaling ships, and from expeditions to pinniped rookeries. Marine mammals, like their terrestrial kin, give birth to live young (figure 12.28). The young of cetaceans, capable swimmers at birth, instinctively surface to breathe. Most pinnipeds are unable to swim at birth so the pups are invariably delivered on land or on ice floes.

The newborn of some marine mammals are relatively large. Gray whale calves weigh in at approximately one ton; blue whales weigh closer to three tons at birth. Still, these newborn mammals are smaller then their parents, and their insulating layers of blubber or fur are not usually well-developed. Several factors compensate for the high surface area: volume ratios and the potentially serious problem of heat loss and body temperature maintenance in

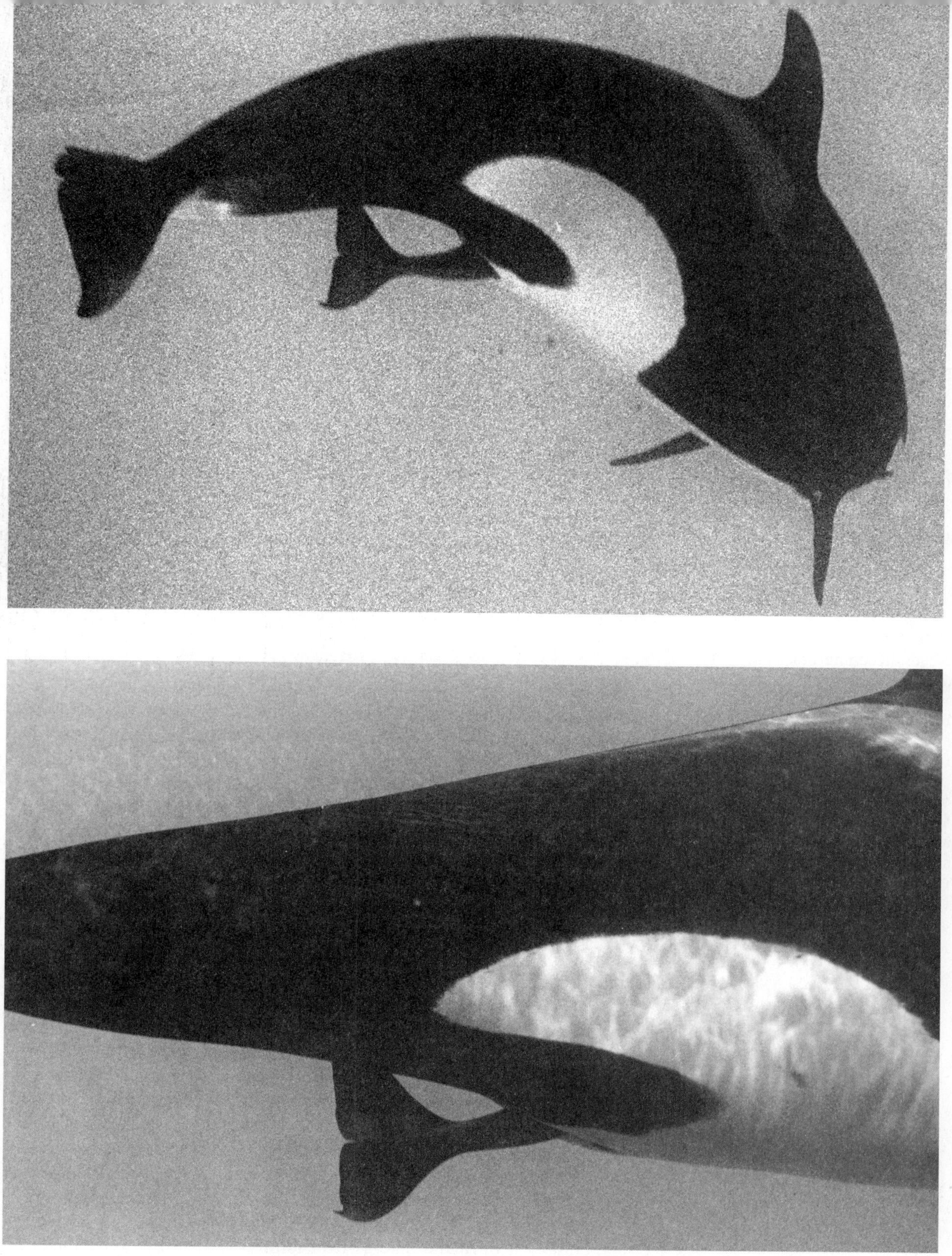

Figure 12.28
A killer whale being born
Courtesy Sea World, Inc., San Diego

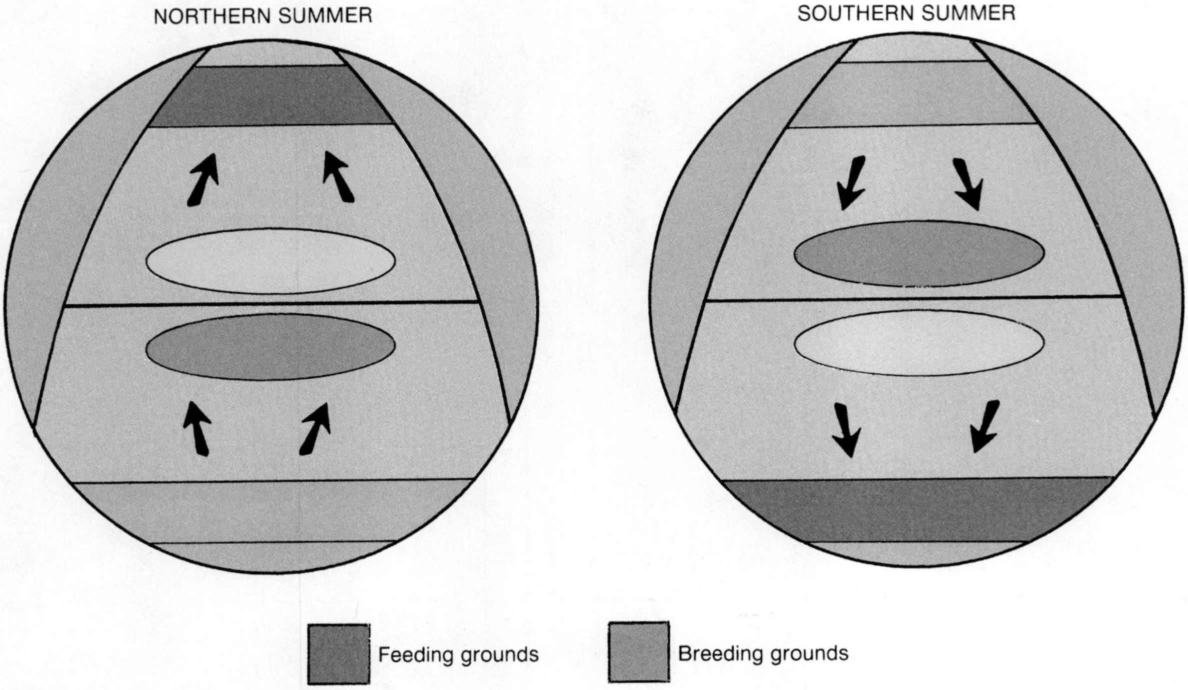

Figure 12.29
Generalized migratory patterns of large whales between summer feeding and winter breeding grounds. Northern and southern populations follow the same migratory pattern but do so six months out of phase with each other. Consequently, northern and southern populations of the same whale species remain isolated from each other, even though both populations approach equatorial latitudes.
Adapted from Mackintosh, 1966

newborn marine mammals. Terrestrial pupping in pinnipeds provides some time for growth before the pups must face their first winter at sea. The larger cetaceans, including the gray whale described in the previous chapter, spend their summers feeding in cold polar and subpolar waters and then undertake long migrations to their calving grounds in tropical and subtropical seas (figure 12.29). In these warm waters, their calves have an opportunity to gain considerable weight before migrating back to their frigid feeding grounds.

The growth rates of the young of some marine mammal species are truly astounding. Weddell seal pups gain 3 kg each day, and elephant seals gain as much as 7 kg/day. Pups of both of these species double their weights within two weeks after birth. Nursing blue whales grow from 3 tons at birth to 23 tons when weaned a scant seven months later (an average weight gain of almost 100 kg a day). These prodigious growth rates are supported by an abundant supply of high-fat milk. Cetacean milk is 25 to 50% fat (cow's milk ranges from 3 to 5% fat). The daily milk yield of a large baleen whale has been estimated at nearly 600 liters (over a half ton). In smaller pinnipeds, two to five liters are more typical. Pinniped milk is also generally high in fat; however, it may be as low as 16% in the California sea lion. In both cetaceans and pinnipeds, the species occupying colder waters consistently produce milk with a high fat content.

The energetic demands made on the female to produce a relatively large offspring and then to supply it with large quantities of fatty milk until it is weaned (usually a few weeks to several months) are exceedingly high. Even the water that goes into the milk imposes additional osmotic stresses that are relieved only with further energy expenditures. Marine mammals have a reasonably long gestation period (several months to a year) and tend to re-

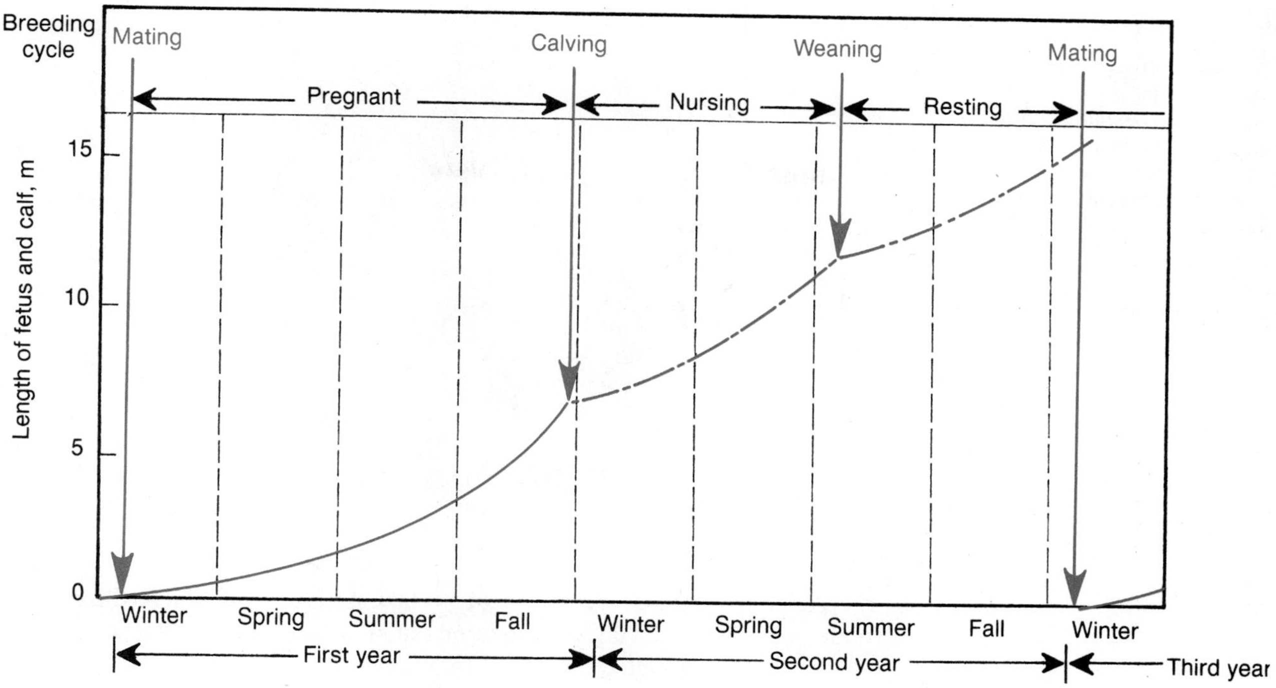

Figure 12.30
The reproductive cycle of female fin whales (*Balaenoptera physalus*) including the accompanying growth of fetus and calf during its period of dependency on the female
Adapted from Mackintosh, 1966

produce not more than once a year. It is typical for the larger whales and at least the walrus, among pinnipeds, to mate only once every two or even every three years.

The breeding cycle of the larger baleen whales is typified by the fin whale. The cycle consists of three parts (figure 12.30). An eleven-month gestation period is culminated by the birth, in tropical waters, of a two-ton calf 6 m long. The calf nurses for six months. During that time, the calf and its mother migrate back to their polar feeding grounds. With food abundant there, the calf is weaned. The female then enters a well-deserved six-month period of rest and recovery. During this feeding period, her fat and blubber reserves are replenished before she migrates back to the winter breeding grounds to mate and begin the cycle again.

The seasons and areas used for breeding by these migratory cetaceans tend to coincide with those used for calving. The same is true for many pinnipeds. The northern fur seal population, numbering about 1.5 million, disperses and forages over much of the North Pacific during the winter. Each summer they congregate in rookeries on the shores of North Pacific islands such as the tiny Pribilof Islands in the Bering Sea. Here both pupping and breeding occur. A few days after giving birth, female fur seals experience a short but intense period of **estrous** during which they are sexually receptive. This brief estrous is the only time during the year that the female ovulates and can become pregnant.

Here a problem arises. A fur seal fetus requires only seven months to develop. Yet seven months after estrous and mating, the pregnant female is far from land somewhere in the wintry North Pacific. These are impossible conditions for delivering a pup that cannot swim. This dilemma is analogous to that experienced by mating sea turtles (discussed on p. 310) and is solved

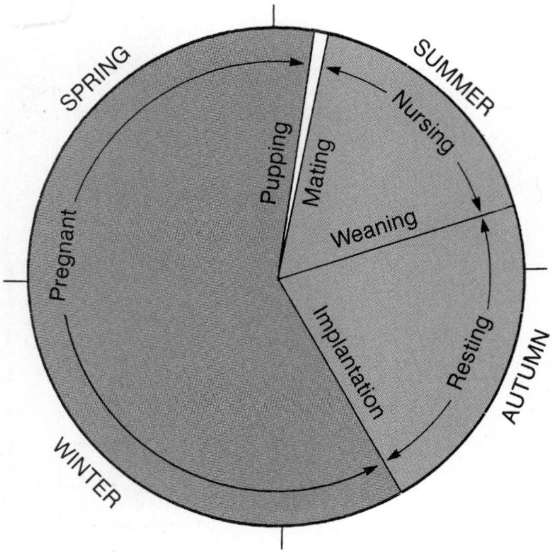

Figure 12.31
The reproductive cycle of the female Pribilof fur seal (*Callorhinus ursinus*). Light blue indicates the period of embryo dormancy; dark blue indicates the period of active fetal growth.

by a reproductive feature—**delayed implantation.** After mating, the fertilized egg undergoes several cell divisions to form a small ball of cells, the **blastocyst.** Unlike the usual course of development for mammalian embryos, for the next four months, the blastocyst lies dormant in the female's uterus. Following the four-month delay, the blastocyst becomes implanted on the inner wall of the uterus, a placental connection develops between the embryo and the uterine wall, and normal embryonic growth and development resume (figure 12.31). About seven months later, after the pregnant female has migrated back to the Pribilof Islands, she delivers a full-term fur seal pup. Delayed implantation is known to occur or is suspected in several other species of pinnipeds as well.

The breeding behavior of fur seals, elephant seals, and sea lions has several notable similarities. In the rookeries, these pinnipeds are extremely gregarious, assembling on the small pupping beaches in unbelievable numbers (figure 12.32). These animals also exhibit a remarkable degree of sexual dimorphism (figure 12.33). The adult males are 3 to 6 times larger than adult females; they have large canines, thick blubber and skin around the neck, special structures for physical and vocal threats, and are quite aggressive toward other males. These exaggerated male characteristics serve one purpose: they secure and hold a group of females and deny other males the opportunity to mate. This behavior imposes a polygynous social order on the species, with relatively few males monopolizing the breeding activities of the population during any one breeding season.

Bartholomew has proposed a model to account for the evolutionary development and maintenance of polygyny and sexual dimorphism in some pinnipeds. He suggests that the two significant features of their amphibious life-style, terrestrial pupping and offshore feeding, have been the determining factors. In the water, these pinnipeds are quite mobile and tend to disperse some distance from the rookery in search of food. Offshore feeding removes the competition for food from the rookery and promotes the fullest use of the few isolated sites that are appropriate as pupping rookeries.

In these congested circumstances, males, even with their very limited mobility on land, can easily contact and mate with several females. As with most mammals, a mature male is physically capable of fertilizing several females. However, the sex ratio of males to females is very nearly 1:1 in all

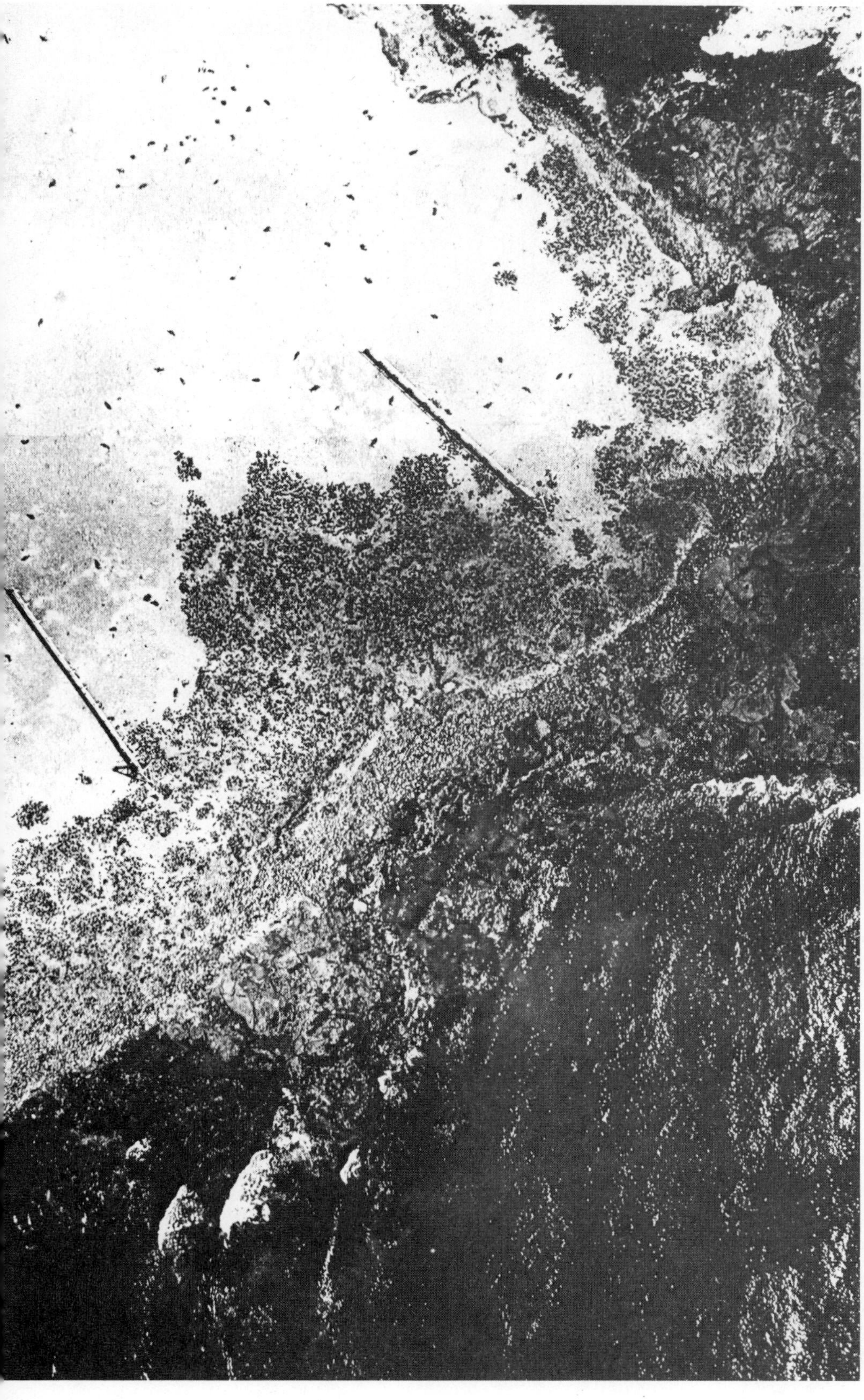

Figure 12.32

Aerial photograph of a crowded fur seal rookery, St. Paul Island, Pribilof Islands in the early 1960s. The clusters of seals near the beach are females, each associated with a breeding bull. The isolated individuals inland (upper left) are bulls that have not yet established harems. The elongated structures are elevated catwalks used for counting and sampling.

Photo by V. Scheffer and K. Kenyon, courtesy Marine Mammal Division, National Marine Fisheries Service

Figure 12.33
Male and female elephant seals display obvious sexual dimorphism. The females lack the elongated nose, enlarged canines, thickened neck, and large size characteristic of sexually mature males.
Courtesy B. Maier, Sea Research

species of mammals; therefore, any male that mates with more than one female must compete for the females by excluding other males from the breeding activities. In fur seals, this competition revolves around the breeding territories. Only the most aggressive and vigorous males successfully establish and maintain breeding territories throughout the breeding season. The remaining males, although sexually mature, are excluded from the breeding activities and banished to bachelor groups around the fringes of the breeding population. Male aggressiveness (toward other males) is controlled in part by **testosterone,** a male sex hormone that also controls the male sex drive. The dual effects of testosterone reinforce the fertility of breeding males. Both male aggressiveness and sex drive are at a peak during the breeding season, a time when the populations in the rookeries are congested.

Successful territorial defense requires that the male fur seal become a permanent feature of the territory for the duration of the breeding season. If a male leaves to feed in the water, he gives up his territory to one of the many "bachelor" males. The males most capable of surviving these breeding fasts (which may last as long as two months) are the larger individuals with extensive fat reserves. The relationship between the large size of males and their reproductive success creates a positive genetic feedback to enhance sexual dimorphism generation after generation. Essentially, the only males that contribute genetic information to subsequent generations are the large, aggressive ones with physical and behavioral traits very different from the traits of females.

To illustrate the differential genetic contributions of male and female polygynous pinnipeds consider that a moderately successful fur seal bull maintains a breeding group of about forty females for an average of five successive years. When unsuccessful matings are taken into account, this male will sire about eighty male and eighty female offspring. Each female during her reproductive lifetime will produce only about three males and three females. Thus, the total genetic contribution of a territorial bull to subsequent generations is about twenty-five times that of each female. This intense selective factor for exaggerated characteristics in male fur seals, elephant seals, and sea lions has led to the most extreme examples of sexual dimorphism of any mammal group.

The gregarious nature and relatively poor terrestrial locomotion of pinnipeds make them easy targets for sealers seeking skins and oil. In the past two centuries, several pinniped species have been severely decimated by commercial slaughters. The northern fur seal population numbered about 2.5 million when discovered by Russian sealers. By 1911, the population was reduced to about 100,000 animals. Protective regulations instituted at that time have allowed the northern fur seal herd to recover to a present population of approximately 1.5 million.

Through the early 1970s, sixty to seventy thousand young Pribilof fur seal males (9% of the total male population) were killed annually for their furs. These three and four year-old males had not yet entered the competition for territories and females, so their furs were undamaged by fighting. Is the impact of harvesting 9% of the males from a population with plenty of excess males really significant? At that time, approximately five hundred thousand pups were born to the Pribilof fur seal herd each year; half were female, half were male. About 14% died from starvation, disease, or by being crushed by adult males before they left the rookery. Another 50% were lost at sea the first winter, leaving about ninety thousand males alive at the end of their first year. By the time the young males reached three years of age, natural causes of mortality had further reduced their numbers to seventy to eighty thousand. When still another sixty to seventy thousand were removed for commercial purposes, the number of males remaining for breeding was relatively small.

It was generally assumed that . . . "the killing of these bachelors does not affect the structure or breeding performance of the herd because of the animals' polygamous habits" (King 1964). That assumption completely ignores the significance of male aggressiveness and competitiveness in the evolution and maintenance of polygyny in pinnipeds. Fur seals have excess males because they are polygynous, but those males are not excess until their reproductive worth has been tested against other males. Potential breeders simply cannot be identified at three or four years of age, and many are slaughtered along with potential nonbreeding males. With competition reduced by the commercial take, the males that do survive have a greatly improved chance of obtaining and keeping a breeding territory regardless of their relative territorial and sexual capabilities. Might the long-term genetic consequences of continued intensive harvesting of the Pribilof fur seal population be too high a price to pay for a fur coat?

The Pribilof fur seal population has been in steady decline since the mid-1950s, in spite of intensive management and a cessation of commercial harvesting since 1972. The genetic effects of previous decades of harvesting have been blamed for the population decline. So has contamination of their insulating fur by crude oil. Another relatively recent hazard is entanglement in fishing nets. Fur seals are curious animals, and will often investigate fixed nets or scraps of lost netting abandoned by expanding fisheries in the northern Pacific Ocean and Bering Sea. Entanglement often means drowning or slow starvation for the unlucky fur seal caught in this flotsam. These are the most likely culprits, but none provides a completely satisfactory explanation for the recent decline in the size of the fur seal population. Numbers increased in the late 1970s, then began to slip again. Presently, Pribilof fur seals use only 25% of the available rookery area used in 1955, and their numbers are continuing to decline.

The northern elephant seal (*Mirounga*) was even more seriously decimated by sealers than was the smaller fur seal. Once distributed from central California to the southern tip of Baja California, this species came under commercial hunting pressure in 1818. A scant half-century later, so few survived that they were not worth hunting. No elephant seals were sighted between 1884 and 1892. In 1892, Townsend discovered eight animals on Isla de Guadalupe, 240 km off the coast of Baja California. Seven were taken for museum specimens. Early census estimates suggest that in the 1890s as few as twenty individuals survived on a single inaccessible beach on Isla de Guadalupe. Beginning with protection afforded the northern elephant seal by Mexico and the United States around the turn of the century, that remnant population slowly recovered. Since then, the northern elephant seal has again spread throughout its former breeding range. The total population has swelled to more than one hundred thousand animals, and the future of this species now seems secure.

Or does it? Is the present northern elephant seal population really as viable and hardy as the pre-exploitation population? Comparisons of twenty-one blood proteins from 159 animals of the "recovered" population suggests that they are not. In marked contrast to proteins of other vertebrate species, no structural differences were demonstrated either between individuals or between separate groups of northern elephant seals breeding on different islands. The lack of structural differences in these proteins points to a complete absence of variation in the genes controlling the synthesis of these proteins. Bonnell and Selander suggest that the absence of genetic variability in the existing northern elephant seal population is the result of a genetic bottleneck when the population was at its low point in the 1890s. It is quite conceivable that, on that isolated beach on Isla de Guadalupe, a lone elephant seal bull dominated the breeding of all the surviving sexually mature females for several years. If so, half the pool of genetic information possessed by the surviving representatives of this species was funneled through a single animal, and the genetic variability presumably inherent in the predecimation population was lost. The rapid recovery of the protected population indicates that genetic variability may not be essential to the short-term survival of this species, possibly because their existence has been cushioned by the relatively uniform and predictable marine environment of the past century. However, this species remains vulnerable to environmental changes occurring in an extended time frame for it may lack the genetic variability necessary to cope with such changing conditions.

Summary

Three classes of air-breathing marine tetrapods, the reptiles, birds, and mammals, have conspicuous groups thriving in the sea. Sea snakes, turtles, marine crocodiles, and large numbers of birds and mammals forage in the sea. Reptiles and birds share several adaptations, including nasal salt glands and uric acid excretion, for life in a salty environment. Marine mammals include two abundant and widespread groups, the cetaceans (whales, porpoises, and dolphins) and the pinnipeds (seals, sea lions and walrus) and the less common sea otters, manatees, and dugong. Each has evolved from a terrestrial mammalian ancestor. In some, the evolutionary adaptations to a marine existence have been extreme. Cetaceans are very streamlined, breathe through a dorsal blowhole, and lack hair and rear legs or flippers. Even so, they are mammals, breathing air, giving birth to live young, and maintaining elevated body temperatures.

To compensate for reduced visibility and their inability to smell underwater, toothed whales (and probably some other groups) have a sophisticated system of echolocation for target detection and orientation.

Air-breathing mammals make several drastic respiratory and circulatory adjustments to prolonged diving, including apneustic breathing, lung collapse, peripheral circulation shutdown, bradycardia, and systemic storage of O_2.

Large size and reduced surface area: volume ratios are obvious adaptations to reduce heat loss. Less apparent but also significant are insulating layers of blubber or fur, countercurrent heat exchangers, and apneustic breathing patterns.

Marine mammals commonly reproduce annually or at even longer intervals. Frequently, birth and mating occur in breeding areas or rookeries. In some pinnipeds that disperse offshore to feed and congregate on isolated rookeries for reproduction, polygyny and sexual dimorphism are extremely well developed.

Review Questions

1. Compare the body-surface area to volume ratio of a whale with that of a copepod. What are the biological implications of these differences?
2. Compare the reproductive cycles and migratory patterns of gray whales and Pribilof fur seals. What purpose does delayed implantation serve in these cycles?
3. Describe how marine mammals store O_2 for use during a deep dive.
4. Describe the obvious sexually dimorphic characteristics exhibited by mature elephant seals or fur seals.
5. What marine mammal adaptations help to avoid the bends and nitrogen narcosis during deep dives?
6. What special features of the life cycle of many pinnipeds probably have led to the evolution of polygyny in this group?

which chara. listed below isn't comm. associated with polygyny is pinipeds

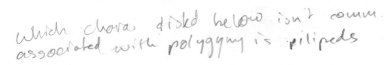

7. List two specific structural features that distinguish each of the following marine mammal groups from the others: baleen whales, toothed whales, sea lions, seals, manatees.
8. Describe the adaptive significance of nasal salt glands and uric acid excretion for reptiles and birds feeding at sea.

Questions for Further Discussion

1. Is your own breathing a voluntary or involuntary response? Can you stop breathing for one minute? For two minutes? For five minutes? Can you voluntarily alter your heartbeat rate or body temperature? Compare your responses to what must occur in a Weddell seal when it is preparing for a long dive.
2. What types of marine birds in your locality are also common in ponds and lakes? In fields? Where do they roost at night?
3. Beginning with the reasonable assumption that cetaceans have evolved from herbivorous terrestrial ancestors, discuss the major structural and physiological adaptations evident in present-day killer whales.
4. What advantages do cetaceans derive from apneustic breathing patterns besides those directly associated with prolonged breath-holding?

Suggestions for Further Reading

Books

Ainley, D. G., et al. 1984. *The marine ecology of birds in the Ross Sea, Antarctica.* Washington, D.C.: American Ornithologists Union.

Alderton, D. 1988. *Turtles and tortoises of the world.* New York: Facts on File, Inc.

Bonner, W. N. 1982. *Seals and man: A study of interactions.* Seattle: University of Washington Press.

Bonner, W. N. 1989. *Whales of the world.* New York: Facts on File, Inc.

Croxall, J. P. 1987. *Seabirds: Feeding ecology and role in marine ecosystems.* New York: Cambridge University Press.

Elsner, R., and B. Gooden. 1983. *Diving and asphyxia: A comparative study of animals and men.* New York: Cambridge University Press.

Gaskin, D. E. 1982. *The ecology of whales and dolphins.* Portsmouth, NH: Heinemann.

Haley, D., ed. 1978. *Marine mammals of eastern North Pacific and Arctic waters.* Seattle: Pacific Search Press.

———. 1984. *Seabirds of the eastern North Pacific and Arctic waters.* Seattle: Pacific Search Press.

Herman, L. M., ed. 1980. *Cetacean behavior: Mechanisms and functions.* New York: John Wiley & Sons.

Kooyman, G. 1989. *Diverse divers: Physiology and behavior.* New York: Springer-Verlag.

Nettleship, D. N., G. A. Sanger, and P. F. Springer, eds. 1985. *Marine birds: Their ecology and commercial fisheries relationships.* Ottawa: Canadian Wildlife Services.

Stirling, I. 1988. *Polar bears.* Ann Arbor, MI: University of Michigan Press.

VanBlaricom, G. R., and J. A. Estes. 1988. *The community ecology of sea otters.* New York: Springer-Verlag.

Articles

Costa, D. 1978. The sea otter: Its interaction with man. *Oceanus* 21(spring):24–30.

Geraci, J. R. 1978. The enigma of marine mammal strandings. *Oceanus* 21 (spring):38–47.

Kooyman, G. L., M. A. Castellini, and R. W. Davis. 1981. Physiology of diving in marine mammals. *Annual Review of Physiology* 43:343–56.

Nelson, C., and K. Johnson. 1987. Whales and walruses as tillers of the seafloor. *Scientific American* 256(2):112–17.

Norris, K. S. 1968. Evoluton of acoustic mechanisms in odontocete cetaceans. *Evolution and Environment,* 297–324.

Owens, D. W. 1980. The comparative reproductive physiology of sea turtles. *American Zoologist* 20:549–63.

Payne, R. S., and S. McVay. 1971. Songs of humpback whales. *Science* 173:585–97.

Pivorunas, A. 1979. The feeding mechanisms of baleen whales. *American Scientist* 67:432–40.

Ray, G. C., J. A. Dobbin, and R. V. Salm. 1978. Strategies for protecting marine mammal habitats. *Oceanus* 21 (spring):55–67.

Scarff, J. E. 1980. Ethical issues in whale and small cetacean management. *Environmental Ethics* 3:241–79.

Wursig, B. 1979. Dolphins. *Scientific American* 240(3):136–48.

Würsig, B. 1988. The behavior of baleen whales. *Scientific American* 258(4):102–7.

Zopal, W. 1987. Diving adaptations of the Weddell seal. *Scientific American* 256(6):100–105.

Fisheries

Chapter 13

Subsistence fishery in Mexico

For much of our history, the seas have been largely immune to the pressures created by the material needs of the land-based human population. Two thousand years ago, the human population of earth was probably between 200 and 300 million people. Survival problems kept life expectancies short. High birthrates were balanced by high death rates; the population grew slowly. Not until 1650, when the Industrial Revolution in Europe brought advances in medicine and technological improvements in food production, did human mortality rates decline and the population double to 500 million. By 1850, the population had doubled to one billion people. Declining death rates continued to accelerate the rate of population growth into the twentieth century. At present, the human population of the world has surpassed five billion people and is projected to surpass seven billion by the end of this century. Of the present population, the United Nations Food and Agriculture Organization (FAO) estimates that at least one-half billion are seriously undernourished. The World Bank places that number nearer to one billion.

The sheer magnitude of the current human population creates enormous demands for food, fiber, minerals, and other commodities that support our modern social fabric. Today, parts of the world ocean are intensively exploited for recreation, military purposes, commercial shipping, fishing, dumping of waste materials, and extraction of gas, oil, and other mineral resources. Although the impact of these activities varies geographically, no portion of the world ocean is isolated from their effects. These effects often transcend national borders as well as the boundaries of many ecological and taxonomic groups. When the biological effects of these societal uses of the sea are large and measurable, they introduce a complex suite of social, political, economic, aesthetic, and biological questions. Often such questions require value judgments that cannot be resolved by scientific means.

The demand for food made by the present human population is enormous and is increasing at a rapid rate. Uncounted millions of people starve to death each year, and hundreds of millions more are deprived of good health and vigor because of inadequate diets. Many people, therefore, regard marine sources of food as a critical part of the solution to present and future food problems.

Fishing is a multibillion-dollar global industry. In 1980, the global import/export trade in fishery commodities was in excess of 30 billion dollars. Most fish are sold for human consumption, but an appreciable portion is also used for livestock fodder, pet foods, and industrial products.

The impact of fishing practices on the stability, and even the continued existence, of some of these marine populations has been severe. These practices have become an area of increasing concern since a relatively small number of species make up the bulk of the world fish harvest. These species have borne the brunt of the human population's demands for seafood. Some species have been eliminated from traditional fishing grounds, while others face the imminent possibility of biological extinction.

A *Brief Survey of* Marine Food *Species*

The raw material of the fishing industry includes a number of species of bony and cartilaginous finfish, many mollusks and crustaceans (shellfish), a variety of other aquatic animals (from worms to whales), and even some marine plants. Each year the FAO compiles and publishes global fishery catch statistics. Figure

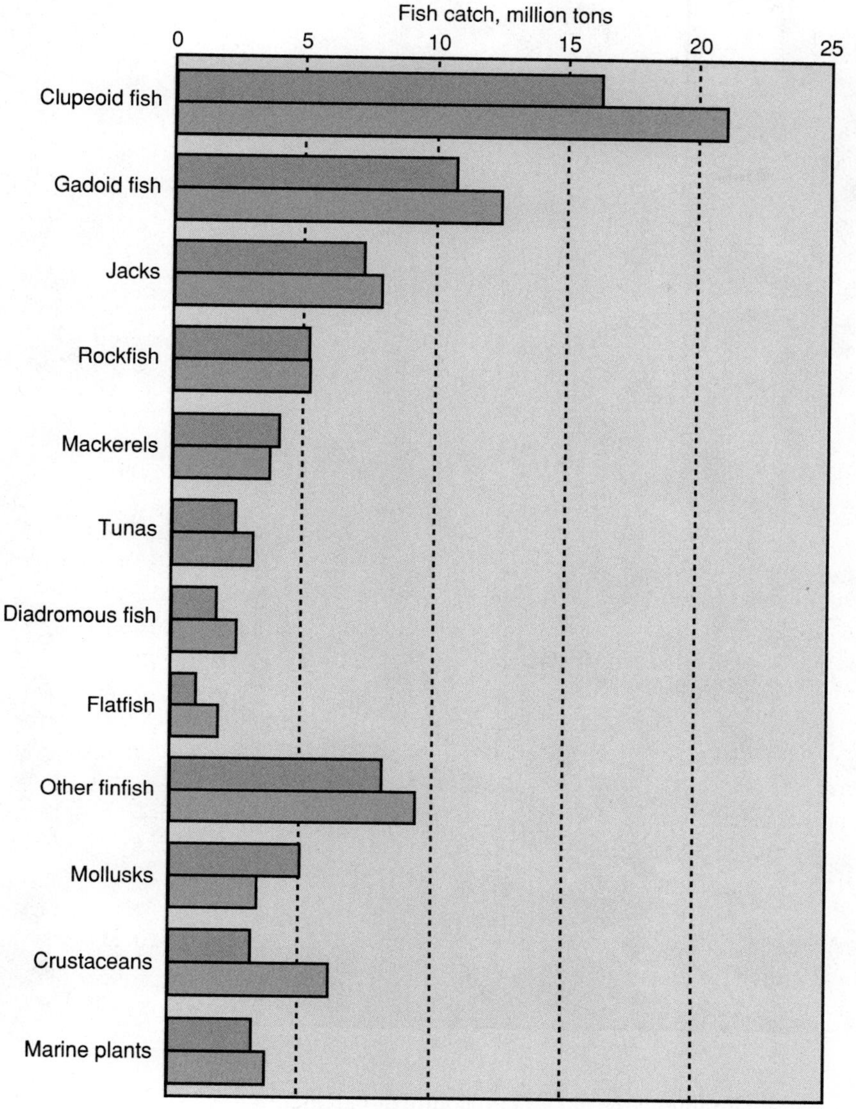

Figure 13.1

Global marine and estuarine harvest by major categories for 1980 (blue bars) and 1985 (green bars)

From FAO catch and landing statistics

13.1 summarizes catch results for 1980 and 1985. The annual catch size has varied somewhat; however, the relative ranking of each group has remained reasonably constant from year to year.

The clupeoid fish, including anchovies (figure 13.2), anchovetas, herrings, sardines, pilchards, and menhaden are very abundant and account for about one-third of the total commercial catch. A single species, the Peruvian anchoveta (*Engraulis ringens*), provided nearly 19%, or more than 13 million tons, of the total 1970 catch, but extensive overfishing caused the fishery to collapse a few years later. The herring catch is an important part of the North Atlantic fishing industry. In the last decade, other herring fisheries in the South Atlantic and North Pacific oceans have been expanding. At its peak in the 1930s, the California sardine industry was landing over 500 thousand tons annually. The menhaden catch yields approximately one million tons annually, largely from the Atlantic Ocean and the Gulf of Mexico.

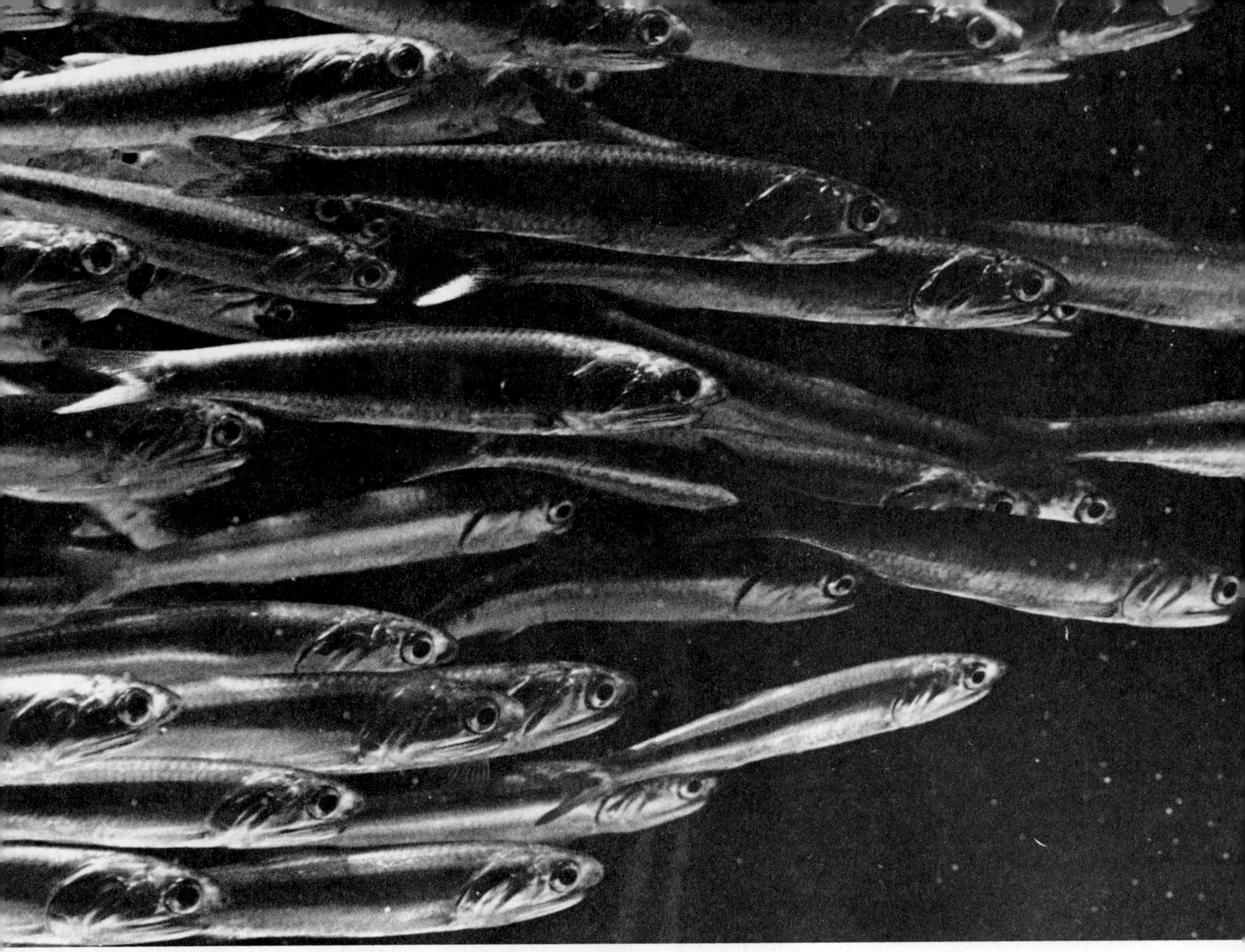

Figure 13.2
The northern anchovy, *Engraulis mordax*
Courtesy National Marine Fisheries Service

The huge size of the clupeoid fish catch is not reflected in its dollar value as an economic commodity or its significance as a source of protein in human nutrition. Nearly all anchovies, anchovetas, and menhaden and much of the herrings, sardines, and pilchards caught are reduced to fish meal to be used as an inexpensive protein supplement in livestock and poultry fodder. As fish meal, clupeoid fish make only indirect contributions to the human diet.

Clupeoid fish are found in shallow coastal waters and in upwelling regions. Their schooling behavior (figure 13.3) simplifies catching techniques and reduces harvesting expenses. Large purse seines (which may be 600 m long and 200 m deep) are used to surround and trap entire schools. Once encircled, the fish are ladled into the ship's hold. Most clupeoid fish are small, with an average adult length of between 15 and 25 cm. Their small size, however, is compensated for by other characteristics that enhance their economic usefulness. These fish are equipped with fine gill rakers that enable them to feed on small organisms close to the base of marine food chains. Mature Peruvian anchovetas feed principally on chain-forming diatoms and other relatively large phytoplankton aggregations. Herring generally feed on herbivorous zooplankton (see fig. 2.11).

Figure 13.3

A school of anchovies (dark mass) in unusually shallow water nearshore at La Jolla, California. (Note the many surfers at top of photo.) The school is approximately 30 m long.

Courtesy J. Squires, National Marine Fisheries Service

The combined catch of cod, pollack, hake, and other gadoid fish has remained fairly constant for the past two decades. Gadoid fish usually live on or near the bottom, are larger than clupeoid fishes, and feed at higher trophic levels. Fishing operations for these species are concentrated on continental shelves and other shallow areas. Cod are caught in the coastal waters of many North Atlantic nations. The Alaskan pollack are caught by Japanese and Soviet trawler fleets in shallow regions of the Gulf of Alaska and the Bering Sea. Fishing by these two nations increased the catch of Alaskan pollack from one million tons in 1965 to over six million tons in 1985. Several species of hakes abound on the continental shelves of many oceans. They have long been prized by Japanese and Soviet fishing fleets, but have only recently gained favor in the United States, where they are usually marketed as whitefish.

Redfish, bass, sea perch, and other rockfish also live near the bottom. No single species of this group dominates the catch statistics, yet the combined 1985 catch amounted to over five million tons. Sold fresh or frozen, most of these fish are popular fish-market items.

Horse and jack mackerel are primarily pelagic carnivores that generally feed on smaller anchovy-sized fish and invertebrates. Mackerel resemble tuna in form, but they seldom exceed 30 to 40 cm in length. The fisheries for these mackerel groups are scattered in coastal and offshore waters.

Tuna are the largest of the commercial species discussed here. Tuna weighing over 100 kg are not unusual, but most range from 5 to 20 kg. Yellowfin, bigeye, albacore, and skipjack tuna account for the majority of tuna catches. Tuna are often the top carnivores in complex food chains and may be separated from the primary producers by seven or more trophic levels. These fish are active predators of smaller, more abundant animals, especially clupeoid fishes and sauries, and are captured in or near nutrient-rich waters where forage fish abound.

United States tuna fishermen rely heavily on long-range purse seiners to harvest schooling species of tuna, especially skipjack and yellowfin tuna (figure 13.4). Yellowfin tuna exhibit a strong but poorly understood behavioral association with some small subtropical dolphins *(Stenella)*. Since dolphins are easily visible at the sea surface, purse seining of yellowfin tuna is simply a matter of setting the nets around a dolphin school with the assumption (usually correct) that a school of yellowfin tuna is just below. In 1972 alone, this practice led to the deaths of over three hundred thousand dolphins, which were captured along with the tuna by the United States tuna-fishing fleet. Since then, tighter restrictions on both design and operation of purse seining, imposed by the 1972 U. S. Marine Mammal Protection Act, have reduced annual dolphin mortality due to purse seining to about twenty thousand for the United States tuna fleet. Much of this apparent reduction, however, reflects a widespread move of the fleet to foreign registry, places where their actions are not subject to U. S. regulations.

To counter the adverse publicity associated with this high dolphin mortality in 1990, several large tuna processing companies announced new policies to buy and market only "dolphin-safe" tuna, tuna caught without setting purse seines on dolphin schools. It remains to be seen whether these policies can be effectively monitored by the tuna-consuming public.

To exploit the more widely dispersed bluefin, tropical yellowfin, and bigeye tuna, laborious longline fishing methods are also used. The tuna aggregate in a narrow zone of relatively high primary productivity that straddles the equator in the eastern half of the Pacific Ocean (see fig 5.26). These large predators feed on sardines, myctophids, crustaceans and other small fish, who in turn graze on the smaller zooplankton. Since 1950, the Japanese longline fishery of the equatorial Pacific Ocean has rapidly developed into the most valuable oceanic fishery of the Pacific Ocean. The longline gear consists of floating mainlines that extend as far as 100 km along the surface. Hanging from each mainline are about two thousand equally spaced vertical lines that terminate with baited hooks. Once a longline set is in place, fishers move along the mainline, remove hooked tuna, and rebait and replace the hooks.

In recent years, many fisheries have begun using gill nets. Designed to entangle fish in the net fabric, these large rectangular nets are either anchored to shore or allowed to drift. Although effective at entrapping fish, they are also invisible and indiscriminant killers of nontarget species. These nets are fast becoming major causes of mortality for some species of sharks and many sea bird and marine mammal populations (see box 9).

Major Fishing Areas of the World Ocean

The shallow water over continental shelves and near-surface banks encourages rapid regeneration of critical nutrients in the photic zone. These nutrients are prevented from escaping into deeper water and accumulating below the upper mixed layer where return to the surface requires a much longer time. High levels of production by phytoplankton in neritic waters are further enhanced

Box 9 *Drift Nets*

Each night in the North Pacific Ocean, up to 60,000 km of ghost drift nets (enough to cross the Pacific Ocean from San Francisco to Tokyo eight times) are set to catch 300,000 metric tons of squid, tuna, and other prized fish with an annual value of 600 million dollars. These nets, also known as gill nets, are made of fine, transparent, almost invisible, monofilament line and can be up to 50 km long and 10 m deep. This method of catching fish is sometimes referred to as "strip mining the seas" because it takes an enormous toll on many species in order to harvest a few. Each year, the nets inadvertently kill tens of thousands of nontarget fish, birds, and mammals that become entangled in the net fabric. Drift nets may be implicated in the recent decline of some North Pacific marine mammal populations.

Drift nets are set at night to catch DSL followers. Fishing for some species with drift nets is more fuel-efficient than either trawling or seining and is thus preferred. Presently, driftnetting activities are concentrated in the Pacific by Japan, South Korea, and Taiwan, and driftnetting is expanding rapidly into the Atlantic. The direct impact of driftnet fishing is compounded by the thousands of km of net panels lost or discarded each year. The monofilament material does not rot, and so floating net panels may continue to drift, killing nontarget animals for years before finally being washed ashore.

The United States Drift Net Monitoring, Assessment and Control Act of 1987 attempted to curb the problems associated with driftnet fisheries. This act requires Japan's North Pacific driftnet fleet to mark its nets and stop discarding unusable nets in United States controlled waters. This was a first step in resolving the problem, but many believe that the only solution is to ban drift nets entirely. The United Nations passed a resolution in December, 1989, to ban all driftnetting by 1992 unless high seas driftnetting nations begin an effective conservation program. But the resolution is not binding on non-member driftnetting nations such as Taiwan. Until some effective agreement is reached that is binding on all nations involved in driftnet fisheries, the waste and over-exploitation will continue.

Drift net and victim
Courtesy Greenpeace

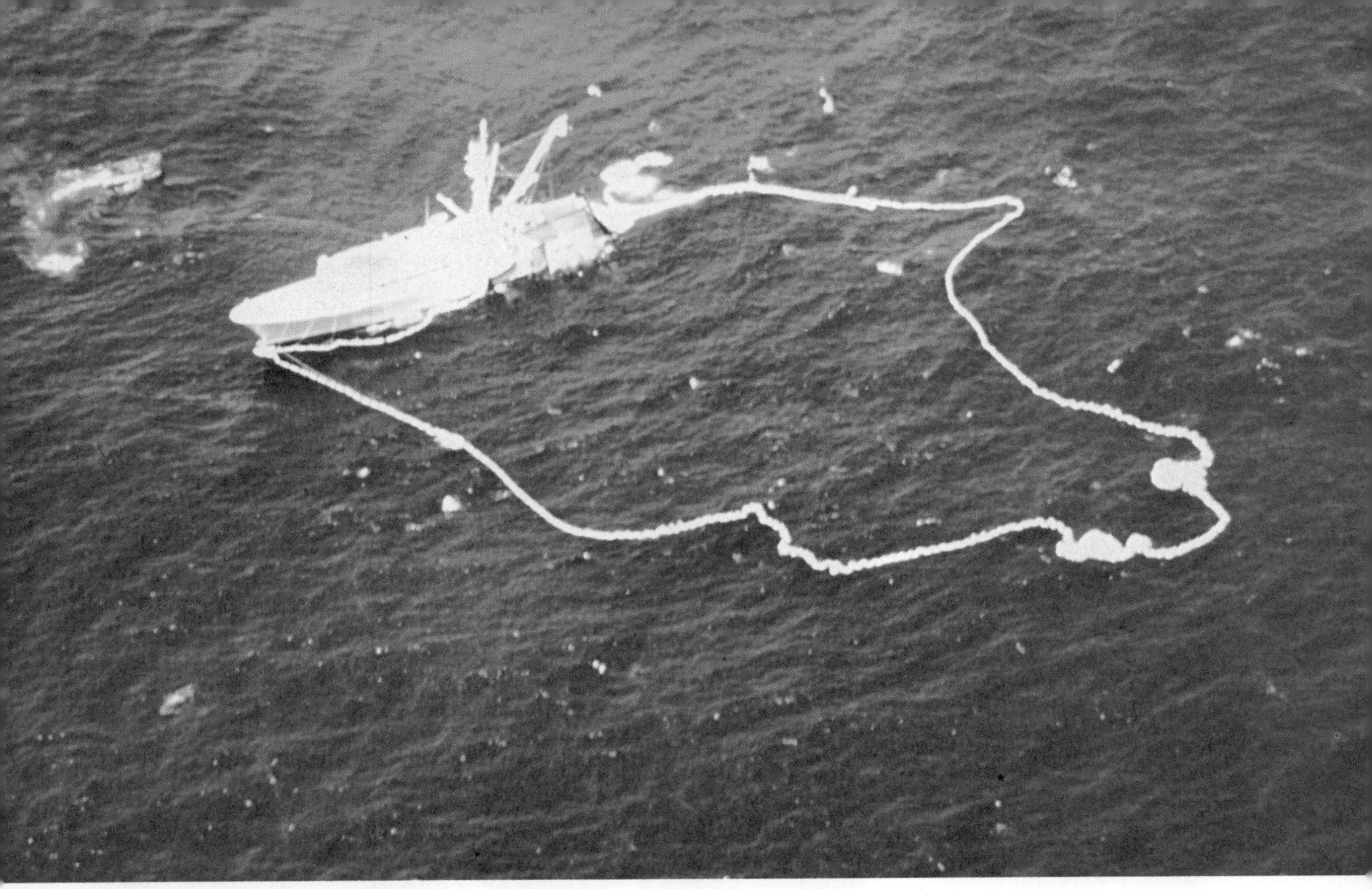

Figure 13.4
A tuna seiner with a school of tuna trapped within its purse net
Courtesy National Marine Fisheries Service

because the resulting animal production is "crowded" into a water column usually less than 200 m deep. In contrast, organic material produced over deep-ocean basins must be shared by the many consumers thinly dispersed through several thousands of meters of water.

Bottom fish and benthic invertebrates, presently constituting nearly 15% of the total catch, are most easily taken in these shallow, near-shore waters. Halibut, flounder, sole, and other flatfish are benthic species commonly caught in shallow waters using bottom trawls. High prices and stable markets for these fish have resulted in extensive fishing of most known stocks. The North Atlantic that has been subject to heavy fishing pressures for decades and is seriously overfished. About 90% of the marine catch is taken from continental shelves and overlying neritic waters, a region representing less than 8% of the total oceanic area.

Other major fishing areas are centered in regions of upwelling where abundant supplies of critical nutrients from deeper waters are returned to the photic zone. Upwelling may, depending on the locality, occur sporadically, on a seasonal basis, or continually throughout the year. (Mechanisms of Antarctic, equatorial, and coastal upwelling were described in chapter 5.)

The nutrient-rich waters surrounding the Antarctic continent sustain a tremendous amount of primary production. Yet, with the exception of the near-defunct pelagic whaling industry, no large fishery has yet developed in Antarctic waters. Long distances to processing facilities and the absence of nearby population centers have had a restraining effect on the successful exploitation of this upwelling region.

Table 13.1
Human Food from Land and Ocean Production Systems, 1985

Food Types	Categories of Production	Food Production, in 10^6 tons Land	Ocean
Plants	Gathering	150	3
	Farming	3500	1
Animals	Hunting	120	73
	Herding	680	2
Total		4450	79
		Less That Used for Fish Meal	−24
		For Human Consumption	55 + 5

Compiled from FAO Production Yearbook and Yearbook of Fisheries Statistics 1985, and Ryther 1981.

Regions of coastal upwelling are most apparent along the west coasts of Africa and North and South America (see chapter 5) but occur to lesser degrees along the coastlines. High yields of commercial species result from increased rates of primary production over shallow bottoms. The greatest concentrations of clupeoid fish, are found in regions of coastal upwelling: Peruvian anchoveta from the Peru Current upwelling area, pilchard from a similar area in the Benguela Current off the west coast of South Africa, and, prior to a drastic decline in the 1940s, sardines from the California Current. The Peruvian and Benguelan upwelling systems also support huge flocks of cormorants, pelicans, penguins, and other seabirds.

Behavioral and physiological responses by fish to currents, water temperature fluctuations, and other environmental factors are not well understood. Some evidence exists to indicate that such responses play a significant role in spatially concentrating commercially useful species. The success of those who seek these fish is in part dependent upon applying what they know of these migratory routes to the practical problems of locating these fish at sea.

A *Perspective on* Marine Sources *of* Food *for* Humans

Humans are omnivores. We obtain nourishment from a tremendous variety of plants and animals. Yet the staples of the human diet can be narrowed down to three types of plants and four groups of animals. The plant staples include cereals (rice, wheat, corn, and other cereal grains), vegetables, and fruits, nuts, and berries. Beef, poultry (plus the milk and egg products of these animals), pork, and fish provide the major share of the food to satisfy the carnivore in us. It is important to understand just how significant the present marine contribution of food is to the total human diet and how meaningful it may be in the future.

Table 13.1 compares categories of plant and animal foods from both terrestrial and oceanic production systems based on the state of technology used in the production of each food category. Plant production is separated into gathering, the casual use of untended wild plants (figure 13.5) and farming, the agricultural tending of domesticated plant species. Comparable categories

Figure 13.5
A kelp harvester in operation. As the harvester moves backward, the kelp is cut below the sea surface and then pulled up the stern loading ramp.
Courtesy Kelco, a division of Merck Pharmaceuticals

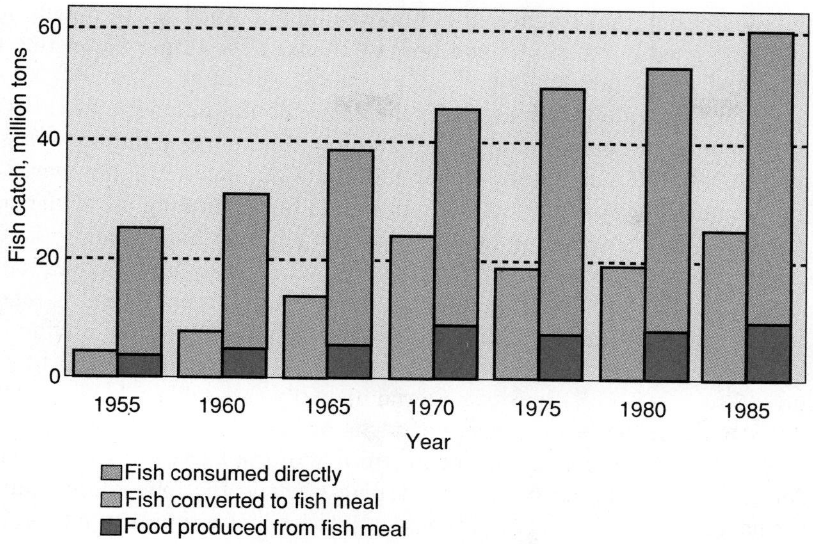

Figure 13.6
Disposition of the world fish catch, 1955–1985
From FAO catch and landing statistics

for animals are used: hunting of wild animals and herding of genetically improved, controlled domesticated animals. These terms are also applied to marine food items. Only a very few marine plants are presently farmed, while oysters, some clams, and a few other marine animals are "herded." Table 13.1 lists the 1985 food production statistics for each of the four production categories for land and ocean. Production statistics for wild plants and wild animals grown on land can only be approximated. The remaining figures are compiled annually by the FAO.

The information presented in table 13.1 forces some uncomfortable, yet undeniable conclusions. The majority of the seafoods harvested are animals three or four trophic levels above the primary producers. In terrestrial agricultural systems, plants are harvested and losses to higher trophic levels are avoided. Furthermore, marine animals consist of wild, unimproved stocks that are hunted rather than controlled and domesticated. Although technologically advanced ships, nets, and fish-finding gear may be used, little of the monetary gains have been reinvested to improve fish stocks.

Another disturbing trend in the use of living marine resources has developed in the past four decades. In 1950, 90% of the world catch was consumed directly, and only 10% was reduced to fish meal for use as a protein supplement for domestic livestock. By 1970, the fish meal fraction had increased to about a third of the world catch (figure 13.6). Assuming the entire 24 million tons of fish reduced to meal in 1985 were fed to pigs and chickens with trophic efficiencies of 20%, only 5 million additional tons of edible pork and poultry was produced. So the actual amount of human food derived from the 1985 fish catch was not the total catch of 79 million tons. Instead, it was nearer 60 million tons; 55 million tons of edible fish and 4 million tons of livestock raised on fish meal derived from 24 million tons of fish.

Long food chains, unsophisticated production systems, and expanding industrial uses of marine organisms all severely limit the capacity of marine food production. The marine environment just does not produce very much food; for the past several decades, only slightly more than 1% of the food consumed by the world human population came from the sea. The likelihood of greatly increasing that fraction of our marine diet depends on the magnitude of still unharvested fish stocks and how we manage the future harvesting of these stocks.

Our total global fish catch for the three decades following World War II have increased about 6% a year. The global human population was expanding at about 2% each year for the same period. Since 1970, however, the gains have been a more modest 1.4% per year. Is the leveling off of the size of the global fish catch an indication that the global fishing industry is approaching some limit on further growth? Not necessarily, but this question is not easily answered. The ultimate limit on marine sources of food is established by the rate of photosynthesis in marine plants. The marine production system begins at the first trophic level with a net production of 200 to 250 billion (2 to 2.5 $\times 10^{11}$) tons of material annually (see table 5.1).

Because neither markets nor techniques are available for economically harvesting phytoplankton, the magnitude of the harvesting fish harvest is determined by: (1) the number of trophic levels in the food chain leading to the harvestable fish, and (2) the efficiency with which animals at one trophic level utilize food derived from the previous trophic level.

The potential commercial value of a fish or other animal is, to a large degree, a function of its size. These animals must be a certain minimum size before commercial exploitation is economically feasible. In addition, the size of the organisms at the base of marine food chains is an essential feature in establishing the number of steps in the food chain. Food chains based on smaller phytoplankton cells (such as those in subtropical gyres) generally consist of a greater number of trophic levels, as do food chains leading to large fish such as tuna (see figure 10.18).

In general, phytoplankton cells decrease in size from greater than 100 μm in coastal and upwelled waters to less than 25 μm in the open ocean. Several moderate-sized zooplankton species such as *Euphausia pacifica,* which function as herbivores in coastal North Pacific waters, must move one step up the food chain and assume a carnivorous mode of feeding in offshore waters because the phytoplankton there are too small to be captured. Other forms of oceanic zooplankton occupying the third trophic level are no more than 1 or 2 mm in length. Virtually all species of herbivorous copepods in the open ocean are preyed upon by chaetognaths that, in turn, become food for small fish.

Thus, in the open ocean environment, three or four trophic levels are required to produce animals only a few cm in length. In an examination of the relationship between photosynthesis and fish production in the open sea, Ryther has estimated that food chains leading to tuna, squid, and other commercially important oceanic species consist of an average of five trophic levels. Ryther also estimated that the average number of trophic levels in the food chains of commercial species is 3 in coastal waters and 1.5 for upwelling areas. The latter number is low because many clupeoid fish taken from upwelling areas graze directly on phytoplankton without any intermediate trophic levels.

Accurate estimates of ecological efficiencies in marine food chains are difficult to achieve. Efficiency factors are based on the growth of organisms which is, in turn, a function of food assimilation minus waste and metabolic costs (such as respiration and locomotion). These factors vary widely between species, between individuals of the same species, and between various stages in the life cycle of a species. Young growing individuals often exhibit efficiencies as high as 30%, but their ecological efficiencies decline to nearly 0% at

Table 13.2
Estimates of Fish Production for the Marine Production Provinces. (Net annual primary production based on table 5.1.)

Province	*N.A.P.P. 10^9 Tons*	*Trophic Levels*	*Trophic Efficiency*	*Fish Production 10^6 Tons*
Open ocean	209	5	10	2
Coastal	68	3	15	230
Upwelling	1	1.5	20	120
Total	278			352

Compiled from Ryther 1969 and sources for table 6.1.

maturity. Senile individuals may even exhibit negative efficiency factors. Thus, efficiency estimates for populations composed of a variety of age groups can be little more than reasonably intelligent guesses. It is even more difficult to approximate the ecological efficiencies of entire trophic levels consisting of a diverse group of animal types, each with its own peculiar age structure and growth rate. Basing his estimates on an assumed maximal potential trophic efficiency of 30%, Ryther assigned ecological efficiency factors of 10% to the oceanic province, 15% to coastal regions, and 20% to areas of upwelling.

Armed with the estimates of net phytoplankton production listed in table 5.1 and repeated in part in table 13.2, the number of trophic levels, and the efficiency of exchange between the trophic levels of each marine production province, we can estimate the total potential production of fish from the sea (last column, table 13.2) to be about 350 million tons annually.

How do these estimates compare with actual production statistics of a well-known fishery? Consider the Peruvian anchoveta fishery, an area of coastal upwelling approximately 50 km × 1,200 km. Using the methods developed by Ryther, this area can be expected to produce about 20 million tons of anchoveta each year. The commerical harvest of this species in 1970 was slightly over 13 million tons, near or possibly even over the capacity of this fishery. In addition, predation by tuna, squid, and about 5 million seabirds probably accounted for an annual consumption of another 8 to 10 million tons of anchoveta. Combined, commercial landings and natural predation of the Peruvian anchoveta reach approximately 22 million tons each year. Ryther's estimate of 20 million tons is sufficiently accurate to justify the use of his predictive methods.

The prediction of a potential annual production of about 350 million tons of animals is not equivalent to an actual harvest of that magnitude: Losses to birds, larger fish, and other predators are significant in some fisheries. Additionally, human preferences for some species of fish will cause other species to remain underutilized. Finally, to maintain a continuing supply of raw materials, the fishing industry must take care to allow a reasonably large fraction (generally one-half to two-thirds) of utilized fish stocks to escape and reproduce so that harvesting can continue on a **sustained yield** basis.

Thus, using existing fishing methods to harvest presently exploited types of seafoods, the resource potential exists to double or, at best, triple our present global fish catch. But a two- or three-fold increase of the 1% that seafood contributes to our present diet is still a very small portion of our total food needs, and continued increases in the human population will surely offset much of those gains in future fisheries production. Two other possibilities for increasing our future seafood harvests will be discussed in the following paragraphs.

Mariculture

Mariculture, the application of farming techniques to grow, manage, and harvest marine animals and plants, may vary from simple enhancement of natural populations by releasing hatchery-reared juvenile fishes to intensive captive maintenance of species for their entire life span. As the numbers in table 13.1 indicate, farming of marine plants and animals presently contributes little to the total of marine food production.

Fish farming has been practiced for centuries in southeast Asia, Japan, and China. Mullets and milkfish are grown in shallow estuarine ponds where they graze on algae, detritus, and small animals. Estuaries, salt marshes, and other productive coastal habitats offer a tremendous potential for cultivating fish in closed pond systems. Yet it is unlikely that "feedlot" production of inexpensive marine organisms will soon be a reality. Intensive mariculture activities modify the nature of an estuary or salt marsh. For each fish pond installed, a portion of the native fish and shrimp populations already contibuting to previously estalished local fisheries will be displaced or denied access to these productive coastal waters.

Salmon ranching in Japan, the U.S.S.R., and in the United States has grown rapidly in the past two decades. Salmon smolts raised in hatcheries begin the prolonged ocean phase of their life cycle at release points and return to these points two to four years later. An adult return equal to 1 to 2% of the smolts released is now being achieved. In 1980, these three countries released a total of about 3 billion smolts, at least 30 million are expected to return to their release sites for easy capture and processing. Schemes to use the high seas to graze other species of pelagic fish will remain impractical as long as the "farmer" cannot be assured that others will refrain from harvesting his/her fish after they have grown.

For practical reasons, mariculturists must confine their activities to coastal waters. In special circumstances, polluting nutrients from sewer treatment plants or hot water from coastal power generating stations could be used beneficially. Diverted into fish ponds, nutrients and the warm water could enhance the growth of primary producers to feed the fish. But these are special circumstances. More commonly, mariculture programs are, and will continue to be, restricted by adverse problems of coastal pollution and habitat destruction and by competing uses for the same land.

Moving down the Food Chain

The ideal species for mariculture are plants at the first trophic level or algal grazers, detritus feeders, and other omnivores not far removed from the primary producers. Oysters, mussels, abalones, lobsters, and small amounts of red algae are grown in controlled environments. Even genetic selection for improved survival and faster growth is being employed on a limited basis. But mariculture is a costly business; it is and probably will be restricted to expensive luxury food items that generate large returns on investments. Captive-raised oysters and lobsters add little to the diets of most people on earth and certainly nothing to the diets of those who most need it.

In theory, if we could harvest what fish eat rather than harvesting the fish themselves, a tenfold increase in the harvest could be realized because one trophic level and its associated energy loss would be eliminated. Rather than contemplating limits of 100 or 200 million tons of fish, we could look forward to harvesting one or two billion tons of marine food each year. Serious problems, however, block this path to greatly increased marine harvests. Almost without exception, animals occupying lower trophic levels are smaller and more dispersed than the animals now harvested.

Although the technological developments necessary to harvest the zooplankton and smaller fish that comprise these lower trophic levels are not insurmountable, they may not be worthwhile. These smaller, more dispersed animals are more difficult to harvest; the additional energy needed to collect these small food items may exceed the energy gained from the additional harvest. It is likely to continue to be more efficient for us to wait until the larger animals have eaten the smaller ones.

To provide one example, a century ago, the phytoplankton crop around the Antarctic continent supported a tremendous assemblage of zooplankton, particularly the krill *Euphausia superba* (figure 10.7). In turn, krill fed large populations of blue, fin, and humpback whales. With these whale populations now seriously reduced, they no longer serve as intermediaries to harvest the krill for us. Fisheries scientists from several countries, led by Japan and the U.S.S.R., are test-harvesting krill with an eye to expanded future production. Preliminary estimates of an annual sustained harvest of 100 million and even 200 million tons have been reported for this one species alone. The potential of such massive harvesting is a complex issue with several ramifications unrelated to food production.

A major problem inhibiting the use of krill is what to do with it once it is caught. There is little demand for fresh or frozen krill. It is nutritious, but few people will buy it in its natural form. Most plans for using krill include some sort of processing to disguise it or to convert it to an odorless, powdered protein concentrate. The protein concentrate could then be mixed with grain flour to make high-protein breads, pastas, rice cakes, tortillas, or almost any other common food item.

The energy costs involved in catching krill, processing it to a palatable form, and transporting it to markets in the Northern Hemisphere will be enormous. Had the Antarctic stocks of great whales been properly managed while they thrived, humans might now indirectly derive more benefit from krill through a controlled harvest of the whales. Excepting mariculture, the potential for harvesting krill and other exotic organisms low in the food web is presently marginal at best. If any hope exists for massive increases in food production for the immediate future, it lies with improving techniques for terrestrial crop production using immediately available techniques to grow well-known crops already in demand by society.

The Problems of Overexploitation

Commercial and subsistence fishing represents a form of predation that has predictable effects on the prey species. When fishing of new stocks begins, initial catches are generally large and include a high proportion of large fish.

Continued or increased fishing pressure tends to reduce the average size and sometimes the abundance of the stock. If the fishing effort is matched to the growth and reproductive potential of the stock, then a **maximum sustainable yield** of fish can be caught year after year without causing major upsets in the stock abundance. Too often, though, the fishing pressure becomes much greater than the stock can withstand. Losses to fishing and natural predators together exceed recruitment of young animals, and populations decline. These declines are quickly reflected in reduced catches.

Numerous examples of overfished stocks can be found in most segments of the fishing industry. Most of the popular species of halibut, plaice, cod, ocean perch, herring, and salmon of the North Altantic and Pacific oceans are being or already have been overexploited. So are many of the warm-water tuna stocks and most of the large whales. The two examples discussed in the following paragraphs are sufficient to demonstrate some of the problems created by overfishing activities that seem in direct conflict with the fishing industry's own best interests.

The Peruvian Anchoveta

The Peruvian anchoveta (*Engraulis ringens*) is a typical clupeoid fish similar to the anchovy shown in figure 13.2. It is a small, fast-growing filter-feeder that schools in the upwelling areas of the Peru Current. The first commercial use of the anchoveta was indirect; from the time of the Incas, droppings or **guano deposits** from the nesting colonies of seabirds that fed on anchoveta have been collected and used as a major source of fertilizer. These seabirds, primarily Peruvian boobies, brown pelicans, and guanay cormorants (figure 13.7) annually converted about four million tons of anchoveta to an inexpensive fertilizer widely used by Peru's subsistence farmers.

Commercial exploitation of the Peruvian anchoveta for reduction to fish meal began in 1950. The next year, 7,000 tons were landed. After 1955, the growth of the fishery was explosive (figure 13.8); over 2 million tons were landed in 1960. By 1970, the catch of this one species had surpassed 13 million tons, almost one-fifth of the entire world fish harvest for that year. Nearly all the catch was taken by local fishermen and reduced to fish meal and oil for export.

Accompanying the meteoric rise in commercial anchoveta catches was a drastic drop in the number of guano birds that depended on the anchoveta for food. From 28 million in 1956, the guano bird population was reduced to 6 million during the El Niño year of 1957 (see chapter 5). With upwelling blocked by the intrusion of a surface layer of warm tropical water, plankton populations were dramatically reduced, anchoveta died or moved, and the guano birds quickly starved. After four years without an El Niño, the bird population had rebounded to 17 million, only to be hit by another El Niño in 1965. That time the bird population plummeted to 4 million, and it has not recovered.

A substantial base of biological information was collected during the development and growth of the Peruvian anchoveta fishery. With the advantages this information base provided, proper management procedures were expected to ensure a large and continuous harvest from this immense stock. The Instituto del Mar del Peru, an advisory panel of fishery experts, projected a maximum sustainable yield of approximately 9.5 million tons annually. At the time, the reduced bird populations were taking less than one million tons each

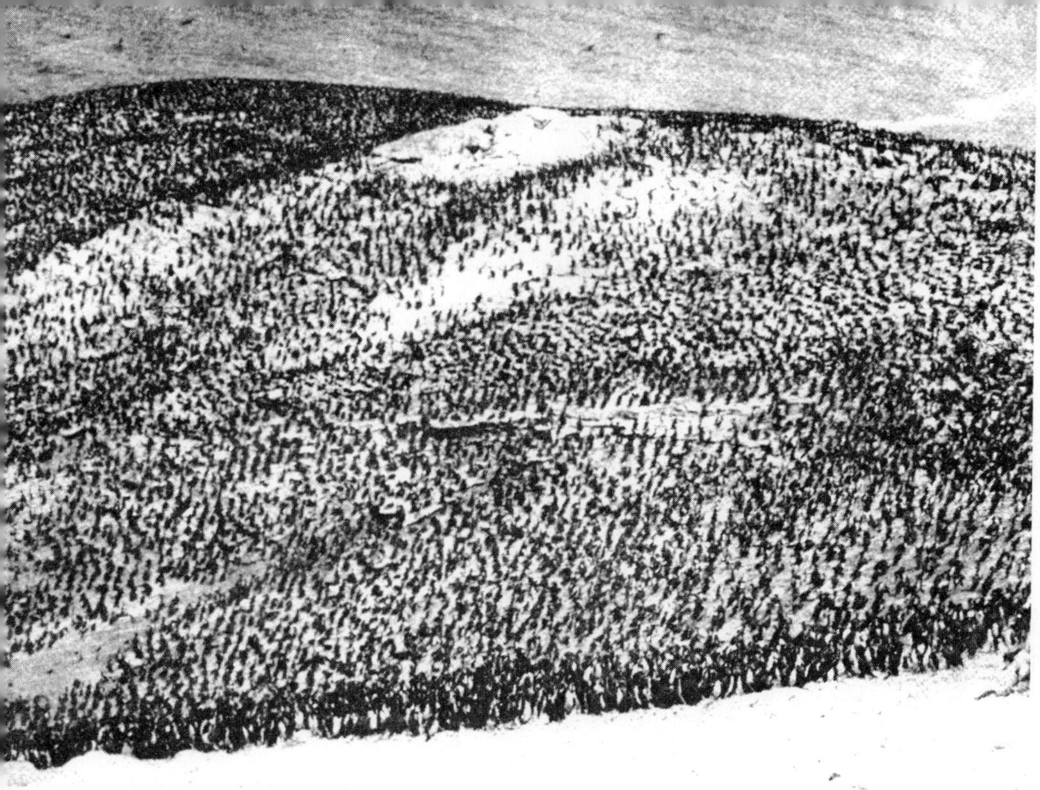

(a)

(b)

Figure 13.7

(*a*) Guanay cormorants (*Phalocrocorax*) at their nests on an island off the coast of Peru. (*b*) A close-up of the crater-shaped nests of the Guanay cormorant.

From Murphy, 1925

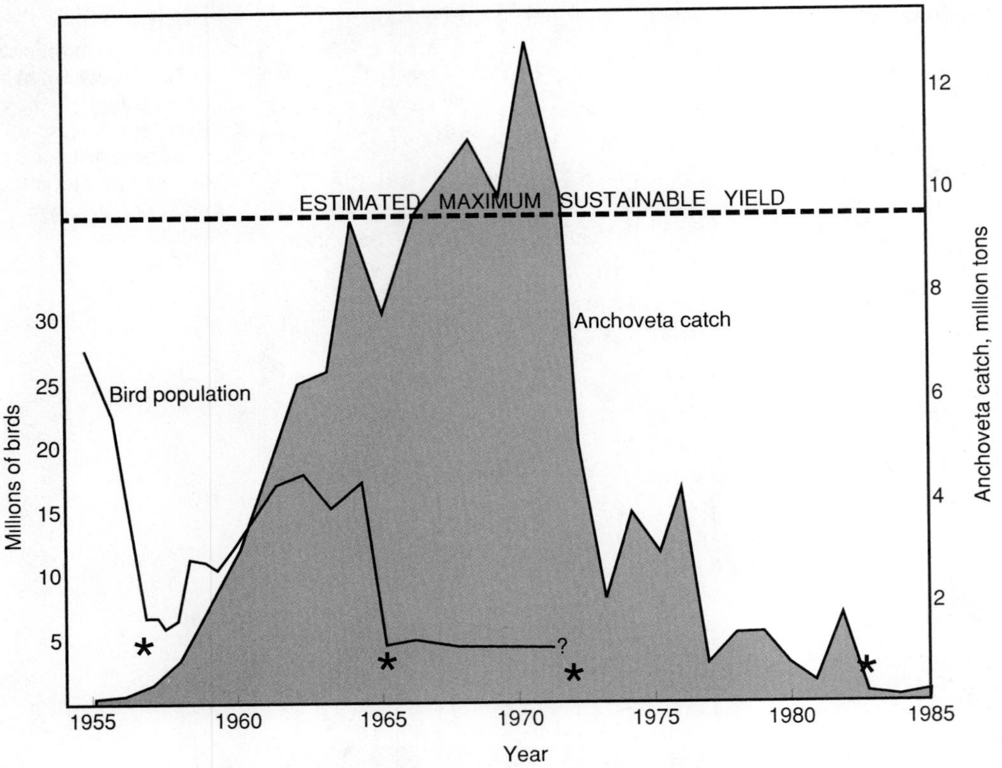

Figure 13.8
Changes in the guano bird population and the anchoveta fish catch (stippled) along the northwest coast of South America. Asterisks indicate El Niño years.
Adapted from Schaefer, 1970, and FAO catch and landing statistics

year. Tonnage reports alone, however, are inadequate and sometimes misleading. As the fishing pressure increased over the decade of the 1960s, the average size of fish being caught decreased, and the number needed to make a ton increased sharply. By 1970, small anchoveta were taken with such efficiency that 95% of the juvenile fish recruited into the population were captured before their first spawning.

A glance at figure 13.8 shows that the catches of anchoveta for 1967 through 1971 exceeded the predicted maximum sustainable yield by at least one million tons each year. The industry and the regulatory agencies responsible for managing the anchoveta stocks had ample warning of what was to come. In 1972, sampling surveys indicated the anchoveta stocks had been severely depleted and recruitment of juvenile fish was poor. As expected, the 1972 catch dropped to little more than 5 million tons, less than half that of the previous year. Even worse was 1973, with an estimated catch of less than 2 million tons. During the next two years, there was a slight improvement, but the yield was still less than 4 million tons each year. Apparently, the fishing pressures of the previous decade were too much for this tremendous stock of fish, and it finally collapsed. Even in the late 1980s, this species and the huge bird populations that once relied on it have shown no sign of recovery to pre-1970 levels.

The Great Whales

The history of the whaling industry has been a long and tragic one. Aboriginal hunting of coastal whales for food has occurred for several thousands years. In the eighteenth and nineteenth centuries, whaling took a new turn. Pelagic whales became major items of commerce as demand for their oil grew and whaling became a profitable commercial enterprise. Ships from a dozen nations combed the oceans for whales that could be killed with hand harpoons and lances. Right, bowhead, and gray whales were favorite targets, for they swam slowly and, once killed, they floated conveniently at the sea surface. In his famed *Moby Dick,* Herman Melville questioned the future of these great whales, faced, as they were, with

> . . . omniscient look-outs at the mastheads of the whale-ships, now penetrating even through Behring's straits, and into the remotest secret drawers and lockers of the world; and the thousand harpoons and lances darting along all the continental coasts; the moot point is, whether Leviathan can long endure so wide a chase, and so remorseless a havoc.

By the end of the nineteenth century the gray whale, both species of right whales, and the bowhead were on the verge of extinction. Under strict international protection, the gray whale has since recovered, but the number of bowheads and right whales remains very low.

The era of modern whaling was initiated in the late nineteenth century with the cannon-fired harpoon equipped with an explosive head. The explosive harpoon was so devastatingly effective that even the large rorquals, the blue and fin whales, were taken in large numbers. These whales had previously been ignored by whalers with hand harpoons, for they were much too fast to be overtaken in sail- or oar-powered boats. The subsequent rapid decline of the whale stocks in the North Atlantic and Pacific oceans forced ambitious whalers to seek new and untouched whaling areas. They found the Antarctic, the rich feeding grounds of the largest populations of whales. The discovery of the Antarctic whale populations touched off seven decades of slaughter unparalleled in the history of whaling.

Aided by pelagic factory ships fitted with stern ramps to haul the whale carcasses aboard for processing, the kill of large rorquals rose dramatically. From 176 blue whales in 1910, the annual take climbed to almost 30,000 in 1931 (figure 13.9). After the peak year of 1931, blue whales became increasingly scarce. Blue whale catches declined steadily until they were commercially insignificant by the mid-1950s. In 1966, only 70 blue whales were killed in the entire world ocean. Only then, when substantial numbers could no longer be found to turn a profit, was the hunting of blue whales banned in the Southern Hemisphere.

The trend of increasing then rapidly declining annual catches, shown by the blue whale curve in figure 13.9, is distressingly similar to that of the Peruvian anchoveta fishery. But the ruthless exploitation of the great whales did not halt with the near extinction of the blue whale. As the blue whale populations gave out, whalers switched to the smaller, more numerous fin whales, catches of which skyrocketed to over 25,000 whales each year for most of the 1950s. But by 1960, the fin whale catch began to plummet, and whaling pressure was diverted to even smaller sei whales. The total sei whale population probably never exceeded 60,000. One third of the sei whale population was killed in 1965 alone. Whaling pressure quickly pushed the catches of this species far beyond a maximum sustainable yield. By the late 1960s, sei whales had followed their larger relatives to commerical extinction, and the whaling effort was shifted to the minke whale, an 8 to 9 m long miniature version of a blue whale (figure 12.13).

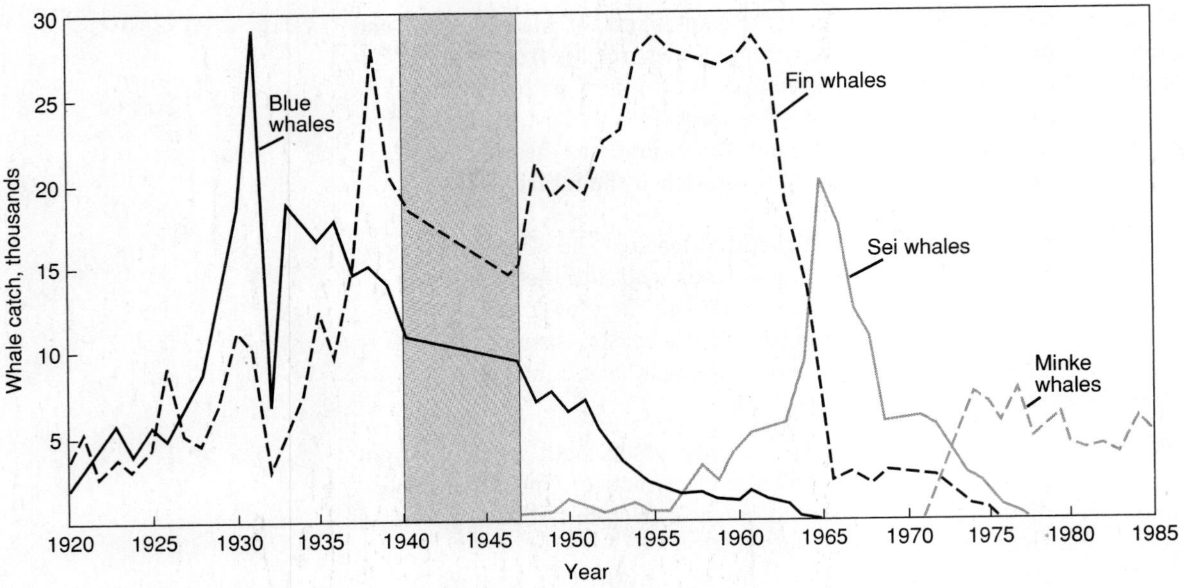

Figure 13.9
FAO catch and landing statistics of blue, fin, sei, and minke whales in the Antarctic, 1920–1985

As early as 1940, whaling nations were faced with undeniable evidence that some stocks of pelagic whales were seriously overexploited. In 1948, twenty whaling nations established the International Whaling Commission (IWC) to oversee the utilization and conservation of the world's whale resources. Unfortunately, the IWC had neither inspection nor enforcement powers. Only once during the 1963 to 1973 decade did the whaling industry actually manage to actually catch the quotas established for it by the IWC. The quotas were, in effect, not quotas at all, as there were no longer enough whales to fill them. In 1974, the IWC, under pressure from several national governments and international conservation organizations, adopted a new set of management procedures for several geographically localized stocks of whales. Under these procedures, all species of baleen whales in the Antarctic except the minke are classified as protected stocks, and no harvesting is allowed. Four species, the blue, gray, humpback, and right whales are protected in all oceans.

In spite of the increased take of minke whales in the Antarctic since 1970, their numbers and the numbers of Antarctic penguins, seals, and fish that rely (as did the now depleted stocks of larger baleen whales) on the Antarctic krill, *Euphausia superba,* have increased appreciably. With the larger whale species so efficiently removed from Antarctic food chains, these smaller, commercially less attractive species responded to the reduced competition with increased growth and maturity rates. The age at sexual maturity of Antarctic minke whales, for instance, has declined from over 15 years in the 1930s to about 7 years at present. Similar changes are seen in other krill-eating species as well.

To some, the severe depletion of the large pristine stocks of krill-eating baleen whales led to the naive assumption that, without these whales, a large "surplus" of krill exists for our harvesting. Such an assumption ignores the evidence that a new equilibrium has developed in krill-based food chains. Minke whales, birds, and seals now play larger roles than they did a century ago.

This is not a unique situation, for many fish stocks depleted by excessive harvesting pressures have been replaced with other (and, from a commercial point of view, often less desirable) species. These new species assemblages, by their very existence in niches previously occupied by the exploited stocks, serve as a barrier to the recovery of those stocks.

It is presently impossible to predict the fate of either the great whales or the Peruvian anchoveta. Of the two, the anchoveta has better survival and recovery potential. Anchoveta mature very rapidly, often spawning within their first year. Once mature, each female deposits nine to twenty-four thousand eggs each year for two or three years. However, the road to recovery for a large, slowly reproducing species such as the blue whale is fraught with unanswered questions. Can the few thousand remaining blue whales scattered over the world ocean encounter each other frequently enough to mate, reproduce, and add to their decimated numbers at a sufficient rate? Will additional blue whales meet stiff competition from other animals for food and other resources appropriated from the whales during their tragic decline? And most importantly, if the population begins to increase, will humans refrain from exploiting it so that it can secure a more solid grip on survival? The reproductive resiliency of the great whales is largely unknown. They may bounce back. The gray whale did, but the right and bowhead whales still have not.

In 1982, the IWC approved a five-year moratorium, to go into effect at the onset of the 1985–1986 whaling season, on the commercial killing of large whales. This moratorium was seen as a critical first step in assessing the impact of nearly a century of intense hunting of oceanic whale stocks. At the same time, it would give declining whale populations an opportunity to stabilize. Even after it went into effect, the moratorium was opposed by several nations with long whaling histories, espeically Japan, Norway, and Iceland. These nations lobbied repeatedly for permits to take whales (particularly fin and minke whales) for scientific research purposes. When permits were denied, Japanese whaling companies repeatedly went whaling for Antarctic minkes anyway.

With the recent increase in the size of their population, minke whales play a relatively new role as a major predator of Antarctic krill; and given the history of the whaling industry during this century, it should not be surprising to find that a nation anticipating substantial harvests of krill in the near future would strive to retain the means of controlling those species that would best compete with such a commerical venture. The five-year moratorium against whaling is due to expire as this book goes to print. How the international community handles this delicate problem in the months and decades ahead will be a serious test of our biological wisdom as well as our political will.

The Tragedy of Open Access

Why have fishing enterprises and fishing nations repeatedly exploited the fish resources on which they depend to the point that returns on their fishing effort decline and too often disappear? Even with the maze of legal and economic considerations involved, incentives for these apparently self-defeating actions are not difficult to find. Salmon, tuna, whales, and other oceanic species are unowned resources belonging to no single nation or individual. They exist outside the jurisdictional limits of all nations and are therefore open to access by any nation. Historically, the concept of **open access** to the high seas evolved in the sixteenth and seventeenth centuries when the right to navigate freely was more crucial than the freedom to fish. But as coastal fish stocks were depleted, fishermen became increasingly dependent on distant stocks in international waters. They eventually discovered that the freedom to fish on the high seas was fundamentally different from the freedom to navigate. Unlike navigation, fishing activities remove a valuable commodity from a common resource pool at the expense of all, including those who do not fish.

Ideally, it is assumed that oceanic resources are unowned and open to access for all people. But with today's advancing pace of technology, some nations achieve the ability to exploit these resources more quickly than others. If the fishing activities of one nation fail to catch these unowned oceanic species, some other nation soon will. In species after species, such attitudes have led to inevitable and predictable results: increased competition between fishing nations for limited resources, duplication of effort, declining fishing efficiency, and, of course, overfishing.

Once in the net, a school of fish is no longer the property of all people; it belongs instead to those who set the net and haul the fish aboard. All people and all nations share the cost of losing the fish, the great whales, and the other marine animals that have nearly disappeared because of overfishing. Yet the short-term profits derived from overfishing are not similarly shared. This is Hardin's concept of the "tragedy of the commons." The tragedy of this situation is that it best rewards those who most heavily exploit and abuse the unprotected living resources of the open ocean.

International Regulation of Fisheries

Without controls to limit the access of fishermen to fish populations in international waters, concerned nations have created regulatory commissions similar to the IWC. These commissions are charged with the responsibility of governing the management and harvest of regional fish stocks. The International Commission for the Northwest Atlantic Fisheries, for instance, includes Canada, Denmark, France, Germany, Iceland, Italy, Norway, Poland, Spain, U.S.S.R., the United States, and the United Kingdom. The regulations established by this commission do not carry the weight of international law, but they are binding on member nations. Even so, they have failed to halt serious overfishing of the cod and ocean perch stocks of the northwest Atlantic.

Other commissions, particularly those regulating the halibut and salmon fisheries in the North Pacific, have been much more successful. Their success, however, is now creating new problems. Too many additional fishing boats from the United States, Canada, Korea, Japan, and the U.S.S.R. are being attracted to these well-managed fisheries. Under these additional fishing pressures, management problems are magnified, profits of individual fishermen are diminished, and the possibilities for overexploitation are greatly enhanced.

In the early 1970s, at the Third United Nations Conference on the Law of the Sea, the prospects for a single international convention to regulate open-ocean fish stocks seemed uncertain. The United States government was under pressure from its own coastal fishing interests to extend United States jurisdiction for fisheries out to 200 miles. They could see the distant-water fishing fleets of the U.S.S.R., Japan, and West Germany taking huge harvests just off their shores. The United States ended its traditional policy of oppo-

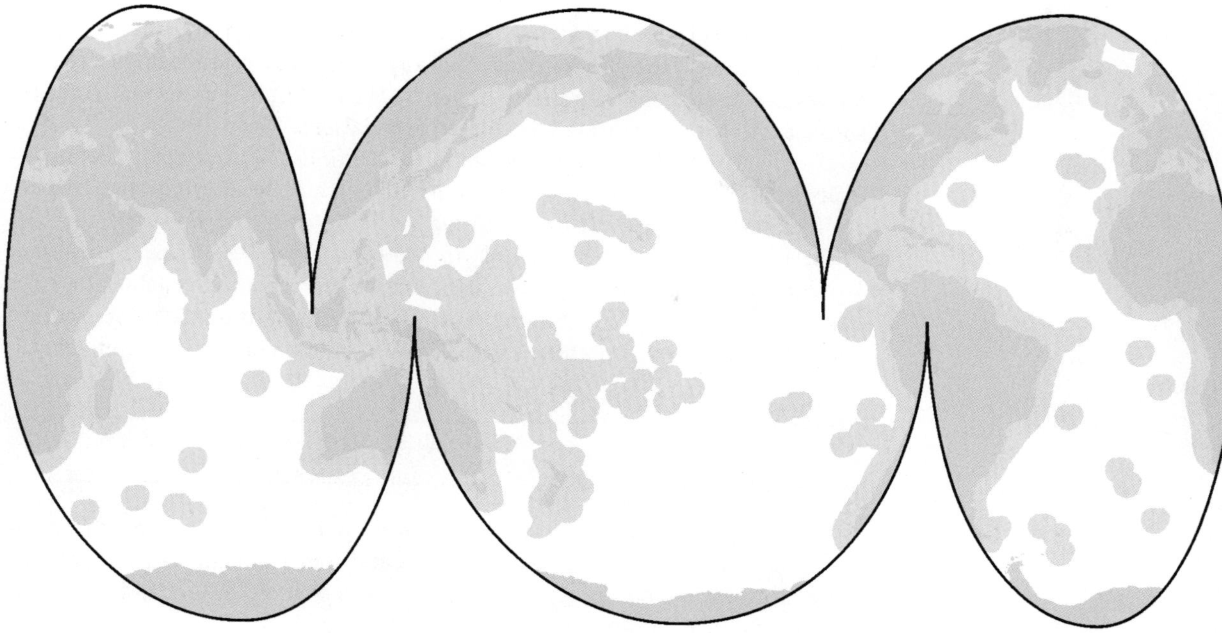

Figure 13.10
Worldwide extent of the 200-mile exclusive economic zones sanctioned by the United Nations

sition to extended zones of control for coastal nations in 1974. In 1976, the United States passed the Fisheries Conservation and Management Act. Under this act, the United States assumed exclusive jurisdiction over fisheries management in a zone extending 200 miles to sea. Entrance of foreign fishing vessels into this Exclusive Economic Zone (E.E.Z.) is allowed on a permit basis only, and then the fishers are allowed to harvest only fish stocks with sustained yields greater than the harvesting capacity of American fishers.

In 1982, the United Nations Conference on the Law of the Sea produced a new draft Law of the Sea Treaty that was to go into effect 12 months after ratification by at least 60 nations. When the draft treaty was produced, the United States, a strong supporter of United Nations treaty development process for nearly a decade, declined to ratify it, leaving the United States isolated from most other nations of the world on this crucial international treaty. The United Nations treaty includes many of the key features found in the United States Fisheries Conservation and Management Act, in particular, a 200-mile-wide exclusive economic zone granting coastal nations sovereign rights with respect to natural resources (including fishing), scientific research, and environmental preservation. Additionally, the United Nations treaty obliges nations to prevent or control marine pollution, to promote the development and transfer of marine technology to developing nations, and to settle peacefully disputes arising from the exploitation of marine resources.

The imposition of 200–mile-wide EEZs by essentially all coastal nations of the world dramatically changes the concept of open access for most of the world's continental shelves, coastal upwelling areas, and major fisheries lying within 200 miles of some nations' shorelines (figure 13.10). This treaty is notably silent regarding the Antarctic upwelling area, for territorial claims on the Antarctic continent are not recognized. Commercial ventures there, including either whale or krill harvesting, must be consistent with the goals of the recent convention for the Conservation of Antarctic Marine Living Resources; namely, the "maintenance of the ecological relationships between harvested, dependent, and related populations of Antarctic marine living resources and the restoration of depleted populations."

The waters around the Antarctic continent represent the last relatively unspoiled large marine ecosystem on earth. The international cooperation demonstrated so far in protecting its living resources has been unusual in the long history of our attempts to protect marine resources. The waters around this remote continent can continue to serve both as a laboratory for improving understanding of living marine systems and as a model for creating approaches to preserving those resources as a common heritage of humankind.

Summary

The variety of marine organisms taken for human food is large, including finfish, shellfish, other invertebrates, whales, and some marine plants. Commercial fishing efforts are generally concentrated in shallow waters and upwelling regions and near ocean current or thermal boundaries.

Presently, slightly more than 1% of the total human diet comes from the sea, and most of that tonnage is wild-caught marine animals. Estimates of future yields suggest that the present harvest of marine food may be tripled or quadrupled.

One of the problems that is limiting present and future marine food harvests is overexploitation of exisiting living marine resources. The Peruvian anchoveta and the stocks of great whales are vivid examples of commercial overexploitation followed by collapse of the stocks. Open access and the absence of realistic, binding regulations to govern the harvest of unowned marine resources continue to promote overexploitation with little regard to its ultimate consequences.

Some optimistic possibilities, including mariculture and the use of krill, still exist. Yet the basic problem remains: The human population continues to increase in size. The mere existence of that human population will have an increasingly detrimental impact on the yield of food from the sea.

Review Questions

1. Describe some of the ways in which human efforts to increase food production on land have reduced the potential yields of food from the sea.
2. List three structural or behavioral features of anchovy, herring, and other clupeoid fish that explain why they account for such a large portion of the total world fish catch.
3. List three specific biological reasons why the oceans, which cover over 70% of the earth's surface, produce only about 1% of the total human food supply.
4. Describe the fate of the Peruvian anchoveta fishery from the mid-1950s to the present. What impact do you think the collapse of that fishery has had on the price of market eggs in Europe? On the abundance of pelican eggs in Peru?

Questions for Further Discussion

1. Most of the world's important fishing areas are located in relatively shallow waters, especially along western coasts of continents. Discuss physical, chemical, biological, and economic factors in your answer.
2. Discuss the conditions which cause 99.8% of the world's plant mass to be on land even though the oceans cover over 70% of the earth's surface.
3. Discuss the factors which limit the contribution of marine sources of food (for humans) to less than 2% of the total volume of food consumed by the present human popluation.

Suggestions for Further Reading

Books

Beddington, J. R., R. J. H. Beverton, and D. M. Lavigne. 1985. *Marine mammals and fisheries*. Boston, MA: George Allen and Unwin.

Bell, F. W. 1978. *Food from the sea: The economics and politics of ocean fisheries.* Denver: Westview Press.

Caddy, J. F., ed. 1988. *Marine invertebrate fisheries: Their assesment and management*. New York: Wiley-Interscience.

Crutchfield, J. A., and G. Pontecorvo. 1969. *The Pacific salmon fisheries: A study of irrational conservation.* Baltimore: Johns Hopkins Press.

Gulland, J. A. 1971. *The fish resources of the ocean.* Surrey, England: Fishing News (Books) Ltd.

Idyll, C. P. 1978. *The sea against hunger.* New York: Thomas Y. Crowell.

Rothschild, B. J., ed. 1983. *Global fisheries: Perspectives for the 1980s.* New York: Springer-Verlag.

Articles

Adey, W. H. 1987. Food production in low-nutrient seas. *Bioscience* 37(5):340–48.

Bardach, J. 1987. Aquaculture. *Bioscience* 37(5):318–19.

Beddington, J. R., and R. M. May. 1982. The harvesting of interacting species in a natural ecosystem. *Scientific American* (Novermber):62–69.

Borgese, E. M. 1983. The law of the sea. *Scientific American* (March):42–49.

Cushing, D. H., and R. R. Dickson. 1976. The biological response in the sea to climatic changes. *Advances in Marine Biology* 14:1–122.

Eberstadt, N. 1986. Population and economic growth. *Wilson Quarterly* 10:95–127.

Fye, P. M. 1982. The law of the sea. *Oceanus* 25(4):7–12.

Harlan, J. R. 1976. The plants and animals that nourish man. *Scientific American* (September):89–97.

Horn, M. H., and R. N. Gibson. 1988. Intertidal fisheries. *Scientific American* 258(1):64–70.

Laws, R. M. 1985. The ecology of the Southern Ocean. *American Scientist* 73:26–40.

Robinson, M. A., and A. Crispoldi. 1975. Trends in world fisheries. *Bioscience* 18:23–29.

Ross, R. M., and L. B. Quetin. 1986. How productive are Antarctic krill? *Bioscience* 36:264–69.

Rudloe, J., and A. Rudloe. 1989. Shrimpers and sea turtles: A conservation impasse. *Smithsonian* 29(9):45–55.

Ryther, J. H. 1981. Mariculture, ocean ranching, and other culture-based fisheries. *Bioscience* 31:223–30.

Schaefer, M. B. 1970. Men, birds, and anchovies in the Peru Current—dynamic interactions. *Transactions of the American Fisheries Institute* 99:461–67.

Scarff, J. E. 1980. Ethical issues in whale and small cetacean management. *Environmental Ethics* 3:241–79.

Walsh, J. P. 1981. U.S. policy on marine pollution. *Oceanus* 24(1):18–24.

Ocean Pollution

Chapter 14

Oiled beach, Prince William Sound

Photo by J. Harvey

Throughout this book, an assumption has been made that pristine ocean waters are essential for the maintenance of healthy marine communities. This assumption is being put to a global test. Each year our growing human population generates an enormous burden of domestic and industrial wastes. Most of this population lives in coastal regions, and adjacent coastal waters have long been used as natural and nearly cost-free disposal sites for unwanted effluvia. Initially, these wastes may be dumped into rivers, down sewers, or up smokestacks, but ultimately, most wastes make their way to the ocean. The world ocean has a large but finite capacity to assimilate these waste materials without apparent degradation of water quality. However, that capacity can be exceeded if ocean mixing processes are not sufficient to dilute or disperse wastes, creating localized water quality problems and subsequent biological disturbances.

Municipal and industrial wastewater discharges (including urban runoff and storm drain and sewer overflows), land-based agriculture and forest harvest activities, ocean-based activities related to dredging, marine mining, drilling for and shipping of oil and gas, and direct ocean dumping are all sources of ocean pollutants. Hot water from power generation plants and nutrients from agricultural runoff and sewage outfalls (particularly phosphates and nitrogen compounds) can promote growth rates of all marine organisms; but when they are discharged into semienclosed estuaries, bays, or lagoons, they often become serious pollutants. It is paradoxical that some of the worst pollutants are the pesticide and fertilizer products used to enhance food production on land, and that some of the most obvious disturbances appear in marine species harvested for human consumption.

Waste materials discharged into ocean waters can be considered pollutants if they have measurable adverse effects on natural populations (table 14.1). These pollutants include a variety of suspended solids, organic compounds, and inorganic nutrients that deplete dissolved oxygen. Other, more persistent contaminants such as heavy metals, pesticides, radioactive wastes, and petroleum products head the list of substances that, even at low concentrations, can adversely affect the health of marine organisms and the integrity of their natural ecological relationships. Once in the ocean, persistent contaminants accumulate in marine organisms, and those accumulations are magnified as they are transferred up food chains.

Heavily polluted waters may create direct human health risks, risks associated with eating seafood contaminated with disease-producing microorganisms and toxic substances. But even at lower concentrations, marine organisms provide us with clues signaling serious physiological or habitat disturbances. Like the living resources of the sea, the ocean itself is a resource shared by most nations on earth. It serves as a valuable and often misused global disposal site for waste substances either too plentiful or too dangerous to store on land. The following discussion will describe a few substances with known serious consequences for marine life, highlighting the critical links between waste disposal, the biological integrity of marine communities, and our own health and well-being.

Sewage

A major source of coastal pollutants, human sewage, fouls bays and beaches with both toxic and nontoxic pollutants. Although billions of dollars have been invested in sewage treatment plants to treat wastewater, new and growing

Table 14.1
A Summary of the Sources and Effects of Some Marine Pollutants

Pollutant	Sources	Effects
Particulate material	Dredged material, sewage, erosion	Smothers benthic organisms, clogs gills and filters, reduces underwater light
Dissolved nutrients	Sewage agricultural runoff	Phytoplankton blooms, decreased dissolved oxygen
Toxics	Pesticides, industrial wastes, oil spills, antifouling paint	Increased incidence of disease, contaminated seafood, immune system suppression, reproductive failure
Oil	Tankers, drill sites, urban and industrial wastes	Smothering, clogging of gills, matting of fur or feathers, toxic effects
Marine debris	Garbage, ship wastes, fishing gear	Physical injuries, mutilations, increased mortality

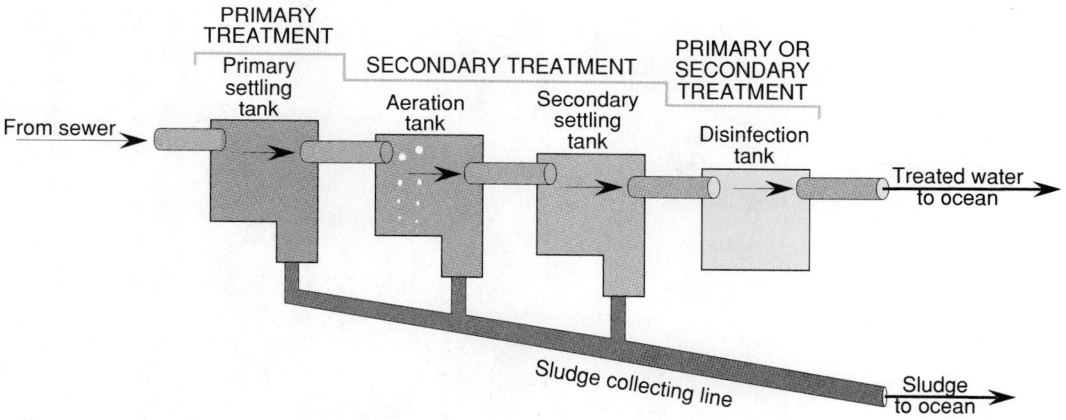

Figure 14.1
Diagram of the steps in a secondary sewage treatment plant. At each step, there is some discharge of materials to the ocean.
Adapted from Duedall, 1990

coastal communities have increased the amount of discharge into oceans and estuaries. The United States Office of Technology Assessment has identified thirteen hundred major industries and six hundred municipal wastewater treatment plants that discharge into the coastal waters of the United States. Typical secondary wastewater treatment is intended to separate solids and to reduce the amount of organic matter (which contributes to biochemical oxygen demand), nutrients, pathogenic bacteria, toxic pollutants, detergents, oils, and grease. In the United States, most ocean discharges of wastewater are supposed to meet secondary treatment standards (figure 14.1). However, many still do not. This problem is much greater in heavily populated developing coastal countries. In many of these countries, discharge of raw sewage and poorly treated sludge directly into estuaries and coastal ocean waters is the norm.

Figure 14.2
Barged sewage sludge being dumped at sea
Courtesy Greenpeace

About 15% of the 300 million tons of sewage sludge produced in the United States each year is discharged into coastal ocean waters through outfall pipelines or from barges. The term **sludge** describes the mix of solids that is the end product of municipal wastewater treatment. Sludge is not unlike detritus from marine sources in its general composition and nutritional value. It has, under ideal conditions, some nourishment value to zooplankton and benthic detritus feeders. But the present rate of dumping in shallow waters off the coasts of most major urban areas is enormous, and the capacity of those areas for accepting additional sludge is already or will soon be exceeded.

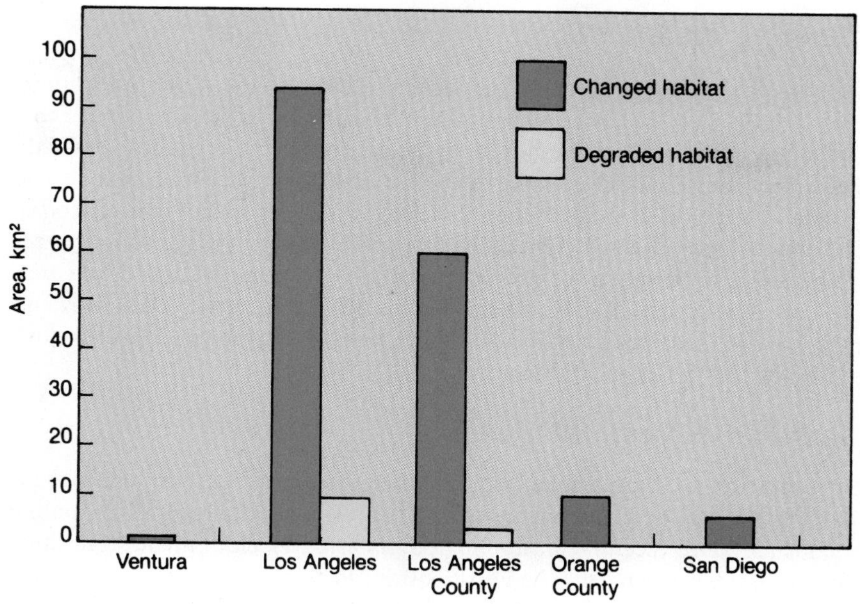

Figure 14.3
Extent of areas changed or degraded by five major sewage outfalls in the southern California Bight, 1978–1979
Data from Mearnes, 1981

Along the northeastern United States coast, sewage sludge is barged to offshore sites for dumping (figure 14.2). By 1992, when New York City is required to cease ocean dumping, about 25 million wet tons of sludge will have been dumped at a site 160 km east of the New Jersey coast. With a water depth of 2400 m, sludge dumped at this site was expected to disperse and dissolve completely before reaching the bottom. When this site was visited by researchers in the submersible *Alvin* in 1989, it was apparent that appreciable amounts of sludge particles were reaching the seafloor, and that these particles were contaminated with heavy metals and human sewage bacteria. The impact of these contaminants on benthic communities is still under study.

Even marine communities near small population centers are not immune from the impact of sewage effluents. The coral reefs of Kaneohe Bay, Hawaii, have suffered extensive damage since 1950. By 1975, two-thirds of the bay's coral reefs had been destroyed, partly by the direct action of the sewage and partly by the smothering effects of a large green alga (*Dictyosphaeria*) whose growth had been stimulated by the increase in sewage-derived nutrients.

In southern California, sludge containing about one-quarter of a million tons of solids is discharged through thirty ocean outfalls each day. At sites near southern California outfalls, concentrations of trace metals, DDT, and PCBs are often increased severalfold in bottom sediments and in larger benthic invertebrates. Measurable changes in species diversity and biomass of benthic infauna and kelp beds can be found, but these changes depend on the rate of discharge and the degree of treatment prior to release. The impact of these heavy loads of nutrients and contaminants is only now beginning to be studied properly, and the picture they present is not simple. Increased abundance of fish and benthic invertebrates have been noted in the vicinity of some outfalls; at others, benthic communities have been noticeably degraded. DDT and PCBs have been shown to enter marine food chains and find their ways through many trophic levels to distant sites. Of the five major sewer outfalls emptying into the Southern California Bight, two have caused obvious degradation in several square km around the outfall site. Together the five outfalls have significantly changed or degraded nearly 200 km² (figure 14.3).

Toxic Pollutants

Many toxic substances enter the sea through sewer systems, but others originate as industrial discharges. For many toxic substances, we do not yet know how to determine their extent or fate in the marine environment or to evaluate their effects on marine life. Some of the better-known trace metals and toxic chemicals include mercury, copper, lead, and chlorinated hydrocarbons. Chlorinated hydrocarbons, synthetic chlorine-containing compounds, are created for use as pesticides or are byproducts of the manufacture of plastics. They are among the most persistent and harmful of all toxic substances and include well-known products like chlordane, lindane, heptachlor, DDT, dioxins, and PCBs (polychlorinated biphenyls).

Anti-Fouling Paints

For centuries, boat hulls have been sheathed in copper or other metals to attempt to retard the attachment and growth of barnacles and other fouling organisms. More recently, antifouling paints using biocides made from these metals have been applied. The latest entrant in this race to find a substance to block fouling organisms is tributyltin (TBT). Paints with TBT are more effective and last longer than older copper-based antifouling paints. However, TBT leaches from boat hulls into harbor waters, but in amounts virtually undetectable with present analytical techniques. Yet even in these very low concentrations (a few parts per trillion), TBT harms nontarget organisms such as oysters and clams. TBT is known to deform oyster shells and cause chronic reproductive failure in a variety of shellfish species. In 1987, the United States Congress passed the Antifouling Paint Control Act that classified TBT as a restricted pesticide and severely limited its use and the amount that could be used in paints. Since TBT eventually degrades to less toxic forms in the marine environment, these new restrictions have already led to decreased concentrations in estuaries and bays.

DDT

By virtue of its long and widespread use, DDT and its effects on marine life have been well-documented. Dichloro-diphenyl-trichloroethane (DDT) was the first of a new class of synthetic chlorinated hydrocarbons. It became available for public use in 1945 and quickly gained international acceptance as an effective killer of most serious insect threats: houseflies, lice, mosquitoes, and several crop pests. In spite of these obvious benefits, the use of DDT has been banned in the United States and in some other nations. Several unfortunate characteristics have transformed DDT from a benefactor to an ecological nightmare.

DDT is a persistent pesticide; it does not break down or lose its toxicity rapidly. Once in seawater, DDT is rapidly absorbed by suspended particles. Because it is nearly insoluble in water, measurable levels of DDT in seawater are practically nonexistent. Yet DDT contamination from land and air has been so pervasive that it can be found in nearly all parts of the world ocean. Antarctic penguins, arctic seals, Bermuda petrels, and fish everywhere have accumulations of DDT in their fatty tissues.

DDT is quite soluble in lipids. Fatty tissues and oil droplets concentrate the DDT absorbed on suspended particles in seawater. Phytoplankton and, to a much lesser extent, zooplankton are the initial steps in DDT's entry

Figure 14.4
Transfer of DDT to and within marine food webs (arrows). DDT is absorbed by phytoplankton and then concentrated at each step in the food web.
Adapted from Epel and Lee, 1970

into marine food webs. Fish, birds, and other predators eventually consume this plankton and its load of DDT, concentrating the toxin in their fatty tissues. At each step in the food web, further concentration or **bioaccumulation** occurs (figure 14.4). Eventually the DDT reaches the top carnivores.

In the 1960s, a serious DDT contamination in the Los Angeles coastal area was centered around the Los Angeles County sewer outfall at Whites Point. The source of most of the DDT was traced to a chemical plant that produced most of the world's supply of DDT. Wastes produced in the manufacture of this pesticide were washed into the sewer system at rates exceeding 100 tons a year. For comparison, the entire Mississippi River drainage system each year added only ten tons of DDT to the waters of the Gulf of Mexico. Concentrations of DDT in marine animals occasionally exceeded the permissible limits for human consumption (5 ppm) established by the United States Food and Drug Administration, and some lots of canned kingfish, jack mackerel, and other species of fish were seized and could not be distributed.

Marine birds suffered the most devastating effects of DDT poisoning. As fish-eating predators, they are sometimes four or five trophic levels removed from the phytoplankton which initially absorbs the DDT. The bioaccumulation of DDT that occurred at each trophic level assured these predatory birds of high DDT loads in their food. DDT and its residues block normal nerve functions in vertebrates. A few birds were found dead from extremely high concentrations of DDT. DDT also interferes with calcium deposition during the formation of egg shells in birds. The egg shells of birds with high DDT loads were very thin and fragile. They frequently broke when laid or failed to support the weight of adult birds during incubation. The broken eggs lay in abandoned nests, mute testimony to the insidious effects of DDT.

The brown pelican (*Pelecanus occidentalis*) is a common sight along both coasts of the United States and Mexico. Nesting colonies of these birds exist on islands along the warmer coasts. A decline in the number of brown pelicans along southern California in the late 1960s was traced to reproductive failures caused by DDT-induced eggshell thinning. In one nesting colony of three hundred pelicans on Anacapa Island (off the southern California coast), twelve intact eggs were laid in 1969. Of those twelve, only three hatched. Some adult birds were sitting on damaged eggs. Others already had abandoned nests littered with remnants of thin-shelled and broken eggs.

DDT from the Los Angeles County sewer outfall was cited as being responsible for the local reproductive failure of the brown pelican and other fish-eating bird. Since the United States banned DDT in 1972, the massive doses of DDT released into California coastal waters by the Los Angeles sewer system have been reduced by 90% and its devastating effects on seabird reproduction are slowly diminishing. Yet DDT is still being used in other parts of the world and some is carried to the ocean each year. By itself, DDT is a threat to the continued existence of several species of marine animals. But it is only symptomatic of the greater danger posed by the many other persistent toxins of which we know even less.

Dioxins

Dioxins are another group of chlorinated compounds gaining international notoriety. The most potent dioxin is TCDD, which is toxic to birds and aquatic life at concentrations of a few parts per quadrillion. Because dioxins, like DDT, are fat-soluble and stable, dioxins bioaccumulate readily and are suspected of causing cancers, developmental malformations, and immune system and reproductive difficulties.

Dioxins enter the marine environment from many sources, but most arrive in the effluent from pulp and paper manufacturing plants that chlorinate wood pulp to produce bleached paper. Trace levels of dioxins have been found in tissues of fish collected near pulp and paper mills. Although the concentrations do not affect fish, the bioaccumulation of dioxin may affect human health if the fish are consumed. Some European paper-producing countries such as Sweden are working to reduce the amounts of dioxin discharged into the Baltic Sea by finding alternative bleaching techniques that do not use chlorine processes and by producing unbleached paper products. More studies to determine the extent and effect of dioxin in marine waters are currently underway.

PCBs

The North Sea, surrounded as it is by many of Europe's industrialized nations, experiences some of the highest levels of marine pollution anywhere. High on the list of these pollutants are dioxins and PCBs. During the summer of 1988, over seventeen thousand common and grey seals died of a viral infection that swept the Baltic, Wadden, and North Seas. By the time it runs its course, this epidemic may kill as many as 80% of some North Atlantic populations of common and grey seals. Stressed seals exhibit symptoms such as lesions, encephalitis, peritonitis, osteomyelitis, and premature abortions.

The source of this epidemic has not been established with any certainty, nor has an absolute link between this viral outbreak and any specific pollutant been demonstrated. However, PCBs in the seals' food is strongly sus-

Figure 14.5
Oil-soaked murre after the *Exxon Valdez* oil spill
Courtesy J. Harvey

pected because there is strong experimental evidence that indicates that low concentrations of PCBs (and possibly dioxins as well) lead to suppression of the immune systems of harbor seals. PCBs also interfere with implantation in seals, leading to fewer births and lower birth weights. Seal pups born of PCB-contaminated mothers may still be confronted with higher mortality rates and suppressed immune system problems.

To examine the extent of the pollution in the Baltic Sea, the seven-nation Helsinki Convention is developing a pollution monitoring and control strategy. In the Pacific Rim nations, similar efforts are underway through the Pacific Basin Consortium on Hazardous Waste Research to identify and study pollutants present in the Pacific Ocean and to develop joint international partnerships to reduce existing and manage future marine pollutants.

Oil on Water

Torrey Canyon (1967), Santa Barbara (1969), *Amoco Cadiz* (1978), and *Exxon Valdez* (1989)—these catastrophic oil spills engender a concern for the marine environment as no invisible contaminant can. Spilled oil floats on seawater and provides a constant reminder of its presence until it is washed ashore or evaporates. Large volumes of oil suffocate benthic organisms by clogging their gills and filtering structures or fouling their digestive tracts. Marine birds and mammals suffer heavily as their insulating fur or feathers become oil-soaked and matted (figure 14.5), and they lose insulation and buoyancy.

On March 22, 1989, the supertanker *Exxon Valdez* ran aground on Bligh Reef in Alaska's Prince William Sound (figure 14.6). The grounding punched holes in eight of the eleven cargo tanks and three of the seven segregated ballast tanks. The result was the largest oil spill to date in United States waters (242,000 barrels or nearly 40,000,000 liters). The spill occurred in an area noted for its rich assemblages of seabirds, marine mammals, fish, and other wildlife. It was one of the most pristine stretches of coastal waters in the United States, with specially designated natural preserves such as the Kenai Fjords and Katmai National Park.

Figure 14.6

The supertanker, *Exxon Valdez,* after running aground on Bligh Reef in Prince William Sound, April, 1989

Courtesy J. Harvey

The area of the spill, because of its gravel and cobble beaches, was particularly sensitive to oil. In places, the thick, tarry crude oil penetrated over a meter below the beach surface. High winds, waves, and currents in the days following the accident quickly spread oil over 26,000 km^2. The toll on wildlife was devastating. Over thirty-three thousand dead birds were recovered, and hundreds of sea otters, seals, sea lions, and other marine mammals, as well as many thousands of the commercial and noncommercial fish, were killed. Traditional fishing and cultural activities of the native communities in Prince William Sound were halted for the year, creating enormous social and economic costs.

With the United States government encouraging more exploration for new seafloor oil deposits to reduce its dependency on foreign imported oil, the risks from oil spills are likely to increase substantially. To prepare for such disasters, particularly after the *Exxon Valdez* oil spill, coastal states are trying to improve oil spill contingency plans and are experimenting with oil dispersants to mitigate the environmental effects of future oil spills.

In spite of the spectacular nature of major spills from tankers or offshore drilling and production platforms, more oil actually enters the marine environment in an average year in runoff from urban streets and parking lots, from leaking underground storage tanks and improperly dumped waste oil and in bilge water from nearly every freighter, fishing vessel, and military ship afloat. The numerous sources and more mundane aspect of these oil pollutants make them more difficult to manage than a single dramatic spill of the same volume of oil from a wrecked tanker.

Marine Debris

Until recently, marine debris was considered to be of minor importance when compared to other pollutants. Problems caused by marine debris, however, may rival or exceed those resulting from some better known pollutants, including oil. By definition, marine debris is any manufactured object discarded in the marine environment. When dumped, it may sink to the sea floor, remain suspended at mid-depths, or float at the surface and eventually be carried ashore by winds and waves.

Prior to the Marine Plastics Pollution Research and Control Act of 1987 (MARPOL), which directs the United States Environmental Protection Agency to find ways to stop plastics pollution, the primary source of marine debris was the massive dumping of garbage at sea by foreign and domestic merchant ships, military and fishing vessels, and recreation boats. Merchant ships generate an estimated 110,000 tons of marine debris yearly and fishing vessels another 340,000 tons. The practice of dumping garbage at sea has been legal because no alternatives were practical. The effects have worsened due to the increase in nonbiodegradable products that float after being dumped. Recently, nonbiodegradable medical wastes in the form of used syringes and vials have been washing up on some of our beaches, apparently dumped illegally at sea.

Even though the amount of debris dumped every day is slowly being reduced with garbage compactors aboard ships and recycling or disposal opportunities in ports ashore, much plastic and other nonbiodegradable garbage continues to be dumped in the sea. This debris harms marine life, damages vessels, and eventually litters beaches. Because these materials decompose very slowly, they will continue to float at the sea surface, carried by currents to harm marine life and litter our beaches for years to come.

Fishing Gear

The world's commercial fishing fleet contributes over 100,000 tons of accidentally lost nets, pots, traps, and setlines, and deliberately discarded pieces of damaged fishing gear each year. The shift since 1940 from the use of natural fibers to virtually nonbiodegradable synthetic fibers for the construction of nets and other fishing gear has made commercial fisheries a major contributor to marine plastic pollution. The largest potential for lost and discarded fishing gear occurs in the North Pacific Ocean, where vessels of many nations operate under adverse climatic conditions. Since 1978, new gill net fisheries for squid have been developed by Japan, the Republic of Korea, and Taiwan in the Central-North Pacific. Over a million kilometers of gill net are now set annually by the squid fisheries. These nets constitute a large potential source of derelict gear which, if lost, continue to drift for thousands of km. Birds, mammals, and other animals that surface frequently are especially susceptible to entanglement in the floating net fabric or other plastic debris (figure 14.7). One recent survey of antarctic fur seals on Bird Island, South Georgia, indicated that, even on that remote island, nearly 1% of the seals were entangled in synthetic debris. Most of the seals entangled were wearing "neck collars" made of plastic strapping (59%) or fishing line and net material (29%). A large proportion of these seals exhibited signs of physical injury, and an unknown number of animals presumably died after contact with floating debris.

Figure 14.7
Beached gray whale, with drift-net fabric wrapped around its tail

Plastics

Plastics constitute as great an environmental threat as all the other kinds of debris combined. Although plastics may break up into smaller pieces, they degrade much more slowly than most other kinds of debris, and most plastics float. Concentrations of plastics tend to be highest in the Northern Hemisphere, where ship traffic is the heaviest, where most plastics manufacturers and fabricators are located, and where more intensive recreational use is made of beaches.

Common plastic products include jugs, bottles, buckets, bags, sheeting, eating utensils, the yokes that hold six-packs of beverage containers together, life preservers, buoys, fish nets, fish net floats, fishing line, rope, styrofoam cups, and styrofoam packing material. Suspension beads, the raw material used by fabricators of plastic products, have become a ubiquitous component of debris. They can now be found in surface waters, in sediments, and on beaches around the world.

Even the most casual observer is sometimes overwhelmed by the startling array of plastic litter encountered on isolated beaches. A recent three-hour collection effort by over two thousand volunteers of SOLV (Save Oregon from Litter and Vandalism) yielded over 26 tons of plastic debris. Most of the debris was believed to have been washed ashore and not to have been left behind

Figure 14.8
One of several posters used in campaigns to reduce marine plastic debris
Courtesy Oregon State University Extension Sea Grant

by beachgoers. Included in the litter were 48,898 chunks of styrofoam larger than a baseball, 2,055 bands used for strapping boxes and other kinds of cargo, 6,117 pieces of rope, 1,442 six-pack yokes, 4,787 plastic bottles and other containers, 1,097 pieces of synthetic fishing gear, 4,090 plastic bags or plastic sheets, and 5,339 plastic food utensils. The effort by SOLV proved so successful that it has become a model (figure 14.8) for annual clean-up efforts in many other coastal states.

Concluding Thoughts: Developing A Sense of Stewardship

With the human population of the world's coastal plains expected to increase by 50% in the next fifteen years, our continued use of the seas as a safe disposal site for the unwanted byproducts of our civilization depends on a better understanding of the consequences of our intrusion on the workings of marine ecosystems. We may be the only species on earth capable of understanding the motives and consequences of our actions. Yet, the history of our economic involvement with marine populations has repeatedly demonstrated a serious lack of practical awareness to the fundamental disturbances our intervention causes in these natural systems. In our scramble for food, sport, and profit from the sea, we have repeatedly, and often with disastrous results, violated existing ecological relationships and invented new ones. We are positioning ourselves with increasing frequency at the tops of heavily exploited marine food chains that are contaminated with the very substances we are afraid to dispose of near our homes. It would be wise to heed the plights of pelicans and seals as sensitive indicators of what might be in store for us if we continue our unthinking and uncaring contamination of the world ocean.

Hopefully, as we approach the twenty-first century, we can learn to leave some old and wasteful habits behind. It will not be easy or simple, but each one of us must develop a sense of stewardship toward the world ocean and its resources that is reflected in our personal as well as our political decisions. By better understanding the fate we are shaping for the world ocean, we may yet be able to

> . . . harmonize our civilization with the environ
> So that our children see our wisdom
> Not inherit our wastes.

Wastes and the Ocean, by Momiji

Summary

Our growing human population generates an enormous burden of domestic and industrial waste that ultimately makes its way to the ocean. Municipal and industrial wastewater discharges (including urban runoff and storm, drain, and sewer overflows), land-based agriculture and forest harvest activities, ocean-based activities related to dredging, marine mining, drilling for and shipping of oil and gas, and direct ocean dumping are all sources of marine pollutants.

Even at low concentrations, some waste can adversely affect the health of marine organisms and the integrity of their natural ecological relationships. Already, some habitats have been significantly changed or degraded.

Toxic pollutants, including antifouling paints, DDT, dioxins, and PCBs enter marine food chains at low trophic levels, and at each step in the food web, become more concentrated. Oil and marine debris (especially fishing gear and plastics) float on the sea surface and eventually create additional nontoxic problems on beaches, reefs, and intertidal areas.

Each one of us must develop a sense of stewardship toward the world ocean and its resources. By caring about and understanding the workings of the world ocean, we may yet be able to minimize further degradation of an integral part of our biosphere.

Review Questions

1. List two types of marine pollutants that may have simultaneous benefits as well as harmful effects on the organisms they contact.
2. List two characteristics of plastic debris that make it an ever-increasing problem in the marine environment.
3. What specific and positive actions can you personally take to reduce some of the marine pollution problems described in this chapter?

Questions for Further Discussion

1. Describe why fat-soluble toxins, such as DDT and dioxins, become more concentrated in tissues of animals at each higher trophic level in marine food chains. List the trophic levels leading to a North Atlantic grey seal contaminated with PCBs.
2. Why is spilled oil particularly harmful to marine birds and mammals?

Suggestions for Further Reading

Books

Charney, J. I., ed. 1982. *The new nationalism and the use of common spaces: Issues in marine pollution and the exploitation of Antarctica.* Lanham, MD: Rowman and Littlefield Publications.

Moriarity, F. 1983. *Ecotoxicology: The study of pollutants in ecosystems.* New York: Academic Press.

Articles

Alexander, M. 1981. Biodegradation of chemicals of environmental concern. *Science* 211:132.

Champ, M. A., and F. L. Lowenstein. 1987. The dilemma of high-technology antifouling paints. *Oceanus* 30(3):69–77.

Croxall, J. P., S. Rodwell, and I. L. Boyd. 1990. Entanglement in man-made debris of Antarctic fur seals at Bird Island, South Georgia. *Marine Mammal Science* 6:221–33.

Cushing, D. H., and R. R. Dickson. 1976. The biological response in the sea to climatic changes. *Advances in Marine Biology* 14:1–122.

Eberstadt, N. 1986. Population and economic growth. *Wilson Quarterly* 10:95–127.

Farmington, J. 1985. Oil pollution: A decade of monitoring. *Oceanus* 28(3):2–12.

Fye, P. M. 1982. The law of the sea. *Oceanus* 25(4):7–12.

Goldwater, L. J. 1971. Mercury in the environment. *Scientific American* 224 (May): 15–21.

Mearns, A. J. 1981. Effects of municipal discharges on open coastal ecosystems. In: *Marine environmental pollution* by R. A. Geyer, ed. Amsterdam: Elsevier.

Oceanus. 1990. Special issue on ocean disposal. 33(2).

Peakall, D. B. 1970. Pesticides and the reproduction of birds. *Scientific American* 222 (April):72–78.

Turner, M. H. 1990. Oil Spill: Legal strategies block ecology communications. *Bioscience* 40:238–42.

Wilbur, R. J. 1987. Plastic in the North Atlantic. *Oceanus* 30(3):61–68.

Appendix A

The Metric System

Table A.1
Common SI Prefixes

				Decimal Notation		Exponential Notation
Micro* (μ)	=	one millionth	=	0.000001	=	10^{-6}
Milli (m)	=	one thousandth	=	0.001	=	10^{-3}
Centi (c)	=	one hundredth	=	0.01	=	10^{-2}
Deci (d)	=	one tenth	=	0.1	=	10^{-1}
Basic unit	=	one	=	1	=	1
Deka (dk)	=	ten	=	10	=	10
Hecto (h)	=	one hundred	=	100	=	10^2
Kilo (k)	=	one thousand	=	1,000	=	10^3
Mega*	=	one million	=	1,000,000	=	10^6

The Systéme International d'Unitès (SI), commonly known as the metric system, is internationally accepted as the system of measure for reporting scientific and engineering data. This system is widely used because of its simplicity and ease of conversion. Unlike the English system that we commonly use, the three basic SI units for distance, volume, and mass (weight) are closely interrelated. Each basic unit is related to the others by a simple equality, making it relatively easy to convert from one unit to another (table A.1).

The basic unit of distance measure is the **meter (m);** the meter is slightly longer than a yard. The meter, like all other basic units of the SI, is subdivided into smaller units by factors of ten. The next smaller distance unit is the **decimeter (dm),** or 0.1 m. Each decimeter is further subdivided into 10 **centimeters (cm).** Further subdivisions or multiples of the meter provide the distance units listed in table A.2.

*These prefixes have been adopted by general usage and are not part of the original metric system. Mega has no accepted abbreviation.

Table A.2
Distance

Nannometer (nm)	=	0.000000001	meter
Micrometer (μm)	=	0.000001	meter
Millimeter (mm)	=	0.001	meter
Centimeter (cm)	=	0.01	meter
Decimeter (dm)	=	0.1	meter
Meter (m)		1	meter
Kilometer (km)	=	1,000	meters

Table A.3
Area

Square millimeter (mm^2)	=	0.000001	square meter
Square centimeter (cm^2)	=	0.0001	square meter
Are (a)	=	100	square meters
Hectare (ha)	=	10,000	square meters
Square kilometer (km^2)	=	1,000,000	square meters

Table A.4
Volume

Milliliter (ml)	=	0.001	liter	=	1 cm^3
Liter (ℓ)	=	1	cubic decimeter	=	1,000 cm^3
Cubic centimeter (cm^3)	=	0.000001	cubic meter	=	1 ml
Cubic decimeter (dm^3)	=	0.001	cubic meter	=	1 ml

Two types of SI units are employed to measure area. Some are simply squared distance measures, such as **square meters (m^2)** and **square centimeters (cm^2)**. Other SI units are exclusively for area measure. They are listed in table A.3.

Two separate, but related, systems of units are also used for volume measure. Some are based on the cube of distance measures, other on the **liter** (ℓ) and its subdivisions. Some of the more common volume units are listed in table A.4.

Table A.5
Mass or Weight

Milligram (mg)	=	0.001	gram
Gram (g)	=	1	gram
Kilogram (kg)	=	1,000	grams
Metric ton	=	1,000,000	grams

Table A.6
SI-English Unit Equivalents

1 meter	=	39.37	inches
1 inch	=	2.54	centimeters
1 mile	=	1.6	kilometers
1 kilometer	=	0.62	mile
1 pound	=	453.6	grams
1 kilogram	=	2.2	pounds
1 liter	=	1.06	liquid quarts
1 liquid quart	=	0.95	liter

The basis for all SI units of mass is the **gram (g).** Other mass units derived from multiples or subdivisions of the gram are listed in table A.5.

Some of the more commonly used SI-English unit equivalents are included in table A.6. Until using the SI becomes automatic, it may be helpful to learn a few of these equivalents so that you may quickly develop a mental concept of the magnitude of the units you are considering.

Appendix B

Some Basic Elements and Atoms

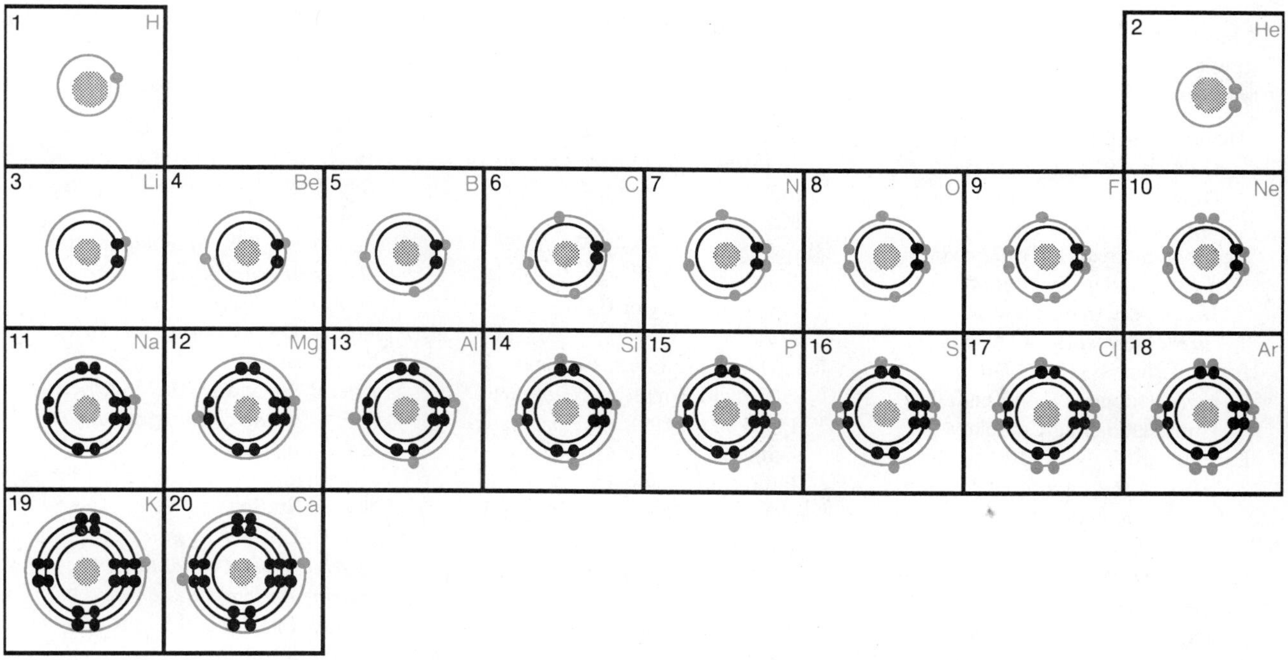

A List of Biologically Important Elements

Element	Symbol	Typically Forms	No. Covalent Bonds	Ionic Charge
Hydrogen	H	molecules and ions	1	+1
Carbon	C	molecules	4	–
Nitrogen	N	molecules	3	–
Oxygen	O	molecules	2	–
Sodium	Na	ions	–	+1
Magnesium	Mg	ions	–	+2
Chlorine	Cl	ions	–	−1
Potassium	K	ions	–	+1
Calcium	Ca	ions	–	+2

Appendix C

Regional Field and Identification Guides for Marine Organisms

I have not personally used all of these guides and cannot vouch for their applicability or accuracy. I would appreciate hearing from you about problems with any of these or about other guides to add to this list.

Abbott, Isabella A., and E. Yale Dawson. 1978. *The seaweeds.* Dubuque, IA: Kendall/Hunt Publishing Company.

Audubon Society. 1981. *The Audubon Society field guide to North American seashore creatures.* New York: A. A. Knopf.

Booth, Ernest S. 1982. *The mammals.* Dubuque, IA: Kendall/Hunt Publishing Company.

Eschmeyer, W. N., and E. S. Herald. 1983. *A field guide to Pacific coast fishes.* Boston: Houghton Mifflin Co.

Gotshall, D. W. 1988. *Marine animals of Baja California.* Marina del Rey, CA: Western Marine.

Gotshall, D. W., and L. L. Laurent. 1979. *Pacific Coast subtidal marine invertebrates, a fish-watcher's guide.* Monterey, CA: Sea Challenger.

Halstead, B. W. 1988. *Poisonous and venomous marine animals of the world.* Burbank, CA: Darwin Publications.

Hinton, S. 1987. *Seashore life of Southern California.* Berkeley, CA: University of California Press.

Jahn, Theodore Louis, Eugene Cleveland Bovee, and Florence Floed Jahn. 1978. *The protozoa.* Dubuque, IA: Kendall/Hunt Publishing Company.

Kaplan, E. H. 1984. *A field guide to southeastern and Caribbean seashores: Cape Hatteras to the Gulf Coast, Florida, and the Caribbean.* Boston: Houghton Mifflin Co.

Kozloff, E. N. 1987. *Marine invertebrates of the Pacific Northwest.* Seattle: University of Washington Press.

Lehmkuhl, Dennis M. 1979. *The aquatic insects.* Dubuque, IA: Kendall/Hunt Publishing Company.

Lippson, A. J., and R. L. Lippson. 1984. *Life in the Chesapeake Bay.* Baltimore: Johns Hopkins University Press.

Littler, D. S. 1989. *Marine plants of the Caribbean: A field guide from Florida to Brazil.* Washington, D.C.: Smithsonian Institution Press.

Morris, B. F., and D. D. Mogelberg. 1973. *Identification manual to the pelagic Sargassum fauna.* Cambridge, MA: Bermuda Biological Station.

Smith, D. L. 1977. *A guide to marine coastal plankton and marine invertebrate larvae.* Dubuque, IA: Kendall/Hunt Publishing Company.

Stokes, F. J. 1984. *Diver's and snorkeler's guide to the fishes and sea life of the Caribbean, Florida, Bahamas, and Bermuda.* Philadelphia: Academy of Natural Sciences Press.

Selected References

General Works

This list may also be used as a guide for library acquisitions.

Books

Borgese, E., and N. Gisburg, eds. 1985. *The ocean yearbook.* Chicago: University of Chicago Press.

Briggs, J. C. 1974. *Marine zoogeography.* New York: McGraw-Hill.

Cushing, D. H., and J. J. Walsh. 1976. *The ecology of seas.* Philadelphia: W. B. Saunders.

*Cloud, P. 1988. *Oasis in space: Earth history from the beginning.* New York: W. W. Norton & Co., Inc.

Duxbury, A. C., and A. B. Duxbury. 1991. *An introduction to the world's oceans.* Dubuque, IA: Wm. C. Brown Publishers.

Gross, M. G. 1982. *Oceanography: A view of the earth.* Englewood Cliffs, NJ: Prentice-Hall.

Hardy, A. H. 1971. *The open sea: Its natural history.* Part I: "The world of plankton." Part II: "Fish and fisheries." Boston: Houghton Mifflin.

Hersey, J. B., ed. 1968. *Deep-sea photography.* Baltimore: Johns Hopkins Press.

Hill, M. N., ed. 1982–83. *The sea: Ideas and observations on progress in the study of the seas,* 3 vols. New York: Interscience Publishers.

Idyll, C. P. 1976. *Abyss: The deep sea and the creatures that live in it.* New York: Thomas Y. Crowell.

Levinton, J. S. 1982. *Marine ecology.* Englewood Cliffs, NJ: Prentice-Hall.

Mader, S. S. 1990. *Biology.* Dubuque, IA: Wm. C. Brown Publishers.

Marshall, N. B. 1980. *Deep-sea biology: Developments and perspectives.* New York: Garland S.T.P.M. Press.

Niesen, T. M. 1982. *The marine biology coloring book.* New York: Harper and Row.

Sieburth, J. M. 1975. *Microbial seascapes: A pictorial essay on marine micoorganisms and their environments.* Baltimore: University Park Press.

Steele, J. H., ed. 1973. *Marine food chains.* Edinburgh, Oliver and Boyd.

Steele, J. H. 1974. *The structure of marine ecosystems.* Cambridge, MA: Harvard University Press.

Steele, J. H., ed. 1978. *Spatial pattern in plankton communities.* New York: Plenum Press.

Valentine, J. W. 1973. *Evolutionary ecology of the marine biosphere.* Englewood Cliffs, NJ: Prentice-Hall.

Vernberg, W. B., and F. J. Vernberg. 1972. *Environmental physiology of marine animals.* New York: Springer-Verlag.

Vernberg, W., ed. 1974. *Symbiosis in the sea.* Columbia, SC: University of South Carolina Press.

Zenkevitch, L. 1963. *Biology of the seas of the U.S.S.R.* New York: John Wiley.

Periodicals

American Naturalist
American Zoologist
Biological Bulletin
Bioscience
Bulletin of Marine Science
Copeia
Crustaceana
Deep-Sea Research
Ecology
Estuaries
Estuaries and Coastal Marine Science
Fishery Bulletin
Journal of Experimental Marine Biology and Ecology
Journal of the Fisheries Research Board of Canada
Journal of Ichthyology
Journal of the Marine Biological Association, U.K.

Journal of Marine Research
Journal of Plankton Research
Limnology and Oceanography
Marine Biology
Marine Mammal Science
Oceanography and Marine Biology, an Annual Review
Oceanus
Oikos
Pacific Science
Scientific American (frequently contains articles pertaining to marine life)
Veliger

Chapter 1

Baker, J. J., and G. E. Allen. 1981. *Matter, energy and life: An introduction to chemical concepts.* Reading, MA: Addison-Wesley.

Berner, R. A., and A. C. Lasaga. 1989. Modelling the geochemical carbon cycle. *Scientific American* 260(3):74–81.

Bogdanov, D. V. 1963. Map of the natural zones of the ocean. *Deep-Sea Research* 10:520–23.

Broecker, W. S. 1983. The ocean. *Scientific American* 249 (September) 146–60.

Broeker, W. S., et al. 1985. Does the ocean-atmosphere system have more than one stable mode of operation? *Nature* 315:21–26.

Dietrich, G. 1980. *General oceanography.* New York: Wiley-Interscience Publishers.

Dietz, R. S., and J. C. Holden. 1970. Reconstruction of Pangaea: Breakup and dispersion of continents, Permian to present. *Journal of Geophysical Research* 75:4939–56.

Flessa, K. W. 1975. Area, continental drift and mammalian diversity. *Paleobiology* 1:189–94.

Gordon, A. L. 1986. The Southern Ocean and global climate. *Oceanus* 26(2):34–44.

Jones, P. D., and T. M. L. Wigley. 1990. Global warming trends. *Scientific American* 263(2):84–91.

Macdonald, K. C., and B. P. Luyendyk. 1981. The crest of the East Pacific Rise. *Scientific American* 244(5):100–116.

Moore, III, B., and B. Bolin. 1986. The oceans, carbon cycle, and global climate change. *Oceanus* 29(4):16–26.

Munk, W. H. 1950. *Origin and generation of waves.* Proceedings First Conference on Coastal Engineering. Berkeley, CA: Council on Wave Research.

Pickard, G. L., and W. J. Emory (eds.). 1982. Descriptive Physical Oceanography. New York: Pergamon Press.

Post, W. M., et al. 1990. The global carbon cycle. *American Scientist* 78(4):310–26.

Rand McNally Atlas of the Oceans. 1977. Chicago, IL: Rand McNally & Company.

Rasmusson, E. M. 1985. El Niño and variations in climate. *American Scientist* 73:168–77.

Scrutton, R. A., and M. Talwani, eds. 1982. *The ocean floor. Bruce Heezen commemorative volume.* New York: Wiley Interscience.

Southward, A. J. 1964. The relationship between temperature and rhythmic cirral activity in some Cirripedia considered in connection with their geographical distribution. *Helgol. wiss. Meersuntersuch.* 10:391–403.

Chapter 2

Allen, T. F. H., and T. B. Starr. 1982. *Hierarchy: Perspectives for ecological complexity.* Chicago, IL: The University of Chicago Press.

De Duve, C. 1984. *A guided tour of the living cell.* New York: W. H. Freeman and Company.

Groves, D. I., J. S. R. Dunlop, and R. Buick. 1981. An early habitat of life. *Scientific American* 245: 64–73.

Guttman, B. S. 1976. Is "levels of organization" a useful biological concept? *Bioscience* 26:112–13.

Hutchinson, G. E. 1961. The paradox of the plankton. *American Naturalist* 95:137–45.

Landry, M. R. 1976. The structure of marine ecosystems: An alternative. *Marine Biology* 35:1–7.

Levinton, J. S. 1982. *Marine ecology.* Englewood Cliffs, N.J.: Prentice-Hall.

Lewin, R. A. 1982. Symbiosis and parasitism—definitions and evaluations. *Bioscience* 32:254.

Mader, S. S. 1990. *Biology.* Dubuque, IA: Wm. C. Brown Publishers.

Miller, R. S. 1967. Pattern and process in competition. *Advances in Ecological Research* 4:1–74.

Murphy, G. I. 1968. Pattern of life history and the environment. *American Naturalist* 102:391–403.

Roughgarden, J. 1972. Evolution of niche width. *American Naturalist* 106:683–718.

Schoener, T. W. 1974. Resource partitioning in ecological communities. *Science* 185:27–29.

Sinclair, M. 1988. *Marine populations: An essay on population regulation and speciation.* Seattle, WA: University of Washington Press.

Valentine, J. W. 1973. *Evolutionary ecology of the marine biosphere.* Englewood Cliffs, NJ: Prentice-Hall.

Van Valen, L. 1974. Predation and species diversity. *Journal of Theoretical Biology* 44:19–21.

Williams, G. C. 1966. Natural selection, the costs of reproduction and a refinement of Lack's principle. *American Naturalist* 100:687–90.

Wolfe, S. L. 1981. *Biology of the Cell.* Belmont, CA: Wadsworth Publishing Co.

Chapter 3

Alexander, R. M. 1979. *The invertebrates.* New York: Cambridge University Press.

Barnes, R. D. 1980. *Invertebrate zoology*. Philadelphia: Saunders College/Holt, Rinehart and Winston.

Brady, H. B. 1884. Report on the foraminifera dredged by H. M. S. *Challenger*, vol. 9, (*Zoology*): 1–814.

Brusca, R. C., and G. J. Brusca. 1986. *Invertebrates*. Sunderland, MA: Sinauer Associates.

Capriulo, G. M. 1989. *Ecology of marine protozoa*. New York: Oxford University Press.

Hickman, C. P., Jr. et al. 1984. *Integrated principles of zoology*. St. Louis: Mosby College Publishing.

Mader, S. S. 1987. *Evolution, diversity, and the environment*. Dubuque, IA: Wm. C. Brown Publishers.

McMahon, T. A., and J. T. Bonner. 1984. *On size and life*. New York: W. H. Freeman and Company.

Muscatine, L., and H. M. Lenhoff, eds. 1974. *Coelenterate biology: Reviews and new perspectives*. New York: Academic Press.

Richardson, J. 1986. Brachiopods. *Scientific American* (September): 100–106.

Russell-Hunter, W. D. 1979. *A life of invertebrates*. New York: Macmillan.

Sebens, K. P. 1977. Habitat suitability, reproductive ecology and the plasticity of body size in two sea anemone populations (*Anthopleura elegantissima* and *A. xanthogrammica*). Ph.D. Dissertation. Seattle: University of Washington.

Stanley, S. M. 1975. *A theory of evolution above the species level*. Proceedings of the National Academy of Science U.S.A. 72:646–50.

Valentine, W. 1978. The evolution of multicellular plants and animals. *Scientific American* (September) 140–58.

Williams, A. B. 1984. *Shrimps, lobsters, and crabs of the Atlantic coast*. Washington, DC: Smithsonian Institution Press.

Chapter 4

Austin, B. 1988. *Marine Microbiology*. New York: Cambridge University Press.

Bold, H. C., and M. J. Wynne. 1978. *Introduction to the algae*. Englewood Cliffs, NJ: Prentice-Hall.

Boney, A. D. 1975. *Phytoplankton*. London: E. Arnold.

Carr, N. G., and B. A. Whitton. 1983. *The biology of cyanobacteria*. Berkeley, CA: University of California Press.

Chapman, A. R. O. 1979. *Biology of seaweeds*. Baltimore: University Park Press.

Dawes, C. J. 1981. *Marine botany*. New York: John Wiley & Sons.

Dawson, E. Y. 1966. *Marine botany, an introduction*. New York: Holt, Rinehart and Winston.

Dring, M. J. 1983. *The biology of marine plants*. London: E. Arnold.

Estes, J. A., and J. F. Palmisano. 1974. Sea otters: Their role in structuring nearshore communities. *Science* 185:1058–60.

Goering, J. J., and P. L. Parker. 1972. Nitrogen fixation by epiphytes on sea grasses. *Limnology and Oceanography* 17:320–23.

Hargraves, P. E., and F. W. French. 1983. Diatom resting spores: significance and strategies. In: *Survival strategies of the algae*. Edited by G. A. Fryxell, pp. 49–68. New York: Cambridge University Press.

Jeffries, R. L. 1981. Osmotic adjustment of the response of halophytic plants to salinity. *Bioscience* 31:42–46.

King, R. J., and W. Schramm, 1976. Photosynthetic rates of benthic marine algae in relation to light intensity and seasonal variations. *Marine Biology* 37:215–22.

Koehl, M. A. R., and S. A. Wainwright. 1977. Mechanical adaptations of a giant kelp. *Limnology and Oceanography* 22:1067–71.

Krogmann, D. W. 1981. Cyanobacteria (blue-green algae)—Their evolution and relation to other photosynthetic organisms. *Bioscience* 31:121–24.

Lembi, C. A., and J. R. Waaland, eds. 1988. *Algae and human affairs*. New York: Cambridge University Press.

Lipps, J. H. 1970. Plankton evolution. *Evolution* 24:1–22.

Lobban, C. S., and M. J. Winne, eds. 1982. *The biology of seaweeds*. Berkeley, CA: University of California.

Mann, K. H. 1972. Ecological energetics of the seaweed zone in a marine bay on the Atlantic coast of Canada. *Marine Biology* 14:199–209.

McPeak, R. H., and D. A. Glantz. 1984. Harvesting California's kelp forests. *Oceanus* 27(1):19–26.

Moll, R. A. 1977. Phytoplankton in a temperate-zone salt marsh: Net production and exchanges with coastal waters. *Marine Biology* 42:109–18.

Moore, R. E. 1977. Toxins from blue-green algae. *Bioscience* 27:797–802.

Okada, H., and A. McIntyre. 1977. Modern coccolithophores of the Pacific and North Atlantic oceans. *Micropaleontology* 23:1–55.

Paasche, E. 1968. Biology and physiology of coccolithophorids. *Annual Review of Microbiology* 22:71–86.

Phleger, C. F. 1971. Effect of salinity on growth of a salt-marsh grass. *Ecology* 52:908–11.

Pickett-Heaps, J. 1976. Cell division in eucaryotic algae. *Bioscience* 26:445–50.

Platt, T., and W. K. W. Li, eds. 1986. Photosynthetic picoplankton. *Can. Bull. Fish. Aquatic Sci.* 214:583.

Pomeroy, L. W. 1974. The ocean's food web, a changing paradigm. *Bioscience* 24:499–504.

Ranwell, D. S. 1972. *Ecology of salt marshes and sand dunes*. London: Chapman and Hall.

Scagel, R. F., et al. 1980. *Nonvascular plants.* Belmont, CA: Wadsworth.

Schmitz, K., and C. S. Lobban. 1976. A survey of translocation in Laminariales (Phaeocophyceae). *Marine Biology* 36:207–16.

Walsby, A. E. 1977. The gas vacuoles of blue-green algae. *Scientific American* (August):90–97.

Werner, D., ed. 1977. *The biology of diatoms.* Berkeley, CA: University of California Press.

Chapter 5

Bainbridge, R. 1957. Size, shape and density of marine phytoplankton concentrations. *Biological Review* 32:91–115.

Baker, J. D., and W. S. Wilson. 1986. Spaceborne observations in support of earth science. *Oceanus* 29(4):76–85.

Boatman, E. S., et al. 1987. Today's microscopy. *Bioscience* 37: 384–94.

Boney, A. D. 1975. *Phytoplankton.* London: E. Arnold.

Bougis, P. 1976. *Marine plankton ecology.* New York: Elsevier.

Brown, O. B., et al. 1985. Phytoplankton blooming off the U.S. East Coast: A satellite description. *Science* 229:163–67.

Duffy, J. E., and M. E. Hay. 1990. Seaweed adaptations to herbivory. *Bioscience* 40(5):368–75.

Fleming, R. H. 1939. The control of diatom populations by grazing. *Journal du Conseil Permanent International pour l'Exploration de la Mer* 14:210–27.

Jenkins, W. J., and J. C. Goldman. 1985. Seasonal oxygen cycling and primary production in the Sargasso Sea. *Journal of Marine Research* 43:465–91.

Malone, T. C. 1971. The relative importance of nannoplankton and net plankton as primary producers in tropical oceanic and neritic phytoplankton communities. *Limnology and Oceanography* 16:633–39.

Mann, K. H. 1973. Seaweeds: Their productivity and strategy for growth. *Science* 182:975–81.

Marshall, H. G. 1976. Phytoplankton density along the eastern coast of U.S.A. *Marine Biology* 38:81–89.

Perry, M. J. 1986. Assessing marine primary productivity from space. *Bioscience* 36:461–67.

Philander, G. 1989. El Niño and La Niña. *American Scientist* 77(5):451–59.

Qasim, S. Z., P. M. A. Bhattuthiri, and V. P. Devassy. 1972. The effect of intensity and quality of illumination on the photosynthesis of some tropical marine phytoplankton. *Marine Biology* 16:22–27.

Raymont, J. E. G. 1980. *Plankton and productivity in the oceans.* Volume 1: Phytoplankton. New York: Pergamon Press.

Russell-Hunter, W. D. 1970. *Aquatic productivity.* New York: Macmillan.

Ryther, J. H. 1969. Photosynthesis and fish production in the sea. *Science* 166:72–76.

Ryther, J. H., and C. S. Yentsch, 1957. Estimation of phytoplankton production in the ocean from chlorophyll and light data. *Limnology and Oceanography* 2:281–86.

Saffo, M. B. 1987. New Light on seaweeds. *Bioscience* 37(9): 654–64.

Smayda, T. J. 1970. The suspension and sinking of phytoplankton in the sea. *Oceanography and Marine Biology,* Annual Review 8:353–414.

Smith, W. O., Jr., and D. M. Nelson. 1986. Importance of ice edge phytoplankton production in the southern ocean. *Bioscience* 36:251–57.

Steele, J. H., ed. 1973. *Marine food chains.* Edinburgh: Oliver and Boyd.

Steeman Nielsen, E. 1952. Use of radioactive carbon (C^{14}) for measuring organic production in the sea. *Journal du Conseil Permanent International pour l'Exploration de la Mer* 18:117–40.

Steeman Nielsen, E. 1975. *Marine photosynthesis.* Amsterdam: Elsevier.

Venrick, E. L., J. A. McGowan, and A. W. Mantyla. 1973. Deep maxima of photsynthetic chlorophyll in the Pacific Ocean. *Fishery Bulletin* 71:41–52.

Walsh, J. J. 1975. A spatial simulation model of the Peru upwelling ecosystem. *Deep-Sea Research* 22:201–36.

Whittaker, R. H., and G. E. Likens. 1973. "Carbon in the biota." In: *Carbon and the Biosphere.* Edited by G. M. Woodwell, E. V. Pecan, Technical Information Center, U.S. Atomic Energy Commission, Oak Ridge, TN.

Chapter 6

Barnes, R. S. K. 1974. Estuarine biology. *Studies in biology,* no. 49. Baltimore: University Park Press.

Botton, M. L., and H. H. Haskin. 1984. Distribution and feeding of the horseshoe crab. *Limulus polyphemus,* on the continental shelf off New Jersey. *Fishery Bulletin* 82(2):383–89.

Britton, J. C. 1989. *Shore ecology of the Gulf of Mexico.* Dallas: Texas Press.

Cloern, J., and F. Nichols. 1985. *Temporal dynamics of an estuary.* Boston: Kluwer Academic.

Costlow, J. D., and C. G. Bookhout. 1959. The larval development of *Callinectes sapidus* Rathbun reared in the laboratory. *Biological Bulletin* 116:373–96.

Durbin, A., and E. Durbin. 1974. Grazing rates of the Atlantic Nemhaden *Brevoortia tyrannus* as a function of particle size and concentration. *Marine Biology* 33:265–77.

Ernst, W. G., and J. G. Morin, eds. 1984. *The environment of the deep sea.* Englewood Cliffs, NJ: Prentice-Hall.

Garrison, D. 1976. Contribution of the net plankton and nannoplankton to the standing stocks and primary productivity in Monterey Bay, California, during the upwelling season. *Fishery Bulletin* 74:183–94.

Heinle, D. R., R. P. Harris, J. F. Ustach, and D. A. Flemer. 1977. Detritus as food for estuarine copepods. *Marine Biology* 40:341–53.

Johnson, D. R. 1985. Wind-forced dispersion of blue crab larvae in the Middle Atlantic Bight. *Continental Shelf Research* 4:425–37.

Johnson, D. R., B. S. Hester, and J. R. McConaugha. 1984. Studies of a wind mechanism influencing the recruitment of blue crabs in the Middle Atlantic Bight. *Continental Shelf Research* 3:425–37.

Lippson, J. A., and R. L. Lippson. 1984. *Life in the Chesapeake Bay.* Baltimore: The Johns Hopkins University Press.

Marshall, H. G. 1980. Seasonal phytoplankton composition in the lower Chesapeake Bay and Old Plantation Creek, Cape Charles, Virginia. *Estuaries* 3:207–16.

McLusky, D. S. 1971. *Ecology of estuaries.* London: Heinemann Educational Books, Ltd.

McRoy, C. P., and C. Helfferich. 1977. *Seagrass ecosystems.* New York: Marcel Dekker, Inc.

Miller, J. M., and M. L. Dunn. 1980. Feeding strategies and patterns of movement in juvenile estuarine fishes. In: *Estuarine perspectives.* Edited by V. S. Kennedy. New York: Academic Press.

Milliman, J. 1989. Sea levels: Past, present, and future. *Oceanus* 32(2):40–43.

National Wildlife Foundation. 1989. *A citizen's guide to protecting wetlands.* Washington, D.C.: National Wildlife Foundation.

Nichols, F., et al. 1986. Temporal dynamics of an estuary: San Francisco Bay. *Science* 231(4738):567–73.

Phillips, R. C. 1978. Seagrasses and the coastal marine environment. *Oceanus* 21:30–40.

Remane, A. 1934. Die Brackwasserfauna. *Zoologischer Anzeiger.* Supplementband 7:34–74.

Selander, R., S. Yang, R. Lewontin, and W. Johnson. 1970. Genetic variation in the horseshoe crab (*Limulus polyphemus*), a phylogenetic "relic." *Evolution* 24:402–14.

Siry, J. V. 1984. *Marshes of the ocean shore.* Austin: Texas A & M University Press.

Teal, J., and M. Teal. 1974. *Life and death of the salt marsh.* New York: Ballantine.

Tyler, M. A., and H. H. Seliger. 1978. Annual subsurface transport of a red tide dinoflagellate to its bloom area: Water circulation patterns and organism distributions in the Chesapeake Bay. *Limnology and Oceanography* 23:227–46.

Valiela, I., and J. Teal. 1979. The nitrogen budget of a salt marsh ecosystem. *Nature* 280:652–56.

Warner, W. W. 1976. *Beautiful swimmers.* Boston: Little, Brown and Company.

Williams, A. B. 1974. The swimming crabs of the genus. *Callinectes* (Decapoda: Portunidae). *Fishery Bulletin* 72:685–798.

Zedler, J., T. Winfield, and D. Mauriello. 1978. Primary productivity in a southern California estuary. *Coastal Zone* 3:649–62.

Chapter 7

Arp, A. J., and J. J. Childress. 1983 Sulfide binding by the blood of the hydrothermal vent tube worm *Riftia pachyptila. Science* 219:295–97.

Childress, J., H. Felback, and G. Somero. 1987. Symbiosis in the deep sea. *Scientific American* 256(5):114–20.

Corliss, J. B., et al. 1979. Submarine thermal springs on the Galapagos Rift. *Science* 203:1073–83.

Dayton, P. K., and R. R. Hessler. 1972. Role of biological disturbance in maintaining diversity in the deep sea. *Deep Sea Research* 19:199–208.

Grahame, J., and G. M. Branch. 1985. *Reproductive patterns of marine invertebrates.* Scotland: Aberdeen University Press.

Gray, J. S. 1974. Animal-sediment relationships. *Oceanography and Marine Biology* (Annual Review) 12:223–61.

Hessler, R. R., J. D. Isaacs, and E. L. Mills. 1972. Giant amphipod from the abyssal Pacific Ocean. *Science* 175:636–37.

Higgins, R. P., and H. Thiel eds. 1988. *Introduction to the study of meiofauna.* Washington, D.C.: Smithsonian Institution Press.

Isaacs, J. D., and R. A. Schwartzlose. 1975. Active animals of the deep-sea floor. *Scientific American* (October): 84–91.

Marshall, N. B. 1980. *Deep sea biology: Developments and perspectives.* New York: Garland S.T.P.M. Press.

Menzies, R. J., R. Y. George, and G. T. Rowe. 1973. *Abyssal environment and ecology of the world oceans.* New York: John Wiley.

Rex, M. A. 1973. Deep-sea species diversity: Decreased gastropod diversity at abyssal depths. *Science* 181:1051–53.

Rokop, F. J. 1974. Reproductive patterns in the deep-sea benthos. *Science* 186:743–45.

Sanders, H. L. 1968. Marine benthic diversity: A comparative study. *American Naturalist* 102:243–82.

Sanders, H. L., and R. R. Hessler. 1969. Ecology of the deep-sea benthos. *Science* 163:1419–24.

Scheltema, R. S. 1971. Larval dispersal as a means of genetic exchange between geographically separated populations of shallow-water benthic marine gastropods. *Biological Bulletin* 140:284–322.

Sebens, K. P. 1985. The ecology of the rocky subtidal zone. *American Scientist* 73:548–57.
Sokolova, M. N. 1970. Weight characteristics of meiobenthos in different regions of the deep-sea trophic areas of the Pacific Ocean. *Okeanologia* (in Russian) 10:348–56.
Strathman, R. 1974. The spread of sibling larvae of sedentary marine invertebrates. *American Naturalist* 108:29–44.
Thorson, G. 1950. Reproduction and larval ecology of marine bottom invertebrates. *Biological Review* 25:1–45.
Thorson, G. 1957. "Bottom communities." In: *Treatise on marine ecology and paleoecology,* edited by J. W. Hedgepeth, Geological Society of America, Vol. 1, Ecology, 461–534.
Thorson, G. 1961. Length of pelagic life in marine bottom invertebrates as related to larval transport by ocean currents. In: *Oceanography, AAAS,* edited by M. Sears, 455–74.
Underwood, A. J. 1974. On models for reproductive strategy in marine benthic invertebrates. *American Naturalist* 108:874–78.

Chapter 8

Armstrong, R. A., and R. McGehee. 1980. Competitive exclusion. *American Naturalist* 115:151–70.
Brafield, A. E. 1978. Life in sandy shores. *Studies in biology* no. 89. London: Edward Arnold.
Carson, R. L. 1979. *The edge of the sea.* Boston: Houghton Mifflin Co.
Connell, J. H. 1961. The influence of interspecific competition and other factors on the distribution of the barnacle *Chthamalus stellatus. Ecology* 42:710–23.
Dayton, P. K. 1971. Competition, disturbance, and community organization: The provision and subsequent utilization of space in a rocky intertidal community. *Ecological Monographs* 41:351–89.
Denny, M. W. 1985. Wave forces on intertidal organisms: A case study. *Limnology and Oceanography* 30:1171–87.
Eltringham, S. K. 1972. *Life in mud and sand.* New York: Crane, Russak & Co.
Epel, D. 1977. The program of fertilization. *Scientific American* (November): 129–38.
Harger, J. R. E. 1972. Competitive coexistence among intertidal invertebrates. *American Scientist* 60:600–607.
Hayes, F. R. 1964. "The mud-water interface." In: *Oceanography and Marine Biology,* an Annual Review. Edited by Harold Barnes, vol. 2:122–45. New York: Hafner Press.
Hoar, W. S. 1983. *General and comparative physiology.* Englewood Cliffs, NJ: Prentice-Hall.
Lewis, J. H. 1964. *The ecology of rocky shores.* London: English Universities Press.
Lubchenco, J. 1978. Plant species diversity in a marine intertidal community: Importance of herbivore food preference and algal competitive abilities. *American Naturalist* 112:23–39.
McIntyre, A. D. 1969. Ecology of marine meibenthos. *Biological Review* 44:245–90.
Menge, B. A. 1975. Brood or broadcast? The adaptive significance of different reproductive strategies in the two intertidal sea stars *Leptasterias hexactis* and *Pisaster ochraceus. Marine Biology* 31:87–100.
Moore, P. G., and R. Seed. 1986. *The ecology of rock coasts.* New York: Columbia University Press.
Newell, R. C. 1979. *Biology of intertidal animals.* Faversham, Kent, U.K.: Ecological Surveys, Ltd.
Palmer, J. D. 1974. *Biological clocks in marine organisms: The control of physiological and behavioral tidal rhythms.* New York: Interscience Publishers.
Reise, K. 1985. *Tidal flat ecology.* New York: Springer-Verlag.
Ricketts, C., J. Calvin, and J. W. Hedgepeth. 1986. *Between Pacific tides.* Revised by D. W. Phillips. Stanford, CA: Stanford University Press.
Sanders, H. L. 1968. Marine benthic diversity: A comparative study. *American Naturalist* 102:243–82.
Sebens, K. P. 1983. The ecology of the rocky subtidal zone. *American Scientist* 73:548–57.
Whitlatch, R. B. 1981. Patterns of resource utilization and coexistence in marine intertidal deposit-feeding communities. *Journal of Marine Research* 38:743–65.

Chapter 9

Adey, W. H. 1978. Coral reef morphogenesis: A multidimensional model. *Science* 202:831–37.
Barlow, G. W. 1972. The attitude of fish eye-lines in relation to body shape and to stripes and bars. *Copeia* 1:4–12.
Birkeland, C. 1989. The Faustian traits of the crown of thorns starfish. *American Scientist* 77(2):154–63.
Chamberlain, J. A. 1978. Mechanical properties of coral skeleton: Compressive strength and its adaptive significance. *Paleobiology* 4:419–35.
Dana, T. F. 1975. Development of contemporary Eastern Pacific coral reefs. *Marine Biology* 33: 355–74.
Darwin, C. 1962. *The structure and distribution of coral reefs.* Berkeley, CA: University of California Press.
Endean, R. 1983. *Australia's Great Barrier Reef.* New York: The University of Queensland Press.
Falkowsky, P. G., et al. 1984. Light and the bioenergetics of a symbiotic coral. *BioScience* 34:705–9.

Fankboner, P. V. 1971. Intracellular digestion of symbiotic zooxanthellae by host amoebocytes in giant clams (Bivalvia: Tridachnidae), with a note on the nutritional role of the hypertrophied siphonal epidermis. *Biological Bulletin* 141:222–34.

Fox, D. L. 1979. *Biochromy: Natural Coloration of Living Things.* Berkeley: University of California Press.

Goreau, T. F., N. I. Goreau, and C. M. Yonge. 1971. Reef corals: autotrophs or heterotrophs? *Biological Bulletin* 141:247–60.

Grigg, R. W. 1982. Darwin Point: A threshold for atoll formation. *Coral Reefs* 1:29–34.

Halstead, B. W., P. S. Auerbach, and D. R. Campbell. 1990. *A colour atlas of dangerous marine animals.* Boca Raton, FL: CRC Press.

Jackson, J. B. C., and T. P. Hughes. 1985. Adaptive strategies of coral-reef invertebrates. *American Scientist* 73:265–74.

Jones, O. A., and R. Endean, eds. 1976. *Biology and geology of coral reefs.* Vols I and II. New York: Academic Press.

Kaplan, E. H. 1988. *A field guide to coral reefs of the Caribbean and Florida including Bermuda and the Bahamas.* Boston: Houghton Mifflin Co.

Limbaugh, C. 1961. Cleaning symbiosis. *Scientific American* (August): 42–49.

Losey, G. S., Jr. 1972. The ecological importance of cleaning symbiosis. *Copeia* 4:820–33.

Mariscal, R. N. 1972. Behavior of symbiotic fishes and sea anemones. In *Behavior of Marine Animals.* Edited by H. E. Winn and B. L. Olla. New York: Plenum Publishing.

Muscatine, L., and J. W. Porter. 1977. Reef corals: Mutualistic symbiosis adapted to nutrient-poor environments. *Bioscience* 27:454–60.

Odum, H. T., and E. P. Odum. 1955. Trophic sructure and productivity of a windward coral reef community on Eniwetok Atoll. *Ecological Monographs* 25:291–320.

Porter, J. W. 1976. Autotrophy, heterotrophy, and resource partitioning in Caribbean reef-building corals. *American Naturalist* 110:731–42.

Sale, P. F. 1974. Mechanisms of coexistence in a guild of territorial reef fishes. *Marine Biology* 29:89–97.

Schener, P. J. 1977. Chemical communication of marine invertebrates. *Bioscience* 27:644–68.

Schuhmacher, H., and H. Zibrowius. 1985. What is hermatypic? *Coral Reefs* 4:1–9.

Shlesinger, Y., and Y. Loya. 1985. Coral community reproductive patterns: Red Sea versus the Great Barrier Reef. *Science* 228:1333–35.

Scott, R. D., and H. R. Jitts. 1977. Photosynthesis of phytoplankton and zooxanthellae on a coral reef. *Marine Biology* 41:307–15.

Sorokin, Y. I. 1972. Bacteria as food for coral reef fauna. *Oceanology* 12:169–77.

Stoddart, D. R. 1973. Coral reefs: The last two million years. *Geography* 58:313–23.

Thresher, R. E. 1984. *Reproduction in reef fishes.* Neptune City, NJ: T.H.F. Publications.

Chapter 10

Allan, J. D. 1976. Life history patterns in zooplankton. *American Naturalist.* 110:165–80.

Alldredge, A. 1976. Appendicularians. *Scientific American* (July):94–102.

Alldredge, A. L., and L. P. Madin. 1982. Pelagic tunicates: Unique herbivores in the marine plankton. *Bioscience* 32:655–63.

Barham, E. G. 1966. Deep scattering layer migration and composition: Observations from a diving saucer. *Science* 151:1399–1403.

Boden, B. P., and E. M. Kampa. 1967. *The influence of natural light on the vertical migrations of an animal community in the sea.* Symposium of the Zoological Society of London 19:15–26.

Boyd, C. M. 1976. Selection of particle sizes by filter-feeding copepods: A plea for reason. *Limnology and Oceanography* 21:175–79.

Bright, T., et al. 1972. Effects of a total solar eclipse on the vertical distribution of certain oceanic zooplankters. *Limnology and Oceanography* 17:296–301.

Brinton, E. 1962. "The distribution of Pacific euphausiids." Bulletin. Scripps Institution of Oceanography 8:51–270.

Frost, B.W. 1972. Effects of size and concentration of food particles on the feeding behavior of the marine planktonic copepod Calanus pacificus. *Limnology and Oceanography* 17:805–15.

Gilmer, R. W. 1972. Free-floating mucus webs: A novel feeding adaptation for the open ocean. *Science* 176:1239–40.

Lam, R. K., and B. W. Frost. 1976. Model of copepod filtering response to changes in size and concentration of food. *Limnology and Oceanography* 21:490–500.

Mauchline, J., and L. R. Fisher. 1969. The biology of euphausiids. *Advances in Marine Biology* 7:1–454.

Porter, K. G., and J. W. Porter. 1979. Bioluminescence in marine plankton: A coevolved antipredation system. *American Naturalist* 114:458–61.

Richman, S., D. R. Heinle, and R. Huff. 1977. Grazing by adult estuarine calanoid copepods of the Chesapeake Bay. *Marine Biology* 42:69–84.

Rubenstein, D. I., and M. A. R. Koehl. 1977. The mechanisms of filter feeding: Some theoretical considerations. *American Naturalist* 111:981–94.

Russel, R. S. 1935. On the value of certain planktonic animals as indicators of water movements in the English Channel and North Sea. *Journal of the Marine Biological Association,* U.K. 20:309–32.

Russell-Hunter, W. D. 1969. *Biology of higher invertebrates.* New York: Macmillan.

Sheldon, R. W., et al. 1972. The size distribution of particles in the ocean. *Limnology and Oceanography* 17:327–40.

Silver, M. W., A. L. Shanks, and J. D. Trent. 1978. Marine snow: Microplankton habitat and source of small-scale patchiness in pelagic populations. *Science* 201:371–73.

Smith, O. L., et al. 1971. Resource competition and an analytical model of zooplankton feeding on phytoplankton. *American Naturalist* 109:571–91.

Steele, J. H., ed. 1973. *Marine food chains.* Edinburgh: Oliver and Boyd.

Steele, J. H. 1976. "Patchiness." In: *Ecology of the Seas.* Edited by D. H. Cushing and J. J. Walsh. Oxford, U.K.: Blackwell Scientific Publications.

Turner, J. T., P. A. Tester, and W. F. Hettler. 1985. Zooplankton feeding ecology. *Marine Biology* 90:1–8.

Vlymen, W. J. 1970. Energy expenditure of swimming copepods. *Limnology and Oceanography* 15:348–56.

Waickstead, J. H. 1976. Marine zooplankton. London: E. Arnold.

Zaret, T. M., and J. S. Suffern. 1976. Vertical migration in zooplankton as a predator avoidance mechanism. *Limnology and Oceanography* 21:804–13.

Chapter 11

Alexander, R. McNeill. 1988. *Elastic mechanisms in animal movement.* New York: Cambridge University Press.

Blake, R. W. 1983. *Fish locomotion.* New York: Cambridge University Press.

Bond, C. E. 1979. *Biology of fishes.* Philadelphia: W. B. Saunders Co.

Carey, F. G. 1973. Fishes with warm bodies. *Scientific American* (February): 36–44.

Carr, A. 1965. The navigation of the green turtle. *Scientific American* (May): 79–86.

Compagno, L. J. V. 1988. *Sharks of the order Carcharhinoformes.* Princeton: Princeton University Press.

Cushing, D. H. 1968. *Fisheries biology.* Madison, WI: University of Wisconsin Press.

Denton, E. J., and J. P. Gilpin-Brown. 1973. Flotation mechanisms in modern and fossil cephalopods. *Advances in Marine Biology* 11:197–268.

Ege, V. 1939. A revision of the genus *Anguilla* Shaw, a systematic, phylogenetic, and geographical study. *Dana Reports* 3:1–256.

Fierstine, H. L., and V. Walters. 1968. Studies in locomotion and anatomy of scombroid fishes. *Southern California Academy of Science,* Memoirs 6:1–34.

Hardin-Jones, F. R. 1968. *Fish migration.* London: Edward Arnold.

Hasler, A. D. 1966. *Underwater guideposts: Homing of salmon.* Madison WI: University of Wisconsin Press.

Hasler, A. D., A. T. Sholz and R. M. Horrall. 1978. Olfactory imprinting and homing in salmon. *American Scientist* 66:347–54.

Hoar, W. W. 1983. *General and comparative physiology.* Englewood Cliffs, NJ: Prentice-Hall.

Kalmijin, A. J. 1977. The electric and magnetic sense of sharks, skates, and rays. *Oceanus* 20:45–52.

Kanwisher, J., and A. Ebling. 1957. Composition of swim bladder gas in bathypelagic fishes. *Deep-Sea Research* 4:211–17.

Koch, A. L., A. Carr, and D. W. Ehrenfeld. 1969. The problem of open-sea navigation: The migration of the green turtle to Ascension Island. *Journal of Theoretical Biology* 22:163–79.

Koehn, R. K. 1972. Genetic variation in the eel, a critique. *Marine Biology* (Berlin) 14:179–81.

McGowan, J. A. 1972. "The nature of oceanic ecosystems." In: *The Biology of the Oceanic Pacific.* Edited by C. B. Miller. Corvallis: Oregon State University Press.

Marshall, N. B. 1966. *The life of fishes.* New York: Universe Books.

Nicol, J. A. C. 1989. *The eyes of fishes.* New York: Oxford University Press.

O'brien, W. J., H. I. Browman, and B. I. Evans. 1990. Search strategies in foraging animals. *American Scientist* 78:152–60.

Partridge, B. L. 1982. The structure and function of fish schools. *Scientific American* 246:114–23.

Pennisi, E. 1989. Much ado about eels. *Bioscience* 39:594–98.

Pike, G. C. 1962. Migration and feeding of the gray whale (*Eschrichtius gibbosus*). *Journal of the Fisheries Research Board of Canada* 19:815–38.

Robertson, D. R. 1972. Social control of sex reversal in a coral-reef fish. *Science* 177:1007–9.

Rommel, S. A., Jr., and J. D. McCleave. 1972. Oceanic electric fields: Perception by American eels? *Science* 176:1233–35.

Royce, W., L. S. Smith, and A. C. Hartt. 1968. Models of oceanic migrations of Pacific salmon and comments on guidance mechanisms. *Fishery Bulletin* 66:441–62.

Schmidt, J. 1923. Breeding places and migrations of the eel. *Nature* (London) 111:51–54.

Shapiro, D. Y. 1987. Differentiation and evolution of sex change in fishes. *Bioscience* 37(7):490–97.

Smith, R. J. F. 1985. *The control of fish migration.* New York: Springer-Verlag.

Tucker, D. W. 1959. A new solution to the Atlantic eel problem. *Nature* (London) 183:495–501.

Warner, R. R. 1973. Ecological and evolutionary aspects of hermaphroditism in the California sheephead. *Pimelometopon pulchrum.* Ph.D. Dissertation. San Diego: University of California.

Warner, R. R. 1984. Mating behavior and hermaphroditism in coral reef fishes. *American Scientist* 72:128–36.

Webb, P. W. 1984. Form and function in fish swimming. *Scientific American* 251:72–82.

Chapter 12

Ainley, D. G., et al. 1984. *The marine ecology of birds in the Ross Sea, Antarctica.* Washington, D.C.: American Ornithologists Union.

Alderton, D. 1988. *Turtles and tortoises of the world.* New York: Facts on File, Inc.

Anderson, H. T., ed. 1969. *The biology of marine mammals.* New York: Academic Press.

Baker, R. C., R. Wilke, and C. H. Baltzo. 1970. The northern fur seals. *Bureau of Commercial Fisheries,* U.S. Fish and Wildlife Service, Circular 336.

Bartholomew, G. A. 1970. A model for the evolution of pinniped polygyny. *Evolution* 24:546–59.

Berta, A., C. E. Ray, and A. R. Wyss. 1989. Skeleton of the oldest known pinniped. *Enaliarctos mealsi. Science* 244:60–62.

Bonnell, M. L., and R. K. Selander. 1974. Elephant seals: Genetic variation and near extinction. *Science* 184:908–9.

Bonner, W. N. 1982. *Seals and man: A study of interactions.* Seattle: University of Washington Press.

Bonner, W. N. 1989. *Whales of the world.* New York: Facts on File, Inc.

Brown, D. H., D. K. Caldwell, and M. C. Caldwell. 1966. Observations on the behavior of wild and captive false killer whales, with notes on associated behavior of other genera of captive delphinids. *Contributions in Science,* Los Angeles County Museum 95:1–32.

Croxall, J. P. 1987. *Seabirds: Feeding ecology and role in marine ecosystems.* New York: Cambridge University Press.

Elsner, R., and B. Gooden. 1983. *Diving and asphyxia: A comparative study of animals and men.* New York: Cambridge University Press.

Fish, J. F., J. L. Sumich, and G. L. Lingle. 1974. Sounds produced by the gray whale, *Eschrichtius robustus. Marine Fisheries Review* 36:38–45.

Gaskin, D. E. 1982. *The ecology of whales and dolphins.* Portsmouth, NH: Heinemann.

Herman, L. M., ed. 1980. *Cetacean behavior: Mechanisms and functions.* New York: John Wiley & Sons.

Kellogg, W. N. 1961. *Porpoises and sonar.* Chicago: University of Chicago Press.

King, J. E. 1964. *Seals of the world.* London: British Museum of Natural History.

Klinowska, M. 1988. How brainy are cetaceans? *New Scientist.*

Kooyman, G. L., M. A. Castellini, and R. W. Norris. 1981. Physiology of diving in marine mammals. *Annual Review of Physiology* 43:343–56.

Laws, R. M. 1961. Reproduction, age and growth of southern fin whales. *Discovery Reports* 31:327–486.

Mackintosh, N. A. 1966. "The distribution of southern blue and fin whales." In: *Whales, dolphins, and porpoises.* Edited by K. S. Norris. Berkeley, CA: University of California Press.

Nelson, C., and K. Johnson. 1987. Whales and walruses as tillers of the sea floor. *Scientific American* 256:112–117.

Nemoto, T. 1959. Food of baleen whales with reference to whale movements. *Scientific Reports of the Whales Research Institute* (Tokyo) 14:149–290.

Norris, K. S., ed. 1966. *Whales, dolphins, and porpoises.* Berkeley, CA: University of California Press.

Norris, K. S. 1968. Evolution of acoustic mechanisms in odontocete cetaceans. *Evolution and Environment* 297–324.

Norris, K. S., and G. W. Harvey. 1972. "A theory for the function of the spermaceti organ of the sperm whale (*Physeter catodon*)." In: *Animal Orientation and Navigation,* pp. 397–417. Washington, D.C.: National Aeronautics and Space Administration.

Pierotti, R., and C. A. Annett. 1990. Diet and reproductive output in seabirds. *Bioscience* 40:568–74.

Pivorunas, A. 1979. The feeding mechanisms of baleen whales. *American Scientist* 67:432–40.

Rice, D. W., and A. A. Wolman. 1971. "The life history and ecology of the gray whale (*Eschrichtius robustus*)." American Society of Mammalogists, special Publication No. 3.

Ridgway, S. H., ed. 1972. *Mammals of the sea: Biology and medicine.* Springfield, IL: Charles C. Thomas.

Schevill, W. E. 1974. *The whale problem, a status report.* Cambridge. MA: Harvard University Press.

Stirling, I. 1988. *Polar bears.* Ann Arbor, MI: University of Michigan Press.

Strauss, M. B. 1970. Physiological aspects of mammalian breath-hold diving: A review. *Aerospace Medicine* 41:1362–81.

VanBlaricom, G. R., and J. A. Estes. 1988. *The community ecology of sea otters.* New York: Springer-Verlag.

Würsig, B. 1988. The behavior of baleen whales. *Scientific American* 258(4):102–7.

Würsig, B. 1979. Dolphins. *Scientific American* (March):136–48.

Zopal, W. 1987. Diving adaptations of the Weddell seal. *Scientific American* 256(6):100–105.

Chapter 13

Adey, W. H. 1987. Food production in low-nutrient seas. *Bioscience* 37(5):340–48.

Bardach, J. 1987. Aquaculture. *Bioscience* 37(5):318–19.

Beddington, J. R., R. J. H. Beverton, and D. M. Lavigne. 1985. *Marine mammals and fisheries.* Boston: George Allen and Unwin.

Beddington, J. R., and R. M. May. 1982. The harvesting of interacting species in a natural ecosystem. *Scientific American* (November):62–69.

Bell, F. W. 1978. *Food from the sea: The economics and politics of ocean fisheries.* Denver: Westview Press.

Borgese, E. M. 1983. The law of the sea. *Scientific American* (March): 42–49.

Caddy, J. F., ed. 1988. *Marine invertebrate fisheries: Their assessment and management.* New York: Wiley-Interscience.

Cushing, D. H. 1981. *Fisheries biology.* Madison, WI: University of Wisconsin Press.

Cushing, D. H., and R. R. Dickson. 1976. The biological response in the sea to climatic changes. *Advances in Marine Biology* 14: 1–122.

Emery, K. O., and C. O. Iselin. 1967. Human food from ocean and land. *Science* 157:1279–81.

Food and Agricultural Organization of the United Nations. 1982. *Atlas of the living resources of the seas.* Rome: Department of Fisheries (FAO).

Food and Agricultural Organization of the United Nations. *Yearbook of fisheries statistics, catches, and landings.* [Rome:] Department of Fisheries (FAO).

Fye, P. M. 1982. The law of the sea. *Oceanus* 25(4):7–12.

Gulland, J. A. 1971. *The fish resources of the ocean.* Surrey, England: Fishing News (Books) Ltd.

Harlan, J. R. 1976. The plants and animals that nourish man. *Scientific American* (September):89–97.

Holt, J. S. 1969. Food resources of the ocean. *Scientific American* (September):178–94.

Horn, M. H., and R. N. Gibson. 1988. Intertidal fisheries. *Scientific American* 258(1):64–70.

Laws, R. M. 1985. The ecology of the Southern Ocean. 1985. *American Scientist* 73:26–40.

Murphy, R. C. 1925. *Bird islands of Peru.* New York: G. P. Putnam and Sons.

Robinson, M. A., and Crispoldi, A. 1975. Trends in world fisheries. *Bioscience* 18:23–9.

Ross, R. M., and L. B. Quetin. 1986. How productive are Antarctic krill? *Bioscience* 36:264–69.

Rothschild, B. J. ed. 1983. *Global fisheries: Perspectives for the 1980s.* New York: Springer-Verlag.

Rudloe, J., and A. Rudloe. 1989. Shrimpers and sea turtles: A conservation impasse. *Smithsonian* 29(9):45–55.

Ryther, J. H. 1969. Photosynthesis and fish production in the sea. *Science* 166:72–76.

Ryther, J. H. et al. 1972. Controlled eutrophication—increasing food production from the sea by recycling human wastes. *Bioscience* 22:144–52.

Ryther, J. H. 1981. Mariculture, ocean ranching, and other culture-based fisheries. *Bioscience* 31:223–30.

Scarff, J. E. 1980. Ethical issues in whale and small cetacean management. *Environmental Ethics* 3:241–79.

Schaefer, M. B. 1970. Men, birds, and anchovies in the Peru Current—dynamic interactions. *Transactions of the American Fisheries Institute* 99:461–67.

Chapter 14

Alexander, M. 1981. Biodegradation of chemicals of environmental concern. *Science* 211:132.

Blus, L., et al. 1971. Eggshell thinning in the brown pelican: Implications of DDE. *Bioscience* 21:1213–15.

Champ, M. A., and F. L. Lowenstein. 1987. The dilemma of high-technology antifouling paints. *Oceanus* 30(3):69–77.

Charney, J. I., ed. 1982. *The new nationalism and the use of common spaces: Issues in marine pollution and the exploitation of Antarctica.* Lanham, MD: Rowman and Littlefield Publications.

Cox, J. L. 1972. DDT in marine plankton and fish in the California Current. *CalCOFI Reports* 16:103–11.

Croxall, J. P., S. Rodwell, and I. L. Boyd. 1990. Entanglement in man-made debris of Antarctic fur seals at Bird Island, South Georgia. *Marine Mammal Science* 6:221–33.

Eberstadt, N. 1986. Population and economic growth. *Wilson Quarterly* 10:95–127.

Epel, D., and W. L. Lee. 1970. Persistent chemicals in the marine ecosystem. *The American Biology Teacher* 207–11.

Farmingon, J. 1985. Oil pollution: A decade of monitoring. *Oceanus* 28:2–12.

Goldwater, L. J. 1971. Mercury in the environment. *Scientific American* 224 (May): 15–21.

Johnston, R., ed. 1977. *Marine pollution.* New York: Academic Press.

Mearns, A. J. 1981. Effects of municipal discharges on open coastal ecosystems. In: *Marine Environmental Pollution.* R. A. Geyer, ed. Amsterdam: Elsevier.

Moriarity, F. 1983. *Ecotoxicology: The study of pollutants in ecosystems.* New York: Academic Press.

Oceanus. 1990. Special issue on ocean disposal. 33(2).

Peakall, D. B. 1970. Pesticides and the reproduction of birds. *Scientific American* 222 (April): 72–78.

Risebrough, R. W., et al. 1967. DDT residues in Pacific seabirds: A persistent insecticide in marine food chains. *Nature* 216:389–91.

Turner, M. H. 1990. Oil Spill: Legal strategies block ecology communications. *Bioscience* 40:238–42.

Walsh, J. P. 1981. U.S. Policy on marine pollution. *Oceanus* 24(1):18–24.

Wilbur, R. J. 1987. Plastic in the North Atlantic. *Oceanus* 30(3):61–68.

Wurster, C. E. 1968. DDT reduces photosynthesis by marine phytoplankton. *Science* 159:1474.

Appendix

La Maraic, A. 1973. *The complete metric system with the international system of units (SI).* Somers, New York: Abbey Books.

Glossary

A

absorptive feeding a means of taking up dissolved food material through specialized organs or across the body wall

abyssal plains flat, sediment-covered areas in the ocean basin usually 3,000 to 5,000 m deep

accessory pigment one of several nongreen photosynthetic pigments found in marine plants that absorbs light energy from the center of the visible light spectrum and transfers it to the green pigment chlorophyll

acrorhagi nematocyst-armed defensive structures of anemones

adenosine triphosphate (ATP) a complex organic compound composed of adenosine and three phosphates, which serves in short-term energy storage and conversion in all organisms

aerobic respiration cellular respiration occurring in the presence of oxygen

air sacs lateral branches of the nasal passages of smaller toothed whales; sources of echolocation sounds

alcoholic fementation a form of anaerobic respiration in which sugar is degraded to alcohol and CO_2 and energy is released

algal ridge low, jagged coral ridge common on the windward side of coral reefs

alveoli minute air sacs in the lungs of vertebrates

amebocyte motile cells within sponges that have the shape or properties of an amoeba

amniotic egg egg of reptiles, birds, and mammals, containing an embryo that develops within an amniotic membrane

anadromous an animal (such as a salmon) that spends much of its life at sea and then returns to a freshwater stream or lake to spawn

anaerobic respiration cellular respiration occurring in the absence of oxygen

androgen in vertebrates, a male sex hormone

anoxic without oxygen

aorta large artery carrying blood away from the heart

aphotic zone the portion of the ocean where the absence of sunlight prohibits plant growth

apneustic breathing breathing pattern exhibited by marine mammals in which several rapid breaths alternate with a prolonged cessation of breathing

areolus a structural unit of diatom frustules

asexual reproduction reproduction by a single individual involving fission, budding, or fragmentation

aspect ratio index of propulsive efficiency obtained by dividing the square of a fish's fin height by the fin area

atom smallest particle of any element that expresses the properties of that element

atmosphere a unit of pressure equal to 14.7 $lbs/in.^2$ and equivalent to the pressure created by a 10 m column of water

atoll a ring-shaped chain of coral reefs from which a few low islands project above the sea surface

autosome a chromosome not designated as a sex chromosome

auxospore the naked cell of a diatom after the frustule has been shed

B

baleen rows of comblike material that project from the outer edges of the upper jaws of filter-feeding whales

bar-built estuary a type of estuary formed behind a coastal barrier, or bar

barrier reef a coral reef separated from the shore by a lagoon

benthic pertaining to the sea bottom and the organisms that inhabit the bottom

benthos marine organisms that live in or on the sea bottom

biantitropical distribution a pattern of a species' geographical distribution that extends across comparable bands of latitude in both the Northern Hemisphere and the Southern Hemisphere

bioaccumulation increasingly concentrated accumulation of substances, especially pollutants, at successively higher trophic levels in food chains

biological clock an innate time sense found in most organisms

biological succession the gradual replacement, through time, of one group of species in a community by others

bioluminescence production of visible light by living organisms

blade the flattened, usually broad, leafy structure of seaweeds

blastocyst in mammals, a small ball of cells representing an early stage of embryonic development

bloom a dense concentration of phytoplankton that occurs in response to optimum growth conditions

bradycardia marked slowing of the heartbeat rate during a breath-hold dive

broadcast spawners marine animals that reproduce by releasing eggs and sperm into the water

bronchi the paired ventilatory tubes of a vertebrate that branch into each lung at the lower end of the trachea

buttress seaward face of a coral reef, extending from a depth of about 20 m to just below the low-tide line

byssal thread a strong elastic fiber used by mussels to attach themselves to a solid substrate

C

calorie a unit of heat energy equivalent to the amount of energy required to change the temperature of 1 g of water 1° C

carnivore an animal that preys on other animals

carpospore spores produced by the carposporophyte form of red algae

carposporophyte a generation of plants, unique to red algae, that produces carpospores

caudal fin an enlarged fin at the posterior end of most fish

caudal peduncle the area where the caudal fin joins the rest of a fish's body

cell wall a supportive structure that encloses the cells of most plants, bacteria, and fungi

cephalization the evolutionary process of increasing specialization of the head, especially the brain and sense organs

cerata fingerlike projections along the dorsal sides of some nudibranches

chloride cell a specialized gill cell of bony fish that excretes chloride

chlorophyll the green photosynthetic pigment of plants, protists, and monerans

chromatophore surface pigment cell found in many animals that expands and contracts to produce changes in color and appearance

chromosome a subcellular structure that contains the genetic information of the cell

cilia numerous short hairlike cellular projections used for locomotion or transport

circadian rhythm a cycle of activity or behavior that recurs about once a day

circalunadian rhythm a cycle of repeating activity each lunar day, or 24.8 hours

cleaning symbiosis a form of mutualism in which one partner picks external parasites and damaged tissue from the other partner

clones genetically identical group of individuals derived from a single individual

coccolith a small calcareous plate imbedded in the cell wall of coccolithophores

coastal plain estuary an estuary created by flooding a coastal river valley with seawater

commensalism a symbiotic relationship in which the symbiont benefits without seriously affecting the host one way or another

community an assemblage of interacting populations living in a particular locale

conduction the molecular transfer of heat through a medium

consumer an organism that consumes and digests other organisms to satisfy its energy and material needs

continental boundary current a surface ocean current flowing generally north or south along a continental edge

continental drift the gradual movement of continents in response to seafloor spreading processes

continental shelf the relatively smooth underwater extension of the edge of the continent that slopes gently seaward to a depth of about 200 m

continental slope the relatively steep portion of the sea bottom between the outer edge of the continental shelf and the deep ocean basin

convection the transfer of energy by the flow or mixing of a liquid or gas

convective mixing the vertical mixing of water masses driven by wind stresses or density changes at the sea surface

corallite the calcareous skeletal cup in which a coral polyp sits

Coriolis effect the apparent change in direction of a moving object (to the left in the Southern Hemisphere and to the right in the Northern Hemisphere) due to the rotation of the earth

countercurrent an ocean current that flows directly back into another current

countershading the coloration pattern found in pelagic animals, with the upper surfaces darkly pigmented and the sides and ventral surfaces silvery or only lightly pigmented

critical depth the depth at which primary production equals plant respiration

cropper a deep-sea animal in which the roles of predator and deposit feeder have merged

cypris the final larval stage of a barnacle

cytoplasm the internal fluid environment of a cell

D

dark reaction that part of the photosynthetic process that, in the absence of light, utilizes preformed ATP and $NADPH_2$ to synthesize complex organic molecules

decomposer an organism that consumes and breaks down dead organic material

deep scattering layer one or more layers of midwater marine animals that reflect and scatter the sound pulses of echo sounders

delayed implantation a pattern in the reproductive cycle of some mammals causing the blastocyst to remain dormant in the female's uterus for some time before implantation on the uterine wall

delta a low-lying sediment deposit often found at the mouth of a river

density ratio of the mass of a substance to its volume

deposit feeder an animal that engulfs masses of sediments and processes them through its digestive tract

detritus excrement and other waste products of all types of organisms, including their remains after death

diadromous an animal that migrates between fresh water and saltwater; includes both anadromous and catadromous fish

diffusion the transfer of substances along a gradient from regions of high concentrations to regions of low concentrations

diploid cells that contain two of each type of chromosome characteristic of its species

diurnal tide a tidal pattern with one high tide and one low tide each lunar day

dive reflex the suite of internal responses, including bradycardia and peripheral circulation shutdown, that occurs during dives by an air-breathing vertebrate

E

ectotherm an animal whose body temperature is controlled by external heat sources

electron negatively charged subatomic particle in orbit around the nucleus of an atom

element fundamental forms of matter

elver a juvenile eel

emergent plant community marine plant community existing above sea level

endoplasmic reticulum a system of folded membranes within the cytoplasm of eucaryotic cells

endotherm an animal whose body temperature is established by internal sources of heat

enzyme protein catalyst that regulates a particular chemical reaction

epifauna benthic animals that crawl about on the sea bottom or sit firmly attached to it

epipelagic zone the upper 200 m of the oceanic province

epiphyte a plant that attaches itself to other plants or animals without parasitizing them

epitheca the larger portion of a diatom frustule

estrogen the female sex hormone in vertebrates

estrous the period of highest sexual receptivity (or "heat") in some female mammals that coincides with the time of egg release by the ovary

estuary the portion of the mouth of a river in which there is substantial mixing of fresh water and seawater

eucaryotes cells characterized by an organized nucleus and other membrane-bound subcellular structures

euryhaline an organism capable of withstanding a wide range of salinities

evolutionary adaptation the changes occurring in a population of individuals over many generations by processes of natural selection

external auditory canal the sound channel connecting the external and middle ears

F

fecundity the number of offspring an organism can produce in a given time span

feedback mechanisms control mechanisms in organisms and communities in which a change in a given factor either inhibits or stimulates processes controlling the production, release, or use of that factor

fertilization the fusion of two haploid gametes to produce a diploid zygote

fetch the extent of the ocean over which winds blow to create waves

finlet small median fin on the dorsal and ventral sides of the rear parts of tuna and similar fish

fjord a deep coastal embayment caused by glacial erosion

flagellum whiplike structure used by cells for locomotion

flocculate a process by which dissolved substances come out of solution and aggregate together to form macroscopic particles

flushing time the time required for all of the water of an estuary to be completely exchanged

food chain a diagrammatic representation of trophic relationships

food web a diagrammatic representation of the complete set of trophic relationships of an organism

form drag hydrodynamic drag on an organism caused by its cross-sectional area

frictional drag the resistance created by an animal's body surface when it moves through a fluid medium

fringing reef a large coral-reef formation that closely borders the shoreline

frustule the siliceous wall of a diatom; consists of two halves

fucoxanthin a golden or brown pigment characteristic of Phaeophyta, Chrysophyta, and Pyrrophyta

G

gamete an egg or sperm cell

gametophyte a gamete-producing haploid plant

gestation period the portion of the reproductive cycle in a female mammal extending from fertilization to birth of its offspring

gill arch in fish, the skeletal supporting structure of a gill

grana flattened saclike structures inside chloroplasts containing chlorophyll and other photosynthetic enzymes

gross primary production the total amount of photosynthesis accomplished in a given period of time

guano the droppings from seabird nesting colonies

gyre the large loop of interconnected surface ocean currents within a single ocean basin, usually spanning 20 to 30° in latitude

H

halophyte flowering plants that are tolerant to complete submergence in seawater

haploid cell a cell containing only one of each type of chromosome characteristic of its species

haptera short, sturdy rootlike structures that form the holdfast of seaweeds

heat capacity the measure of heat energy required to change the temperature of 1 g of a substance 1° C

hemocyanin an oxygen-binding pigment found in the blood of several kinds of invertebrates

hemoglobin an oxygen-binding red blood pigment found in vertebrates and some invertebrates

herbivore an animal adapted to feed on plants

hermaphrodite an animal that has the sex organs of both sexes

heterotroph an organism that is unable to synthesize its own food from inorganic substances and must utilize other organisms for nourishment

high tide the highest level reached by the rising tide

holdfast a structure that attaches seaweeds to the sea bottom or to other substrates

holoplankton species of zooplankton that remain in the plankton throughout their lives

homeostasis tendency of living organisms to maintain a steady state in their internal environmental conditions, including body temperature, blood sugar level, and metabolic rate

homeotherm an animal, such as a bird or mammal, that maintains precisely controlled internal body temperatures using its own heating and cooling mechanisms

host one member of the host-symbiont pairing characteristic of all symbiotic relationships

hydrogen bond a weak bond formed by the attractive force between the charged ends of water molecules and other charged molecules or ions

hyperosmotic a water medium with a higher concentration of ions than that of another solution separated by a selectively permeable membrane

hypoosmotic a water medium with a lower concentration of ions than that of another solution separated by a selectively permeable membrane

hypotheca the smaller portion of a diatom frustule

I

infauna animals that live within the sediment of the sea bottom

interstitial animal an animal that occupies the spaces (interstices) between sediment particles

ion an electrically charged atom or molecule formed by gaining or losing one or more electrons

ionic bond in crystalline structures, an atomic bond formed between adjacent oppositely charged ions

iridocyte a fish skin cell that contains reflecting crystals of guanine

isohaline having the same salinity

isosmotic a water medium with the same concentration of ions as another solution separated by a selectively permeable membrane

K

kelp a group of large brown seaweeds

kingdom the largest taxonomic category of classification, consists of several closely related phyla or divisions

L

labyrinth organ one of a pair of equilibrium organs in vertebrates that contains three fluid-filled semicircular canals

langmuir cells parallel pairs of counter-rotating ocean convection cells driven by surface winds

last glacial maximum (LGM) the time of the maximum extent of the last major continental glacial advance in the Northern Hemisphere, about 18,000 years ago

latent heat of fusion the heat that must be extracted from a liquid to freeze it to a solid at the same temperature. For water, it is 80 cal/g

latent heat of vaporization the heat energy required to convert a liquid to a gas at the same temperature. For water, it is 540 cal/g

latitude the angular distance north or south of the equator of a position on the earth's surface; measured in °

leptocephalus larva leaf-shaped transparent larva of some eels

light reaction that part of the photosynthetic process that, in the presence of light, captures energy to form ATP and $NADPH_2$ to be used to synthesize complex organic molecules in the dark reaction

limiting factor any factor necessary for the growth or health of an organism that limits further growth if in insufficient supply

lipid a class of organic compounds, including fats, oils, waxes, and steroids

littoral the intertidal zone

longitude the angular distance of a position on the earth's surface east or west of the Greenwich Prime Meridian; measured in °

low tide the lowest level reached by the falling tide

M

macrofauna benthic animals larger than about 0.5 mm

mangal a tropical community of mangrove plants and associated organisms

mariculture the collective techniques applied to grow marine organisms in captive, controlled situations

maximum sustainable yield the maximum level of fishing effort that a fish stock can withstand without causing major upsets in the abundance of its stock

meiofauna benthic animals intermediate in size between macrofauna and microfauna

meiosis a process of cellular division that reduces the chromosome number by half

meristematic tissue within some seaweeds, specific tissue sites where most cell division for growth occurs

meroplankton larval forms of benthic and nektonic adults that are temporary members of the plankton community

mesopelagic zone the portion of the pelagic division that extends from the bottom of the epipelagic zone to about 1,000 m

metabolism collectively, all the biochemical processes occurring in a living organism

microatoll a small, flat, atoll-shaped coral structure generally found in protected coral lagoons

microfauna benthic animals smaller than about 0.1 mm

mitochondria in eucaryotes, a subcellular organelle that conducts cellular respiration

mitosis a process of cell division resulting in two descendant cells genetically indentical to their parent cell

mixed semidiurnal tides tidal pattern during a lunar day with unequal high tides and unequal low tides

molecule a particle of matter consisting of two or more atoms bound by covalent bonds

mortality the rate at which individuals of a population die

mutualism a type of symbiotic relationship in which both the symbiont and the host benefit from the association

myoglobin a red muscle pigment with a strong chemical affinity for oxygen (similar to that of hemoglobin)

myomere one of a series of muscle segments along the trunk of vertebrates, especially fish

N

nanoplankton phytoplankton with cell sizes smaller than 60 μm mesh opening of a fine-mesh silk plankton net

nauplius microscopic free-swimming planktonic stage of barnacles and some crustaceans

neap tides sets of moderate tides that alternate with spring tides and recur every two weeks

nekton large, actively swimming marine animals

neritic pertaining to the portion of the marine environment that overlies the continental shelves

neuromast a mechanosensory cell found in vertebrates

neuston planktonic organisms living (usually floating) at or on the sea surface

niche the functional role of an organism as well as the suite of physical and chemical factors that limit its range of existence

nitrogen fixation conversion by bacteria and cyanobacteria of atmospheric N_2 to other forms of nitrogen used by eucaryotic plants

nitrogen narcosis the narcotic effect of high concentrations of N_2 experienced by divers after prolonged breathing of air under pressure

nuclear membrane the membrane surrounding the nucleus of eucaryotic cells

nucleus the membrane-bound central structure of eucaryotic cells that contains the chromosomes

O

oceanic pertaining to the portion of the marine environment that overlies the deep ocean basins

olfaction ability to detect and identify chemicals dissolved in air or water by using olfactory sensory cells

open access the concept of international law that permits free access by any nation to marine resources existing outside national jurisdictions

osmoregulator an organism that osmoregulates

osmosis diffusion of material across a selectively permeable membrane

osmotic conformers organisms that tolerate large variations of internal ionic concentrations without serious damage

osmotic pressure in hypoosmotic conditions, the internal fluid pressure that develops from the osmotic inflow of water

oviparity a condition which describes the habit of releasing eggs which later hatch

ovoviviparity an intermediate condition between viviparity and oviparity in which the eggs are incubated inside the mother until hatching

ozone O_3, formed by the action of ultraviolet light acting on atmospheric O_2

P

Pangaea the supercontinent that consisted of all the present land masses prior to their breakup and subsequent drift to their present positions

parasitism a type of symbiotic relationship in which the parasite lives on or in the host and benefits at the expense of the host

pelagic pertaining to the waters of the ocean and the organisms which inhabit the water column

pen in squids, a thin, chitinous structure extending the length of the mantle tissue

period in ocean waves, the time required for two successive waves to pass a reference point

pH a numerical scale from 0 to 14 that is used to represent the H ion concentration of a water solution

pheromone a chemical substance used for communication between organisms of the same species

photic zone the portion of the ocean where light intensity is sufficient to accommodate plant growth

photophores an animal's light-producing organs

photosynthesis the biological synthesis of organic material from inorganic substances using light as an energy source

phycobilin a type of pink or blue accessory photosynthetic pigment found in cyanobacteria and red algae

physoclist swim bladder in fish, a swim bladder lacking an air passage to the esophagus

physostomous swim bladder in fish, a swim bladder with an air passage or duct to the esophagus

phytoplankton microscopic photosynthetic members of the plankton

picoplankton the small sized groups of phytoplankton with cells less than 2 micrometers in width

pinocytosis channel a channel through which cells actively engulf liquids or small particles of food

plankton free-floating, usually minute, organisms of the sea

planula the planktonic larval form of some corals

plasma membrane the selectively permeable outer membrane of a cell

plate tectonics the collective geologic processes that move the crustal plates of the earth and cause continental drifting and seafloor spreading

pleopods abdominal paired appendages in crustaceans

pneumatic duct in fish, the connection between the esophagus and swim bladder

pneumatocyst gas-filled float present in several types of kelp plants

pneumatophore a gas-filled float used by some siphonophores to maintain buoyancy in the water

poikilotherm an organism whose body temperature varies with and is largely controlled by environmental temperatures

polar easterlies winds that blow from east to west at very high latitudes

pollen the small fertilizing structure of flowering plants that contain the male gamete

polygyny a type of social and breeding organization in which a male is dominant over and mates with several females

population a group of freely interbreeding organisms of the same species

predator a carnivorous animal that feeds by killing other animals

predictive model a somewhat simplified representation of a physical process that yields information with predictive value

primary producer organisms that synthesize material by photosynthesis or chemosynthesis

primary production the synthesis of organic material from inorganic molecules

procaryotes bacteria and cyanobacteria that lack the structural complexity and defined nucleus found in eucaryotes

producer an organism, usually photosynthetic, that contributes to the net primary production of a community

protein a long-chain polymer of amino acids that functions as enzymes or as structures in cells

proton a positively charged subatomic particle found in the nucleus of any atom

protozoea an early developmental stage of some crustaceans

R

raphe a groove in the frustules of pennate diatoms through which cytoplasm extends for locomotion

red tide a bloom condition in which some species of dinoflagellates produce toxins that may cause serious morality to other forms of marine life

reef massive near-shore deposits of coral skeletal material

reef flat the portion of a coral reef that extends behind the algal ridge to the island

rhizome the horizontal underground stem of sea grasses

ribosome a small, subcellular organelle involved in protein synthesis

rods light-sensitive cells of the retina found in vertebrates; responsible for vision in dim light and noncolor vision

S

salinity a measure of the total amount of dissolved ions in seawater

saturation light intensity the light intensity that maximizes the photosynthetic rate

saxitoxin a paralytic toxic produced by dinoflagellates, that accumulates in the butter clam (*Saxadoma*)

scavenger an animal that feeds on the dead remains of other animals and plants

school a well-defined social organization of marine animals consisting of a single species with all members of a similar size

seafloor spreading a global process of oceanic crust moving away from ridge and rise systems where it formed

seamount an undersea volcano

secondary lamella a small extension of a gill filament containing blood capillaries for gas exchange

selectively permeable membrane a membrane that is permeable to small molecules, usually H_2O, O_2, and CO_2, but not permeable to larger molecules or ions

semidiurnal tides tidal patterns with two high tides and two low tides each lunar day

septa a thin structure separating internal parts of organisms

sequential hermaphrodite an animal that first functions as one sex and then changes to the opposite sex as it increases in age

sex chromosome one of a pair of chromosomes whose composition determines gender

sexual reproduction a mode of reproduction involving the production of gametes by meiosis, followed by a fusion of the gametes in fertilization

shelf break the outer edge of the continental shelf, typically 100 to 200 m deep

siphon tubelike structure of mollusks used to take in and expel water from the mantle cavity

siphuncle a central tubelike tissue connecting the chambers of shelled cephalopods such as *Nautilus*

smolt a young salmon just before it migrates downstream and out to sea

spermaceti organ a large organ in the forehead of sperm whales that is filled with a fine-quality liquid or waxy spermaceti oil

sporangium a special plant cell or structure that produces spores

sporophyte a spore-producing diploid plant

spring tides extremely high tides and low tides that alternate with neap tides and recur every two weeks

standing crop total amount of plant or animal material in an area at any one time

statocyst a gravitationally-sensitive vesicle lined with sensory cells and containing dense bodies; found in many invertebrates

stenohaline an organism that only tolerates exposure to slight variations in salinity

stigma a structure on the female part of a flower on which pollen grains are received and germinate

stipe the flexible, stemlike structure found in the large seaweeds

stroma the part of the chloroplast containing the enzymes for the dark reactions of photosynthesis

submergent plant community a marine plant community restricted to subtidal environments

surface current long-term directional flow of water at the sea surface

surface tension the mutual attraction of water molecules at the surface of a water mass that creates a flexible molecular "skin" over the water surface

suspension feeder an animal that uses a filtering device or sticky mucus to obtain plankton or detritus from the water

symbiont the beneficiary of a symbiotic relationship

symbiosis an intimate and prolonged association between two (or more) organisms in which at least one partner obtains some benefit from the relationship

T

taxonomy the process of classifying organisms according to their evolutionary relationships

temperature a relative intensity measure of the condition caused by heat

testosterone in vertebrates, a male sex hormone

tidal range vertical distance between high and low tides

tide a long period wave noticeable as a periodic rise and fall of the sea surface along coastlines

trace element an element needed for normal metabolism but available only in minute amounts from the environment

trachea windpipe

trade winds subtropical winds that blow from northeast to southwest in the Northern Hemisphere and from southeast to northwest in the Southern Hemisphere

trench deep area in the ocean floor, generally deeper than 6,000 m

trophic pertaining to feeding or nutrition

trophic level the position of an organism or species in a food chain

trophosome an internal, symbiotic bacteria-filled organ of the giant tube worm, *Riftia*

turbulence random, nonlaminar flow of a fluid

turnover rate the rate at which members of a population or community replace themselves

tympanic bulla bony case in the middle ear that encloses the sound-processing structures of mammals

U

ultraplankton phytoplankton with cells between 2 and 5 micrometers in width

upwelling the process that carries nutrient-rich subsurface water upward to the photic zone

uric acid the main nitrogenous excretory product in birds, reptiles, some invertebrates, and insects.

V

vacuole a liquid or food-filled cavity within a cell

vena cava the major vein returning blood to the heart of vertebrates

vertical migration daily or seasonal movement of small marine animals between the photic zone and midwater depths

villi small fingerlike projections of tissue that increase surface area and improve secretion and absorption

viscosity the resistance of water molecules to external forces that would separate them

viviparity a condition describing the act of giving birth to live young

W

wave a periodic, travelling undulation of the sea surface

westerlies winds that blow primarily from the west in the mid-latitudes

X

xanthophyll a group of yellow or golden photosynthetic pigments

Z

zoea an early larval stage of many crustaceans

zooplankton animal members of the plankton

zooxanthellae symbiotic unicellular dinoflagellates found in corals, sea anemones, mollusks, and several other types of marine animals

zygote the product of the fusion of two gametes to produce a diploid single cell

Taxonomic Index*

*Italicized page numbers refer to figures in text.

U

V

Z

Subject Index*

A

*Italicized page numbers refer to figures in text.

D

E

F

G

H

N

R

S

T